W9-DHX-947

# Argentina

# WORLD BIBLIOGRAPHICAL SERIES

General Editors:
Robert G. Neville (Executive Editor)
John J. Horton

Robert A. Myers                    Ian Wallace
Hans H. Wellisch          Ralph Lee Woodward, Jr.

**John J. Horton** is Deputy Librarian of the University of Bradford and currently Chairman of its Academic Board of Studies in Social Sciences. He has maintained a longstanding interest in the discipline of area studies and its associated bibliographical problems, with special reference to European Studies. In particular he has published in the field of Icelandic and of Yugoslav studies, including the two relevant volumes in the World Bibliographical Series.

**Robert A. Myers** is Associate Professor of Anthropology in the Division of Social Sciences and Director of Study Abroad Programs at Alfred University, Alfred, New York. He has studied post-colonial island nations of the Caribbean and has spent two years in Nigeria on a Fulbright Lectureship. His interests include international public health, historical anthropology and developing societies. In addition to *Amerindians of the Lesser Antilles: a bibliography* (1981), *A Resource Guide to Dominica, 1493–1986* (1987) and numerous articles, he has compiled the World Bibliographical Series volumes on *Dominica* (1987) and *Nigeria* (1989).

**Ian Wallace** is Professor of German at the University of Bath. A graduate of Oxford in French and German, he also studied in Tübingen, Heidelberg and Lausanne before taking teaching posts at universities in the USA, Scotland and England. He specializes in contemporary German affairs, especially literature and culture, on which he has published numerous articles and books. In 1979 he founded the journal *GDR Monitor*, which he continues to edit under its new title *German Monitor*.

**Hans H. Wellisch** is Professor emeritus at the College of Library and Information Services, University of Maryland. He was President of the American Society of Indexers and was a member of the International Federation for Documentation. He is the author of numerous articles and several books on indexing and abstracting, and has published *The Conversion of Scripts* and *Indexing and Abstracting: an International Bibliography*. He also contributes frequently to *Journal of the American Society for Information Science, The Indexer* and other professional journals.

**Ralph Lee Woodward, Jr.** is Chairman of the Department of History at Tulane University, New Orleans, where he has been Professor of History since 1970. He is the author of *Central America, a Nation Divided*, 2nd ed. (1985), as well as several monographs and more than sixty scholarly articles on modern Latin America. He has also compiled volumes in the World Bibliographical Series on *Belize* (1980), *Nicaragua* (1983), and *El Salvador* (1988). Dr. Woodward edited the Central American section of the *Research Guide to Central America and the Caribbean* (1985) and is currently editor of the Central American history section of the *Handbook of Latin American Studies*.

VOLUME 130

# Argentina

Alan Biggins

*Compiler*

## CLIO PRESS

OXFORD, ENGLAND · SANTA BARBARA, CALIFORNIA
DENVER, COLORADO

© Copyright 1991 by Clio Press Ltd.

All rights reserved. No part of this publication may be reproduced, stored in any retrieval system, or transmitted in any form or by any means, electronic, mechanical, photocopying or otherwise, without the prior permission in writing of the publishers.

British Library Cataloguing in Publication Data

Biggins, Alan
Argentina. – (World bibliographical series; v. 130)
I. Title    II. Series
016.982

ISBN 1–85109–109–2

Clio Press Ltd.,
55 St. Thomas' Street,
Oxford OX1 1JG, England.

ABC-CLIO,
130 Cremona Drive,
Santa Barbara,
CA 93117, USA.

Designed by Bernard Crossland.
Typeset by Columns Design and Production Services Ltd, Reading, England.
Printed and bound in Great Britain by
Billing and Sons Ltd., Worcester.

# THE WORLD BIBLIOGRAPHICAL SERIES

This series, which is principally designed for the English speaker, will eventually cover every country (and many of the world's principal regions), each in a separate volume comprising annotated entries on works dealing with its history, geography, economy and politics; and with its people, their culture, customs, religion and social organization. Attention will also be paid to current living conditions – housing, education, newspapers, clothing, etc.– that are all too often ignored in standard bibliographies; and to those particular aspects relevant to individual countries. Each volume seeks to achieve, by use of careful selectivity and critical assessment of the literature, an expression of the country and an appreciation of its nature and national aspirations, to guide the reader towards an understanding of its importance. The keynote of the series is to provide, in a uniform format, an interpretation of each country that will express its culture, its place in the world, and the qualities and background that make it unique. The views expressed in individual volumes, however, are not necessarily those of the publisher.

## VOLUMES IN THE SERIES

1 *Yugoslavia*, John J. Horton
2 *Lebanon*, Shereen Khairallah
3 *Lesotho*, Shelagh M. Willet and David Ambrose
4 *Rhodesia/Zimbabwe*, Oliver B. Pollack and Karen Pollack
5 *Saudi Arabia*, Frank A. Clements
6 *USSR*, Anthony Thompson
7 *South Africa*, Reuben Musiker
8 *Malawi*, Robert B. Boeder
9 *Guatemala*, Woodman B. Franklin
10 *Pakistan*, David Taylor
11 *Uganda*, Robert L. Collison
12 *Malaysia*, Ian Brown and Rajeswary Ampalavanar
13 *France*, Frances Chambers
14 *Panama*, Eleanor DeSelms Langstaff
15 *Hungary*, Thomas Kabdebo
16 *USA*, Sheila R. Herstein and Naomi Robbins
17 *Greece*, Richard Clogg and Mary Jo Clogg
18 *New Zealand*, R. F. Grover
19 *Algeria*, Richard I. Lawless
20 *Sri Lanka*, Vijaya Samaraweera
21 *Belize*, Ralph Lee Woodward, Jr.
23 *Luxembourg*, Carlo Hury and Jul Christophory
24 *Swaziland*, Balam Nyeko

25 *Kenya*, Robert L. Collison
26 *India*, Brijen K. Gupta and Datta S. Kharbas
27 *Turkey*, Merel Güçlü
28 *Cyprus*, P. M. Kitromilides and M. L. Evriviades
29 *Oman*, Frank A. Clements
31 *Finland*, J. E. O. Screen
32 *Poland*, Richard C. Lewański
33 *Tunisia*, Allan M. Findlay, Anne M. Findlay and Richard I. Lawless
34 *Scotland*, Eric G. Grant
35 *China*, Peter Cheng
36 *Qatar*, P. T. H. Unwin
37 *Iceland*, John J. Horton
38 *Nepal*, John Whelpton
39 *Haiti*, Frances Chambers
40 *Sudan*, M. W. Daly
41 *Vatican City State*, Michael J. Walsh
42 *Iraq*, A. J. Abdulrahman
43 *United Arab Emirates*, Frank A. Clements
44 *Nicaragua*, Ralph Lee Woodward, Jr.
45 *Jamaica*, K. E. Ingram
46 *Australia*, I. Kepars
47 *Morocco*, Anne M. Findlay, Allan M. Findlay and Richard I. Lawless

*For Susan, Alistair and Laurence*

# Contents

## Contents

# Contents

# Contents

# Introduction

Argentina is Latin America's second largest and second most powerful nation, but it is not yet a grand player on the world stage, although it was once a considerable economic power. The country is perhaps least known for the spectacular range and beauty of its natural scenery, and perhaps best known for its folkloric manifestations, the gaucho and the tango, for its twin exports of beef and wheat, for the political excesses of the 1970s and for the Falklands War of 1982. Argentines have always felt themselves destined for greatness and, while they have at their disposal the most favourable natural resources imaginable, endemic political and institutional instability continually dashes their potential.

Argentina is a representative federal republic consisting of twenty-two provinces, the Federal District including the capital city of Buenos Aires, and the national territory of Tierra del Fuego. The President is nominated by an electoral college for a six-year term. The national parliament is composed of two houses: the Chamber of Deputies (254 members elected by universal suffrage for terms of four years) and a Senate (46 members, two Senators from each province elected by the provincial parliaments for nine-year terms). Ninety per cent of the population are officially Roman Catholic; a further two per cent of the population are Protestant and another two per cent Jewish (Buenos Aires has the second largest Jewish community in the Americas after New York).

Argentina is the third largest country in Latin America in terms of population, 32 millions, and is highly urbanized, with four-fifths living in cities of 100,000 or more and a third living in the city of Buenos Aires on the huge River Plate estuary. Between 1857 and 1930, over six million people emigrated to Argentina, most of them from

Western Europe (four-fifths from Italy and Spain alone), but also considerable numbers of Jews from Russia and Poland and Arabs from Syria and Lebanon. The country prides itself on its European heritage: there is a famous saying that an Argentine is an Italian who speaks Spanish and thinks he is English. But Argentina has another, less obvious, face. In the north, at least half the people are *mestizos*, two per cent of the population. Descendants of the 300,000 Indians at the time of the Conquest now make up less than one per cent of the total population; they live in small farming communities on the country's borders: the foothills of the Andes in the south, the Chaco and the northwest provinces of Salta and Jujuy. On the other hand, there remains little trace of the few thousand Negro slaves who were brought to serve as domestic servants and labourers during the colonial period. Buenos Aires is one of the great cosmopolitan cities of the world and its European architecture and culture have earned it the label 'the Paris of South America'. But the capital and other cities of the eastern seaboard are also surrounded by shanty-towns, known as *villas miserias*, inhabited by thousands of migrant workers from the interior and from neighbouring countries, attracted by the hope of finding work in service and manufacturing industries. There are great social and economic contrasts between the pampas and the interior provinces; in terms of population and economic development, Buenos Aires has long been as important as all the other regions combined.

Argentina has low birth and death rates and enjoys one of the best-developed health and social-security systems in Latin America. Infant mortality is low and life expectancy high; there is a high level of food consumption (Argentines eat a large amount of their own beef) and an above-average daily calorie intake, although malnutrition is common in the shanty-towns. Argentina has one of the highest adult-literacy levels in Latin America, but state education, free and compulsory up to the age of fourteen, has lost much of its earlier excellence, with high drop-out and truancy rates.

The land and climate are good and the country is self-sufficient in food and energy. The pampas produce the best wheat and cattle (sixty millions of them) anywhere in the world; sugar and tobacco thrive in the north, and the south has sheep and rich supplies of (largely untapped) minerals, including enough oil for the country's needs. Manufacturing industries produce iron and steel, cars, textiles, machinery and transport equipment, and industrial chemicals. Hydroelectric power supplies half the country's energy needs; there are two nuclear power stations and a third is due for completion in 1995. Most of Argentina's exports of wheat, maize, meat, wool, hides and skins, are sent to Europe, the rest of Latin America, the United

States, the Soviet Union, China and Japan. The country also has a well-educated and well-qualified labour force, and produces skilful doctors and engineers. Argentina's trades-union movement is well developed and independent, Peronist-dominated and highly bureaucratic. The country is distinguished in the arts and there has been a welcome resurgence in cultural activity since 1983. The works of prose writers Jorge Luis Borges, Julio Cortázar and Manuel Puig are known internationally. The Colón Theatre in Buenos Aires is the finest opera house in Latin America (and one of the greatest in the world), Alberto Ginastera a musical composer of international distinction, and tango-singer Carlos Gardel remembered for his later films made in Hollywood. Argentine sports figures are household names – racing drivers Juan Fangio and Carlos Reutemann, tennis players Guillermo Vilas and Gabriela Sabatini, footballer Diego Maradona.

**Geography**

Argentina presents a range of physical features and climates unrivalled anywhere in Latin America. It is the second largest country in South America after Brazil and the eighth largest in the world, with an area of 1,083,714 square miles, making it about seven-and-a-half times the size of Great Britain and a third the size of the United States. From north to south, wedge-shaped Argentina extends about 2,300 miles, from east to west some 1,000 miles. In addition, it claims some 481,750 square miles of islands in the south Atlantic (the Falkland Islands, South Georgia and South Sandwich Islands) and a segment of the Antarctic. It shares common boundaries with five countries: Chile to the west, Bolivia and Paraguay to the north, Brazil to the northeast and Uruguay to the east. Within these boundaries Argentina's climate and land types display great variety.

The country consists of four principal geographical regions. The core pampas region is a huge semi-circle of flat prairies with a radius of 500 miles in which the country's agricultural and manufacturing production is concentrated. It is a fertile plain with few rivers and almost no hills to break the monotony. The second region, the Northwest and Cuyo, contains mountain ranges which reach their highest point in Mount Aconcagua (nearly 23,000 feet), high plateaux and undulating hills and valleys. The third region is the Northeast, which includes the subtropical scrub forests of the Chaco, and Mesopotamia, a hot and rainy area lying between the rivers Uruguay and Paraná. One of the continent's most spectacular sights are the Iguazú Falls in the far corner of Misiones province on the border with

Brazil; at 230 feet the falls are slightly higher than Niagara and half as wide again. The fourth natural area comprises Patagonia and Tierra del Fuego. Patagonia stretches 1,000 miles from the Colorado river down to the Beagle Channel; a cold, rainy and windy region, it contains some fertile valleys, but the almost treeless vegetation consists largely of clumpy grass. Tierra del Fuego is an island of 15,000 square miles at the tip of South America; the eastern half belongs to Argentina, the western half to Chile. Argentine Tierra del Fuego contains the world's most southerly town, Ushuaia, and reaches its southernmost point in stormy Cape Horn.

## History

The name 'Argentina' (from the Latin *argentum*, silver) was used by the first Spanish explorers as a synonym for the River Plate (Río de la Plata), since they believed that it led to the silver mines later discovered in Upper Peru, modern Bolivia. Buenos Aires was settled permanently in 1580 and Argentina's northwest colonized simultaneously by Spaniards crossing the Andes from Chile and Peru. Until the creation of the Viceroyalty of the Río de la Plata – modern-day Argentina, Bolivia, Paraguay and Uruguay – in 1776, Argentina remained a neglected outpost of the Spanish empire, the northwest supplying food, horses and mules to Upper Peru, and Buenos Aires dependent for legal trade on the Viceroyalty of Peru while deriving much of its revenue from contraband. The invasions of Buenos Aires by British troops in 1806 and 1807 – they and their reinforcements were twice defeated by a local militia – were a most significant event in Argentine history: the citizens of Buenos Aires realized that the Spanish Crown could not defend them, and the brief British administration gave them a taste for free trade. On 25 May 1810 the Spanish Viceroy was deposed and an independent national government in a United Provinces of the River Plate declared.

But the country was torn by bitter rivalry between Buenos Aires and the provinces of the north and west: the former wanted to dominate a centralized ('unitarian') state, the latter wanted local autonomy within a 'federal' structure. Between 1828 and 1852, the country was ruled by the tyrant Juan Manuel de Rosas, *caudillo* (chieftain) of Buenos Aires province. In 1853 the Argentine Confederation, with its temporary capital in Paraná, enacted a national constitution, modelled on that of the United States of America; it has remained the country's basic set of laws. Buenos Aires joined the union in 1861.

The foundations of modern Argentina were laid between 1862 and 1880. Large-scale immigration was encouraged under the watchword 'to govern is to populate', at a time when the nascent agricultural economy was in great need of skilled labour, and foreign trade and investment fostered with a Europe that represented all that was 'civilized'. The country's population soared from 1,200,000 in 1852 to 8 millions in 1914. The introduction of the refrigerator ship in 1876 galvanized Argentina's modern meat industry; beef could now be shipped to Britain, then Argentina's greatest market, in exchange for Britain's manufactured goods. British engineers, financed by British capital, built and managed most of Argentina's public utilities, including the railway system which had the slaughterhouses, meat-packing plants and the port of Buenos Aires at its centre. By 1914 Argentina exported half the world's beef, making it the richest country in Latin America and the tenth richest in the world. The country was at the peak of its prosperity.

In 1916 Hipólito Yrigoyen, leader of the Radical Party, became Argentina's first universally elected president. His Unión Cívica Radical, founded in 1891, was the country's first political party to enjoy a mass following, that of middle-class urban immigrants. The military coup of 1930 marked the beginning of the long cycle of interventions in modern Argentine history by an increasingly politicized military establishment.

Among the group of army officers which seized power in 1943 was a young colonel, Juan Domingo Perón. He was appointed Minister of War and Vice-President of the republic; more significantly, he also became Minister for Labour and Social Welfare, a position he used to build up unprecedented support among the working class. He controlled the unions but gave the workers minimum wages and paid holidays, and also introduced long-overdue reforms in health care, state pensions and social security. The widowed Perón married Eva Duarte, an ambitious radio actress who became the perfect partner for him, combining feminine charm with ruthless demagoguery. 'Evita' won the hearts of the poorest people by building schools, hospitals and clinics, although much of the public and private funds she collected through her Social Welfare Foundation was spent extravagantly. She died of cancer in 1952 at the age of 33. Perón's first administration was a military–worker alliance in the classic fascist mould; after he was re-elected in 1951 he moved to the right, censoring the media, 'intervening' the universities, persecuting the churches and imprisoning, torturing and exiling his opponents. The armed forces removed him in September 1955.

Efforts were now made to 'de-Peronize' Argentina and weaken the Peronist grip on the unions, although the exiled Perón and the memory of 'saint' Evita remained powerful forces in Argentine politics over the next eighteen years. Stagnation, inflation and unemployment dogged the country from 1955 to the early 1970s; multinational, especially United States, companies began to dominate the economy. The late 1960s saw the beginnings of urban terrorism – political assassinations and kidnappings – by extreme left-wing, mostly middle-class, youths influenced by the Cuban Revolution. The two principal guerrilla groups were the Montoneros (representing the Peronist left) and the Trotskyite People's Revolutionary Army (ERP). In March 1973, the military called elections in which the Peronist Party was again allowed to stand. Perón's proxy, Héctor Cámpora, won and promptly stepped down to allow Perón to return and win fresh elections. Perón died in July 1974, at the age of 78, after only nine months as president, to be succeeded by his third wife and vice-president, María Estela (Isabel) Martínez de Perón, a former cabaret dancer. With the Peronist movement split into extreme left and right factions locked in civil war, and inflation out of control, the armed forces in 1976 forced Isabel to resign, an event which was greeted with almost universal relief.

A military junta began a 'process of national reorganization' to stamp out revolutionary Peronism. Political and trades-union activity, the media and higher education were strictly controlled, but it was the more extreme methods employed by the military that so shocked the world. In addition to those known killed, during the 1976-82 counterinsurgency 'crusade', between 10,000 and 15,000 people (some put the figure as high as 30,000) were held without trial, tortured, killed and their bodies disposed of. In most cases the authorities denied that they were holding any suspects at all; prisoners therefore simply 'disappeared' – Argentina has given the world the word *desaparecido*. Many thousands more went into exile.

In April 1982, the third junta leader, General Leopoldo F. Galtieri, tried to deflect criticism and exploit nationalist sentiments by invading the British Falkland Islands, which Argentina has claimed (this is said, not entirely jokingly, to be the one cause that all Argentines agree upon) as part of its territory since the *Islas Malvinas* were seized and settled by Britain in 1833. Two months later a British Task Force recaptured the islands. The Argentine military was discredited, Galtieri was hurriedly replaced by a caretaker president, and by October 1983 popular pressure had led to elections for a civilian government.

Raúl Alfonsín, a lawyer and leader of the Radical Party, was elected president. Democracy was restored; thousands of exiles returned from abroad. A commission was set up to investigate the deaths of civilians which had taken place during the 'process', and in 1985 the various junta leaders were tried and imprisoned for human-rights crimes (although Alfonsín later called a 'full stop' to further trials). His stabilization plans for controlling inflation failed as badly as the military's monetarist programme before him.

New and peaceful elections were held in May 1989; they were won by the Peronist Carlos Saúl Menem, a flamboyant second-generation Syrian who served two terms as governor of La Rioja province. He overturned his electioneering rhetoric and has astonished everyone by acting in a most un-Peronist way, declaring that Argentina will become a corporate capitalist coalition, and vowing to cut inflation and encourage economic growth with austerity measures. Perhaps his boldest initiative, apart from his promise to fight corruption at all levels of society and to reduce widespread tax evasion, has been to sell inefficient and loss-making state enterprises, thereby helping to reduce Argentina's longstanding foreign debt ($60b in early 1991). He has restored normal diplomatic and trading relations with Great Britain despite his previous threat to spill more blood in order to recapture the Falkland Islands. Like Alfonsín before him, Menem has called for national reconciliation on the question of human-rights abuses during the 'dirty war' in the late 1970s. Although he was himself imprisoned for five years by the military, he has pardoned the members of the 1976-83 juntas, the officers involved in military uprisings in 1987-88, and fifty guerrillas gaoled in the 1970s.

The country's future stability and prosperity depend more than ever before on the establishment of a solid consensus between the political parties, industrial and commercial employers, landowners, union leaders, the working people and, last but not least, the unpredictable military establishment. Only then will an Argentina tainted with the image of a politically immature and divided society attract the foreign investment it needs to help build a prosperous one. The armed forces are still the key ingredient and the risk of their intervening yet again will be prevented chiefly by the ability of the young democracy to succeed economically.

*The bibliography*

This bibliography attempts to give even coverage to a wide range of subjects on Argentine history, life and culture. Since it is *selective* the compiler's choice of items for inclusion has necessarily been very subjective. The table of contents follows the pattern set by earlier volumes in the World Bibliographical Series, with the addition of a number of sections and subsections of particular Argentine interest: the gaucho, the tango, the railways, the city of Buenos Aires, the Falkland Islands, the military, human rights, inflation and debt. There is a vast array of publications in English on Argentina in certain areas such as history, politics, the economy and literature;

accordingly, very few items in Spanish have been included in these sections, indicating only that the English-language literature is adequate as an introduction to their study, and not that Argentine titles are without merit. Spanish-language materials – nearly 340 main items – *have* been included when there were no or few equivalent studies in English. Although the compiler believes this to be a fair compromise in a work intended primarily for the English speaker, he hopes that the interested reader with Spanish will make the effort to seek out Argentine publications to supplement the works listed here. The section on science and technology is regrettably short since the area is peculiarly deficient in good general studies in both Spanish and English.

Wherever possible, recently published titles have been preferred. Of the 1350 main works recorded in the bibliography (over 250 more are referred to in the annotations), eighty per cent were published after 1960, and forty-three per cent since 1980. However, just over two hundred items (one-fifth of the total) published between 1900 and 1950 have been included where it was felt that their subject-matter, authoritativeness or historical interest were important. In addition, nearly fifty classic items published during the nineteenth century are listed, most of them in the section devoted to travellers' tales. One essential English-language work from 1774 (item no. 109) was included since this is also available in two twentieth-century reprint editions.

The compiler has chosen to end the History section at 1976, the year in which the second Peronist administration was ended by another military intervention. Studies of the period since 1976 will be found under Government and Politics, as will the related questions of human rights and the military institution itself. The bibliography went to press just as books and significant articles in English on the present administration of President Carlos Menem were being published. The first of these, a journal article which came to the compiler's attention too late to include as a separate entry, is mentioned in the annotation to item no. 599. A title's predominant subject has determined its place in the bibliography: hence agricultural history is to be found under Agriculture, urban population under Population, and so on. One area warrants a special note: the Falkland Islands, or Islas Malvinas as they are known in Argentina. There is a voluminous literature on the 1982 war and its aftermath, much of it concerned with the military campaign; the compiler was therefore placed in the unenviable position of having to choose what in his opinion were the dozen or so most representative titles to accompany his choice of works on the sovereignty issue.

The items in each section have been arranged alphabetically by title. Bibliographies have been placed in the final Bibliography section, not with their relevant subject sections. Theses and dissertations have not been included. Very little cross-referencing between sections has been made since it is expected that the table of contents and the subject index will guide the reader to the material on any particular topic.

*Acknowledgements*

Most of the material included in this bibliography was consulted in libraries belonging to the University of London: the British Library of Political and Economic Science, Institute of Latin American Studies, University College and University of London Library. More specialized material was located in a number of other libraries of the University: Institute of Advanced Legal Studies, Institute of Archaeology, Institute of Education, Institute of Historical Research, Heythrop College, King's College, London School of Hygiene and Tropical Medicine, School of Oriental and African Studies and Warburg Institute. Certain other specialized and rare items were available only in four branches of the British Library: British Museum (Natural History), Humanities and Social Sciences (British Museum Library), Information Sciences Service (Library Association) and the Aldwych and Holborn branches of the Science Reference and Information Service. Other libraries in London whose collections proved invaluable were the Hispanic and Luso-Brazilian Council, Royal Geographical Society, Royal Institute of British Architects and Wellcome Institute for the History of Medicine. I wish to record my thanks to the staffs of these libraries, and in particular to Claire Diamond, Alison Hill, Patricia Noble and Robin Price. The few items not traced in London libraries were obtained through the United Kingdom's excellent inter-library-loan system. The British Library Document Supply Centre, Boston Spa, supplied a number of books and photocopies from its own stock and secured loans from the Bodleian Library, Oxford, and from Cambridge University. Finally, some material was borrowed directly from other British university libraries, notably Essex and Glasgow.

A number of academic colleagues advised me on the choice of titles for inclusion in the bibliography, and gave me the benefit of their expert subject knowledge: Dr Roger Gravil, Professor William V. Jackson, Dr John King, Professor John Lynch, Dr Oliver Marshall, Ing. Juan Carlos Nicolau, Dr George Philip, Dr Ian Roxborough and Dr David Sheinin (who also read and commented on several sections of the manuscript). Thanks are also due to the following for providing details of their own and other publications:

## Introduction

Mr Nick Caistor, Dr Valerie Fifer, Mr Dereck Foster, Mr George Gibson of the Anglo-Argentine Society, Mr Andrew Graham-Yooll and Mrs Gillian Peiro. The map was drawn by Mr Tim Aspden, Department of Geography, University College London. Miss Valerie Cooper read the manuscript and made many helpful recommendations concerning the text. I owe an enormous debt of gratitude above all to the late Dr Harold Blakemore, former Secretary of the Institute of Latin American Studies, University of London, and compiler of the *Chile* volume in the World Bibliographical Series. He encouraged and guided me from start to finish, and provided me with notes on a hundred titles, parts of which I have incorporated in the annotations. Any errors or omissions remaining in the bibliography, in spite of the help offered so generously by all of the above, are my responsibility. Dr Robert Neville and his staff at the Clio Press were extremely patient and cooperative, especially during the later stages of the project. My final thanks are to my family, whose support meant everything.


*Alan Biggins*
*London*
*May 1991*

# The Country and its People

1 **Argentina.**
Nick Caistor. Oxford: Macmillan Children's Reference, 1990. 96p. map.
(World in View).
This is the most recent, and perhaps the best, introduction to Argentina for younger
readers. Its nine chapters cover geography, prehistory and history to 1989, agriculture,
industry, transport, 'Argentina today' (work in the city and on an *estancia*, housing,
health and welfare, youth, education, religion), sports and the arts, and prospects for
Argentina's future. The colour and black-and-white photographs are well chosen and
of good quality.

2 **Argentina.**
W. A. Hirst. London: T. Fisher Unwin, 1910. 308p. bibliog. (The South
American Series).
The first nine chapters summarize Argentine history and geography. The following
thirteen chapters look at Buenos Aires and other parts of the country (Bahía Blanca,
Patagonia, Paraná, Rosario, Santa Fe, the Chaco and the cities of the north),
'Argentine life in town and country', political conditions, the armed forces, religion,
education, journalism and literature, industry, agriculture and livestock farming,
finance and commerce, and the railways. There is a final chapter of information for
English travellers. Sixty-four photographs are included.

3 **Argentina.**
Marion Morrison, illustrated by Ann Savage. Basingstoke, England:
Macmillan Children's Books, 1989. 46p. maps.
This is an attractively produced introduction to the country for schoolchildren,
illustrated with many colour photographs and drawings, covering geography, flora and
fauna, history, industry, transport, family life, 'life on the ranch', food and shopping,
leisure activities, schooling, the arts and the media.

## The Country and its People

4 **Argentina.**
George Pendle. London: Adam & Charles Black, 1957. 88p. map.
bibliog. (The Lands and Peoples Series).
A perceptive little book for younger readers, still suitable despite its date. Its nineteen
chapters deal selectively with the land and people, history (colonial, the English
invasions of 1806-7, San Martín's campaigns, Yrigoyen and Perón), British and Welsh
settlers, the pampa (with an excursion to the town of Pilar), the city and suburbs of
Buenos Aires, the River Paraná, Misiones, Tierra del Fuego – and the Falkland
Islands, which Argentina claims as part of its territory.

5 **Argentina: a country study.**
Edited by James D. Rudolph. Washington, DC: American University,
Foreign Area Studies Division, 1985. 3rd ed. 402p. maps. bibliog. (Area
Handbook Series).
Earlier editions of this 'attempt to treat in a compact and objective manner the
dominant social, political, and national security aspects of contemporary Argentine
society' were published in 1969 and 1974. After a brief country profile, signed chapters
deal in depth with the historical setting, society and environment, the economy,
government and politics, and national security. The last chapter discusses the armed
forces, nuclear development and capabilities, the war against subversion and the
Falklands War. This is perhaps the best single introduction to the country.

6 **Argentina and Chile.**
Brian Elliott. South Melbourne, Australia; London: Macmillan, 1988.
30p. maps. (The Americas).
This is a very basic children's introduction to the two countries, in parallel layout on
each page. There are fourteen sections, with good photographs, dealing with
geography, flora and fauna, the people and their language, history, constitution and
government, industry, trade and commerce, transport and communications, agriculture, education, religion, architecture and housing, sports and recreation, culture and
festivals.

7 **Argentina and her people of to-day: an account of the customs,
characteristics, amusements, history and advancement of the Argentinians,
and the development and resources of their country.**
Nevin O. Winter. Boston, Massachusetts: L. C. Page, 1911. 421p. map.
After describing Buenos Aires and the regions, the author, who uses both first-hand
knowledge of Argentina and 'the works of the leading writers upon that country',
devotes chapters to the people at play, education and the arts, religion, industry and
trade, the railways and the armed forces. 'At the present time Argentina stands at the
head of all the republics south of the United States in commercial importance . . . The
people are energetic, resourceful and ambitious.'

8 **Argentina and Uruguay.**
Gordon Ross. London: Methuen, 1917. 308p. map.
The author was a financial editor of the Buenos Aires *Standard*. Fourteen chapters
deal with history and politics; immigration, racial elements and social conditions;
national, provincial and municipal government; Buenos Aires; finance and commerce;

railways and ports; the provinces and National Territories; agriculture and forestry; literature and the arts. There are very brief sections on Montevideo and Uruguay's interior. The book is illustrated with twelve photographs.

9   **Argentina 1880.**
Buenos Aires: SS&CC Ediciones, 1982. 120p.

One hundred full-page sepia photographs from private collections depict 'city and country' (mainly buildings, usually in Buenos Aires) and 'characters and customs' (including gauchos, occupations – water-vendor, orange-seller, washerwoman – and General Roca on his conquest of the desert), between 1870 and 1890. The photographers, where known, were H. G. Olds, E. C. Moody, Christiano Junior, Samuel Boole, Antonio Pozzo and others. See also *Imágenes del Río de la Plata: crónica de la fotografía rioplatense, 1840-1940.*

10   **Argentina in pictures.**
Prepared by E. W. Egan.   Minneapolis, Minnesota: Lerner
Publications, Geography Department, 1988. rev. ed. 64p. maps. (Visual
Geography Series).

Intended for classroom use, this is described as an 'introduction to the geography, history, government, people, and economy of the second largest South American country'. An informative text accompanies eighty-three attractive colour and black-and-white photographs.

11   **Argentina, 1930-1960.**
Compiled by Jorge A. Paíta, with the collaboration of Julia Helena
Acuña (et al.).   Buenos Aires: Sur, 1961. 447p.

High-quality essays on all aspects of Argentine life during the period under review, by noted contributors, including politics (Roberto Cortés Conde), agriculture (José A. Martínez de Hoz), industry and finance (Walter Beveraggi Allende), the sciences (José Babini) and mass culture (José Enrique Miguens). Other chapters cover population, foreign relations, education, public services, the arts, religion and ethics.

12   **Argentina, Paraguay & Uruguay.**
Axel Hornos.   Camden, New Jersey: Thomas Nelson, 1969. 223p. map.
bibliog. (World Neighbors).

The section on Argentina, with seventy-two photographs, fills one-half of this guide for the younger reader. Descriptions of Buenos Aires, the pampas, Mendoza, the northern provinces and Patagonia are interspersed with some history of each region and interviews with 'today's Argentines': students, typical families, farmers and *estancieros* (estate-owners), an engineer, a teacher, and the owner of a *rotisería*.

13   **Argentina, past & present.**
W. H. Koebel.   London: Adam & Charles Black, 1914. 2nd ed. 465p.
map.

William Henry Koebel was a prolific author of books on Argentina, Chile, Paraguay and Uruguay. This follows the familiar pattern of British guidebooks on Argentina during the period of expansion before 1930: a regional tour and analyses of Argentine social and cultural life, politics and economics, with usually a chapter on the British community and its contribution to Argentine development, accompanied by a large number of photographs. The author also published *Modern Argentina: the El Dorado of today; with notes on Uruguay and Chile* (London, 1907) and *The new Argentina* (New York, 1923).

14 **Argentina: physical features, natural resources, means of communication, manufactures and industrial development.**
   George J. Mills.   London: Pitman, 1914. 209p. maps. (South American Handbooks).

Although the purpose of the volume is not stated, it was clearly intended as a practical guidebook for the British or North American businessman or traveller. Sixteen chapters describe the country's history, constitution, geography and natural history, population, commercial laws, finance and banking, inland transport and communications, ports and harbours, agriculture and forestry, mining, exports and imports. There is an appendix of useful information and a list of principal towns and cities.

15 **The Argentine Republic: its physical features, history, fauna, flora, geology, literature & commerce.**
   A. Stuart Pennington.   London: Stanley Paul, 1910. 352p. map.

The book, by a twenty-year resident of the country, is described as a 'collection of facts and not a mere record of feelings or opinions', on history, geography and geology, society, government, flora and fauna, industry and agriculture, Buenos Aires and the provinces, 'life in Argentina', and a good chapter on literature, journalism and politics, which quotes a number of poems in the original Spanish.

16 **The Argentine Republic, written in German by Richard Napp, assisted by several fellow-writers, for the Central Argentine Commission on the Centenary Exhibition at Philadelphia.**
   Richard Napp.   Buenos Aires: Sociedad Anónima, 1876. 463p. maps.

An encyclopaedic but unillustrated survey of the country in twenty-five chapters, covering history, geography, geology, flora and fauna, mineral resources, industry, agriculture, communications, the economy, commerce, education and the press, scientific institutions, religion, the armed forces, the Indian population, immigration and agricultural colonization, and the provinces.

17 **The Argentines: how they live and work.**
   Dereck H. N. Foster.   Newton Abbot, England: David & Charles; New York: Praeger, 1972. 150p. map. (How They Live and Work).

This is one of the better introductory guides to Argentina for both young people and adults, although obviously dated in parts. It covers geography, history, population, religion, federal and local government, currency, taxation, the police, justice, the armed forces, housing, food and drink, social security and health, the modern economy, education, transport, the arts and recreation. There is also a short (and mildly humorous) section of 'hints for visitors'.

18 **Cómo somos los argentinos.** (What we Argentines are like.)
Delfín Leocadio Garasa. *Journal of Inter-American Studies*, vol. 7,
no. 3 (July 1965), p. 363-74.
An impartial short essay on the national character by an Argentine academic, who says
that the average Argentine is prone to mental laziness, lack of foresight, melancholy,
nostalgia, vanity, nationalism, pride, scepticism and complaining. He is also non-
individualistic, sensitive, generous, elegant, fond of sports and gambling, 'an enemy of
violence' and 'not given to noisy shows of emotion'. Argentina is an insecure nation
because it needs time to digest and assimilate its imported culture. If the intention was
to describe Argentines to an English-speaking audience it is a pity that the article was
not translated.

19 **Handbook of the River Plate; comprising the Argentine Republic,**
**Uruguay and Paraguay.**
Michael George Mulhall, Edward T. Mulhall. Buenos Aires: Standard
Printing Office; London: Edward Stanford, 1863-92. maps.
E. T. Mulhall emigrated to Argentina from Ireland in 1855 and his brother followed in
1861. They founded a newspaper, *The Standard*, in 1861, which they used to attract
British capital and immigrants to the country. The six editions of the *Handbook* had
the same purpose (see the many advertisements at the back). Besides being a useful
guidebook to the regions, it contained valuable information for the potential investor
on agriculture, banking, commerce and mining.

20 **El hombre que está solo y espera.** (The man who stands alone and waits.)
Raúl Scalabrini Ortiz. Buenos Aires: Tráfico, 1931. 200p.
The author described this famous essay as a 'psychological and aesthetic guide to
Buenos Aires': the musings of a *porteño* (Buenos Aires man), standing on a street
corner 'between Corrientes and Esmeralda streets', on the Argentine character
(individualistic and egocentric), friendship, women, the life of an immigrant in the
capital, language, politics and (adumbrating Scalabrini's future nationalistic writings)
foreign investment. The title is teasingly ambiguous, since *espera* can also mean
'hopes'. There have been many reprints.

21 **Illustrated descriptive Argentina.**
Henry Stephens. New York: Knickerbocker Press, 1917. 763p. map.
This is a useful compilation of 377 black-and-white photographs arranged by province
and showing mainly public buildings, monuments and street scenes. Some of the
captions are valuable but many could have benefited from expansion. Most of the
photographs were taken by the author; the rest are by H. G. Olds ('the pioneer
landscape photographer of Buenos Aires'), Chute & Brooks of Rosario and A. A.
Kirwin of Tucumán.

22 **Inside South America.**
John Gunther. London: Hamish Hamilton, 1966. 610p. maps. bibliog.
There are three penetrating chapters on Argentina. 'Backdrop to Argentina'
summarizes the country's history to 1943, geography, population, 'how Argentina
differs from Brazil', the economy and national sensitiveness. 'From the Colonel to the
General' completes the history between Perón ('a combination of idealism and

5

trickery') and Onganía. 'Buenos Aires' describes the city, the *porteño* character and language, a 'handful' of other cities (Rosario, San Carlos de Bariloche, Salta, Córdoba), foreign policy, the Communists, 'lords of the land and other groups' (the Church and the Army), labour and trade unionism, and meetings with a student, an American banker and Jorge Luis Borges.

## 23 An introduction to Argentina.
Robert J. Alexander. London: Pall Mall Press; New York: Praeger, 1969. 197p. map. bibliog.

A comprehensive introduction to the country's geography, history (emphasizing the modern period since the first Perón administration), economy, politics and government, people and society, education, the arts and entertainment, and international relations. The author concludes optimistically: 'Argentina may well become a country admired and studied as an example of how to resolve grave economic, social, and political problems rather than as a case study of errors and evils to be avoided.'

## 24 The land and people of Argentina.
Elvajean Hall. Philadelphia; New York: J. P. Lippincott, 1960. 128p. map. (Portraits of the Nations Series).

The first fourteen chapters provide an elementary view of Argentina's geography and wildlife, and of significant events in Argentina's history; the last seven chapters look at aspects of the gaucho, life on an *estancia*, Buenos Aires, family life, education, holidays and recreation.

## 25 Latin America and the Caribbean: a handbook.
Edited by Claudio Véliz. London: Anthony Blond, 1968. 840p. maps. bibliog.

In part one, James C. Hunt (Argentina, p. 4-20) summarizes the country's history to 1966 and the modern economy, and provides a short directory of basic information. There is much on Argentina in the following four sections dealing with politics and international relations, economics (including a useful case study, 'The industrialization of Argentina', p. 597-604, by Ezequiel Gallo and Jorge Katz, covering 1870-1965), social background and contemporary arts.

## 26 Let's go to Argentina.
Keith Lye. London: Franklin Watts, 1986. 32p. map.

Twenty-eight well-chosen photographs illustrate an attractive junior text covering geography, energy, agriculture, industry, Buenos Aires, Salta, Mar del Plata, Iguazú, Lake Nahuel Huapí, education and sport. There is also a section on the Falkland Islands.

## 27 Let's visit Argentina.
Garry Lyle, John C. Caldwell. London: Burke, 1983. 96p. map.

This is a well-written text for the older primary-school pupil. Three chapters deal with Argentina's history to 1982, two with regional geography, and the remainder describe society and modern life in Argentina (education, religion, food and sports). The thirty-eight photographs are rather poor.

28 **Pepe of Argentina.**
Betty Cavanna, photographs by George Russell Harrison. London:
Chatto & Windus, 1962. 71p. (Around the World Today Books).
Teenage Pepe lives in a two-room brick house in a suburb of Córdoba with his parents,
sister and two brothers. Pepe is seen spending his habitual weekend at his
grandmother's farm, at school, and working as a kitchen boy at a summer school in
San Carlos de Bariloche. After much debate about his future career, he decides that he
will take over the the farm when he is ready.

29 **¿Qué es la Argentina?** (This is Argentina.)
Guillermo Ara, Romulado Brughetti (et al.). Buenos Aires:
Columba, 1970. 362p. (Colección Esquemas, 100).
A basic introduction to the country – economy, religion, education, art and
literature, philosophy, science, folklore – by nine Argentine specialists in their
respective subjects, illustrated by thirty-one photographs. The prologue is by Jorge
Luis Borges.

30 **Ramón writes.**
Basil Thomson. Buenos Aires: Buenos Aires Herald, 1979. 160p.
These are the fictitious letters of 'a fairly advanced and confident but careless student'
of English, written in a hilarious Spanglish which the author says 'in those days was
referred to as Irish-Porteño', or 'Irish-Argentinisms'. Just over 150 Ramón 'letters'
appeared sporadically in the *Buenos Aires Herald*, Argentina's English-language daily,
between October 1949 and December 1976, and followed his progress as 'student,
would-be playboy, lover, family man, estanciero, dreamer and reluctant worker'.
There are eleven cartoons by Peter Woolcock and an appreciation of Basil Thomson,
who died in 1977, by Robert Cox, former editor of the *Herald*. The author considers
that the two classic Ramonisms are 'it touches to me' ('it is my turn to . . .') and 'we
pinched gum' ('our car had a puncture').

31 **The River Plate Republics: Argentina, Paraguay, Uruguay.**
J. Halcro Ferguson and the editors of *Life*. New York: Time-Life
Books, 1965. 160p. maps. bibliog. (Life World Library).
An excellent collection of black-and-white photographs is complemented by an
informative text covering history, politics, the economy and the arts by Ferguson, a
former Latin American correspondent of the London *Observer*. Just two chapters out
of ten on these 'three nations linked by great rivers' are devoted to Paraguay and
Uruguay.

32 **The South American sketches of R. B. Cunninghame Graham.**
Selected and edited, with an introduction, notes, glossary, and
bibliography, by John Walker. Norman, Oklahoma: University of
Oklahoma Press, 1978. 292p. bibliog.
Cunninghame Graham (1852-1936), horseman, politician, linguist and writer, was the
son of an aristocratic Scottish soldier and a Spanish mother, and a friend of W. H.
Hudson and Joseph Conrad. In 1870, when only seventeen, he set out on an
unsuccessful ranching venture in Argentina, where he acquired the material for his
future writings. Thirty of his sketches and short stories (sixteen set in Argentina, the

rest in Uruguay, Paraguay, Brazil, Colombia and Venezuela), depicting gauchos, Indians and other pampas characters, are here reprinted from eleven of his published collections. Graham died on a final pilgrimage to Buenos Aires at the age of eighty-four. A. F. Tschiffely (see *This way southward: a journey through Patagonia and Tierra del Fuego*) wrote an affectionate life, *Don Roberto* (London: Heinemann, 1937).

## 33 Those perplexing Argentines.
James Bruce. New York: Longmans, Green, 1953. 362p.

'No other country in Latin America is more important to the United States today than Argentina.' Bruce, who was US ambassador to Argentina, 1947-49, here presents a generally sympathetic picture of the Argentine people, 'their collective personality, as it were'. After an assessment of the Argentine character, other chapters deal with government and politics, Buenos Aires and other cities, immigration, labour, agriculture and industry, the gaucho, the landowners and the middle class, marriage and the family, the Church, education, the press, arts and recreation, and international relations, with special reference to the United States.

## 34 The Times book on Argentina.
London: Times Publishing Company, 1927. 332p. map.

Published in the year that British diplomatic representation in Argentina was raised to embassy status, and two years after the Prince of Wales's visit to the country, this describes itself as 'a small volume containing essential data relating to the country's principal features – geographical, political, financial, productive, industrial and commercial'. The text is printed in double columns and is packed full of information. There are fourteen plates and many tables.

## 35 Twentieth century impressions of Argentina: its history, people, commerce, industries, and resources.
Director-in-chief, Reginald Lloyd. London: Lloyd's Greater Britain Publishing Co., 1911. 850p. maps.

This is a deluxe oversized volume, with hundreds of illustrations, published to commemorate Argentina's centenary. Seventy-one chapters, some signed, of between one and ten pages, describe every aspect of the land, people, political and social institutions, economic life and pastimes.

## 36 X-ray of the pampa.
Ezequiel Martínez Estrada, translated by Alain Swietlicki. Austin, Texas; London: University of Texas Press, 1971. 415p. (Texas Pan American Series).

Martínez Estrada (1895-1964), an essayist, poet, novelist and playwright, originally published *Radiografía de la pampa* in 1933. Thomas F. McGann writes in his introduction: 'As an X-ray strikes through all human substance, so this great book . . . penetrates the experience of the people of Argentina'. As 'part history, part essay in social psychology, part prophecy', this legendary attack on the social, cultural and political dislocation of the early 1930s is still evoked as a valid statement on today's Argentina.

# Geography

## General

37  **Argentina.**
Richard P. Momsen. Garden City, New York: Nelson Doubleday,
1970. 64p. maps. (American Geographical Society. Around the World
Program).
This is a brief geography textbook suitable for shoolchildren. Part one summarizes the
country's history and then looks at agriculture in general, the railways and the province
of Buenos Aires. Part two takes a region-by-region approach. There are twenty-eight
colour plates.

38  **La Argentina: geografía general y los marcos regionales.** (Argentina:
a general and regional geography.)
Edited by Juan A. Roccatagliata. Buenos Aires: Grupo Editorial
Planeta, 1988. 783p. maps. bibliog.
A good modern economic geography – detailed, comprehensive, well illustrated and
documented – by a team of expert Argentine authorities, including Raúl C. Rey
Balmaceda. The economy, population, natural resources, agriculture, industry,
urbanization, transport and communications, trade and commerce are given a general
treatment in part one and regional in part two.

39  **La Argentina: suma de geografía.** (Argentina: a complete geography.)
Edited by Francisco de Aparicio, Horacio A. Difrieri. Buenos Aires:
Ediciones Peuser, 1958-63. 9 vols. maps. bibliog.
A monumental, encyclopaedic treatment of the country's geography, printed clearly
with hundreds of maps, diagrams, photographs and facsimiles. Volume one reviews the
historical literature, the general territory, regional geology and natural resources;
volume two covers climate, hydrography, the sea and coasts; volume three orography,
phytogeography and zoogeography; volume four soils and agriculture; volume five

9

flora, fauna, forests and natural parks; volume six mining, industry and trade; volume seven the population, urbanization, rural settlement and transport; volume eight a succinct history of Argentina's development, health and nutrition, cartography and toponymy; volume nine the urbanization of Buenos Aires and other cities, geomagnetism, sixty-one aerial photographs and an index to the whole work.

### 40 The Argentine Republic: its development and progress.
Pierre Denis, translated by Joseph McCabe. London; New York: T. Fisher Unwin, 1922. 296p. maps. bibliog.

An introduction to the regional economic geography of the country, in which the author has 'endeavoured to indicate the essential aspects of colonization in modern Argentina: the conquest of the soil by man, the exploitation of its natural resources, the development of agriculture and cattle-breeding, and the growth of the population and enlargement of the urban centres'. This was an outstanding study in its day.

### 41 The climate of Argentina, Paraguay and Uruguay.
Fritz Prohaska. In: *Climates of Central and South America*. Edited by Werner Schwertdfeger. Amsterdam; Oxford; New York: Elsevier Scientific Publishing, 1976, p. 13-112. maps. bibliog. (World Survey of Climatology, vol. 12).

The following aspects are discussed for each of the principal regions of Argentina: wind, cloudiness, duration of sunshine, global radiation, temperature, humidity, precipitation and thunderstorms. There are fifty-four tables and thirteen figures.

### 42 Climate of the Argentine Republic.
Walter G. Davis. Buenos Aires: Printing Office of the Argentine Meteorological Office, 1910. 111p. maps.

Davis, then head of Argentina's National Meteorological Office, discusses the country's climate according to four climatic zones (Littoral, Mediterranean, Andean and Patagonian): atmospheric pressure, temperature, rain, humidity, evaporation, wind, cloudiness and the state of the sky. There are about a hundred tables in the text and an appendix of forty-four maps, graphs and bar charts.

### 43 Description géographique et statistique de la Confédération Argentine.
(Geographical and statistical description of the Argentine Confederation.)
Jean-Antoine Victor Martin de Moussy. Paris: Librairie de Firmin Didot, 1860-73. 3 vols and atlas.

The French geographer Martin de Moussy lived in Argentina from 1841 until his death in 1869. His detailed but occasionally unreliable geography and statistical summary of what was then known as the Argentine Confederation (1853-62) deals with hydrography, orography, geology and mineralogy, climate, vegetation and agriculture (volume one), fauna, population (including physiology, pathology and hygiene), industry and commerce, communications, government and administration, law, religion and education (volume two), a detailed survey of the provinces under the above categories and a collection of historical documents, 1500-1864 (volume three). The dense text is difficult to read and there are unfortunately very few tables.

44   **Geografía de la República Argentina.** (Geography of Argentina.)
     Federico A. Daus, with the collaboration of Roberto García Gache,
     cartography by José Cantos.   Buenos Aires: Angel Estrada, 1954.
     2 vols. maps.

This is a sound descriptive physical geography, though obviously dated in its economic
geography, containing many maps, figures and (poorly reproduced) photographs.
Published in the same year, a comprehensive geographical dictionary whose population
data are based on the 1947 census is: *Diccionario geográfico argentino* (Buenos Aires:
Instituto Geográfico Militar, 1954. 8 vols).

45   **The grasslands of Latin America.**
     G. M. Roseveare.   Aberystwyth, Wales: Imperial Bureau of Pastures
     and Field Crops, 1948. 291p. maps. bibliog. (Bulletin, 36).

Argentina figures largely in this study of natural grasslands and grazings, plant cover,
soils, climate and stockraising. There are separate sections on the Humid Pampa, the
western dry Pampa and *monte* (scrubland), Entre Ríos, Corrientes, the Chaco and
Patagonia. There is an index of grass genera and species.

46   **International river boundaries in the Argentine Republic.**
     Alfredo de las Carreras.   *International Relations*, vol. 9, no. 1 (May
     1987), p. 56-63. bibliog.

Noting that almost all of Argentina's borders have been established by reference to
geographical landmarks, and all by treaty or arbitration, the author deals in turn with
the River Plate basin (serving as Argentina's boundary with Uruguay), the River
Uruguay (Brazil and Uruguay), the Paraná (Paraguay), the Paraguay (Paraguay), the
Pilcomayo (Paraguay and Bolivia), rivers of the Andes mountain range and the glaciers
in the south (Chile), and other coterminous rivers.

47   **Latin America.**
     Preston E. James, C. W. Minkel, assisted by Eileen W. James.   New
     York; Chichester, England; Brisbane, Australia; Toronto; Singapore:
     Wiley, 1986. 5th ed. 578p. maps. bibliog.

The chapter on Argentina (p. 416-49) is an excellent introduction to the country's
physical, economic, political and social geography, arranged by main regions: the
Northwest, Mesopotamia, the Chaco, Patagonia and the Humid Pampa.

48   **Latin America: a regional geography.**
     Gilbert J. Butland.   London: Longman, 1972. 3rd ed. 464p. maps.
     bibliog. (Geographies: an Intermediate Series).

Part four of this student geography deals with the River Plate republics. Chapter
eighteen (p. 313-53) treats Argentina region by region (Northwest, Chaco and
Northeast, Pampa and Entre Ríos, Patagonia), subdivided by climatic variations and
economic development.

49 **Latin America: an economic and social geography.**
John P. Cole. London: Butterworths, 1975. 2nd ed. 470p. maps.
bibliog.
In contrast to most geographies of the country, the chapter on Argentina (p. 316-38) is
organized by theme and not by region: demographic and physical features, agriculture,
energy, mining and industry, regions and regional problems, and future prospects.

50 **Latin America: countrysides and united regions.**
Robert S. Platt. New York; London: Whittlesey House, 1943. 564p.
maps.
In a collection of 'simple field studies' carried out in 1930 and all published previously
in various journals, Argentina is represented (p. 353-88) by six: two *estancias* and an
immigrant farm on the humid pampa, an orchard in the Paraná Delta, a sheep ranch
on the dry pampa of northern Patagonia, and a vineyard in Mendoza.

51 **The River Plate republics.**
J. Colin Crossley. In: *Latin America: geographical perspectives.*
Edited by Harold Blakemore, Clifford T. Smith. London; New York:
Methuen, 1983, p. 383-455. 2nd ed. maps. bibliog.
The chapter is predominantly about Argentina, with only small sections on Uruguay
and Paraguay, and adopts a thematic and chronological, rather than a regional,
approach: colonial period to 1852; the integration of Argentina into the world
economy, 1852-1930; changes in demography, agriculture and industry, 1930-60; the
move towards balanced development after 1960 (demography, energy, transport,
industry, agriculture and land use, and innovations such as mechanization and soil
management).

52 **South America.**
David C. Money. London: University Tutorial Press, 1976. 6th ed.
331p. maps. bibliog. (Advanced Level Geography Series).
A good introductory text dealing with 'each country in its natural setting, describing its
resources and man's development of these resources'. Argentina (p. 166-207) is divided
into the following sections: broad physical divisions, climates and vegetation, peoples
and settlement and the regions (including, inevitably, the Falkland Islands). There are
fourteen maps, fifteen tables and six plates.

53 **South America.**
Arthur S. Morris. London: Hodder & Stoughton, 1987. 3rd ed. 285p.
maps. bibliog.
Two short chapters on Argentina (p. 128-50) begin with an introduction to the physical
geography and the historical pattern of land settlement and economic development,
and go on to describe the regions: Buenos Aires and the Pampas area, Patagonia,
Cuyo, the Northwest, Chaco and the Northeast. Subjects covered uniformly within
region are the modern economy, agriculture, urban centres and industry. There is also
a short survey of regional planning.

# Regional

54 **The Argentine Colorado – interprovincial rivalries over water resources.**
Arthur S. Morris. *Scottish Geographical Magazine*, vol. 94, no. 3 (Dec. 1978), p. 169-80. maps.

Five provinces (Buenos Aires, La Pampa, Neuquén, Río Negro and Mendoza) share the thousand-kilometre-long River Colorado along its course from the Andes to the Atlantic. The article describes interprovincial rivalries over rights to water since 1911, notably upstream Mendoza province's desire to divert the river for its own irrigation and power needs, an issue over which the national government had to arbitrate in 1976. The water use of each of the five provinces is discussed.

55 **The cultural determinants of entrepreneurship and economic development: a case study of Mendoza Province, Argentina, 1861-1914.**
William J. Fleming. *Journal of Economic History*, vol. 39, no. 1 (March 1979), p. 211-24.

Examines the role played by the extended family, individualism and the patron–client relationship on the one hand, and the entrepreneurial class on the other, in the economic development of Mendoza. The author concludes that 'the elite provided the kind of exemplary commitment to economic growth, the government added the supportive public policies, and the society in general demonstrated that ability to initiate and accept change . . . essential to modernization and development'. For a wider consideration of the regional geography of the Cuyo region, see his *Region versus nation: Cuyo in the crosscurrents of Argentine development, 1861-1914* (Tempe, Arizona: Arizona State University, Center for Latin American Studies, 1987. 82p.).

56 **The development of the upper valley of the Río Negro and its periphery within the Comahue region, Argentina.**
Mabel Manzanal, César A. Vapñarsky. In: *Small and intermediate urban centres: their role in regional and national development in the Third World.* Edited by Jorge E. Hardoy, David Satterthwaite. London; Sydney; Auckland, New Zealand; Toronto: Hodder & Stoughton in association with the International Institute for Environment and Development, 1986, p. 18-79. maps. bibliog.

The Comahue region encompasses the provinces of Río Negro and Neuquén and the county of Patagones in Buenos Aires Province. The chapter describes population concentration and economic development in an intensively cultivated and irrigated strip of 700 square kilometres, the counties of General Roca and Confluencia in the Upper Valley of Río Negro and Neuquén, between 1879 and 1980. The Upper Valley's northwest periphery is dominated by two major urban centres of oil and gas exploration, Viedma and Carmen de Patagones.

57 **Development strategy for Cuyo, Argentina.**
William V. Ackerman. *Annals of the Asociation of American Geographers*, vol. 65, no. 1 (March 1965), p. 36-47. maps.

Measuring economic activity, housing quality and internal migration indices to determine the state of development of the two provinces of Cuyo (Mendoza and San Juan), the author finds that the province of Mendoza is better developed and proposes that other development axes for Mendoza should be centred on San Rafael/General Alvear, San Martín and Tinuyán; and that, since San Juan province has many economically lagging departments, planning for northern Cuyo should be organized around Greater San Juan.

58 **Historia de la provincia de Buenos Aires: su panorama de 460 años, 1516-1978.** (History of the province of Buenos Aires, 1516-1978.)
Exequiel C. Ortega. Buenos Aires: Editorial Plus Ultra, 1978. 333p. maps. bibliog. (Historia de Nuestras Provincias, 4).

A chronological, geographical history, charted by twenty-two good maps, of the gradual evolution of the more than 120 *partidos* (districts or counties) of the province of Buenos Aires beyond the federal capital.

59 **The historical-political geography of the Humid Pampa to 1850.**
Rolf Sternberg. *Montclair Journal of the Social Sciences*, vol. 3, no. 2 (fall 1974), p. 97-125. maps.

Describes three phases of the occupancy of the Humid Pampa: the pre-European era of the few thousand nomadic Indians (Puelche, Querandí and Guaraní); the economic activities of the early white settlers (1527-1810), in the main providing animal products to the mining enterprises in Upper Peru; and the rise to political and economic pre-eminence of Buenos Aires, 1810-50. For a continuation of this article, see *Occupance of the humid pampa, 1856-1914*. Two similar but much older essays by Oscar Schmieder are still useful: 'Alteration of the Argentine Pampa in the colonial period', *University of California Publications in Geography*, vol. 2, no. 10 (27 Sept, 1927), p. 303-21; and 'The Pampa – a naturally or culturally induced grass-land?', *ibid.*, vol. 2, no. 8, p. 255-70. See also Walter S. Tower, 'The Pampa of Argentina', *Geographical Review*, vol. 5, no. 4 (April 1918), p. 293-315.

60 **Northern Patagonia: character and resources. Volume I: a study of the elements of development in the region tributary to the national railway from Port San Antonio to Lago Nahuel Huapí and the extension to Valdivia, Chile; including the Andean Lake District.**
Ministerio de Obras Públicas, Comisión de Estudios Hidrológicos, Buenos Aires. New York: Scribner Press, 1914. 464p. maps.

This 'topographic, geological, and economic' survey of the Pampas and Andes of northern Patagonia describes the principal topographic features of the region and local descriptions of the constituent regions, including their natural resources and industries. Bailey Willis, author of *A Yankee in Patagonia* (q.v.), was Director of the Comisión de Estudios Hidrológicos, 1911-14. Volume two was never published.

61 **Occupance of the Humid Pampa, 1856-1914.**
Rolf Sternberg. *Revista Geográfica* (Mexico), no. 76 (June 1972),
p. 61-102. maps. bibliog.

During the second half of the nineteenth century the Humid Pampa 'became the main productive center of the nation, replacing the band between Córdoba and Salta'. This striking change was brought about by the influx of European immigrants who supplied the manpower for the early farm colonies and, after 1880, became tenant farmers on the large *estancias*. See also *The historical-political geography of the Humid Pampa to 1850*.

62 **Patagonia, windswept land of the south.**
Roger Perry. New York: Dodd, Mead, 1974. 126p. map.

Written in a straightforward style suitable for children, the book describes both Chilean and Argentine Patagonia: the early native Indians; the first explorers (Magellan to Darwin, 1520-1826); the history, physical geography and wildlife of the eastern steppes from Lake Nahuel Huapí down to Río Gallegos, the Andean fjords and glaciers, and the Isla Grande of Tierra del Fuego; and the modern economy of Patagonia (sheep, mining and tourism).

63 **The periphery and the environment: three case-studies in Argentina and Brazil (1870-1970).**
Brian A. Thomson. *International Social Science Journal*, vol. 30, no. 3 (1978), p. 498-535. map.

Describes three cases of regional development planning: Santiago del Estero (1870-1920), Resistencia, capital of Chaco Province (1930-70), and northwest Paraná, Brazil (1940-74). The two Argentine cases 'were phased into the [international-market] system at a later date through the Buenos Aires space'. Santiago del Estero was 'a handicapped social space', neither provided with the necessary infrastructure nor attracting investment. By contrast, the Chaco was unoccupied territory when the expansion of the wet Pampas began; by 1968, 'Resistencia accounted for 51 per cent of the province's population, 32 per cent of its new product and 60 per cent of its commercial activity', with accompanying infrastructural and environmental problems.

64 **The quebracho region of Argentina.**
William D. Durland. *Geographical Review*, vol. 14, no. 2 (April 1924), p. 227-41. maps.

The heartwood of the quebracho tree yields an extract used in the manufacture of tannin. It is so abundant and of such high quality in northern Argentina (most of the provinces of Santiago del Estero and Salta and parts of Santa Fe) and southern Paraguay to permit commercial exploitation. There are accounts of the geography (including the varieties of forest) and colonization of the region, and of the timbering process itself.

65 **Regional development in Argentina: administrative and organisational problems.**
José M. Dagnino Pastore, A. C. Sturzenegger, P. E. Andrien. In: *Multidisciplinary aspects of regional development: annual meeting of directors of development training and research institutes, Montpellier, 7th-12th September, 1968.* Paris: Development Centre of the Organisation for Economic Co-operation and Development, 1969, p. 193-213. map.
This chapter describes the work of the National System of Development Planning and Action (created in September 1966) with regard to relations between national, provincial and municipal authorities, organization within the regions, problems of infrastructure and finance. Three regional development agencies (Federal Investment Council, Bermejo River National Commission, Buenos Aires Colorado Valley Development Corporation) provide case studies.

66 **Regional disparities and policy in modern Argentina.**
Arthur S. Morris. Glasgow: University of Glasgow, Institute of Latin American Studies, 1975. 16p. maps. bibliog. (Occasional Papers, 16).
'Apart from a brief flirtation with growth pole policy and fairly consistent expressions of concern for the regional pattern, Argentine economic policy has in outward appearance had only a modest regional component.' There was no enunciated regional policy before the 1960s; polarized development in the form of industrial parks was the trend after 1965, but these growth poles were often 'too loose a set of small towns'. Using data from the 1965 and 1971 five-year plans, the author shows that regional planning tends to favour the central metropolitan region.

67 **Ring around the city.**
Winthrop P. Carty. *Américas*, vol. 33, no. 2 (Feb. 1981), p. 3-8.
In 1970 a young lawyer and urban planner, Guillermo Domingo Laura, noticed that there was almost no housing in the riverside areas of the Reconquista river encircling Greater Buenos Aires. His efforts led to the creation of the Metropolitan Area Green Belt, Southeast (CEAMSE), a state enterprise which began building a green belt (*cinturón ecológico*) of recreational parks, ninety miles long and covering 115 square miles, on swampy ground along the river's course reclaimed by refuse landfill, thereby solving the city's problem of pollution from refuse incineration.

# Geology

68 **Argentine volcano viewed from space.**
Peter Francis. *Geographical Magazine*, vol. 55, no. 3 (March 1983), p. 142-7. map.
The Cerro Galán Caldera, a single volcano with a rim rising to 5,200 metres altitude and a crater 40 kilometres across at its longest diameter, had been unknown until observed by the Skylab spacecraft in 1973. See also the same author's 'The Cerro

Galán Caldera, Argentina', *Earthquake Information Bulletin* (Reston, Virginia), vol. 14, no. 2 (1982), p. 124-33.

69 **Descripción geológica de la Patagonia.** (The geology of Patagonia.)
Egidio Feruglio. Buenos Aires: Imprenta y Casa Editora Coni, 1949-50. 3 vols. maps. bibliog.

This, the first comprehensive geology of Patagonia, was the result of research undertaken after 1927 by the author and other geologists on behalf of the state oil company, Yacimientos Petrolíferos Fiscales. Many maps, cross-sections and plates enrich this attractively presented work.

70 **Geología regional argentina.** (The regional geology of Argentina.)
Edited by Armando F. Leanza. Córdoba, Argentina: Academia Nacional de Ciencias de Córdoba, 1972. 869p. maps. bibliog.

The proceedings of the First Simposio de Geología Regional Argentina (Córdoba, 1969), held to commemorate the Academy's 100th anniversary, containing thirty-one chapters on all regions of the country by distinguished Argentine geologists. The proceedings of the Second Symposium held in 1976 (published 1979-80, 2 vols) contain fifty-four chapters, updating the 1972 volume and adding several new studies.

71 **Guía paleontológica argentina.** (Palaeontological guide to Argentina.)
Buenos Aires: Consejo Nacional de Investigaciones Científicas y Técnicas, 1963-79. 19 vols. maps. bibliog.

This is a series of detailed catalogues of fossils, organized in three parts according to the main fossil-bearing strata – Palaeozoic, Mesozoic and Cainozoic. The first seven Palaeozoic volumes are credited to Hildebranda A. Castellaro (1-4), Arturo J. Amos (5-6) and Carlos A. Menéndez (7).

72 **Meteorites and craters of Campo del Cielo, Argentina.**
William A. Cassidy, Luisa M. Villar, Theodore E. Bunch, Truman P. Kohman, Daniel J. Milton. *Science*, vol. 149, no. 3688 (3 Sept. 1965), p. 1055-64. maps.

The findings of a 1962-63 Argentine-US expedition to the site of a strewnfield and crater field 150 kilometres south of Gancedo, Chaco province. The 5,800-year-old iron meteorite fell in a seventeen-kilometre straight line leaving at least nine impact craters (five described here for the first time) with diameters of 20-100 metres. There are seven photographs.

73 **The mineral and other resources in the Argentine Republic (La Plata) in 1869.**
F. Ignacio Rickard. London: Longmans, Green, 1870. 323p.

Major Rickard, who claimed to be a British subject but who may have been a German engineer, was at the time Government Inspector General of Mines. This is an official translation of his 1869 report to the Minister of the Interior, Dalmacio Vélez Sarsfield, describing the small-scale mining industries (mainly copper and silver) in the provinces of San Luis, Mendoza, San Juan, La Rioja, Catamarca, Tucumán, Santiago del Estero and Córdoba. Rickard also published a more popularized account of his experiences: *A mining journey across the Great Andes; with explorations in the silver mining districts of the provinces of San Juan and Mendoza, and a journey across the pampas to Buenos Aires* (London: Smith, Elder, 1863. 314p.).

### 74 Mineral survey in the Andean Cordillera, Argentina.
New York: United Nations Development Program, 1968. 176p. maps.

A joint Argentine-United Nations team prospected for metallic mineral deposits in 130,000 square kilometres of the Argentine Cordillera in the provinces of San Juan, Mendoza and Neuquén, during 1963-66. This barren, unpopulated area had previously been thought to have no economic potential, but the survey found 'large, low-grade copper mineralization of the porphyry copper type' in the northern part of the prospect area, opposite Chile's southern copper belt.

### 75 Sheep farming and erosion in Patagonia.
John F. Bergmann. In: *International aspects of development in Latin America: geographical perspectives. Proceedings of the Conference of Latin Americanist Geographers. Volume 6: Selected papers and abstracts from the 7th General Session held in El Paso, Texas, October 20-24, 1976.* Edited by Gary S. Elbow. Muncie, Indiana: CLAG Publications, 1977, p. 65-74. maps.

Naturally high winds and seventy-five years of intensive over-grazing by sheep (and goats) have contributed to severe erosion of the Patagonian sheep pastures, 'in extreme cases to complete removal of all vegetation cover'. He recommends that 'stocking rates must be reduced, pastures fenced and managed on a rotation basis'.

### 76 Soils of Argentine. [sic]
Juan Papadakis. *Soil Science*, vol. 95, no. 5 (May 1963), p. 356-66. map. bibliog.

The author considers soils under eight natural regions – grassland (pampa), mid-latitude thorny woodland, subtropical dry woodland and parkland, subtropical forest, western desert, temperate mountainous forest, sub-Antarctic summer grassland, and Antarctic subglacial desert – and describes their climate, vegetation, and the formation, classification and characteristics of their soils. Reference is made to the twenty-four soil classification regions, with their subregions, shown on the map.

# Maps, atlases and gazetteers

### 77 Argentina: official standard names approved by the United States Board on Geographic Names.
Washington, DC: Department of the Interior, Office of Geography, 1968. 699p. map. (Gazetteer, 103).

An alphabetical gazetteer of 48,000 geographical names and features: standard names (unapproved variant names cross-referenced), up to seventy-five different designations as to what the name refers to (for example, ford, railway station, volcano), their latitude/longitude and the administrative division to which they belong. There is also a glossary of nearly 200 generic terms.

78  **Atlas de la República Argentina.** (Atlas of Argentina.)
Buenos Aires: Instituto Geográfico Militar, 1989. 6th ed. 81p. maps.

Consists of thirty-six colour maps, thirty with overlay sheets, of the provinces and major cities, supplemented by graphs and tables giving further physical and socioeconomic information, and a glossary of terms. There is no index. The Instituto Geográfico Militar, a technical branch of the Argentine Army, published the first edition in 1965.

79  **Atlas del desarrollo territorial de la Argentina.** (Atlas of the territorial development of Argentina.)
Patricio H. Randle.  Buenos Aires: OIKOS, 1981. 3 vols. maps.

The comprehensive atlas contains 313 pages of colour maps (scale 1:10,000,000) of the whole country showing: historical developments 1502-1978; administrative, juridical and ecclesiastical units; agricultural production; urbanization and population growth; and communications infrastructure. The *Memoria* (247p.) provides sources and explanatory notes, and the *Serie de estadísticas históricas* (283p.) supporting statistical data for 1895-1977.

80  **Atlas geográfico de la República Argentina.** (Geographical atlas of Argentina.)
Buenos Aires: Editorial Nuevo Mundo, 1986. 127p. maps.

Coloured maps of each province are followed by pages of historical and demographic and economic statistical data, with more colour illustrations.

81  **Atlas: geografía histórica de la pampa anterior.** (Historical-geographical atlas of Greater Buenos Aires.)
Patricio H. Randle, Nélida Gurevitz.  Buenos Aires: Editorial Universitaria de Buenos Aires, 1971. 2 vols. maps.

The *pampa anterior* is the immediate hinterland of the city of Buenos Aires, corresponding roughly to Greater Buenos Aires. Volume one is the explanatory *Memoria descriptiva*. The atlas contains thirty-six coloured maps showing land distribution, population, agricultural and livestock use, and transport development for the national census years 1869, 1895, 1914, 1947 and 1960.

82  **Atlas histórico de la República Argentina.** (Historical atlas of Argentina.)
Compiled and edited by José Juan Biedma and drawn by Carlos Beyer.
Buenos Aires: Angel Estrada, 1909. 56p.

A classic historical atlas, with explanatory text, containing nineteen colour facsimiles of a total of twenty-nine maps and plans, beginning with Martin Behaim's 1492 map of the world and progressing though the early discoveries and the Viceroyalties of Peru and the Río de la Plata to the British invasions (1806-7), the wars of independence (1810-25), the civil and Indian wars (1814-61) and the Paraguayan War (1865-70).

**Geography.** Maps, atlases and gazetteers

83 **Atlas total de la República Argentina.** (Complete atlas of Argentina.)
   Edited by Elena Chiozza, Ricardo Figueira. Buenos Aires: Centro
   Editor de América Latina, 1981-83. 6 vols.

A comprehensive atlas combining maps, text, photographs and Landsat images, in separate volumes: *Atlas físico* (2 vols), *Atlas político*, which includes demographic maps based on the 1980 census, *Atlas económico* (2 vols), and *Atlas de la actividad económica* (economic resources, agriculture and livestock).

84 **Carta de suelos de la República Argentina.** (Map of the soils of
   Argentina.)
   Buenos Aires: Instituto Nacional de Tecnología Agropecuaria, 1970- .

Twenty-seven sheets of this series, scale 1:100,000, have been published.

85 **Carta topográfica de la República Argentina.** (Topographical map
   of Argentina).
   Buenos Aires: Instituto Geográfico Militar, 1939- .

A set of seventy 'ordnance survey' maps, scale 1:500,000. The IGM also produces similar maps, scale 1:250,000 (1951- , about one-half of the projected 231 sheets so far published), scale 1:100,000 (1911- , one-half of the 1900 or so sheets to date), and scale 1:50,000 (1906- , one-sixth of the 7197 sheets to date).

86 **Guía de la República Argentina para investigaciones geográficas.**
   (Geographer's research guide to Argentina.)
   Prepared by the Instituto Geográfico Militar Argentino. Buenos Aires:
   Instituto Panamericano de Geografía e Historia, 1983. 297p. maps.
   bibliog.

In three parts: cartography (maps for each of sixteen organizations, notably the Instituto Geográfico Militar, Servicio de Hidrografía Naval and the Servicio Geológico Nacional, show the areas for which maps produced by them are available); land surveys (geodesy); and a bibliography and list of Argentine libraries specializing in geography. The guide includes aerial photographs and satellite images.

87 **Mapa ecológico de la República Argentina.** (Ecological map of
   Argentina.)
   Buenos Aires: Fundación Agro-Palermo, 1983.

Measuring 84 by 40 cm (scale 1:5,000,000), this single-sheet map has indexes of ecological groups by region and subregion and a 20-page accompanying booklet in Spanish, French and English ('Argentina: its ecological reality').

88  **Mapa geológico de la República Argentina.** (Geological map of
    Argentina.)
    Compiled by Víctor A. Ramos, Abel H. Pesce (et al.). Buenos Aires:
    Ministerio de Economía, Secretaría de Industria de Minería,
    Subsecretaría de Minería, 1982.

One map on two sheets each measuring 86 by 91 cm, scale 1:2,500,000. The Servicio
Geológico Nacional (SGN) produced a geological map (scale 1:500,000) in 1964, a
*Mapa hidrogeológico* (scale 1:5,000,000) in 1963, a *Mapa geotécnico* (three sheets,
scale 1:2,500,000) in 1978, and an ambitious *Carta geológico-económica* (scale
1:200,000), about a quarter of whose projected 700 or so sheets have been produced
since 1932.

89  **Los planos más antiguos de Buenos Aires, 1580-1880.** (The earliest maps
    of Buenos Aires, 1580-1880.)
    Alfredo Taullard.  Buenos Aires: Jacobo Peuser, 1940. 266p. maps.

Thirty-five plans and maps, eighteen folding, from Juan de Garay's 1583 plan of the
city of Buenos Aires to an 1888 map of the Federal Capital.

90  **República Argentina.** (Argentina.)
    Buenos Aires: Instituto Geográfico Militar, 1981.

A complete single-sheet map of the country (scale 1:5,000,000) and measuring 83 by 40
cm. Relief is shown by shading and spot heights. There is an inset map showing
political divisions. The IGM has also published maps to scales 1:10,000,000 (1980) and
1:2,500,000 (1986, 2 sheets).

91  **República Argentina: red caminera principal.** (Main road map of
    Argentina.)
    Buenos Aires: Automóvil Club Argentina, Area de Cartografía Vial y
    Turística, 1984.

A single road map showing provincial boundaries (scale 1:4,000,000, 97 by 57 cm,
folding to 21 by 11 cm). On the reverse are text, a map showing distances from Buenos
Aires, an index, and a list of ACA's hotels and service stations.

# Travel guides

92  **Argentina.**
    Edited and produced by Deirdre Hall, directed and designed by Hans
    Hoefer.  Singapore: APA Publications, distributed by Harrap, 1988.
    325p. maps. bibliog. (Insight Guides).

Partly a general introduction to the country, partly a travel guide, this consists of
thirty-five chapters by a team of writers, in three sections: 'Welcome, history &
geography', 'Places & features', and 'Travel tips'. The 'features' include the tango, the
Welsh in Patagonia, flora and fauna, sports, wine, the gaucho and some archaeology.
There are over 230 excellent colour photographs.

93 **Argentina: a travel survival kit.**
Alan Samagalski. Hawthorn, Australia: Lonely Planet, 1989. 216p.
maps. bibliog.
Another in Lonely Planet's guides for the low-budget traveller, in chapters covering: facts about the country, essential information and practical tips for the visitor, getting there, travelling within the country, Buenos Aires, Misiones and the Northeast, the Andean provinces, Patagonia and Tierra del Fuego. There are nearly fifty good maps and town plans.

94 **Backpacking in Chile & Argentina.**
Edited by Clare Hargreaves, with contributions by Clare Hargreaves, Hilary Bradt, John Pilkington, John and Christine Myerscough, Nick Cotton. Chalfont St Peter, England: Bradt Publications; Edison, New Jersey: Hunter Publishing, 1989. 2nd ed. 185p. maps. bibliog.
The first edition, published in 1980, included the Falkland Islands, now dropped from this edition. 'The best walking areas in Chile and Argentina tend to be around the Andes which forms the border, so the book wanders between the two countries, moving north to south.' One-third of the book contains general information. The walks are illustrated with eighteen trekking maps. 'Argentina should be hiked in winter (May to October) since the summer rains wash out the trails.' There is useful information on health, national parks, natural history and edible fruits, greens and fungi. Mountaineers should consult *Mountaineering in the Andes: a sourcebook for climbers*, by Jill Neate (London: Expedition Advisory Centre, 1987, [n.p.]); this contains a topography and climbing history (Argentina, p. 50-90), a 'peak gazetteer' (Argentina, p. 152-69) and a full bibliography.

95 **Birnbaum's South America 1990.**
Stephen Birnbaum, Alexandra Mayes Birnbaum. Boston, Massachusetts: Houghton Mifflin, 1989. 864p. maps.
Arranged in three sections: 'The cities', with a twenty-page section on Buenos Aires; 'Diversions', containing information on sports, entertainment and cultural activities in Argentina; and 'Directions', including seven itineraries across Argentina and a chapter on the Falkland Islands (p. 479-526).

96 **Buenos Aires.**
Directed and designed by Hans Hoefer, edited and produced by Kathleen Wheaton. Buenos Aires: APA Publications, 1988. 233p. maps. (Insight City Guides).
Between an eighty-page introduction to the history and people of the city and ten pages of travel tips there are thirty-two chapters on 'Places and features' (p. 96-212) covering transport, cultural and sporting activities, shopping, hotels and restaurants in the city centre and suburbs.

97 **Fodor's 90 South America.**
Edited by Kathleen McHugh, Alice Thompson.   New York; London:
Fodor's Travel Publications, 1989. 629p. maps.
The latest edition of this annual guide includes practical 'facts at your fingertips'
followed by a regional guide (Buenos Aires, Iguazú Falls, the Northwest, Mendoza,
Patagonia, Bariloche, Tierra del Fuego) and information on travel, accommodation,
restaurants, cultural activities, sports and entertainment, and shopping.

98 **Michael's guide: Argentina, Chile, Paraguay & Uruguay.**
Michael Shichor.   Tel Aviv, Israel: INBAL Travel Information, 1987.
225p. maps.
An introduction contains all the usual practical information for all four countries. The
section on Argentina, p. 59-129, follows a familiar regional approach: Buenos Aires,
the Iguazú Falls, the North, the Central region, the Lake District, Patagonia and
Tierra del Fuego. A reprint with a new cover was misleadingly issued as a '1990
edition'.

99 **South America on a shoestring.**
G. Crowther.   South Yarra, Australia; Berkeley, California: Lonely
Planet Publications, 1986. 3rd ed. 736p. maps.
Largely superseded by *Argentina: a travel survival kit* (q.v), but still worth consulting
for some of the unusual towns that it singles out as its 'cheapest places to see, travel,
eat and stay': Buenos Aires, Bariloche, Calafate, Comodoro Rivadavia, Córdoba,
Iguazú Falls, Jujuy, La Quiaca, Mendoza, Posadas, Puerto Madryn, Río Gallegos, Río
Grande and Ushuaia.

100 **1991 South American handbook.**
Edited by Ben Box.   Bath, England: Trade and Travel Publications,
1989. 1150p. maps.
Without doubt the best single travel guide to the region, now in its sixty-seventh
edition. The section on Argentina (p. 39-195) contains an introduction, an eleven-
region survey and ten pages of information for visitors, including a warning about the
increase in street crime. Everything from car hire to the address of the Argentine
Chess Club is covered.

# Travellers' Accounts

## General

101 **South America rediscovered.**
Tom B. Jones. Minneapolis, Minnesota: University of Minnesota Press; London: Oxford University Press, 1949. 285p. maps. bibliog.
A classic guide to the sources 'that were available to the reading public of Great Britain and the United States in the nineteenth century' and that may be employed to 'reconstruct southern South America as foreigners saw it in the years from 1810 to 1870'. Chapters 2-4 (p. 19-78) relate to Argentina: 'Buenos Aires', 'Westward Ho!' (journeys overland across the pampas from Buenos Aires to Chile and Peru) and 'The Conquest of the River Plate, 1853-1870'. This is a very readable social history of the land, people and political and economic institutions which makes no apology for 'the levity which has crept into these pages. There is humor in the travelers' tales'. The bibliography, p. 241-58, contains some brief annotations. Extracts from earlier British visitors' accounts of Buenos Aires are contained in Octavio C. Battolla, *Los primeros ingleses en Buenos Aires, 1780-1830* (Buenos Aires: Editorial Muro, 1928. 173p.). An interesting anthology of travellers of the eighteenth century is Juan Mühn, *La Argentina vista por viajeros del siglo XVIII* (Buenos Aires: Huarpes, 1946. 159p. [Biblioteca Enciclopédica Argentina, vol. 7]).

# Before 1900

**102  Across Patagonia.**
Lady Florence Caroline Dixie, with illustrations from sketches by Julius
Beerbohm.  London: Richard Bentley, 1880. 251p.
'Precisely because it was an outlandish place and so far away, I chose it.' Lady Dixie
visited Patagonia with seven companions, including her husband, her two brothers and
the illustrator, Julius Beerbohm, an engineer who had in 1877 made his own journey
through the region and published his *Wanderings in Patagonia; or, Life among the
ostrich-hunters* (London: Chatto & Windus, 1879. 278p.). Her journey of one thousand
miles on horseback took forty-four days in early 1879 and her account is sometimes a
rather monotonous description of the 'dreary landscape' and 'many a discomfort – the
earthquake, the drenching rains, the scorching sun, the pitiless mosquitoes, and the
terrible blasting winds'.

**103  Argentina and the Argentines: notes and impressions of a five years'
sojourn in the Argentine Republic, 1885-90.**
Thomas A. Turner.  London: Swan Sonnenschein, 1892. 370p.
Many sharp and often scathing observations are to be found in this 'series of "Notes"
or sketches of Argentina and the Argentines', which amount to virtually a handbook
on all aspects of the country: geography, the political system and bureaucracy, the
economy (he witnessed the financial crisis of 1890), taxation and banking, the
professions, the railways, health, education and the press, crime, women and the
family, entertainments, the British in Argentina and the Argentine character. There
are excellent descriptions of Buenos Aires and its suburbs, and La Plata.

**104  Argentine, Patagonian, and Chilian sketches, with a few notes on
Uruguay.**
Charles Edmond Akers.  London: Harrison & Sons, 1893. 190p.
Akers was a correspondent for the London *Times* and parts of the book appeared
originally in *The Standard* of Buenos Aires, 1891-92. Like Turner (*Argentina and the
Argentines* [q.v.]), he describes with some sarcasm the effects of the crash of 1890. In
addition, there are chapters on the city of Buenos Aires and its inhabitants, and the
provinces to the south and south-west of the capital (salt deposits near Carmen de
Patagones, Río Negro, Lake Nahuel Huapí, the Andes crossing to Valdivia and a
Patagonian *estancia*).

**105  At home with the Patagonians: a year's wanderings over untrodden
ground from the Straits of Magellan to the Río Negro.**
George Chaworth Musters.  London: John Murray, 1871. 322p. map.
Musters had been fascinated with Patagonia ever since reading Charles Darwin's
*Journal of researches into the geology and natural history of the various countries
visited by H.M.S. Beagle . . .* (q.v.). He crossed to Patagonia from the Falkland
Islands in April 1869, riding on horseback from Punta Arenas northeast to Santa Cruz,
up the Andes via Esquel to Lake Nahuel Huapí and east to Carmen de Patagones from
where he sailed to Buenos Aires. He was treated well by Tehuelche Indians and
chapter five describes their manners and customs. He enters the historical debate
concerning their mythical height ('Are they giants or not?'): 'The average height of the
Tehuelche male members of the party with which I travelled was rather over than

under 5 feet 10 inches'. There is a modern reprint (New York: Greenwood Press, 1969).

## 106 Brazil and the River Plate, 1870-76.
William Hadfield.   Sutton, England: W. R. Church; London: Edward Stanford, 1877. map.

This volume updates the author's earlier *Brazil, the River Plate and the Falkland Islands* (London, 1854) and *Brazil and the River Plate in 1868* (London, 1869). Hadfield, who first visited Argentina in 1853, was variously secretary to the Buenos Ayres Great Southern Railway and South American Steam Navigation Company, and editor of the *South American Journal* (London). He visited Buenos Aires, Rosario and Córdoba. There are assessments of Argentine banks, the telegraph service, the country's mineral resources, and diplomatic and consular relations with Great Britain.

## 107 Buenos Ayres and Argentine gleanings: with extracts from a diary of Salado exploration in 1862 and 1863.
Thomas Joseph Hutchinson.   London: Edward Stanford, 1865. 321p. maps.

Hutchinson, who was British Consul at Rosario, states that the object of his book was 'to give a description of those parts of the Argentine Republic which I have visited, and to supply statistics as well as other details on the important subjects of immigration, sheep farming, and cotton cultivation'. Apart from the many personal observations on Buenos Aires, Rosario, Paraná, Santa Fe, the Chaco, Tucumán, Córdoba and (notably) Santiago del Estero, there are frequent and valuable statistics for 1860-62 throughout, and hints for the prospective immigrant, including the text of the land law of 1862. Appendix five contains the account of his 'Río Salado navigation', a Foreign Office mission to ascertain whether the wild cotton growing in the Salado Valley 'might best be collected and forwarded to England'.

## 108 Buenos Ayres, and the Provinces of the Rio de la Plata: from their discovery and conquest by the Spaniards to the establishment of their political independence. With some account of their present state, trade, debt, etc.; an appendix of historical and statistical documents; and a description of the geology and fossil monsters of the Pampas.
Sir Woodbine Parish.   London: John Murray, 1852. 434p. 2nd enlarged ed. map.

The author was the first British chargé d'affaires in Buenos Aires (1823-31) and a friend of the dictator Juan Manuel de Rosas. The first two parts provide the historical background to 1827, part three a valuable summary of the history and existing conditions of the interior provinces, and part four an essay on the country's trade and public debts, 1822-52. Chapter nine and the appendix are a valuable source of vital and meteorological statistics from 1770 to 1847 (Parish was a keen geologist and a Fellow of the Royal Society). Population, transport, agriculture, cattle-raising, the gaucho, immigration, women, priests, lawyers and the military are some of the topics covered in this scholarly classic. The second edition adds mainly older historical detail to the first edition of 1839.

109  **A description of Patagonia, and the adjoining parts of South America; containing an account of the soil, produce . . . &c., of those countries; the religion, government, policy, customs, dress, arms, and language of the Indian inhabitants; and some particulars relating to Falkland's Islands.**
Thomas Falkner.   Hereford, England: C. Pugh, 1774. 144p. map.
Falkner (1707-84), a doctor born in England of Irish parents, travelled to the River Plate in 1831 for health reasons, converted to Catholicism and served as a Jesuit missionary in the Paraguayan reductions, in Córdoba and in Patagonia. He remained among the Patagonian Indians until his return to England after the expulsion of the Jesuits in 1767. Although his account was heavily edited before publication, it remains a classic description of the country and of the manners and customs of the native inhabitants of Patagonia. It includes a short grammar and vocabulary of the Moluche language. Two modern facsimile editions have been published (Chicago: Armann & Armann, 1935; New York: AMS Press, 1976).

110  **Far away and long ago: a history of my early life.**
W. H. Hudson.   London: J. M. Dent; Boston, Massachusetts: E. P. Dutton, 1918. 332p.
William Henry Hudson's parents, originally from Devon, had married in Boston and settled in Argentina in 1832. Hudson, the third of six children, was born in 1841 on an *estancia* 'quaintly named *Los Veinte-cinco Ombúes*, which means the Twenty-five Ombú Trees', in Quilmes, south of Buenos Aires. When he was six the family moved to another farm near Caseros, where he recalls hearing the battle in which Rosas was defeated in 1852. This charming book describes the first fifteen years of his life: his father and mother, the children's three eccentric schoolmasters, the elder brother who introduced him to Darwin's works, the farm's gaucho workers, their weird and wonderful neighbours (many of them British), and the wildlife he saw around him.

111  **A five years' residence in Buenos Ayres, during the years 1820-1825: containing remarks on the country and inhabitants; and a visit to Colonia del Sacramento. By an Englishman. With an appendix, containing rules and police of the port of Buenos Ayres, navigation of the River Plate &c., &c.**
George Thomas Love.   London: G. Hebert, 1827. 2nd ed. 176p.
Love was director and editor of *The British Packet and Argentine News*, a Buenos Aires English-language newspaper (1826-52). He divides his book into three sections: the port city of Buenos Aires, its foreign residents, and the native (or 'creole') and Spanish residents. He is informative on matters of commerce (especially custom-house regulations), education, religion and other social matters. 'I came to Buenos Ayres somewhat prejudiced, expecting to observe illiberality and bigotry, in place of the many amiable qualities of which I have found them [the Argentines] possessed.'

112 **Forty years in the Argentine Republic.**
Arthur E. Shaw. London: Elkin Mathews; Buenos Aires: Mitchell's
Book Store, 1907. 229p.

In 1864 'an old friend of my father's offered to take me, at the age of sixteen, out there
and "make a man of me"'. His first job was as member of a surveying party for the
Central Argentine Railway, and he remained in railway and tramway engineer-
ing/surveying work – on which he is very informative – throughout most of the country
for the rest of his life.

113 **Gleanings and remarks: collected during many months of residence at**
**Buenos Ayres, and within the upper country; with a prefatory account of**
**the expedition from England, until the surrender of the Colony of the**
**Cape of Good Hope, under the joint command of Sir D. Baird, G.C.B.,**
**K.C., and Sir Home Popham, K.C.B.**
Alexander Gillespie. Leeds, England: B. Dewhirst, 1818. 342p.

Major Gillespie served during the second British invasion of Buenos Aires (1807) and
although he includes some details of the campaign he concentrates on the community
aspects of life in the city as seen by a prisoner of war and has left us acute comments
on the people's social customs and amusements. He does not say much about the city's
institutions. When he and other captives were moved to the 'upper country' as far as
Córdoba 'to preserve us from a disorderly populace', he describes the pampas as he
goes.

114 **The great silver river: notes of a residence in Buenos Ayres in 1880 and**
**1881.**
Sir Horace Rumbold. London: John Murray, 1890. 366p.

Rumbold was British consul-general in Chile before becoming envoy extraordinary to
Argentina, 1879-81. His descriptions of the city and province of Buenos Aires are
interspersed with an account of a steamer trip up the Uruguay River as far as Misiones.
The second edition updates the first (1887) with a chapter on the 'present commercial
position of the country', in which he notes the progress made in the eight years since
he was last in the country, but warns of signs of 'an impending financial crisis, which
are becoming more marked even as I write'.

115 **Idle days in Patagonia.**
W. H. Hudson. London: Chapman & Hall, 1893. 256p.

In later life Hudson, who had settled in London in 1869, returned to Patagonia on a
year-long scientific mission to a hostile region which served as a breeding-place for
many birds: 'the passion of the ornithologist took me. Many of the winged wanderers
with which I had been familiar from childhood in La Plata were visitors, occasional or
regular, from this grey wilderness of thorns'. He was 'idle' for some of the time after
he accidentally shot himself in the knee with a revolver. There are twenty-seven
illustrations by Alfred Hartley and J. Smit.

116    Journal of researches into the geology and natural history of the various
       countries visited by H.M.S. Beagle, under the command of Captain
       Fitzroy, R.N., from 1832 to 1836.
       Charles Darwin.    London: Henry Colburn, 1839. 615p. maps.
Darwin was the best-known British visitor to Argentina in the early nineteenth
century. His journal describes the *Beagle*'s voyage from the Cape Verde Islands, via
South America, to Tahiti and Mauritius. He visited Bahía Blanca, Buenos Aires, Santa
Fe, Santa Cruz, Tierra del Fuego and the Falkland Islands, describing everything he
saw, from the land and the people to – most famously – the geology, flora and fauna.
In Río Negro Province he visited the military encampment of Juan Manuel de Rosas,
'a man of an extraordinary character'; 'in conversation he is enthusiastic, sensible, and
very grave'.

117    Journey from Buenos Ayres, through the provinces of Cordova,
       Tucuman, and Salta, to Potosi, thence by the deserts of Caranja to
       Arica, and subsequently, to Santiago de Chili and Coquimbo,
       undertaken on behalf of the Chilian and Peruvian Mining Association, in
       the years 1825-26.
       Joseph Andrews.    London: John Murray, 1827. 2 vols.
The first volume (312 pages) and the first two chapters of volume two are devoted to
Argentina. Andrews has left us some very good descriptions of the contemporary
political scene and local conditions and customs as well as of the Famantina mines in
La Rioja province. Unlike Francis Bond Head (*Rough notes taken during some rapid
journeys across the pampas and among the Andes* [q.v.]), who thought that mining
profits would be cut by the cost of importing machinery, Andrews, the agent of a
British mining firm, insisted that capital was needed to get the mines working
productively. There is a modern reprint (New York: AMS Press, 1971).

118    La Plata, the Argentine Confederation, and Paraguay. Being a narrative
       of the exploration of the tributaries of the River La Plata and adjacent
       countries during the years 1853, '54, '55, and '56, under the orders of
       the United States Government.
       Thomas Jefferson Page.    New York: Harper; London: Trübner, 1859.
       632p. map.
Page was a naval officer and commander of a United States scientific mission sent out
in 1853 to explore and survey the Paraná River and its tributaries. Between 1853 and
1856 he travelled some 8,000 miles by land and water through the Argentine
Confederation and Paraguay. He visited the *estancia* of General Urquiza on an
excursion to Gualeguaychú in Entre Ríos. Page was impressed by the rapid growth and
vitality of the towns along the Paraná, contrasting with Santiago's 'aspect of decay':
Paraná, capital of the Confederation from 1852 to 1861, and Rosario, which by 1856
had become a strong competitor with the port of Buenos Aires. He concluded that the
rivers he inspected were suitable for steam navigation: 'The time is only postponed
when steamers will enter Corrientes, Rosario, and Buenos Ayres, freighted with the
products of the North and West.'

119 **El Lazarillo: a guide for inexperienced travelers between Buenos Aires and Lima. 1773.**
Concolorcorvo, translated by Walter D. Kline.   Bloomington, Indiana: Indiana University Press, 1965. 315p. map. (Unesco Collection of Representative Works. Latin-American Series).

'Concolorcorvo', the pseudonym of Alonso Carrió de la Vandera (or Bandera, c1715-c1778) was a native of Gijón, Spain. He falsely identified himself as Don Calixto Bustamante Carlos Inca, invented a false place of publication (his native Gijón) and a false date (1773) for his *El Lazarillo de ciegos caminantes*, famous as a contemporary guidebook and as a literary masterpiece in the picaresque style; the book served also as an official report on the mail service between Buenos Aires and Lima. Some passages here have been cut and others edited, but otherwise the translation, based on the 1942 Buenos Aires edition, admirably preserves 'the charmingly awkward and unpolished style' of the original. Carrió was always careful to ascertain the number of inhabitants in each place he visited and the book is noted for its 'census' of Buenos Aires (2,200 inhabitants in 1770).

120 **Letters from Paraguay: describing the settlements of Montevideo an [sic] Buenos Ayres; the presidencies of Rioja Minor, Nombre de Dios, St. Mary and St. John &c. &c. With the manners, customs, religious ceremonies, &c. of the inhabitants. Written during a residence of seventeen months in that country.**
John Constanse Davie.   London: G. Robinson, 1805. 293p.

Davie, a wealthy man disappointed in a love affair, 'resolved to travel'. Taken ill off Buenos Aires, he convalesced for seventeen months in the Jesuit convent of St Dominic, during which time he wrote down his observations in the form of letters to a friend in London. The Argentine letters, dated between June 1797 and May 1798, contain detailed descriptions of Buenos Aires in the 1790s. He did not like the city: 'there is nothing in it worth describing', complaining constantly of its dirtiness. After recovering his health he visited the Jesuit missions in Paraguay. His later journeys to Mendoza and Chile are recorded in the posthumous *Letters from Buenos Ayres and Chili* (London: R. Ackermann, 1819).

121 **Letters on South America; comprising travels on the banks of the Paraná and Rio de la Plata.**
John Parish Robertson, William Parish Robertson.   London: John Murray, 1843. 3 vols.

The Robertsons were Scottish merchants who lived and traded in Uruguay, Brazil, Peru and Argentina from 1806 to the 1830s, but 'were scarcely ever a month at a time, in the same place'. The letters, which are addressed to General William Miller, 'Field Marshal of Peru', describe the later experiences of the brothers as traders in Argentina. 'Buenos Ayres, for the first twenty years that the English knew it, – that is, from 1810 to 1830 –, might really be called a delightful place. From the political causes [Rosas] there has been a sad change for the worse, in the construction of its society, from 1830 down to the present day.' Very entertaining on foreign residents, especially the British, in Buenos Aires and Corrientes.

122  **Life among the giants; or, The captive in Patagonia: a personal narrative.**
Benjamin Franklin Bourne.  Boston, Massachusetts: Gould & Lincoln; London: Henry Vizetelly, 1853. 233p.

In 1850 the author left New Bedford for California via Cape Horn to join the gold rush. Landing at the Straits of Magellan to shoot wild game, he was captured by 'black-looking giants', nomadic Patagonian Indians. For just over three months before he managed to escape, he was forced to move about with the tribe on their hunting excursions. He describes the average height of the Indians as 'nearly six and a half feet', their habits as 'not only filthy, but indolent to the last degree . . . They never go on a hunting expedition till there is nothing more to eat'.

123  **My life in the Argentine Republic.**
Charles Darbyshire.  London: Frederick Warne, 1918. 140p.

Darbyshire first went to Argentina in 1852 (in time to describe the siege of Buenos Aires in that year) to work for an English export house dealing in salted hides and tallow. He paid a visit to General Justo José de Urquiza, president of the Argentine Confederation 1854-60, on his *estancia* near Concepción del Uruguay: 'He was extremely annoyed at what he was pleased to call the ingratitude of the "porteños" (natives of Buenos Aires) after delivering them from the thraldom of Rosas.' Rather a lightweight book, but interesting on British *estancia* conditions; Darbyshire married into an Entre Ríos cattle and sheep family and his brothers were sheep farmers in Buenos Aires province. He left the country in 1869 and paid a last visit in 1893-94.

124  **Narrative of a journey across the cordillera of the Andes, and of a residence in Lima, and other parts of Peru, in the years 1823 and 1824.**
Robert Proctor.  London: Archibald Constable [and] Hurst, Robinson, 1825. 374p.

Proctor, an agent for a British loan to Peru, arrived in Buenos Aires in 1823. This diary of his journey on which he was accompanied by his wife, infant son and three servants, is a highly readable one. The Argentine section of the journal (p. 1-60) describes the departure from Buenos Aires, the towns and gaucho inhabitants of the pampas, and the cities of San Luis and Mendoza.

125  **Paraguay, Brazil, and the Plate: letters written in 1852-1853.**
Charles Blachford Mansfield, with a sketch of the author's life by the Rev. Charles Kingsley, Jr.  Cambridge, England: Macmillan, 1856. 504p. map.

Two-fifths of the book relates to Argentina, which Mansfield (1819-55), a chemist by profession, visited between August and November 1952, spending his time between the city and outskirts of Buenos Aires and a journey up the River Paraná to Rosario and Corrientes, where for six weeks he was plagued by fleas. Buenos Aires is described thus: 'there is something most delicious about the air of this place, notwithstanding the horrible stenches from the putrid flesh all about the town'; Urquiza: 'a very respectable English farmer-like, honest-looking man'; the pampa: 'I was impressed at the quantity of animal life'. From Corrientes he travelled on to Asunción by pack-horse. There is a modern reprint (New York: AMS Press, 1971).

126 **Picturesque illustrations of Buenos Ayres and Monte Video, consisting of twenty-four views: accompanied with descriptions of the scenery, and of the costumes, manners, &c. of the inhabitants of those cities and their environs.**
Emeric Essex Vidal.    London: R. Ackermann, 1820. 115p.

This is a famous set of aquatints which have been endlessly reproduced in later works, containing general views and portraits of the inhabitants of Buenos Aires (the landing-place, the fort, the square and market-place, a church, the customs-house, a slaughter-house, a water cart, milk boys, a beggar on horseback) and of the pampas (farms and a *pulpería* [public house], Indians and gauchos, mules and waggons, soldiers, an ostrich hunt and horse race). Vidal was purser on HMS *Hyacinth* which visited the River Plate. Several handsome Argentine facsimile editions have been published this century.

127 **Pioneering in the pampas: or the first four years of a settler's experience in the La Plata camps.**
Richard Arthur Seymour.    London: Longmans, Green, 1870. 2nd ed. 180p. map.

In the area of Frayle Muerto (now Bella Vista, halfway between Rosario and Córdoba), Seymour and his friend Frank went out to seek their fortune between 1865 and 1888. They bought 24,000 acres in Indian country and a prefabricated iron house, and proceeded to build up a modest sheep ranch. They had many English neighbours and a stream of visitors from England. Seymour is not too sympathetic towards the native peons, although he does say that 'the lowest gaucho has a wonderful advantage over the most respectable English labourer in manner and address'. He later expanded into wheat and cattle farming and employed English farm-hands from his native Warwickshire. Apart from the monotonous life, enlivened by horse-races, 'our worst trouble of all has been the incursions of the Indians' and he encourages his fellow-countrymen to settle in the country.

128 **Report of journeys across the Andes and pampas of the Argentine Provinces.**
Archibald MacRae.    Washington, DC: A. O. P. Nicholson, 1855. 300p. maps. (US Naval Astronomical Expedition to the Southern Hemisphere during the years 1849-'50-'51-'52. Vol. 2).

Volume one of the report of this scientific expedition – Chile, by James Melville Gillis – was also published in 1855. Lieutenant MacRae left Santiago and took sixty days to cross the Andes to Mendoza and San Luis by the Upsallata Pass, making observations but breaking his mountain barometer in the process. Returning to the United States, he volunteered to retrace the route at his own expense, which he did in 1853, returning finally in March 1854. His criss-crossing of the Andes through various mountain passes is described in the first seven chapters, the scientific observations on pages 69-82. There is much good-humoured comment on the local people, scenery and wildlife.

129  **Rough notes taken during some rapid journeys across the pampas and among the Andes.**

Francis Bond Head.　London: John Murray, 1828. 3rd ed. 321p.

Captain Head served in the Royal Engineers (1811-25) before becoming manager of the Río de la Plata Mining Association (1825-26). Leaving his family in Buenos Aires, Head crossed the pampas from east to west four times in order to survey the company's mines near Upsallata in west-central Argentina and over the Andes in Chile; the book ends with his advising against investment in the mines. A fine horseman, 'Galloping' Head, as he is often called, is a shrewd commentator of the Argentine character and the political scene: he felt for the downtrodden gaucho, Indian and Negro, he writes lovingly of animals and scathingly of Catholicism. Head later became Lieutenant-Governor of Upper Canada (1835-38). The book was reprinted under the title *Journeys across the pampas and among the Andes* (edited by C. Harvey Gardiner. Carbondale, Illinois: Southern Illinois University Press, 1967), and there is a good summary of the work and of Head's career in John Walker's 'From the Argentine plains to Upper Canada: Sir Francis Bond Head, gaucho apologist and costumbrist of the pampa', *NorthSouth: Canadian Journal of Latin American Studies*, vol. 5, no. 9 (1980), p. 97-120.

130  **Sketches of Buenos Ayres and Chile.**

Samuel Haigh.　London: J. Carpenter and Son, 1829. 316p. map.

Describes two visits made by the author to Buenos Aires in 1817 and 1821. An account of his visit to Peru in 1825 was added to the earlier work in *Sketches of Buenos Ayres, Chile, and Peru* (London: Effingham Wilson, 1831). A merchant-adventurer, Haigh was a friend of the first British consul to the United Provinces of the Río de la Plata, Woodbine Parish, and of General William Miller, a veteran of the South American wars of independence, to whom he dedicates a 'memoir' in chapter one. This is a sympathetic and colourful account of Buenos Aires, the pampas, Luján, San Luis, Mendoza and the Andes crossing to Chile.

131  **South American journals, 1858-59.**

George Augustus Peabody, edited from the original manuscript by John Charles Phillips.　Salem, Massachusetts: Peabody Museum, 1937. 209p. map.

The introduction by Peabody's editor and friend, Phillips, states that 'the expedition . . . was undertaken as a sporting adventure, and he makes no claim to be aiding science'. Nevertheless, this is a lively description of the River Plate (and to a lesser extent Chile) which the author, apparently a man of leisure who had been admitted to the bar but who never practised law, visited with three companions.

132  **Travels in Buenos Ayres, and the adjacent provinces of the Rio de la Plata. With observations, intended for the use of persons who contemplate emigrating to that country; or, embarking capital in its affairs.**

J. A. B. Beaumont.　London: James Ridgway, 1828. 270p. map.

Intended as a guide 'to draw the attention of the British public to the advantages of Buenos Ayres for agricultural emigrants', this is a detailed geographical survey of the province of Buenos Aires, concentrating upon its agricultural and commercial potential, together with slightly sour comments on the political, social and cultural life of the capital. Beaumont was invited by the Buenos Aires government to superintend British immigration to the country ('*men* and *money* are the avowed wants of the government of Buenos Ayres') and he established two settlements on the west bank of the Paraná and in Entre Ríos, described in chapters 7-8. The appendix reproduces the 'Treaty of amity, commerce, and navigation' between Great Britain and the United Provinces of the Río de la Plata (1825).

133 **Travels in Chile and La Plata, including accounts respecting the geography, geology, statistics, government, finances, agriculture, manners and customs, and the mining operations in Chile. Collected during a residence of several years in these countries.**
John Miers.   London: Baldwin, Cradock & Joy, 1826. 2 vols. maps.

The first 300 pages of the first volume describe the author's journey across the pampas to Mendoza, with observations also on Córdoba and San Juan, en route to Chile via Villavicencio and the Upsallata Pass (crossing which his pregnant wife nearly died). The remainder of volume one and the whole of volume two are devoted to Chile where he was involved in unsuccessful mining ventures. An engineer and botanist, Miers was later commissioned by the Buenos Aires government to install machinery for a mint. There is a modern reprint (New York: AMS Press, 1970).

134 **Travels in South America, during the years 1819-20-21; containing an account of the present state of Brazil, Buenos Ayres, and Chile.**
Alexander Caldcleugh.   London: John Murray, 1825. 2 vols. maps.

Chapters 5-10 of volume one concern Buenos Aires, Santa Fe, Córdoba, San Luis and Mendoza. The author, who was a promoter of the Anglo-Chilian Mining Company and therefore said to be a deadly rival of Joseph Andrews (see *Journey from Buenos Ayres, through the provinces of Cordova, Tucuman, and Salta, to Potosi* . . .), 'endeavoured to collect every fact which relates to the government, the resources and the prospects of the countries which he visited', not forgetting food, modes of dress, the arts, houses, education, the press, the public library (forerunner of the National Library), religion and justice, Indians and slaves.

135 **Travels into Chile, over the Andes, in the years 1820 and 1821, with some sketches of the productions and agriculture; mines and metallurgy; inhabitants, history, and other features, of America; particularly of Chile, and Arauco.**
Peter Schmidtmeyer.   London: Longman, Hurst, Rees, Orme, Brown & Green, 1824. 378p. map.

The author travelled in a two-wheeled carriage (*birlocho*) from Buenos Aires across the pampas to San Luis, Mendoza and over the Andes to Chile by way of the Upsallata Pass. His observations on social and economic matters, geography, wildlife and pampas Indians are valuable and the illustrations are exceptional. He also provides a plan of the post road between Buenos Aires and Santiago and the distances between towns.

136  **A trip across the Pampas of Buenos Aires (1836-1837).**
Platon Alexandrovich Chikhachev, translated from the Russian by Jack
Weiner.   Lawrence, Kansas: University of Kansas, Center of Latin
American Studies, 1967. 63p. map. bibliog. (Occasional
Publications, 8).

A slight but unique account of a journey in 1837 from Valparaíso to Buenos Aires via
Santiago, Mendoza and San Luis by 'a Russian aristocrat, a geographer and something
of a gadfly' (introduction), twenty-four years old at the time. The account, said to be
based heavily on Head (q.v.) was originally published in a Russian geographical
journal in 1844. The whole journey took forty days; he took only four days between
Santiago and Mendoza and galloped across the pampas covering an average of sixty
miles a day. In Montevideo he re-embarked on the same British frigate which had
dropped him off in Chile.

137  **Twenty-four years in the Argentine Republic; embracing the author's
personal adventures, with the civil and military history of the country,
and an account of its political condition, before and during the
administration of Governor Rosas; his course of policy; the causes and
character of his interference with the government of Monte Video, and
the circumstances which led to the interposition of England and France.**
John A. King.   London: Longman, Brown, Green & Longmans;
Philadelphia: D. Appleton, 1846. 324p.

Colonel King, a native of New York, enlisted in the Buenos Aires militia at the age of
fourteen in 1817. While not a very profound work (it emphasizes military matters and
has been criticized as naïve, not to say ignorant and deceitful, on political affairs), it
does nevertheless present a fascinating picture of a soldier of fortune who led an
adventurous life with the armies of liberation in northern Argentina before 1837. A
certain Thomas R. Whitney prepared the text from King's account. There is a recent
reprint (New York: AMS Press, 1971).

138  **Two thousand miles' ride through the Argentine provinces: being an
account of the national products of the country, and habits of the people;
with a historical retrospect of the Rio de la Plata, Monte Video, and
Corrientes.**
William MacCann.   London: Smith, Elder, 1853. 2 vols. map.

MacCann spent 1848 in Argentina. He visited a number of *estancias* and was struck by
the fact that, within a radius of 150 miles south and southeast of Buenos Aires, the
country was 'one vast sheep-walk' in the hands of English, Irish and Scottish farmers.
A ride as far as the Indian frontier via the towns of Tandil and Chascomús, a river-trip
up the Paraná and Uruguay, Rosario, Santa Fe and Córdoba, are all described. The
dictator Rosas, whom he knew well, is painted in an unusually favourable light. He is
gently critical of native Argentines: 'the resources of the country are altogether
neglected for want of an industrious population', whereas 'the prospect of reward to
British capital and industry is most favourable'.

139   **La vie et les moeurs à La Plata.** (Life and manners in Argentina.)
Emile Daireaux.   Paris: Hachette, 1889. 2nd rev. ed. 2 vols. maps.
Daireaux (1843-1916), who spent ten years in Argentina, here records the old customs
of a society which had been changed irreversibly by European immigration. He also
describes the country's commerce, industry and agriculture, and, being a lawyer and
journalist, he is especially interested in the legal system and the press. This is one of
the best social and economic descriptions of Argentina in the second half of the
nineteenth century.

140   **Voyage à Buénos-Ayres et à Porto-Alègre, par la Banda-Oriental, les
missions d'Uruguay et la province de Rio-Grande-do-Sul. (De 1830 à
1834.) Suivi de considérations sur l'état du commerce français à
l'extérieur, et principalement au Brésil et au Rio-de-la-Plata.** (A journey
to Buenos Ayres and to Pôrto Alegre, by way of the Banda Oriental,
the Uruguayan missions and the Province of Rio-Grande-do-Sul. [From
1830 to 1834.] Followed by observations on the state of French foreign
trade, principally with Brazil and the River Plate.)
Arsène Isabelle.   Le Havre: J. Morlent, 1835. 618p. map.
Chapters six to twelve contain one of the most complete descriptions of Buenos Aires
in the 1830s – its buildings, government and police force, manufactures, commerce, sea
and river navigation, and its inhabitants' customs. The author makes plain his dislike
for the dictator Rosas.

141   **Voyage of Ulrich Schmidt to the rivers La Plata and Paraguai.**
Ulrich Schmidt, with notes and an introduction by Luis L.
Domínguez.   In: *The conquest of the River Plate (1535-1555).*
London: Hakluyt Society, 1891, p. 1-91. map. bibliog.
Ulrich Schmidt (or Schmidel, c1510-c1570) was a Bavarian soldier and agent for
Flemish merchants established in Seville, who accompanied Pedro de Mendoza's
expedition to the River Plate and was present at the first founding of Buenos Aires in
1536. This is his exciting account of adventures in the River Plate, 1535-52. The first
German edition was published in Frankfort-on-Main in 1567. The volume also contains
'The commentaries of Alvar Núñez Cabeza de Vaca', who succeeded Mendoza as
*adelantado* (governor) of Buenos Aires.

142   **Voyage to South America, performed by order of the American
Government, in the years 1817 and 1818, in the frigate 'Congress'.**
Henry Marie Brackenridge.   Baltimore, Maryland: John Toy, 1819.
2 vols. map. (A Collection of Modern and Contemporary Voyages &
Travels. Third Series: New Voyages and Travels, vol. 3, no. 6).
A London edition, with a slightly different title and with chapters arranged differently,
was published in 1820. Brackenridge, a lawyer, was secretary to a team of
commissioners sent to study the political situation in South America. The mission also
visited Brazil and Chile but this is primarily a description of the United Provinces of
the Río de la Plata – the country, inhabitants, administrative structure and economy.

143 **Voyages dans l'Amérique Latine méridionale depuis 1781 jusqu'en 1801; contenant la description géographique, politique et civile du Paraguay et de la rivière de la Plata; l'histoire de la découverte et de la conquête de ces contrées; des détails nombreux sur leur histoire naturelle, et sur les peuples sauvages qui les habitent; le récit des moyens employés par les Jésuites pour assujéter et civiliser les indigènes.** (Travels in South America between 1781 and 1801; containing descriptions of the geographical, political and civil state of Paraguay and the River Plate; a history of the discovery and conquest of those countries; and numerous details on their natural history and on the savage peoples who inhabit them, recounting the methods employed by the Jesuits to subjugate and civilize the Indians.)
Félix de Azara.  Paris: Dentu, 1809. 4 vols and atlas.

A classic description of the River Plate's natural history and inhabitants by a Spanish military engineer sent to the region in 1780 as a member of the commission surveying the boundary between Spanish and Portuguese America. His work provided information which was used by those responsible for the land development pursued in the next century. A Spanish translation, *Viajes por la América meridional*, with a useful introduction and notes, was published by Espasa-Calpe in 1923.

# Twentieth century

144 **The amazing Argentine: a new land of enterprise.**
John Foster Fraser.  London: Cassell, 1914. 291p.

Twenty-three chapters describe impressions gleaned on a tour of the country, concerning the city and province of Buenos Aires, railway development, the settlement of the land, industry, agriculture (including the sugar industry of the northeast) and livestock, constitution and government, Rosario, Córdoba, Bahía Blanca, Mendoza and the Andes. In a final section, Fraser considers Argentina's bright future despite difficulty in 'breaking through and away from the old Spanish habits'. There are fifty-four photographs.

145 **Among the gauchos.**
Hugo Backhouse.  London: Jarrolds, 1950. 208p.

The author arrived in Argentina at the age of sixteen, 'armed with a pile of introductions from my father to various business houses interested in camp affairs', and spent many years working on *estancias* near Bahía Blanca, in Santa Fe province and in the *sierras* of Córdoba. His fellow workers, sports (including rodeos and polo), hunting and wildlife are described, with fifty paintings and drawings by the author.

Travellers' Accounts. Twentieth century

146 **The Argentina of to-day.**
L. E. Elliott. London: Hurst & Blackett, 1927. 284p. map.
A rail journey through Argentina (appropriately, the map is of the railway network),
from the Straits of Magellan to the Bolivian border, provided the material for this
encyclopaedic guide to Argentina in the 1920s, with historical background and thirty-
four photographs added. He devotes much space to Argentina's natural resources and
export trade of meat and wheat. In chapter two there is an interview with 'a page of
living history', a ninety-six-year-old Anglo-Argentine who remembered Charles
Darwin's visit to the country and had known Juan Manuel de Rosas.

147 **Argentine tango.**
Philip Guedalla. London: Hodder & Stoughton, 1932. 254p.
A lyrical, elegantly written travel book on Argentina in seven sections, each of which
bears the name of a tango step. He combines historical flashbacks (the English
invasions: 'Argentines reflect with a comfortable glow that the victory was theirs and
that, after all, the English paid their country the supreme compliment of invasion')
with descriptions of the contemporary scene: the railways, the Sociedad Rural
agricultural show, the French and British communities ('Argentina is the one foreign
country in the world where England has made herself at home'), meetings with men of
letters and with General Uriburu in Government House, and interludes on an *estancia*
and in Mendoza.

148 **Between Maule and Amazon.**
Arnold J. Toynbee. London: Oxford University Press, 1967. 154p.
maps.
The British historian wrote a number of travel books on South and Central America.
These are brief observations on a trip made to Argentina, Brazil and Chile in 1966.
Chapters 12-17 (p. 48-73) recall the Paraná river, Buenos Aires and Salta ('Argentina's
two worlds'), Jujuy and Humahuaca, Santiago del Estero, Tucumán and Mendoza.
There is also a chapter on the Falkland Islands.

149 **Chaco chapters.**
Winifred Revill. London: Hodder & Stoughton, 1947. 192p. map.
Between November 1938 and 1945 the author and her husband represented the South
American Missionary Society among the Mataco Indians of the Argentine Chaco – at
Santa María, on the Argentine bank of the river Pilcomayo bordering Bolivia. Her
book is a charming reconstruction of life with the Indians and white neighbours,
though some will no doubt find it condescending towards the Mataco, 'a backward
tribe of Indians who still live a primitive existence fishing, hunting, and gathering wild
fruits' and who migrate to the sugar canefields during the harvest months.

150 **The condor and the cows.**
Christopher Isherwood. London: Methuen, 1949. 195p. maps.
bibliog.
This is a diary of the famous English novelist's trip with William Caskey (who took the
photographs) to South America. The guests of a refugee friend from Isherwood's
Berlin days, they spent some two months in Buenos Aires, on *estancias* near Mar del
Plata and on the Ramakrishna Mission in Bella Vista, an hour from the capital. He
finds Buenos Aires 'both very modern and very old-fashioned'. He meets the writer

38

Victoria Ocampo but fails to gain an introduction to Eva Perón. There are shrewd comments on tensions between Perón, Great Britain, the United States and Nazi Germany.

### 151 The conquest of Fitzroy.
Marc Antonin Azéma, translated by Katharine Chorley, Nea Morin.
Fair Lawn, New Jersey: Essential Books; London: André Deutsch, 1957. 237p. maps.

An account of the French ascent, led by the author, of Mount Fitzroy in the Patagonian Andes, between December 1951 and February 1952. The mountaineering history of Fitzroy (from 1916) is sketched, together with a description of the surrounding areas.

### 152 The countries of the King's Award.
Thomas Hungerford Holdich. London: Hurst & Blackett, 1904. 420p. map.

Colonel Sir Thomas Holdich, a vice-president of the Royal Geographical Society, was a member of the British Tribunal of Arbitration on the Argentine-Chilean boundary question which was resolved by the Award of King Edward VII in November 1902. As well as describing the history and outcome of the award, and the geography of the disputed area (Patagonia and Tierra del Fuego), Holdich comments on the Argentine people, their industries, railways and sea ports, *estancias* and armed forces.

### 153 En Argentine: de Buenos-Aires au Gran Chaco. (In Argentina: from Buenos Aires to the Gran Chaco.)
Jules Huret. Paris: E. Fasquelle, 1913. 529p.

Huret was a French journalist who lived for some time in Buenos Aires and contributed articles to *La Nación*. These are his penetrating impressions of society and culture in Buenos Aires, Tucumán, Salta, Chaco, Corrientes, Misiones and Entre Ríos. In the same year he published a second volume of observations, this time on southern Buenos Aires province, Córdoba, Mendoza and Río Negro: *En Argentine: de la Plata à la Cordillère des Andes* (546p. map).

### 154 Fat man in Argentina.
Tom Vernon. London: Michael Joseph, 1990. 262p. maps.

Eighteen-stone Vernon, a writer and broadcaster, is well known for his BBC radio series *Fat man on a bicycle*, in which he toured France, Norway and Britain. A two-part television programme on his Argentine bicycle journey was show on British television in autumn 1990. He restricts himself to two areas: the central pampas (Luján westward to Córdoba) and northern Patagonia (south and then east from Bariloche, ending at Rawson on the Atlantic coast), with a final chapter on Salta. He has often amusing encounters with first-generation Welsh, English, Irish, French and German settlers and their descendants. There are thirty photographs.

### 155 From the Falklands to Patagonia: the story of a pioneer family.
Michael James Mainwaring.   London; New York: Allison & Busby,
1983. 288p. maps. bibliog.

Shepherd William Halliday emigrated from Dumfries in Scotland to the Falkland
Islands in 1862 and went from there to join the Welsh sheep-farming community in
Patagonia. In 1966 the author met Mabel, William's last surviving child, 'still living in
the wooden house in which she had been born in 1888'. The book quotes extensively
from the family's various diaries and reproduces nearly one hundred photographs. A
remarkable story of struggle against many hardships, and with interesting accounts of
the pioneers' Tehuelche neighbours.

### 156 Hoo Hooey: an Argentine Arcady, and how I came there.
H. J. Muir.   London: Country Life, 1947. 277p.

We are told little about the author, except that he was born in Warwickshire in 1884
and that he emigrated to Argentina on an impulse after seeing a poster advertising
assisted passages to the country. Within six hours of arriving in Buenos Aires he was
off to become assistant manager at a country railway station. From there he progressed
to estate manager on an Anglo-Argentine saw-mill in Salta province and two sugar
plantations in Jujuy ('pronounced Hoo Hooey') province, where he was succeeded by
his brother; he was also appointed police commissioner in both places. A valuable
record of the violent but loyal gauchos, other English emigrants and the plantations'
Indian casual labourers.

### 157 In Patagonia.
Bruce Chatwin.   London: Jonathan Cape, 1977. 204p. maps. bibliog.

'In my grandmother's dining-room there was a glass-fronted cabinet and in the cabinet
a piece of skin.' It had belonged to the brontosaurus skeleton shipped to the Natural
History Museum by Chatwin's grandmother's cousin, the sailor Charley Milward, who
found the remains in a glacier. Starting at the Museum of Natural History of La Plata
in December 1974, Chatwin follows Milward's trail through Argentine Patagonia and
Chilean Tierra del Fuego, meeting mainly first-generation immigrants: English, Welsh,
Scottish, German, Spanish, Russian, Swedish, Arab and Boer. There are historical
flashbacks to various episodes in the region's history, including a lengthy reconstruction of the career of Butch Cassidy and the Sundance Kid – he claims to find
their log cabin and hears several first-hand accounts of their activities.

### 158 El Jimmy, outlaw of Patagonia.
Herbert Childs.   Philadelphia: J. B. Lippincott; London: Hutchinson,
1936. 399p. map.

James ('Santiago') Radbone was born in Berkshire, England, in 1874. Having 'got
mixed up with a girl' he emigrated to Patagonia to work on a sheep farm in 1892 partly
'to hush the matter up, and partly for adventure's sake'. After a hard and colourful life
in the region (at one time on the run from the Chilean police), amongst gauchos,
fellow-Britons and Indians (he married a Tehuelche and there is much here on the
tribe's lifestyle and customs), Radbone asked Robert Le Moyne Barrett (q.v.) to find
someone to write his biography; Barrett in turn contacted Childs. This book of
Jimmy's reminiscences – part reported speech, part third-person narrative – is a
wonderful picture of frontier life.

159 **Land of tempest: travels in Patagonia, 1958-62.**
Eric Shipton.   London; New York: Hodder & Stoughton, 1963. 224p.
maps.

Shipton's glaciological and botanical expeditions to the volcanoes and glaciers of the Patagonian Andes took him to Lakes San Martín, Viedma and Argentino in Argentina, and to Lake O'Higgins in Chile. The second half of the book is set in Chilean Tierra del Fuego south of Punta Arenas. There are twenty-four photographs.

160 **Letters from the Argentine.**
Francis Herron.   New York: G. P. Putnam's Sons, 1943. 307p. map.

Herron, a young United States journalist, visited Argentina from December 1941 to August 1942. These are the letters which he wrote to Walter S. Rogers, Director of the Institute of Current World Affairs, New York, 'simple accounts of what I saw, experiences I had and the activities in which I was engaged while studying provincial Argentina' (Santa Fe, Mendoza, Córdoba, the northwest and Chaco). He records his conversations with mainly Argentine academics and students, and in Córdoba has an interesting meeting with Carl C. Taylor, author of *Rural life in Argentina* (q.v.).

161 **Mischief in Patagonia.**
H. W. Tilman.   Cambridge, England: Cambridge University Press, 1957. 185p. maps.

In 1955-56 the author sailed in his small boat *Mischief* from England through the Strait of Magellan to Puerto Bueno in southern Chile; he and his two companions then crossed the ice-cap – the Calvo Glacier in Chile and the Bismarck Glacier in Argentina – to Lago Argentino and back, a journey of six weeks. The book is largely confined to details of sailing and mountain climbing.

162 **The old Patagonian express: by train through the Americas.**
Paul Theroux.   London: Hamish Hamilton, 1979. 340p. maps.

A diary of Theroux's train journey from Boston to Esquel in Patagonia; the last five chapters (p. 280-340) are set in Argentina, and start with the crossing from Bolivia to Tucumán ('the ultimate provincial town, self contained and remote') via La Quiaca, Humahuaca and Jujuy on *El Panamericano*. In the north he 'liked the look of Argentina. The landscape was wide open and fertile'. He then catches *La Estrella del Norte* ('North Star') to Buenos Aires (which depressed him), the *Lagos del Sur* ('Lakes of the South') to Ingeniero Jacobacci and the 'old Patagonian express' (ironically a very slow steam train, fourteen hours) to Esquel. He writes shrewdly and wittily both of being a traveller and of the people he meets: a German hitch-hiker, a party of meat salesmen, Jorge Luis Borges (to whom he reads Poe and Kipling), the station master at Ingeniero Jacobacci, and a Welsh boy on the 'Patagonian express'.

163 **Pampa grass: the Argentine story told by an American pioneer.**
Diego Newbery.   Buenos Aires: Editorial Guarania, 1953. 244p.

A simply told but eventful account, transcribed by his son, of a three-year visit to the interior of Argentina, interspersed with historical background. A dentist by profession, the author in 1877 visited his brother Ralph (after whose famous pilot son the Jorge Newbery airport outside Buenos Aires was named), who had set up a dental practice in the Argentine capital. He went to Corrientes and Bahía Blanca by boat, Rosario and Córdoba by train, Salta by herding 200 pack mules there. In Jujuy he teamed up with

Domingo Pérez, a local politician on the run, with whom he narrowly evaded capture by a military search-party.

### 164 The real Argentine: notes and impressions of a year in the Argentine and Uruguay.
J. A. Hammerton.   New York: Dodd, Mead, 1915. 453p.

'The chief fault of most writers on the Argentine is the indiscriminate praise they shower around, their fulsome flattery of the country.' For him, Argentina is a land of pain, Buenos Aires a city of sham: 'everything that met one's eyes was mean, or makeshift'. His caustic but perceptive eye roves over street life, social life, business life, the Argentine at home, the British colony, life in the 'camp' and provincial towns. His observations on Uruguay follow on pages 379-437. The British edition was published as *The Argentine through English eyes, and a summer in Uruguay* (London: Hodder & Stoughton, 1916).

### 165 The river and the people.
Gordon Meyer.   London: Methuen, 1965. 223p.

From cosmopolitan Buenos Aires the book moves up the Paraná River to Corrientes and thence into the Paraguayan Chaco. Meyer paints a fascinating portrait of the *porteño* (Buenos-Airean) character ('extreme individual maturity and political infantility'), and especially of rich women and their attitudes to marriage. He lived in South America for many years, and also published a novel and three novellas set in Argentina: *Sweet water and bitter* (London: Methuen, 1962) and *Death in the campo* (Methuen, 1963).

### 166 The sand, the wind and the sierras: days in Patagonia.
Mollie Robertson, illustrated by Maurice Wilson.   London: Geoffrey Bles, 1964. 253p. map.

The autobiography of a girl who spent her childhood (9 to 15 years) in the foothills of the Andes on two different Patagonian ranches owned by 'the Company'. Apart from her taciturn father and strong-willed mother, she had only animals, the farm's Tehuelche and Chilean workers and eccentric European storekeepers for company; she describes them all with charming simplicity. 'It is difficult to realise the utter isolation in the great distances between ranches which then existed in this part of Patagonia.' Despite the dusty climate and monotonous food, she was heartbroken when the time came for the family to return to England after the First World War.

### 167 South America: observations and impressions.
James Bryce.   New York: Macmillan, 1920. rev. ed. 611p. maps.

This is the travel diary of a four-month trip to South America. Chapter nine (p. 315-48) describes Lord Bryce's stay in Buenos Aires. In contrast to Peru, Bolivia and Chile, which he had visited beforehand, 'in the River Plate regions there is (except along the Andes and in the far north) little natural beauty, and nothing that recalls the past'. After contemplating local society, the European immigrants and ranching activities, he concludes that 'Argentina is the United States of the Southern Hemisphere' and that 'seldom has nature lavished gifts upon a people with a more bountiful hand'.

168 **South America to-day.**
Georges Clemenceau.   London: T. Fisher Unwin; New York: G. P.
Putnam's Sons, 1911. 315p.
This former Prime Minister of France had no trouble communicating with the
Argentine people since 'every one here understands French'. He found 'a large public
of European culture and wide intelligence, eager to hear what any European might
have to say'. The book emphasizes Argentina, with four chapters on Uruguay and
Brazil. He visited Rosario and Tucumán, but devotes most space to Buenos Aires and
the 'camp', where he enjoyed game-shooting and equestrian sports.

169 **This way southward: a journey through Patagonia and Tierra del Fuego.**
A. F. Tschiffely.   London: Heinemann; New York: W. W. Norton,
1940. 354p. maps.
Tschiffely, a Swiss writer who taught in schools in England and Argentina, had
previously made an epic 10,000-mile journey from Buenos Aires to Washington on two
creole horses, Macha and Gato, in 1925-28. This was published as *Tschiffely's ride*
(London: Heinemann, 1933), a very popular book in its day. He returned to Argentina
in 1937, was reunited with his two horses, and then set out to cover seven thousand
miles by car down the Patagonian Atlantic coast, through Chilean Tierra del Fuego, up
the Andean side of Patagonia to Bahía Blanca and back to Buenos Aires, 'without a
single breakdown'. There are over eighty good photographs, many of them of Ona,
Yahgan and Tehuelche Indians.

170 **Through the heart of Patagonia.**
H. Hesketh Prichard.   London: Heinemann; New York: D. Appleton,
1902. 346p. maps.
'The original motive with which these travels were undertaken lay in a suggestion . . .
that the prehistoric Mylodon might still survive hidden in the depths of the forests of
the Southern Andes.' Hesketh's scientific expedition on horseback in search of the
giant ground sloth left Rawson in September 1900, zigzagged down to Santa Cruz,
spent a few months in the Andean *cordillera* near Lake Argentino and then crossed
eastwards to Río Gallegos from where the party sailed for Punta Arenas. They finally
left Patagonia in June 1901 after a total journey of 2,000 miles, having come across 'no
single scrap of evidence of any kind which would support the survival of the Mylodon'.
The accounts of shooting for food become rather monotonous, but there are valuable
chapters and an appendix on Tehuelche manners, legends and hunting methods. Other
appendices describe the discovery by Francisco P. Moreno of the remains of the
Mylodon in 1874, and flora and fauna.

171 **Uttermost part of the earth.**
E. Lucas Bridges.   London: Hodder & Stoughton, 1948. 558p. maps.
Stephen (Esteban) Lucas Bridges was the son of Thomas and Mary Bridges, the first
white missionaries to settle amongst the Yahgan Indians at Ushuaia, southern Tierra
del Fuego, in 1871. In 1887, when Stephen was twelve, his parents founded the
Estancia Harberton, a sheep and cattle farm named after Mary's birthplace in Devon,
twenty-five miles east of Ushuaia; they also had 100 acres of land on Picton Island. The
book combines autobiography, anthropology and natural history with the early
missionary history of the region. There is so much detail on Indian culture (including a
retelling of several Ona myths) that an index of Indian characters is needed. An

43

appendix relates the remarkable story of Thomas's Yamana-English dictionary of 23,000 words, the manuscript of which was finished in 1879, almost stolen by an unscrupulous Dr Cook, retrieved and given to the British Museum in 1939. A facsimile of the first edition (Austria, 1933) was published in Buenos Aires in 1987.

172 **Voice from the wilderness.**
R. G. Thompson. London: Macdonald, 1947. rev. ed. 238p.

In 1938 the author went to southern Paraguay and the Argentine province of Misiones 'to seek and find those tens of thousands of men, women and children who had fled from threatened frontiers, from wars and rumours of wars and collapsing economies, to seek peace and the right to live'. In Part two, 'El Dorado' (p. 119-214) he visits the communities of the 150,000 settlers who, between the World Wars, migrated to the Alto Paraná between Posadas and the Iguazú Falls: Bonpland (a Polish settlement), El Dorado (German) and Victoria (British). Thompson wrote an earlier, disappointing, travel book, *Argentine interlude: the first roll of a rolling stone* (London: Duckworth, 1931).

173 **A Yankee in Patagonia, Edward Chace: his thirty years there, 1898-1928.**
Robert Le Moyne Barrett, Katharine Ruth Ellis Barrett. Boston, Massachusetts; New York: Houghton Mifflin; Cambridge, England: W. Heffer & Sons, 1931. 349p. maps.

'Who is Chace? Just a Yankee, cast ashore in . . . Santa Cruz – a sailor and sheep-driver, whose lazo or gun never missed its mark, who did not know fear, but gave his whole heart and thirty years of his life to Patagonia.' Chace, a carpenter on a Boston schooner, went to Patagonia in 1898 to look over abandoned whaling grounds in the South Shetlands, and stayed. The Barretts interviewed him in New England; their book indeed 'retains all the spontaneity, fragrance and colour of the original tale' of his life among the Indians, sheep drivers, wild cattle, ostriches, guanacos and pumas.

174 **A Yankee in Patagonia. (A bit of autobiography.)**
Bailey Willis. Stanford, California: Stanford University Press, 1947. 152p. maps.

Beginning in 1910 Willis, Professor of Geology at Stanford University and working for the US Geological Survey, 'chanced on an opportunity to promote the welfare of the Argentine people by telling them what a rich and promising province lay neglected in the Patagonian Cordillera of the Andes'. Until the First World War interrupted his scientific missions, he 'explored, and continued exploring, planning highways, railways, cities, and colonization'.

# Flora and Fauna

## General

**175 Argentina protects its wildlife treasures.**
William G. Conway, photographs by Des and Jen Bartlett. *National Geographic*, vol. 149, no. 3 (March 1976), p. 290-320. maps.
Consists of two photo-essays: a system of wildlife reserves and parks established by the Department of Tourism and Wildlife in Chubut, where new roads, new industries and growing towns are threatening wildlife; and the mammals and birds along a 200-mile stretch of the Patagonian coast.

**176 Cameos from the silver-land; or the experiences of a young naturalist in the Argentine Republic.**
Ernest William White. London: John van Voorst, 1881. 2 vols. map.
An expedition made with the intention of correcting the 'at times absurd, at others biassed' notions of Argentina held by the English. The author visited the whole of Argentina, apart from Patagonia and Tierra del Fuego, chiefly on 'steamers, railways, diligencies, carts', but also covering about 1,200 miles on mule. As well as giving a wealth of detail on all classes of animals and plant life (he includes their scientific names), he is also interesting on Argentine life, society and institutions.

**177 The naturalist in La Plata.**
W. H. Hudson. London: Chapman & Hall, 1892. 388p.
Most of the twenty-four chapters gathered together here were first published in a variety of natural history and other journals. Pumas, skunks, wasps, dragon-flies, mosquitoes, spiders, humming-birds, crested screamers, woodhewers, vizcachas, guanacos, horses and cattle are described beautifully by this famous British naturalist (1841-1922), who was born and lived in Argentina until 1874. Hudson also writes more generally on such topics as 'animal weapons', fear in birds, mimicry and warning

45

colours in grasshoppers, the death-feigning instinct, and music and dancing in nature. The twenty-eight illustrations are by J. Smit.

178 **Naturalistas argentinos durante la dominación hispánica.** (Argentine naturalists of the colonial period).
Guillermo Fúrlong Cárdiff. Buenos Aires: Editorial Huarpes, 1948. 438p. (Cultura Colonial Argentina, 7).

Over 200 naturalists, from Diego García (fl. 1526) to independence (1810), are chronicled in minute detail by this prolific Jesuit historian of the River Plate. There are over 300 contemporary illustrations by Pedro Montenegro, José Sánchez Labrador (the most industrious of the colonial River Plate naturalists), Florián Baucke and others.

179 **Notes on the natural history of the Strait of Magellan and West coast of Patagonia, made during the voyage of H.M.S. 'Nassau' in the years 1866, 67, 68 & 69.**
Robert O. Cunningham. Edinburgh: Edmonston & Douglas, 1871. 517p. map.

Cunningham was the naturalist on a three-year survey of Chilean and Argentine Patagonia and Tierra del Fuego, the River Gallegos, the southern Chilean Pacific coast and the Falkland Islands. He encountered Patagonian Indians and contributed to the debate concerning the existence of Patagonian 'giants': 'the men being rarely less than five feet eleven inches in height, and often exceeding six feet by a few inches'.

180 **Los parques nacionales de la Argentina y otras de sus áreas naturales.** (The national parks of Argentina and other areas of outstanding natural beauty.)
Francisco Erize, Marcelo Canevari, Pablo Canevari, Gustavo Costa, Mauricio Rumboll. Madrid: Instituto de Cooperación Iberoamericana [and] Instituto de Caza Fotográfica y Ciencias de la Naturaleza, 1981. 224p. bibliog.

In 1981 Argentina had eighteen national parks and other *monumentos naturales* covering 27,500 square kilometres (just under one per cent of the total area of the country), protected by a new law of 1980. This beautifully illustrated book describes, region by region, the parks' physical features and the wildlife found in them. A map would have been useful. See also the earlier *Los parques nacionales argentinas* (Buenos Aires: Guillermo Kraft, 1945), with black-and-white photographs by Herbert Kirchhoff.

181 **Piedras de Afilar: the unfulfilled dream of a 19th-century Scottish botanist in South America.**
Oliver Dawe. Haddington, Scotland: Charles Skilton, 1988. 167p. map. bibliog.

The biography of John Gillies, a Scottish doctor who settled in Mendoza, bought a huge tract of land 'the size of Kent', called Piedras de Afilar (Spanish for 'whetstones'), on which he tried unsuccessfully to found an agricultural colony of immigrants from Scotland. Gillies was also a keen amateur botanist, and the book describes his extensive field trips in the area and his contribution to Argentine botanical knowledge. After his death in 1834 his heirs spent many years establishing title to the land; the family sold the estate in 1951.

182  **To the River Plate and back: the narrative of a scientific mission to South America, with observations upon things seen and suggested.**
W. J. Holland.   New York; London: Knickerbocker Press, 1913. 387p.
Replicas of a skeleton of the dinosaur *Diplodocus Carnegiei* belonging to the Carnegie Museum were presented to the national museums of various European countries, starting with the British Museum in 1905. President Roque Sáenz Peña asked Andrew Carnegie to present one to the Museum of Natural History in La Plata, and Holland, Director of the Carnegie Museum, was instructed to take the replica there. This book records that mission, his tour of the country and his observations of birds, animals and flowers.

183  **The whispering land.**
Gerald Durrell, with illustrations by Ralph Thompson.   London: Rupert Hart-Davis, 1961. 235p.
The famous naturalist gives a lively and entertaining account of a visit to two regions of Argentina (Patagonia and Jujuy) to bring back specimens of birds and animals for the Jersey Zoo. On the Valdés peninsula he encounters elephant seals, guanacos, Darwin's rhea and the hairy armadillo; at Deseado the penguin colonies and the Patagonian hare. In Jujuy he is able to buy many specimens from the locals: parrots, rabbits, wild pigs, pumas, vampire bats, pigmy owls, nocturnal monkeys and peccaries. In *The drunken forest* (London: Rupert Hart-Davis, 1956. 238p.) he describes a two-month trip to Tierra del Fuego and Paraguay with the (unsuccessful) aim of collecting ducks and geese.

184  **The wilds of Patagonia: a narrative of the Swedish expedition to Patagonia, Tierra del Fuego and the Falkland Islands in 1907-1909.**
Carl Skottsberg (et al.).   London: Edward Arnold, 1911. 336p. maps.
Skottsberg, a lecturer at the University of Uppsala, was botanist on this three-man Swedish Magellan Expedition accompanied by two geologists. The book contains mainly scientific details of wildlife but includes valuable commentaries on such matters as the German colonists of Lake Argentino, and the Andes and Beagle Channel boundary disputes with Chile.

# Flora

185 **Flora de la provincia de Buenos Aires.** (The flora of the province of
Buenos Aires.)
Edited by Angel Lulio Cabrera. Buenos Aires: Instituto Nacional de
Tecnología Agropecuaria, 1963-70. 6 vols. (Colección Científica del
INTA. Tomo 4, parte 1-6).

Twenty-eight contributors have here produced a detailed and richly illustrated
inventory of 'all the species of vascular plants which grow naturally in the province of
Buenos Aires, in the Federal Capital and on Martín García Island [in the River Plate
estuary]'; some imported and cultivated plants growing spontaneously are also
included. See also the same author and Elsa Matilde Zardini's concise *Manual de la
flora de los alrededores de Buenos Aires* (Buenos Aires: Editorial Acme, 1978. 2nd ed.
755p.), describing 138 species of flowers which grow within a 50-kilometre radius of the
capital.

186 **Flora of Tierra del Fuego.**
David M. Moore. Oswestry, England: Anthony Nelson; St Louis,
Missouri: Missouri Botanical Garden, 1983. 396p. maps. bibliog.

An authoritative work based on studies undertaken by the author since 1961 and
illustrated with eight colour plates and 282 line drawings credited to R. N. P. Goodall,
Flora Patagónica and S. Parkinson (1745?-71). Seven types of vegetation are identified.
Families and species of the flora are described systematically and their geographical
affinities (native, alien) indicated. The appendices list the flora's Spanish, English and
Indian names (and uses, in the last case).

187 **Great botanical gardens of the world.**
Edward Hyams, William MacQuitty. London: Nelson, 1969. 288p.
map.

The text is by Hyams, the splendid photographs by MacQuitty. 'The Botanical Garden
of Buenos Aires [Jardín Botánico 'Carlos Thays', p. 266-8] can no longer be called
"great"; but in the past it did important work in the botany of South American plants.'
In 1892 Carlos Thays, Argentina's 'Capability' Brown, created the garden, covering
fifteen acres in the heart of Buenos Aires, with 721 species of Argentine plants.
Although the garden ran a very good training school for professional gardeners, by
1969 it had become badly neglected. Thays wrote his own guide to the garden: *El
Jardín Botánico de Buenos Aires* (Buenos Aires: Peuser, 1910. 180p.).

188 **Guía de flores argentinas : Argentine flowers.**
Florence Woodgate Konczewska. Buenos Aires: Editorial Albatros,
1976. 64p.

Forty-six flowers, one per page and each illustrated (not too clearly) in colour
photographs, are described in a bilingual Spanish-English text. There is an index and a
glossary of Spanish and English terms used. Scientific names are also given.

189 **Hongos argentinos.** (Argentine mushrooms.)
J. Raithelhuber.   Buenos Aires: Compañía Impresora Argentina,
1974. vol 1. bibliog.
There are some 1,600 species of mushroom in Argentina. Volume one of a projected
three volumes describes the 181 species (both edible and poisonous) to be found in the
Federal Capital and province of Buenos Aires: their common and scientific names,
habitat, description, smell and taste, and whether edible (the author even includes
three recipes). There are six pasted-in colour photographs, twenty plates of drawings,
and good indexes.

190 **The natural vegetation of Nahuel Huapí National Park, Argentina.**
E. J. Wilhelm, Jr..   *Geographical Knowledge* (Kanpur-2, India),
vol. 1, no. 2 (July 1968), p. 74-84. map. bibliog.
This brief article describes the complexity of the natural vegetation to be found in the
Nahuel Huapí National Park, where at least five vegetation formations can be
distinguished: 'the montane series, the temperate (Valdivian) rain forest, the
mesophytic forest, the central transition series, and the Patagonian steppe'.

191 **Pollen flora of Argentina: modern spore and pollen types of**
**Pteridophyta, Gymnospermae, and Angiospermae.**
Vera Markgraf, Héctor L. D'Antoni.   Tucson, Arizona: University of
Arizona Press, 1978. 208p. map. bibliog.
A comprehensive, illustrated directory of the 374 species of pollen flora types occurring
in Argentina. The pollen morphological keys for identification of the pollen grains are
divided into four plant geographical regions (Amazonic [subtropic forest of NW and
NE Argentina], Chaqueño, Andean-Patagonic and Subantarctic), followed by a
description of the spore and pollen types of the families referred to in the title, pollen
morphological keys and three alphabetical indexes (family and species, species,
common names).

192 **The potatoes of Argentina, Brazil, Paraguay, and Uruguay: a**
**biosystematic study.**
John Gregory Hawkes, J. P. Hjerting.   Oxford: Clarendon Press,
1969. 525p. maps. bibliog. (Annals of Botany Memoirs, 3).
Intended for taxonomists, geneticists and plant-breeders, and based on collecting
expeditions and experimental work in England and Denmark, this impressive study of
the wild and indigenous cultivated tuber-bearing *Solanum* species combines a full
discussion of the taxonomic concepts and methods with a detailed catalogue of
individual species, their distribution, habitat, breeding behaviour, etc. There are 150
black-and-white photographs and many sketches and tables.

193 **Survey of Argentine medicinal plants – folklore and phytochemical screening.**
A. L. Bardoni, M. E. Mendiondo, R. V. D. Rondina, J. D. Coussio.
*Lloydia*, no. 35 (1972), p. 69-80; *Economic Botany*, vol. 30, no. 2 (April-June 1976), p. 161-85. bibliog.

A two-part catalogue of more than 100 of Argentina's 700 native medicinal and toxic plant species; those selected are used as popular medicines. The tables give their common name, habitat, medicinal use, preparation method, chemical composition and the results of phyochemical screening. For a fuller directory in Spanish see Martín Toursarkissian, *Plantas medicinales de la Argentina: sus nombres botánicos, vulgares, usos y distribución geográfica* (Buenos Aires: Editorial Hemisferio Sur, 1980. 178p.).

# Fauna

194 **Amphibians of Argentina.**
José Miguel Cei.   Florence, Italy: Università degli Studi di Firenze, 1980. 609p. maps. bibliog. (Monitore Zoologico Italiano. New Series. Monografía, 2).

The main sections in this scholarly field guide are the 'Key to identification of amphibians' (p. 99-147) and the 'Description of the species of amphibians with remarks on their life history and biology' (p. 149–end). There are 24 colour plates and over 200 black-and-white drawings and photographs. Chapter one reviews the historical literature and describes the amphibians' general morphophysiological characteristics. See also the same author's 'Additional notes to *Amphibians of Argentina*: an update, 1980-1986' in *Monitore Zoologico Italiano*, N. S., vol. 21, no. 3 (1987), p. 209-72. A pocket field guide to amphibians is José M. Gallardo's *Anfibios argentinos: guía para su identificación* (Buenos Aires: Biblioteca Mosaico, 1987. 98p.).

195 **Arbovirus investigations in Argentina, 1977-1980.**
M. S. Sabattini, C. J. Mitchell, T. P. Monath (et al.).   *American Journal of Tropical Medicine and Hygiene*, vol. 34, no. 4 (July 1985), p. 937-75. maps. bibliog.

Included here are four studies of the ecology of the 'epizootics of equine encephalitis', a joint project between the Institute of Virology of the University of Córdoba and the Division of Vector-Borne Viral Diseases, Centers for Disease Control, Fort Collins, Colorado. The focus is upon Santa Fe province, where the mosquito-borne virus, observed since 1908, has occurred most frequently. Human cases of the disease have been rare.

196 **Aves argentinas: guía para el reconocimiento de la avifauna bonaerense :
A field guide to the birds of Buenos Aires Province.**
Tito Narosky, illustrated by Darío Izurieta.    La Plata, Argentina:
Asociación Ornitológica de La Plata, 1978. 128p. bibliog.
According to the author, more than 300 species of birds (one-third of the country's
total number of species) are to be found in the province of Buenos Aires. He provides
for each bird: common and scientific names, length, seasonal presence (resident,
migratory), habitat, abundance (rare, scarce, common, abundant), behaviour and a
general description. The text is bilingual.

197 **Las aves argentinas: una guía de campo.** (A field guide to the birds of
Argentina.)
Claës Christian Olrog.    Buenos Aires; Tucumán, Argentina:
Universidad Nacional de Tucumán, Instituto Miguel Lillo, 1959. 343p.
map. bibliog.
This is a well-illustrated guide to the native and seasonal migrant birds of Argentina, a
total of 904 species and subspecies. There is a small, basic water-coloured sketch and a
standard description for each bird: common and scientific names, appearance and
distinguishing features, size, behaviour, song, where commonly found and at what time
of year, distribution (with a distribution sketch map) and its subspecies. An index of
common names is provided. There is a modern reprint (Buenos Aires: Administración
de Parques Nacionales, 1984. 349p.). The same author has produced a revised but
unillustrated directory of birds: *Nueva lista de la avifauna argentina* (Tucumán,
Argentina: Fundación Miguel Lillo, 1979. 324p. [Opera Lilloana, 27]).

198 **Aves marinas del Río de la Plata y aguas vecinas del Océano Atlántico.**
(Marine birds of the River Plate estuary and the neighbouring waters of
the Atlantic Ocean.)
Rodolfo Escalante, illustrated by Víctor García Espiell.    Montevideo,
Uruguay: Barreiro y Ramos, 1970. 199p. bibliog.
The River Plate contains a rich supply of plankton which attracts marine birds in large
numbers. This guide covers the Argentine coast of Buenos Aires and Río Negro
provinces, Uruguay and the southern Brazilian coast. For each bird there is a brief
description for identification, geographical distribution, nesting and general habits.
There are eight plates of drawings, and an index of common and scientific names.

199 **A biogeographic analysis of the mammals of Salta Province, Argentina:
patterns of species assemblage in the Neotropics.**
Ricardo A. Ojeda, Michael A. Mares.    Lubbock, Texas: Texas Tech
University Press, 1989. 66p. maps. bibliog. (Texas Tech University
Museum. Special Publication, 27).
Salta Province in northwestern Argentina, a tropical-temperate region of 155,000
square kilometres, 'is one of the most diverse regions in South America, from the
standpoint of the types of major habitats it contains'. The authors examined 1,028
specimens from the area and recorded '112 species, 78 genera, 28 families, and nine
orders of mammals' within 8 vegetationally defined macrohabitats; and they assess the
taxonomic and ecological resemblance between them and conclude that there are two

major clusters, the 'aridlands' and 'forests' fauna. There are no illustrations of the mammals themselves. Definitely not for the general reader.

200 **Birds of La Plata.**
W. H. Hudson.    London: J. M. Dent; New York: E. P. Dutton, 1920.
2 vols.

'The matter contained in this work is taken from the two volumes of the *Argentine Ornithology*, published in 1888-9, and was my first book on the subject of bird life.' It is also a companion volume to *The naturalist in La Plata* (q.v.). According to Hudson, about one-quarter of South American bird species are to be found in Argentina, with about half that number in the River Plate area. Although 'the species known to me personally number 233', Hudson describes 84 exclusively neotropical species: tanagers, troupiads, tyrant-birds, plant-cutters, woodhewers, ant-birds, gallito birds, humming-birds, screamers, courlans, jacanas, seed-snipe, tinamus and rheas.

201 **The birds of South America.**
Robert S. Ridgely, Guy Tudor, with the collaboration of William L. Bown.    Oxford: Oxford University Press, 1989- . 4 vols. map. bibliog.

Over 3,100 bird species are either resident or migrant in South America. Volume one of this four-volume set, devoted to the Oscine Passerines, is described as 'the first modern field handbook for all the true songbirds', encompassing some 750 species. The text is by Ridgely, the thirty-one coloured drawings (there are no photographs) by Tudor. After chapters on habitats, biogeography, migration and conservation, the main section describes the birds according to types. Each entry, typically half a page, gives the common and scientific names, size and physical description, similar species, habitat and behaviour, song and range (also shown on a shaded map). Volumes 2-4 will cover the Suboscine Passerines (landbirds) and Nonpasserines (waterbirds). There is no geographical index.

202 **Butterflies of the neotropical region.**
Bernard Laurence D'Abrera.    Melbourne, Australia: Lansdowne Editors, in association with E. W. Classey [vol. 1]; Ferny Creek, Australia: Hill House [vol. 2]; Black Rock, Australia: Hill House [vols 3-5], 1981-88. 5 vols. maps. bibliog.

Butterflies from the Caribbean Sea as far south as the province of Misiones (northeast Argentina) are displayed in this beautifully produced large-format series, totalling 877 pages and consisting chiefly of life-size colour illustrations. The volumes are grouped according to families. The author has also produced a pocket-sized volume, *Butterflies of South America* (Ferny Creek, Australia: Hill House, 1984. 256p.).

203 **Enciclopedia de las aves argentinas.** (Encyclopaedia of Argentine birds.)
Martín Rodolfo de la Peña.    Santa Fe, Argentina: Librería y Editorial Colmegna, 1978-79. 321p. bibliog.

A useful directory of Argentina's 948 identified species of birds, in eight fascicules organized according to the country's four ornithological regions (subtropical, Chaco-Pampean, Andean-Patagonian, Antarctic), and giving common and scientific names, length, colouring, habits, habitat, geographical distribution, and details of nests found by the author. The black-and-white photographs are rather poorly reproduced. There is an index of common names.

204  **Fauna argentina.** (Fauna of Argentina.)
Tucumán, Argentina: Centro Editor de América Latina, 1988. 5 vols. maps. bibliog.
No general editor is credited for this well-produced series. There are volumes for mammals, birds, amphibians and reptiles, fishes and insects, each consisting of some 200 pages of text, colour photographs and scientific drawings.

205  **Fauna de agua dulce de la República Argentina.** (Freshwater fauna of Argentina.)
Buenos Aires: Fundación para la Educación, la Ciencia y la Cultura, 1970- .
An irregular series of very technical publications covering all freshwater creatures: fish, mammals, birds, insects, etc. The present editor is Raúl Adolfo Ringuelet.

206  **Guía de los mamíferos argentinos.** (A guide to the mammals of Argentina.)
Claës Christian Olrog, M. M. Lucero.  Tucumán, Argentina: Fundación Miguel Lillo, 1980. 151p. maps. bibliog. (Instituto Miguel Lillo. Miscelánea, 69).
Part one discusses the mammals in their biological, anatomical and ecological contexts. Part two describes and illustrates (with thirty-six black-and-white drawings) the twelve species, and provides distribution maps. There are indexes of common and scientific names.

207  **A guide to the birds of South America.**
Rodolphe Meyer de Schauensee.  Wynnewood, Pennsylvania: Livingston Publishing for the Academy of Natural Sciences of Philadelphia; Edinburgh: Oliver & Boyd, 1970. 470p. maps. bibliog.
This is a systematic aid to identification recording all 2,924 species, belonging to 865 genera and 93 families, regularly found in South America. It gives their physical characteristics, range and habitat. The same author and Eugene Eisenmann have produced *The species of birds of South America with their distribution* (Narberth, Pennsylvania: Livingston, 1966. 577p.).

208  **Illustrated field guide to abundant marine fish species in Argentine waters.**
Matthias Stehmann.  *Mitteilungen aus dem Institut für Seefischerei* (Hamburg: Bundesforschungsanstalt für Fischerei), no. 23 (1979), p. 1-152. bibliog.
This is described as a 'revised and completed reprint', the first edition having been published in April 1978. The text is rather poorly reproduced from typescript but it contains much valuable information in (stilted) English. 'The author has selected those species which are abundant on the Patagonian shelf . . . and which . . . arc or may be

of commercial interest'. Most species are illustrated with 132 black-and-white drawings and poor photographs. There are indexes to the fishes' names in English, Spanish and German.

209 **Keys to the bats of Argentina.**
Arthur M. Greenhall, Rexford D. Lord, Elio Massoia. Ramos Mejía, Argentina: Pan American Zoonoses Center, 1983. 103p. bibliog. (Special Publication, 5).

Not designed specifically for the specialist, this provides identification of forty-six species of bats 'of well-documented occurrence in Argentina': a list of species, scientific and common names, taxonomic and zoogeographical comments, and the key section itself (consisting of brief physical descriptions, p. 17-23) followed by fifty-seven black-and-white photographs (p. 25-91).

210 **Lista de los peces de agua dulce de la Argentina.** (A list of the freshwater fishes of Argentina).
Hugo L. López, Roberto C. Meani, Amalia M. Miquelarena. Buenos Aires: Instituto de Limnología 'Dr Raúl A. Ringuelet', 1987. 50p. bibliog. (Biología Acuática, 12).

There have been certain changes in the taxonomy of certain groups since Ringuelet's *Los peces argentinos de agua dulce* (1967) and the authors' purpose is to update the latter's work and to list newly recorded species. Full historical citations are given. There are no illustrations.

211 **Observations on the birds of Argentina, Peru, Uruguay, and Chile.**
Frank Alexander Wetmore. Washington, DC: Government Printing Office, 1926. 448p. map. (Smithsonian Institution. United States National Museum. Bulletin, 133).

Wetmore, Assistant Secretary of the Smithsonian Institution, was sent to the region by the US Department of Agriculture's Biological Survey between May 1920 and May 1921. This is an annotated catalogue, with field observations, of the birds observed and collected. There are forty photographs of terrain and nests, but none of birds.

212 **Peces antárticos del sector argentino.** (Fishes of Argentine Antarctica.)
Norberto Bernardo Bellisio. Buenos Aires: Secretaría de Marina, Servicio de Hidrografía Naval, 1964-67. 5 vols. maps. bibliog.

Reports of the Argentine Navy's Antarctic Expeditions (Campañas Navales Antárticas), 1962-67, giving details of certain species examined off Antarctica and the South Orkney Islands.

213    **Peces marinos de la Argentina y Uruguay.** (Marine fishes of Argentina
       and Uruguay.)
       Roberto C. Menni, Raúl A. Ringuelet, Raúl H. Aramburu.    Buenos
       Aires: Hemisferio Sur, 1984. 359p. map. bibliog.

The South Atlantic is rich in marine fauna – 300 known genera, 400 species. The
detailed catalogue of marine fishes appears on pages 81-209, the plates on pages 257-
334. A review of the existing literature, a glossary and indexes of scientific and
common names complete the volume.

214    **South American birds: a photographic aid to identification.**
       John S. Dunning, with the collaboration of Robert S. Ridgely.
       Newtown Square, Pennsylvania: Harrowood Books, 1987, 351p. maps.

This book, which apparently took twenty-five years to produce, 'describes all the birds
likely to be seen in interior South America including the freshwater lakes'. The birds,
all of which were netted and photographed against natural foliage, are arranged
according to 74 family orders and their more than 2,700 species, and the entries
include: scientific and English names, preferred habitat and foliage type, length and
physical description. There is a small distribution map against each of the excellent
illustrations.

# Archaeology and Prehistory

215 **Additional petroglyphs in the central Humahuaca Valley.**
Alicia A. Fernández Distel.  *Latin American Indian Literatures*,
vol. 7, no. 1 (spring 1983), p. 81-90. map. bibliog.
A description of petroglyphs found by the author between 1972 and 1978 in the
Rodero Gorge, Jujuy province, adding to the discoveries described by Eric Borman in
1908; with three pages of drawings and a brief history of archaeological excavations in
the area. The petroglyphs, representing the human figure, date from the last period of
Humahuaca culture before the Inca horizon (AD 1210-1400).

216 **Advances in Andean archaeology.**
Edited by David L. Browman.  The Hague; Paris: Mouton, 1978.
580p. maps. bibliog.
This volume consists of papers from the Ninth International Congress of Anthropo-
logical and Ethnological Sciences (Chicago, 1973) and contains four chapters of
Argentine interest: Víctor A. Núñez Regueiro, 'Considerations on the periodizations
of northwest Argentina', p. 453-84; Myriam Noemí Tarragó, 'Paleoecology of the
Calchaquí Valley, Salta Province, Argentina', p. 485-512; José Antonio Pérez,
'Concerning the archaeology of the Humahuaca Quebrada', p. 513-24; Elena Perrotta
and Clara Podestá, 'Contribution to the San José and Santa María cultures, northwest
Argentina', p. 525-51.

217 **Advances in the archeology of the pampa and Patagonia.**
Luis Abel Orquera.  *Journal of World Prehistory*, vol. 1, no. 4 (Dec.
1987), p. 333-413. maps. bibliog.
An excellent overview dealing with two distinctive 'cultural-adaptive traditions': the
terrestrial hunter-gatherers who occupied the whole of the pampa and most of
Patagonia, and the maritime hunter-gatherers (Magellan Fueguian canoe Indians)
occupying only the southern tip of Patagonia ('both adaptations were achieved by the
end of the fifth millennium B.C.'). It describes the early complexes of the pampa and
northern and central Patagonia (notably the Los Toldos and Magellan phases, the

earliest documented examples). Seven sites and fifteen artefacts (including examples of rock art) are illustrated and there are four tables of radiocarbon dates.

218 **The Alamito culture of northwestern Argentina.**
Víctor A. Núñez Regueiro. *American Antiquity*, vol. 35, no. 2 (April 1970), p. 133-40. map. bibliog.
In two parts: a detailed description of the site (Campo del Pucará, a broad valley about 100 kilometres north of the city of Catamarca) and its artefacts, and a comparison of the Alamito culture of the fourth century BC (named after a small village near the sites and discovered in 1858) with other cultures. The inhabitants' settlement pattern, burial customs, food and social organization are discussed, and there are illustrations of a typical site, a stone sculpture and pottery whistles.

219 **An analysis of Santa María urn painting and its cultural implications.**
Ronald L. Weber. *Fieldiana: Anthropology*, new series, no. 2 (25 Nov. 1981), p. 1-32. (Field Museum of Natural History, Chicago. Publication, 1326).
The author traces the development of urn design and painting through the five phases of the Santa María culture. He concludes that the burial urns were 'clearly made under the influence of the Inca during the occupation of northwest Argentina in the last half of the fifteenth century'. The urns are uniform in shape but 'carry the most complex designs of any South American vessels'. Body, neck and nose designs are illustrated.

220 **Archaeological researches in the department of La Candelaria (Prov. Salta, Argentina).**
Stig Rydén. *Etnologiska Studier* (Gothenborg: Eleanders Boktryckeri Aktiebolag), no. 3 (1936), 327p. maps. bibliog.
The department of La Candelaria occupies the southeastern portion of Salta province. After a description of the fifteen sites excavated by the author in 1932, there is a detailed description of the artefacts – burial urns of Diaguita origin, sixteen other types of clay vessels, stone and earthenware objects other than vessels, and shell, bone and metal objects. Finally, the prehistoric culture of the area is discussed together with an account of modern native pottery-making and grain stores.

221 **Argentina indígena & prehistoria americana.** (Indigenous Argentina and prehistory of Latin America.)
Dick Edgar Ibarra Grasso. Buenos Aires: Tipográfica Editora Argentina, 1967. 685p. maps. bibliog.
Although there is some treatment of present-day Indians, most of the book is concerned with the prehistoric origin and development of cultural elements in Argentina (physical anthropology, ethnology, ethnography and linguistics) and is illustrated with hundreds of photographs and drawings of artefacts, many previously unpublished. There is constant comparison with the Indian cultures of neighbouring countries.

222 **Arte argentino antes de la dominación hispánica / Argentine art before the Hispanic domination.**
Giancarlo Puppo.    Seattle, Washington: University of Washington Press, 1981. 276p.

Some 250 superb photographs (a few in colour) of pottery, metal, stone and other objects, arranged according to ten cultural categories, accompanied by a bilingual text and chronological chart. A beautifully produced book, suitable for art historians as well as archaeologists, which demolishes the myth that Argentina had no significant pre-Hispanic art. The artefacts are from public museums and private collections, and many have not been illustrated before.

223 **Arte precolombino de la Argentina: introducción a su historia cultural.**
(Pre-Columbian art of Argentina: an introduction to its cultural history.)
Alberto Rex González.    Buenos Aires: Filmediciones Valero, 1977. 469p. maps. bibliog.

A superbly illustrated study of pre-Columbian cultures through their art which complements Giancarlo Puppo's *Arte argentino antes de la dominación hispánica* (q.v.). The art and culture (rock art and stone sculpture, cave paintings, metalwork, music) are subdivided according to six culturally stylistic areas – Pampa, Patagonia and Tierra del Fuego; the Sierras Centrales; the Northwest; the Quebrada de Humahuaca and Puna; Santiago del Estero; the Littoral and Chaco – and period – early (500 BC – AD 650), middle (AD 650-850) and late (AD 850-1480).

224 **Catalogue of fossil hominids. Part 3: Americas, Asia, Australasia.**
Edited by Kenneth Page Oakley, Bernard Grant Campbell, Theya Ivitsky Molleson.    London: Trustees of the British Museum (Natural History), 1975. 217p. maps.

Three sites in Argentina are described by Thomas Carl Patterson and Junius B. Bird on pages 3-5: Candonga Cave (cranium of a young girl, near Salsipuedes, Córdoba province), Fontezuelas (nearly complete female skeleton, northern Buenos Aires province) and Intihuasi Cave (partial remains of five skeletons, San Luis province). Data are given for site location, chronological age, artefacts, physical measurements, etc.

225 **Chaco pottery and Chaco history, past and present.**
Niels Fock.    In: *Akten des 34. Internationalen Amerikanistenkongresses, Wien, 18-25 Juli 1960.*    Vienna: Verlag Ferdinand Berger, 1962, p. 477-84. map. bibliog.

In 1958 the author and his wife made an expedition to the western, arid half of the Argentine Chaco immediately south of the Río Bermejo. In four sites, he found four ceramic styles bearing no resemblance to those of modern Mataco Indians, and three different forms of direct and secondary urn burial which differed from the modern Mataco habit of simple interment or burial on platforms. (For more on burial forms, see his 'Inca imperialism in northwest Argentina, and Chaco burial forms', *Folk*, vol. 3 [1961], p. 67-90.) Methods of pottery firing, ornamentation and cord decoration are described, and there is a drawing of a flat-bottomed bowl.

226 **Copper and copper alloys in ancient Argentina.**
G. A. Fester. *Chymia: annual studies in the history of chemistry*,
vol. 8 (1962), p. 21-31.
A rather crude (compared with the more northern) metallurgical culture stretching
from the highlands of Peru to northwestern Argentina produced utensils from copper
and bronze. A laboratory study of copper (and a few brass) objects excavated in the
Valley of Hualfín, near Belén in Catamarca province, and belonging to the Museum of
La Plata, revealed their chemical composition and method of manufacture.

227 **Cultural development in northwestern Argentina.**
Alberto Rex González. In: *Aboriginal cultural development in Latin
America: an interpretative review.* Edited by Betty J. Meggers,
Clifford Evans. Washington, DC: Smithsonian Institution, 1963,
p. 103-17. map. bibliog. (Smithsonian Miscellaneous Collections,
vol. 146, no. 1. Publication, 4517).
This is a useful summary of the archaeology of northwest Argentina, describing the
early pre-ceramic and the later agricultural and pottery-making cultures after 500 BC.
He concludes that 'more clearly than any other part of aboriginal Latin America, this
region appears to deserve the label of a melting pot, into which elements of very
different origins [from the altiplano and the tropical forests] were fused together to
produce a unique and characteristically local result'. The map shows the location of
archaeological sites, but there are unfortunately no illustrations of artefacts.

228 **The felinic complex in northwest Argentina.**
Alberto Rex González. In: *The cult of the feline: a conference in pre-
Columbian iconography, October 31st and November 1st, 1970.*
Edited by Elizabeth P. Benson. Washington, DC: Dumbarton Oaks
Research Library and Collections, 1972, p. 117-38. bibliog.
The iconography of the feline – in metalwork, pottery and stone carving – occurs
mainly in the Tafí and Condorhuasi cultures of the early period, and reaches its peak
'in frequency and in artistic and technological development' in the La Aguada culture,
found in the Calchaquí Valley to the north of San Juan province, around AD 850.
The article is illustrated.

229 **Historia de la arqueología argentina.** (History of Argentine
archaeology.)
Jorge Fernández. Mendoza, Argentina: Asociación Cuyana de
Antropología, 1982. 320p. map. bibliog. (Anales de Arqueología y
Etnología).
This is concerned with the study of Argentine archaeology, which can be divided into
five periods since the 'archaic or documentation' phase (1516-1871): the 'heroic phase'
(1872-1900), the development of archaeological studies in the university (1901-25,
1925-49), and of 'scientific' (1950-60) and modern scientific/professional archaeology
(since 1960). It includes a survey of the literature of the chief archaeological regions
and artefact/site types. There is a good bibliography of 1,937 items.

230 **An introduction to American archaeology. Vol. 2: South America.**
Gordon R. Willey. Englewood Cliffs, New Jersey: Prentice-Hall,
1971. 559p. maps. bibliog. (Prentice-Hall Anthropology Series).
A highly detailed and well-illustrated technical review of the status of archaeological
research. Chapter seven, 'Eastern and southern South America' (p. 452-78), contains
three sections of Argentine interest: 'The Chaco area', 'The Pampean area' and 'The
Fueguian area'. Each describes the natural setting, languages and tribes, and cultural
traditions.

231 **Inventory of radiocarbon dates from southern Patagonia and Tierra del
Fuego.**
Omar R. Ortiz-Troncoso. *Journal de la Société des Américanistes*,
vol. 67 (1980-81), p. 185-211. map. bibliog.
Radiocarbon dates for Patagonia have been known since 1951. This paper gives a
detailed tabular inventory of 160 radiocarbon measurements on samples from the two
areas, Argentine and Chilean Patagonia and Tierra del Fuego. The samples are
grouped into four categories (archaeological and glaciological samples and samples
related to volcanism and changes in sea level) and the following information is given:
site name, laboratory number, type of material dated, age, bibliographical reference.

232 **The La Aguada culture of northwestern Argentina.**
Alberto Rex González. In: *Essays in pre-Columbian art and
archaeology.* Edited by Doris Z. Stone (et al.). Cambridge,
Massachusetts: Harvard University Press, 1964, p. 389-420. map.
bibliog.
La Aguada culture materials have been found chiefly in the provinces of La Rioja and
Catamarca, but also at a few sites in Salta, Tucumán and San Juan. The author
summarizes the debate concerning the terms Draconian and Barreales as cultural or
ceramic styles. (The former was first used by Lafone Quevedo in 1892 when he noted
that certain painted figures resembled dragons; the latter is named after a culture at
Los Barreales, province of San Juan, first described by Salvador Debenedetti in 1917.)
Both cultures are assessed in terms of their society and artefacts. González suggests
that 'Argentina is a culture of Andean origin', citing such elements as advanced
metalwork and elaborate ceramics as evidence.

233 **Lowland Argentine archeology.**
George D. Howard, Gordon R. Willey. New Haven, Connecticut:
Yale University Press; London: Oxford University Press, 1948. 42p.
bibliog. (Yale University Publications in Anthropology, 39).
A volume covering the pampas and the northeast (including the basins of the Paraná
and Uruguay rivers), consisting of two papers: 'Northeast Argentina' (Howard) and
'The Argentine pampa' (Willey, an expansion of his chapter, 'Archeology of the
Greater Pampa', in *Handbook of South American Indians* [q.v.]). The methodology is
the same as that used in *Northwest Argentine archeology* (q.v.), which this volume
complements: definition of the ceramic styles, cultures and periods, and description of
the major sites. Based exclusively on the existing published literature, with eight pages
of plates.

234 New data on the archaeology of the Haush, Tierra del Fuego.
Anne Chapman, Thomas R. Hester. *Journal de la Société des Américanistes*, vol. 62 (1973), p. 185-208. map. bibliog.

The Haush were a hunter-gatherer people inhabiting the far eastern shore of the Isla Grande of Argentine Tierra del Fuego until the end of the nineteenth century and quite different culturally from the neighbouring Selk'nam and Yámana tribes. The artefacts found at eight sites along the shoreline were chiefly chipped-stone and bone blades and projectile points, of which there are some good photographs. A good description of the canoe-Indian cultures of southern Chilean Tierra del Fuego, but with relevance to the Argentine part of the island, is: Fredrik Barth, 'Cultural development in southern South America: Yahgan and Alkaluf vs. Ona and Tehuelche', *Acta Americana*, vol. 6, nos 3-4 (July-Dec. 1948), p. 192-9. See also P. W. Steager, 'The Yahgan and Alcaluf: an ecological description', *Kroeber Anthropological Society Papers* (Berkeley: University of California, Department of Anthropology), no. 32 (1965), p. 69-77.

235 **Northwest Argentine archeology.**
Wendell C. Bennett, Everett F. Bleiler, Frank H. Sommer. New Haven, Connecticut: Yale University Press; London: Oxford University Press, 1948. 160p. maps. bibliog. (Yale University Publications in Anthropology, 38).

Within each of four regions, covering 'the entire province of Jujuy and the northern mountainous section of the adjacent province of Salta to the east', the following elements are traced: major pottery styles and artefact complexes, major sites, cultures and periods. An excellent synthesis of the published literature, while the authors' analysis and interpretation are original. There are twelve pages of plates and twenty-six figures in the text.

236 **A note on the antiquity of bronze in N. W. Argentina.**
Alberto Rex González. In: *Actas del XXXIII Congreso Internacional de Americanistas, San José, 20-27 julio 1958.* San José, Costa Rica: [n.p.], 1958; Nendeln, Liechtenstein: Kraus Reprint, 1978, vol. 2, p. 384-97. bibliog.

Forty-two bronze specimens (bracelets, bells, chisels, axes, needles, tweezers and 'three probable ornaments'), thirty-nine belonging to the Barreales culture ('either the Ciénaga or Aguada phase') and three from the Condorhuasi culture, are described in turn but unfortunately not illustrated. All the objects were found in tombs and are now part of the B. M. Barreto collection in the Museo de La Plata. Their age, chemical composition, hardness and tensile strength are given.

237 **Pre-Columbian metallurgy of northwest Argentina: historical development and cultural process.**
Alberto Rex González. In: *Pre-Columbian metallurgy of South America: a conference at Dumbarton Oaks, October 18th and 19th, 1975.* Edited by Elizabeth P. Benson. Washington, DC: Dumbarton Oaks Research Library and Collections, 1979, p. 133-202. maps. bibliog.

Despite being inhabited primarily by agricultural, pottery-making groups, northwest Argentina was 'an early center of pre-Columbian metallurgical production, notable both in quality and quantity'. Tin, copper, silver and gold were used. This metallurgical production is described according to period (early, middle, late, Inca) and region (Puna, Valliserrana, Selvas Occidentales, La Aguada). There are twenty-five photographs and drawings and a map showing the most important mines in the region.

238 **The prehistory of NW Argentina: the Calchaquí Valley Project, 1977-1981.**
Gordon C. Pollard. *Journal of Field Archaeology*, vol. 10 (1983), p. 11-32.

A study of twenty-four sites by the author and Pío Pablo Díaz, Director of the Museo Arqueológico de Cachi, in the semi-arid Calchaquí Valley of the Andean region of southern Salta Province. The ceramics discovered, of which there are seventeen illustrations, date from AD 1000-1300 and show a strong Inca influence. See also the same author's 'The bronze artisans of Calchaquí', *Early Man*, vol. 3, no. 4 (1981), p. 27-33.

239 **Preliminary report on archaeological research in Tafí del Valle, N. W. Argentina.**
Alberto Rex González, Víctor A. Núñez Regueiro. In: *Akten des 34. Internationalen Amerikanistenkongresses, Wien, 18-25 Juli 1960.* Vienna: Verlag Ferdinand Berger, 1962, p. 485-96. bibliog.

'Tafí del Valle has an outstanding and almost unique characteristic within the archaeology of northwest Argentina: its monoliths or menhirs, sometimes 4m. long and exceeding 3 tons in weight.' The Tafí culture flourished some 1500 years ago. This study is based on excavations in early 1960 at the two most important Tafí Valley sites, El Mollar and La Plaza.

240 **Los pueblos y culturas indígenas del Litoral.** (Aboriginal peoples and cultures of the Argentine littoral.)
Antonio Serrano. Santa Fe, Argentina: Editorial Castellví, 1955. 124p. maps.

A classic study of the archaeology and ethnography of the early civilizations of the area bordering the Paraná and Uruguay rivers (present-day provinces of Santa Fe, Entre Ríos, Corrientes, Misiones, Formosa and Chaco, some 400,000 square kilometres), emphasizing the Chané, Charrúa, Toba, Guaraní and Guayaná tribes. Artefacts are illustrated by fifty (rather poor) black-and-white photographs.

241 **Rock art in western Argentina: the Andean region of Cuyo.**
Juan Schobinger. *Latin American Indian Literatures*, vol. 4, no. 1
(spring 1980), p. 64-9. bibliog.

To date, sixty-five rock-art sites, all in mountainous areas, have been identified in the
Cuyo region (provinces of Mendoza, San Juan and San Luis). There are two distinct
sectors: northern rock art, with clear Andean connections, and southern rock art, with
both Patagonian and Andean links. All of Cuyo rock art (there are two pages of
drawings of motifs) has 'magico-religious' associations.

242 **Rock art of the National Nahuel Huapí Park.**
Jorge Fernández. *Latin American Indian Literatures*, vol. 7, no. 2
(fall 1983), p. 202-9. bibliog.

The Nahuel Huapí Park is a large natural reserve where 'prehistoric sites with rock art,
especially pictographs, abound'. This article describes the well-preserved, 'essentially
abstract', paintings of Las Mellizas, a rocky hollow on the northeastern shore of Lake
Traful, and includes an inventory and two pages of drawings.

243 **Rock paintings in Argentina.**
M. Inez Hilger, Margaret Mondloch. *Anthropos*, vol. 57 (1962),
p. 514-23. map. bibliog.

Despite the title, this article deals exclusively with the Vega Valley site near San
Martín de los Andes, Neuquén province, although there is some comparison with
northern (Ando-Peruvian) and Patagonian rock paintings, and other nearby sites in
Neuquén and Chubut are mentioned. The paintings are found on exposed outcrops of
smooth flat rock, on rougher angular surfaces, and on cave walls. 'All are painted
directly on the surfaces; none is engraved. Several symbols form a horizontal line;
others form a group, indiscriminately placed.'

244 **Rock-paintings of northwest Córdoba.**
G. A. Gardner, with the collaboration of S. E. Gardner. Oxford:
Clarendon Press, 1931. 147p. map. bibliog.

The following sites were studied between 1921 and 1928: Agua de la Pilona, La
Aguada, Cerro Casa del Sol, Cerro Veladero and Cerro Colorado. The rock paintings,
executed by ancient Comechingón Indians, represent humans, animals and geometrical
figures. The authors conclude that 'the paintings are not idle daubings; that they are
something more than expressions of artistic feeling; that certain of them may be
records of some kind, or representations of remarkable events, while others may have
a symbolical, religious, or magical significance'. There are 25 photographs, 172 traced
figures and 44 colour sketches of the principal groups of paintings.

245 **A seriation of the late prehistoric Santa María culture of Northwestern Argentina.**
Ronald L. Weber. *Fieldiana: Anthropology*, vol. 68, no. 2 (26 Jan. 1978), p. 49-98. bibliog.

This is an attempt to establish a useful chronology, on stylistic grounds, for a collection of Santa María burial urns in the Field Museum of Natural History, Chicago. The urns have three distinctive segments: base, mid-section and neck. The seriation charts show the occurrence of different base, body, neck and handle shapes; of five phases of body shape; and of thirteen types of ornamentation.

# History

## General

**246  Argentina.**
    H. S. Ferns.   London: Ernest Benn; New York: Praeger, 1969. 284p.
    maps. bibliog. (Nations of the Modern World).
A reliable and readable (indeed, deliberately 'argumentative') introduction to
Argentine history from the beginnings of the Spanish colony to the régime of General
Juan Carlos Onganía (1966-70), with over half the text devoted to the modern period
since 1930. The chapter on 'The politics of a free society' is very revealing on the
Argentine character ('nothing is settled about Argentine life'). There are twenty-eight
well-chosen black-and-white illustrations.

**247  Argentina.**
    George Pendle.   London; New York; Toronto: Oxford University
    Press, 1963. 3rd ed. 212p. maps. bibliog.
The author of this introductory history was a remarkable British businessman who
owned one of the best private libraries on Latin America in the United Kingdom and
wrote a number of works on the continent which are distinguished by a wide
knowledge of the literature and a lucid, evocative style. Though inevitably dated, his
volume on Argentina still repays reading, not least for its account of the first Perón
period, 1945-55, when the author lived in Buenos Aires for much of the time. This
third edition was reprinted (with corrections) in 1965. Issued under the auspices of the
Royal Institute of International Affairs.

248 **Argentina, a city and a nation.**
James R. Scobie. New York: Oxford University Press, 1971. 2nd ed. 323p. maps. bibliog. (Latin American Histories).

The author's untimely death in 1981 deprived Argentine history of one of its most distinguished authorities in the United States and one of its finest interpreters in the English-speaking world as a whole. This exemplary history – political, economic, social and cultural, with emphasis on 'the country's formative years', the nineteenth century – is highly recommended. 'From metropolis and village, *porteño* (of the port, hence, of Buenos Aires) and provinces, finally emerged a nation.' The work also contains a splendid annotated 'selective guide to the literature on Argentina', p. 266-302.

249 **Argentina, 1516-1987: from Spanish colonization to the Falklands War and Alfonsín.**
David Rock. London: I. B. Tauris; Berkeley, California: University of California Press, 1987. 511p. maps. bibliog.

This has become the standard one-volume history of Argentina, written by a leading British authority on Argentine political history. It is a substantial account of 'economic issues and politics, supplemented by brief discussions of the social order', and focusing on the twentieth century. It tries to answer the question, 'What went wrong? Why has Argentina failed to realize its promise?'. The author's answer is somewhat controversial: Argentina is 'a classically "colonial" society' and he blames early 'structural imbalances and distortions that were to affect its later development'.

250 **Argentina: illusions and realities.**
Gary W. Wynia. New York; London: Holmes & Meier, 1986. 207p.

A useful survey of the modern period of Argentine history, from Perón in the 1940s, through the following military and civilian régimes, to the congressional elections of 1985. In 1983-84 the author 'witnessed a long-repressed people resurrect themselves and try harder than ever to deal with the real rather than the illusory world confronting them'; what they lack is 'an ability and a willingness to regulate their combative urges in the political arena'.

251 **Argentina in the twentieth century.**
Edited by David Rock. London: Duckworth, 1975. 230p. maps.

A valuable collection of eight essays originating from a symposium at the University of Cambridge. The work is divided logically into three sections: A. G. Ford, Roger Gravil and Colin Lewis on British and United States trade and investment and Argentine economic development, 1880-1965; the editor and Walter Little on the conservative élite 1912-30, the 'popular origins' of Peronism 1930-45, and the 'survival and restoration' of Peronism 1943-73; and Ian Rutledge and Jorge Fodor on the sugar-cane industry of Salta and Jujuy 1930-43 (the former's chapter revised in *The integration of the highland peasantry into the sugar cane economy of northern Argentina, 1930-43* [q.v.]) and Perón's policies for agricultural exports 1946-48.

252 **Argentina, sociedad de masas.** (Argentina, mass society.)
Torcuato S. di Tella, Gino Germani, Jorge Graciarena (et al.). Buenos
Aires: Editorial Universitaria de Buenos Aires, 1965. 2nd ed. 284p.
map. bibliog. (Biblioteca de América. Temas: Sociología).
A collection of essays on twentieth-century Argentina by a distinguished team of
Argentine and foreign sociologists, historians and economists. In two parts: a historical
analysis of the formation of the modern nation (the 1880s, early industrialization 1870-
1914, immigration, the Radical Party 1890-1916, stages in economic development); and
a more theoretical examination of the factors contributing to the country's 'institutional
crisis' (political participation, the party system, social structures, the military).

253 **The Argentine Republic.**
Ysabel Fisk Rennie. New York: Macmillan, 1945. 431p. map. bibliog.
Despite the original date of publication this remains a valuable introduction to
political, economic and social developments from the end of the Rosas régime in 1853
to the revolution of June 1943 presaging the rise of Perón. The work is based on a wide
range of secondary sources. There is a modern reprint (Westport, Connecticut:
Greenwood Press, 1975).

254 **The fitful republic: economy, society, and politics in Argentina.**
Juan E. Corradi. Boulder, Colorado: Westview Press, 1985. 175p.
map. bibliog.
A useful short interpretation of the various strands of the economy, notably agrarian
and industrial groups, in Argentina's modernization (or, rather, its 'lack of steady
economic growth and political stability'). It begins with the colonial period but
concentrates on the period after 1930 and especially the 1970s. Argentine history has
been plagued by a 'persistent swing between tyranny and tumult'.

255 **Historia argentina.** (History of Argentina.)
Edited by Tulio Halperín Donghi. Buenos Aires: Editorial Paidós,
1972. 8 vols. maps. bibliog.
There is a bewildering number of multi-volume histories of Argentina in Spanish, all of
them of uneven quality. This, edited by the outstanding Argentine historian of his
generation, is one of the best; its contributors include Carlos Sempat Assadourian,
José C. Chiaramonte, Ezequiel Gallo, Roberto Cortés Conde and Javier Villanueva. It
is chronological in arrangement and well illustrated.

256 **Historia argentina contemporánea, 1862-1930.** (History of
contemporary Argentina.)
Buenos Aires: Academia Nacional de la Historia, 1963-67. 7 vols.
This work continues the *Historia de la nación argentina* (q.v.). Written by a
distinguished team of contributors, it covers political, economic, cultural and regional
history. It is arranged chronologically, and is well illustrated and well indexed. Two
substantial historical journals are published by the Academy: the annual *Boletín* (1924- )
and the half-yearly *Investigaciones y ensayos* (1966- ). A popularized monthly
magazine, analogous to the British *History Today*, is *Todo es historia*, edited by Félix
Luna (1967- ).

257 **Historia de la nación argentina (desde los orígenes hasta la organización definitiva en 1862).** (History of the Argentine nation, from the beginnings to its unification in 1862.)
Edited by Ricardo Levene. Buenos Aires: Academia Nacional de la Historia, 1963. 3rd ed. 15 vols.

An 'official' political history edited by one of Argentina's most famous historians (1885-1959) and continued by the previous item (q.v.). The editor has published a useful one-volume history in English: *A history of Argentina*, translated and edited by William Spence Robertson (Chapel Hill, North Carolina: University of North Carolina Press, 1937. 565p., reprinted by Russell & Russell, New York, 1963). A well-illustrated but rather poorly documented history by a group of conservative historians is *Historia de la Argentina*, edited by Vicente D. Sierra (Buenos Aires: Unión de Editores Latinos, 1956-80. 10 vols. of a projected 15).

258 **Historia integral argentina.** (Complete history of Argentina.)
Edited by Haydée Gorosteguí de Torres. Buenos Aires: Centro Editor de América Latina, 1970-72. 10 vols. bibliog.

A 'popular' but well-researched set of monographs by a team of expert contemporary historians, summarizing political, economic and social history from 1800. Includes extracts from historical documents. A partial reprint was issued in three volumes in 1980.

259 **The historiography of the Río de la Plata area since 1830.**
Joseph Barager. *Hispanic American Historical Review*, vol. 39, no. 4 (Nov. 1959), p. 588-642.

Discusses major trends in historiography (two have predominated: liberal and conservative), bibliographical aids, lacunae ('there are so many gaps in the history of the Río de la Plata area that it is a fertile field for research') and prospects for the future. Partly a continuation of Ricardo Caillet-Bois, 'La historiografía', in *Historia de la literatura argentina*, edited by Rafael A. Arrieta (Buenos Aires: Ediciones Peuser, vol. 6, 1960, p. 19-198), itself a continuation of Rómulo D. Cárbia, *Historia crítica de la historiografía argentina, desde sus orígenes en el siglo XVI* (La Plata: Universidad de La Plata, Facultad de Humanidades y Ciencias de la Educación, 1939. 2nd ed. 483p.).

260 **A history of Argentine political thought.**
José Luis Romero, introduction and translation by Thomas F. McGann. Stanford, California: Stanford University Press; Oxford: Oxford University Press, 1963. 274p. maps. bibliog.

More a history of 'major political and economic themes' than a study of formal political ideas, 1530 to 1955. The author divides Argentine historical development into three stages: colonial, nineteenth-century 'creole' and present-day 'alluvial', and identifies three competing ideologies: authoritarianism, liberalism and (after 1880) popular democracy. The author is strongest on the nineteenth century; his treatment of the 1943-55 period has been criticized for its rather one-sided anti-Peronism.

261 **A house divided: Argentina, 1880-1980.**
Eduardo Crawley. London: C. Hurst, 1984. 472p. map.
Written by an Argentine journalist who works in London, this history of modern
Argentina is aimed less at the academic specialist than at the intelligent general reader.
It is soundly based on a wide range of secondary sources, journals, periodicals and
newspapers, as well as on the author's personal correspondence and interviews with
many important figures who took part in the events described in its pages. Nine-tenths
of the book is devoted to the period 1930-80, especially the 1970s, with a short
epilogue on the 1982 Falklands War and the return to democracy in 1983-84. Central to
the book is the story of Perón and the 'many attempts by his adversaries to eradicate
peronismo or usurp its legacy'. Highly anecdotal but reliable.

262 **A socioeconomic history of Argentina, 1776-1860.**
Jonathan C. Brown. Cambridge, England: Cambridge University
Press, 1979. 302p. maps. bibliog. (Cambridge Latin American Studies,
35).
Despite its broad title, this well-researched study is concerned primarily with the city
and province of Buenos Aires, from the foundation of the Viceroyalty of the Río de la
Plata to the dawn of modernization. It focuses on the region's agricultural production
and international trade, especially in hides and woollens. There is a case-study of the
prominent Anchorena landowning family and one chapter is devoted to the other
interior provinces. The author rejects the 'dependency' theory of Argentine
development by showing that foreign merchants were always reliant upon local
suppliers, transport and processing plants; and that Argentina exported to a number of
countries, including non-industrial countries such as Cuba and Brazil.

# Discovery and colonial period (1516-1810)

263 **The conquest of the River Plate.**
R. B. Cunninghame Graham. London: William Heinemann, 1924.
313p. map. bibliog.
Cunninghame Graham's writings on Latin America, like those of his friend W. H.
Hudson, have been unjustly neglected since his death; this is perhaps his best-known
historical work on a region he knew well as a cattle-rancher and horse dealer. In
Graham's characteristic literary style it tells the epic story of 'some of the conquerors
of the River Plate as human beings'. It opens with the first discovery of the River Plate
estuary by Juan de Solís in 1516 and ends with the second, and permanent, founding of
the city of Buenos Aires by Juan de Garay in 1580. Although the conquest was not as
dramatic as were the conquests of Peru and Mexico, it nevertheless 'shows up in high
relief the dauntless courage, patience in hardships, and contempt of death to be
observed in all the Spaniards of those days who passed to the New World'. The volume
was reprinted by Greenwood Press (New York, 1968).

264 **Economic growth and regional differentiations: the River Plate region at the end of the eighteenth century.**
Juan Carlos Garavaglia. *Hispanic American Historical Review*, vol. 65, no. 1 (Feb. 1985), p. 51-89. maps.

An analysis of economic growth between 1786 and 1802 in three River Plate regions (Tucumán, Cuyo and the Littoral-Banda Oriental [Uruguay] region), based on tithe-collection statistics. During the period, Tucumán showed the highest growth index of all the regions, increasing by 246 per cent, followed by Santa Fe with 153 per cent and Buenos Aires with only 35 per cent. However, Buenos Aires and the Banda Oriental were the dominant areas, concentrating on wheat production. There was a significant growth of cattle-raising activity in the 'Nuevo Littoral' area (Santa Fe and Entre Ríos) and around the city of Córdoba.

265 **The genesis of economic attitudes in the Río de la Plata.**
Mario Rodríguez. *Hispanic American Historical Review*, vol. 36, no. 2 (May 1956), p. 171-89.

This classic article is concerned primarily with the contraband trade in the region during the late seventeenth century. Buenos Aires flourished on contraband trade, despite the Spanish Crown's efforts to curb the practice. In 1680 the Portuguese established the fort of Colônia do Sacramento on the River Plate estuary opposite Buenos Aires with the principal aim of competing for the lucrative sale of cattle hides to Europe. Urged on by Platine cattlemen, the Buenos Aires authorities besieged and attacked Colônia several times, but Colônia continued contraband trading sporadically for another hundred years.

266 **Indian warfare on the pampa during the colonial period.**
Alfred J. Tapson. *Hispanic American Historical Review*, vol. 42, no. 1 (Feb. 1962), p. 1-28.

A well-written account of the confrontation between Spanish settlers and the Indian population in the hinterland, with emphasis on the eighteenth century. The pampa Indians – Querandí, Puelche, Tehuelche and Pehuenche – stubbornly refused to share their lands and cattle, and inflicted raids (*malones*) and occasional massacres on the white settlers. From the 1750s the Indians were contained by a string of forts established along the frontier in the provinces of Buenos Aires, Santa Fe, San Luis, Córdoba and Mendoza. The last major raid of the colonial era was on Luján in 1780 in which over one thousand Indians took part.

267 **Las invasiones inglesas al Río de la Plata, 1806-1807.** (The British invasions of the River Plate, 1806-1807.)
Juan Beverina. Buenos Aires: Círculo Militar, 1939. 2 vols. maps. (Círculo Militar. Biblioteca del Oficial).

A well-documented account of one of the most significant events in Argentina's history. The first, unauthorized invasion of Buenos Aires was carried out by 1,600 men led by Sir Home Popham and William Carr Beresford, then returning from an expedition against the Dutch in Cape Town. Two months later, a local militia under the leadership of Santiago Liniers, a French-born Spanish naval officer, overwhelmed the British occupying troops. This is known in Argentina as the *Reconquista*. A second expedition to recapture the city in 1807 left England under General John Whitelocke; the British troops took Montevideo but suffered heavy losses as they converged through the streets of Buenos Aires and were forced to evacuate. The invasions discredited the Spanish authorities and restored local pride and self-reliance; independence was not far off. Almost as good a history of the invasions is Carlos Roberts, *Las invasiones inglesas del Río de la Plata (1806-1807) y la influencia inglesa en la independencia y organización de las provincias del Río de la Plata* (Buenos Aires: Jacobo Peuser, 1938. 458p.). A remarkable reconstruction of the events, as described in diary form by an imaginary actor, is Alberto M. Salas, *Diario de Buenos Aires, 1806-1807* (Buenos Aires: Editorial Sudamericana, 1981. 680p.). For first-hand accounts of participants in the invasions and of the court-martial of General Whitelocke, see the five works listed in the volume on Uruguay by Henry Finch (1989), Volume 102 in the World Bibliographical Series.

268 **Liberation in South America, 1806-1827: the career of James Paroissien.**
R. A. Humphreys. London : Athlone Press, 1952. 177p. maps.
Paroissien, an English physician of French Huguenot parents, played an important part in the Argentine independence movement. He sailed for Buenos Aires on hearing news of the first British invasion in 1806, and spent eighteen months in Montevideo trading and aiding the second invasionary force. After a year in Brazil and imprisonment for involvement in a plot to bring Queen Carlota of Portugal to Buenos Aires with the idea of forming a constitutional monarchy, Paroissien joined the liberating expedition to Upper Peru. He remained with the army in the north, becoming director of the newly established gunpowder factory in Córdoba (1812-15); by 1816 he was chief surgeon to San Martín's Army of the Andes. After 1820 and until his death he was mainly involved with the liberating armies of the future republics of Peru, Bolivia and Chile.

269 **Power, corruption, and commerce: the making of the local administrative structure in seventeenth-century Buenos Aires.**
Zacarías Moutoukias. *Hispanic American Historical Review*, vol. 68, no. 4 (Nov. 1988), p. 771-801.
The author demonstrates that Spanish colonial local government in Buenos Aires, and the city's garrison, were financed from illegal commerce: 'by resorting, on the one hand, to *navíos de registro*, or ships licensed to sail outside the regular fleet system, and, on the other hand, to shipments of silver from Potosí, the so-called *situado*'. Smuggling gave rise to a powerful and frequently corrupt oligarchy of public officials, merchants and military men; 'the wealth of the merchants consolidated royal power'.

270 **Spanish colonial administration, 1782-1810: the intendant system in the Viceroyalty of the Río de la Plata.**
John Lynch. London: Athlone Press; Fair Lawn, New Jersey: Essential Books, 1958. 335p. maps. bibliog. (University of London Historical Studies, 5).
This is a study of the origin, establishment and organization of the intendant system, one of the most important of the Bourbon administrative reforms; it is based heavily on material in the Archive of the Indies in Seville. In 1782 the newly created Viceroyalty of the River Plate was divided into eight intendancies: Buenos Aires, Salta del Tucumán (modern Tucumán, Santiago del Estero, Catamarca and Jujuy), Córdoba (Córdoba, San Juan, San Luis, Mendoza and La Rioja), Paraguay, and (in Upper Peru, modern Bolivia) La Plata, Cochabamba, La Paz and Potosí. The eight intendants had clearly defined powers in the departments of finance, justice, war and general

71

administration. The intendancies had the paradoxical effect of stimulating the desire of Argentines for more liberty from Spain, and 'helped to precipitate the collapse of the imperial regime'. There is a later reprint (New York: Greenwood Press, 1970).

271 **Structure and profitabilty of royal finance in the Viceroyalty of the Río de la Plata in 1790.**
Herbert S. Klein. *Hispanic American Historical Review*, vol. 53, no. 3 (Aug. 1973), p. 440-69.
An examination of the annual records of the network of treasury offices (*cajas reales*) deposited in the Tribunal Mayor de Cuentas (principal accounts office) of Buenos Aires reveals that two-thirds of the royal income from the River Plate was generated by the port of Buenos Aires and the Indian and mining region of Upper Peru; most of Buenos Aires's trade was itself shipped to Upper Peru. The primary sources of government revenue were taxes on mining (32.1 per cent), on commerce (21.8 per cent) and Indian tribute (21 per cent). The single largest expense of the royal government in the Viceroyalty was 'the maintenance of its own civil, military, religious, and military bureaucracy'. The two full appendices list royal income and expenditure by region.

# Independence and the Rosas dictatorship (1810-52)

272 **Argentine dictator: Juan Manuel de Rosas, 1829-1852.**
John Lynch. Oxford: Clarendon Press; New York: Oxford University Press, 1981. 414p. map. bibliog.
Rosas (1793-1877) is, perhaps Perón apart, the most controversial figure in Argentina's post-independence history, seen by admirers as the first incarnation of Argentine nationalism and, somewhat unwittingly, as a forger of national unity, and by his detractors as a brutal tyrant. This brilliant portrait of the man and his times by a leading authority on Argentine history in the early modern period, based on extensive archival research, is the definitive work on him in English. Rosas, whose personal rule of terror as governor of Buenos Aires between 1829 and 1852 was ended by his defeat at the battle of Caseros, died in exile in Southampton, England, in 1877; his remains were repatriated to Argentina in 1990.

273 **Carlos de Alvear, man of revolution: the diplomatic career of Argentina's first minister to the United States.**
Thomas B. Davis, Jr. Durham, North Carolina: Duke University Press, 1955. 305p.
Carlos María de Alvear (1789-1852) is best known for his military victories in the wars of independence and the war against Brazil (1825-27). This volume, however, is concerned primarily with his diplomatic career, set against a background which provides a good general history of the period. He was twice appointed Minister Plenipotentiary to the United States, briefly in 1824-25 and then as Rosas's representative between 1838 and 1852. When Alvear failed to negotiate a settlement of

the Falkland Islands problem, he requested his return to Buenos Aires; this was refused and he remained an unwilling resident (although loyal to Rosas) until his death in 1852, just after Urquiza's victory over Rosas at Caseros. Alvear's grandson, Marcelo T. de Alvear, was president 1922-28. The work was reprinted by Greenwood Press (New York, 1968).

274 **David Curtis DeForest and the revolution of Buenos Aires.**
Benjamin Keen.  New Haven, Connecticut: Yale University Press, 1947. 186p. bibliog. (Yale Historical Publications. Miscellany, 46).
DeForest (1774-1825) first arrived in Buenos Aires in 1802; 'there he learned to trade "in the smuggling way"'. He witnessed the British invasions, became 'an outfitter of patriot privateers that made heavy inroads on Spanish commerce', and built up a fortune from the slave trade and his own privateering. He repeatedly asked to be made United States consul in Buenos Aires; Supreme Director Juan Martín de Pueyrredón appointed him unofficial consul-general in 1818, after which he retired to his native Connecticut and devoted his last years to the promotion of cultural relations between the United States and Argentina.

275 **The economic aspects of Argentine federalism, 1820-1852.**
Miron Burgin.  Cambridge, Massachusetts: Harvard University Press, 1946. 304p. bibliog. (Harvard Economic Studies, vol. 78).
This scholarly study of the economic factors that influenced the development of Argentine regionalism during Rivadavia's administration (1820-29) and the Rosas dictatorship has, in many respects, still not been superseded in the range and interpretation of source materials. It covers land policy, agriculture and cattle raising, commerce and industry, public debt, banking, protectionism and federal finances.

276 **Foreign intervention in the Río de la Plata, 1835-50: a study of French, British, and American policy in relation to the dictator Juan Manuel de Rosas.**
John F. Cady.  Philadelphia; London: University of Pennsylvania Press, 1929. 296p. maps. bibliog.
France's naval blockade of Buenos Aires between 1838 and 1840 began over Argentina's discriminatory treatment of its citizens and 'the question of equal status with the British'. The Anglo-French blockade of Buenos Aires (1845-47) was provoked by Rosas's own blockade of Montevideo, partly intended to force River Plate trade through Buenos Aires. By contrast, the policy of the North American government during this period was 'clearly one of non-interference'.

277 **Historia de Belgrano y de la independencia argentina.** (The story of Belgrano and Argentine independence.)
Bartolomé Mitre.  Buenos Aires: Estrada, 1927. 6th ed. 4 vols.
Mitre (1821-1906) was not only an outstanding public figure and president of the republic from 1862 to 1868, but also a distinguished historian. His classic study of the life and times of General Manuel Belgrano (1770-1820), the great patriot leader and military hero of the wars of independence, was first published in 1857. A good biography of Mitre himself is William H. Jeffrey, *Mitre and Argentina* (New York: Library Publishers, 1952. 290p.).

278  **Life in the Argentine Republic in the days of the tyrants; or, Civilization and barbarism.**
Domingo Faustino Sarmiento, translated by Mrs Horace Mann.   New York: Hurd and Houghton, 1868; New York: Hafner, 1961. 400p.

*Facundo; o, La civilización y la barbarie* was first published in serial form in Chile in 1845, while Sarmiento was in exile from the dictatorship of Juan Manuel de Rosas. It is partly a biography of Juan Facundo Quiroga, strong man (*caudillo*) of La Rioja province, and a thinly disguised attack on Rosas himself, but is best known as (in the description of the *Historical dictionary of Argentina* [q.v.]), 'a profound and colorful sociological and geographical study of the land and historic roots that produced the gaucho mentality that [Sarmiento] considers largely responsible for the anarchy, civil wars, and resulting tyranny'. He extols 'civilization', represented by the best of European values, and condemns the 'barbarism' of indigenous creole culture. The translation, by the wife of an American educationalist who helped to form Sarmiento's own ideas on education, has stood the test of time.

279  **The life of Sarmiento.**
Allison Williams Bunkley.   Princeton, New Jersey: Princeton University Press; London: Oxford University Press, 1952. 566p. bibliog.

The outstanding biography in English of perhaps the most distinguished Argentine statesman of the nineteenth century, Domingo Faustino Sarmiento (1811-88), educationalist, writer and president of the republic from 1868 to 1874. The biography was reprinted in 1969 by Greenwood Press (New York). The author emphasizes Sarmiento's intellectual formation before 1852 and his considerable literary output, and she has edited a collection of his writings: *A Sarmiento anthology* (Princeton, New Jersey, 1948; reprinted by Kennikat Press, New York, 1972. 337p.).

280  **La lucha por la consolidación de la nacionalidad argentina, 1852-1862.**
(The struggle for nationhood: Argentina, 1852-1862.)
James R. Scobie.   Buenos Aires: Librería Hachette, 1964. 425p. bibliog. (Colección El Pasado Argentino).

The text was originally written (but unfortunately never published) in English and translated for this edition. It is the account of a critical decade between the end of the Rosas dictatorship – eight years of conflict between Buenos Aires and the provinces which 'finally confirmed the domination of Buenos Aires over the rest of the country' – and the eventual political reorganization of the republic under Bartolomé Mitre. The littoral's economic dominance in wool production and foreign trade is also discussed.

281  **Martín Güemes: tyrant or tool? A study of the sources of power of an Argentine caudillo.**
Roger M. Haigh.   Fort Worth, Texas: Texas Christian University Press, 1968. 77p. maps. bibliog. (Texas Christian University Monographs in History and Culture, 3).

Güemes belonged to one of Salta province's leading families which in 1810 was faced with the dilemma of recognizing the junta in Buenos Aires or the one in Spain. 'The salteños chose to recognize Buenos Aires, and the royalist reaction was sudden and intense. The kinship élite found themselves committed to a struggle that threatened their existence.' In 1815 Güemes was elected governor by the same élite which 'was looking for a leader who would provide stability, military security, a measure of self-government, and who was acceptable to the group'. The author concludes that he was in fact the tool, 'merely the agent', of the dominant group, but he proved a successful military leader and was popular with the people. He was killed during a royalist invasion in 1821.

282 **Politics, economics and society in Argentina in the revolutionary period.**
Tulio Halperín Donghi, translated by Richard Southern.    Cambridge,
England; New York; Melbourne, Australia: Cambridge University
Press, 1975. 425p. bibliog. (Cambridge Latin American Studies, 18).
This impressively researched but difficult study by a distinguished modern Argentine historian is essential reading on a highly complex period, 1806 to 1820. The author's stated purpose was 'to trace the vicissitudes of a political élite created, destroyed and then created again by war and revolution'. It is primarily a political history, set against the background of the economic uncertainty following the wars of independence, and with a discussion of the contemporary social structure. Unusually, the urban élite of the viceregal era was replaced by a rural landowning élite.

283 **Reform and reaction in the Platine provinces, 1810-1852.**
David Bushnell.    Gainesville, Florida: University Presses of Florida,
1983. 182p. bibliog. (University of Florida Monographs. Social
Sciences, no. 69).
The author examines the processes of constitutional, legal, institutional, religious and social change during this period of great upheaval, by analysing contemporary decrees, laws, constitutions and miscellaneous regulations. He treats his subject within three sub-periods (the Rivadavian reforms and after, 1810-21; the 'apogee of Buenos Aires liberalism' and liberal innovations in the other provinces, 1821-27; and the 'reaction' of the Rosas dictatorship, 1835-52); and within six geographical zones (five Argentine regions and Uruguay).

284 **Rivadavia y su tiempo.** (The life and times of Rivadavia.)
Ricardo Piccirilli.    Buenos Aires: Ediciones Peuser, 1960. 2nd ed.
3 vols.
Bernardino Rivadavia (1780-1845) was the dominant figure in Argentina's early post-independence history from 1811 to 1827. He was the key minister to successive presidents before becoming briefly president of the United Provinces, 1826-27. He was the instigator of daring and sometimes controversial administrative reforms and attempted to impose a unitarist constitution on the divided provinces.

285 **The River Plate republics from independence to the Paraguayan War.**
John Lynch.    In: *Cambridge history of Latin America. Vol. 3: From
independence to c.1870.*    Edited by Leslie Bethell.    Cambridge,
England: Cambridge University Press, 1985, p. 615-76. map. bibliog.
An excellent introduction to the political and economic history of Argentina, Uruguay and Paraguay during the half-century between 1820 and 1870. The period was dominated by the rise of the *estancia* and provincial *caudillos* (chieftains), the dictator Rosas, the division of Argentina into Buenos Aires and the Argentine Confederation

of thirteen provinces under Urquiza, the constitution of 1853, and the presidencies of Mitre and Sarmiento.

### 286   The Spanish American revolutions, 1808-1826.

John Lynch.   New York: Norton, 1986. 2nd ed. 448p. maps. bibliog.

A classic work which is distinguished by a profound knowledge of the sources and a lucid style. Chapter two (p. 38-88) is devoted to the political, military and economic events in Argentina: the British invasions of 1806-7, the May 1810 revolution and the declaration of independence in 1816 by the 'United Provinces of South America', the uneasy relations between Buenos Aires and the interior provinces, the administration of Bernardino Rivadavia, and the economy and society on the eve of the Rosas dictatorship.

# National consolidation and expansion (1852-1930)

### 287   La Argentina del ochenta al centenario. (Argentina, 1880-1910.)

Edited by Gustavo Ferrari, Ezequiel Gallo.   Buenos Aires: Editorial Sudamericana, 1980. 927p. maps. (Colección Historia y Sociedad).

A wide-ranging collection of more than fifty essays covering the period from 1880 to the centenary year 1910 (or 1914-16 in some chapters), by a distinguished group of mainly Argentine and British political and economic historians. The volume is arranged in five sections: political 'antecedents' of the period, presidents and certain other key figures between 1880 and 1910, economy and society, international relations and cultural life.

### 288   Argentina from the First World War to the revolution of 1930.

David Rock.   In: *Cambridge history of Latin America, Vol. 5: c.1870 to 1930.*   Edited by Leslie Bethell. Cambridge, England: Cambridge University Press, 1986, p. 419-52. bibliog.

An excellent introductory essay on a key period of modern Argentine history by the leading British historian of the 'Radical years'. The author subdivides his contribution under the following headings: 'The war and postwar economy', 'War and postwar politics', and 'The military coup of 1930'. 'Politically the years between 1916 and 1930 witnessed the first and also the most prolonged of Argentina's many abortive experiments with representative democracy'; economically the period 'witnessed overall a continuation of Argentina's prewar economic prosperity based on the growth of its export sector'.

### 289 Argentina: society and politics, 1880-1916.
Ezequiel Gallo. In: *Cambridge history of Latin America. Vol. 5: c.1870 to 1930.* Edited by Leslie Bethell. Cambridge, England: Cambridge University Press, 1986, p. 359-91. bibliog.

An excellent overview of the period between the presidency of General Julio A. Roca and the military coup of 1930, during which Argentina 'enjoyed several decades of relative political unity and stability . . . This in turn resulted in, and was to some extent a consequence of, fundamental changes in the demographic and social structure of the country' – a massive influx of immigrants, rapid social mobility leading to a great expansion of the middle sectors, and the beginnings of organized labour.

### 290 The breakdown of democracy in Argentina, 1916-30.
Peter H. Smith. In: *The breakdown of democratic regimes. Part 3: Latin America.* Edited by Juan J. Linz, Alfred Stepan. Baltimore, Maryland: Johns Hopkins University Press, 1978, p. 3-27.

'In 1930 the armed forces, in collaboration with civilian elements and with the apparent support of the populace, pulled off a military coup. Argentine democracy was overthrown.' The author of this convincing account of the origins of the 1930 coup argues that the breakdown of democracy was the product of 'a crisis in legitimacy' intensified by economic problems. It broke down 'because of the *kind* of socioeconomic development which took place in Argentina and the *sequence* between socioeconomic and political change'. The ruling Radical Party refused to share power and 'conservatives came to see democracy as dysfunctional and therefore illegitimate'; they found willing allies in the armed forces.

### 291 The conquest of the desert.
Alfred Hasbrouck. *Hispanic American Historical Review*, vol. 15, no. 2 (May 1935), p. 195-228.

The first three-quarters of the nineteenth century saw a continuous 'making and breaking of treaties' with the pampa Indians. The final conquest of the so-called Argentine 'desert' (the semi-arid but mostly fertile pampas) was planned and executed by General Julio A. Roca. At the start of the campaign, 1875, the total population of the pampa Indians north of the Río Negro was about 12,000; by 1878 only 2,000 remained. By 1885 the conquest was complete and 20,000 square leagues of rich territory had been reclaimed for future colonization. Roca was hailed as a hero and elected president in 1880. The classic history in Spanish is Juan C. Walther, *La conquista del desierto: síntesis histórica de los principales sucesos ocurridos y operaciones militares realizadas en la Pampa y Patagonia contra los indios (años 1527-1885)* (Buenos Aires: EUDEBA, 1970. 3rd ed. 597p.). For a useful brief summary, see F. J. McLynn, 'The frontier problem in nineteenth-century Argentina', *History Today*, vol. 30 (Jan. 1980), p. 28-32.

292 **Counterrevolution in Argentina, 1900-1932: the Argentine Patriotic League.**
Sandra McGee Deutsch. Lincoln, Nebraska; London: University of Nebraska Press, 1986. 319p. bibliog.
Whereas previous studies of counterrevolution (defined as 'opposition to liberalism, democracy, feminism, and the various strains of leftism') have concentrated on the coup of 1930, this work traces the roots of counterrevolutionary sentiment back to 1900. 'The key events that triggered its formation were the labor mobilizations of 1909-10 and particularly 1919-21'. The ultra-conservative Liga Patriótica Argentina, the focus of this study, was founded after the violent labour strikes culminating in the bloody 'tragic week' of 1919; it had the aim of counteracting 'bolshevism' and educating the immigrant working class, and became 'the first significant, long-lasting counterrevolutionary organization' and one of the country's most powerful political associations during the 1920s. It was 'primarily antileftist, not antiliberal', and its membership broader than previously thought.

293 **The failure of democracy in Argentina, 1916-1930: an institutional perspective.**
Anne L. Potter. *Journal of Latin American Studies*, vol. 13, no. 1 (May 1981), p. 83-109.
'Before 1912 the oligarchy ruled; between 1912 and 1930, the middle class ruled; after 1930, the conservative oligarchy was restored to power.' The author traces the causes of the revolution of 1930 by examining previous writers' explanations for the failure of democracy in 1930. The standard cause given is that the Radical Party's conservative opposition intervened because it was afraid of losing its political power; the author suggests that underlying the events of 1929-30 was 'an institutional system that made them possible . . . on the one hand, the separation of powers and the fixed presidential term, and, on the other, the federal system and the power of intervention'. Taken together, they created an intolerable situation 'in which the President was able to deny all political space to opposing parties or movements'.

294 **Farmers in revolt: the revolutions of 1893 in the province of Santa Fe, Argentina.**
Ezequiel Gallo. London: Athlone Press, 1976. 97p. map. bibliog. (University of London. Institute of Latin American Studies. Monographs, 7)
The author describes the history of agricultural colonization in the province of Santa Fe (see also *La pampa gringa: la colonización agrícola en Santa Fe, 1870-1895*) and the three colonists' rebellions which took place in February, July and September of 1893. The most militant colonies were those with the largest proportion of Swiss immigrants. The colonists' demands were moderate: they 'sought no more than a reduction or elimination of the taxes which burdened the production and marketing of grain'. They showed a preference for the recently created Radical Party, which supported their uprisings; afterwards the central region of Santa Fe was one of the main electoral strongholds of Radicalism. The colonists' struggles yielded few practical results; 'the grain tax was not lowered nor was the right to vote in municipal elections restored to foreigners'. In June 1912, the farmers of Alcorta, a village in Santa Fe province, stopped work in the fields, demanding lower rents and contractual improvements; the conflict spread throughout the whole of the southern part of Santa Fe province and became the first great agrarian strike in Argentine history. See

Eugenia Scarzanella, '"Corn fever": Italian tenant farming families in Argentina',
*Bulletin of Latin American Research*, vol. 3, no. 1 (Jan. 1984), p. 1-23.

295    **The growth of the Argentine economy, c.1870-1914.**
Roberto Cortés Conde.    In: *Cambridge history of Latin America. Vol.
5: c.1870 to 1930.*    Edited by Leslie Bethell.    Cambridge, England:
Cambridge University Press, 1986, p. 327-57. map.
A short but exemplary summary of Argentina's period of dynamic economic
transformation, emphasizing the factors of production – land, labour and capital – and
the phases of growth: 1880-90, 1890-1900 and 1910-12. Rapid economic growth, at an
annual rate of five per cent except for the years 1890-95, was achieved by the
exploitation of staples, 'agricultural and cattle products which found an outlet in
international markets'; the more intensive use of labour 'also permitted a better
distribution of income and an increase in demand'.

296    **The origins of the Paraguayan War.**
Pelham Horton Box.    Urbana, Illinois: University of Illinois Press, 1930.
345p. maps. bibliog. (University of Illinois Studies in the Social
Sciences, XV, nos 3-4).
The Paraguayan War (1865-70), or War of the Triple Alliance, fought between
Argentina, Brazil and Uruguay on the one hand and Paraguay on the other, was a
significant event in the growth of Argentine nationality in the last century. The
immediate cause of the war was political strife in Uruguay; Brazil and Argentina
backed one faction and the Paraguayan president Francisco Solano López the other,
declaring war on Brazil and invading the Argentine territories of Misiones and
Corrientes. Paraguay lost half its male population in the bloody five-year war which
ensued. There is a modern reprint (New York: Russell & Russell, 1967).

297    **Politics in Argentina, 1890-1930: the rise and fall of Radicalism.**
David Rock.    Cambridge, England: Cambridge University Press,
1975. 315p. bibliog. (Cambridge Latin American Studies, 19).
This is both a study of the origins and early development of the Radical Party,
Argentina's first major popular movement, from the time of its foundation in 1891 to
the overthrow of the third Radical government in the military coup of 1930, and also
the definitive history in English of that period. Another of the book's central themes is
the 'political inter-relationship' between the four major social and economic groups:
the landed and commercial élite of the pampas region, foreign capital (predominantly
British), and the urban middle and working classes, both mainly in the city of Buenos
Aires. Radicalism failed principally to overcome the problem of political instability; it
manifested the difficulties of 'applying a system of power-sharing in a society markedly
biassed towards elitism and entrenched privilege'.

298    **The province of Buenos Aires and Argentine politics, 1912-1943.**
Richard J. Walter.    Cambridge, England: Cambridge University Press,
1985. 244p. bibliog. (Cambridge Latin American Studies, 53).
A carefully researched study in Argentine political history, providing a detailed
account of provincial politics in the country's wealthiest, largest and most populous
province. The period was dominated by the Radical Party (Unión Cívica Radical),
which governed from 1916 to 1930, a period of 'expanded citizen participation in

politics and reasonably honest elections'; and by the Partido Conservador between 1930 and 1943, a period of 'more sporadic citizen participation and less than honest elections'. During this century Buenos Aires has contained between twenty-five and forty per cent of all the country's voters and a similar proportion of national congressmen; an understanding of the political role of Buenos Aires is therefore vital to an understanding of Argentine national politics. The book explores the long history of political disputes between province and nation; during the last century the governors of Buenos Aires had powers rivalling those of the national government and the province is still a major political force.

299 **South America and the First World War: the impact of the war on Brazil, Argentina, Peru and Chile.**
Bill Albert, with the assistance of Paul Henderson. Cambridge, England: Cambridge University Press, 1988. 388p. bibliog. (Cambridge Latin American Studies, 65).

In many respects the war 'marked a major economic, political, social and cultural watershed' for all four nations. The volume is arranged by country within four main themes: foreign trade, finance, manufacturing industry and the labour movement. The author asks why Argentina, whose commodities were in such great demand and whose foreign trade was averaging twenty-five per cent of gross domestic product between 1915 and 1924, did not gain more economic advantage than it did during the war; even so, the war stimulated economic nationalism and acted as a catalyst to Argentina's manufacturing industry 'by dramatically demonstrating both the weakness and dependence of the national economy in general and of industry in particular'. The urban working class, 'propelled by the world and domestic capitalist crises' brought on by the war 'had fully emerged as a legitimate and powerful factor in the Argentine political equation'.

# Conservatism and the rise of populism (1930-46)

300 **Argentine diary: the inside story of the coming of fascism.**
Ray Josephs. New York: Random House, 1944. 358p. map.

This is the diary kept by the author, an American journalist, during his residence in Argentina from the beginning of 1943 to the end of January 1944. It vividly records, and at considerable length, his impressions of events in the country: the evolving political picture under chief executive Ramón S. Castillo who was replaced on 4 June 1943 by a military coup headed by General Pedro Pablo Ramírez, himself to be succeeded in March 1944 by General Edelmiro Farrell. Perón is first mentioned on 18 June 1943, as a leading figure in the group of army colonels which carried out the coup a fortnight before. His rise is charted in fascinated detail. This is how he is described on 3 December: 'Perón's strong sense of showmanship, his Goering-like uniforms and his constant smile hide a relentless drive which insures getting what he's after'. The book ends with this statement: 'Today Argentina and Bolivia head the fascist parade in Latin America. But they march to a tune played by the band in Madrid and the time is called in Berlin.' The book was published in an English edition by Victor Gollancz in 1945.

301 **Argentine riddle.**
Félix J. Weil. New York: John Day, 1944. 297p. map.
A study of Argentina's political, social and (especially) economic development during the 1930s and 1940s, by a former official of President Agustín P. Justo's finance minister, 1932-34. 'I wanted to show how Argentina is now at the crossroads, with a battle royal raging between the new industrialization and the old vested agrarian interests.' General Farrell had recently taken power and the author foresaw with misgiving that Perón would soon replace him.

302 **Estudios sobre los orígenes del peronismo.** (Studies in the origins of Peronism.)
Miguel Murmis, Juan Carlos Portantiero (vol. 1), Marta Panaia, Ricardo Lesser, Pedro Skupch (vol. 2). Buenos Aires: Siglo XXI, 1971-73. 2 vols.
Volume one consists of two essays, originally published as working papers by the Instituto Torcuato di Tella, on industrial growth and class alliances between 1930 and 1940, and on the labour movement before 1945. The four essays in volume two, generally unsympathetic towards Perón, consider the decline of British 'hegemony' and the rise of United States influence in Argentina, 1914-47, and the military's policy towards industry, 1943-47.

303 **Latin America and the Second World War.**
R. A. Humphreys. London: Athlone Press, 1981-82. 2 vols.
(University of London. Institute of Latin American Studies.
Monographs, 10-11).
Based on published and unpublished documents of the foreign ministries of the United Kingdom, the United States and Germany, and on contemporary Latin American newspapers, this is an outstanding history of the experiences of the Latin American states during the Second World War, during which the author was attached to the British Foreign Office. One-third (p. 129-202) of volume two deals with Argentina. Successive Argentine presidents after 1941 maintained the country's traditional policy of neutrality during the war and refused to join the United States and most of the other Latin American nations in declaring war against the Axis powers until as late as March 1945.

304 **Prologue to Perón: Argentina in depression and war, 1930-1943.**
Edited by Mark Falcoff, Ronald H. Dolkart. Berkeley, California; London: University of California Press, 1975. 236p. maps. bibliog.
The volume reprints seven previously published essays by Argentine and United States scholars – including the editors and Arthur P. Whitaker, Javier Villanueva, Joseph S. Tulchin and Gustavo Sosa-Pujato – which discuss political and economic developments, foreign policy, 'intellectual currents', popular culture and the provinces. The period 1930-43 spanned 'two Argentinas': an 'outpost of Europe in South America' in 1930; by 1943 'rent by all the classic cleavages of early industrial society, divisions compounded by a personalistic political movement and the full range of contemporary social and spiritual maladies'.

305 **Revolution before breakfast: Argentina 1941-1946.**
Ruth and Leonard Greenup. Chapel Hill, North Carolina: University of North Carolina Press, 1947. 266p. map.

A journalistic account of the 1943 revolution and 'how it grew', covering such miscellaneous topics as food and eating out, the Argentine character (and especially the people's *picardía criolla*, native trickery), 'gambling and drinking and sin', the Second World War and German influence, the police state, social classes, United States ambassador Spruille Braden and the 1946 presidential elections ('the case of the clean ballot'), Perón ('Latin superman'), education, the arts and media, and Argentine attitudes towards the United States.

306 **Why Perón came to power: the background to Peronism in Argentina.**
Edited by Joseph R. Barager. New York: Alfred A. Knopf, 1968. 274p. bibliog. (Borzoi Books on Latin America).

The Borzoi series of readings from a wide variety of sources on particular Latin American issues and problems was aimed primarily at students. This volume consists of twenty-two selections from Domingo F. Sarmiento to George Pendle, half of them extracts from items listed in this bibliography, and each prefaced by the editor. Part one supplies the historical background: the conflict between Buenos Aires and the interior, the transformation of social and political structures in the early twentieth century, and the intervention of the military in 1943. Part two considers Perón's 'winning and consolidation of power'; and part three includes three essays 'in retrospect'.

# The first Peronist administration (1946-55)

307 **Eva Perón.**
Nicholas Fraser, Marysa Navarro. London: André Deutsch; New York: W. W. Norton, 1980. 214p. bibliog.

This is the most complete biography of Eva Perón to date, the joint work of a British journalist and an Argentine historian who has specialized in the subject. It is based on a detailed reading of primary and secondary sources, including over one hundred personal interviews. It recounts Eva Perón's small-town origins, her early career as an actress and her elevation at the age of twenty-four to mistress of Juan Domingo Perón in 1944 (they married in late 1945). Marysa Navarro contributes a feminist study of Eva's charisma and feminine qualities which proved the perfect complement to her husband: she served as a bridge between Perón and the people, convincing the poor of his intentions to protect and employ them. See also Navarro's 'Evita's charismatic leadership', in *Latin American populism in comparative perspective*, edited by Michael L. Conniff (Albuquerque, New Mexico: University of New Mexico Press, 1982, p. 47-66), and *Evita* (Buenos Aires: Corregidor, 1981. 371p.).

308 **Eva Perón: the myths of a woman.**
Julie M. Taylor. Chicago: University of Chicago Press; Oxford:
Basil Blackwell, 1979. 175p. bibliog. (Pavilion Series in Social
Anthropology).
A detailed anthropological study of three myths surrounding the life and career of Eva
Perón propagated by her supporters and enemies: the Peronist 'Lady of Hope' (her
purity, maternal and wifely roles), the anti-Peronist 'woman of the black myth' (using
the powers of her sex to dominate instead of to protect), and 'Eva the revolutionary', a
myth developed by the Left during the 1960s and 1970s. Myths one and three were
supposed to have emanated from the working class (which idolized her), but the author
argues that they are a middle-class idealization of how the working class felt about her.
The author also includes a general biography of Eva (p. 34-71) and considers the role
of women in Argentine society.

309 **Evita, first lady: a biography of Eva Perón.**
John Barnes. New York: Grove Press; London:
Fontana/Collins, 1978. 195p.
The author was editor of the *Buenos Aires Herald* 1955-59 and *Newsweek*'s
correspondent in Buenos Aires 1970-73. His biography is journalistic in style and
rather sensationalist but nevertheless remarkably comprehensive in scope: Eva's
birth in the small provincial town of Los Toldos in 1919, her charitable but
manipulative work among the *descamisados* ('shirtless' workers), her sensational
'Rainbow Tour' of European capitals, her death from cancer in 1952 at the age of
thirty-two, and the return of her embalmed body from a cemetery in Italy to Buenos
Aires in 1972. Inspired by the famous musical of the same name is an excellent
collection of photographs accompanied by a racy but creditable text by W. A.
Harbinson: *¡Evita! A legend for the seventies*, designed by Mike Ricketts (London:
W. H. Allen, 1977. 128p.).

310 **Juan Domingo Perón: a history.**
Robert J. Alexander. Boulder, Colorado: Westview Press, 1979.
177p. bibliog.
This short and fair-minded – though ultimately unflattering – portrait of Perón is
intended as an interpretive essay 'rather than a scholarly treatise' – a 'tentative
assessment' of the man based on the author's observations and interviews with leading
politicians, businessmen and union leaders. The author gives Perón credit for
recognizing the importance of the manufacturing sector for the country's future
economic progress and for extending economic, social and political benefits to the
working class; he criticizes his dictatorial methods, neglect of agriculture and poor
conduct of financial affairs. The appendix consists of the notes of an interview with the
exiled Perón in Madrid in September 1960. Still one of the best accounts of the first
Perón regime at the height of the leader's powers is the same author's *The Perón era*
(New York: Columbia University Press, 1951; London: Victor Gollancz, 1952. 239p.).

311 **Leader and vanguard in mass society: a study of Peronist Argentina.**
Jeane J. Kirkpatrick. Cambridge, Massachusetts; London: MIT Press,
1971. 262p. (M.I.T. Studies in Comparative Politics).

Written by a former United States ambassador to the United Nations, this is a study of
the Peronist movement based on a national political-attitude survey of 2,014 adults
in towns of 2,000 or more inhabitants, conducted between October and December
1965. The author distinguishes between 'core Peronists', who continued to show strong
personal support for Perón ten years after his overthrow, perhaps 18.1 per cent of the
population, and 'pro-Peronists', the more numerous 36.6 per cent who supported the
movement generally. Not suprisingly, core Peronists 'comprised part of the working
class, identified with the whole of it, and made demands in the name of the whole that
exceeded the demands of the whole class'; by contrast, pro-Peronists overlapped
considerably in social terms with Radical Party supporters. The conclusion is that
Argentines are 'a tranquil people governed by agitated rulers'. For analyses of the
social foundation of Peronist support during 1946-55, see *Peronism in Argentina: the
social base of the first regime, 1946-1955*.

312 **Party and state in Peronist Argentina, 1945-1955.**
Walter Little. *Hispanic American Historical Review*, vol. 53, no. 4
(Nov. 1973), p. 644-62.

The author speculates on Argentina's lack of an effective political party between 1946
and 1955, and the resulting imposition of Perón's brand of personalist rule. This was
achieved in two stages. From 1946 to 1948, the Peronist movement was split
ideologically between the 'autonomously-inclined syndicalist wing of Peronism and a
variety of nationalist and opportunist factors', and the former faction won. After 1949,
Perón failed 'to transcend the vulgar personalism achieved by his victory over the
working class representatives and create an effective mass party'.

313 **Perón: a biography.**
Joseph A. Page. New York: Random House, 1983. 594p. bibliog.

This is the definitive biography, the first full-length political history of Perón and his
era, painstakingly researched by a professional lawyer and very readable, although the
personality of his subject comes out rather flat. 'There was much to dislike in Perón –
the cynicism, the utter disdain for truth, the lack of principle, the selfishness, the
irresponsibility'; 'his greatness was contextual only . . . his stature owes much to the
mediocrity of his competitors and those who came after him'; and 'to his credit he
legitimized the aspirations of millions of Argentines previously excluded from civil
life'. Eight pages of photographs are included.

314 **Perón and after.**
Fritz L. Hoffmann. *Hispanic American Historical Review*, vol. 36,
no. 4 (Nov. 1956), p. 510-28; vol. 39, no. 2 (May 1959), p. 212-33.

The end of Perón's two successive presidencies in 1955 not only unleashed a flood of
publications on the man and his régime in Argentina itself; it also saw the appearance
in that country of works by Argentine exiles and English-speaking writers which had
previously been banned. These two articles survey that literature and provide
interesting contemporary comment on Perón's nearly ten-year rule and the legacy it
left. Among the subjects treated in the reviewed literature are the tyranny of the
régime, the Church–state clash, the economy and the oil question, education, labour,

the constitution, the 1955 revolution against Perón and the succeeding Frondizi government.

315 **Perón and the enigmas of Argentina.**
Robert Crassweller.   New York; London: W. W. Norton, 1987. 432p.
map. bibliog.
The author was a former Latin American adviser to the International Telephone and Telegraph Company. His is a well-illustrated and entertaining biography, and he has tried to explain the enigma presented by the man and his movement. Perón's popularity with the masses is seen as stemming from an 'intuitive identity and community that united the leader and a majority of the nation in a tenacious relationship of quite unusual loyalty'. Peronism is defined as an authoritarian, populist movement, with elements of nationalism, pauperism and the cult of strong individual leadership; 'Perón's achievements flowed from his personification of Argentina's Hispanic and Creole civilization'.

316 **Peronism in Argentina: the social base of the first regime, 1946-1955.**
Ernest Spencer Wellhofer.   *Journal of Developing Areas*, vol. 11,
no. 3 (April 1977), p. 335-56.
The first Peronist administration has generated a mass of literature concerning the social base of its support in the 1946 and 1954 elections at district and national level. This article is a useful summary of existing studies, notably those by Peter Smith, Gino Germani, Walter Little and Peter Snow. The present author concludes that 'the regime's support base included all social groups and was dependent on neither the mobilization of the less experienced voters nor the tangible gratifications of public policy to its 1946 supporters'. See also Walter Little, 'Electoral aspects of Peronism, 1946-1954', *Journal of Interamerican Studies & World Affairs*, vol. 15, no. 3 (Aug. 1973), p. 267-84; Peter H. Smith, 'The social base of Peronism', *Hispanic American Historical Review*, vol. 52, no. 1 (Feb. 1972), p. 55-73; and Peter H. Snow, 'Social mobilization, political participation, and the rise of Juan Perón', *Political Science Quarterly*, vol. 84, no. 1 (March 1969), p. 30-49.

317 **Perón's Argentina.**
George I. Blanksten.   Chicago, Illinois: University of Chicago Press;
London: Cambridge University Press, 1953. 478p. bibliog.
This study was for many years the basic work on Perón's first government. It is a detailed analysis of Perón's coming to power, his ideology and his strategy. Blanksten, a political scientist, spent nine months in Argentina researching the book, which was condemned as 'espionage'. He was declared *persona non grata* and the preface includes the warning that 'it has not been easy for me to be objective about contemporary Argentine politics, but I have tried'.

318 **Política y cultura popular: la Argentina peronista, 1946-1955.** (Politics
and popular culture: Peronist Argentina, 1946-1955.)
Alberto Ciria.   Buenos Aires: Ediciones de la Flor, 1983. 357p.
bibliog.
This ambitious recreation of the Perón years analyses: the ideology of Peronism, the role of Congress, the political parties, and the impact of Peronism on education and popular culture, but the last occupies only a small part of the book.

319 **The woman with the whip: Eva Perón.**
Mary Foster Main. Garden City, New York: Doubleday, 1952. 286p.
This is a well-written but undocumented biography of the last years of Eva Perón's life (1944-52) which is generally critical of its subject but at times surprisingly sympathetic. It has become famous as a contemporary denunciation of Eva's unscrupulousness in the use of power and incidentally of the position of women in Argentine society. The author used the pseudonym María Flores. A revised edition was published in 1980 (New York: Dodd Mead. 288p.) with the title *Evita: the woman with the whip*. Also rather notorious, though equally 'unscholarly' and sometimes inaccurate, is Fleur Cowles's lively comparison of the careers of Eva Perón and Encarnación, the wife of Juan Manuel de Rosas: *Bloody precedent: the Perón story* (New York: Random House; London: Frederick Muller, 1952. 253p.).

# Civilian and military governments (1955-76)

320 **Argentina under Perón, 1973-76: the nation's experience with a labour-based government.**
Guido di Tella. London: Macmillan; New York: St Martin's Press, 1983. 246p. bibliog.
The author briefly discusses previous régimes from Perón's first administration in the 1940s but reserves the bulk of his treatment for the 1973-76 period, when Juan Domingo Perón was actually in office for only ten months. The emphasis is on the political economy: di Tella was deputy minister of economic affairs under Isabel Perón from August 1975 to January 1976. He provides a unique insider's assessment of the various long-range and short-term economic reforms introduced, and of the major economic issues of the period: investment, profits, trade and inflation. Although the author is a Peronist he is not blind to Peronism's shortcomings, especially the political mismanagement which led to hyperinflation, terrorist violence and, ultimately, the 1976 military coup.

321 **Argentine upheaval: Perón's fall and the new regime.**
Arthur P. Whitaker. New York: Praeger; London: Atlantic Press, 1956. 179p. (University of Pennsylvania. The Foreign Policy Research Institute Series, 1).
This is a study of the turbulent events of the second half of 1955: the three-month crisis from the abortive naval revolt against Perón on June 16 to his overthrow on September 19, General Eduardo Lonardi's three-week caretaker government which followed and General Pedro E. Aramburu's November army coup. The account takes us to 1 December. The author also considers the 'important international implications' of Aramburu's foreign policy, especially for the United States, and the volume neatly complements his 1954 study, *The United States and Argentina* (q.v.). See also *Permanent crisis and the failure to create a democratic regime: Argentina, 1955-66.*

322 **Bureaucratic authoritarianism: Argentina, 1966-1973, in comparative perspective.**
Guillermo O'Donnell. Berkeley, California; Los Angeles; London: University of California Press, 1988. 338p.

The author calls this an 'empirical investigation into the political and economic processes in Argentina between June 1966 and March 1973'. His near-definitive historical account of the period is compared to the conditions in Brazil after 1964, Uruguay and Chile after 1973 and Argentina (again) after 1976, and concludes that the country between 1966 and 1973 displayed symptoms of 'the implantation, social impact, and collapse of a type of state I have termed bureaucratic-authoritarian' (see *Modernization and bureaucratic-authoritarianism: studies in South American politics*).

323 **Juan Perón and the reshaping of Argentina.**
Edited by Frederick C. Turner, José Enrique Miguens. Pittsburgh, Pennsylvania: University of Pittsburgh Press, 1983. 268p. (Pitt Latin American Series).

A varied collection of essays by Argentine, United States, Brazilian and Spanish scholars, which attempts to show the diverse aspects of Peronism and its effects on Argentine society. While frequently critical, the writers are all 'strongly convinced of the importance of Peronism'. Among the topics discussed are Eva Perón, Juan Domingo Perón's relations with the trades unions and the Church, his attempted incomes policy, the continuance of working-class support for Perón and the presidential elections of September 1973 which returned him briefly to power.

324 **Permanent crisis and the failure to create a democratic regime: Argentina, 1955-66.**
Guillermo O'Donnell. In: *The breakdown of democratic regimes. Part 3: Latin America*. Edited by Juan J. Linz, Alfred Stepan. Baltimore, Maryland; London: Johns Hopkins University Press, 1978, p. 138-77.

In three parts: 'some aspects of Argentina's historical legacy', in which the author reviews the chief protagonists of the previous one hundred years since national unification: the landed oligarchy, the middle class and the urban popular sector. In part two, he examines the 'social setting' of the economically turbulent 1955-66 period: per capita income, foreign exchange, industry and inflation. During this period the military 'became the most effective channel for the satisfaction of sectoral demands'; there were numerous attempted military coups, 'but none had changed the existing political system'. General Juan C. Onganía's successful 1966 army takeover differed from earlier coups in that this time the armed forces had 'no intention of convoking elections or returning government to political parties in the foreseeable future'; it was 'a conscious effort to change the existing political system by the inauguration of a bureaucratic-authoritarian regime'. For O'Donnell's detailed political study of bureaucratic-authoritarianism, see *Modernization and bureaucratic-authoritarianism: studies in South American politics*, and *Bureaucratic authoritarianism: Argentina, 1966–1973, in comparative perspective*.

325 **The return of Eva Perón, with The killings in Trinidad.**
V. S. Naipaul. London: André Deutsch; New York: Knopf, 1980.
227p.

The title chapter, p. 95-170, describes the famous novelist's impressions of the Argentine political scene between 1972 and 1977; it appeared originally in the *New York Review of Books*. Naipaul writes of the lingering poisonous effects on the people of the mythical figure of 'saint' Eva Perón, who died in 1952: 'she was expensively embalmed, and now [in 1972] her corpse is with Perón at the Iron Gate', the Madrid suburb from where the exiled former president 'dictates peace terms with the military regime of Argentina'. The country was in despair but 'someone holds out hope' and 'the return of Perón, or the triumph of Peronism' was anticipated. He writes of the economy ('the peso has gone to hell'), and witnesses the political terror of March 1977 ('the guerrillas still raid and rob and blow up' and the police 'reply to terror with terror. They, too, kidnap and kill, they torture'). He visits a shanty-town and a brothel, both symbols of Argentina's tragedy and 'sense of despair', and elicits the opinions of a trade-union leader, a civil-rights lawyer, a publisher-bookseller, a film-maker, a waiter in Mendoza and a political commentator.

# Population

326 **Argentina.**
Horacio D. Gregoratti, Carlos Luzzetti. In: *Population policy in developed countries*. Edited by Bernard Berelson. New York: McGraw-Hill, 1974, p. 427-44.

A survey of the demographic and environmental factors which have tended to cause only moderate population growth in Argentina compared to neighbouring countries (except Uruguay): fertility rates, age structure (in 1970, only 29.3 per cent of the population was under fourteen years of age), reduced migration, modern urban life-styles, the influence of the mass media, high per capita income (the growing middle classes tend to practise voluntary family planning), the shortage of housing and the expense of educating a family's children. The authors also describe the methods of birth control used in Argentina and the position of the government and other influential groups on population growth.

327 **Aspectos demográficos de la urbanización en la Argentina: 1869-1960.**
(Demographic aspects of urbanization in Argentina, 1869-1960.)
Zulma L. Recchini de Lattes. Buenos Aires: Instituto Torcuato Di Tella, Centro de Investigaciones Sociales, Programa de Actividades Demográficas, 1973. 99p. map. bibliog. (Serie Naranja: Sociología).

This mainly descriptive study, with thirty-eight tables and fourteen graphs, begins with a consideration of the general trends in the history of Argentina's urbanization process, and then details the rates of urban migration by age and sex between 1869 and 1960. By 1960 Buenos Aires contained almost one-half of the country's total urban population even though, after 1914, there was a slight decentralization of the urban population from the pampean region to other areas. The study reveals that there were more women and adults in the cities than in the countryside, that net migration to the large cities represented more than two-thirds of their total growth after 1947, and that Buenos Aires and Mendoza had received most interprovincial migrants, whereas other cities had grown through rural–urban intraprovincial migration.

Population

328    **Buenos Aires, puerto del Río de la Plata, capital de la Argentina: estudio crítico de su población, 1536-1936.** (Buenos Aires, River Plate port, capital of Argentina: a critical study of its population, 1536-1936.) Nicolás Besio Moreno.    Buenos Aires: Talleres Gráficos Tuduri, 1939. 500p. maps. bibliog.

An impressive chronological history of birth, marriage and mortality rates in Buenos Aires, including valuable examinations of the sources used by the author (chronicles and other first-hand accounts, city censuses). There are also chapters on migration, the slave trade and epidemics. A classic study, though some of the figures have since been found to be suspect.

329    **Demographic consequences of international migratory movements in the Argentine Republic, 1870-1960.** Zulma L. Recchini de Lattes.    In: *Proceedings of the World Population Conference, Belgrade, 30 August – 10 September 1965. Vol. 4: Selected papers and summaries: migration, urbanization, economic development.*    New York: United Nations, Department of Economic and Social Affairs, 1967, p. 211-15.

A study of the direct influences of immigration – 'which, according to existing records, amounted in the course of a century (from 1857 to 1960) to 5,094,874 persons' – on the size, sex–age structure and geographical distribution of the population, and on the fertility rate (53.2 per 1,000 in 1870-80, 24.1 in 1950-60). 'In the absence of international migration, the population would have been approximately 27 per cent smaller than it actually was in 1895, 46 per cent smaller in 1914, and 52 and 55 per cent smaller respectively in 1947 and 1960.' See also the same author and Alfred E. Lattes's *Migraciones en la Argentina: estudio de las migraciones internas e internacionales, basado en datos censales, 1869-1960.*

330    **Estimaciones de la población de Buenos Aires en 1744, 1778 y 1810.** (Estimates of the population of Buenos Aires in 1744, 1778 and 1810.) Lyman L. Johnson.    *Desarrollo Económico*, vol. 19, no. 73 (April-June 1979), p. 107-19. bibliog.

Based on a new examination of data obtained from parish birth and burial registers, the author's research found larger populations than those given in the enumerations (*padrones*) of 1744 (originally 11,600, Johnson estimates at least 11,620 and at most 14,525), 1778 (24,363, Johnson at least 29,920, at most 37,400) and 1810 (42,872, Johnson at least 37,400, at most 76,450). The chief reason given for the underestimates is the failure to count the free black population. See also *Population and space in eighteenth century Buenos Aires.*

331　**Evolución demográfica argentina de 1810 a 1869.** (The evolution of Argentina's population, 1810-1869.)
Ernesto J. A. Maeder.　Buenos Aires: Editorial Universitaria de Buenos Aires, 1969. 68p. (Temas de EUDEBA: Estadística).

An important compilation of demographic data: a history and description of the demographic sources available followed by the recorded populations, official and non-official, of the nation and provinces between 1810 and 1869. A companion volume to the next item.

332　**Evolución demográfica argentina durante el período hispano, 1535-1810.** (The evolution of Argentina's population during the Hispanic period.)
Jorge Comadrán Ruiz.　Buenos Aires: Editorial Universitaria de Buenos Aires, 1969. 120p. (Temas de EUDEBA).

Like the previous item, to which it forms a companion volume, this is a short but classic study of population growth covering: the native Indians, the early conquest and settlements, the growth of the city and the countryside, and the first foreign immigrants. There are numerous small tables throughout. For Argentina's native population before the conquest, see Jane Pyle, 'A reexamination of aboriginal population estimates for Argentina', in *The native population of the Americas in 1492*, edited by William M. Denevan (Madison, Wisconsin: University of Wisconsin Press, 1976, p. 181-204).

333　**Evolution of fertility in Argentina and Uruguay.**
Ana M. Rothman.　In: *International Population Conference / Congrès International de Population, London, 1969*.　Liège, Belgium: International Union for the Scientific Study of Population, 1971, vol. 1, p. 712-32. bibliog.

Between 1869 (the date of the first census) and 1960 the Argentine population increased sixteen times, while the Uruguayan population grew twenty times between 1852 and 1963. By 1960, their gross reproduction rates had reached values under 1.5, while in the rest of Latin American the rates exceeded 2.0, and were in some cases as high as 3.0. Based on corrected census figures for the period, the study measures gross and net reproduction rates, age-specific fertility rates, and the relation between fertility levels and various socioeconomic indicators.

334　**Fertility levels and differentials in Argentina in the nineteenth century.**
Jorge L. Somoza.　*Milbank Memorial Fund Quarterly*, vol. 46, no. 3, part 2 (July 1968), p. 53-71. bibliog.

The Argentine population increased dramatically between 1869 and 1914, owing to a combination of mass immigration and high fertility and decreasing mortality levels; thereafter, fertility declined sharply. 'It has been estimated that the level of fertility of the population of Argentina around 1895 was equivalent to six children ever born per woman at the end of the child-bearing period of life.' Fertility was uniform throughout the regions, but in Buenos Aires it was well below the rest of the country. The differentials studied are: native and foreign-born women, urban and rural women, mothers' literacy rates.

# Population

335 **The growth and structure of a provincial community of poncho weavers, Belén, Argentina, 1678-1869.**
Esther Hermitte.  In: *Peasants, primitives, and proletarians: the struggle for identity in South America.*  Edited by David L. Browman, Ronald A. Schwarz. The Hague: Mouton, 1979, p. 49-72. bibliog.

Belén, in the northwestern province of Catamarca, has been an important centre of textile production since its foundation in 1678. Today, most of the labour force is still involved in the manufacture of ponchos and shawls of vicuña and llama wool; significantly, its production is controlled by women, while the men are involved in agriculture. Using city, provincial and national censuses, this chapter describes Belén's demographic growth and social structure, 1756-1869. For a more detailed analysis of the role of women in the community, see the same author's 'Ponchos, weaving, and patron-state relations in northwest Argentina', in *Structure and process in Latin America: patronage, clientage and power systems*, edited by Arnold Strickon and Sidney M. Greenfield (Albuquerque, New Mexico: University of New Mexico Press, 1972, p. 159-77).

336 **Migration and population imbalance in the settlement hierarchy of Argentina.**
Richard J. Wilkie.  In: *Environment, society, and rural change in Latin America.*  Edited by David A. Preston. Chichester, England; New York: John Wiley, 1980, p. 157-84. maps. bibliog.

Argentina's unbalanced urban–rural population distribution is demonstrated graphically by the fact that since 1950 nearly one-half of the population has been concentrated in the five largest cities (Buenos Aires, Rosario, Córdoba, La Plata and Mendoza). Three phenomena are examined: the major shift of population from rural to urban areas after 1940; interprovincial migration; and local-level migration, with a case-study of Aldea San Francisco, a small community of 200 inhabitants in Entre Ríos province. For a detailed study of Aldea San Francisco, see *Toward a behavioral model of peasant migration: an Argentine case of spatial behavior by social class level* (item no. 346).

337 **Migration, population change, and ethnicity in Argentina.**
Alfredo E. Lattes.  In: *Migration and urbanization: models and adaptive strategies.*  Edited by Brian M. Du Toit, Helen I. Sofa. Chicago, Illinois: Aldine, 1975, p. 117-41. bibliog. (World Anthropology, 8).

Using census data exclusively, the author focuses on international immigration and internal migration, first, as determinants of the Argentine population in 1869, and second, as long-term factors in the size, spatial distribution and composition of the population between 1869 and 1960. Before 1914, immigration was the main factor of growth; after 1914, natural increase was the main factor, but provincial depopulation then occurred through internal migration.

338 **La mortalidad en Buenos Aires entre 1855 y 1960.** (Mortality in Buenos Aires, 1855-1960.)
María S. Müller.   Buenos Aires: Instituto Torcuato Di Tella, Centro de Investigaciones Sociales. Centro Latinoamericano de Demografía, 1974. 141p. bibliog. (Serie Naranja: Sociología. Programa de Actividades Demográficas).

Life expectancy in 1960 was more than double that in 1855 (70.7 years compared with 32.2). Detailed tables give mortality rates by age, sex and age, and ethnic origin. They reveal that mortality rates fell more sharply for young people than for old, and that during the period 1887-1914 (figures are not available for other years) foreign-born Argentines had a higher life expectancy than native-born.

339 **La mortalidad en la Argentina: evolución histórica y situación en 1970.** (Mortality in Argentina: historical evolution and situation in 1970.)
María S. Müller.   Buenos Aires: Centro de Estudios de Población, 1978. 111p. bibliog.

After an analysis of mortality trends for the period 1870-1970, broken down by sex and age and by four main regions (Buenos Aires, the Littoral provinces, Cuyo and the Northwest) as well as for the country as a whole, the main section and appendix present detailed mortality tables for 1961-70 according to the same differentials.

340 **La población de Argentina.** (The population of Argentina.)
Compiled by Zulma Recchini de Lattes, Alfredo E. Lattes.   Buenos Aires: Ministerio de Economía, Secretaría de Estudios de Programación y Coordinación Económica, Instituto Nacional de Estadística y Censos, 1975. 212p. maps. bibliog. (Serie Investigaciones Demográficas, 1. Committee for International Coordination of National Research in Demography Series).

A collection of seven expert studies summarizing some of the more detailed monographs reviewed elsewhere in this section: Lattes on population growth and its spatial distribution between 1870 and 1970; changes in the composition of the population (age, sex, origin) by Susana Schkolnik and Edith A. Pantelides; urbanization, the economically active population (Recchini de Lattes); projections to the year 2000 (32.9 million) by Recchini de Lattes and María J. Elsa Cerisola.

341 **La población de Buenos Aires: componentes demográficos del crecimiento entre 1855 y 1960.** (The population growth of Buenos Aires, 1855-1960.)
Zulma L. Recchini de Lattes.   Buenos Aires: Instituto Torcuato Di Tella, 1971. 189p. map. bibliog. (Publicación del Programa Población y Sociedad. Serie Naranja: Sociología).

Considers the effects of immigration, migration and natural growth on the population of the city of Buenos Aires and its metropolitan area, mainly between 1855 and 1960 (during which time the population expanded five times to a total of seven millions), but also between 1580 (the city's second founding) and 1855 (by which time the population had increased sevenfold). For a study of the population of the province of Buenos Aires during roughly the same period, see Nicolás Sánchez Albornoz, 'Rural population and depopulation in the province of Buenos Aires, 1869-1960', in *Population and economics*, edited by Paul Duprez (Winnipeg, Canada: University of Manitoba Press, 1970, p. 315-34).

342 **Population geography of Argentina.**
Robert J. Tata. *Revista Geográfica* (Mexico City), no. 85 (June 1977), p. 79-95. maps.

Argentina 'boasts the demographic characteristics of an advanced nation': a highly urbanized population (70 per cent of the population living in cities larger than 20,000 inhabitants, producing a low overall population density, and only 18 per cent of the labour force working in agriculture), a comparatively low national growth rate of 1.4 per cent, and low birth and death rates.

343 **Recent changes in the distribution of population in Argentina.**
Ross N. Pearson. In: *Papers of the Michigan Academy of Science, Arts, and Letters*, vol. 49, part 2: Social Science. Edited by R. A. Loomis. Ann Arbor, Michigan: University of Michigan Press, 1964, p. 367-81. maps.

An analysis of the changing patterns of population distribution in Argentina using data from the previous two national population censuses (1947 and 1960). During this period the population increased by 25.9 per cent, the metropolitan region of Buenos Aires by 32 per cent. A similar study by the same author appeared as: 'Mapping population change in Argentina', *Revista Geográfica* (Rio de Janeiro), vol. 33, no. 59 (July-Dec. 1963), p. 63-77.

344 **The rural population of Argentina to 1970.**
Richard W. Wilkie. In: *Statistical abstract of Latin America*. Edited by James W. Wilkie, Peter Reich. Los Angeles, California: UCLA Latin American Center Publications, vol. 20 (1980), p. 562-80.

Examining data for dispersed settlements and villages of between 100 and 2,000 inhabitants, the author finds that the dispersed rural population declined sharply between 1947 and 1960 and less sharply between 1960 and 1970, whereas the village population (4.6 per cent of the population) actually increased during the former period. Overall, the rural population declined steadily from 62.5 per cent in 1895 to 21.3 per cent in 1970, the lowest level for any Latin American country.

345 **Theory and method in a study of Argentine fertility.**
Aaron V. Cicourel. New York: John Wiley, 1974. 212p. bibliog. (A Wiley-Interscience Publication).

A detailed socio-psychological, not medical, study of the factors affecting the fertility and sexual habits of a sample of 252 Buenos Aires families. The author is frankly self-critical when evaluating the methodology he uses. Tables indicate the socioeconomic characteristics of the women interviewed and their attitudes to family size and planning.

346 **Toward a behavioral model of peasant migration: an Argentine case of spatial behavior by social class level.**
Richard W. Wilkie. In: *Population dynamics of Latin America: a review and bibliography. Papers presented at the second General Session of the Conference of Latinamericanist Geographers, Boston, Massachusetts, April 17, 1971.* Edited by Robert N. Thomas. East Lansing, Michigan: CLAG Publications, 1973, p. 83-114. bibliog.

In 1966-67 the author interviewed 530 present and former inhabitants of Aldea San Francisco in Entre Ríos province, a small and isolated community of 298 peasants (58 households) descended from Volga Germans who first settled the area in the 1870s. He presents a detailed picture of the community by social class and sex, and also tries to discover what motivated the out-migrants to leave. He finds that, on average, 'the middle-class has the highest ranking in dynamic migration behavior'. The migrants' specific 'mistrust of the environment' which caused them to leave Aldea San Francisco is dealt with in the author and Jane Riblett Wilkie's 'Environmental perception and migration behavior: a case study in rural Argentina', in *Internal migration systems in the developing world, with special reference to Latin America*, edited by Robert N. Thomas, John M. Hunter (Cambridge, Massachusetts: Schenkman, 1980, p. 135-51). See also *Migration and population imbalance in the settlement hierarchy of Argentina*.

# Women

347 **Las argentinas de ayer y hoy.** (The Argentine woman, yesterday and
today).
Lily Sosa de Newton.   Buenos Aires: Librería y Editorial
L. V. Zanetti, 1967. 237p. bibliog.
After a chronological treatment of the role of women in Argentina's history from the
colonial period to the present day, the remaining five chapters, mainly covering 1800
onwards, are concerned with the early feminist movement, girls' and women's
education, women writers, women in the arts and sciences, and women at work.

348 **The Argentine woman: her social, political and economic role.**
N. Eriksson.   *Review of the River Plate*, vol. 52, no. 3840 (21 Dec.
1972), p. 959-61, 985-8.
A useful short article, with twenty-two statistical tables, concerning the position of
women in Argentine society, especially the demographic characteristics of the female
population, the education of women and the female labour force. The Argentine
woman 'is moving away from the Hispanic-Latin American life style that still persists in
the countryside, and towards greater participation in labour, financial and political
affairs'.

349 **The challenge of constructing civilian peace: women and democracy in
Argentina.**
María del Carmen Feijóo.   In: *The women's movement in Latin
America: feminism and the transition to democracy*.   Edited by Jane S.
Jaquette. Boston, Massachusetts; London: Unwin Hyman, 1989,
p. 72-94.
Women, 'motivated by "private" emotions of loss', played a central role in the popular
movement against the military régimes of 1976-83. The most prominent women's
groups were the Mothers of the Plaza de Mayo (formed in April 1977), the National
Movement of Housewives (in July 1982 women in Buenos Aires, Quilmes, Rosario and

Córdoba staged 'purchasing' strikes and demonstrations against high prices), and the various feminist groups, most of which were dissolved after the 1976 coup. However, the limited power women attained in 1983 has declined and 'women are still largely absent from conventional politics'. Another version of this paper may be found in the same author and Mónica Gogna's 'Women in the transition to democracy', in *Women and social change in Latin America*, edited by Elizabeth Jelin (Geneva: United Nations Research Institute for Social Development; London: Zed Books, 1990, p. 79-114).

350  **Domestic workers in Buenos Aires.**
Mónica Gogna.  In: *Muchachas no more: household workers in Latin America and the Caribbean.*  Edited by Elsa M. Chaney, Mary Garcia Castro.  Philadelphia: Temple University Press, 1989, p. 83-104. bibliog. (Women in the Political Economy.)
This is a rare study of Argentine domestic women workers, based on secondary sources, classified advertisements and interviews conducted in the late 1970s, which finds that most of them are young, poorly educated and migrant women. The article discusses access to domestic employment, legal status, working conditions, salaries, job stability and relations between worker and employer.

351  **Dynamics of the female labour force in Argentina.**
Zulma Recchini de Lattes.  Paris: Unesco, 1983. 98p. bibliog. (Women in a World Perspective).
An examination of the connection between working women, their age, marital status and family structure, through a cohort analysis of the data from the 1947, 1960 and 1970 national population censuses. Four areas of Argentina, each with different social, demographic and economic characteristics, were studied: Buenos Aires, Misiones, Río Negro and Neuquén, and Salta. See also *The impact of education on the female labor force in Argentina and Paraguay*.

352  **Education, philanthropy, and feminism: components of Argentine womanhood, 1860-1926.**
Cynthia Jeffress Little.  In: *Latin American women: historical perspectives.*  Edited by Asunción Lavrin.  Westport, Connecticut; London: Greenwood Press, 1978, p. 235-53. (Contributions in Women's Studies, 3).
Explores the ways in which some groups of Argentine women were able to 'break away from the Spanish tradition of sheltered womanhood' and to participate in the country's social and economic life before 1926 (when the Civil Code improved their rights), through their involvement in philanthropic activities, in education and in the early feminist movement. Women's associations, conferences and notable individual feminists are mentioned.

353  **The female vote in Argentina, 1958-1965.**
Paul H. Lewis.  *Comparative Political Studies*, vol. 3, no. 4 (Jan. 1971), p. 425-41. bibliog.
Since women and men used separate polling stations between 1958 and 1965, data are available on how women actually voted. A higher proportion of women than men were found to have voted, women tended to support the more conservative parties, and

'working-class women were more radical than upper-class men and about as radical as middle-class men. Still, women tended to be more conservative than men of the same social class'.

### 354 ¡Feminismo! The woman's [sic] movement in Argentina from its beginnings to Eva Perón.
Marifran Carlson.   Chicago, Illinois: Academy Chicago Publications, 1988. 224p. bibliog.

This is the first book-length study of feminism in Argentina, surveying the early participation of (mainly upper-class) women in the charitable work of the Sociedad de Beneficencia (Benevolent Society, founded in 1823), women's education in the nineteenth century, the National Council of Women (1910), the links with socialism and the Free-Thought movement (1900-10), the International Feminist Congress (1910), and the position of women during the conservative (1928-43) and Perón administrations.

### 355 The impact of education on the female labor force in Argentina and Paraguay.
Catalina H. Wainerman.   In: *Women's education in the Third World: comparative perspectives*.   Edited by Gail P. Kelly, Carolyn M. Elliott.   Albany, New York: State University of New York Press, 1982, p. 264-79.

Using data from Argentina's 1970 and Paraguay's 1972 national population censuses, the effects of education and family conditions on the supply of women to the labour force are calculated. It is found that among women with husbands 'education plays the role of overcoming the negative influence of family burdens' and encourages them to seek work. The chapter was first published in a special issue of *Comparative Education Review*, vol. 24, no. 2, part 2 (June 1980), p. S180-95. Other aspects of women's participation in Argentina's occupational structure are to be found in the same author's (with Ruth Sautú and Zulma Recchini de Lattes) 'The participation of women in economic activity in Argentina, Bolivia, and Paraguay: a comparative study', *Latin American Research Review*, vol. 15, no. 2 (1980), p. 143-51; and (with Recchini de Lattes) 'Marital status and women's work in Argentina: a cohort analysis', *Genus*, vol. 34, nos 3-4 (1978), p. 23-41.

### 356 Juana Manso – Argentine feminist.
Jim Levy.   Bundoora, Australia: La Trobe University, Institute of Latin American Studies, 1977. 16p. (Occasional Papers, no. 1).

Juana Paula Manso de Noronha (1819-75) was a feminist educational reformer. In 1859 President Sarmiento appointed her headmistress of the first co-educational primary school in Buenos Aires, and in 1865 she became editor of *Anales de la Educación Común*, Argentina's first educational journal. She promoted women's education as the most effective route to their emancipation, as well as changes in the legal system.

357 **Migrant careers and well-being of women.**
Judith Friedenberg, Graciela Imperiale, Mary Louise Skovron.
*International Migration Review*, vol. 22, part. 2, no. 82 (summer 1988),
p. 208-25. bibliog.
In 1980 there were 69,000 Argentines living in the United States, forty-three per cent
of whom had arrived after 1970 – initially professionals and technicians but increasingly
manual workers after 1965. This is an examination of the 'psychosocial adjustment' of
112 Argentine women migrants, from a broad range of social classes, who were living
in New York City in 1981-82. Women, especially those without children and household
help, were found to be generally more psychologically demoralized than Argentine
male migrants. Contrary to expectations, unmarried women were equally as
demoralized as married women.

358 **La mujer argentina.** (The Argentine woman.)
Héctor Iñigo Carrera. Buenos Aires: Centro Editor de América
Latina, 1972. 116p. bibliog. (La Historia Popular. Vida y Milagros de
Nuestro Pueblo, 91).
The twenty-four illustrations suggest a history of female fashions through the ages, but
this is in fact a short, popularized study, based on secondary sources, from early
travellers to modern sociologists, of the Argentine woman's social and economic
history.

359 **La mujer en la pampa (siglos XVIII y XIX).** (The Argentine woman on
the pampa in the eighteenth and nineteenth centuries.)
María Teresa Villafañe Casal. La Plata, Argentina: Talleres Gráficos
de Angel Domínguez e Hijo, 1958. 104p. bibliog.
A study of some of the 'neglected' women in Argentina's history, the women who
contributed to the expansion of the pampa: soldiers' women, rural women
(landowners, peasants, colonizers), female healers, store-owners, mail-carriers,
schoolteachers – and even the unfortunate women captured by Indians.

360 **No God, no boss, no husband: anarchist feminism in nineteenth-century
Argentina.**
Maxine Molyneux. *Latin American Perspectives*, vol. 13, no. 1
(winter 1986), p. 119-45. bibliog.
An examination of the anarchist-feminist tendency within the Anarchist movement in
1890s Argentina, and in particular of the small, clandestine newspaper *La Voz de la
Mujer* (Woman's Voice), one of the first recorded instances in Latin America of the
'fusion of feminist ideas with a revolutionary and working-class orientation'. It first
appeared in January 1896, was distributed (by men) mainly in Buenos Aires, La Plata
and Rosario, and ran to nine issues for only a year.

361 **Sociocultural factors mitigating role conflict of Buenos Aires professional women.**
Nora Scott Kinzer. In: *Women cross-culturally: change and challenge.* Edited by Ruby Rohrlich-Leavitt. The Hague; Paris: Mouton, 1975, p. 181-97. bibliog. (World Anthropology).

A 1967 questionnaire study of a sample of 125 professional women employed full-time in fields traditionally considered to be 'masculine' professions (law, medicine, pharmacy, biochemistry, architecture, engineering and agronomy), revealed that each of these women came from supportive high-status families where the father was the role model, was 'socialized to be independent and non-nurturant', well educated, married with one or two children cared for by domestic servants, and working in a 'subordinate position' for low pay yet satisfied with her job. For a more detailed description of the sample and methodology used, see the same author's 'Women professionals in Buenos Aires' in *Female and male in Latin America: essays*, edited by Ann M. Pescatello (Pittsburgh, Pennsylvania: University of Pittsburgh Press, 1973, p. 159-90).

362 **The status of women in Argentina.**
Kathleen B. Tappen. Washington, DC: US Office of the Coordinator of Inter-American Affairs, Research Division, Social and Geographic Section, 1944. 22p. bibliog.

Using statistics for 1939-41, this is, according to Knaster (see *Women in Spanish America: an annotated bibliography from pre-conquest to contemporary times*), a general overview of the Argentine woman: economic and social conditions, occupational opportunities, political and civil rights, marriage, suffrage activities, labour and maternity legislation, education, organizations working for women's rights, and women's life and work in Buenos Aires and the interior.

363 **Women and crime: Buenos Aires, 1757-97.**
Susan Migden Socolow. *Journal of Latin American Studies*, vol. 12, no. 1 (May 1980), p. 39-54.

This article is based on the records of seventy criminal cases brought before two municipal courts in the city of Buenos Aires and the rural areas within a 145-mile radius. Artisan and lower-class women were found to be the usual victims or accomplices of violent interpersonal crimes – physical abuse, wife-beating, rape, kidnapping and haircutting committed in the home by family, friends, acquaintances or neighbours.

364 **Women, peonage, and industrialization: Argentina, 1810-1914.**
Donna J. Guy. *Latin American Research Review*, vol. 16, no. 3 (1981), p. 65-89.

The author argues that while men enjoyed the economic opportunities brought about by industrialization, women remained as domestic servants for merchants and ranchers in primitive cottage industries. These industries were an important component of the economies of the north, west and centre of the country, but they declined with the onset of industrialization and the growth of the coastal region after 1870.

365 **Women workers and the class struggle: the case of Argentina.**
Nancy Caro Hollander. *Latin American Perspectives*, vol. 4, nos 1/2
(1977), p. 180-93. bibliog.
A feminist, polemical study of the position of women under Peronism (1946-55), when
they won significant democratic rights and improvements in their work conditions and
wages. Women were chiefly mobilized through the *unidades básicas* (women's centres
in poor neighbourhoods) and the Peronist Women's Party. However, 'the ideology of
the Peronist women's movement was not profoundly radical enough to totally
challenge the established role of women'. Largely a reworking of the same author's
'Women: the forgotten half of Argentine history', in *Female and male in Latin
America: essays*, edited by Ann M. Pescatello (Pittsburgh, Pennsylvania: University of
Pittsburgh Press, 1973, p. 141-58), and 'Si Evita viviera . . .', *Latin American
Perspectives*, vol. 1, no. 3 (fall 1974), p. 42-57.

366 **The working woman in the Argentine economy.**
Blanca Stábile. *International Labour Review*, vol. 85, no. 2 (Feb.
1962), p. 122-8.
Describes the increasing role played by women in various sectors of the economy and
their employment conditions: equality of pay, the provision of nurseries and
kindergartens, legislation governing women's employment, vocational and educational
training (the expanding labour market needing more women), and maternity benefits
and protection. The author calls upon women to participate increasingly in the trade
unions, professional organizations, non-governmental women's bodies and politics.

**Women of the world: Latin America and the Caribbean.**
*See* item no. 948.

# Immigration and Colonization, Nationalities and Minorities

## General immigration

367 **Argentina as an immigration country.**
Juan F. Marsal. *Migration*, vol. 1, no. 4 (Oct.-Dec. 1961), p. 17-35.
The chief features of Argentine immigration were its planning by politicians and 'the distinguished Creole minority', the huge numbers entering the country between 1870 and 1930, its regional and urban concentration, its demographic concentration (mainly young Italian and Spanish males) and its concentration in certain occupations and social strata (new and expanding secondary and tertiary industries, leading to the formation of the 'new urban middle classes and the industrial proletariat'). A study of the first century of immigration by one of the first directors of the Argentine immigration office is Juan A. Alsina's *La inmigración en el primer siglo de la independencia* (Buenos Aires: Felipe S. Alsina, 1910. 231p.).

368 **The dynamics of Argentine migration (1955-1984): democracy and the return of expatriates.**
Edited by Alfredo E. Lattes, Enrique Oteiza, with the collaboration of Jorge Graciarena. Geneva: United Nations Research Institute for Social Development; Buenos Aires: Centro de Estudios de Población, 1987. 142p. map. bibliog. (UNRISD Report, no. 86.13).
Part one focuses on the general emigration of Argentines – for political, educational, economic and social reasons – during the last three decades, and includes detailed statistical and literature surveys. Part two examines the perception of Argentine immigrants in two host countries, Mexico and Venezuela, and by the Argentine press. Lattes estimates the total number of expatriates at approximately 547,000 in 1984, only a few of whom acquired formal refugee status. Most Argentines abroad were concentrated in the United States, Israel, Venezuela, Spain, Britain, Canada and Australia, in that order. With the return to democracy in 1983, a large number of political exiles began to return. See also *Return to Río de la Plata: response to the return of exiles to Argentina and Uruguay.*

369 **Historia de la colonización agrícola en Argentina.** (History of
agricultural colonization in Argentina.)
Roberto Schopflocher.   Buenos Aires: Editorial Raigal, 1955. 96p.
bibliog. (Colección Campo Argentino, 2).

A succinct history of land settlement, 1820s to the present: government support for the
private promoters, the economic, legal and agricultural factors influencing colonization, and some of the actual colonies established.

370 **Immigration and nationalism: Argentina and Chile, 1890-1914.**
Carl E. Solberg.   Austin, Texas; London: University of Texas Press,
1970. 222p. 2 maps. bibliog. (Institute of Latin American Studies. Latin
American Monographs, no. 18).

A comparative study of the 'nationalist reaction against immigration that swept
Argentina and Chile early in the twentieth century', contrasting with the earlier
general welcoming of the immigrants. Mass urban immigration (shortsighted land
policies discouraged settling on the land) gave rise to social, economic and political
changes 'that weakened the monopoly of power the landed elites had held'; the élite
then 'attempted to use cultural nationalism to justify its continued dominance'. This
monograph is based on wide-ranging sources, including newspapers.

371 **Marriage patterns and immigrant assimilation in Buenos Aires, 1882-
1923.**
Samuel L. Baily.   *Hispanic American Historical Review*, vol. 60, no. 1
(Feb. 1980), p. 32-48.

Using the *Anuario estadístico* of the city of Buenos Aires for the period, this analysis of
marriage patterns among Argentines, Italians and Spaniards refutes the melting-pot
theory propagated by José Luis Romero and Gino Germani: 'approximately two out of
every three Italian and Spanish males who married before 1900 found Italian and
Spanish spouses' and 'assimilation – as measured by inter-marriage – did not take place
very rapidly or completely at all'.

372 **Mass immigration and modernization in Argentina.**
Gino Germani.   In: *Masses in Latin America.*   Edited by Irving Louis
Horowitz.   New York: Oxford University Press, 1970, p. 289-330.

Reprinted from *Studies in Comparative International Development*, vol. 2, no. 11
(1966), p. 165-82, this is concerned with the demographic, economic, social and
cultural effects of mass immigration, 1853-1947. The dependence of industry on
European immigrants during the formative stages of industrialization (1880-1930) is
examined in Oscar Cornblit's 'European immigrants in Argentine industry and
politics', in *The politics of conformity in Latin America*, edited by Claudio Véliz
(London; New York; Toronto: Oxford University Press, 1967, p. 221-48.).

## Immigration and Colonization, Nationalities and Minorities. General immigration

373  **Migraciones en la Argentina: estudio de las migraciones internas e internacionales, basado en datos censales, 1869-1960.** (Migration in Argentina: a study of internal and international migration, based on census data, 1869-1960.)
Zulma L. Recchini de Lattes, Alfredo E. Lattes.  Buenos Aires: Instituto Torcuato Di Tella, Centro de Investigaciones Sociales, 1970. 333p. maps. (Serie Naranja: Sociología).
A full commentary on the growth and spatial distribution of migration to and within Argentina, supported by eighty tables and nearly forty graphs. Analyses net migration (by Argentines and non-Argentines, total and by province, by sex and age) and interprovincial and interdepartmental migration.

374  **Mobility and integration in urban Argentina: Córdoba in the Liberal era.**
Mark D. Szuchman.  Austin, Texas; London: University of Texas Press, 1980. 236p. maps. bibliog. (Institute of Latin American Studies. Latin American Monographs, no. 52).
Traces the lives of some 4,000 (mainly Spanish and French) immigrants after their arrival in Córdoba, Argentina's major interior city, between 1870 and 1914, assessing their level of integration into the new society. Emphasis is given to their occupational and residential mobility and their educational and marriage patterns. There was significant out-migration from the city; those immigrants who stayed found little opportunity of vertical mobility within a rigid social system.

375  **La pampa gringa: la colonización agrícola en Santa Fe, 1870-1895.**
(Foreign settlers on the pampa: agricultural colonization in the province of Santa Fe, 1870-1895.)
Ezequiel Gallo.  Buenos Aires: Editorial Sudamericana, 1983. 457p. maps. bibliog. (Colección Historia y Sociedad).
A scholarly account of the foundation of agricultural colonies by mostly individual Italian peasant immigrants or private companies, in the wheat-exporting province of Santa Fe; 360 colonies were founded between 1856 and 1895. There is a chapter on the violent colonists' revolts of 1877-94 (see also *Farmers in revolt: the revolutions of 1893 in the province of Santa Fe, Argentina*). Another excellent work on the subject is Oscar Luis Ensinck, *Historia de la inmigración y la colonización en la provincia de Santa Fe* (Buenos Aires: Fundación para la Educación, la Ciencia y la Cultura, 1979. 359p.)

376  **Peopling the Argentine pampa.**
Mark Jefferson.  New York: American Geographical Society, 1926. 211p. maps. (Research Series, 16).
This is a classic text, illustrated with over forty plates, on the European colonization of Santa Fe and Entre Ríos provinces in the nineteenth century. Esperanza, the first-ever colony, just north of Santa Fe city, was founded with 200 Swiss families in 1856. The author, a geographer, had first-hand experience of colonies in Tucumán and Córdoba. He includes a chapter on the railways' contribution to agriculture in the region. There is a modern reprint (Port Washington, New York: Kennikat Press, 1971).

377 **Pioneer settlement in northeast Argentina.**
Robert C. Eidt. Madison, Wisconsin; Milwaukee, Wisconsin;
London: University of Wisconsin Press, 1971. 277p. maps. bibliog.
Another work on land settlement, this time in Misiones province, formerly a part of
Corrientes and made a National Territory in 1881, from the seventeenth-century Jesuit
missions to the present. The author describes the development of European
*latifundismo*, government sponsorship of colonization, and private foreign colonization
companies. He contrasts the private *Waldhufen* (long, narrow forest-farm villages) and
public *damero* (grid-pattern) settlement patterns. There are ten plates.

378 **Return to Río de la Plata: response to the return of exiles to Argentina
and Uruguay.**
Lelio Mármora, Jorge Gurrieri. Hoya Station, Washington, DC:
Georgetown University, Center for Immigration Policy and Refugee
Assistance, Hemispheric Migration Project, 1988. 39p.
In 1981 the Argentine press began to focus attention on political exiles after the
Association of Argentines in Foreign Countries published a report which counted
2,125,000 expatriates. Political exiles, mostly from the 'Peronist left', began returning
to Argentina during the last years of the military dictatorship. The most important
non-governmental organizations for reintegration were the Office of Solidarity for
Argentine Exiles (OSEA, formed of the leaders of human rights organizations) and
the National Commission for the Return of Argentines Abroad (CNREA). There was
a 'near-absence of the Argentine government from the integration process', the
programmes were limited to short-term advisory status, and there was an 'indifferent
response' on the part of the various sectors of society, a vague and often prejudiced
image of the returned exiles.

379 **Rural life in Argentina.**
Carl C. Taylor. Baton Rouge, Louisiana: Louisiana State University
Press, 1948. 464p. maps. bibliog.
In 1942-43 the author travelled 20,000 miles throughout Argentina and interviewed
over 120 farm families on behalf of the United States Departments of Agriculture and
State. This is both a valuable history of agriculture and land colonization and a classic
textbook on rural sociology focusing on landownership, tenant farming and the
farmers' standards of living. There are seventeen photographs.

380 **Sugar and seasonal labor migration: the case of Tucumán, Argentina.**
John A. Kirchner. Chicago, Illinois: University of Chicago,
Department of Geography, 1980. 174p. maps. bibliog. (Research
Papers, no. 192).
Describes the plantation economy of Tucumán, Argentina's most important sugar-
producing province; the sugar harvest (*zafra*); and the seasonal migration of labour to
the harvest from Santiago del Estero and Salta, and from Tucumán itself. The work is
based on over 100 case-studies of workers in thirteen labour camps.

# Immigration from neighbouring South American countries

### 381 Argentine experience in the field of illegal immigration.
Juan Manuel Villar. *International Migration Review*, vol. 18, no. 3 (fall 1984), p. 453-73. maps. bibliog.
Argentina has a long history of illegal immigration from Bolivia, Paraguay, Chile, Uruguay and Brazil. During the 1970s, the number of immigrant workers from these countries decreased, mainly because of a decline in their purchasing power and stricter immigration controls. Many foreigners settled legally in the country after the amnesty decree of January 1974, but fewer than after the Migration Regulations of 1965, when 150,000 aliens were allowed to settle. Also summarizes illegal immigration since 1914.

### 382 Extranjeros en la Argentina: cuantía y continuidad de los flujos migratorios limítrofes, 1970-1985. (Foreigners in Argentina: the extent and regularity of migratory flows from neighbouring countries, 1970-1985.)
Graciela M. de Marco. *Estudios Migratorios Latinoamericanos* (Buenos Aires), vol. 1, no. 3 (Aug. 1986), p. 323-50.
The author estimates that a minimum of 859,723 immigrants entered Argentina from all areas between 1970 and 1985, and calculates the numbers of immigrants from neighbouring countries settling both temporarily and permanently between 1970 and 1985.

### 383 Immigrant workers in the Buenos Aires labor market.
Adriana Marshall. *International Migration Review*, vol. 13, no. 3 (fall 1979), p. 488-501. bibliog.
During the 1960s about seventy per cent of foreign immigrants (about 217,000) sought work in the Buenos Aires metropolitan area. The article analyses them by sex ratios, age structure, rates of participation in the labour force (higher than for native Argentines) and occupation (they were concentrated mainly in unstable and poorly paid manual jobs, especially construction, domestic service and manufacturing). Three categories of migrant workers are studied: from neighbouring countries, internal and international.

### 384 La incorporación paraguaya y brasileña en el nordeste argentino.
(The assimilation of Paraguayans and Brazilians in northeast Argentina.)
Julio César Espínola. *Revista Paraguaya de Sociología*, vol. 19, no. 53 (Jan.-April 1982), p. 135-44. bibliog.
Significant immigration from Paraguay to the northeast along the rivers Paraguay and Paraná began in the 1890s, became large-scale after 1947 and dried up in the 1970s. The author estimates the number of permanent Paraguayans at 100,000, and estimates the number of Brazilian farmer-immigrants, concentrated along the rivers Uruguay and Paraná, at 50,000. Paraguayan immigrants, involved in agriculture, construction and other industries, were found to be better assimilated than Brazilian. See also F. de P. Oliva, 'Paraguayan workers in Buenos Aires: hope and despair', *Migration Today*, no. 18 (1974), p. 18-26.

385 **Shifting patterns in migration from bordering countries to Argentina: 1914-1970.**
Juan M. Carrón. *International Migration Review*, vol. 13, no. 3 (fall 1979), p. 475-87. bibliog.

Betweeen 1914 and 1947, immigrants from bordering countries tended to settle in interior provinces which were then enjoying economic, especially agricultural, growth. Between 1947 and 1960, there was a drift to the Buenos Aires area, but the majority remained in the interior, then declining economically. After 1960, the movement towards Buenos Aires became more pronounced; here the migrants found work in the more stagnant areas of the economy.

386 **Workers from the north: plantations, Bolivian labor, and the city in northwest Argentina.**
Scott Whiteford. Austin, Texas: University of Texas Press, 1981. 189p. maps. bibliog. (Institute of Latin American Studies. Monographs, no. 54).

An ethnographic study of the Bolivian villagers who every June migrate to the large sugar plantations of Salta and Jujuy for the five- to seven-month harvest, their families, recruitment, work and living conditions on the plantations, and the workers' community and its uneasy relationship with its trade union. Between harvests, many of the Bolivian workers find labouring work and temporary residence in the city of Salta.

# Immigration from outside the Americas

387 **And here the world ends: the life of an Argentine village.**
Kristin Hoffman Ruggiero. Stanford, California: Stanford University Press, 1988. 226p. bibliog.

A case-study of everyday life in the tiny village of Colonia San Sebastiano, near La Paz in the province of Entre Ríos, founded in 1888 by Protestant Waldensians from the French-Italian Alps whose descendants in 1980 constituted three-quarters of the 1,000 inhabitants. Five chapters describe the history of the village, its agriculture and the community's social and family life and institutions.

388 **The Arabs in Tucumán, Argentina.**
María Elena Vela Ríos, Roberto Caimi. In: *Asiatic migrations in Latin America*. Edited by Luz M. Martínez Montiel. Mexico City: Colegio de México, 1981, p. 125-46. bibliog.

Relatively little has been written about the Arab community in Argentina, which numbers between 600,000 and 800,000, but this group has now attracted attention since the rise to the presidency of Carlos Saúl Menem, of Syrian descent. The first Arabs came to Argentina in 1868, although the first official entry was not until 1896, and became modest merchants; most Arabs (predominantly Syrians and Lebanese – the authors also include Ottomans and Turks in their discussion) settled in Buenos Aires,

**Immigration and Colonization, Nationalities and Minorities.**
Immigration from outside the Americas

followed by the northeast. In Tucumán, the Arab population is around 53,000. The classic early study, published in 1910, is Alejandro Schamun, *La colectividad siria en la Argentina* (reprinted by Editorial del Polígono, 1983).

389 **Las asociaciones polacas en Misiones, 1898-1938.** (Polish associations in Misiones, 1898-1938.)
Danuta Lukasz. *Estudios Latinoamericanos* (Warsaw), no. 8 (1981), p. 169-88.

The first Polish immigrants to Argentina arrived in 1897. This article traces the community organization (cultural, educational, religious and economic) of Polish residents in the province of Misiones, from the first cooperative store in the parish of Azara (1906) to the creation of a provincial-wide Education Council in 1937.

390 **Les aveyronnais dans la pampa: fondation, développement et vie de la colonie aveyronnaise de Pigüé – Argentine, 1884-1974.** (Aveyron settlers on the pampa: the foundation, growth and life of the Aveyron colony of Pigüé, Argentina, 1884-1974.)
Jean Andreu, Bartolomé Bennassar, Romain Gaignard. Toulouse, France: Privat, 1977. 325p. maps. bibliog.

In December 1884 forty French families from the Villefranche de Rouergue area on the River Aveyron reached Pigüé, 130 kilometres north of Bahía Blanca in the province of Buenos Aires, and began farming 27,000 hectares of land acquired by contract in France. The book charts the colonists' early difficulties and eventual prosperity, their slow adaptation to Argentine society (they remain faithful to their French origins) and their community organizations.

391 **La colectividad italiana en la Argentina.** (The Italian community in Argentina.)
Luis Mercadante. Buenos Aires: Alzamor Editores, 1974. 293p. bibliog. (Colección del Sol).

Sixteen chapters include a chronology of Italian immigration; the contribution of Italians to the labour force, industry, literature, journalism and the arts; and their associations, welfare organizations, cultural activities and publications. Contains a good name index.

392 **Cómo fue la inmigración irlandesa en la Argentina.** (Irish immigration in Argentina.)
Juan Carlos Korol, Hilda Sábato. Buenos Aires: Plus Ultra, 1981. 214p. maps. bibliog. (Colección Esquemas Históricos, 33).

The Irish were one of the earliest immigrant groups in Argentina: between 10,500 and 11,500 arrived during the nineteenth century, most of them before 1880, and many participated in Buenos Aires province's sheep-breeding industry, then the most dynamic sector of the economy. This an excellent study of the community's demographic, economic and social structures, 1869-95; by the latter year the total number of Irish and Irish-Argentines was 18,617.

393 **The desert and the dream: a study of Welsh colonization in Chubut, 1865-1915.**
Glyn Williams.   Cardiff: University of Wales Press, 1975. 230p. maps. bibliog.

The definitive history of the first fifty years of the famous Welsh colony in Patagonia to 1915, when active immigration virtually ceased. It describes conditions in Wales, the early history of Patagonia, the arrival of the poorly prepared settlers and the development of the colony, whose first permanent settlement was Rawson. The relationship between the settlers and the native Indians is well described. The book includes twelve photographs. An excellent fictionalized account of one man's experiences in the Welsh colony is Richard Llewellyn's *Up, into the singing mountain* (London: Michael Joseph, 1963).

394 **The Dutch colony in Tres Arroyos, Argentina: a particular case of ethnic group maintenance.**
C. F. Jongkind.   *International Migration*, vol. 23, no. 3 (Sept. 1985), p. 335-47.

Over 10,000 Dutch immigrants entered Argentina before 1940. The Tres Arroyos colony, 500 kilometres south of Buenos Aires, was formed by two waves of immigrants from Holland: 4,000 poor farmers in 1889, and a group of wealthier farmers' sons in 1924 who married the daughters of the first settlers. They have retained a strong Dutch character to this day and are seen as a closed community, with a 'high level of participation in organizations such as the Dutch school, the agrarian co-operative and the Reformed Church'.

395 **Los eslavos en Misiones: consideraciones en torno al número y a la distribución geográfica de los campesinos polacos y ucranianos (1897-1938).** (The Slav community in Misiones: a study of the number and geographical distribution of Polish and Ukrainian peasants, 1897-1938.)
Ryszard Stemplowski.   *Jahrbuch für Geschichte von Staat, Wirtschaft und Gesellschaft Lateinamerika*, vol. 19 (1982), p. 320-90. maps.

Slav immigration to Argentina began in 1897 when fourteen families from Galicja in Austria-Hungary went to live in Misiones. By 1941 there were 176,000 Ukrainian and Polish Slavs living in the province, 140,000 of them engaged in agriculture. This is a study of their demographic history and colonies. See also *Ukrainians in Argentina: a Canadian perspective*.

396 **The forgotten colony: a history of the English-speaking communities in Argentina.**
Andrew Graham-Yooll.   London: Hutchinson, 1981. 318p. map. bibliog.

An entertaining history by a Scots-Argentine of the many British, Irish and North American contributions to Argentina's development. 'British influence in Argentina was greatest in four fields: commerce, education, transportation and sports', but British missionaries, mercenaries, doctors, churchmen and travellers also appear here. Today the British community is one of the most numerous outside the Commonwealth. The bibliography is rightly described by the author as among the best on the subject.

**Immigration and Colonization, Nationalities and Minorities.**
Immigration from outside the Americas

See also Michael G. Mulhall, *The English in South America* (Buenos Aires: Standard Office; London: E. Stanford, 1878) and Juan P. Bailey's 'Inmigración y relaciones étnicas: los ingleses en la Argentina', *Desarrollo Económico*, vol. 18, no. 72 (Jan.-March 1979), p. 539-58. A nationalistic account of the Falkland Islands dispute which contains a brief section on the little-studied emigration of Falklanders ('kelpers') to Patagonia, is Haroldo Foulkes, *Los kelpers en las Malvinas y en la Argentina* (Buenos Aires: Ediciones Corregidor, 1983. 189p.). See also *The land that England lost: Argentina and Britain, a special relationship.*

397  **Los franceses en la Argentina/Les français en Argentine.** (The French in Argentina.)
Edited by Manrique Zago.    Buenos Aires: Manrique Zago Ediciones, 1986. 191p.

A photo-study, with a parallel Spanish and French text, of the French involvement in Argentina's history: investment, education, industry, aviation, culture, art, science and fashion.

398  **German Buenos Aires, 1913-1933: social change and cultural crisis.**
Ronald C. Newton.    Austin, Texas; London: University of Texas Press, 1977. 225p. bibliog. (Texas Pan American Series).

Middle-class German immigrants formed a small but important group in the Buenos Aires business community during the period. In 1914 the community numbered only 45,000; the author estimates German-speaking immigration at 130,000-140,000 between 1919 and 1932. The community was 'relatively homogeneous educationally, culturally and linguistically' but after 1918 was split by resentment between old and new immigrants, 'between monarchists and fascists on the one hand, and republicans, socialists and defenders of Weimar on the other'. Between 1933 and 1945, some 43,000 (mainly Jewish) German, Austrian and other West European refugees from Nazism fled to Argentina but received hostile treatment from the Argentine right-wing press; see Newton's 'Indifferent sanctuary: German-speaking refugees and exiles in Argentina, 1933-1945', *Journal of Inter-American Studies and World Affairs*, vol. 24, no. 4 (Nov. 1982), p. 395-420.

399  **Hacer la América: autobiografía de un inmigrante español en la Argentina.** ('Making it' in South America: the autobiography of a Spanish immigrant in Argentina.)
Juan F. Marsal.    Buenos Aires: Editorial del Instituto Torcuato Di Tella, 1969. 445p. (Serie Naranja: Sociología).

Marsal, a well-known sociologist, edited this extraordinary autobiography of 'J.S.', an anonymous Catalan who went out to Argentina in 1927 to better his lot, leaving behind his wife and daughter. He became a carpenter in Buenos Aires and Santiago del Estero, and a roving photographer in Entre Ríos and Misiones. In 1959, by now in poor health, he returned home at the request of his marrried daughter. Marsal contributes a useful study of Spanish immigration to Argentina and the return of immigrants to Spain.

400 **La inmigración italiana en la Argentina.** (Italian immigration to
Argentina.)
Compiled by Fernando Devoto, Gianfausto Rosoli. Buenos Aires:
Editorial Biblos, 1985. 270p. map. (Colección Historia. Serie
Mayor, 3).

One of the best accounts of Italians in Argentina: their integration into local society,
their community and cultural associations, and their contributions to the political and
labour movements. See also Francis Korn (ed.), *Los italianos en la Argentina* (Buenos
Aires: Fundación Giovanni Agnelli, 1983. 141p.) and the two photo-studies with
bilingual Spanish-Italian text edited by Manrique Zago: *Argentina, la otra patria de los
italianos/Argentina, l'altra patria degli italiani* (Buenos Aires: Manrique Zago
Ediciones, 1983. 215p.), and *Los italianos en la Argentina en los últimos cincuenta
años, 1937-1987/Gli italiani in Argentina negli ultimi cinquant'anni, 1937-1987* (same
publisher, 1987. 191p.)

401 **La inmigración sirio-libanesa en la Argentina: una aproximación.**
(Syrian-Lebanese immigration in Argentina: an assessment.)
Jorge O. Bestene. *Estudios Migratorios Latinoamericanos*, vol. 3,
no. 9 (Aug. 1988), p. 239-68.

Analyses the causes for their emigration, their numbers and spatial distribution in the
host country, professions, institutions, religious and social life, and social cohesive-
ness. A Syrian-Lebanese community which established itself in northern Santiago del
Estero province between 1900 and 1930 is studied in Alberto Tasso, 'Migración e
identidad social: una comunidad de inmigrantes en Santiago del Estero', *Estudios
Migratorios Latinoamericanos*, vol. 2, nos 6-7 (Aug.-Dec. 1987), p. 321-36.

402 **Japanese agricultural colonization: a new attempt at land opening in
Argentina.**
Robert C. Eidt. *Economic Geography*, vol. 44, no. 1 (Jan. 1968),
p. 1-20. bibliog.

Formal Japanese agricultural settlement in Argentina dates from 1957, when the first
colonies were established in Misiones and Mendoza provinces. This article reviews
Japanese immigration in general and provides a case-study of the *Luján 'B'* colony at
Garulapé, Misiones. Japanese immigration from a specific locality, the Ryukyu Islands,
is the subject of James Lawrence Tigner's 'The Ryukyuans in Argentina', *Hispanic
American Historical Review*, vol. 47, no. 2 (May 1967), p. 203-24. The first Ryukyuans
settled in Buenos Aires in 1886; by the 1950s the community numbered 10,000, the
third largest Japanese community in Latin America after Brazil and Peru.

403 **One family, two worlds: an Italian family's correspondence across the
Atlantic, 1901-1922.**
Edited, with an introduction by Samuel L. Baily, Franco Ramella,
translated by John Lenaghan. New Brunswick, New Jersey; London:
Rutgers University Press, 1988. 251p. maps.

Oreste Sola emigrated from Biella in northern Italy to Buenos Aires at the age of
seventeen and his brother Abele joined him eleven years later. This is a collection of
208 of the 351 surviving letters written by sons and parents spanning the years 1901-22,
providing us with 'unique insight into the Italian community and especially the Biellesi

of Buenos Aires', who worked predominantly in the textile mills in the suburb of Belgrano at the turn of the century. See also Baily's 'The adjustment of Italian immigrants in Buenos Aires and New York, 1870-1914', *American Historical Review*, vol. 88, no. 2 (April 1983), p. 281-305; and, on pages 306-46 of the same journal, Herbert S. Klein's 'The integration of Italian immigrants into the United States and Argentina: a comparative analysis'.

404 **Plainsmen of three continents: Volga German adaptation to steppe, prairie, and pampa.**
Timothy J. Kloberdanz. In: *Ethnicity on the Great Plains.* Edited by Frederick C. Luebke. Lincoln, Nebraska: University of Nebraska Press for the University of Nebraska-Lincoln, Center for Great Plains Studies, 1980, p. 54-72.
Volga German settlers have colonized three of the world's major grasslands: the Russian steppes, the North American Great Plains and the South American pampas. The first Argentine colony was founded in the province of Buenos Aires in 1878, and went on to play an important part in Argentina's grain production. A book-length study of the same community is Olga Weyne's *El último puerto: del Rhin al Volga y del Volga al Plata* (Buenos Aires: Instituto Torcuato Di Tella, 1987. 305p.).

405 **Spanish immigration in Argentina.**
Antonio Lago Carballo. *Migration News*, 9th year, no. 1 (May-June 1960), p. 9-11.
'Argentina has always been the main outlet for Spanish emigration, and Spanish immigrants in that country are outnumbered only by Italians.' The period of greatest Spanish immigration (but compare next item) was 1901-20, when 1,243,000 immigrants arrived; the Spanish Civil War and Second World War interrupted the flow, but it soon regained its former impetus, with a further 232,000 Spaniards entering Argentina between 1945 and 1959. The Spanish Civil War drove many intellectuals to Argentina; their contribution to the publishing industry, journalism and the arts is described in Blas Matamoro, 'La emigración cultural española durante la posguerra de 1939', *Cuadernos Hispanoamericanos*, no. 384 (June 1982), p. 576-90.

406 **Spanish immigration to Argentina, 1870-1930.**
Alicia Vidaurreta de Tjarks. *Jahrbuch für Geschichte von Staat, Wirtschaft und Gesellschaft Lateinamerikas*, vol. 19 (1982), p. 285-319.
Spanish immigrants accounted for 31.11 per cent of the net immigration into Argentina during the period. It reached its lowest point between 1881 and 1885 (9.1 per cent) and its highest between 1920 and 1930 (68 per cent); compare previous item. This is a well-documented article with detailed statistics. 'Spaniards had the strongest foreign influence on Argentine customs, habits and arts . . . [and] reached their lowest level of participation in Argentine life in the political sphere.'

407 **The story of the Irish in Argentina.**
Thomas Murray. New York: P. J. Kennedy & Sons, 1919. 514p.
bibliog.

A chronological history, from the first Irishman to tread on Argentine soil, Thomas Fehily (or Field), a Jesuit missionary, in 1586. The book emphasizes the Irish military involvement in Argentina's nineteenth-century wars, the Irish participation in sheep-farming ('which has been for them and for the Republic a source of great wealth and advancement'), and the Irish community churches. Eduardo A. Coghlan has compiled a mammoth set of statistics on the Irish in Argentina, 1822-95: *El aporte de los irlandeses a la formación de la nación argentina* (Buenos Aires: Imprenta 'El Vuelo de Fénix', 1982. 670p.); and a genealogy of the most prominent Irish families: *Los irlandeses en la Argentina: su actuación y descendencia* (Buenos Aires: Librería Alberto Casares, 1982. 963p.)

408 **Las tierras de los ingleses en la Argentina (1870-1914).** (British landowners in Argentina, 1870-1914).
Eduardo José Míguez. Buenos Aires: Editorial de Belgrano, 1985.
348p. bibliog.

A good study of major British family *estancias* in Argentina, most of which were public companies. One of them, the Santa Fé Land Company, is the subject of Campbell P. Ogilvie (ed.), *Argentina from a British point of view; and notes on Argentine life* (London: Wertheimer, Lea & Co., 1910. 277p.); the seventeen 'notes' are reflections on life in the 'camp' (open country) by British workers.

409 **Ukrainians in Argentina: a Canadian perspective.**
Oleh W. Gerus. *Journal of Ukrainian Studies*, vol. 11, no. 2 (1986),
p. 3-18.

The number of Ukrainians living in Argentina in 1986 is estimated at between 200,000 and 220,000, nearly one per cent of the total population. This article documents their immigration and settlement between 1897 and 1950, their community organizations and religious life. Their greatest contribution has been the transformation of harsh subtropical territories into productive croplands, notably in Misiones (see *Los eslavos en Misiones: consideraciones en torno al número y a la distribución geográfica de los campesinos polacos y ucranianos* (1897-1938)) and the Chaco. They have largely preserved their cultural identity in this rural environment.

410 **Yugoslav immigrant experiences in Argentina and Chile.**
Víctor C. Dahl. *Inter-American Economic Affairs*, vol. 28, no. 3
(winter 1974), p. 3-26. bibliog.

Yugoslav emigration to Argentina originated in the 1840s when Dalmatian sailors jumped ship in Buenos Aires. In 1965 there were an estimated 130,000 persons of Yugoslav stock in the country, compared with over 20,000 in Chile and over 40,000 in Brazil. During the 1890s an active Croatian cultural and intellectual movement developed and throughout this century nationalist Yugoslavs, dominated by Croatians, have 'reacted spiritedly to homeland political events'. Serbo-Croatian-language newspapers and literature in Argentina are also discussed.

# The Jews

411 **Antisemitism in Argentina: the Jewish response.**
Judith Laikin Elkin.   In: *Living with antisemitism: modern Jewish responses*.   Edited by Jehuda Reinharz.   Hanover, New Hampshire; London: Published for Brandeis University Press by University Press of New England, 1987, p. 333-48.

A comprehensive discussion of antisemitism in Argentina, which makes many challenging statements. The 'antisemitism built into society' by its principal institutions (the Church, the military, the traditional landowning élite and the labour unions) 'forms the context in which antisemitic acts can be carried out with impunity, since they are acceptable to large sectors of the Argentine public'; the Jewish community, represented mainly by the Delegación de Asociaciones Israelitas Argentinas (DAIA), has 'no leverage with these institutions at all'; 'the best of Argentine liberalism extends total acceptance to Jews, but at the cost of assimilation. This is a price the organized community will not pay'. See also Sandra McGee Deutsch, 'The Argentine Right and the Jews, 1919-1933', *Journal of Latin American Studies*, vol. 18, no. 1 (May 1986), p. 113-34.

412 **Argentina y la historia de la inmigración judía (1810-1950).** (Argentina's history of Jewish immigration, 1810-1950.)
Haim Avni.   Jerusalem: Editorial Universitaria Magnes, Universidad Hebrea de Jerusalén/AMIA Comunidad de Buenos Aires, 1983. 593p. map. bibliog.

This is the best single account of Jewish immigration to Argentina, covering such topics as agricultural colonies, community organizations, antisemitism, and the return of emigrants to Israel. Two illustrated celebrations of Argentine Jewry are *Judíos & argentinos + judíos argentinos*, edited by Manrique Zago (Buenos Aires: Manrique Zago Ediciones, 1988. 288p.), and the same publisher's bilingual *Pioneros de la Argentina, los inmigrantes judíos/Pioneers in Argentina, the Jewish immigrants* (1982, 216p.).

413 **Colonia Barón Hirsch: a Jewish agricultural colony in Argentina.**
Morton D. Winsberg.   Gainesville, Florida: University of Florida Press, 1964. 71p. maps. (University of Florida Monographs. Social Sciences, no. 19).

At the height of the mass migration of Jews from Eastern Europe, Baron Maurice de Hirsch, a Bavarian by birth, created the charitable Jewish Colonization Association and purchased land for emigration in Canada, the United States, Brazil and Argentina. The first Argentine colony was established in Santa Fe province in 1891; in all, twelve JCA colonies were founded in the country before 1936. This paper treats in detail the 273,000-acre Colonia Barón Hirsch (1905), 325 kilometres southwest of Buenos Aires, and the problems it faced. See also the same author's three-part 'Jewish agricultural colonization in Entre Ríos, Argentina', *American Journal of Economics and Sociology*, vol. 27, no. 3 (July 1968), p. 285-95; vol. 27, no. 4 (Oct. 1968), p. 423-8; vol. 28, no. 2 (April 1969), p. 179-91.

**414 From pale to pampa: a social history of the Jews of Buenos Aires.**
Eugene F. Sofer. New York: Holmes & Meier, 1982. 165p. bibliog.

The Jewish community of Buenos Aires is the largest in Latin America and contains four-fifths of all Argentine Jews. This book samples 1,600 cases of East European (Ashkenazi) Jews between 1895 and 1939, mapping their residential concentration, professional mobility and community organization within the city, against a background of national politics and antisemitism. A recent work focusing on the institutional workings of several key Zionist and religious organizations in Buenos Aires is Victor A. Mirelman, *Jewish Buenos Aires, 1890-1930: in search of an identity* (Detroit, Michigan: Wayne State University Press, 1990. 300p.).

**415 Israeli ecstasies/Jewish agonies.**
Irving Louis Horowitz. New York: Oxford University Press, 1974. 244p.

Chapter eight (p. 133-67) is entitled 'Organization and ideology of the Jewish community of Argentina', and effectively summarizes the author's earlier journal articles on the Jewish community before about 1960. It deals with immigration ('adaptation without integration'), 1905-40, and the community's impressive range of voluntary organizations. He ends with a provocative set of conclusions and a postscript on the status of the community in 1969.

**416 Jewish communities in frontier societies: Argentina, Australia, and South Africa.**
Daniel Judah Elazar, with Peter Medding. New York; London: Holmes & Meier, 1983. 357p. bibliog.

Part two (p. 61-134), is devoted to the three distinct groups of Argentine Jews (Ashkenazi, Sephardic and German) who form 'the fourth or fifth largest diaspora community' (South Africa is the eighth, Australia the eleventh or twelfth). The authors examine the organizational structures of their community, the differences between their culture and the host society's, and prospects for the future.

**417 The Jewish gauchos of the pampas.**
Alberto Gerchunoff, translated by Prudencio de Pereda. London; New York: Abelard-Schuman, 1959. rev. ed. 169p.

Gerchunoff (1884-1950), the journalist son of Russian-Jewish immigrants, was only twenty-five when he published *Los gauchos judíos* (of which this is a translation), dedicted to Baron de Hirsch (see item no. 413). These twenty-five tragi-comic stories about the imaginary Jewish colony of Rajil in Entre Ríos province at the turn of the century are parable-like, with a strong pastoral feeling.

**418 The Jewish presence in Latin America.**
Edited by Judith Laikin Elkin, Gilbert W. Merkx. Boston, Massachusetts; London; Sydney; Wellington: Allen & Unwin, 1987. 338p. (Thematic Studies in Latin America).

Contains five chapters on Argentine Jewry: Víctor A. Mirelman on Sephardic immigration to Argentina before the Nazi period; two chapters on antisemitism: Bernard Segal, 'Jews and the Argentine center: a middleman minority', and Carlos H. Waisman, 'Capitalism, socialism, and the Jews: the view from Cabildo [a right-wing

Catholic publication, 1920s-1983]'; Leonardo Senkman, 'Argentine culture and Jewish identity'; and Israel Even-Shoshan, 'Informal Jewish education in Argentina'.

419    **The Jews of Argentina: from the Inquisition to Perón.**
Robert Weisbrot.    Philadelphia: Jewish Publication Society of America, 1979. 348p. bibliog.
This work is in three parts: the early settlers (their origins, the organization of their communities); their culture (Zionism, literature, religion, education); and the host country (acculturation, antisemitism). Despite their 'eminently successful acculturation, Jews never have achieved full acceptance or security in their adopted land', and 'a new generation of native-born Jews is rapidly jettisoning its East European traditions and, in the process, Judaism itself'.

# Indigenous population

420    **Los aborígenes argentinos: síntesis etnográfica.** (Indians of Argentina: an ethnographic summary.)
Antonio Serrano.    Buenos Aires: Editorial Nova, 1947. 288p. map. bibliog. (Biblioteca Americanista).
A classic review of the ethnohistory and archaeology (but emphasizing the ethnographic features) of the Indians of seven regions: northwest, Chaco, littoral area, central Andes, centre, pampas and Patagonia, and Tierra del Fuego. There are 164 photographs and drawings, chiefly of artefacts, and a detailed index of tribes.

421    **Los aborígenes de la Argentina: ensayo socio-histórico-cultural.**
(The Indians of Argentina: a social, historical and cultural essay.)
Guillermo E. Magrassi.    Buenos Aires: Ediciones Búsqueda, 1987. 140p. bibliog. (Colección 'Desde Sudamérica').
A short but valuable account of the history and present conditions of the various Indian tribes of Tierra del Fuego, the pampa, Patagonia, the littoral provinces and Mesopotamia (between the Uruguay and Paraná rivers), the Chaco and the northwest. It includes the texts of five legends from three of these regions and fifty-five historical and contemporary photographs. An essential journal containing regular articles in English on indigenous populations in Argentina is the *IWGIA Newsletter* (Copenhagen: International Work Group for Indigenous Affairs, 1971- . quarterly). The IWGIA also publishes a series of *Documents*. See no. 21 (Nemesio J. Rodríguez, *Oppression in Argentina: the Mataco case*. 1975. 30p.) and no. 46 (Nicolás Iñigo Carrera, *'Violence' as an economic force: the process of proletarianisation among the indigenous people of the Argentinian Chaco, 1884-1930*. 1982. 50p.).

422    **Antropología argentina.** (Anthropology of Argentina.)
Ciro René Lafón.    Buenos Aires: Editorial Bonum, 1977. 190p. map. bibliog.
A cultural history of the various Indian tribes of five principal regions (northwest, northeast, centre, Patagonia and Tierra del Fuego), and a systematic classification of

the remaining groups which retain pre-Hispanic cultural characteristics. Northwest Indians are the most conservative, maintaining many archaic cultural traits from the time of the conquest. Not perhaps for the general reader, and there are no illustrations, footnotes or index.

423  **Drama and power in a hunting society: the Selk'nam of Tierra del Fuego.**
Anne Chapman.   Cambridge, England; New York: Cambridge University Press, 1982. 201p. maps. bibliog.

In the 1960s there were only eight surviving members of the Selk'nam (or Ona) tribe of Tierra del Fuego which had numbered 3,500-4,000 in 1880 when the 'White man suddenly began to colonize their land'. After two chapters on the tribe's history and socioeconomic structure, chapters 3-9 describe in detail the Hain (or *kloketen*) ceremony in which young men were initiated into adulthood.

424  **From nomadism to sedentary agriculture.**
Jacob A. Loewen.   *América Indígena*, vol. 26, no. 1 (1966), p. 27-42.

Two Chaco tribes, the Lengua and Chulupí, largely lost their hunting-gathering tradition through reliance on food supply from Mennonite settlers who arrived in 1928. When the trans-Chaco highway was built in 1960, the two tribes, of whom the Chulupí were the most vociferous, demanded land, agricultural equipment and private family dwellings. The subsequent settlement programme, launched in 1961, is described.

425  **Handbook of South American Indians.**
Edited by Julian H. Steward.   Washington, DC: US Government Printing Office, 1946-59.   7 vols. maps. bibliog. (Smithsonian Institution. Bureau of American Ethnology. Bulletin, 143).

Fourteen chapters on the archaeology, culture, language, population, natural environment, territory and tribal divisions of native Argentine Indians are to be found in the first two volumes of this classic and still reliable work: 'the marginal tribes' of the north and south, and 'the Andean civilizations'. A facsimile reprint was issued by Cooper Square (New York) in 1963.

426  **Indian tribes of the Argentine and Bolivian Chaco: ethnological studies.**
Rafael Karsten.   Helsinki: Finska Vetenshaps-Societeten, 1932. 236p. map. bibliog. (Societas Scientiarum Fennica. Commentationes Humanorum Litterarum, vol. IV, no. 1).

Consists of ethnological material collected in 1911-13 along the Pilcomayo river which forms the Argentine-Bolivian border, among the Argentine Mataco Indians, the Bolivian Chorote and the Toba of both countries. He describes their political and economic structures, warfare, social organization, religion and mythology, dances and language; and he includes forty-two photographs, musical examples and a glossary of Toba terms. There is a modern reprint (New York: AMS Press, 1979).

## Immigration and Colonization, Nationalities and Minorities.
## Indigenous population

427 **The Indians of Tierra del Fuego.**
Samuel K. Lothrop. New York: Museum of the American Indian,
Heye Foundation, 1928. 244p. map. bibliog. (Contributions, vol. 10).
In 1924-25 the author spent three months among the foot Indians (Ona and Haush)
and canoe Indians (Yahgan, Alcaluf) of the southern shore of Tierra del Fuego. He
details their archaeology, language, dress and ornamentation, encampments, tools,
weapons and hunting methods, social organization, amusements, religion and
mythology.

428 **Into another jungle: the final journey of the Mataco?**
Ariel Dorfman. *Grassroots Development*, vol. 12, no. 2 (1988),
p. 2-15. map.
Dorfman, a Chilean writer, visited the village of El Sauzalito, in the dry scrub Chaco
forest bordering the Bermejo river; here, with the initial help in 1973 of the Instituto
del Aborigen (Bureau of Indian Affairs), a successful programme has been
implemented for helping the Mataco to develop a number of agricultural projects
through an Asociación Comunitaria.

429 **The Mataco of northern Argentina.**
Samuel Shapiro. *Journal of Interamerican Studies*, vol. 2, no. 4 (Oct.
1960), p. 443-8.
An account of the use of Indian (mostly Mataco) seasonal labour on Argentina's
second-largest sugar mill, San Martín del Tabacal, in the Chaco. Conditions on the mill
were considered fairly good, but the Mataco worked less and were paid less than the
other tribes, and the author suggests improvements: pure water, decent housing and
better medical care.

430 **La movilidad del indígena y el mestizaje en la Argentina colonial.**
(Indian mobility and racial mixture in colonial Argentina.)
Ricardo Zorraquín Becú. *Jahrbuch für Geschichte von Staat,
Wirtschaft und Gesellschaft Lateinamerikas*, vol. 4 (1967), p. 61-85.
Considers the spontaneous and forced migrations of Indian tribes during the Spanish
empire, the legislation governing the Indian populations, their confinement to villages
(reductions), and especially the social conditions of the racially mixed *mestizos*, who
were rejected by both Spaniards and Indians.

431 **Las organizaciones indígenas en la Argentina.** (Indian organizations in
Argentina.)
Andrés Serbín. *América Indígena*, vol. 41, no. 3 (July-Sept. 1981),
p. 407-34. bibliog.
This is a history and contemporary assessment of the federations representing the
largest groups of Argentina's 150,000 Indians (Colla, Toba, Chiriguano, Mataco,
Mapuche, Mocoví, Pilagá, Chorote, Chané, Chulupí and Tehuelche) and their
relations with provincial and state governments. The first federation, the Centro
Indígena de Buenos Aires, was formed in 1968, followed by a number of powerful
regional federations in the early 1970s, among them the Confederación Indígena
Neuquina, the Federación Indígena del Chaco, and similar federations for Tucumán,
the Federal Capital and Greater Buenos Aires, Salta, Formosa and Santa Fe. A

national Comisión Coordinadora de Instituciones Indígenas de la Argentina (CCIIRA) was created in 1970.

432 **Las poblaciones indígenas de la Argentina: su origen – su pasado – su presente.** (The Indian peoples of Argentina: their origin, past and present.)
Salvador Canals Frau.    Buenos Aires: Editorial Sudamericana, 1953. 575p. maps. bibliog.

A good general survey of the pre-Hispanic origins of the native Argentine Indians, and a description of twenty-two contemporary pampean and Andean tribes: their physical appearance, language and lifestyle (economy, hunting and agriculture, kinship and religion), illustrated with over 150 photographs and drawings of their habitats, arts and crafts. The situation of the Indians in 1960 is covered by 'Panorama de la población indígena', *Boletín Indigenista* (Mexico), vol. 20 (1960), p. 10-18. The Indian population was counted again in 1978; Argentina then had 398,000 indigenous people, or 1.5 per cent of the total population; see Enrique Meyer, Elio Masferrer, 'La población indígena de América en 1978', *América Indígena*, vol. 39, no. 2 (April-June 1979), p. 217-337.

433 **The situation of the Indians in the Argentine: the Chaco area and Misiones province.**
Miguel Alberto Bartolomé.    In: *The situation of the Indian in South America*.    Edited by Walter Dostal.    Geneva: World Council of Churches, 1972, p. 218-51. map. bibliog.

For each group of Indians (Chané, Chiriguano, Chorote, Chulupí, Mataco, Mbya or Guaraní, Mocoví, Pilagá and Toba), the author describes its history, location and settlements, agricultural and hunting economy, other sources of work, language and social structure, religion, relationships with other tribes and the white population, and position in national life. A brief final section reviews Indian organizations and legislation, and anthropological research.

434 **Los tobas argentinos: armonía y disonancia en una sociedad.** (The Toba of Argentina: harmony and dissonance in an Indian society.)
Elmer S. Miller.    Mexico City: Siglo Veintiuno, 1979. 175p. map. bibliog.

A synthesis of the author's earlier writings on the Toba, and a revised translation of *Harmony and dissonance in Argentine Toba society* (New Haven, Connecticut: Human Relations Area Files, 1980). The 18,000 Toba live mainly in the Argentine provinces of the Chaco and Formosa, with a further 1,000 in the Bolivian and Paraguayan Chaco. The book is divided into three sections: harmony (the Tobas' balanced relationship with nature before the conquest), disharmony (the first disruptive contacts with European colonists), and new harmony (their successful integration of Pentecostalism into their shamanistic practices).

**A reexamination of aboriginal population estimates for Argentina.**
*See* item no. 332.

# Black population

435 **The African experience in Spanish America: 1502 to the present day.**
Leslie B. Rout, Jr. Cambridge, England: Cambridge University
Press, 1976. 404p. bibliog. (Cambridge Latin American Studies, 23).

Chapter seven discusses that 'historical curio', the Negroid population in the River
Plate countries. The section on Argentina (p. 185-97) describes the abolition of slavery
(in 1813 all children born to black slave women were declared *libertos* and the further
importation of slaves was prohibited, but abolition was not absolute until the passing of
the 1853 Constitution); the treatment of the race question in the writings of Juan B.
Alberdi, Domingo F. Sarmiento, Carlos O. Bunge and José Ingenieros; and the
position of the Afro-Argentine since abolition (he 'has not disappeared entirely. As of
1971 perhaps 3,500 lived in the city of Buenos Aires and its suburbs').

436 **The Afro-Argentines of Buenos Aires, 1800-1900.**
George Reid Andrews. Madison, Wisconsin: University of Wisconsin
Press, 1980. 286p. map. bibliog.

In 1778, blacks constituted about a third of the population of Buenos Aires, in 1838
over a quarter, and in 1887 only two per cent. The author examines the four
explanations usually given for their disappearance, and finds supporting evidence for
the first three: their disproportionate losses in nineteenth-century wars, their
progressive 'whitening' though miscegenation, their higher mortality rates and the
abolition of the slave trade in 1813. There is a discussion of racism in Argentine history
and chapters on the black contribution to the arts and black mutual-benefit and
political organizations.

437 **Manumission in colonial Buenos Aires, 1776-1810.**
Lyman L. Johnson. *Hispanic American Historical Review*, vol. 59,
no. 2 (May 1979), p. 258-79.

During the period covered, 1,482 manumissions were recorded, mainly of Negro slaves
(who accounted for more than eighty per cent of the slave population in 1810), and in
nearly sixty per cent of these cases freedom was purchased by the individual slave or
his family. Female black slaves and mulattos had some advantage in the manumission
process. Negroes and mulattos dominated many of the city's petty entrepreneurial
occupations; see also Arnold Strickon's 'The impact of racial discrimination on black
artisans in colonial Buenos Aires', *Social History*, vol. 6, no. 3 (Oct. 1981), p. 301-16.

438 **The negro in the Viceroyalty of the Río de la Plata.**
Irene Diggs. *Journal of Negro History*, vol. 28, no. 3 (July 1951),
p. 281-301.

The article is mainly concerned with Argentina (pages 287-90 refer to the Banda
Oriental, modern Uruguay): the slave trade between 1580 and the end of the viceregal
period; the employment of blacks as soldiers, domestic servants, artisans and in
professional occupations; and the Negro impact on language, culture and the arts.

439  **La población negra y mulata de la ciudad de Buenos Aires, 1810-1840.**
(The black and mulatto population of Buenos Aires, 1810-1840.)
Marta B. Goldburg.  *Desarrollo Económico*, vol. 16, no. 61 (April-
June 1976), p. 75-99.

A demographic study, with detailed tables of Buenos Aires's 1836 and 1838 city
censuses, enabling the author to suggest that the black population in 1810 was higher
than the censuses indicated. High mortality rates among the black population, a low
proportion of males to females, intermarriage with whites and a deterioration in the
slaves' quality of life after emancipation, were the chief causes of the gradual decrease
in the black population.

440  **La trata de negros en el Río de la Plata durante el siglo XVIII.**
(The black slave trade in the River Plate in the 18th century.)
Elena F. Scheuss de Studer.  Buenos Aires: Universidad de Buenos
Aires, 1958. 378p. maps. bibliog. (Facultad de Filosofía y Letras.
Publicaciones del Instituto de Historia Argentina 'Doctor Emilio
Ravignani', 101).

The most complete history of the slave trade, with seventeen statistical tables and as
many plates. The author provides figures for the number of slaves introduced to
Buenos Aires between 1742 and 1806 from Brazil (12,473) and directly from Africa
(13,460), and points to substantial French and English involvement in the contraband
trade in slaves.

# The Gaucho

441   **The gaucho.**
Photographs by René Burri, text by José Luis Lanuza, foreword by
Jorge Luis Borges.   New York: Crown Publishers; London:
Macdonald, 1968. 181p.

Fifty-five pages of text on the history of the gaucho as portrayed by British and
Argentine writers (illustrated with line drawings by A. Güiraldes and paintings by Juan
León Pallière) are followed by 122 pages of black-and-white photographs and a
Spanish-English glossary of gaucho terms. The photographs show the gaucho at work
(roundup, herding, branding, horsebreaking, riding equipment) and taking his
relaxation.

442   **El gaucho: Argentina–Brasil–Uruguay.** (The gaucho: Argentina, Brazil
and Uruguay.)
Emilio A. Coni, preliminary study by Beatriz Bosch.   Buenos Aires:
Solar/Hachette, 1969. 2nd ed. 320p. (Biblioteca 'Dimensión
Argentina').

The author was described by Slatta (*Gauchos and the vanishing frontier* [q.v.]) as 'a
fervent *anti-porteño* federalist' who insisted that the province of Santa Fe was the
gaucho's homeland. He deliberately sets out to 'demolish some myths' with this
controversially unsympathetic history of the gaucho, 1617 to the present, which
includes an account of the early development of the cattle industry, the etymology of
the word *gaucho*, and the gaucho in literature. This 'second' edition is a reprint of the
posthumous first edition of 1945.

443 **The gaucho: cattle hunter, cavalryman, ideal of romance.**
Madaline Wallis Nichols. Durham, North Carolina: Duke University Press, 1942. 152p. bibliog.
'This book tells how the highly disreputable gauchos emerged from the background of a pastoral society and how those gauchos came to win honour', from the portrayal of the gaucho as a 'colonial bootlegger whose business was contraband trade in cattle hides' to the 'romantic use of the gaucho as a literary and artistic theme'. There is a good bibliographical essay on pages 67-144, but the scholarly text itself is regrettably short. The 1968 reprint (New York: Gordina Press) contained a new introduction.

444 **The gaucho: his changing image.**
S. Samuel Trífilo. *Pacific Historical Quarterly*, vol. 33 (1964), p. 395-403.
A brief but well-documented survey of the gaucho in history; the etymology of the word *gaucho* and how it 'changed from one of opprobrium to one of praise'; and the 'only really objective descriptions' of the gaucho in the nineteenth-century writings of foreign, especially British, travellers.

445 **Gauchos and the vanishing frontier.**
Richard W. Slatta. Lincoln, Nebraska; London: University of Nebraska Press, 1983. 271p. bibliog.
The best single source on the historical and literary gaucho, emphasizing the violence of rural life in nineteenth-century Buenos Aires province, the unreliability of seasonal ranch work, the gaucho's forced conscription into the army, his losing battle against modernization and the legal restrictions placed upon him, culminating occasionally in his xenophobic attacks on immigrant colonists, and, finally, his emergence as a mythological figure.

446 **Historia social del gaucho.** (A social history of the gaucho.)
Ricardo Rodríguez Molas. Buenos Aires: Centro Editor de América Latina, 1982. 302p. bibliog. (Capítulo. Biblioteca Argentina Fundamental, 159. Serie Complementaria: Sociedad y Cultura, 11).
Attacking the tendency to glamorize the miserable conditions endured by the nineteenth-century inhabitant of the pampa, the author attempts to present a more honest picture of the gaucho's 'feudal past' and 'difficult present' from the sixteenth century to 1910. This is a revision of the 1968 edition published by Ediciones Maru.

447 **Last of a breed: the gauchos.**
Robert Laxalt, photographs by O. Louis Mazzatenta. *National Geographic*, vol. 158, no. 4 (Oct. 1980), p. 478-501. map.
There are eleven colour photographs in this popularly written article on modern Argentine 'gauchos', showing their distinctive dress and performing their daily work, on three *estancias* in Buenos Aires, Corrientes and Salta provinces. There are also brief glimpses of their equivalents in Paraguay and Brazil.

# Language

448 **Concerning the phonemes of standard *porteño* Spanish.**
David W. Foster.   In: *Three essays on linguistic diversity in the Spanish-speaking world: the U.S. Southwest and the River Plate area.* Edited by Jacob Ornstein. The Hague; Paris: Mouton, 1975, p. 61-70. (Jana Linguarum. Series Practica, 174).
A detailed, comprehensive study of the six main sound systems in Buenos Aires Spanish. The author criticizes the limitations of Vladimir Honsa's structural-linguistics approach ('The phonemic systems of Argentinian Spanish', *Hispania*, vol. 48, no. 2 [May 1965], p. 275-83), favouring an interpretation through generative linguistics.

449 **Diccionario de argentinismos de ayer y de hoy.** (Dictionary of Argentinisms, yesterday and today.)
Diego Abad de Santillán.   Buenos Aires: Tipográfica Editora Argentina, 1976. 1000p.
The major dictionary of Argentine vocabulary, acknowledging the many sources used in its compilation, recording over 11,000 words and phrases. Many entries, such as *gaucho* and *tango*, are treated in immense detail, and most are illustrated by quotations. The compiler states that the work complements his *Gran enciclopedia argentina* (q.v.), which itself includes many popular phrases and expressions.

450 **Diccionario de voces extranjeras usadas en la Argentina.** (Dictionary of foreign words used in Argentina.)
José Gobello.   Buenos Aires: Fundación Federico Guillermo Brochet, 1988. 223p. bibliog.
A unique dictionary of foreign words ('which do not corrupt our Spanish, but enrich it'), from *abat-jour* to *yuppie*, imported from Arabic, Dutch, English, French, Greek, Guaraní, Hungarian, Italian (including some of its dialects) and Norwegian.

451 **Diccionario de voces y expresiones argentinas.** (Dictionary of Argentine words and phrases.)
Félix Coluccio.   Buenos Aires: Editorial Plus Ultra, 1985. 334p.
bibliog. (Temas Argentinos, 8).

In this corrected and enlarged edition, the quotations illustrating the terms included (which he categorizes as vulgar, popular and *lunfardo*, or Buenos Aires slang) are taken from a wide range of sources, chiefly gaucho novels and Argentine newspapers.

452 **Diccionario del hampa y del delito. Lunfardo latinoamericano. Drogadicción. "Punk". Insurrección. Mitología. Voces vulgares y populares.** (Dictionary of crime and the underworld, *lunfardo*, drug addiction, punk, terrorism, folklore, vulgar and popular expressions.)
Raúl Tomás Escobar.   Buenos Aires: Editorial Universidad, 1986. 345p. bibliog.

A wide-ranging selection of terms whose nature is perfectly described in the title. There are also expressions from the world of horse-racing, the 'pop' culture in general, and a number of imports from Bolivia, Brazil, Chile, Uruguay and Central America.

453 **Diccionario del lenguaje campesino rioplatense; contiene alrededor de tres mil voces y locuciones, aclaradas y comentadas.** (Dictionary of River Plate rural speech, containing some three thousand words and phrases, fully explained.)
Juan Carlos Guarnieri.   Montevideo, Uruguay: Editorial Florensa y Lafón, 1968. 144p.

This is a new version of the compiler's *Nuevo vocabulario campesino rioplatense* (1957), emphasizing the vocabulary of cattle-ranching, gaucho horsemanship and flora and fauna (many of the last are of Guaraní and Quechua origin). He is strong on etymology and he has included many interesting regionalisms.

454 **Diccionario del lenguaje rioplatense.** (Dictionary of the language of the River Plate area.)
Juan Carlos Guarnieri.   Montevideo, Uruguay: Ediciones de la Banda Oriental, 1979. 199p.

The introduction to the long vocabulary contains a good description of the history of country (*gauchesco*) and city underworld (*lunfardo*) popular speech.

455 **Diccionario lunfardo y de otros términos antiguos y modernos usuales en Buenos Aires.** (Dictionary of *lunfardo* and other old and modern terms used in Buenos Aires speech.)
José Gobello.   Buenos Aires: A. Peña Lillo, 1975. 234p. bibliog.

This is probably the best dictionary of Buenos Aires jargon, *lunfardo*, by the founder-Secretary of the Academia Porteña del Lunfardo. He ascribes several linguistic levels to the more than 3,000 terms listed, from 'elevated' to the obscene and criminal, and adds many quotations from literary and other sources. The bibliography includes over 350 items.

456 **El elemento italiano en el habla de Buenos Aires y Montevideo.** (The Italian element in the speech of Buenos Aires and Montevideo.) Giovanni Meo-Zilio, Ettore Rossi. Florence, Italy: Valmartina, 1970. 183p. bibliog. (Centro di Richerche Storiche, Filosofiche, Letterarie e Linguistiche per l'America Latina. Richerche Rioplatensi, 1).

River Plate Spanish is the richest in Italianisms. The authors trace the influence of Italian national and regional speech, listing some 500 terms. They also include notes on the spelling and pronunciation of Italian surnames in the region.

457 **English influence on the common speech of the River Plate.** Américo Barabino. *Hispania*, vol. 33, no. 2 (May 1950), p. 163-5.

Lists about fifty words derived from English and American companies, Hollywood and (especially) sport, which have created new words or which are used with a special meaning (for example, 'goal' as the origin of *golero*, 'goalkeeper').

458 **El español de la Argentina: estudio destinado a los maestros de las escuelas primarias.** (The Spanish of Argentina: for primary-school teachers.) Berta Elena Vidal de Battini. Buenos Aires: Consejo Nacional de Educación, 1966. 2nd ed. 214p. maps.

A comprehensive and well-documented study of Argentine Spanish based on personal research in five linguistic regions (littoral, northeast, northwest, Cuyo and centre), summarizing regional linguistic differences, pronunciation, morphology and syntax. The fourteen large colour maps are clear and helpful. This is called volume 1, but further volumes appear not to have been published. A valuable piece of work which deserves a wider audience than the one for which it was designed.

459 **The French influence on the Spanish of the River Plate.** Paul V. Cassano. *Orbis*, vol. 21, no. 1 (1972), p. 174-82.

An evaluation of the main phonological influences on River Plate Spanish, affecting oral vowels, nasalized vowels and consonants. There are phonemic diagrams and charts of the segmental phonemes of French and Argentine Spanish.

460 **El habla del boliche: diccionario del lenguaje popular rioplatense; contiene alrededor de cuatro mil voces y locuciones, aclaradas y comentadas.** (Bar speech: a dictionary of popular River Plate speech, containing about four thousand words and phrases, fully explained.) Juan Carlos Guarnieri. Montevideo, Uruguay: Editorial Florensa y Lafón, 1967. 212p.

Briefly defines the meaning and etymology of 4,000 words, idioms and proverbs registered here: rural and *lunfardo*, tango and foreign derivations. The compiler notes the large number of Quechua words (surprisingly more than Guaraní) and the slight Brazilian-Portuguese influence.

461  **Identification of Argentine Spanish vowels.**
Miguelina Guirao, Ana M. Borzone de Manrique.  *Journal of
Psycholinguistic Research*, vol. 4, no. 1 (Jan. 1975), p. 17-25. bibliog.

An attempt to create a 'simple but representative map of the acoustic spectrum of the
vowels of Argentine Spanish', which showed similarities with American English vowels
but no correlation with the cardinal vowels. A sound analyser was used to convert
recorded speech into spectograms which were then plotted into the five figures
reproduced here.

462  **The influence of Italian on the phonology of the Spanish of Argentina.**
Paul V. Cassano.  *Forum Italicum*, vol. 8, no. 4 (Dec. 1974),
p. 557-73.

This article looks at the ways in which Italian vowels and consonants have influenced
their Argentine-Spanish counterparts. See also Herman James, Julio Ricci, 'The
influence of locally spoken Italian dialects on River Plate Spanish', *Forum Italicum*,
vol. 1, no. 1 (1967), p. 48-59.

463  **Lunfardo, Argentina's unknown tongue.**
John D. Grayson.  *Hispania*, vol. 47, no. 1 (March 1964), p. 66-8.

*Lunfardo* began as a thieves' cant from the Buenos Aires underworld, but 'emerged
from the waterfront to permeate the everyday speech of . . . all *porteños*, if only
humorously'. The author discusses its enormous vocabulary, enriched by foreign loan-
words and coinage by metaphor (*ventana*, window, for 'eye'), vesre ('*revés*', word-
reversal) and syllable displacement (*diome* for 'medio'), with a sample of quotations
from some of the writers who have used it as a medium of expression.

464  **El lunfardo de Buenos Aires.**
José Barcia.  Buenos Aires: Editorial Paidós, 1973. 173p. (Biblioteca
del Hombre Contemporáneo, vol. 241).

A well-written, undocumented book for the non-specialist by a former president of the
Academia Porteña del Lunfardo. The vocabulary (p. 151-73) defines about 1,000
words and phrases and there are quotations from *lunfardo* writers.

465  **Sobre el origen y uso del *che* argentino.**
Amalia C. Dishman.  *Hispania*, vol. 65, no. 1 (March 1982), p. 93-7.
bibliog.

The word *che* is known internationally as the nickname of the Argentine-born guerrilla
leader Ernesto Guevara. This article explores its disputed origin (probably the
Tehuelche for 'man'), gives fifteen examples of its use (as emphasis, exclamation, and
so on), and shows its linkage with *vos*, the popular River Plate form of *tú*, 'you'. Angel
Rosenblat, in 'Origen e historia del '*che*' argentino', *Filología*, vol. 8 (1962), p. 325-401,
argues for the derivation of Argentine and Spanish-Valencian *che* from old Spanish
¡ce!, 'hey!'.

# Language

### 466 South American Indian languages: retrospect and prospect.
Edited by Harriet E. Manelis Klein, Louisa R. Stark.   Austin, Texas:
University of Texas Press, 1986. 863p. bibliog.

Part three is devoted to the indigenous languages of southern and eastern South America. In chapter eighteen (p. 691-731), Klein surveys the current status of the nine families of Argentina's indigenous languages; chapter nineteen (p. 732-52) is a history of the Quechua language in Santiago del Estero ('still fairly vigorous, especially in comparison to the state of the language in the rest of northwest Argentina where it is on the verge of extinction'); and chapter twenty (p. 753-83) by Christos Clairis looks at 'Indigenous languages of Tierra del Fuego'.

### 467 Spanish in the Americas.
Eleanor Greet Cotton, John M. Sharp.   Washington, DC:
Georgetown University Press, 1988. 378p. bibliog. (Romance
Languages and Linguistics Series).

In this guide to Latin American dialectology, chapter seventeen (p. 242-75) surveys the River Plate region. 'Phonologically, Buenos Aires dominates most of Uruguay as well as the entire eastern half of Argentina, from 300 miles to the north all the way down to the southernmost tip.' There is a sampling of Argentine vocabulary of Spanish, Italian, Portuguese, French, North American and British origin; and two examples of *cocoliche* (see *Cocoliche: the art of assimilation and dissimulation among Italians and Argentines*); extracts from Nemesio Trejo's 1905 farce, *Los políticos*, and from a recent issue of the daily *La Prensa*.

### 468 Spanish pronunciation in the Americas.
D. Lincoln Canfield.   Chicago, Illinois; London: University of Chicago
Press, 1981. 118p. maps. bibliog.

There are references to Argentine Spanish in the introductory chapters. The chapter on Argentina (p. 23-7) emphasizes three distinctive features of Argentine Spanish: the gradual levelling of 'll' and 'y', regional differences in the trilled 'r', and the aspiration of the final 's', more common in men than women.

### 469 A transformational analysis of Spanish *se*.
David William Foster.   *Linguistics*, no. 64 (1970), p. 10-25.

An examination of the transformational forms of the pronoun *se*, 'one of the most ubiquitous morphs in the Spanish language', based on Argentine Spanish. It is used as a substitute for *le* and *les*, with intransitive and transitive verbs, as a truly reflexive pronoun, and as the nominal object or subject.

470 **Vocabulario y refranero criollo.** (Vocabulary and collection of native proverbs.)
Text and original drawings by Tito Saubidet. Buenos Aires: Editorial Guillermo Kraft, 1943. 421p.

A handsomely produced dictionary of rural (predominantly gaucho) speech and folklore, but also much more: a veritable encyclopaedia of all things connected with the rural life, illustrated by the author's seventeen charming coloured paintings and many black-and-white line drawings of, for example, riding apparel, farm equipment, wildlife and cockfighting. Based on a twelve-year study in the towns of Tapalqué (where the author was born) and Azul, in southern Buenos Aires province.

# Philosophy and Intellectual Thought

471 **A century of Latin-American thought.**
William Rex Crawford. Cambridge, Massachusetts: Harvard
University Press, 1961. rev. ed. 322p. bibliog.

In this study of thirty-five nineteenth- and twentieth-century Latin American
*pensadores*, chapter two, 'Independence and nationhood', discusses the political
thought of Esteban Echeverría, Juan Bautista Alberdi and Domingo F. Sarmiento;
chapter five, 'Positivism and idealism in Latin America', examines nine Argentine
thinkers: Agustín Enrique Alvarez Suárez, Carlos O. Bunge, Alcides Arguedas,
Joaquín V. González, José Ingenieros, Alejandro Korn, Manuel Ugarte, Manuel
Gálvez and Ricardo Rojas. There is a 1966 reprint (New York: Praeger).

472 **Cincuenta años de filosofía en la Argentina.** (Fifty years of philosophy in
Argentina.)
Luis Farré. Buenos Aires: Ediciones Peuser, 1958. 362p.

A reliable history of philosophy, 1900-50: themes (positivism and anti-positivism,
materialism, existentialism, Catholic philosophy), thinkers (including Rodolfo Rivarola,
Carlos Baires, Carlos O. Bunge, Aníbal Ponce, Juan B. Justo, Alejandro Korn,
Coriolano Alberini, Francisco Romero), the first Congreso Nacional de Filosofía
(1949), and a number of contemporary philosophers. There is an index of names but
no bibliography, although the footnotes are full.

473 **La filosofía en la Argentina.** (Philosophy in Argentina.)
Juan Carlos Torchía Estrada. Washington, DC: Unión Panamericana,
1961. 305p. bibliog. (Departamento de Asuntos Culturales. División de
Filosofía y Letras. Pensamiento de América).

A study of the relationship between philosophical ideas and Argentine culture: colonial
scholasticism and its successors – secular 'ideology', romanticism, positivism, and
contemporary philosophy.

474 **La filosofía en la Argentina actual.** (Philosophy in Argentina today.)
Alberto Caturelli. Buenos Aires: Editorial Sudamericana, 1971.
2nd ed. 373p. bibliog.

A well-documented and well-indexed history of Argentine philosophy from colonial times, in eleven thematic chapters, with an emphasis on more contemporary thought and especially the author's own specialization, *filosofía cristiana*. A more recent introduction is Hugo E. Biagini, *Panorama filosófico argentino* (Buenos Aires: Editorial Universitaria de Buenos Aires, 1985. 135p.).

475 **Francisco Romero on problems of philosophy.**
Marjorie S. Harris. New York: Philosophical Library, 1960. 115p.

Francisco Romero (1891-1962) was born in Seville but went to Argentina at an early age. He is one of the foremost intellectuals of the Positivist school. This is a presentation of Romero's views on the explanation of certain fundamental problems of philosophy (which interested him more than the development of an actual philosophical system), with illustrative quotations from twelve of his major works.

476 **Influencias filosóficas en la evolución nacional.** (The influence of philosophy on national development.)
Alejandro Korn. Buenos Aires: Editorial Claridad, 1936. 231p.
(Colección Claridad: 'Obras de Alejandro Korn').

The biobibliographical introduction by Luis Aznar (p. 3-20) discusses the career and importance of Korn (1860-1936), Argentina's leading antipositivist. Like Torchía Estrada (see *La filosofía en la Argentina*), Korn attempts to set Argentina's philosophical history in the context of national cultural development. Largely undocumented. See also William Jackson Kilgore, 'Latin American philosophy and the place of Alejandro Korn', *Journal of Interamerican Studies*, vol. 2, no. 1 (Jan. 1960), p. 77-82.

477 **Intellectual precursors of conservative nationalism in Argentina, 1900-1927.**
David Rock. *Hispanic American Historical Review*, vol. 67, no. 2 (May 1987), p. 271-300.

Pre-nationalism, or 'traditionalism', emerged as a reaction against positivism. Its leading figures were Manuel Gálvez, Ricardo Rojas and Leopoldo Lugones. There was a growing politicization of the traditionalists after 1916, 'as they shifted into general opposition to popular democracy, and in doing so, set the stage for the rise of *nacionalismo*'; 'at this point the movement appeared to subsist largely on negatives – anticommunism, anti-Semitism, *antiyrigoyenismo*'. The article analyses the chief ingredients of the writings of the leading traditionalists. A good introduction to nationalism is Marysa Navarro Gerassi, *Los nacionalistas* (Buenos Aires: Jorge Alvarez, 1968).

478  José Ingenieros, Argentine intellectual historian: *La evolución de las ideas argentinas.*
Paul S. Holbo.    *The Americas*, vol. 21, no. 1 (July 1964), p. 20-35.
Ingenieros (1877-1925) was born in Italy but his parents brought him to Argentina when a child. Holbo provides a brief historical sketch followed by critical comments on Ingenieros's major work, *La evolución de las ideas argentinas* (1918-20, 2 vols), a philosophical/sociological/political study of Argentina 1810-52. A lifelong Socialist, Ingenieros 'left no doubt about his enmity toward religion', and the work is filled with provocative observations about specific events in Argentine history, and 'astute comments on great social phenomena'.

479  Latin American philosophy in the twentieth century: man, values, and the search for philosophical identity.
Edited by Jorge J. E. Gracia.    Buffalo, New York: Prometheus Books, 1986. 269p. bibliog. (Frontiers of Philosophy).
Includes short biographies/critiques and extracts in English from the works of five Argentine philosophers: Francisco Romero, *Theory of man* (from the full translation, Berkeley, California: University of California Press, 1964); Risieri Frondizi, *The nature of the self: a functional interpretation* (from the full translation, Carbondale, Illinois: Southern Illinois University Press, 1971); Carlos Astrada, *Existencialismo y crisis de la filosofía* (Buenos Aires, 1963); Alejandro Korn, *Apuntes filosóficos* and *Axiología* (from *Obras completas*, La Plata, 1938); Arturo Andrés Roig, from *Filosofía actual en América Latina* (Mexico City: Grijalbo, 1976).

480  Latin American social thought: the history of its development since independence, with selected readings.
Harold Eugene Davis.    Washington, DC: University Press of Washington, 1966. 2nd ed. 560p. bibliog.
Within a chronological arrangement of the principal phases in social thought – enlightenment and independence, liberalism and utilitarianism, positivism, and twentieth-century trends – there are short biographical notes and extracts in English from the works of the following: Mariano Moreno, Esteban Echeverría, Juan Bautista Alberdi, Domingo F. Sarmiento, Agustín Enrique Alvarez Suárez, José Ingenieros, Manuel Gálvez and Ricardo Rojas.

481  Nacimiento y desarrollo de la filosofía en el Río de la Plata, 1536-1810.
(The birth and development of philosophy in the River Plate, 1536-1810.)
Guillermo Fúrlong Cárdiff.    Buenos Aires: Editorial Guillermo Kraft, 1952. 758p. bibliog. (Publicaciones de la Fundación Vitoria y Suárez, 2).
A comprehensive history of colonial philosophy, chiefly in Argentina, in three sections: seventeenth- and eighteenth-century scholasticism, dominated by the University of Córdoba; the effects of the expulsion of the Jesuits and the introduction of cartesianism; the influence of eclecticism and encyclopaedism, and the political thought of the representatives of the independence movement of 1810.

482 **Philosophical analysis in Argentina.**
Eduardo Rabossi. In: *Philosophical analysis in Latin America*.
Edited by Jorge J. E. Gracia, Eduardo Rabossi, Enrique Villanueva,
Marcelo Dascal. Dordrecht, Netherlands: D. Reidel, 1984, p. 17-23.
(Synthese Library, vol. 172).
Argentine philosophical analysis was influenced by Bertrand Russell and G. E. Moore
in England and the Vienna Circle in Austria. Its origins are traced back to the short-
lived but influential periodical *Minerva* (1944-45), founded by Mario Bunge. The
movement took off when Bunge was appointed full professor of the philosophy of
science at the University of Buenos Aires in 1956, but suffered a setback when the
universities were 'intervened' by the armed forces in 1966; since 1970 the movement
has had to struggle against waves of Marxism and 'catechistic Thomism'.

483 **Race in Argentina and Cuba, 1880-1930: theory, policies, and popular
reaction.**
Aline Helg. In: *The idea of race in Latin America, 1870-1940*.
Edited and with an introduction by Richard Graham. Austin, Texas:
University of Texas Press, 1990, p. 37-69. (Institute of Latin American
Studies. Critical Reflections on Latin America Series).
Explores the European-influenced 'scientific racism' of three leading Argentine
intellectuals: statesman and educator Domingo F. Sarmiento, 'who in the 1880s,
pointed to race as accounting for a multitude of Latin American problems'; lawyer and
educationalist Carlos Octavio Bunge, author of *Nuestra América* (1903), a book almost
forgotten today but famous at the time, which also ascribed Latin America's key
problem to its ethnic composition; and physician and sociologist José Ingenieros. By
the end of the nineteenth century, 'the themes of blacks, Indians, and miscegenation
were losing their currency in favor of the debates regarding immigrants'.

484 **Ricardo Rojas and the emergence of Argentine cultural nationalism.**
Earl T. Glauert. *Hispanic American Historical Review*, vol. 43, no. 1
(Feb. 1963), p. 1-13.
Ricardo Rojas (1882-1957) – poet, literary historian, educator and dramatist – was the
leading exponent of cultural nationalism in Argentina. *La restauración nacionalista*
(1909) first expressed the thesis that 'Argentina, faced with the threat of invasion by
foreign influence and ideas, needed to develop a collective conscience based on her
own traditions'. The development of this philosophy is traced in his later philosophical
works: *Blasón de plata* (1910), *La argentinidad* (1916), *Eurindia* (1924, a synthesis of
his earlier ideas); and in his historical biographies of San Martín and Sarmiento: *El
santo de la espada* (1933) and *El profeta de la pampa* (1945).

485 **Sociology in Argentina.**
Hobart A. Spalding, Jr. In *Positivism in Latin America, 1850-1900:
are order and progress reconcilable?* Edited and with an introduction
by Ralph Lee Woodward. Lexington, Massachusetts: D. C. Heath,
1971, p. 50-9. (Problems in Latin American Civilization).
Positivism formed the intellectual base of Argentine sociology, which, unlike its
European counterpart, lacked universality, being concerned almost exclusively with
national events and themes: descriptions or analyses of Argentine individual or

collective psychology, the national character and contemporary society, were all favourite themes. There are two pages on José Ingenieros and short extracts by Juan Bautista Alberdi and José Luis Romero (from the latter's *A history of Argentine political thought* [q.v.]). See also the same author's *Argentine sociology from the end of the nineteenth century to World War One* (Buenos Aires: Instituto Torcuato Di Tella, Centro de Investigaciones Sociales, 1976. 2nd ed. 19p. Documento de Trabajo, 52), which discusses the work of other sociologists – Francisco and José María Ramos Mejía, Juan Agustín García, Carlos O. Bunge, Juan Nicolás Matienzo, Lucas Ayarragaray and Agustín Alvarez.

486 **Three Argentine thinkers.**
Solomon Lipp. New York: Philosophical Library, 1969. 177p. bibliog.
After a brief general summary of the history of Argentine philosophy, the development of Argentine philosophical thought is traced through the works of José Ingenieros ('the greatest representative of the Spencer-Darwin synthesis'), Alejandro Korn ('the last representative of the generation of 1880 . . . – that group which . . . exercised a decisive influence on the economic and cultural development of Argentina'), and Francisco Romero (whose 'principal interest concerned the nature and function of the person'). There are lengthy quotations from the major works.

# Religion

## Christian religions

### 487 Argentina and the Papacy, 1810-1927.
Almon R. Wright. *Hispanic American Historical Review*, vol. 18, no. 1 (Feb. 1938), p. 15-42.

The history of conflicts between the Argentine government and the Vatican and its delegates and envoys – Rivadavia's ecclesiastical reforms, clashes over patronage of the clergy, the establishment of archbishoprics, civil marriage and religious education, and the appointment of Argentina's first ambassador to the Holy See in 1927.

### 488 Argentine liberalism and the Church under Julio Roca, 1880-1886.
Lee Bruce Kress. *The Americas*, vol. 30, no. 3 (Jan. 1974), p. 319-40.

An account of the battle of wills between the Church and the liberal government of Julio Roca, and especially the Minister of Justice, Religion and Public Instruction, Eduardo Wilde, for whom religion was 'a cloud of foolishness with an odor of incense'. The main points of dispute were Wilde's establishment of a civil registry and lay teaching in the schools, and his sensational expulsion of the papal nuncio, Luis Mattera, who had become embroiled in Catholic–Protestant unrest in Córdoba.

### 489 Catholic radicalism and political change in Argentina.
Michael Dodson. In: *Religion in Latin American life and literature*. Edited by Lyle C. Brown, William F. Cooper. Waco, Texas: Markham Press Fund, 1980, p. 316-30.

Describes the actions of the *Movimiento de Sacerdotes para el Tercer Mundo* (Movement of Priests for the Third World, founded May 1968), during the presidency of Juan Carlos Onganía, 1966-70. The *tercermundistas* were 'humanist socialists', influenced by the French worker-priests of the 1950s and the Second Vatican Council (1962). They were active in the worker-student strikes of May-June 1969 and were successful in 'effecting immediate short run political change'. For the movement's later activities, see the same author's 'Priests and Peronism: radical clergy and Argentine politics', *Latin American Perspectives*, vol. 1, no. 3 (fall 1974), p. 58-72; and John T. Deiner, 'Radicalism in the Argentine Catholic Church', *Government and Opposition*, vol. 10, no. 1 (winter 1975), p. 70-89.

490 **Catholicism, nationalism, and democracy in Argentina.**
John J. Kennedy. Notre Dame, Indiana: University of Notre Dame Press, 1958. 219p. (International Studies of the Committee on International Relations).

An evaluation of the role of Catholicism in the life of the Argentine nation, from 1810 to the end of the first Peronist regime (1955): not a study of Church–state relations but of 'a considerable body of Argentine social and political thought that can be called Catholic', especially the two great formative periods of Argentine history which also produced the most significant Catholic nationalist writing, 1810-30 and 1853-90. After 1900, Catholic writing becomes 'more formally philosophic', but there is a final chapter on the Church's involvement in recent social and political conflicts. Also useful on the modern period is Arthur P. Whitaker, 'Nationalism and religion in Argentina and Uruguay', in *Religion, revolution, and reform: new forces for change in Latin America*, edited by William V. D'Antonio and Frederick B. Pike (New York: Praeger; London: Burns & Oates, 1964, p. 73-90).

491 **Church and State in Buenos Aires in the seventeenth century.**
Eduardo R. Saguier. *Journal of Church and State*, vol. 26, no. 3 (autumn 1984), p. 491-514.

Explores the 'contradictory nature' of the colonial Church, which provoked differences between bishops, regular and secular clergy, and religious orders; in particular the mechanisms by which the ecclesiastical bureaucracy, gradually becoming more independent from royal patronage, 'manipulated the state and controlled the social structure'.

492 **Church and State in Latin America: a history of politico-ecclesiastical relations.**
John Lloyd Mecham. Chapel Hill, North Carolina: University of North Carolina Press, 1966. rev. ed. 465p. bibliog.

Chapter ten, 'The State-Church in Argentina' (p. 225-51), describes the position of the Roman Catholic Church during the nineteenth century. 'After the passage of lay education and civil marriage laws in the 1880's religion ceased to be a political issue.' The narrative then jumps to Perón's well-known conflicts with the Church, after which 'the Church was restored to the *status quo ante* 1943'. Today, Roman Catholicism 'occupies a somewhat anomalous middle ground between the position of a full-fledged state church and separation'.

493 **Church–State relations in Argentina in the twentieth century: a case study of the Thirty-second International Eucharistic Congress.**
Jesús Méndez. *Journal of Church and State*, vol. 27, no. 2 (spring 1985), p. 223-43.
A 'stance of benevolent impartiality was a wise one for the Church to take' in the early days of the post-1930 military administration. This article sets out in detail the planning and actual ceremonies of the Eucharistic Congress which was celebrated in various parts of Buenos Aires, 10-14 October 1934, 'amidst intense feelings of civil camaraderie, Catholic fervor, and spiritual reconciliation'. The author notes the pro-Hispanic sympathies of the organizing committee.

494 **Disciples of Christ in Argentina, 1906-1956: a history of the first fifty years of mission work.**
J. Dexter Montgomery. St Louis, Missouri: Bethany Press, 1956. 180p. maps. bibliog.
The work of the Argentine branch of the Protestant-evangelical Disciples of Christ began in 1906 with the opening of a mission in the Buenos Aires suburb of Belgrano. Further missions and 'preaching points' were established in other towns of Buenos Aires province and in northern Chaco province. By 1929 an Argentine Central Council of Disciples Churches had been created. The author, who spent eighteen years with the church in Argentina, here describes its achievements and the missionaries themselves.

495 **Don't cry for me.**
Katharine Makower. London; Sydney; Auckland, New Zealand; Toronto: Hodder & Stoughton, 1989. 197p. map. bibliog.
A partisan book, with a misleading title, honouring the work and staff of the South American Missionary Society (SAMS) among Toba and Mataco Indians in the northern Chaco (Salta and Formosa provinces) since 1914, and describing its health, educational and agricultural programmes. The author defends the British SAMS against 'anthropologists' criticisms of missionary activity among tribal people', which, she says, are more justifiably applied to its North American counterparts. Includes a useful history of earlier missionary activity in the area.

496 **Education and the Church–State clash in Argentina: 1954-1955.**
Virginia W. Leonard. *Catholic Historical Review*, vol. 66, no. 1 (Jan. 1980), p. 34-52.
Half of this article covers Church-state relations during the whole of the first Perón period, 1943-55. By 1954, the one institution not controlled by Perón was the Roman Catholic Church, although 'it acted on the whole as a prop to his government'. Perón now attacked the Church's most sensitive area by ending government support for private Catholic schools and suppressing religious education in the state schools. He was excommunicated in June 1955; this provoked an unsuccessful coup and, in turn, the sacking of churches by Peronist mobs. A fuller narrative of the 1954-55 Church-state crisis is Pablo Marsal S., *Perón y la iglesia* (Buenos Aires: Ediciones Rex, 1955. 157p.). Leonard's book-length study of the Roman Catholic Church's educational role, examining in particular the contentious issues of catechism in state schools and the recognition of private Catholic universities, is: *Politicians, pupils, and priests: Argentine education since 1943* (New York: Peter Lang, 1989. 456p.).

497 **The Evangelical Church in the River Plate republics (Argentina and Uruguay): a study of the economic and social basis of the Evangelical Church in Argentina and Uruguay.**
John Merle Davis.   New York; London: International Missionary Council, Department of Social and Economic Research and Counsel, 1943. 119p.
The study is limited to 'representative types' of Evangelical churches in Buenos Aires city and province, the provinces of Santa Fe and Entre Ríos, and Uruguay. There is an emphasis on the churches' congregations, pastors and financial resources.

498 **Foreign missionaries in Argentina, 1938-1962: a study of dependence.**
Ernest S. Sweeney.   Cuernavaca, Mexico: Centro Intercultural de Documentación (CIDOC), 1970. 361p. (Sondeos, no. 68).
Both Catholic and Protestant missionaries are surveyed. Protestant churches had a membership of 38,293 in 1938, growing to 414,323 in 1961; and 844 Argentine and 680 foreign church workers in 1957, compared with 4,303 Catholic missionaries in 1961. Their influence is everywhere: 'in schools, hospitals, seminaries, parishes and publishing houses. This foreign enterprise is one of the most striking socio-religious developments in the history of the Republic'.

499 **Historia de la iglesia en la Argentina.** (A history of the Church in Argentina.)
Cayetano Bruno.   Buenos Aires: Editorial Don Bosco, 1966-81. 12 vols. maps. bibliog.
A comprehensive, well-indexed and beautifully illustrated history from the colonial period to 1900. A useful one-volume history, covering 1516-1962, is Juan Carlos Zuretti's *Nueva historia eclesiástica argentina, del Concilio de Trento al Vaticano II* (Buenos Aires: Itinerarium, 1972. 528p.); for the colonial period, 1536-1810, see Rómulo D. Cárbia's *Historia eclesiástica del Río de la Plata* (Buenos Aires: Alfa y Omega, 1914. 2 vols).

500 **Man, milieu, and mission in Argentina: a close look at church growth.**
Arno W. Enns.   Grand Rapids, Michigan: William B. Eerdmans, 1971. 258p. map. bibliog.
In 1971 there were approximately seventy-four distinct Evangelical religious bodies working in Argentina. This is a historical study of the beginnings and growth of ten of the principal Protestant Evangelical churches which in 1967 had a combined community of 932,220. Twenty graphs and tables show the size and growth rates of the denominations.

501 **New Catholic encyclopedia.**
Prepared by an editorial staff at the Catholic University of America, Washington, DC.   New York: McGraw-Hill, 1967. 15 vols.
Volume one contains a useful synthesis of Argentine church history (p. 779-85) by Guillermo Fúrlong Cárdiff and a profile of the private Catholic University of Argentina, Buenos Aires, by O. N. Derisi (p. 785).

502 **Records of the Scottish settlers in the River Plate and their churches.**
James Dodds. Buenos Aires: Grant & Sylvester, 1897. 460p.
The Scottish community in Argentina dates from 1825, with the founding of the Monte
Grande colony near Buenos Aires; its members were staunch Presbyterians, often
obtaining money from Scotland for their new churches. This book focuses on the
ministers and activities of the St Andrew's Scotch Presbyterian Church (the leading
Scottish church, opened 1835), St John's (Quilmes), St Andrew's (Chascomús) and
other rural churches in Buenos Aires province. There are sixteen photographs.

503 **Religious liberty in Argentina during the first Perón regime, 1943-1955.**
David F. D'Amico. *Church History*, vol. 46, no. 4 (Dec. 1977),
p. 490-503.
The title conceals the article's true emphasis, the restriction of *Protestant* liberties
during the Perón years, with the connivance of the Roman Catholic Church. Three
areas were affected: 'freedom to propagate their views by radio broadcasts; freedom to
move and act without the government checking their personnel, finances, and
property; and freedom to buy property and erect church buildings in certain areas of
the country'.

504 **The River Plate republics: a survey of the religious, economic and social
conditions in Argentina, Paraguay and Uruguay.**
Webster E. Browning. London; New York: World Dominion Press,
1928. 139p. maps.
The book deals chiefly with the history of Evangelical missions and churches in the
area, and mostly in Argentina, with a chapter on the emergence of Protestant
Christianity.

505 **Toward a pious republic: Argentine social Catholicism in Córdoba,
1895-1930.**
Arthur F. Liebscher. *Journal of Church and State*, vol. 30, no. 3
(autumn 1988), p. 549-67.
During the 1890s, the Church began to engage in *acción social*, social activism
embracing various charitable works. A number of Cordoban Catholic organizations,
formed to bolster this social action programme, is examined, notably the Catholic
People's Union, a federation of charities for immigrant workers, which ceased
operation in 1928 having 'turned into an aristocratic organization with little grass roots
support'. 'Despite its elevated intentions, social Catholicism could not compete with
politicians and unions in winning working-class allegiance.' One success story was the
Asociación Obrera de la Sagrada Familia (Holy Family Workers' Association), serving
railway workers and said to be still active.

506 **A vision of hope: the churches and change in Latin America.**
Trevor Beeson, Jenny Pearce. London: Fount Paperbacks, Fontana,
1984. 290p. map. bibliog.
A study produced under the auspices of the British Council of Churches. The chapter
on Argentina (p. 100-22) disappointingly devotes half of its space to background
political and economic history; only five pages remain for sketches of three churches:
Roman Catholic (including the Movement of Priests for the Third World), Protestant

(including missionary work) and Pentecostal. There is a useful general list of contact addresses at the end of the book.

507 **Witness to the truth: the complicity of Church and dictatorship in Argentina, 1976-1983.**
Emilio F. Mignone, translated by Phillip Berryman.    Maryknoll, New York: Orbis, 1988. 162p.

This is a condemnation of the failure of the Catholic hierarchy to take a coordinated stand against human rights violations during the so-called 'dirty war'; only four of the country's more than eighty bishops did so, even though two bishops and sixteen priests were themselves victims. The author singles out Archbishop Antonio José Plaza of La Plata, 'who most obviously and uninhibitedly has been identified with the military dictatorship and its methods of repression'. The author's own daughter disappeared in May 1976. In this translation of the author's *Iglesia y dictadura* (Buenos Aires, 1986), the foreword is by Adolfo Pérez Esquivel (see *Christ in a poncho: testimonials of the nonviolent struggles in Latin America*).

**The political and economic activities of the Jesuits in the La Plata region: the Hapsburg era.**
*See* item no. 852.

# Non-Christian religions

508 **Folk literature of the Chorote Indians.**
Edited by Johannes Wilbert, Karin Simoneau.    Los Angeles: University of California, UCLA Latin American Center Publications, 1985. 400p. map. bibliog. (UCLA Latin American Studies, vol. 60).

After the Chaco War (1932-35) the Mataco-speaking Argentine Chorote left their settlements on the left bank of the Pilcomayo and established themselves in villages on the right bank, where they were evangelized by Anglican and Pentecostal missionaries. Two of these 150 oral mythic narratives, here in English translation, were collected by the Swedish anthropologist Erland von Nordenskiöld; the rest were recorded by Edgardo J. Cordeau and others from the University of Buenos Aires between 1969 and 1977. The motif indexes are by narrative, topical, alphabetical, and distribution by motif group.

509 **Folk literature of the Mataco Indians.**
Edited by Johannes Wilbert, Karin Simoneau.    Los Angeles: University of California: UCLA Latin American Center Publications, 1982. 507p. map. bibliog. (UCLA Latin American Studies, vol. 52).

The introduction by Niels Fock contains a useful ethnographic and cultural history of the Mataco people of the Gran Chaco. The 207 narratives are reprinted from the collections of five anthropologists (Italian, Danish, English, Swedish and Spanish) and are grouped by theme: star mythology and cosmogony origins, cataclysms, the trickster, animals, and unclassified. A short study of the Mataco language, based on extracts from the Mataco (Anglican) New Testament, is Joseph Biddulph, *Mataco language of northern Argentina* (Pontypridd, Wales: Languages Information Centre, [n.d.]. 20p.).

510  **Folk literature of the Selknam Indians: Martin Gusinde's collection of Selknam narratives.**
Edited by Johannes Wilbert. Los Angeles: University of California, UCLA Latin American Center Publications, 1975. 266p. maps. bibliog. (UCLA Latin American Studies, vol. 32).

A translation of volume one of Martin Gusinde's monumental three-volume *Die Feuerland-Indianer* (1931-74); the other two volumes dealt with the Yámana (q.v.) and Alkaluf Indians. This volume includes the text of fifty-nine myths and legends of the extinct Selk'nam, in two sections: prominent personages and other subjects (habitat, the flood, ancestors, deeds of shamans, the guanaco and other animals, wood spirits, the *klokoten* initiation rite). The motif indexes are by narrative and alphabetical. The introduction includes an account of Gusinde, a German Catholic priest, who made four expeditions to Tierra del Fuego in 1918-24.

511  **Folk literature of the Tehuelche Indians.**
Edited by Johannes Wilbert, Karin Simoneau. Los Angeles: University of California, UCLA Latin American Center Publications, 1984. 266p. map. bibliog. (UCLA Latin American Studies, vol. 59).

Contains 110 narratives, contributed by ten collectors, on cosmology, the *élal* (culture hero), man and culture, plants, animals and extraordinary creatures. The introduction traces the history of the Patagonian Tehuelche from foot to mounted hunters and their loss of territory to the Mapuche Indians and the Europeanization of the pampa after the War of the Desert (1879-83). Since 1900 the Tehuelche have 'undergone a process of genocide and cultural disintegration which has led to their present-day demise'. See Glyn Williams, 'An ecological perspective of socioterritorial organization among the Tehuelche in the nineteenth century', in *Peasants, primitives, and proletarians: the struggle for identity in South America*, edited by David L. Browman and Ronald A. Schwarz (The Hague: Mouton, 1979, p. 75-105).

512  **Folk literature of the Toba Indians. Vol. 1.**
Edited by Johannes Wilbert, Karin Simoneau. Los Angeles: University of California, UCLA Latin American Center Publications, 1982. 597p. map. bibliog. (UCLA Latin American Studies, vol. 54).

The Toba live in over sixty scattered settlements in the eastern Chaco and Formosa provinces of northern Argentina. This collection contains a total of 199 narratives and tale fragments recorded between 1912 and 1980 by seven anthropologists, chiefly Alfred Métraux (ninety-three myths collected 1933-39, taken from his *Myths of the Toba and Pilagá Indians of the Gran Chaco*. Philadelphia: American Folklore Society, 1946) and Roberto D. Terán (sixty-five texts collected 1975-80 and published here for the first time). The myths concern star mythology, cataclysms, origin stories, the trickster, animals, heroes and legendary beings, extraordinary creatures and places. A few Bolivian Toba myths are included.

513 **Folk literature of the Yamana Indians: Martin Gusinde's collection of Yamana narratives.**
Edited by Johannes Wilbert. Berkeley, California: Los Angeles; London: University of California Press, 1977. 308p. maps. bibliog. (UCLA Latin America Studies, vol. 40).

A translation of volume two of Gusinde's *Die Feuerland-Indianer* (see item no. 510), consisting of sixty-six, slightly rewritten and rearranged, oral narratives from the extinct Yámana, or Yahgan, tribe of Tierra del Fuego. In two sections: 'how the world came to be' (heaven and earth, culture heroes), and myths and legends (explanatory myths, shamans, spirits and ogres).

514 **Shamans, power symbols, and change in Argentine Toba culture.**
Elmer S. Miller. *American Ethnologist*, vol. 2, no. 3 (Aug. 1975), p. 477-96. bibliog.

The Tobas' adoption of Pentecostalism (see *Los tobas argentinos: armonía y disonancia en una sociedad*) has attracted the interest of a number of anthropologists. The confrontation with Christian symbolism disrupted traditional Toba symbolism – as expressed in cosmology, shamanism and sorcery – and their understanding of 'power'. See also Miller's 'The Argentine Toba Evangelical religious service', *Ethnology*, vol. 10, no. 2 (April 1971), p. 149-59; Jacob A. Loewen, Albert Buckwater and James Kratz, 'Shamanism, illness and power in Toba church life', *Practical Anthropology*, vol. 12, no. 6 (Nov.-Dec. 1965), p. 250-80; and William D. and Marie F. Reyburn, 'Toba caciqueship and the Gospel', *International Review of Missions*, vol. 45, no. 178 (April 1956), p. 194-203.

# Social Structures and Social Conditions

515 **Becoming modern: individual change in six developing countries.**
Alex Inkeles, David H. Smith.   Cambridge, Massachusetts: Harvard
University Press; London: Heinemann Educational, 1974. 437p.
bibliog.
Interviews were conducted with nearly 6,000 men from three continents – Argentina
and Chile represent South America – in an effort to determine 'the process whereby
people move, from being traditional to becoming modern personalities'. The contexts
and causes of modernity against which the interviewees were assessed were: home
background, education, factory experience, influence of the mass media, farmers'
experience of agricultural cooperatives, urban non-industrial employment, the
'quantity and quality' of urban experience, and rural-versus-urban origin.

516 **Buenos Aires, vida cotidiana y alienación.** (Buenos Aires, daily life and
alienation.)
Juan José Sebreli.   Buenos Aires: Ediciones Siglo Veinte, 1964. 183p.
A famous and controversial Marxist interpretation of the attitudes towards their daily
lives of four classes of Buenos Aires society: the upper classes (*las burguesías*, living in
the *barrio del norte*, northern districts), the middle classes, the 'lumpen' on the city's
outskirts, and the working classes (*obreros*) in the crowded tenements of the city
centre.

517 **Carlos Felipe: kinsman, patron, and friend.**
Arnold Strickon.   In: *Structure and process in Latin America:
patronage, clientage, and power systems*.   Edited by Arnold Strickon,
Sidney M. Greenfield.   Albuquerque, New Mexico: University of New
Mexico Press, 1972, p. 43-70.
This is a case-study of Carlos Felipe (a pseudonym) in his various social roles: as
member of a well-to-do family proud of its anti-Peronism, as manager of one of his
family's business operations (and, in the same context, as employer), and as a friend to

the sons of prominent middle-class families in the rural neighbourhood where he manages his family's cattle ranch. 'Unlike his brothers, Carlos had not become his father's assistant. Drawing on the fortunes of his family, he had gone his own way – that of a *niño bien*, a playboy, a racer of automobiles and horses.'

518 **Changing criminal patterns in Buenos Aires, 1890 to 1914.**
Julia Kirk Blackwelder, Lyman L. Johnson. *Journal of Latin American Studies*, vol. 14, no. 2 (Nov. 1982), p. 359-79.

An analysis of crimes against persons and property, public drunkenness and disorderly behaviour, recorded in the *Anuario estadístico de la ciudad de Buenos Aires*, 1883-1914, a period when the city grew five-fold and overcrowding and family disorganization encouraged high levels of public-order offences, committed mostly by day labourers. Police effectiveness declined and juvenile delinquency increased in equal proportions.

519 **La clase alta de Buenos Aires.** (The upper class of Buenos Aires.)
José Luis de Imaz. Buenos Aires: Universidad de Buenos Aires, Instituto de Sociología, 1962. 86p. map. (Colección Estructura. Investigaciones y Trabajos).

A classic 1959 questionnaire survey of a sample of twenty-five upper-class members of the capital's Jockey Club: family background and relationships, number of children, occupation, political activity and attitudes, and social life.

520 **La clase media de la ciudad de Buenos Aires: estudio preliminar.**
(The middle class of Buenos Aires: a preliminary study.)
Gino Germani. *Desarrollo Económico*, vol. 21, no. 81 (April-June 1981), p. 109-27.

Reprint from a pioneering article which first appeared in 1942, analysing the number and occupations of the city's middle class between 1895 and 1936, during which time it grew by 361 per cent. In 1895, the middle class represented 35 per cent of the city's total work-force; it accounted for 45.9 per cent in 1936, by which year 20.5 per cent were either employers or self-employed, chiefly in industry, commerce and services; and 25.4 per cent were classed as employees. By contrast, the working class represented 54.1 per cent in 1936.

521 **Class and kinship in Argentina.**
Arnold Strickon. In: *Contemporary cultures and societies of Latin America*. Edited by Dwight B. Heath, Richard Adams. New York: Random House, 1965, p. 324-41.

A comparison of the kinship organization of an 'estancia elite' and its gaucho (*criollo*) workers in a cattle community about 180 miles southwest of Buenos Aires. The *estanciero* preserves his property-owning status through vertical family lineage, whereas the *criollo*'s laterally extended family 'increases the probability that at least one of them will be in a position to be of service to him in time of need'. Reprinted from *Ethnology*, vol. 1, no. 4 (Oct. 1962), p. 500-15.

522   **A cross-national study of Buenos Aires and Chicago adolescents.**
Robert James Havighurst, María Eugenia Dubois, Michael
Csikszentmihalyi, Russell Doll.   Basel, Switzerland; New York:
S. Karger, 1965. 80p. (University of Chicago. Committee on Human
Development. Bibliotheca 'Vita Humana', fasc. 3).
Sociological and psychological tests were administered to pupils of differing social
classes from a variety of schools and colleges in Buenos Aires. Five principal
conclusions were formed: Buenos Aires youths are less self-assertive than their
Chicago counterparts, less resistive to authority, less 'instrumental' and 'expressive in
their orientation to the world', less interested and active in heterosexual relations, and
see themselves as generally less active than Chicago youth.

523   **Delinquency in Argentina: a study of Córdoba's youth.**
Lois B. DeFleur.   Pullman, DC: Washington State University Press,
1971. 164p. maps. bibliog.
A detailed analysis was made of a sample of 5,453 cases of delinquency tried before
Córdoba's Juvenile Court over a four-year period, and sixty-three offenders
interviewed in prison. Much of the delinquency was carried out in 'relatively small,
stable, and cohesive, but somewhat loosely organized' gangs of boys of the same age
and status 'oriented toward immediate hedonistic gratifications'. Chapter two is a good
summary of Córdoba's early population history and political-economic development.

524   **Differentiation among the urban poor: an Argentine study.**
Alison M. MacEwan.   In: *Sociology and development*. Edited by
Emanuel de Kadt, Gavin Williams.   London: Tavistock Publications,
1974, p. 197-226.
A case-study, conducted 1964-68, of the 1,168 squatters of Las Canaletas, a shanty-
town in San Pedro, a small riverside town (population 25,000) 190 miles from Buenos
Aires. Differences in the residents' social status were measured by occupation and
income, types of dwellings, material possessions, education and kinship patterns. The
author examines the last factor in more detail in 'Kinship and mobility on the
Argentine pampa', *Ethnology*, vol. 12, no. 2 (April 1973), p. 135-51.

525   **Eclipse of an aristocracy: an investigation of the ruling elites of the city
of Córdoba.**
Juan Carlos Agulla, translated by Betty Crouse.   Montgomery,
Alabama: University of Alabama Press, 1976. 151p.
Traces the decline of the Cordoban aristocracy (high-ranking politicians, the legal
profession, university administrators) in four key years: 1924, 1937, 1951 and 1960.
The loss of power of the pre-1918 'doctoral' aristocracy (lawyers, doctors, clerks of the
high courts of justice) is attributed to industrialization (which attracted the talents of
what Agulla calls the 'available' aristocracy but not the traditional) and the formation
of the new middle classes.

526 **Estructura social de la Argentina: análisis estadístico.** (The social structure of Argentina: a statistical analysis.)
Gino Germani. Buenos Aires: Editorial Raigal, 1955. 278p.
(Biblioteca Manuel Belgrano de Estudios Económicos).

A well-documented analysis, with 110 supporting tables, of the country's population and socioeconomic structures (work-force by industry, social classes, education, political attitudes), based on census and other official statistical data. See also *Política y sociedad en una época de transición: de la sociedad tradicional a la sociedad de masas.*

527 **Evolución histórica de la estratificación social en la Argentina.**
(Historical development of social stratification in Argentina.)
Sergio J. Bagú. Buenos Aires: Universidad de Buenos Aires,
Facultad de Filosofía y Letras, Instituto de Sociología, 1961. 87p.
(Trabajos e Investigaciones. Publicación Interna, 36).

The author considers that Argentina's society has passed through three stages of development: 'unified', as was the nation, in 1880, 'articulated' between 1880 and 1930, and 'directed' since 1930. The country's social strata are equated with four areas of national life: the distribution of the work-force within economic production (agriculture, industry, business and commerce), consumption (housing, health and other public services), knowledge (education and literacy) and power (the economic and political élite, the judiciary, the armed forces).

528 **Family, kinship and work among rural proletarians in Tucumán, Argentina.**
Hebe M. C. Vessuri. In: *Family and kinship in Middle America and the Caribbean: proceedings of the 14th seminar of the Committee on Family Research of the International Sociological Association, Curaçao, September 1975.* Edited by Arnaud F. Marks, René A. Römer.
Willemstad, Curaçao: Institute of Higher Studies in Curaçao;
Leiden, Netherlands: Royal Institute of Linguistics and Anthropology, Department of Caribbean Studies, 1978, p. 181-226. bibliog.

A study of permanent and transient workers on a sugar estate, Colonia Cevil Hueco, near the city of Tucumán, northwest Argentina. It focuses on their families, their relationships with the local community and the role of work and seasonal migration in relation to both. During the harvest, the 'family works as an efficient team'.

529 **Family relations in Argentina: diachrony and synchrony.**
Catalina H. Wainerman. *Journal of Family History*, vol. 3, no. 4 (winter 1978), p. 410-21. bibliog.

An assessment of the 'authoritarian or egalitarian character of interpersonal relations' of families in modern Buenos Aires and more traditional Catamarca, using an unusual indicator: the use of 'pronominal address in dyadic interaction (specifically, symmetrical and asymmetrical interchanges of the variants *vos*, *tú*, and *usted* of the second person singular pronoun)'. The author finds greater egalitarianism in Buenos Aires, while the 'frequency of asymmetrical usage between generations in 1970 Catamarca resembles that prevailing in Buenos Aires fifty years earlier', and 'today's difference between Catamarca and Buenos Aires is similar to the one existing between 1900 and 1950 among Buenos Aires families'.

### 530 History of an Argentine passion.
Eduardo Mallea, translated, with an introduction and annotations, by Myron I. Lichtblau. Pittsburgh, Pennsylvania: Latin American Literary Review Press, 1983. 184p. bibliog. (Explorations).

Novelist Eduardo Mallea first published this long poetic essay in 1937. According to the introduction, 'Mallea's "passion" . . . is his deep feeling for Argentina', a condemnation of 'the Argentina of the 1930s dominated by a conservative, even repressive oligarchy that has betrayed the fundamental truth and moral order on which the country was built'. He contrasts the visible ('the materialistic, ostentatious, false veneer that the country, especially Buenos Aires, lives with from day to day') and the invisible ('what Mallea would like the country to become, what the country once was').

### 531 Migración y marginalidad en la sociedad argentina. (Migration and marginality in Argentine society.)
Mario Margulis. Buenos Aires: Paidós, 1968. 207p. bibliog. (Biblioteca América Latina. Serie Menor, 10).

Sociological essays on migration, containing a case-study of migrants from a depressed agricultural area (Chilecito, La Rioja province), to an uncertain future in the workers' quarters of Greater Buenos Aires.

### 532 Notable family networks in Latin America.
Diana Balmori, Stuart F. Voss, Miles Wortman. Chicago; London: University of Chicago Press, 1984. 290p. bibliog.

Guatemala and Mexico are the other countries represented in this study based on notarial records and family papers. Balmori's chapter on Argentina (p. 129-84) focuses on three generations of 154 prominent Buenos Aires families, selected from the membership of the Sociedad Rural and Jockey Club: the family business, professions and public offices pursued by their members, marriage and property. 'The first generation bought land on which the second generation created and merged estancias; . . . the second generation merged the cattle estancia and the urban trading post; . . . members of the third generation were professional people and therefore did not live on the estancias or run them.'

### 533 Order, family, and community in Buenos Aires, 1810-1860.
Mark D. Szuchman. Stanford, California: Stanford University Press, 1988. 307p. bibliog.

'The underlying thesis of this book is that the dynamics in the relations between citizen and state were generated by a commonly desired objective: the reestablishment of law and order after the period of social and political turbulence that began with the Revolution of 1810.' The author uses family history to reconstruct the daily experiences of the 'common people' (the *gente de pueblo,* whom he contrasts with the well-to-do, the *gente decente*). Main chapters discuss the criminal justice system, children's education and the city's changing demographic structure.

534 **Paraná: social boundaries in an Argentine city.**
Rubén E. Reina.    Austin, Texas; London: University of Texas Press,
1973. 390p. maps. bibliog. (Institute of Latin American Studies. Latin
American Monographs, no. 31).

Paraná, capital of Entre Ríos province since 1883, was capital of the Argentine
Confederation between 1853 and 1861 and 'in that role the city social structure was
modified'. Today's population (over 100,000 in the year the study was written) is the
product of mass immigration before 1895: Italians, Russians, Germans, British, Swiss
and Middle Easterners. This is a description of the way of life of the middle-class
inhabitants of Paraná; the city has only a small group of non-middle-class families. The
city contains many of the basic Argentine national characteristics but is of 'less urban
sophistication than the industrial cities of Buenos Aires or Córdoba'.

535 **Política y sociedad en una época de transición: de la sociedad tradicional
a la sociedad de masas.** (Politics and society in an age of transition from
traditional to mass society.)
Gino Germani.    Buenos Aires: Paidós, 1962. 266p. bibliog.
(Biblioteca de Psicología Social y Sociología).

A well-documented application of the 'structural-functional' theory of social organization, by one of Argentina's leading sociologists, to the problems inherent in the process
of transition from a traditional agricultural to a modern industrial society, with specific
studies of Argentine mass immigration, the family, and political participation under
totalitarian, specifically Peronist, government. Germani developed this theme in his
other major work, *Sociología de la modernización* (1969). For a partial synthesis in
English, see his *Social modernization and economic development in Argentina* (Geneva:
United Nations Research Institute for Social Development, 1970. 75p. Report, 70.6).
See also *Estructura social de la Argentina: análisis estadístico*.

536 **Public culture and the management of ethnic diversity: an Argentine
case.**
Kenneth J. Ackerman.    *Cultures et Développement*, vol. 3, no. 3
(1971), p. 375-413.

The pseudonymous agricultural trade-centre of 'Brilho' (founded 1928), Misiones
province, has an ethnically mixed population of 15,000 – *criollos* (professionals and
local-government workers, chiefly Poles, Germans, Swedes, Paraguayans, Brazilians,
Turks and Jews) and *extranjeros* ('outsider' farmers and businessmen). The author
shows how the various *criollo* nationalities, especially the Germans, view each other,
and presents examples of 'inter-ethnic encounters': a *criollo* justice of the peace hears a
case of *extranjero* (Ukrainian) family litigation, and the relations between a *criollo*
household and its *extranjero* neighbours.

537  **Social mobility rates in Buenos Aires, Montevideo and São Paulo: a preliminary comparison.**
Bertram Hutchinson.  *América Latina* (Rio de Janeiro), vol. 5, no. 4 (Oct.-Dec. 1962), p. 3-18.

An examination of social status and mobility in the three cities, based on a hierarchical ranking of 154 occupations, predominantly industrial, reduced to six status categories (professional down to unskilled), with a closer comparison between the manual/non-manual and upper/middle/lower categories. The study reveals that Buenos Aires and Montevideo 'offered conditions more conducive to social mobility, especially upward mobility, than has São Paulo', and 'the reduction in the relative size of the lowest status category [semi-skilled and unskilled manual] appears greatest in Buenos Aires'.

538  **Three Latin American sociologists: Gino Germani, Pablo Gonzales [sic] Casanova, Fernando Henrique Cardoso.**
Joseph A. Kahl.  New Brunswick, New Jersey; Oxford: Transaction Books, 1988. 2nd ed. 215p. bibliog.

An attempt to illuminate the rapid growth of sociology and political science in Latin America immediately after the Second World War by examining the careers and major writings of three leading sociologists: Germani (Argentina, 'the senior scholar of the three', p. 23-73), González Casanova (Mexico) and Cardoso (Brazil). Germani was born in Rome in 1911, moved to Argentina in 1934, and became professor of sociology and head of the Institute of Sociology at the University of Buenos Aires in 1955. He has been a Harvard professor since 1966. This second edition has a new introduction by Peter B. Evans.

539  **White slavery, public health, and the Socialist position on legalized prostitution in Argentina, 1913-1936.**
Donna J. Guy.  *Latin American Research Review*, vol. 23, no. 3 (1988), p. 60-80.

In 1875 the Buenos Aires municipal council legalized female prostitution within authorized bordellos; in 1903, the city had 8,000-10,000 prostitutes, many of them evading registration. This article documents the Socialist Party's campaign against white slavery in the city, beginning with Socialist Deputy Alfredo Palacios's anti-pimping law of 1913 and culminating in the abolition of legalized prostitution in 1936. Efforts to protect Jewish women from prostitution are described in Víctor A. Mirelman, 'The Jewish community versus crime: the case of white slavers in Buenos Aires', *Jewish Social Studies*, vol. 46, no. 2 (spring 1984), p. 145-68. A famous exposé of the white slave trade by Frenchman Albert Londres is *The road to Buenos Ayres* (London: Constable, 1928. 125p.); this is a sensationalized version of the findings of the League of Nations Committee on the International Traffic in Women and Children, which visited Buenos Aires in 1924.

540 **Youth in Argentina: between the legacy of the past and the construction of the future.**
Cecilia Braslavsky.    *CEPAL Review* (Santiago, Chile), no. 29 (Aug. 1986), p. 42-54. bibliog.

A survey of young people aged fifteen to twenty-four years, based on the 1960, 1970 and 1980 national population censuses: their number and regional distribution (between one-third and one-half lives in rural areas), the situation of young women, the key role of the family in the 'socialization' of young people, their educational levels, and the world of work. Young people constitute one-sixth of the Argentine population (4,553,104 in 1980) and their numbers are growing. Seventy-four per cent of youth worked for a living in 1983, most of them as skilled industrial workers.

# Health and Medicine, Social Welfare and Social Services

## Health and medicine

541 **Age of menarche in urban Argentinian girls.**
H. Lejárraga, F. Sanchirico, M. Cusminsky. *Annals of Human Biology*, vol. 7, no. 6 (Nov.-Dec. 1980), p. 579-81. bibliog.
A representative sample of 6,494 girls aged eight to nineteeen from the city of La Plata (46.2 per cent of the city's total of 22,800 in this age group) revealed a mean age of menarche of 12.53 ± 0.05 years. In 1971, Lejárraga, Cusminsky and Elsa P. Castro calculated the mean age of puberty in La Plata's total population aged eight to twelve: see 'Age of onset of puberty in urban Argentinian children', *Annals of Human Biology*, vol. 3, no. 4 (July 1976), p. 379-81.

542 **Child psychology in Argentina.**
Mauricio Knobel. *Journal of Clinical Child Psychology*, vol. 4, no. 2 (summer 1975), p. 7-9. bibliog.
Two-thirds of this article is devoted to a useful general survey of the practice of psychology in Argentina: 'There are no unified teaching criteria, no professional status and orientation, no legal status, no true psychological identity.' The author then describes the pioneers in the development of child psychology and the teaching of child analysis, which is dominated by psychoanalytic techniques. 'There is no official status of child psychologist' and 'salaries are so low that it is essential to get into private practice to survive'.

**Health and Medicine, Social Welfare and Social Services.**
Health and medicine

543 **Coronary heart disease mortality and coronary risk factors in Argentina.**
Julia H. Hauger-Klevene, Emma C. Balossi. *Cardiology*, vol. 74, no. 2 (1987), p. 133-41.
Since 1960 there has been a marked increase in deaths through coronary heart disease in Argentine men and women aged 35-64. In 1978, heart diseases, headed by CHD, were responsible for 42.4 per cent of all deaths, and Argentine men had one of the highest CHD mortality rates in the world (603.9 per 100,000). The three major coronary risk factors are high cholesterol (Argentines are famed for their high red-meat intake), blood pressure and cigarette smoking.

544 **Cuando murió Buenos Aires, 1871.** (When Buenos Aires died: 1871.)
Miguel Angel Scenna. Buenos Aires: Ediciones La Bastilla, 1974. 503p. (Serie A Sangre y Fuego).
Yellow-fever epidemics afflicted Buenos Aires in 1852, 1859 and, most seriously, 1871, when more than 14,000 (half the city's population) died in four months, sometimes at the rate of 500 a day. Many Argentines at the time blamed immigrants for the outbreak. This is an exhaustive account of how the city's health services were paralysed and how the government and citizens mobilized to fight the epidemic. The appendix lists the number of deaths per day, 27 January–31 May.

545 **Decrease in the prevalence of infection by *Trypanosoma Cruzi* (Chagas' disease) in young men of Argentina.**
E. L. Segura, A. C. Pérez (et al.). *Bulletin of the Pan American Health Organization*, vol. 19, no. 3 (1985), p. 252-64. map.
Chagas' disease, transmitted by triatomine bugs and causing fever with frequent inflammation of the heart muscles, is most common in northern, central and western provinces of Argentina. In 1981 the blood samples of 212,614 military conscripts (virtually all eighteen-year-old Argentine males) were tested for TC antibodies; the results showed a decline in the national prevalence of TC infection of about forty per cent compared with the results of similar tests made in 1964-69 (5.8 per cent compared with 10.3 per cent). The decline is due to the use of insecticides (but see *Pesticides in intensive cultivation: effects on working conditions and workers' health*) and better public-health screening.

546 **Democracy, authoritarianism, and health in Argentina.**
José Carlos Escudero. *International Journal of Health Services*, vol. 2, no. 4 (1981), p. 559-72.
A condemnation of the health policies of military régimes in Argentina since 1955, contrasted with Perón's 'democratic' régime (when the number of hospital beds nearly doubled, compared with only a seven per cent increase from 1955 to 1969). Other examples (reduced public-health expenditure, 'fee charging for performance of health activities', increased mortality and malnutrition, irregular access to health services, a lack of concern with preventive medicine, and inadequate dental care, as well as political murder, 'disappearance' and torture) are cited to support the argument.

547 **Distribution of hereditary blood groups among Indians in South America. VII: In Argentina.**
G. Albin Matson, H. Eldon Sutton, Jane Swanson, Abner Robinson.
*American Journal of Physical Anthropology*, new series, vol. 30, no. 1 (Jan., March, May 1969), p. 61-84. map. bibliog.

Blood specimens were taken from 945 full-blooded Indians of the Diaguita, Mataco, Chiriguano, Choroti, Toba, Chané, Chulupí and Araucanian tribes, and tested for blood groups and other factors. Group O was found to be consistently high, with the Toba, Choroti and Mataco exhibiting 100 per cent frequency; this is not uncommon for isolated, putatively full-blooded Indian populations in Middle and South America. Eleven detailed tables are included.

548 **The distribution of tetanus in Argentina.**
Vicente E. Mazzáfero, Mario Boyer, Alvaro Moncayo-Medina.
*Bulletin of the Pan American Health Organization*, vol. 15, no. 4 (1981), p. 327-32. map.

Tetanus occurs most frequently in the subtropical provinces of Catamarca, Corrientes, Chaco, Formosa, Jujuy, Misiones, Salta, Santiago del Estero and Tucumán. National data for 1965-77 show varying annual rates of infection between 1.2 and 1.7 cases per 100,000 (with a high of 3.1 per 100,000 in 1967); data for Buenos Aires show a large number of deaths from tetanus in newborn babies (9-17 deaths per 100,000 live births).

549 **The ecology of malnutrition in eastern South America.**
Jacques Meyer May, Donna L. McLellan. New York: Hafner Press; London: Collier Macmillan, 1974. 558p. maps. bibliog. (Studies in Medical Geography, vol. 13).

Chapter five of this five-country survey, 'The Republic of Argentina' (p. 483-545), contains a disproportionate amount of background information before describing agricultural policies (1966-73), foreign aid programmes, the production and supply of food (adequate), diet (per capita calorie intake is high), and nutritional disease (low, but goitre and obesity – 'malnutrition with hypernutrition' – among low-income pregant women are common). Yet 'there must be below-par diets in many of the *villas miserias*'.

550 **Historia de la farmacia argentina.** (History of pharmacy in Argentina.)
Francisco Cignoli. Rosario, Argentina: Librería y Editorial Ruiz, 1953. 403p. bibliog.

A well-documented history, with a full name index, of the development of pharmacy from its primitive beginnings to the present, including its teaching in the universities, professional publications and the modern pharmaceutical industry.

551 **Historia de la medicina en el Río de la Plata desde su descubrimiento hasta nuestros días, 1512-1925.** (The history of medicine in the River Plate, from discovery to the present day, 1512-1925.)
Eliseo Cantón. Madrid: Imprenta G. Hernández y Galo Sáez, 1928. 6 vols. bibliog.
A well-illustrated chronological history of the practitioners and institutions of medicine, mainly from 1810. Volume two includes a full discussion of the Protomedicato (Medical Examining Board, created 1779), which regulated all medical and public-health activities during the viceregal period and beyond.

552 **Historia general de la medicina argentina.** (A general history of medicine in Argentina.)
Antonio Aguilar (et al.). Córdoba, Argentina: Universidad Nacional de Córdoba, Dirección General de Publicaciones, 1976-80.
2 vols. bibliog.
A comprehensive history of all branches of medicine, but lacking an index and bibliography, though well footnoted. Also useful are the brief synthesis to 1950, *Panorama histórico de la medicina argentina*, by Alicia Elena Casais de Corne, Fiz Antonio Fernández and Julio Lardies González (Buenos Aires: Todo es Historia, 1977. 147p.); and *Historia de la medicina argentina: tres conferencias*, confined to colonial medicine, by José Luis Molinari (Buenos Aires: Imprenta López, 1937. 147p.).

553 **HIV-1 infection in intravenous drug abusers with clinical manifestations of hepatitis in the city of Buenos Aires.**
Marcelo Díaz Lestrem, Hugo Fainboim (et al.). *Bulletin of the Pan American Health Organization*, vol. 23, nos 1-2 (1989), p. 35-41.
Ninety-nine intravenous drug users, four of them homosexual/bisexual – with an average age of twenty-one years, eighty-nine per cent of them male – were tested for hepatitis and HIV infection in Buenos Aires hospitals between December 1986 and September 1987. Eighty-seven subjects were suffering from various forms of hepatitis, mainly hepatitis B, and forty-seven were infected with HIV-1.

554 **Hunger and monetarism in Buenos Aires, 1976-1983: a food systems approach.**
Warwick Armstrong. *Boletín de Estudios Latinoamericanos y del Caribe*, no. 45 (Dec. 1988), p. 29-49. bibliog.
The case of Buenos Aires under the last military régime is an 'excellent illustration of systematic hunger'. Yet food production, though 'dominated strongly by transnational corporations', actually rose during 1976-83. The author analyses food-consumption patterns, 1973-84, and blames 'monetarist-military strategy' for malnutrition among low-income groups; he is irritated by those in the *villas miserias* who choose unhealthy (and more expensive) convenience food.

555 **Incidence of childhood cancer in La Plata, Argentina, 1977-1987.**
Ricardo Drut, Ana Hernández, Daniel Pollono. *International Journal of Cancer*, vol. 45, no. 6 (15 June 1990), p. 1045-7. bibliog.
La Plata has 151,085 children aged 0-14. The incidence of malignant tumours in children, 1977-87, was 106.5 per million (127.4 for males, 83.4 for females). Leukaemia (30.5 per cent), lymphoma (15.2 per cent) and tumours of the central nervous system (14.1 per cent) accounted for sixty per cent of all tumours. This is similar to the Latin American pattern but different from North America and Europe where brain tumours rank second.

556 **Liver cirrhosis mortality in Argentina: its relationship to alcohol intake.**
Julia H. Hauger-Klevene, Emma C. Balossi. *Drug and Alcohol Dependence*, vol. 19, no. 1 (1987), p. 29-33.
Rates of liver cirrhosis mortality increased significantly in both sexes between 1962 and 1970 and declined (except for men aged 35-44 years) between 1970 and 1978. However, 'the age-adjusted mortality rate persisted in 1978 at a level significantly higher than in 1962'. In 1978-79, liver cirrhosis was the fifth cause of death for the age group 45-64. This is attributed to the high intake of alcohol: Argentina has the world's fourth-highest wine consumption per inhabitant, and beer and whisky consumption has also risen.

557 **La medicina popular.** (Popular medicine.)
Hugo E. Ratier. Buenos Aires: Centro Editor de América Latina, 1972. 109p. (Vida y Milagros de Nuestro Pueblo. La Historia Popular, 87).
A short, illustrated survey of popular medicine: home remedies and cures, patent medicines, country *curanderos* ('curers'), bone-setters and other unofficial practitioners.

558 **Médicos argentinos.** (Argentine physicians.)
Osvaldo Loudet. Buenos Aires: Editorial Huemul, 1966. 238p.
A gallery of medical doctors, surgeons, physiologists, neurologists, forensic doctors and others, mainly of the nineteenth century. Unfortunately, it is poorly documented and has neither index nor illustrations. See also Guillermo Fúrlong Cárdiff's informative *Médicos argentinos durante la dominación hispánica* (Buenos Aires: Editorial Huarpes, 1947. 311p.).

559 **Pesticides in intensive cultivation: effects on working conditions and workers' health.**
Elena L. Matos, Dora I. Loria, Nelson Albiano, Norma Sobel, Elisa C. de Buján. *Bulletin of the Pan American Health Organization*, vol. 21, no. 4 (1987), p. 405-16.
Two groups of greenhouse workers from the province of Buenos Aires were studied, April-December 1983. Both groups made indiscriminate use of a wide range of pesticides, took inadequate protective measures, and experienced a wide range of acute and chronic intoxication symptoms.

560 **Prevalencia de desórdenes mentales en el área metropolitana de la República Argentina.** (The prevalence of psychiatric disorders among the population of Greater Buenos Aires.)
Graciela Di Marco. *Acta Psiquiátrica y Psicológica de América Latina* (Buenos Aires), vol. 28, no. 2 (June 1982), p. 93-102. bibliog.

Random interviews (using the Present State Examination technique) with 3,411 adult men and women were conducted September-December 1979 in the Federal District and nineteen *partidos* (districts) of Greater Buenos Aires. Twenty-six per cent (30.8 per cent female, 20.3 per cent male) were found to be suffering from neuroses (especially depression), affective and schizophrenic psychosis, and paranoia. There was a high prevalence among poorer married and unemployed women with young children.

561 **Primary care and the pattern of disease in a rural area of the Argentine Chaco.**
Mary T. Brett. *Bulletin of the Pan American Health Organization*, vol. 18, no. 2 (1984), p. 115-26. map.

A study of the patients (mostly Indians) treated by a missionary clinic in the Chaco village of La Paz, June 1979–May 1980. The major conditions diagnosed were (in this order): respiratory diseases (especially tuberculosis, mainly contracted by Indians); gastrointestinal problems; obstetric, gynaecological and genitourinary infections; minor skin infections; and infectious diseases. There were also cases of hypertension, brucellosis, obesity, epilepsy, cancer and diabetes, occurring only among mestizos and whites.

562 **La psicología en Argentina: pasado, presente y futuro.** (Psychology in Argentina: past, present and future.)
Rubén Ardila. *Revista Latinoamericana de Psicología*, vol. 11, no. 1 (1979), p. 77-91. bibliog.

An interesting overview of the history and current practice of psychology in Argentina, by a visiting Colombian psychologist. He writes of the development of the profession; the archetypal psychologist (a young married woman, with two children and a husband who is also a psychologist or doctor); psychology's unique ideological base and emphasis on psychoanalysis; the growth of experimental psychology since 1970; and professional publications.

563 **La psiquiatría argentina.** (Psychiatry in Argentina.)
Antonio Alberto Guerrino.    Buenos Aires: Editores Cuatro, 1982. 272p. bibliog.

A chronological, illustrated history of mental illness and psychiatric hospitals, practice and study, including a chapter on forensic psychiatry. Also useful is *Historia de la psiquiatría argentina*, by Osvaldo Loudet and Osvaldo Elías Loudet (Buenos Aires: Ediciones Troquel, 1971. 212p.).

564 **Rubella antibodies in female applicants for premarital health certificates in Mar del Plata, Argentina.**
Francisco Pereira, Osvaldo Uez. *Bulletin of the Pan American Health Organization*, vol. 20, no. 2 (1986), p. 179-85.

A group of 781 women aged 15-49 from the General Pueyrredón department of Mar del Plata, who applied to the National Institute of Epidemiology for premarital health certificates during 1981, were screened for rubella antibodies. Twelve per cent of the women lacked rubella-specific antibodies, and were presumably susceptible to infection. The total number of cases of rubella occurring in Argentina in 1981 was 15,194 – about sixty-three cases per hundred thousand.

565 **Salud y política social.** (Health and social policy.)
Aldo Neri. Buenos Aires: Hachette, 1982. 261p.

One of the most quoted Argentine works on the subject in recent years, but in fact a rather repetitive essay on the theoretical organization and financing of public health services as social institutions, with an Argentine case-study (p. 79-261) critical of the health policies of the recent military governments. Some nuggets of information will be gleaned from the text and the eight small tables.

566 **Social class and social mobility in relation to psychiatric symptomatology in Argentina.**
Michael J. Saks, Jane Edelstein, Juris G. Draguns, Toba A. de Fundia. *Revista Interamericana de Psicología*, vol. 4, no. 2 (June 1970), p. 105-21. bibliog.

Over a hundred male and female patients in psychiatric institutions in and around Buenos Aires and Córdoba were analysed for the study. 'Overt, impulsive, and bizarre symptomatology predominated among lower class patients, intermediate levels of socioeconomic status tended toward self-blame and guilt, and the highest groups . . . expressed anxiety, tension, and alienation.'

567 **Social violence and psychoanalysis in Argentina: the unthinkable and the unthought.**
Janine Puget. *Free Associations: Psychoanalysis, Groups, Politics, Culture*, no. 13 (1988), p. 84-140. bibliog.

The violence of the years 1976-83 caused psychological shock to some of the population: some suffered alienation, others 'managed to preserve [their] capacity to think and to perceive the real facts of the external world'. The 'unthinkable' was the 'possible, but intolerable knowledge' of those caught up in the violence (in extreme cases, victims of torture); the 'unthought' was other people's unconscious denial of what was going on around them. Some actual cases are mentioned.

# Social welfare and social services

**568 Medical care under social security in developing countries.**
Geneva: International Social Security Association, 1982. 170p. (Studies and Research, no. 18).

The brief section on Argentina, by Luis Alberto Najun Zaragaza (p. 67-71), describes health care and medical services, the legislation governing social security and the agencies involved, and the financing and benefits of social-security schemes.

**569 Social security in Latin America: pressure groups, stratification, and inequality.**
Carmelo Mesa-Lago. Pittsburgh, Pennsylvania: University of Pittsburgh Press, 1978. 351p. (Pitt Latin American Studies).

A study of social security in Argentina, Mexico, Chile, Peru and Uruguay. The chapter on Argentina describes the four phases in the evolution of the social-security system: 1810-1914, when pensions were available only to privileged groups; 1915-44, when pension coverage was extended to the members of the strongest unions; 1944-54, the Perón years, when the foundations of modern social security were laid; and 1955-74, when benefits became widespread and the system standardized. The four main pressure groups are analysed: the military, civil servants, blue- and white-collar workers, and the self-employed, professionals and entrepreneurs. Finally, the inequalities of the system are discussed.

**570 Social welfare, 1850-1950: Australia, Argentina and Canada compared.**
Edited by D. C. M. Platt. London: Macmillan, 1988. 208p.

The proceedings of a conference held in 1985. There are two chapters on Argentina in part one, 'Charity, health and housing': Carlos Escudé, 'Health in Buenos Aires in the second half of the nineteenth century', and Francis Korn and Lidia de la Torre, 'Housing in Buenos Aires, 1887-1914'. The second part, 'Labour', covers only Canada and Australia. The final part, 'Comparisons', includes H. S. Ferns, 'Argentina and Canada, 1880-1930: problems and solutions in immigrant communities'; Peter Alhadeff, 'Social welfare and the slump: Argentina in the 1930s'; and John Fogarty, 'Social experiments in regions of recent settlement: Australia, Argentina and Canada'. The editor comments: 'More might have been achieved in Argentine social welfare had not Irigoyen's Radicals, in political office continuously from 1916 to 1930, dissociated themselves from everything foreign.'

**571 Social welfare in Latin America.**
Edited by John Dixon, Robert Scheurell. London; New York: Routledge, 1990. 303p. bibliog. (Comparative Social Welfare Series).

The chapter on Argentina, by Irene Queiro Trajalli (p. 1-24), contains a brief history of the social-welfare system, and then considers social security and personal social services for the aged, the disabled, needy families, children and youth, the sick and injured, and the unemployed. 'The welfare system in Argentina is mainly provided for by central, provincial and local governments, labour organisations and charitable private institutions. As a result, some welfare programmes are highly centralised.'

# Politics

## General

572  **Argentina: a country divided.**
Joseph R. Barager.   In: *Political systems of Latin America.*   Edited
by Martin C. Needler.   Princeton, New Jersey: Van Nostrand, 1964,
p. 403-44. bibliog.
A historical introduction to the Argentine political system to 1963, followed by an
contemporary analysis of the country's political parties and interest groups, the
constitution, the structure of national and provincial/local government, economic
policy, and Church–state and foreign relations.

573  **Argentina and the failure of democracy: conflict among political elites,
1904-1955.**
Peter H. Smith.   Madison, Wisconsin: University of Wisconsin Press,
1974. 215p. bibliog.
Part one is a summary of key aspects of twentieth-century political history. Part two is
an investigation of the 'dynamics of decay and failure' of the democratic political
system and the emergence of corporate authoritarianism under Perón, based on a
sophisticated computer analysis of 1,571 members of the Chamber of Deputies: their
background and status, party alignment and voting behaviour as reflected in 1,712 roll-
calls taken between 1904 and 1955. Military interventions tended to follow the
intensification of divisions along party lines. The methodological and statistical tables
occupy half the book.

159

574 **Argentina: the frustration of ungovernability.**
Gary W. Wynia. In: *Politics, policies, and economic development in Latin America.* Edited by Robert Wesson. Stanford, California: Hoover Institution Press, 1984, p. 14-35. (Hoover Press Publication, 306).
An assessment of the adverse effects of Argentine politics since 1930 on economic development: the ungovernability caused by partisan groups and their practice of 'veto politics', and the growth of the Argentine state, with its power of patronage, 'high cost and gross inefficiencies'. The author concludes with one of his many forthright statements: 'One hopes that the Argentine upper class has learned that it cannot run the country as it wishes, that the middle class has discovered that its alienation does it and the nation more good than harm, and that the working class recognizes that if it is to live in a capitalist society, it cannot ignore the demands of those who supply its capital.'

575 **Argentina, 1943-1987: the national revolution and resistance.**
Donald C. Hodges. Albuquerque, New Mexico: University of New Mexico Press, 1988. rev. ed. 342p. bibliog.
Based on interviews with guerrilla leaders and a reading of revolutionary publications, this revised and enlarged edition provides a valuable but partisan documentary of left-wing revolutionary organizations and their armed resistance to military régimes, 1956-73 and 1976-83. It focuses on the Ejército Revolucionario del Pueblo (People's Revolutionary Army), the Montoneros and the Fuerzas Armadas Revolucionarias; the author says that the last were most successful in integrating 'a revolutionary vanguard with the politics of a mass movement [Peronism]'. One author has suggested the 'conspiracy theory' notion that the left-wing terrorism which led to the 'dirty war' against it was orchestrated by the Soviet KGB; be that as it may, it is mentioned here as a counter to the overwhelmingly anti-military literature elsewhere in this bibliography: Pierre F. de Villemarest, *The strategists of fear: twenty years of revolutionary war in Argentina* (Geneva: Editions Voxmundi, 1981. 217p.). See also *Soldiers of Perón: Argentina's Montoneros.* In 1980 the Argentine government published *Terrorism in Argentina*, a 442-page catalogue of guerrilla atrocities, compiled mainly from newspaper reports.

576 **Argentine Radicalism: the history and doctrine of the Radical Civic Union.**
Peter G. Snow. Iowa City, Iowa: University of Iowa Press, 1965. 137p. bibliog.
A scholarly chronological history of the Unión Cívica Radical from its foundation in 1890 to 1964. Factionalism has dogged the party; in 1957 it split into the 'Intransigente' and 'del Pueblo' (People's) Radical Parties. The appendices contain useful tables of election statistics for 1916-63, the composition of the Chamber of Deputies (1912-30), and the UCR's electoral manifestos of 1945, 1960 and 1963. The definitive history to 1957 in Spanish is Gabriel del Mazo, *El radicalismo: ensayo sobre su historia y doctrina* (Buenos Aires: Ediciones Gure, 1957-59. 3 vols). For the later period, see Marcelo Luis Acuña, *De Frondizi a Alfonsín: la tradición política del radicalismo* (Buenos Aires: Centro Editor de América Latina, 1984. 2 vols). See also *Politics in Argentina, 1890-1930: the rise and fall of Radicalism.*

577 **Authoritarianism and the crisis of the Argentine political system.**
William C. Smith.   Stanford, California: Stanford University Press,
1989. 395p. bibliog.

A history of the political economy of Argentina since 1966 – how authoritarian régimes
have failed more spectacularly than civilian to reconcile economic modernization with
liberal democracy – focusing on the major protagonists: the armed forces, 'state
technocratic elites', the dominant industrial and agrarian sectors of the economy,
organized labour, revolutionary organizations and the political parties. He disagrees
with Guillermo O'Donnell's once-influential 'bureaucratic-authoritarianism' approach
(see *Bureaucratic authoritarianism: Argentina, 1966-1973, in comparative perspective*:
'the notion of a close correlation between economic phases and specific political
arrangements cannot be sustained'.

578 **Authoritarianism, fascism, and national populism.**
Gino Germani.   New Brunswick, New Jersey: Transaction Books,
1978. 292p.

An important study by a refugee from Italian fascism of the relationship between social
modernization and authoritarian régimes, a comparison of fascist Italy and Perón's
nationalist-populist régime. Italy manifested classical fascism, with the 'demobilization'
of the lower classes and the middle classes becoming the mass base for the fascist
movement; by contrast, Perón's national populism was founded upon the mass of
labourers who had recently migrated to the cities, while at the same time retaining
some of the middle sectors – union leaders, military officers and industrialists – to
implement his worker mobilization. Germani's theories were fashionable in the 1970s
but his emphasis on internal migration has since been largely discredited by social and
political historians.

579 **Elecciones y partidos políticos en la Argentina: historia, interpretación y
balance, 1910-1966.** (Elections and political parties in Argentina:
history, performance and interpretation, 1910-1966.)
Darío Cantón.   Buenos Aires: Siglo XXI, 1973. 277p. (Sociología y
Política).

An evaluation, with thirty-eight tables, of the country's electoral history after the
Sáenz Peña law of 1912 providing for compulsory male suffrage. Analyses the
proportion of votes recorded in the various electoral districts, political tendencies at
the national and local levels, the percentage of votes cast for each of the parties, the
class base of Peronist and Radical supporters and the factionalism of the Peronist and
Radical parties. Cantón drew heavily on his 1968 *Materiales para el estudio de la
sociología política en la Argentina*, while acknowledging some of its errors.

580 **Historia crítica de los partidos políticos argentinos.** (A critical history of
the political parties of Argentina.)
Rodolfo Puiggrós.   Buenos Aires: Ediciones Corregidor, 1972. 5 vols.

Both a political history of the period, 1890-1945, and a political-party history, by a
Marxist historian, with footnotes but no bibliography. See also Leonardo Paso,
*Historia del origen de los partidos políticos en la Argentina (1810-1918)* (Buenos Aires:

Ediciones 'Centro de Estudios', 1972. 518p.), continued by *Historia de los partidos políticos en la Argentina (1900-1930)* (Buenos Aires: Ediciones Directa, 1983. 574p.).

581 **Los que mandan. (Those who rule.)**
José Luis de Imaz, translated and with an introduction by Carlos A. Astiz, with Mary F. McCarthy. Albany, New York: State University of New York Press, 1970. 279p.

A classic sociological study of the family, educational background and careers of members of Argentina's 'power elites', written for an Argentine readership and originally published in 1964. Presidents, governors and cabinet ministers, political leaders, administrators, the armed forces, large landowners, industrialists, the Church, professional politicians, and union leaders are scrutinized. He concludes that there is no ruling élite, 'even though there are always many individuals who "command"'.

582 **Modernization and bureaucratic-authoritarianism: studies in South American politics.**
Guillermo A. O'Donnell. Berkeley, California: University of California, Institute of International Studies, 1973. 219p. bibliog. (Politics of Modernization Series, 9).

A pioneering work examining the relationship between social and economic modernization and political change, with case-studies of Brazil (where the author had lived) and Argentina after the Second World War. He rejects the theory that democratic politics accompanies modernization in late-industrializing countries and presents his own, now debatable, hypothesis that in Brazil (1964) and Argentina (1966) the military's coalition with industrialists in economic policy formulation ruled out consensus politics. He developed the 'bureaucratic-authoritarian' thesis in his analysis of the following period; see *Bureaucratic authoritarianism: Argentina, 1966-1973, in comparative perspective*.

583 **Parties and power in modern Argentina (1930-1946).**
Alberto Ciria, translated by Carlos A. Astiz with Mary F. McCarthy. Albany, New York: State University of New York Press, 1974. 357p.

A Marxist analysis of the political events of the period (Uriburu to Perón) together with their chief protagonists: political parties, the Church, the military, economic interest groups and the labour movement. Consists of lengthy excerpts from the works of other analysts held together by the author's critical comments.

584 **Party competition in Argentina and Chile: political recruitment and public policy, 1890-1930.**
Karen L. Remmer. Lincoln, Nebraska; London: University of Nebraska Press, 1984. 296p. bibliog.

A convincing politico-historical study of Chile (1891-1924) and Argentina during the Radical era of 1912-30, comparing each country's political leaders and their social backgrounds, party competition, degree of political participation and economic and social-welfare legislation. Chilean politicians remained upper-class, whereas in Argentina party competition resulted in politicians' being drawn increasingly from middle- and lower-class backgrounds; this led to a much broader base of popular support for their parties than in Chile. Well researched and carefully annotated with a large number of detailed statistical tables.

585 **The Peronist Left, 1955-1975.**
Daniel James. *Journal of Latin American Studies*, vol. 8, no. 2 (Nov. 1976), p. 273-96.
After the removal of Perón from power in 1955, 'a "left" emerged . . . as the defender of the working class, anti-capitalist strain of Peronism, looking back to the euphoria of October 1945 and the organization and advances of the working class in the first Peronist government'. The three main elements of this movement were the 'combative' unions (*combativos*), successors to the hard-line (*línea dura*) unions of the 1958-62 Frondizi period and opposed to the 1966-73 military governments; revolutionary Peronism, confined to small marginalized groups; the Peronist Youth (*Juventud Peronista*) strain of revolutionary Peronism, and the guerrilla groups, especially the Montoneros.

586 **The political elite in Argentina.**
Julio A. Fernández. New York: New York University Press, 1970. 133p. bibliog.
Biographical information and a questionnaire survey of 782 major office-holders (the executive, members of Congress and state governors) in the 1958 and 1963 administrations formed the basis for this study of the recruitment and attitudes of the 'political elite'. The political élite is found to be recruited from a wide range of professions and from all regions of the country. While a good education helps, previous political experience is more important. A study of the social background and recruitment of candidates for the legislature and governorship of Mendoza province is Richard Robert Strout, *The recruitment of candidates in Mendoza Province, Argentina* (Chapel Hill, North Carolina: University of North Carolina Press, 1968. 159p.).

587 **Political forces in Argentina.**
Peter G. Snow. New York; London: Praeger, 1979. rev. ed. 166p. map.
Written expressly for undergraduate teaching, this has become a classic history and analysis of the political parties and their electoral support; the armed forces (recruitment, factionalism, the causes of military coups); the labour movement; the Church (Church–state relations, Christian Democrats, Catholic Nationalists, the Catholic left); and students and politics.

588 **The Socialist Party of Argentina, 1890-1930.**
Richard J. Walter. Austin, Texas: University of Texas Press, 1977. 284p. map. bibliog. (Institute of Latin American Studies. Monographs, no. 42).
A descriptive and chronological study of the role of the Partido Socialista in national politics during its most successful period, concentrating on the city of Buenos Aires, where 'the party originated, organized, and enjoyed its greatest strength' and where, between 1912 and 1930, the Socialist and Radical parties were the two main competitors for political office. The book surveys this electoral battle, the principal Socialist leaders (middle-class like their supporters), schisms within the party and its failure to win consistent popular support. The conclusion includes a summary of the party's history after 1930. Since 1955 the party 'has not been able to re-establish

contact with the working class, which has remained firmly Peronist in sympathy and orientation'.

589 **Soldiers of Perón: Argentina's Montoneros.**
Richard Gillespie. Oxford: Clarendon Press; New York: Oxford University Press, 1982. 310p. map. bibliog.

Among the many terrorist groups which sprang up in Argentina in the 1970s, the Montoneros were not only the best known and most numerous but also had the clearest affiliation to Peronism and attachment to its leader. Indeed, the exiled Perón positively encouraged their violent activities, targeted against military personnel, many of whom were assassinated, and businessmen held to ransom. The group first achieved notoriety in 1970 with the abduction and murder of former acting president Pedro Aramburu. But on his return to power in 1973, Perón effectively turned to the right and disavowed his left-wing army which ironically had started out as right-wing Catholic. The merit of this book lies in the author's use of rare sources, including interviews with Montonero leaders, and his comprehensive knowledge of their literature. However, dispassionate readers will soon detect where the author's sympathies lie, despite his protestations of impartiality; see the valuable review and commentary by Celia Szusterman, *Journal of Latin American Studies*, vol. 16, no. 1 (May 1984), p. 157-70.

590 **El voto peronista: ensayos de sociología electoral argentina.** (The Peronist vote: essays in Argentine electoral sociology.)
Edited by Manuel Mora y Araujo, Ignacio Llorente. Buenos Aires: Sudamericana, 1980. 524p. maps. bibliog. (Colección Historia y Sociedad).

An important collection of essays on the social base of electoral support for Peronism (1946-55 and 1973-75), by Argentine and United States scholars: pioneering articles by Peter H. Smith and Gino Germani, criticisms of Germani by Smith, Eldon Kenworthy and Tulio Halperín Donghi, and further chapters by José Luis de Imaz, Manuel Mora y Araujo and Ignacio Llorente. Many are reprinted from the key Argentine journal *Desarrollo Económico*. A detailed statistical survey of voting patterns in Peronist-dominated elections, 1946-73 is *The populist challenge: Argentine electoral behavior in the postwar era*, by Lars Schoultz (Chapel Hill, North Carolina; London: University of North Carolina Press, 1983. 141p.). See also Walter Little, 'The electoral aspects of Peronism, 1946-1954', *Journal of Interamerican Studies and World Affairs*, vol. 15, no. 3 (Aug. 1973), p. 267-84.

**Politics in Argentina, 1890-1930: the rise and fall of Radicalism.**
*See* item no. 297.

**The Province of Buenos Aires and Argentine politics, 1912-1943.**
*See* item no. 298.

**Political parties of the Americas.**
*See* item no. 1281.

# Demilitarization and democracy, 1976-

**591 Argentina hoy.** (Argentina today.)
Compiled by Alain Rouquié. Buenos Aires: Siglo Veintiuno, 1982.
279p. bibliog. (Historia Inmediata).

Seven essays analysing Argentina from Perón's last presidency to the military régime 1976-80: Rouquié on economic stagnation as a cause of military intervention; Ricardo Sidicaro on landowners and agricultural exports; Aldo Ferrer on the economy and Francisco Delich on the labour movement since 1976; Silvia Segal and Eliseo Verón comparing Perón's political doctrines in the 1940s and 1970s; German sociologist Peter Waldmann on guerrilla violence; and the Uruguayan writer Angel Rama on the state of culture in the political climate.

**592 Argentina: the state of transition, 1983-85.**
Andrew Graham-Yooll. *Third World Quarterly*, vol. 7, no. 3 (July 1985), p. 573-93.

A challenging view of Argentine politics and society during the last two decades, focusing on the transition from military to democratic rule – the military, the political parties, the guerrilla groups of the 1970s, human rights and the Falklands War. The author is cautious about the future, warning of Argentina's lack of community spirit. The armed forces 'have become the dominant political party in all but name and are accepted as such by civilians'. Those same civilians are fickle, and 'demand most and offer the least'.

**593 The Argentine elections of 30 October 1983.**
Joe Foweraker. *Electoral Studies*, vol. 3, no. 1 (1984), p. 107-12.

Describes the background, parties, campaign and results of the election in which Raúl Alfonsín and the Radical Party won an absolute majority (52 per cent, Peronists 40 per cent, with a large turnout of 82 per cent of voters). He reminds us that, just two months before the election, the Peronists were still expected to win; however, 'they carried the weight of the past with them'. Equally useful is Torcuato S. di Tella, 'The October 1983 elections in Argentina', *Government and Opposition*, vol. 19, no. 2 (spring 1984), p. 188-92, which focuses on the reasons for the Peronist defeat.

**594 The Argentine process of demilitarization, 1980-83.**
Guillermo Makin. *Government and Politics*, vol. 19, no. 2 (spring 1984), p. 225-38.

The author looks back to 1930 for the causes of the recent militarization of Argentine politics and then studies the reforms forced upon the armed forces after their defeat in the Falklands War, the simultaneous strengthening of the political parties, and the fresh political attitudes ushered in by the calling of elections in 1983. He states optimistically, 'too much has changed since the last coup to make another probable' and 'the weakness of the political parties has been replaced by a much-improved bi-partisan system'.

595 **Democratization and demilitarization in Argentina, 1982-1985.**
Ronaldo Munck. *Bulletin of Latin American Research*, vol. 4, no. 2 (1985), p. 85-93.
In 1983, newly elected President Raúl Alfonsín faced formidable obstacles: one of the worst economic crises the country had ever known, a 'political system deeply altered by the historic defeat of Peronism' and the shadow cast by the memory of the military régime. When he failed to turn round the economy public euphoria quickly changed to disillusionment. The author, who writes in a polemical style, regrets that the 'bulk of the left-wing intelligentsia . . . has jumped onto the Radical bandwagon', and he predicts a growing role for the working class and the trades unions in the unfolding process of democratization.

596 **The fall of the Argentine military.**
George Philip. *Third World Quarterly*, vol. 6, no. 3 (July 1984), p. 624-37.
Reviews the history of military regimes since 1930 before analysing the period since 1976: the 'relatively liberal' Generals Videla and Viola, Galtieri and the fall of the régime, Bignone (chosen deliberately by the armed forces since he had 'no military-political base of his own to preside over a retreat from power'), the October 1983 elections, and prospects for the future. The military 'did in fact move with some political sophistication and their departure from power was comparatively well managed'.

597 **From military rule to liberal democracy in Argentina.**
Edited by Mónica Peralta Ramos, Carlos H. Waisman. Boulder, Colorado; London: Westview Press, 1987. 175p.
A collection of conference papers presented at the University of California, San Diego in February 1984, some revised during 1985, which discusses 'economic, political, and cultural aspects of the transition, from different disciplinary perspectives and theoretical orientations', and concentrates on changes under the military régime rather than during Alfonsín's administration. In part one, the editors, Juan Villarreal, Michael Monteón and David Rock deal with politics and the economy, 1976-83; four papers in part two deal with politics and culture (Juan E. Corradi, Julie M. Taylor, Noé Jitrik and Hector J. Sussman – the last is an interesting explanation of Argentina's failure to promote scientific research and technical innovation during the period).

598 **The land that lost its heroes: the Falklands, the post-war and Alfonsín.**
Jimmy Burns. London: Bloomsbury, 1987. 287p. bibliog.
The author was Argentine correspondent of the London *Financial Times* from early 1982 to 1986. He gives a lively account of the mood of the country during the Falklands ('the people's') War, the junta's behind-the-scenes planning, the inadequate reactions of British diplomacy and intelligence, Alfonsín's rise to power and the new 'democracy at work' (human-rights trials, debt problem, political parties, Church, labour movement). There is a valuable chapter on 'culture's re-birth' (publishing, theatre and cinema).

599 **Latin American Weekly Report.**
London: Latin American Newsletters Ltd, 1979- . weekly.
The best English-language source for current political and economic information on Argentina. It continues *Latin America* (1967-77) and *Latin American Political Report* (1977-79). For economic data and comment, see the same publisher's monthly *Latin American Economy & Business* (Oct. 1990- ), which continues *Latin American Economic Report* (1973-79, 1985-90). These should be supplemented by the monthly political and economic content of *Latin American Regional Reports: Southern Cone* (1979- , ten issues a year) and (from a different publisher) *Latin American Monitor: Southern Cone* (London: Latin American Monitor, 1984- ). Also useful is *El Bimestre Político y Económico* (Buenos Aires: Centro de Investigaciones Sociales sobre el Estado y la Administración, 1982- . five or six issues a year). Each issue contains a two-month chronology of events compiled from current Argentine newspapers and magazines – for example, the August 1990 number reviews the months of May and June – with short articles and commentaries on topical issues. The publishers have recently announced that it may be ceasing publication. Detailed assessments in English of the new Menem administration are now beginning to appear; the first is Torcuato S. di Tella, 'Menem's Argentina', *Government and Opposition*, vol. 25, no. 1 (winter 1990), p. 85-97.

600 **Political transition in Argentina: 1982 to 1985.**
Virgilio R. Beltrán. *Armed Forces and Society*, vol. 13, no. 2 (winter 1987), p. 215-33.
Chronicles the fall of the military government, the 1983 elections, the Radical government's relations with the armed forces (their budget was reduced from 4.2 per cent of GNP in 1978-83 to 2.4 per cent in 1985), the human-rights trials and the government's economic difficulties. See also David Pion-Berlin, *The ideology of state terror: economic doctrine and political repression in Argentina and Peru* (Boulder, Colorado; London: Lynne Rienner, 1989. 227p.), which focuses on 1976-83.

# The military

601 **Argentina: the authoritarian impasse.**
Guillermo Makin. In: *The political dilemma of military regimes*. Edited by Christopher Clapham, George Philip. London; Sydney: Croom Helm, 1985, p. 151-69.
Focuses on the military interventions of 1966 and 1976, with a preliminary essay on the political role of the armed forces since 1890 and a discussion of O'Donnell's theory of bureaucratic-authoritarianism (q.v.). The military régimes of 1955-59 and 1962-63 'may be regarded as attempted Moderator régimes, at least in the sense that the military sought to hand over to civilian politicians untainted by the threat of Peronism', while the 1966-73 and 1976-83 régimes belong with the 'Veto category'. The author wonders whether 1983 heralded in a transient or permanent demilitarization.

602 **Armed forces of Latin America: their histories, development, present strength and military potential.**
Adrian J. English. London: Jane's, 1984. 490p. maps. bibliog.

The section on Argentina (p. 17-67) describes the general structure of the armed forces; the personnel, formations, major units and equipment of the army, navy and air force; paramilitary forces; sources of defence *matériel* supply and current requirements; defence production; and foreign influences. Also invaluable for defence analysts are the annual *The military balance* (London: International Institute for Strategic Studies) and *SIPRI yearbook: world armaments & disarmaments*, produced by the Stockholm International Peace Research Institute (Oxford: Oxford University Press).

603 **Arms production in developing countries: an analysis of decision making.**
Edited by James Everett Katz. Lexington, Massachusetts: Lexington Books, 1984. 370p.

The chapter on Argentina by Jacquelyn S. Porth (p. 53-72) analyses the role of Argentina's military in the context of the country's national-security and foreign-policy considerations, and then discusses the history of the arms industry and the present state of arms production and exports. See also Edward S. Milenky, 'Arms production and national security in Argentina', *Journal of Inter-American Studies and World Affairs*, vol. 22, no. 3 (Aug. 1980), p. 267-88.

604 **The army and politics in Argentina, 1945-1962: Perón to Frondizi.**
Robert A. Potash. Stanford, California: Stanford University Press; London: Athlone Press, 1980. 418p. bibliog.

A sequel to item 605 below, similarly based on an impressive range of sources, including over eighty interviews with leading figures, focusing on officers' personal rivalries and interservice relations, and the military's involvement in political developments. The first section is a masterly history of the Perón period and the book ends with the coup that deposed civilian President Frondizi in 1962. Both volumes have been best-sellers in Argentina.

605 **The army and politics in Argentina, 1928-1945: Yrigoyen to Perón.**
Robert A. Potash. Stanford, California: Stanford University Press, 1969. 314p. map. bibliog.

A major narrative history of the Argentine military, emphasizing the army as an institution and the role of the military in national political life, which should be read in conjunction with Rouquié's work (q.v.) which more successfully explores the latter. Potash expertly analyses the social origins, attitudes and 'role conceptions' of the officer corps (which doubled in size between 1930 and 1945), as well as its political factionalism and internal rifts. By the time of the 1943 coup, many officers 'adopted the view that the political parties were now incompetent and that only a military government could meet the problems of the day. The principal and ultimate beneficiary of this outlook was of course Colonel Juan D. Perón'. Continued by *The army and politics in Argentina, 1945-1962: Perón to Frondizi* (q.v.).

606   Civil-military relations in contemporary Argentina.
      Walter Little.   *Government and Opposition*, vol. 19, no. 2 (spring
      1984), p. 207-24.
Thirteen leading parties contested the 1983 national elections. This article analyses
those parties' attitudes and policies towards the armed forces. Each party's manifesto
declared that the military should be subordinate to civilian governments and their
security function defined; the parties' views on conscription, military expenditure and
the military's earlier human-rights violations are also examined.

607   Democracy, militarism, and nationalism in Argentina, 1930-1966: an
      interpretation.
      Marvin Goldwert.   Austin, Texas; London: University of Texas Press,
      1972. 253p. bibliog. (Institute of Latin American Studies. Latin
      American Monographs, 25).
An evaluation of the Argentine army's social and economic modernization policies. It
was torn between traditional and modern factions: 'integral' (authoritarian economic)
nationalists and 'liberal' nationalists (constitutional free-marketeers). Perón's brand of
popular integral nationalism attempted to 'reconcile social order and traditionalism
with modernization under authoritarian military rule'. The army withdrew its initial
support when the experiment failed and since then has been fiercely anti-Peronist.

608   Disunity and disorder: factional politics in the Argentine military.
      Philip B. Springer.   In: *The military intervenes: case studies in political
      development.*   Edited by Henry Bienen.   New York: Russell Sage
      Foundation, 1968, p. 145-68.
Describes conflicts between two factions of the Argentine army, September 1962 to
June 1966: the Azules ('Blues') and the Colorados ('Reds'). The Azules revolted
against the high command on three issues: they wanted to reduce the power of the
navy, then allied with the Colorados; they believed that the Colorados were destroying
military discipline and the army's hierarchical structure; and that the Colorados wanted
to instal a military dictatorship. After four days of fighting, the victorious Azul leader,
General Juan Carlos Onganía (later president, 1966-70), instigated a purge of the high
command. The author also analyses the social backgrounds of the leading figures: the
Azules were all upper-class cavalry officers, with traditional views on the army as the
'backbone of the nation'. A good discussion of the Azul–Colorado factionalism is also
contained in Charles D. Corbett, *The Latin American military as a socio-political force:
case studies of Bolivia and Argentina* (Miami, Florida: University of Miami, Center for
Advanced International Studies, 1972. 143p.).

609   European military influence in South America: the origins and nature of
      professional militarism in Argentina, Chile and Peru, 1890-1940.
      Frederick M. Nunn.   *Jahrbuch für Geschichte von Staat, Wirtschaft
      und Gesellschaft Lateinamerikas*, vol. 12 (1975), p. 230-52.
In all four countries, training by European (chiefly French and German) military
advisers resulted in the creation of a powerful interest group, the officer corps, and
'stimulation . . . of political interest, and motivation of elitist, professional army
officers to assume responsibility for the conduct of national affairs when they became
convinced that civilians were incapable'. See also George Pope Atkins, Larry V.

Thompson, 'German military influence in Argentina, 1921-1940', *Journal of Latin American Studies*, vol. 4, no. 2 (Nov. 1972), p. 257-74; and Warren Schiff, 'The influence of the German armed forces and war industry on Argentina, 1880-1914', *Hispanic American Historical Review*, vol. 52, no. 3 (Nov. 1972), p. 436-55.

610   **The military in South American politics.**
George Philip.   London: Croom Helm, 1985. 394p. bibliog.

Chapter ten, 'Military governments and military failures in Argentina' (p. 246-74), reviews the activities of the military during the 1966-83 period. '1966 marks a clear turning-point in Argentine history. It was the beginning of a deliberate attempt to impose a new pattern of politics by *dictat*.' The author analyses the social and economic factors which presented difficulties for military governments, and the military's in-built handicaps (inefficient military-run enterprises, insensitivity to 'those sections of civil society not entrenched in heavy bureaucratic organisations', and factional disunity).

611   **Military interventions in Argentina: 1900-1966.**
Darío Cantón.   In: *Military profession and military regimes: commitments and conflicts*.   Edited by Jacques Van Doorn.   The Hague; Paris: Mouton, 1969, p. 241-69.

The landed oligarchy was Argentina's leading élite until 1916, when the military took 'control of the mobilization of the people' and became in effect another oligarchy. The chapter discusses the professionalization of the military, the points of conflict and agreement between the military and the oligarchy, and the military revolts during the period (using the list compiled by Liisa North in her *Civil-military relations in Argentina, Chile and Peru* [Berkeley, California: University of California, Institute of International Studies, 1966. 86p.]. Cantón develops his thesis in *La política de los militares argentinos: 1900-1971* (Buenos Aires: Siglo XXI Editores, 1971. 161p.). Two articles which chart the number and types of military revolts (there were eighteen between 1930 and 1970) are: Gilbert W. Merkx, 'Recessions and rebellions in Argentina, 1870-1970', *Hispanic American Historical Review*, vol. 53, no. 2 (May 1973), p. 285-95; and Rosendo A. Gómez, 'Intervention in Argentina, 1860-1930', *Inter-American Economic Affairs*, vol. 1, no. 3 (Dec. 1947), p. 55-73.

612   **Poder militar y sociedad política en la Argentina.** (The military and politics in Argentina.)
Alain Rouquié, translated by Arturo Iglesias Echegaray.   Buenos Aires: Emecé, 1981-82. 2 vols.

Less strictly narrative than the other major work on the Argentine military, Potash's two volumes (qq.v.), Rouquié's is even more analytical of the army's internal relations, the ideologies of the officer corps, and the military's relations with the major social and economic groups. The military's view of itself as guardian of the state is contrasted with the failure of civilian administrations. This is a translation of *Pouvoir militaire et société politique en République Argentine* (Paris, 1978).

613 **The political economy of Latin American defense expenditures: case studies of Venezuela and Argentina.**
Robert E. Looney. Lexington, Massachusetts: Lexington Books, 1986. 325p. bibliog.

A comparison of Venezuela, a small military spender and minor arms producer, with Argentina, a major military force and a leading arms producer. The first two parts consist of a theoretical 'cross-sectional analysis' of defence spending by Latin American governments followed by the Venezuelan case-study. The section on Argentina occupies pages 209-308. Régime type in Argentina has 'a major impact on the amount and share of resources devoted to defense. Military regimes [between 1961 and 1982] consistently outspent their civilian counterparts on defense and increased the share of defense in the central government budget'. A difficult book because of its econometric-model approach. Two more straightforward analyses are David L. Feldman, 'Argentina, 1945-1971: military assistance, military spending, and the political activity of the Armed Forces', *Journal of Inter-American Studies and World Affairs*, vol. 24, no. 3 (Aug. 1982), p. 321-36; and Mario Esteban Carranza, 'The role of military expenditure in the development process: the Argentine case, 1946-1980', *Ibero Americana*, vol. 12, nos 1-2 (1983), p. 115-66.

# Human rights

614 **Argentina: the military juntas and human rights: report of the trial of the former junta members, 1985.**
London: Amnesty International, 1987. 94p.

Describes the trial before the civilian Federal Court of the nine members of the military juntas during the period 1975-82 when thousands of their opponents disappeared or were tortured and killed. The largest section is devoted to the oral public proceedings – prosecution and defence cases, verdict and sentence, appeals to the Supreme Court. Focusing on the aftermath of the trials is Marcel A. Sancinetti, *Derechos humanos en la Argentina postdictatorial* (Buenos Aires: Lerner, 1988. 344p.).

615 **Christ in a poncho: testimonials of the nonviolent struggles in Latin America.**
Adolfo Pérez Esquivel, edited by Charles Antoine, translated from the French by Robert R. Barr. Maryknoll, New York: Orbis Books, 1983. 139p. bibliog.

The introduction presents a profile of human-rights campaigner Pérez Esquivel. Part one ('The ant and the elephant') is autobiographical. Part two contains 'testimonies of nonviolence' in Argentina, Brazil, Ecuador and Paraguay. The Argentine examples are Pérez's brainchild, the Peace and Justice Service (Servicio Paz y Justicia en América Latina, a lay ecumenical organization working non-violently for basic human rights), and the Mothers of the Plaza de Mayo. The appendix includes his acceptance speech on being presented with the Nobel Peace Prize in 1980.

616 **The disappeared: voices from a secret war.**
John Simpson, Jana Bennett.    London: Robson Books; New York:
St. Martin's Press, 1985. 416p.

The best account in English of the 'dirty war' and the human-rights situation set against
the political and economic background, by two BBC correspondents. Includes a
number of case-studies (the most notorious being those of Jacobo Timerman [q.v.] and
Argentine-Swedish girl Dagmar Hagelin, abducted by mistake but who 'disappeared'
just the same), the Mothers of the Plaza de Mayo, the acquiescence of the Church,
censorship and the brave stand of the *Buenos Aires Herald*, the position of the United
States, the 1978 World Cup, the Falklands War, and criticism of the British Embassy
and successive British governments. An estimated 11,000 people 'disappeared' during
1976-83.

617 **Legal accountability for human rights violations in Argentina: one step
forward and two steps back.**
Alejandro M. Garro, Henry Dahl.    *Human Rights Law Journal*,
vol. 8, nos 2-4 (1987), p. 282-344.

Discusses the trial of the former junta members and the judgment of the Federal
Appeals Court which convicted them, and analyses 'the reversal of the trend [the so-
called 'Full Stop' and 'Due Obedience' laws], which condoned the actions of a huge
number of senior and junior military officers through what amounted to an amnesty for
the vast majority of culprits of the "dirty war"'. See also George C. Rogers,
'Argentina's obligation to prosecute military officials for torture', *Columbia Human
Rights Law Review*, vol. 20, no. 2 (spring 1989), p. 259-308.

618 **The little school: tales of disappearance & survival in Argentina.**
Alicia Portnoy, translated by Alicia Portnoy with Lois Athey and
Sandra Braunstein.    Pittsburgh, Pennsylvania; San Francisco: Cleis
Press, 1986. 136p.

The poignant yet unsensationalized story of one woman who was detained and tortured
by the army between January 1977 and early 1979. She recounts her experiences in
three detention camps (the book's title is taken from the second camp, nicknamed 'La
Escuelita'), her release due to the efforts of the OAS fact-finding mission (q.v.) and
exile in the United States, where she was reunited with her husband and young
daughter who had both also been taken away by the military.

619 **The making of human rights policy in Argentina: the impact of ideas and
interests on a legal conflict.**
Mark Osiel.    *Journal of Latin American Studies*, vol. 18, no. 1 (May
1986), p. 135-80.

Discusses the 1985 trial of the military juntas from the point of view of the chief
'political actors', each of whom had a different conception of the 'social and political
world': President Alfonsín, who tried to make political capital out of the trials; the
human-rights organizations (their 'very moralism and preoccupation with justice at all
costs had [deprived them] of much influence over policy'); and the military, concerned
to achieve the 'most effective way of keeping its members out of jail and fostering the
conditions for a prompt return to power'.

620 **The Mothers of Plaza de Mayo (Línea Fundadora): the story of Renée Epelbaum, 1976-1985.**
Marjorie Agosín, translated by Janice Malloy.  Stanford, Canada: Williams-Wallace, 1989. 121p. bibliog.
Renée Epelbaum's son was abducted in August 1976 as he left the medical school where he was soon to receive his degree in psychiatry (a profession disproportionately victimized during the 'dirty war'); she sent her two younger children to Uruguay for protection, but they were also abducted by a military commando unit. She became one of the founders of the Mothers of the Plaza de Mayo. This is her story as recounted to Marjorie Agosín, a Chilean poet.

621 **Mothers of the disappeared.**
Jo Fisher.  London: Zed Books; Boston, Massachusetts: South End Press, 1989. 168p. bibliog.
The definitive work on the Mothers of the Plaza de Mayo, based on interviews with over forty mothers (and grandmothers) of the disappeared, describing the formation of the organization, its members' varied backgrounds, how they became a formidable force of opposition to the military government, and their undiminished campaigning after the return to democratic rule and frequent criticism even of the Alfonsín administration and other human-rights groups. Another history of the Mothers by the *France-Presse* correspondent during the period is Jean-Pierre Bousquet, *Las locas de la Plaza de Mayo* (Buenos Aires: Fundación para la Democracia en Argentina / El Cid Editor, 1983. 192p.), translated from the French edition of 1982.

622 **Nunca más (never again): a report by Argentina's National Commission on Disappeared People.**
London; Boston, Massachusetts: Faber & Faber, in association with *Index on Censorship*, 1986. 463p.
The National Commission (Comisión Nacional sobre la Desaparición de Personas, CONADEP), also known as the Sábato Commission after its president, the novelist Ernesto Sábato, presented its finding to President Raúl Alfonsín in September 1984. The report consists chiefly (p. 9-385) of testimonies of victims of abduction and torture, and an appraisal of the judiciary during the repression ('the judicial process became almost inoperative as a means of appeal').

623 **Prisoner without a name, cell without a number.**
Jacobo Timerman, translated by Toby Talbot.  New York: Random House, 1980; London: Weidenfeld & Nicolson, 1981. 164p.
Timerman, the Ukrainian-born Jewish publisher/editor of the Buenos Aires daily *La Opinión* which published lists of the disappeared during the 1970s, was arrested by army extremists in April 1977 and held under solitary confinement and house arrest, with periods of torture, for thirty months. His book describes his life and career and, most famously, his ordeal in the clandestine camp known as COT 1 [Tactical Operations Centre] Martínez. His case won international notoriety and he was eventually released and flown to Israel. He is critical of the too-cautious stance of the Argentine-Jewish community towards the human-rights situation.

624 **Report of an Amnesty International mission to Argentina, 6-15 November 1976.**
London: Amnesty International, 1977. 92p.

Political violence increased with the overthrow of the government of María Estela Martínez de Perón in March 1976. A three-man delegation headed by Lord Avebury visited the country to investigate cases of abduction, torture and murder; it was 'severely intimidated and harassed'. The bulk of the report reproduces evidence from prisoners and relatives of missing persons. An appendix lists the names of disappeared persons since March 1976. An enlarged list of the disappeared was issued in 1980: *The 'disappeared' of Argentina: list of cases reported to Amnesty International, November 1974–December 1979*. 136p. (and supplement, 1982). The first-hand accounts of two prisoners in secret detention camps in Buenos Aires are contained in *Testimony on secret detention camps in Argentina* (Amnesty International, 1980. 63p.). Some of the first-hand published accounts of torture are examined in 'Rituals of the modern state: the case of torture in Argentina' by Steven Gregory and Daniel Timerman, *Dialectical Anthropology*, vol. 11, no. 1 (1986), p. 63-72.

625 **Report on the situation of human rights in Argentina.**
Organization of American States, Inter-American Commission on Human Rights. Washington, DC: Organization of American States, General Secretariat, 1980. 294p. (OEA/Ser.L/V/II.49, doc.19, corr.1).

The Commission visited Argentina in September 1979 and interviewed major political, legal and Church figures (including President Videla and his ministers), army and police officers, human-rights organizations, political, professional and labour organizations, and others. The report details instances of 'serious violations of fundamental human rights', but notes that the number of violations decreased after the Commission's visit.

# Constitution and Law

## Constitution

626 **Argentine constitutional history, 1810-1852: a re-examination.**
Joseph T. Criscenti. *Hispanic American Historical Review*, vol. 41,
no. 3 (Aug. 1961), p. 367-412.
A study of political developments and thwarted attempts at constitutional organization
of the Argentine provinces from 1810 – when, having set in train the wars of
independence, these provinces were divided 'by disagreement over their political
future' – to the eventual drafting of the Constitution of 1853.

627 **Argentine constitutional law: the judicial function in the maintenance of
the federal system and the preservation of individual rights.**
Santos Primo Amadeo. New York: Columbia University Press, 1943.
243p. bibliog. (Columbia University. Faculty of Law. Columbia Legal
Studies, 4).
Examines features of Argentine constitutional law 'with special reference to the
role of the judicial department in the maintenance of the federal system and the
protection of human rights'. Part one analyses the making of the 1853 Constitution,
influenced by the United States Constitution of 1787; part two contains an important
chapter on the relationship between the federal government and the provinces,
including various cases of provincial 'intervention' by the federal government; part
three considers the Constitution's provisions for the protection of the individual.

628 **The Argentine constitutional revision of 1949.**
Lucretia L. Ilsley. *Journal of Politics*, vol. 14, no. 2 (May 1952),
p. 224-40.
In 1949 President Perón revised the 1853 Constitution, with the justification that 'only
by constant revision could the benefits which had accrued to the masses since the
revolution of 1943 be carried on effectively'. The article describes the circumstances

leading to the revision and points out the main amendments. This 'Constitución Justicialista' was annulled by President Aramburu in 1956 and the 1853 Constitution reinstated.

629 **Las constituciones de la Argentina (1810-1972).** (The constitutions of Argentina, 1810-1972.)
Compiled, with notes and preliminary study by Arturo Enrique Sampay. Buenos Aires: Editorial Universitaria de Buenos Aires, 1975. 661p.

An introductory essay on the constitutional evolution of the country (p. 1-77) is followed by thirty-seven historic constitutional texts, beginning with the 'Reglamento de la Junta Gubernativa (25 de mayo de 1810)'. Similarly, Faustino J. Legón and Samuel W. Medrano's *Las constituciones de la República Argentina* (Madrid: Ediciones Cultura Hispánica, 1953. 527p.), has a good preface (p. 1-191) to the texts of twenty-six constitutional and organic laws, 1811-1949.

630 **Constitutions of the countries of the world.**
Edited by Albert P. Blaustein, Gisbert H. Flanz. Dobbs Ferry, New York: Oceana Publications, 1970- . bibliog.

Volume one of this regularly updated manual contains the English text of the 110 articles of the Argentine Constitution, 'sanctioned by the Gen. Constitutent Congress on May 1, 1853, as amended and coordinated by the Ad Hoc National Convention on September 25, 1860; and with the amendments made by Conventions of 1866, 1898, and 1957'. Since the Alfonsín administration in 1983 returned essentially to the principles of the 1853 Constitution while making some small changes to its electoral provisions, the translation used here is that by Fortunata Calvo Roth, reprinted from the Pan American Union edition of 1968. Also included are a historical chronology of constitutional developments by Christian García-Godoy, and the text of the 'statute for the process of national reorganization' (1978).

631 **Historia constitucional argentina.** (A constitutional history of Argentina.)
José Rafael López Rosas, prologue by Germán J. Bidart Campos. Buenos Aires: Editorial Astrea, 1977. rev. ed. 707p.

An impartial political history of constitutional law, with an emphasis on the nineteenth century. The author contends that the 1853 Constitution owes little to foreign models and sympathizes with the federalist strain in Argentine history.

632 **Historia constitucional de la República Argentina.** (A constitutional history of Argentina.)
Emilio Ravignani. Buenos Aires: J. Peuser, 1926-30. 3 vols. bibliog.

A classic work on constitutional development, devoted almost entirely to the early nineteenth century, by a noted historian and Radical politician who taught constitutional history at the University of La Plata. His six-volume *Asambleas constituyentes argentinas* (published 1937-40) contains the texts of constitutions together with his commentaries.

633 **Historia de la constitución argentina.** (A history of the Argentine constitution.)
Julio B. Lafont.   Buenos Aires: Editorial F.V.D., 1953. 3rd ed. 2 vols. bibliog.

An important constitutional history to 1880, well documented and with a good bibliography. The appendices to each volume reproduce important historical documents.

634 **Historia institucional argentina.** (An institutional history of Argentina.)
Carlos Sánchez Viamonte.   Mexico City: Fondo de Cultura Económica, 1957. 2nd ed. 229p. (Colección Tierra Firme, 39).

A well-documented history which quotes extensively from contemporary sources – constitutions, government declarations, debates, and the like. There is no general bibliography but the footnotes are detailed.

635 **Historia política y constitucional argentina.** (A constitutional and political history of Argentina.)
Germán José Bidart Campos.   Buenos Aires: EDIAR, 1976. 2 vols. bibliog.

An impressively documented work (the footnotes occupy about a third of the text) covering 1810-1976, written from a traditional 'liberal' and anti-Marxist viewpoint. Volume one, 1810-53, combines straightforward narrative with analysis and is concerned mostly with constitutional developments. Volume two is almost entirely descriptive and stresses political rather than constitutional history.

# Law

636 **American-Argentine private international law.**
Werner Goldschmidt, José Rodríguez-Novás.   Dobbs Ferry, New York: Oceana Publications, published for the Parker School of Foreign and Comparative Law, Columbia University, 1966. 117p. (Bilateral Studies in Private International Law, 15).

A detailed handbook of Argentine private international law and its application under international treaties, specifically with the United States. Chapters are organized under: nationality and domicile, procedure, contracts and other juridical acts, family law, succession and commercial law.

637 **Argentina: adjustment for inflation in Argentine income tax law.**
Jorge Macón.   *Bulletin for International Fiscal Documentation*, vol. 35 (July 1981), p. 295-300.

Describes the methods by which the Argentine tax system has been modified to account for persistently high inflation; 'in doing so it was realized that traditional tax systems are based on the implicit assumption that price levels are stable'. Before 1960

177

income tax laws were rooted in the valuation of capital goods; after 1960 so-called 'price level accounting' and then 'working capital' approaches were applied.

638  **Argentina: divorce at last!**
Mario J. Bendersky.  *Journal of Family Law*, vol. 27, no. 1 (1988-89), p. 1-5.

Describes the provisions and implications of Law No. 23.515 (promulgated 8 June 1987) which legalized divorce in Argentina. Until the enactment of the new law, judicial separation was the only alternative to full divorce; the new law preserved judicial separation but now it could be changed to divorce *ad vinculum* by decision of either or both of the parties. No fewer than fourteen divorce bills were presented before Congress between 1900 and 1954, when Perón introduced absolute-divorce Law 14,394. The law was suspended fourteen months later, after Perón's overthrow. See Donald A. Wiesner, 'Enactment and suspension of absolute divorce in Argentina', *American Journal of Comparative Law*, vol. 9, no. 1 (1960), p. 94-104.

639  **Argentine laws on foreign investments and the transfer of technology.**
Fernando C. Aranovich, John Hewko.  *International Lawyer*, vol. 21, no. 2 (spring 1987), p. 379-96.

An analysis of the provisions of the Argentine Foreign Investments Law (1976) and the Transfer of Technology Law (1981), which ended the previously too-restrictive practices governing both areas. For another view of the investments law, see Ricardo Giacchino, 'Foreign investment under contemporary Argentine law', *American Journal of Comparative Law*, vol. 26, no. 1 (winter 1978), p. 91-101.

640  **The Argentine penal code.**
With an introduction by Ricardo Levene, translated by Emilio González-López, guest editor Frederick W. Danforth, Jr.  South Hackensack, New Jersey: Fred B. Rothman; London: Sweet & Maxwell, 1963. 114p. (American Series of Foreign Penal Codes, 6).

The brief introduction (p. 1-16) gives an account of the history of criminal studies in Argentina and describes the history of the criminal code and its salient features. The English text of the 306 articles of the complete code is then given: general provisions and provisions relating to twelve particular crimes, with an appendix of penal laws relating to minors.

641  **The Argentine Supreme Court: the court of constitutional guarantees.**
Germán José Bidart Campos, translated by William J. Brisk.  Buenos Aires: Allende & Brea, 1982. 143p.

The Corte Suprema de Justicia de la Nación is Argentina's highest court, often called the 'court of constitutional guarantees', denoting its 'role in protecting the individual against governmental abuse'. The text describes the history and workings of the court in relation to Argentine constitutional law. 'One of the most glaring deficiencies in the Court's performance is its characterization of many issues as "political" and therefore non-justiciable.' The Court recognized the military junta after the coup of 1943 but was purged when it became apparent 'that the judiciary would not tolerate the arbitrary governing tactics of the army officers'. See Alan T. Leonhard, 'The 1946 purge of the

Argentine Supreme Court of Justice', *Inter-American Economic Affairs*, vol. 17, no. 4 (spring 1964), p. 73.

642 **Commercial arbitration in Argentina.**
Alejandro E. Fargosi, translated by Alejandro M. Garro. *University of Miami Inter-American Law Review*, vol. 20, no. 3 (summer 1989), p. 687-95.
Commercial arbitration is governed by the codes of civil and commercial procedure promulgated by each province and applied by the federal courts. This is a discussion of the law of arbitration according to the Federal Code of Civil and Commercial Procedure: voluntary and compulsory arbitration, the arbitration process (the parties in dispute, tribunal, award, appeal and enforcement), and arbitration in the Stock Exchange. 'The economic and business reality of Argentina is partially responsible for the infrequent use of arbitration.'

643 **Enciclopedia jurídica OMEBA.** (OMEBA law encyclopaedia.)
Edited by Manuel Essorio y Florit, Carlos R. Obal, Alfredo Bitbol.
Buenos Aires: Editorial Bibliográfica OMEBA, 1954-76. 26 vols.
bibliog.
A comprehensive, well-documented encyclopaedia of international and Argentine law, updated by supplements.

644 **The evolution of petroleum contracts in Argentina – issues of the foreign investor's legal protection.**
Wolfgang J. Müller, Thomas G. Stern. *Journal of Energy & Natural Resources Law*, vol. 7 (1989), p. 189-230. bibliog.
Argentina has frequently changed its energy policy and this has had 'various impacts on the development of contracts'. Considers sixteen petroleum contracts, concluded 1958-87 between the state oil company, Yacimientos Petrolíferos Fiscales, and foreign investors or investor consortia, sometimes with the participation of private Argentine companies. The contracts were for drilling, development, or a combination of exploration and development.

645 **Historia del derecho argentino.** (A history of Argentine law.)
Ricardo Levene. Buenos Aires: Guillermo Kraft, 1945-58. 11 vols.
A monumental history, by one of Argentina's most distinguished historians, of legal and constitutional developments from pre-Columbian times to the Constitution of 1853. It includes the texts of historic documents. A digest, *Manual de historia del derecho argentino*, was first published in 1952 and has seen several later editions.

646 **International encyclopaedia for labour law and industrial relations.**
Edited by R. Blanpain. Deventer, Netherlands: Kluwer, 1977- .
A loose-leaf encyclopaedia, updated regularly. Volume two, 'Labour law', contains a chapter on Argentina (174p.) by A. J. Ruprecht, rewritten by Monica Smith, current to January 1984. In two sections: individual and collective labour relations.

647 **The law and practice of labor arbitration in Argentina.**
Máximo Daniel Monzón, Juan Manuel Salas. *University of Miami Inter-American Law Review*, vol. 21, no. 1 (fall 1989), p. 185-96.

Describes and comments on the laws regulating labour arbitration: the conciliation process ('replete with ambiguities'), arbitration laws (civil and commercial codes), arbitration of individual labour disputes, and the voluntary and compulsory arbitration of collective labour disputes. The author notes that the compulsory arbitration of collective labour disputes has rarely been resorted to.

648 **Lower-class families, women, and the law in nineteenth-century Argentina.**
Donna J. Guy. *Journal of Family History*, vol. 10, no. 3 (fall 1985), p. 318-31. bibliog.

Examines the origins of *patria potestad*, the traditional legal rights which 'élite' male heads of family exercised over wives, children and family employees; nineteenth-century labour legislation (when the state 'chose to regulate the labor market and recruit men for military service and women for public service or domestic employment', poor male family heads lost the right to control their family labour); and the commercial and civil codes. The state did not enact marriage legislation until 1888 or universal military conscription until 1901, but 'it had long been intervening in family matters related to work'; this did not essentially alter the regional impact of family labour 'because it allowed provinces to define work related ordinances'.

649 **The new Argentine antitrust law: competition as an economic policy instrument.**
Guillermo Cabanellas, Wolf Etzrodt. *Journal of World Trade Law*, vol. 17, no. 1 (Jan.-Feb. 1983), p. 34-53.

Argentina has had antitrust legislation for several decades but it had very limited practical application. This is a description of the new Antitrust Law (Ley de Defensa de la Competencia) of August 1980, which forms 'part of a general scheme devised to enhance competition through a more flexible import tariff policy and a lower participation of the public sector in the economy'. Related to this law is the 1981 Transfer of Technology Law (see *Argentine laws on foreign investments and the transfer of technology*).

650 **La organización judicial argentina en el período hispánico.**
(The organization of justice in colonial Argentina.)
Ricardo Zorraquín Becú. Buenos Aires: Editorial Perrot, 1981. 2nd ed. 219p. (Universidad de Buenos Aires. Facultad de Derecho y Ciencias Sociales. Instituto de Historia del Derecho Ricardo Levene. Colección de Estudios para la Historia del Derecho Argentino, 12).

Analyses the development, functions and effectiveness of the various administrative and ecclesiastical law tribunals which operated during the colonial era. It includes good name and subject indexes. The same author published a classic general history of Argentine law: *Historia del derecho argentino* (Buenos Aires: Editorial Perrot, 1966-69. 2 vols).

651 **Repertorio de legislación argentina, años 1862-1970: leyes y decretos nacionales. Actualizados hasta diciembre de 1970.** (Index to Argentine legislation, 1862-1970: national laws and decrees. Updated to December 1970.)
Buenos Aires: Revista de Jurisprudencia Argentina, 1972. 2 vols.
Volume one is a chronological listing of national laws. Volume two groups them by subject. For each law, full volume and page references are given for the location of the full text in the official *Anuario de Legislación* (1853-1970) and in the professional journals *Jurisprudencia Argentina* (1918- ) and *Anales de Legislación Argentina* (1941- ).

652 **The right to choose a name.**
Phanor J. Eder. *American Journal of Comparative Law*, vol. 8, no. 4 (1959), p. 502-7.
According to Argentine law, civil registrars are 'prohibited from inscribing births of persons with first names not expressed in Spanish or not appearing in the calendar or among the names of the Fathers of the Independence'. Describes three cases from 1957 and 1959 in which the fathers had given their children their own first names: 'Zadit' Báez Castro, 'Kirk' Moore and 'Malcolm' King. The Attorney General argued that the free choice of a name was not unconstitutional, but his decisions were overturned by the Supreme Court. The law is still applied, but more flexibly.

653 **A statement of the laws of Argentina in matters affecting business.**
Raúl C. Sanguinetti. Washington, DC: Organization of American States, General Secretariat, 1975. 4th ed. 303p. bibliog.
One in a series providing businessmen, lawyers and others with a summary of the country's basic legislation currently in force. The fourth edition contains extracts from the Constitution and the statutory and regulatory provisions governing forty-two categories of activity, from nationality to fishing. Emphasis is given to commercial, industrial and labour law. A translation of the laws as they applied in the early 1930s is J. A. and E. de Marval (et al.), *Laws of Argentina: with regulations and recent amendments to the commercial code and copyright law* (Buenos Aires: J. A. & E. de Marval, 1933. 1244p.).

# Administration and Local Government

654 **Breve historia del parlamento argentino.** (A brief history of the
Argentine parliament.)
Enrique Bugatti. Buenos Aires: Alzamor Editores, 1974. 220p.
bibliog. (Colección del Alba, vol. 2).

A rather superficial chronological history of the parliaments of the various national
administrations between 1813 and 1974, useful for the gallery of names of key
personalities scattered throughout the text (there is a detailed name index at the back).

655 **The bureaucrats of Buenos Aires, 1769-1810: amor al real servicio.**
Susan Migden Socolow. Durham, North Carolina; London: Duke
University Press, 1987. 356p. bibliog.

A scholarly treatment of the colonial Argentine civil service, its methods of
recruitment and appointment, patterns of advancement, salaries and retirement
benefits. One chapter scrutinizes the bureaucrats' social and family relationships, and
an appendix gives the genealogies of four selected bureaucratic 'clans'. The principal
bureaucratic institutions studied are the Viceroy and his secretariat, Royal Audiencia
(High Court), Tribunal de Cuentas (Royal Auditing Agency), Royal Hacienda
(Exchequer), Royal Renta de Tabaco (Tobacco Monopoly), Aduana (Customs) and
Correo Real (Royal Postal Service).

656 **The federal system of the Argentine Republic.**
Leo Stanton Rowe. Washington, DC: Carnegie Institution of
Washington, 1921. 161p. bibliog. (Publication, 258).

Part one analyses the historical antecedents of the Argentine political and
constitutional system since 1810. Part two analyses the principles and present
organization of the federal system: the executive (President), legislature (Congress),

judiciary, constitutional guarantees to person and property, liberty of speech and of the press, and religious liberty. It also contains the English text of the 1853 Constitution. The author was President of the Pan American Union.

657   **Gobierno y administración de la República Argentina.** (The government and administration of Argentina.)
Segundo V. Linares Quintana.   Buenos Aires: Tipográfica Editora Argentina, 1959. 2nd ed. 2 vols.
An important history of the legal bases of the governmental and administrative systems from 1810, including the constitution, federal government, executive, judiciary, public services, public and municipal law, customs regulations, landholding, taxation, constitutional rights and guarantees, and private property.

658   **Government of the Argentine Republic.**
Austin F. Macdonald.   New York: T. Crowell, 1942. 476p. map. bibliog.
A good account of the structural and legal aspects (but little on the actual practice) of the institutions of Argentine government. Separate chapters discuss political parties and elections, the constitution, the powers of federal and provincial governments, the practice of national 'intervention', the office of President, ministries and other agencies of government, Congress, the legal system, national finance, education, agriculture and industry, labour and social welfare, provincial administration and local government, including that of the city of Buenos Aires.

659   **Latin American legislatures: their role and influence. Analyses for nine countries.**
Edited by Weston H. Agor.   New York; Washington, DC; London: Praeger, 1971. 523p. bibliog. (Praeger Special Studies in International Politics & Public Affairs).
Chapter four, by Lee C. Fennell, 'Congress in the Argentine political system: an appraisal' (p. 139-71), discusses the structure and powers of the national Congress after 1958 and before it was suspended after the military coup of June 1966. There are analyses of the electoral system and the past and present status of Congress, based on four criteria: remuneration of senators and deputies, career patterns of former presidents, interviews with deputies who served 1965-66, and a public opinion survey of 1963. Chapter five, 'Profile variables among Argentine legislators', by Peter Ranis (p. 173-257), presents profiles of seventy-six Deputies from ten political parties according to socioeconomic background and political attitudes.

660   **Local government in Argentina.**
Eileen Harloff, Rubén C. A. Cardón.   *Planning and Administration*, vol. 12, no. 2 (autumn 1985), p. 77-8.
Describes the system of local government in the municipalities (*municipios*), the basic units of government in the provinces. Each municipality has a deliberative body, variously called *consejo deliberante*, *sala de representantes* or *consejo municipal*. Executive authority rests with the *departamento ejecutivo* headed by an *intendente municipal*. Sources of finance vary from province to province. The city of Buenos Aires is divided into fourteen districts, each with a district council (*consejo vecinal*)

composed of nine members (*vocales*) appointed by the mayor with the approval of the municipal council. 'Municipal autonomy and competency are limited, and responsibilities are mainly concerned with matters of general local interest.'

661 **El parlamento argentino en épocas de cambio: 1890, 1916 y 1946.**
(The Argentine parliament in times of change: 1890, 1916 and 1946.)
Darío Cantón. Buenos Aires: Editorial del Instituto Torcuato Di Tella, 1966. 208p. bibliog. (Serie Naranja: Sociología).

Analyses the socioeconomic characteristics and political attitudes of members of both houses of Congress (Senators and Deputies) in three crucial years of change, grouping the data firstly by education, profession, national origin, age and social background, and secondly by political party. One revelation is that few lower-class men entered politics. An appendix compares the findings with similar studies from England, France and the United States.

662 **The parliament of the Argentine nation.**
Antonio J. Macris. *Inter-Parliamentary Bulletin* (Geneva), 66th year, third quarter, no. 3 (1986), p. 145-62.

Whereas executive power is exercised by the President and judicial power by the Supreme Court of Justice, legislative power rests with the two houses of Congress. Forty-six Senators represent the provinces and Federal Capital as 'autonomous political entities'; they serve nine-year terms and two-thirds stand for re-election every three years. Deputies are elected directly by the people they represent; their number depends on the number of inhabitants in each district; they serve four-year terms and one-half stands for re-election every two years. The structure, functions and powers of the Senate and Chamber of Deputies are described in detail. A slightly different version of this article may be found in *Constitutional and Parliamentary Information*, first series, no. 149 (first quarter 1987), p. 3-16. See also the data on Argentina contained in the fourteen thematic tables of *Parliaments of the world: a comparative reference compendium*, prepared by the International Centre for Parliamentary Documentation of the Inter-Parliamentary Union (Aldershot, England: Gower, 1986. 2nd ed.).

663 **The position of the judiciary in the political system of Argentina and Mexico.**
Robert E. Biles. *Lawyer of the Americas*, vol. 8, no. 2 (June 1976), p. 287-318.

Analyses the constitutional and legal constraints on the judiciary, especially the federal supreme courts, focusing on the areas of judicial independence, judicial review, de facto government and states of siege. Political instability has reduced respect for judicial independence, caused frequent major turnovers in the staff of the judiciary, and 'created the necessity for accommodation to unconstitutional regimes'. Nevertheless, criminal justice has been of a fairly high quality and Argentina is one of Latin America's leaders in legal philosophy. Argentina, in particular, has followed the example of the United States in matters of jurisdiction. The courts theoretically exercise a much wider scope of judicial review than the Mexican; they have greatly influenced the development of Argentine constitutional law but in practice made far fewer constitutional decisions. The predominance of de facto governments over the past forty years has weakened and intimidated the courts, but these have been reasonably effective in protecting individual rights. 'On occasion, the courts have even successfully challenged the president.'

664  **Public administration and social changes in Argentina: 1943-1955.**
Jean-Claude García-Zamor.   Rio de Janeiro: Editora Mory / Casa Vallele, 1968. 190p. maps. bibliog.
The first two parts summarize the Perón era and its effects on political and social change. Part three, p. 107-48, details Perón's reorganization of the central, provincial and local government, and of the civil service. During this time, Perón gradually centralized political power in Buenos Aires, made widespread use of intervention in order to consolidate his hold over the provinces, and increased control of municipal and local administration. The author gives details of changes to the training and retirement benefits of civil servants.

# Foreign Relations

665 **Antarctica and South American geopolitics: frozen lebensraum.**
Jack Child. New York; Westport, Connecticut; London: Praeger,
1988. 232p. maps. bibliog.

Argentina's tricontinental geopolitical stance on Antarctica is described on pages
65-104. A first expedition to the region was made in 1881 and the first official claim to a
wedge-shaped sector made in 1939. Argentina's Antarctic history has always had 'an
almost exclusively military thrust', and an ambivalent attitude towards the 1959
Antarctic Treaty. Today Argentine, Chilean and British claims overlap on the
Antarctic Peninsula. Since the Falklands War, Argentina has apparently set aside
'some of the earlier, highly nationalistic geopolitical thinking'.

666 **Argentina and Chile: the struggle for Patagonia, 1843-1881.**
Richard O. Perry. *The Americas*, vol. 36, no. 3 (Jan. 1980),
p. 347-63.

In 1843 Chile established a fort on the Brunswick Peninsula and by the 1870s had
effectively colonized the eastern slopes of the Andes. Argentina, preoccupied with the
River Plate arena, had by the 1840s founded only one colony on the Río Negro, but
now began to take a greater interest in Patagonia. A purely commercial treaty was
agreed in 1856; later boundary negotiations foundered but an 1881 treaty awarded
Chile the Straits of Magellan and Argentina Patagonia. The British government
arbitrated in the Andes border dispute, specifying the border as the highest peaks of
the Andean *cordillera* as far as 52° South by the Award of King Edward VII in 1902.
However, it required another British Boundary Commission to demarcate the entire
frontier; see Major W. D. Rushworth, 'The Argentine-Chilean frontier case, 1965-7',
*The Royal Engineers Journal*, vol. 8, no. 4 (Dec. 1967), p. 291-301. See also *The
Beagle Channel dispute: confrontation and negotiation in the Southern Cone*.

667 **Argentina and the United States, 1810-1960.**
Harold F. Peterson. Albany, New York: State University of New York, 1964. 627p. maps. bibliog.
A scholarly and wide-ranging chronological history of diplomatic relations between the two countries, best for its treatment of the nineteenth century, based on United States, but not Argentine, diplomatic archives. It also contrasts the similarities and differences between the two nations in 1810 and 1960.

668 **Argentina between the great powers, 1939-46.**
Edited by Guido di Tella, D. Cameron Watt. London: Macmillan, in association with St. Antony's College Oxford, 1989. 212p. maps.
A collection of essays on the triangular nature of diplomatic and economic relations between Argentina, Great Britain and the United States, by a group of scholars including Joseph S. Tulchin, Carlos Escudé, Mario Rapoport, Ronald C. Newton, Callum A. MacDonald and Stanley E. Hilton. Argentina antagonized the Allies by staying neutral during the Second World War until as late as March 1945. Carlos Escudé's own *Gran Bretaña, Estados Unidos y la declinación argentina: 1942-1949* (Buenos Aires: Editorial de Belgrano, 1983. 399p.) is a revised Yale doctoral thesis based on British and United States archives. A similar study by another Argentine historian is Mario Rapoport's *Gran Bretaña, Estados Unidos y las clases dirigentes argentinas, 1940-1945* (Buenos Aires: Editorial de Belgrano, 1981. 313p.). Fiercely nationalistic but well researched is the classic work on British economic policy in Argentina by Raúl Scalabrini Ortiz, *Política británica en el Río de la Plata* (Buenos Aires: Editorial Reconquista, 1940. 314p.), first published in 1936, with later editions.

669 **Argentina, the United States, and the inter-American system, 1880-1914.**
Thomas F. McGann. Cambridge, Massachusetts: Harvard University Press, 1957. 330p. (Harvard Historical Studies, vol. 70).
An examination of Argentina's economic, political and cultural relations with the United States in a period when Argentina emerged as the richest country in Latin America. Special features are the analysis of Argentina's role in the inter-American system (the first four Pan American Conferences, 1889-90, 1901-2, 1906 and 1910, the last held in Buenos Aires), the Argentine reaction to the United States' protective tariffs, Theodore Roosevelt's 'big stick' policy and the expansion of US business interests in Argentina.

670 **Argentina's foreign policies.**
Edward S. Milenky. Boulder, Colorado: Westview Press, 1978. 345p. bibliog. (Westview Replica Editions).
This work examines Argentina 'as an independent actor in world affairs'. Separate sections deal with the recent history of diplomacy, emphasizing the years 1973-76: the instruments and economic-military 'capabilities' of foreign policy; the policy-making process itself; relations with the United States; relations with Western Europe, other non-Communist countries, Communist countries and the Third World; relations with other Latin American nations; and multilateral diplomacy (Latin American economic-integration systems, the inter-American system, international organizations). There is no index.

671 **Argentina's foreign policy: 1930-1962.**
Alberto Conil Paz, Gustavo E. Ferrari, translated by John J.
Kennedy. Notre Dame, Indiana; London: University of Notre Dame
Press, 1966. 240p. bibliog.

The authors, from the Universidad del Salvador, Buenos Aires, present a chronological Argentine assessment of the conduct of foreign policy relations during three critical decades in modern Argentine history: the Depression of the 1930s, the Second World War and the Perón decade. Relations with the United States are given prominence. The text is well documented but the index is poor. 'In spite of its ambitious formulation, foreign policy was sown with deep internal contradictions . . . Brazil, after having drawn rich benefits from her collaboration with the United States during the war, was now inventing new techniques to continue obtaining advantages [and] Argentina, again, arrived too late.'

672 **Argentine territorial nationalism.**
Carlos Escudé. *Journal of Latin American Studies*, vol. 20, no. 1
(May 1988), p. 139-65.

Compares Argentine and Chilean shared perceptions of territorial losses at each other's expense, fanned by the media and educational indoctrination: 'In Argentina there is a widespread perception of Chilean expansion at Argentina's expense [south of the river Bío-Bío] and of additional territorial losses elsewhere. In Chile there is a parallel perception of Argentine expansionism [in Patagonia] at Chile's expense.' In fact, Argentina and Chile – and Brazil – have made huge territorial gains, and Argentina's only 'very minor territorial loss' was the Falkland Islands.

673 **The Beagle Channel dispute: confrontation and negotiation in the Southern Cone.**
James L. Garrett. *Journal of Interamerican Studies and World Affairs*,
vol. 27, no. 3 (fall 1985), p. 81-109. maps. bibliog.

Describes the history and mediation of the dispute over the 125-mile-long Beagle Channel and the islands of Picton, Nueva and Lennox south of the Channel: the boundary treaty of 1881, the appointment again (see *Argentina and Chile: the struggle for Patagonia, 1843-1881*) of British arbitration in 1971, the eventual appointment of Pope John Paul II as mediator in 1980, and the treaty establishing a joint boundary and awarding Chile sovereignty over the disputed islands.

674 **Brazilian-Argentine relations in the 1980s: from wary rivalry to friendly competition.**
Wayne A. Selcher. *Journal of Interamerican Studies and World Affairs*, vol. 27, no. 2 (summer 1985), p. 25-53. bibliog.

In May 1980 Brazilian President João Figueiredo made a historic visit to Argentine President Jorge Videla, ending forty years without a summit meeting between the two countries. The article describes Brazilian-Argentine political, economic and security relations since 1970, with speculation about future prospects. From the Brazilian perspective, see Stanley E. Hilton, 'The Argentine factor in twentieth century Brazilian foreign policy strategy', *Political Science Quarterly*, vol. 100, no. 1 (spring 1985), p. 27-51.

675    **Britain and Argentina in the nineteenth century.**
H. S. Ferns.    Oxford: Clarendon Press, 1960. 517p. maps.
A classic survey of political, economic and financial relations between the two countries, by a Canadian scholar. The work begins with an excellent description of the British invasions of the River Plate, 1806-7 ('in many respects the most important event in Argentine history . . . [when] the Argentine Republic was born'), and ends with the Baring Crisis of the 1890s. The book is in itself an expert history of Argentina in the nineteenth century. There is a modern reprint (New York: Arno Press, 1977).

676    **Discreet partners: Argentina and the USSR since 1917.**
Aldo César Vacs, translated by Michael Joyce.    Pittsburgh, Pennsylvania: University of Pittsburgh Press, 1984. 154p. bibliog. (Pitt Latin American Series).
The title is misleading, for only one-quarter of the book is devoted to the period before 1970. Perón signed the first trade agreement with the USSR in 1953 but relations were generally poor until President Lanusse (1970-73) began to 'pursue a realistic policy abroad free from ideological perceptions'. Argentina benefited famously from President Carter's 1980 trade embargo on grain exports to the USSR. There are interesting sections on economic interest groups which favoured close trade relations with the USSR, and the minimal influence of the pro-Soviet Argentine Communist Party. See also Mario Rapoport, 'Argentina and the Soviet Union: history of political and commercial relations (1917-1955)', *Hispanic American Historical Review*, vol. 66, no. 2 (May 1986), p. 239-85.

677    **Geopolitics and conflict in South America: quarrels among neighbors.**
Jack Child.    New York: Praeger, 1985. 196p. maps. bibliog. (Politics in Latin America. A Hoover Institution Series).
Geopolitical ideology is strongest in the South American nations of Argentina, Brazil and Chile. The book includes case-studies of Argentine-Chilean conflict (the Beagle Channel), Argentine-Brazilian power rivalry and conflicting Argentine, Chilean and British interests in the South Atlantic (Falkland Islands, Antarctica). An essential journal dealing with Argentine geopolitical thinking and military strategy is *Estrategia* (Buenos Aires: Instituto Argentino de Estudios Estratégicos y de las Relaciones Internacionales, 1969- , bimonthly, indexed by *HAPI: Hispanic American Periodicals Index* and *Handbook of Latin American Studies* [qq.v.]).

678    **Geopolitics of the Southern Cone and Antarctica.**
Edited by Philip Kelly, Jack Child.    Boulder, Colorado; London: Lynne Rienner, 1988. 273p. maps. bibliog.
Papers on Argentina, Chile, Uruguay, Paraguay, Bolivia and Brazil. Norberto Ceresole and Roberto Russell write on Argentine foreign policy in the region; the buffer states of Bolivia, Uruguay and Paraguay are examined in relation to the River Plate basin by authors from the relevant countries; and there is a final section on Antarctica and the Falkland Islands. For a scholarly defence of Argentina's claims in the South Atlantic, including the Antarctic, see Admiral Jorge A. Fraga, *La Argentina y el Atlántico Sur: conflictos y objetivos* (Buenos Aires: Ediciones Pleamar, 1983. 340p.).

679 **Historia de las relaciones exteriores argentinas (1810-1955).** (A history of Argentina's foreign relations, 1810-1955.)
Isidoro Ruiz Moreno. Buenos Aires: Editorial Perrot, 1961. 430p. bibliog.

A broad historical study of foreign relations, useful for its country-by-country approach, ending with references to Finland, Sweden and Japan (admittedly only a total of thirty-six lines). Other valuable general diplomatic histories by Argentine scholars are Miguel Angel Cárcano, *La política internacional en la historia argentina* (Buenos Aires: Editorial Universitaria de Buenos Aires, 1972-73. 3 vols. in 4); Roberto Etchepareborda, *Historia de las relaciones internacionales argentinas* (Buenos Aires: Editorial Pleamar, 1978. 279p.); and Juan Archibaldo Lanús, *De Chapultepec al Beagle: política exterior argentina, 1945-1980* (Buenos Aires: Emecé, 1984. 571p.).

680 **The influence of Latin American governments on the shaping of United States foreign policy: the case of U.S.-Argentine relations, 1943-1948.**
Albert P. Vannucci. *Journal of Latin American Studies*, vol. 18, no. 2 (Nov. 1986), p. 335-82.

For most of this period the United States 'doggedly maintained that the governments in Argentina were Axis collaborators and Axis emulators. And yet, in the span of five years, U.S. policy with respect to Argentina reversed itself no fewer than seven times.' But Argentina did not become isolated; by 1948 the country was held in high esteem by the international community, Latin America refused to accept the United States' position that Argentina was a 'hemisphere problem', and the United States 'suffered one of its most embarrassing diplomatic defeats'.

681 **The land that England lost: Argentina and Britain, a special relationship.**
Edited by Alistair Hennessy, John King. London: Lester Crook Academic Publishing, 1991. 288p. maps. bibliog.

A comprehensive collection of essays by British, Argentine, Irish and Canadian scholars on political, economic, diplomatic and cultural relations between the two countries. More unusual topics include British travel writing on Argentina, British cultural influence, Borges and England, the English tango craze, British pioneers on Argentina's tropical frontier, and British press reaction to the Peróns.

682 **The limits of hegemony: United States relations with Argentina and Chile during World War II.**
Michael J. Francis. Notre Dame, Indiana; London: University of Notre Dame Press, 1977. 292p. (International Studies of the Committee on International Relations).

Studies Argentine and Chilean domestic politics 'in order to help explain the successes and failures of United States foreign policy'. Chile was dependent on the United States for sales of copper and nitrates, whereas Argentina was still more dependent on Great Britain. The book concludes that 'Washington overextended its influence by trying to dictate Argentina's foreign policy', provoking nationalism in the Argentine military, frustrated over Argentina's failure to become a world leader after 1930; the 1943 coup resulted largely from these political tensions.

683 **The Roosevelt foreign-policy establishment and the 'Good Neighbor': the United States and Argentina, 1941-1945.**
Randall Bennett Woods. Lawrence, Kansas: The Regents Press of Kansas, 1979. 277p. bibliog.

Two groups in the United States Department of State disagreed over the direction of United States foreign policy towards Argentina at the time: the 'Latin Americanists', committed to the Good Neighbor policy of non-interference (Sumner Welles and others); and the 'Internationalists' (Cordell Hull and others), who warned that Argentina was 'Facist, pro-Nazi, anti-United Nations, and expansionist'. The author describes the alternate application of soft- and hard-line punitive measures against Argentina pursued by each group. See also Callum A. MacDonald, 'The politics of intervention: the United States and Argentina, 1941-1946', *Journal of Latin American Studies*, vol. 12, no. 2 (Nov. 1980), p. 365-96. The culmination of the State Department's Argentine policy was the publication just before the 1946 presidential elections of the so-called 'Blue book on Argentina', inspired by Spruille Braden, then Ambassador to Argentina, which produced documentary evidence of Argentine collusion with the Nazis. Its full title is *Consultation among the American Republics with respect to the Argentine situation: memorandum of the United States government* (Department of State, 1946. 131p.). See Roger R. Trask, 'Spruille Braden versus George Messersmith: World War II, the Cold War, and Argentine policy, 1945-1947', *Journal of Interamerican Studies and World Affairs*, vol. 26, no. 1 (Feb. 1984), p. 69-95.

684 **Southern Cone maritime security after the 1984 Argentine-Chilean Treaty of Peace and Friendship.**
Michael A. Morris. *Ocean Development and International Law*, vol. 18, no. 2 (1987), p. 235-54. maps.

Discusses the background of the treaty and each country's military strategy with regard to the Argentine and Chilean Seas, the South Atlantic and the South Pacific. Both have 'long advanced ambitious pretensions to control adjacent ocean space'; 'naval power is the ultimate arbiter . . . and in this respect Argentina holds the advantage'. The Argentine Sea is particularly conflict-prone. The 1984 treaty 'undercut Chilean aspirations in the South Atlantic' but Chile still lays claim to extensive Antarctic territory and has a superior strategic position in the far south: 'Argentina lacks good ports along the Atlantic littoral, and her position south of the Strait of Magellan is precarious'. Chile has been concerned at Argentine penetration into the South Pacific for over a century. Argentina and Chile also differ in their perceptions of allies and adversaries (Soviet Union, Great Britain, United States, Brazil, South Africa).

685 **Strategy in the southern oceans: a South American view.**
Virginia Gamba-Stonehouse. London: Pinter, in association with John Spiers, 1989. 155p. maps. bibliog. (Studies in Contemporary Maritime Policy and Strategy, 1).

Part two, 'Argentina and Brazil in the western South Atlantic' (p. 71-134), assesses the local, regional and international implications of the two countries' geopolitical and strategic policies with regard to the western South Atlantic, how their interests conflict with those of other parties in the region (Chile, Uruguay, South Africa, Great Britain and the Soviet Union), and the implications of the Falklands War. Cooperation between Argentina and Brazil has been chiefly in the nuclear and military fields. The author also discusses policies with regard to fishing (Argentina has signed accords with

191

the Soviet Union and Bulgaria) and oil (unlike Argentina, Brazil obtains most of its oil from under the sea).

686  **The Treaty of Tordesillas and the Argentine-Brazilian boundary settlement.**
Mary Wilhelmine Williams.  *Hispanic American Historical Review*, vol. 5, no. 1 (Feb. 1922), p. 3-23. maps.
A fascinating article on the vexed question of the Argentine-Brazilian boundary. The Treaty of Tordesillas (1494) drew a rough-and-ready vertical boundary 370 leagues west of the Cape Verde Islands; lands to the west of it would belong to Spain, those to the east to Portugal. A description is provided of the various boundary commissions during the following four hundred years, during which Uruguay was made a buffer state between the two countries in 1828, and ending in the award of United States President Grover Cleveland in 1895.

687  **The United States and the Southern Cone: Argentina, Chile, and Uruguay.**
Arthur P. Whitaker.  Cambridge, Massachusetts; London: Harvard University Press, 1976. 464p. maps. bibliog. (American Foreign Policy Library).
The first three chapters summarize the political, economic, social and cultural histories of the three nations. Part four analyses their relationships with the United States from the latter's viewpoint, in Argentina's case from 1810 to 1976 and emphasizing the twentieth century. This work updates the author's earlier *The United States and Argentina* (1954).

688  **United States perceptions of Latin America, 1850-1930: a 'new West' south of Capricorn?**
J. Valerie Fifer.  Manchester, England: Manchester University Press, 1991. 220p. maps. bibliog.
The United States forecast a bright future for the temperate south of South America after 1850: there lay 'progressive Spain'. Argentina's size and pivotal location in the temperate south gave it the most potential in American eyes but in the end the country proved the biggest disappointment, since by 1930 it still displayed the greatest gap between possibilities and performance. The book reveals how American perceptions of progress in South America, and particularly in Argentina, were increasingly influenced by what was being tried and accomplished in the American West. It discusses United States naval and geographical surveys to Argentina, American fact-finding and published literature on the country, and jaundiced American perceptions of Argentina's general lack of Western-style development.

# The Falkland Islands Dispute

## The sovereignty issue

689 **América Latina y la guerra del Atlántico Sur: experiencias y desafíos.**
(Latin America and the war in the South Atlantic: experiences and challenges.)
Edited by Roberto Russell. Buenos Aires: Editorial de Belgrano, 1984. 248p. (Colección Temas de Política Internacional).
Ten essays edited by an Argentine authority on international affairs, reflecting Argentine, Brazilian, Chilean, United States and European reactions to the past and possible future consequences of the Falklands War for the region and for Latin America's international relations.

690 **The Falkland Islands as an international problem.**
Peter J. Beck. London; New York: Routledge, 1988. 211p. maps. bibliog.
A 'work of synthesis', by a foremost British authority on the Anglo-Argentine dispute over the title to the Falkland Islands, which discusses the development of the sovereignty dispute from the British occupation of the islands in 1833 to the 1982 war, and the war itself and its aftermath. The author sets out to correct what he sees as misconceptions in the mass of literature that has appeared since 1982 and suggests the 'need for a transformation in Argentine thinking towards the Malvinas [the Argentine name for the Falklands] and similarly the British government needs to consider its real interests . . . some argue that British interests in Latin America and the wider world might be better served by a policy that moved towards the Argentine point of view, an approach encouraged by an appreciation of the historical and legal weaknesses of British title'.

193

691 **Falkland Islands review: report of a committee of Privy Counsellors.**
Lord Franks, Chairman.   London: HMSO, 1983. 105p. map.
(Cmnd. 8787).

Soon after the conclusion of the Falklands War, the British government appointed a committee 'to review the way in which the responsibilities of Government in relation to the Falkland Islands and their Dependencies were discharged in the period up to the Argentine invasion'. The report presents a summary of the dispute between 1965 and 1979, followed by a detailed examination of the government's policy towards Argentina and the Falkland Islands in the period leading up to the war. To the question 'Could the invasion of 2 April have been foreseen?', the committee's reply was that it was 'satisfied that the Government did not have warning of the decision to invade'.

692 **Falklands/Malvinas: whose crisis?**
Martin Honeywell, Jenny Pearce.   London: Latin America Bureau,
1982. 135p. map. (Special Brief).

A soundly based survey of British policy towards the Falkland Islands from a left-wing standpoint. The authors criticize the British government for exploiting the Falklands economy and supporting Argentina's military régimes, and expose the weaknesses of both countries' claims to the islands.

693 **Falklands, politics and war.**
G. M. Dillon.   London: Macmillan, 1988. 296p.

A detailed analysis of British policy-making towards the Falkland Islands and the political causes of the conflict, which analyses the mass of parliamentary and other evidence concerning the outbreak of the war, 'much of it conflicting', and in particular the role of Prime Minister Margaret Thatcher, other ministers and Whitehall officials. The study ends with the sinking of the Argentine carrier, the *General Belgrano*, on 2 May 1982.

694 **The little platoon: diplomacy and the Falklands dispute.**
Michael Charlton.   Oxford: Basil Blackwell, 1989. 230p.

An 'oral history' of (mainly) British diplomacy towards the Falkland Islands question, consisting of interviews recorded 1985-86 with the men who formulated policy from the time the islands 'once again became an active issue in the 1960s': senior officials in the Foreign Office and Ministry of Defence, their counterparts in Argentina and the United States, and the admirals 'who had the last word'. The interviews were originally broadcast as a series of eight programmes for the BBC's Radio Three. The title refers to 'those subtle underlying determinants of British democracy which Edmund Burke defined as the first principle of public affections, devotion to the "little platoon", the small minority', in this case the Falkland Islanders themselves.

695 **Signals of war: the Falklands conflict of 1982.**
Lawrence Freedman, Virginia Gamba-Stonehouse.   London; Boston,
Massachusetts: Faber & Faber, 1990. 417p. maps. bibliog.

An Anglo-Argentine cooperative work (the authors are professor and Argentine research fellow in the department of war studies at King's College, London) which describes the consequences of Anglo-Argentine 'asymmetry' in the conflict as they unfolded during the first half of 1982: 'Britain was holding doggedly on to islands about which very few people cared, but those few who did cared strongly. In Argentina everybody cared.' The book is a valuable synthesis of the existing literature, drawing also on original material and interviews, but makes no judgement on the sovereignty issue.

696  **Sovereignty in dispute: the Falklands/Malvinas, 1493-1982.**
Fritz L. Hoffmann, Olga Mingo Hoffmann.   Boulder, Colorado; London: Westview Press, 1984. 194p. maps. bibliog. (Westview Special Studies on Latin America and the Caribbean).

A well-written summary, by two North American scholars, of the sovereignty dispute from the sixteenth century to the 1982 war. Half the book is devoted to the period before 1833, when Britain reasserted possession of the islands. The war itself is touched on only lightly. The work is marred by being biased in favour of the Argentine case and by such statements as: 'With its bloodless invasion of the islands, the Argentine government could have called world attention to its discipline as well as its military capacity.'

697  **The struggle for the Falkland Islands: a study in legal and diplomatic history.**
Julius Goebel.   New Haven, Connecticut: Yale University Press, 1982. 482p. maps. bibliog.

The 1982 Falklands War has given rise to an astonishing amount of publications on both sides but there were very few scholarly works in English before that date. Goebel's book, first published in 1927, is an outstanding exception. It is a meticulously researched study of the historical background to the controversy, biased towards the Argentine position, reprinted here with a preface and introduction by J. C. J. Metford. The latter is a reprint of his 'Falklands or Malvinas? The background to the dispute', *International Affairs*, vol. 44, no. 3 (July 1968).

698  **Una tierra argentina: las Islas Malvinas.** (The Malvinas, Argentine territory.)
Ricardo R. Caillet-Bois.   Buenos Aires: Academia Nacional de la Historia, 1982. 453p. 3rd ed. (Biblioteca de Historia Argentina y Americana, 19).

Covering much the same historical period as Goebel (item no. 697) and based on Argentine primary sources. Also useful for a presentation of the Argentine case are Laurio H. Destéfani, *The Malvinas, the South Georgias, and the South Sandwich Islands: the conflict with Britain* (Buenos Aires: Edipress, 1982. 143p.), mainly to 1834; and Ricardo Zorraquín Becú, *Inglaterra prometió abandonar las Malvinas: estudio histórico y jurídico del conflicto anglo-español* (Buenos Aires: Librería Editorial Platero, 1975. 200p.), which stresses Britain's supposed secret promise in 1771 to abandon the islands in return for Spain's restitution of the British naval base it had destroyed in 1770.

# The Falklands War, 1982

**699　The battle for the Falklands.**
Max Hastings, Simon Jenkins.　London: Michael Joseph; New York:
W. W. Norton, 1983. 372p. maps.
The joint work of a British war correspondent and a political editor, this book is
described as 'an interim report on Britain's war in the South Atlantic, based
overwhelmingly on the testimony of the participants, at home and abroad, at sea and
ashore'. The claim is too modest. This is an indispensable document, combining
Jenkins's descriptions of the complex political and diplomatic course of events in
London with Hastings's eyewitness accounts of military operations in the South
Atlantic. The task force succeeded 'in large measure through [Mrs Thatcher's] qualities
of leadership. She is entitled to the credit for both luck and her judgement'.

**700　Los chicos de la guerra: the boys of the war.**
Daniel Kon.　Sevenoaks, England: New English Library, 1983. 188p.
The original Argentine edition, first published in 1982 a few months after the war, was
a best-seller running to eight editions in fifteen months; a successful film was also
released in 1984. It records the testimonies of a cross-section of eight young Argentine
conscripts, all but one of whom served in the front line. See also Carlos M. Túrolo's
*Así lucharon* (Buenos Aires: Editorial Sudamericana, 1982. 327p.), the experiences of
ten young Argentine military officers during the campaign.

**701　Eyewitness Falklands: a personal account of the Falklands campaign.**
Robert Fox.　London: Methuen, 1982. 337p. maps.
Assigned by BBC Radio to the British task force, war correspondent Robert Fox
provides a graphic eyewitness 'account of what the men and women I was with said and
did' during the land campaign. Transcripts of Fox's and Brian Hanrahan's BBC radio
broadcasts from land and sea are contained in the famously titled '*I counted them all
out and I counted them all back': the battle for the Falklands* (London: BBC, 1982.
139p.). Another factual account of the war from the British point of view by
correspondents of the *Observer* and *Times* is Patrick Bishop and John Witherow, *The
winter war* (London: Quartet Books, 1982. 153p.).

**702　The Falkland Islands.**
Ian J. Strange.　Newton Abbot, England: David & Charles, 1984.
328p. 3rd ed. maps. bibliog.
This third edition of the standard history of the Falkland Islands contains two new
chapters: 'The conflict and occupation' (p. 246-89) is an essential eyewitness account of
events in Port Stanley from the Falklanders' point of view; the final chapter describes
the islanders' rehabilitation after the war.

703 **Falklands – the secret plot.**
Oscar Raúl Cardoso, Ricardo Kirschbaum, Eduardo Van der Kooy,
translated by Bernard Ethell.    East Molesey, England: Preston
Editions, 1987. 327p.

Three journalists from the Buenos Aires daily *Clarín* describe the Galtieri junta's
planning of the invasion and its political and diplomatic activities before and after the
war, based on interviews with officials in Buenos Aires, London and Washington,
dramatically reconstructed. The original Argentine edition (1983) was a best-seller.

704 **The Falklands war: the full story.**
Written and edited by Paul Eddy, Magnus Linklater, Peter Gillman.
London: André Deutsch, 1982. 274p. maps.

A solid reconstruction of the causes and the military and diplomatic events of the war,
by members of the *Sunday Times* (London) 'Insight' team.

705 **Malvinas: testimonio de su gobernador.** (Malvinas: the eyewitness
account of its governor.)
Carlos M. Túrolo.    Buenos Aires: Editorial Sudamericana, 1983.
337p.

General Mario Benjamín Menéndez was appointed military commander and governor
of the Falkland Islands after the invasion of 2 April 1982, and it was he who signed the
document of surrender to the British forces three months later. This is the testimony of
his experiences as given to an Argentine reporter in over a hundred hours of interview.

706 **El otro frente de la guerra: los padres de las Malvinas.** (The war's other
front: the Fathers of the Malvinas.)
Dalmiro M. Bustos.    Buenos Aires: Ramos Americana Editora, 1982.
219p.

A psychiatrist by profession, with a conscript son sent to the islands, Dr Bustos
formed a group of soldiers' parents in the city of La Plata with the aim of bolstering the
morale of the Argentine troops at the war, through, among other means, a nightly
radio broadcast beamed to the islands by a local station. While the bulk of the text is
his account of that initiative, the book also contains letters from the soldiers during the
war, their accounts of it when they returned, and the text of the communications sent
by the Parents' Group.

707 **The sinking of the Belgrano.**
Arthur Gavshon, Desmond Rice.    London: Secker & Warburg, 1984.
218p. maps. bibliog.

Together with the circumstances surrounding British intelligence of Argentine
intentions towards the Falklands on the eve of the war, the *Belgrano* affair remains the
most controversial aspect of it. On 2 May 1982, while President Belaúnde of Peru and
United States Secretary-of-State Alexander Haig were negotiating a peace formula, the
Argentine cruiser *General Belgrano* was torpedoed by the British nuclear submarine
*Conqueror* and 368 lives were lost. Two days later, an Argentine Exocet missile struck
the British destroyer *Sheffield* and twenty-one died. So did, with these events, hopes of
a negotiated settlement. The authors' thesis, based on serious research but apparently

**The Falkland Islands Dispute.** The Falklands War, 1982

hindered by a lack of official cooperation, is that the sinking of the *Belgrano* was an unnecessary act, given its position and course outside the British exclusion zone around the islands within which any Argentine ship might legitimately be attacked. The book raises the question as to whether the British government was seriously interested in any solution short of total victory. The thesis is highly controversial and the assertions probably unprovable; but if, as recent evidence suggests, the Galtieri junta had no intention of withdrawing peacefully from the Falklands, the sinking of the *Belgrano* may have been as crucial for the success of the British military campaign as the diplomatic stonewalling was intended to be for the survival of the Argentine generals.

# The Economy and Economic History

## General

708 **Argentina, Australia, and Canada: studies in comparative development, 1870-1965.**
Edited by D. C. M. Platt, Guido di Tella.   London: Macmillan in association with St. Antony's College, Oxford; New York: St. Martin's Press, 1985. 237p.
This collection reflects the modern historiographical and economic interest in comparative studies of national economies. John Fogarty and Guido di Tella examine the pre-1914 phase, when the patterns of development in all three 'regions of recent development' were broadly similar. Carl E. Solberg discusses land tenure, Warwick Armstrong social classes and forces, and Roberto Cortés Conde and Carlos F. Díaz Alejandro post-1914 industrialization. A third set of essays by Charles A. Jones, D. C. M. Platt and Peter Alhadeff examines the financing of economic growth.

709 **Argentina: economic and commercial conditions in the Argentine Republic.**
A. H. Tandy.   London: HMSO, for the Board of Trade, Commercial Relations and Exports Department, 1956. 111p. map. (Overseas Economic Surveys).
Tandy, commercial minister at the British Embassy in Buenos Aires, produced this comprehensive survey of the Argentine economy in the last year of Juan Domingo Perón's first period as president. With its many statistical tables it is an excellent source for the historian and economist, on finance, natural resources, industry, transport and communications, foreign trade and balance of payments. There were earlier surveys by J. G. Lomax (1948. 128p.) and S. G. Irving (1935. 216p.).

710 **Argentina: economic memorandum.**
Washington, DC: World Bank, 1985. 2 vols. map. (A World Bank Country Study).

The report of a World Bank mission to Argentina in June-July 1983, as the country prepared to return to democracy after seven years of military rule. Volume one (278p.) surveys economic policy, public-sector finance, agricultural exports, industry, trade and the financial sector. Volume two (p. 279-409) is a statistical appendix.

711 **Argentina in 1914: the pampas, the interior, Buenos Aires.**
David Rock. In: *Cambridge History of Latin America. Vol. 5: c1870 to 1930.* Edited by Leslie Bethell. Cambridge, England: Cambridge University Press, 1986, p. 393-418. bibliog.

A brief essay which assesses the Argentine economy on the eve of the First World War, generally viewed as marking the beginning of the end of the country's heyday of extraordinary economic development.

712 **Argentina 1990: annual report on government, economy & business.**
London: Latin American Monitor, 1990. 123p. map. bibliog.

One of a series of annual country surveys, this is a concise and detailed source of information on the Argentine economy. There are sections on government, economic policy and indicators, finance, investment, foreign trade and industry. Includes forty-four tables.

713 **The Argentine economy.**
Aldo Ferrer, translated by Marjory M. Urquidi. Berkeley, California; Los Angeles: University of California Press; London: Cambridge University Press, 1967. 239p.

The work of a former Economics Minister and professor of economics at the University of Buenos Aires, this is both a chronological dependency-theory history of the Argentine economy from the sixteenth century and a panorama of the state of the economy in the late 1950s. Argentina's postwar economic difficulties were caused by 'the lack of proper answers to the problems of an agricultural economy in transition to a modern industrial society'. See also his 'The Argentine economy, 1976-1979', *Journal of Interamerican Studies and World Affairs*, vol. 22, no. 2 (May 1980), p. 131-62.

714 **Argentine international trade under inconvertible paper money, 1880-1900.**
John H. Williams. Cambridge, Massachusetts: Harvard University Press, 1920. 282p. bibliog. (Harvard Economic Studies, 22).

A classic study of Argentina's first two decades of economic boom, particularly of its paper money and foreign trade and investment, containing also much relevant information on wages and prices and the balance of payments. At the beginning of this period, paper money was depreciated, 'gold having been driven completely out of circulation', and there was heavy borrowing of foreign capital and a favourable trade balance. The Baring Crisis of 1890-91 produced a depression followed by a dramatic recovery. The work has been reprinted (New York: Greenwood Press, 1969).

715 **The Argentine Republic, 1516-1971.**
H. S. Ferns. Newton Abbot, England: David & Charles; New York: Barnes & Noble, 1973. 212p. map. bibliog. (National Economic Histories).

Intended for undergraduate students and the intelligent layman, this text by a Canadian authority on modern Argentina is a concise chronological introduction to the country's economic evolution. It presents the interesting, if unfashionable, view that Argentina's failure in the modern period to capitalize on its resources and earlier dynamic growth has much to do with its Hispanic cultural inheritance.

716 **Australia and Argentina: on parallel paths.**
Tim Duncan, John Fogarty. Melbourne, Australia: Melbourne University Press, 1984. 203p. maps. bibliog.

An important comparative study which emphasizes the different political traditions of the two countries in seeking to explain their diverse economic evolution. Between 1880 and 1940, Argentina's economic performance was, on the whole, better than Australia's. After 1950 'Argentina made the mistake of milking its top performer [agriculture], thus turning its back on the greatest international economic boom in modern history. It became poor as a result. Australia, by contrast, has conserved its dynamic industries'. See also the series of papers and commentaries edited by John Fogarty, Ezequiel Gallo and Héctor Diéguez, *Argentina y Australia* (Buenos Aires: Instituto Torcuato Di Tella, 1979. 246p.).

717 **Country profile: Argentina.**
London: Economist Intelligence Unit, 1986- . annual. map. bibliog.

A continuation of the EIU's *Quarterly economic review of Argentina, annual supplement*, this provides information on currency, national accounts, employment, wages and prices, agriculture, mining, manufacturing, construction, tourism, transport and communications, finance, foreign trade and foreign debt. The publication is supplemented by the quarterly *Argentina: country report* (1990- ), a monitor of political, economic and business conditions with a statistical supplement.

718 **El desarrollo económico de la Argentina.** (The economic development of Argentina.)
Mexico City: United Nations Economic Commission for Latin America, Departamento de Asuntos Económicos y Sociales. 1959. 3 vols.

The most extensive study of the Argentine economy made to the date of publication, and a rich source of statistics for economic historians. An English summary is 'The problems of economic development in Argentina', *Economic Bulletin for Latin America*, no. 3 (March 1959), p. 13-24. A second ECLA study of the Argentine economy a decade later is *Economic development and income distribution in Argentina* (New York, 1969. 269p.).

719 **La economía argentina.** (The Argentine economy.)
Alejandro E. Bunge. Buenos Aires: Agencia General de Librerías y
Publicaciones, 1928-30. 4 vols.

A classic survey of Argentine economic development from 1810 to 1920, also
interesting as an early example of Argentine economic nationalism.

720 **The economic development of the Argentine Republic in the last fifty
years.**
Ernesto Tornquist & Co.. Buenos Aires: Ernesto Tornquist & Cía,
1919. 328p. maps.

A famous descriptive survey of the Argentine economy at its apogee, prepared for
foreign investors by one of the country's oldest banks. Separate chapters deal with
geography and political organization, population, agriculture and the meat industry,
industries, communications, foreign trade, shipping, commercial and credit institutions, public wealth and finances, and prices and consumption of foodstuffs.

721 **An economic history of Argentina in the twentieth century.**
Laura Randall. New York: Columbia University Press, 1978. 322p.
bibliog.

A comprehensive, if somewhat technical, treatment of economic history by a leading
United States scholar who confronts the dependency theory and ascribes Argentina's
comparative economic failure to internal factors. See also the same author's *A
comparative economic history of Latin America, 1500-1914. Vol. 2: Argentina* (Ann
Arbor, Michigan: University Microfilms International, 1977. 268p.), which devotes a
mere twenty-seven pages to the colonial period.

722 **Essays on the economic history of the Argentine Republic.**
Carlos F. Díaz Alejandro. New Haven, Connecticut; London: Yale
University Press, 1970. 549p. map. (Publication of the Economic
Growth Center, Yale University).

The rather prosaic title might lead the potential reader to underestimate the
importance of this work as a contribution to the scholarly literature on Argentine
economics and economic history. Since publication, however, it has attained the status
of a classic for the depth and weight of its treatment. The focus is on the period after
1930; there is a valuable statistical appendix of 136 tables.

723 **The gold standard, 1880-1914: Britain and Argentina.**
A. G. Ford. Oxford: Clarendon Press, 1962. 200p.

A clinical monetary study, with a large number of graphs, of Argentina's and Britain's
individual economic performances, and only incidentally of their financial and trade
relations, during the classic era of the gold standard. Argentina abandoned the gold
standard in 1885 but rejoined in 1900 and 'remained a member of the club until 1914'.
There is a good Spanish translation with an introduction by Aldo Ferrer: *El patrón oro:
1880-1914. Inglaterra y Argentina* (Buenos Aires: Editorial del Instituto Torcuato Di
Tella, 1966).

724  **Historia económica de la Argentina, 1850-1930.** (An economic history of Argentina, 1850-1930.)
Ricardo M. Ortiz.  Buenos Aires: Raigal, 1955. 2 vols. bibliog.
(Biblioteca Manuel Belgrano).
A detailed and comprehensive study of the period; a highly regarded and widely read text despite the author's Marxist bias.

725  **The international economic position of Argentina.**
Vernon Lovell Phelps.  Philadelphia: University of Pennsylvania Press; London: Oxford University Press, 1938. 276p. bibliog.
A detailed examination of Argentina's import–export trade and foreign investments, especially its relations with the United States, from 1914 to 1937. Between 1910 and 1934 foreign investments in Argentina, mostly from the United States, increased one hundred times; although the country's chief sources of imports were the United States and Britain, after 1920 the United States imposed tariff increases and restricted its own market for Argentine products.

726  **Living within our means: an examination of the Argentine economic crisis.**
Aldo Ferrer.  London: Third World Foundation for Social and Economic Studies; Boulder, Colorado: Westview Publications, 1985. 98p.
The main thrust of this short study by a well-known economist and former Finance Minister is that the country's apparent inability to live within its economic means turns on its future capacity to renegotiate its foreign debt, avoid hyperinflation and somehow unite the nation behind these goals. For an interesting analysis of the situation at the time though somewhat short on prescription, see *Discipline as the central objective of the economic programme of the Argentine government since 1976*. Rodolfo H. Terragno's *The challenge of real development: Argentina in the twenty-first century* (Boulder, Colorado: Lynne Rienner, 1989. 140p.) is a rather philosophical piece by a former Minister of Public Works on the role that science and education should play in the process of economic development.

727  **Multinationals and maldevelopment: alternative development stategies in Argentina, the Ivory Coast and Korea.**
Lawrence R. Alschuler.  Basingstoke, England: Macmillan, 1988. 218p. bibliog.
An analysis of the development strategies of six Argentine régimes, 1946-76, especially in relation to their encouragement of foreign investment, concluding that 'foreign companies are controlling an increasing share of Argentine industrial product, employing a constant (not growing) share of industrial labor, and are transferring their productivity increases to wages proportionately less than national firms do'. For the following period see Daniel Azpiazu, 'Transnational corporations in Argentina, 1976-1983', *CEPAL Review*, no. 28 (April 1986), p. 99-133.

The Economy and Economic History. General

728  **The political economy of Argentina, 1880-1946.**
Edited by Guido di Tella, D. C. M. Platt.   London: Macmillan; New
York: St. Martin's Press, 1986. 217p. map.
An important collection of essays co-edited by the late Christopher Platt, former
professor of Latin American history at St Antony's College, Oxford. Nine scholars,
including the editors, Joseph S. Tulchin, Tulio Halperín Donghi, David Rock, Arturo
O'Connell, Peter Alhadeff, Jorge Fodor and Callum A. MacDonald, discuss such
themes as export policies, currency problems, foreign trade and investment (essentially
Great Britain and the United States), and the agricultural sector. There is a key
chapter by Raúl Prebisch (see *The influence of Raúl Prebisch on economic policy-
making in Argentina, 1950-1962*) on the economic policies of the 1930s and 1940s.

729  **The political economy of Argentina, 1946-1983.**
Edited by Guido di Tella, Rudiger Dornbusch.   Pittsburgh,
Pennsylvania: University of Pittsburgh Press; Basingstoke, England:
Macmillan, 1989. 349p. bibliog. (Pitt Latin American Series).
(St. Antony's Macmillan Series).
Essentially chronological in layout, this valuable set of essays assesses the economic
policies of successive régimes in the period covered. Commentaries by other specialists
are included and there are almost seventy tables. J. C. Portantiero provides an
'overview' of the period and Guido di Tella a postscript to 1986. Di Tella and Carlos
Rodríguez Braun have recently edited some remarkable complementary interpretations of the same period by nearly all of Argentina's living Finance Ministers:
*Argentina, 1946-1983: the economic ministers speak* (the same publishers, 1990).

730  **Reversal of development in Argentina: postwar counterrevolutionary
policies and their structural consequences.**
Carlos H. Waisman.   Princeton, New Jersey: Princeton University
Press, 1987. 329p. bibliog.
A 'sociological interpretation of the reversal of economic and political development' in
Argentina. The study focuses on the 1930s and 1940s, because it was then that
Argentina 'switched development tracks and became an underdeveloped society'. A
future volume on the 1970s is promised. A famous early work which argues that
Argentina's basic problem is 'fundamentally, though not exclusively, social rather than
economic', is Tomás Roberto Fillol, *Social factors in economic development: the
Argentine case* (Cambridge, Massachusetts: MIT Press, 1961. 118p.). See also Susan
and Peter Calvert's *Argentina: political culture and instability* (Basingstoke, England:
Macmillan, 1989. 327p.).

731  **The Review of the River Plate.**
Buenos Aires (Casilla de Correo 294 (Suc. 13-B), 1413 Buenos Aires),
1891- . 2 issues a month.
A long-established English-language publication subtitled 'a journal dealing with
Argentine financial, economic, agricultural, political and shipping afffairs'. Argentina's
foremost Spanish-language economic journal is the quarterly *Desarrollo Económico*,
published by the Instituto de Desarrollo Económico y Social since 1961; it is indexed
by *HAPI: Hispanic American Periodicals Index* and *Handbook of Latin American
Studies* (qq.v.).

732 **The state and capital accumulation in Argentina.**
Guillermo Flichman. In: *The state and capital accumulation in Latin America. Volume 2: Argentina, Bolivia, Colombia, Ecuador, Peru, Uruguay, Venezuela.* Edited by Christian Anglade, Carlos Fortin. Basingstoke, England: Macmillan, 1990, p. 1-31. bibliog. (Latin American Studies Series).

An examination of the Argentine state's efforts (1930s-70s) 'to create necessary conditions for capital accumulation through the regulation of income distribution and the allocation of resources, and through direct participation in productive activities'. The same period is covered in Mónica Peralta Ramos's *Etapas de acumulación y alianzas de clases en la Argentina (1930-1970)* (Buenos Aires: Siglo Veintiuno, 1972. 187p.), a Marxist interpretation of the political effects of capital accumulation on class structure and class interrelations.

733 **The state and underdevelopment in Spanish America: the political roots of dependency in Peru and Argentina.**
Douglas Friedman. Boulder, Colorado; London: Westview Press, 1984. 236p. bibliog. (Westview Replica Edition).

Although influenced by the work of dependency theorists, notably André Gunder Frank, the author takes issue with the view that the developing nations of Spanish America in the late nineteenth century were dependent on world capitalism directed by the United States and Western Europe. He concedes that internal factors, such as political and social-class relations, were no less significant in Peru and Argentina, where state structures needed resources 'to impose order on conflict-ridden societies', and those resources had to come from foreign trade. In short, this is a 'refined dependency' argument, and is a useful contribution to a controversial debate.

# Economic policy

734 **Argentina in the postwar era: politics and economic policy making in a divided society.**
Gary W. Wynia. Albuquerque, New Mexico: University of New Mexico Press, 1978. 289p. bibliog.

This is an important contribution to the unending debate concerning the paradox of Argentina's modern economic development; it focuses upon the formulation and implementation of government policies between 1946 and 1976. The author points to the crucial cause of the 'divided society': by ignoring or alienating the very sectors whose cooperation was essential for the success of its economic policy, each government created economic problems which led in turn to political conflict.

735 **The Argentine economy: policy reform for development.**
Eduardo R. Conesa. Lanham, Maryland; New York; London:
University Press of America, 1989. 124p.

The author reviews successive economic policies after 1930, since when Argentina has experienced economic stagnation and political instability without a consensus on how best to deal with these problems. He also presents his own proposals for resolving them. This book is not for the general reader.

736 **Currency substitution and liberalization: the case of Argentina.**
Ugo Fasano-Filho. Aldershot, England: Gower, 1986. 194p. bibliog.

A study of economic policies since 1959, but focusing on the military government's 1976-81 free-market liberalization programme introduced by Finance Minister José Martínez de Hoz in an effort to reverse the trend of low growth and high inflation. The non-specialist may be deterred by the econometric analysis but chapters 3-5 are more straightforward. Fifty-four tables are included.

737 **Discipline as the central objective of the economic programme of the
Argentine government since 1976.**
Adolfo Canitrot. *World Development*, vol. 8, no. 11 (Nov. 1980),
p. 913-28.

A trenchant brief attack on the 'liberal' economic programme of Finance Minister José Martínez de Hoz, 1976-79. The author notes that, while the military government could count on widespread national concern at the economic crisis, this was a short-term asset only and inherent pressures for industrial expansion and subsidized investments, incompatible with the programme, would re-emerge. This liberalization programme has been the subject of a number of other studies, including: Jan Peter Wogart, 'Combining price stabilization with trade and financial liberalization policies: the Argentine experience, 1976-1981', *Journal of Interamerican Studies and World Affairs*, vol. 25, no. 4 (Nov. 1983), p. 445-76; and Arthur J. Mann, Carlos E. Sánchez, 'Monetarism, economic reform and socio-economic consequences: Argentina, 1976-1982', *International Journal of Social Economics*, vol. 11, nos 3/4 (1984), p. 12-28.

738 **Economic policymaking in a conflict society: the Argentine case.**
Richard D. Mallon, in collaboration with Juan V. Sourrouille.
Cambridge, Massachusetts; London: Harvard University Press, 1975.
264p. bibliog.

An excellent analysis of macroeconomic policymaking from 1948 to 1970, based in part on the author's own experience as an adviser to Argentina's National Development Council 1965-66. 'Decision-makers in Argentina have quite consistently attempted to adopt policy positions that seemed designed to tear society apart rather than to forge new coalitions.'

739 **Economic stabilization in Argentina: the Austral Plan.**
Luigi Manzetti, Marco dell'Aquila. *Journal of Latin American
Studies*, vol. 20, no. 1 (May 1988), p. 1-26.

An appraisal of the plan introduced by President Raúl Alfonsín in June 1985 to combat Argentina's hyperinflation, showing how 'although quite successful and innovative in its initial stages, the Austral Plan eventually collapsed. This was as a result of strong political pressures that induced the government to reactivate the economy and alter its economic strategy when faced with unresolved economic problems'. The pessimistic conclusion has been borne out by subsequent events.

740 **Financing private business in an inflationary context: the experience of Argentina between 1967 and 1980.**
Domingo F. Cavallo, A. Humberto Petrei.  In: *Financial policies and the world capital market: the problem of Latin American countries.*
Edited by Pedro Aspe Armella, Rudiger Dornbusch, Maurice Obstfeld. Chicago; London: University of Chicago Press, 1983, p. 153-85.
(National Bureau of Economic Research. Conference Report).
The authors (Cavallo was director of the Central Bank during the last military régime and is currently Finance Minister) analysed the balance sheets of seventy-eight private firms to discover the effects of anti-inflationary policies on their financial structure. An analysis of the effects of economic policy reforms on manufacturing and agricultural exporting firms between 1976 and 1981 is *Scrambling for survival: how firms adjusted to the recent reforms in Argentina, Chile, and Uruguay,* edited by Vittorio Corbo and Jaime de Melo (Washington, DC: World Bank, 1985. 226p. [Staff Working Papers, 764]).

741 **Inflation stabilization: the experience of Israel, Argentina, Brazil, Bolivia, and Mexico.**
Edited by Michael Bruno, Guido di Tella, Rudiger Dornbusch, Stanley Fischer.  Cambridge, Massachusetts; London: MIT Press, 1988. 419p. bibliog.
This collection of papers and commentaries originated in a conference held in Spain in mid-1987. It contains two rather technical contributions on Argentina: José Luis Machinea and José María Fanelli (p. 111-52) and Alfredo J. Canavese and Guido di Tella (p. 153-90) on President Raúl Alfonsín's anti-inflation Austral Plan of 1985-87.

742 **The influence of Raúl Prebisch on economic policy-making in Argentina, 1950-1962.**
Kathryn Sikkink.  *Latin American Research Review,* vol. 23, no. 2 (1988), p. 91-114.
A well-documented study on the life and times of the outstanding economist Raúl Prebisch (1901-86), an international figure whose reputation in Latin America is analagous to that of J. M. Keynes in English-speaking countries. As Executive Secretary of the United Nations Economic Commission for Latin America (ECLA) from 1948 to 1962, and as Secretary-General of the United Nations Conference on Trade and Development (UNCTAD) from 1964 to 1969, he was a decisive voice and influence in the modern economic history of Latin America. At one time he was special economic adviser to President Eduardo Lonardi and was instrumental in bringing the ECLA mission to Argentina in 1958 (see *El desarrollo económico de la Argentina*). See also 'Raúi Prebisch, 1901-1986: an appreciation', by James H. Street, *Journal of Economic Issues,* vol. 21, no. 2 (June 1987), p. 649-59.

743 **Neoconservative economics in the Southern Cone of Latin America,
1973-1983.**
Joseph Ramos.   Baltimore, Maryland; London: Johns Hopkins
University Press, 1986. 200p. bibliog. (Johns Hopkins Studies in
Development).

A survey of the liberal economic policies of the military régimes of Argentina, Chile
and Uruguay in the decade covered. The author compares and contrasts the three
countries' experiences of free-market policies, and is doubtful that they generated
genuine development: 'at the root of the faulty model lay the antiinterventionist biases
of neoconservative policymakers'. See also Edward C. Epstein, 'Recent stabilization
programs in Argentina, 1973-86', *World Development*, vol. 15, no. 8 (Aug. 1987),
p. 991-1005; and Robert F. Kaufmann, *The politics of debt in Argentina, Brazil, and
Mexico: economic stabilization in the 1980s* (Berkeley, California: University of
California, Institute of International Studies, 1988. 137p. Research Series, no. 72).

# Foreign debt

744 **Argentina's bargaining with the IMF.**
Kendall W. Stiles.   *Journal of Interamerican Studies and World
Affairs*, vol. 29, no. 3 (fall 1987), p. 55-85. bibliog.

Argentina's relations with the International Monetary Fund have been, and remain, a
critical factor in government economic policy, given the country's massive foreign debt.
The article covers the period 1982 to June 1988, and includes a detailed chronology of
the various standby loans made by the IMF. Since 1982 'Argentine governments have
deliberately employed a "bargaining" strategy in their relations with the IMF'. See also
Jorge Marshall, José Luis Mardones S. and Isabel Marshall L., 'IMF conditionality:
the experiences of Argentina, Brazil, and Chile', in *IMF conditionality*, edited by John
Williamson (Washington, DC: Institute for International Economics, 1983, p. 275-
323), which covers the period 1958-77 for Argentina.

745 **Argentina's debt to the Equity Conversion Program.**
Miguel Paz, David J. Tecson.   *Journal of World Trade Law*, vol. 22,
no. 5 (Oct. 1988), p. 81-7.

In January 1988, with a foreign debt of around fifty billion dollars, the Alfonsín
government introduced a 'debt-to-equity conversion programme', through which two
billion dollars of the debt would be converted into equity in the Argentine private
sector over the next five years. As well as eliminating a small part of the external debt,
the plan was intended to stimulate productive investment in the economy. The article
describes how the programme operates and the progress to date: 'guarded optimism
and recognition of a delayed step in the right direction'.

746 **Argentina's foreign debt: its origin and consequences.**
Marcelo Diamand, Daniel Naszewki. In: *Politics and economics of external debt crisis: the Latin American experience.* Edited by Miguel S. Wionczek, in collaboration with Luciano Tomassini. Boulder, Colorado; London: Westview Press, 1985, p. 231-76. (Westview Special Studies in Latin America and the Caribbean).

'Although Argentina's current foreign debt would appear to be partly due to the accumulated indebtedness of three decades, the greater part was incurred under Minister of Finance José Martínez de Hoz', whose stabilization plans (1976-79) are examined in particular detail here. The author attributes the indebtedness to 'increased imports, increased tourism, the flight of capitalism and interest service'. See also Carlos A. Rodríguez, 'Argentina's foreign debt: origins and alternatives', in *Debt, adjustment and recovery: Latin America's prospects for growth and development*, edited by Sebastian Edwards and Felipe Larraín (Oxford; Cambridge, Massachusetts: Basil Blackwell, 1989, p. 181-204.).

747 **The foreign debt of the Argentine Republic.**
Harold Edwin Peters. Baltimore, Maryland: Johns Hopkins University Press; London: Oxford University Press, 1934. 186p. bibliog. (Johns Hopkins University Studies in Historical and Political Science. Extra Volumes: New Series, 21).

A classic study of the evolution of the foreign debt, 1880-1930. Before 1880, provincial borrowing overshadowed that of the national government. Between 1880 and 1889, 'borrowing went on at a tremendous rate, culminating in disaster for both the Argentine and its creditors'. After the First World War the government looked to United States capital; the flotation of a long-term loan was first made in 1924; 'thereafter offerings came rapidly, so that nearly three hundred millions were taken by the national government alone'.

# Inflation

748 **Argentina's most recent inflationary cycle, 1975-85.**
Guido di Tella. In: *Latin American debt and the adjustment crisis.* Edited by Rosemary Thorp, Laurence Whitehead. Basingstoke, England: Macmillan in association with St. Antony's College, Oxford, 1987. p. 162-207. bibliog.

Argentina's recent development has shown 'a pronounced tendency to cycles, not in income so much as prices, each cycle taking the economy to a new and higher level of inflation'. The author describes the behaviour of inflation during the period and suggests remedies. He observes that inflation has been taken so much for granted that 'economic actors are no longer sensitive to any kind of monetary signal, or to assurances about the stability of any set of prices'; ironically, the very predictability of inflation is 'what keeps the economy going'.

749 **Conflict and inflation in Argentina, 1966-1980.**
Rosalía Cortes. The Hague: Institute of Social Studies, 1985. 82p.
bibliog. (Research Report Series, no. 16).

Since the 1950s Argentina has experienced an average inflation rate of twenty-five per cent. This paper charts the effects of successive economic policies on the inflationary process. Also useful is 'Relative price distortions and inflation: the case of Argentina, 1963-1976', by Ke-Young Chu and Andrew Feltenstein, *International Monetary Fund Staff Papers*, vol. 25, no. 3 (Sept. 1978), p. 452-93.

750 **Cuarenta años de inflación en la Argentina: 1945-1985.** (Forty years of inflation in Argentina, 1945-1985.)
Guillermo Vitelli. Buenos Aires: Editorial Legasa, 1986. 239p.
bibliog. (Ensayo Crítico).

A detailed analysis of Argentina'a failure to stabilize prices since the Second World War, focusing on salaries, foreign exchange, interest rates, public-service charges and agricultural and industrial prices. There are over fifty tables in the text and a further ten pages of statistical appendices.

# Finance, Investment and Banking

## Finance and investment

751 **Argentina: business opportunities in the 1980's.**
Prepared and written by Michael Frenchman in collaboration with
Metra Consulting Group and J. P. Ford, International Joint Ventures
Ltd. London: Metra Consulting Group, 1979. 339p. maps.
A comprehensive guide for the investor. Two introductory chapters review the
economy from the Perón era, main industries and services, agriculture, food and
fishing. These are followed by information on investing and trading in Argentina, and a
chapter of general information. The appendices list essential information such as the
top 180 companies, laws of finance and investment, government departments and
commercial bank ratings. Seventy-five tables are included.

752 **Argentina in transition: evaluating business prospects in a new setting.**
Ken Oehlkers. New York: Business International Corporation, 1978.
99p.
There are chapters on Argentina's key industrial sectors, rules for the foreign investor
and operating variables (labour, price controls, import and export controls, credit
financing, foreign exchange and remitting profits). Appendices cover taxation and the
texts of the 1976 and 1977 foreign-investment and transfer-of-technology laws. The
author was the associate editor of *Business Latin America* (see *Latin American Markets*).

753 **Argentina: pros and cons of a long standing presence.**
Mattia Barbera. *Politica Internazionale* (English edition, Florence),
vol. 5, no. 2 (autumn 1986), p. 73-87.
A study of Italian investment in Argentina, 1860-1985, including two case-studies of
Olivetti and Fiat. Olivetti opened its Argentine branch for the production of
typewriters in 1951. Fiat first began operations in 1923, continued to expand until 1976

but began a disinvestment policy in 1982. The other principal Italian industrial firms operating in Argentina are Pirelli, ENI, Montedison, Manelli, SNIA-Viscosa, Branca, Gancia and Catene Regina. Today, Italy ranks fourth of foreign countries investing in the country.

754 **Características y análisis histórico de las inversiones extranjeras en la Argentina, 1930-1973.** (The history and characteristics of foreign investments in Argentina, 1930-1973.)
Daniel Mato, Marta Colman.    Buenos Aires: Editorial El Coloquio, 1974. 135p.

A useful collection of information marred by its consistent attacks on foreign 'imperialism'. The appendices contain a case-study of the automobile industry by Antonio Brailovsky, a critical analysis of the 1973 foreign-investment law, and the texts of this law and five earlier laws (1949-71). Ten tables are included.

755 **Doing business in Argentina.**
Buenos Aires: Price Waterhouse, 1987. 90p.

The financial consultants Price Waterhouse first opened their practice in Argentina in 1913. The four main chapters of this guide describe the investment climate, 'doing business' (exchange controls and restrictions on foreign investment, regulatory agencies, investment incentives, banking and local finance, exporting to Argentina, business entities, labour relations and social security), accounting practices and taxation. There is a supplement (April 1989. 23p.). A recent report which highlights the positive climate for investment opening up under President Menem is: *Investment opportunities in Argentina*, written by Sebastian Doggart, financial editor of the *Buenos Aires Herald*, and others (London: Southern Development Trust, 1991. 104p.).

756 **Evolución monetaria argentina.** (The history of money in Argentina.)
Rafael Olarra Jiménez.    Buenos Aires: Editorial Universitaria de Buenos Aires, 1968. 187p. bibliog. (Temas de EUDEBA. Economía).

A straightforward history, with useful tables, of money and banking 1810-1968, with a review of fiscal policy, especially since 1931.

757 **Foreign finance in Argentina for the first half-century of independence.**
D. C. M. Platt.    *Journal of Latin American Studies*, vol. 15, no. 1 (May 1983), p. 23-47.

Written by the leading authority on the history of Anglo-Latin American commercial relations, this is a challenging refutation of a widely held Argentine view that independent Argentina was really a dependency of Great Britain and, therefore, that the country's political independence was inhibited by its economic weakness. The author shows that the 1824 Baring loan made little impact on the Argentine economy; Rosas opposed foreign trade and capital investment; the cost of the Paraguayan War was met almost entirely within Argentina ('the alternative of foreign borrowing did not exist!'); while public borrowing abroad became important after 1870, private investment in Argentina began much earlier. He concludes that 'until the last decades of the nineteenth century, Argentina was funded largely within the Republic'.

758 **French investments in Argentina and Brazil.**
J. Fred Rippy. *Political Science Quarterly*, vol. 64, no. 4 (Dec. 1949), p. 560-78.

Large-scale French investment in Argentina began in the 1880s. The major investments were in public services, including three French-owned railways, two port companies (one French-owned and the other French-operated), and interests in a gas company and two or three electricity utilities. Next in size were banks and loan companies (ten French-controlled), real estate, agriculture, trading and manufacturing firms, and mining. French and other foreign investments were severely checked when Perón nationalized foreign utilities in the 1940s.

759 **Latin American markets.**
New York: Mortgage Commentary Publications, 1981- . fortnightly.

Formerly published by Financial Times Business Information, London (1981-90), this newsletter provides up-to-date facts and figures on the latest developments in business, finance, trade, the domestic economy, legislation, industry and technology. Also useful on trade and direct investment is *Business Latin America* (New York: Business International Corporation, 1966- ), subtitled 'weekly report to managers of Latin American operations'.

760 **Monetary developments in Argentina, 1852-1865.**
James R. Scobie. *Inter-American Economic Affairs*, vol. 8, no. 2 (autumn 1954), p. 54-83.

An account of monetary developments from the defeat of Rosas to the outbreak of the Paraguayan War, during which time the country experienced budgetary deficits, an unfavourable balance of trade and fluctuating paper currrency. Successive governments met the budgetary deficit 'by internal and external loans and by the printing of paper money, a form of forced loan from the public'.

761 **Money and prices in Argentina, 1935-1962.**
Adolfo César Diz. In: *Varieties of monetary experience.* Edited by David Meiselman. Chicago; London: University of Chicago Press, 1970, p. 69-162. (Economics Research Studies of the Economics Research Center of the University of Chicago).

The year 1935 marks the establishment of the Central Bank and the modern era of banking. Between 1935 and 1962 the economy was subject to fluctuating rates of inflation, unstable economic growth and variable economic policy. This is an econometric study of the demand for and supply of money during the period. The demand for money increased at an average rate of fifteen per cent a year; 'variations in the expected rate of change in prices and in the expected per capita real income explain a very high fraction of the observed variation in per capita real money holdings'; changes in the rate of money supply significantly affected the behaviour of the rate of inflation.

762 **El servicio del capital extranjero y el control de cambios: la experiencia argentina de 1900 a 1943.** (Foreign financial services and exchange control: the experience of Argentina between 1900 and 1943.) Walter M. Beveraggi Allende. Mexico City: Fondo de Cultura Económica, 1954. 238p. bibliog.

A study of the effects of foreign investments and financial services on Argentina's balance of payments and foreign debt.

763 **El sistema financiero argentino.** (The Argentine financial system.) Andrés Nova. Buenos Aires: Selcon Editorial, 1970. 354p. bibliog. (Selección Contable).

Examines official monetary policy, the banking system, non-bank financial institutions (including credit companies) and investment financing, ending with the text of the 1969 law for the regulation of finance companies.

764 **The state and business practice in Argentina, 1862-1914.** Charles A. Jones. In: *Latin America, economic imperialism and the state: the political economy of the external connection from independence to the present.* Edited by Christopher Abel, Colin M. Lewis. London; Dover, New Hampshire: Athlone, 1985, p. 184-98. (University of London. Institute of Latin American Studies. Monographs, no. 13).

After 1862 substantial amounts of capital were raised in London for investment in the newly unified republic. 'The greater part of these funds went to the national government and to the leading provinces and municipalities, or else was invested in major railway enterprises.' Focusing on the cases of the London and River Plate Bank and the River Plate Trust, Loan, and Agency Company, this chapter examines British banking policy towards Argentina, the relations between British financial institutions and Argentine state and public-service banks, and the corporate control of British banks vis-à-vis local decision-making. Although British financial institutions projected a conservative, cautious image, 'managers certainly did break the rules continually' and they were not the sole cause of the Argentine economy's lack of diversification. The author examines British financial institutions – especially banks and the particular case of the London and River Plate Bank – in Santa Fe in his 'Personalism, indebtedness, and venality: the political environment of British firms in Santa Fe province, 1865-1900', *Ibero-Amerikanisches Archiv*, vol. 9, new series, nos 3/4 (1983), p. 381-98.

765 **Summary of business conditions in Argentina (April 1987 edition).** Prepared by Harteneck, López y Cía, Correspondents of Coopers & Lybrand. Buenos Aires: Harteneck, López y Cía, 1987. [n.p.].

Provides an outline of the 'important legislation and operating factors that would affect persons or businesses contemplating investments or operations in Argentina', under these headings: basic laws and regulations governing finance and companies, taxation, joint ventures and temporary union of companies, the financial system, labour and immigration, imports and exports, quotation and tender procedures, and local operating factors. There is an appendix of statistical information.

766 **Who invested in Argentina and Uruguay?**
Charles A. Jones. *Business Archives*, no. 48, vol. 4, no. 4
(Nov. 1982), p. 1-23.

An examination of portfolio investment by seventy-one River Plate joint stock companies in 1895, when their total paid-up share capital amounted to £62 millions. More than half the capital was supplied by only 1,800 individuals, and about one-sixth by only sixty-eight individuals. The companies and their portfolio values are listed in tables and appendices. The author looks more closely at some of these individuals, especially Charles Morrison, who invested over half a million pounds in Argentina and helped found the River Plate Trust, Loan, and Agency Company, in 'Great capitalists and the direction of British overseas investment in the late nineteenth century: the case of Argentina', *Business History*, vol. 22, no. 2 (July 1980), p. 152-69.

# Banking

767 **The Argentine banking crisis of 1980.**
Tomás J. J. Baliño. Washington, DC: International Monetary Fund, Central Banking Department, 1987. 69p. bibliog. (IMF Working Paper, WP/87/77).

In 1980 one of the country's largest banks, the Banco de Intercambio Regional, failed and within a few days three other major banks had to be intervened, two of which were later liquidated. During 1980-82 a total of seventy-one financial institutions were liquidated. This paper examines the problems of the financial system which led to the bank failures, the banking crisis itself and the reaction of the authorities. Twenty-seven tables are included.

768 **The Argentine banking system.**
Julio González del Solar. *Bank of London & South America Quarterly Review*, vol. 6, no. 4 (Nov. 1966), p. 159-86.

Describes the three major reforms of the banking system, 1935-57, the subsequent growth of the banking system and its current structure. The 1935 reform established the Central Bank as a mixed-capital enterprise in which the private banks had a shareholding. The 1946 and 1949 reforms nationalized bank deposits and 'did nothing to adapt the banking system better to the needs of the economy'. The 1957 reform returned deposits to the banks and restored the 'classic banking system' as it had existed in 1935. After 1957 the banking system developed more rapidly than in the previous twenty years, but less rapidly than other sectors of the economy.

769 **Banking structures and sources of finance in South America.**
Edited by Anne Hendrie. London: Financial Times Business Publishing, 1980. 370p. (The Banker Research Unit Publications).

The chapter by Marta Fainboim of Lloyds Bank International (p. 1-29) reviews banking legislation, the Central Bank, banking institutions (commercial, state, private, foreign, investment, development and mortgage banks, the sources and uses of funds), non-banking institutions (finance companies, savings and loan associations, credit cooperatives, insurance companies, and the capital markets), lending practices and exchange controls. There are twelve tables and a list of nine state and twelve private banks.

770  **A century of banking in Latin America: to commemorate the centenary in 1962 of the Bank of London & South America Limited.**
David Joslin.   London: New York; Toronto: Oxford University Press, 1963. 307p. maps.
The study is confined largely to British banks; chapters three and seven are devoted to the London and River Plate Bank, 1862-1914. The bank established its head office in Buenos Aires and later added branches in Rosario, Córdoba, Montevideo and Tucumán. The bank's policies, notable chairmen and relations with domestic state and private banks and other British banks are discussed. In 1918 the bank was bought by Lloyds Bank and in 1923 was amalgamated with the London and Brazilian Bank and London and River Plate Bank to form the Bank of London and South America.

771  **The development of Argentina [sic] commercial banking since 1957.**
Frederick Brooman.   Buenos Aires: Instituto Torcuato di Tella, Centro de Investigaciones Económicas, 1968. 13p. (Documento de Trabajo, 26).
'Since 1957, when Argentina's commercial banks recovered their autonomy after a decade of complete dependence on the Central Bank, there has been a remarkable growth in the number of banking offices.' Using information from the Central Bank's *Guía bancaria de la República Argentina* and *Boletín estadístico* (1964), the author studies this numerical growth (no fewer than thirty-seven new banks came into existence between 1957 and 1963), the distribution of new offices outside the capital itself, banking growth in terms of total assets and deposits, and the reasons for the expansion. Despite the emergence of middle-sized banks, 'the system continues to be dominated . . . by big banks with extensive branch systems'.

772  **A history of money and banking in Argentina.**
Angel M. Quintero Ramos.   Río Piedras, Puerto Rico: University of Puerto Rico, 1965. 346p. bibliog.
A descriptive, chronological study to 1949 – the first work to consider the whole history of money and banking in Argentina – based on a 1950 New York University thesis. At each stage it covers the currency, commercial and central banking, the general economic and political environment, foreign trade and government economic policy. Seventy-six tables are included.

773  **Moneda y bancos en la República Argentina.** (Money and banking in Argentina.)
Jorge A. Difrieri.   Buenos Aires: Abeledo-Perrot, 1967. 381p. bibliog.
A history of money and banking from the colonial period, but especially since 1810. See also Ildefonso F. Cavagna Martínez, *Sistema bancario argentino* (Buenos Aires: Ediciones Arayú, 1954. 493p.), a legal history with useful sections on Perón's banking reforms, international banking agreements and foreign investment.

# Taxation

774 **Argentine provincial tax systems.**
Ernest F. Patterson. *Inter-American Economic Affairs*, vol. 7 no. 3 (winter 1953), p. 37-64.
The most important provincial taxes are the property tax, the stamp tax, the licence tax, the tax on profitable activities, the inheritance tax, and the severance tax (on the exploitation or sale of resources or products). In addition, there are numerous minor taxes 'such as fees for registration of livestock marks and brands, tax on horse races, tax on sale of electricity, fees for measuring land, admission taxes, and the like'. The main features of the principal taxes as applied in representative provinces are described, with extracts from provincial codes.

775 **The tax system of the Argentine national government.**
Ernest F. Patterson. *National Tax Journal*, vol. 5, no. 3 (Sept. 1952), p. 267-74.
Describes the development of the tax structure to 1944 and the principal taxes currently in use: customs duties, internal (excise) taxes, sales tax, income tax, excess-profits and capital-gains taxes, and minor (stamp, licence and property) taxes. The author also makes certain criticisms of the tax system.

776 **Taxation in Latin America.**
Edited by M. A. García Caballero. Amsterdam: International Bureau of Fiscal Documentation, 1970- . 3 vols.
Volume one of this regularly updated looseleaf service contains the country surveys. Argentina (supplement no. 72, Sept. 1988), occupies 92 pages. There is a current tax chart showing current rates of corporate/individual income tax and value-added tax, and a discussion of the tax system, followed by detailed sections on the present provisions for taxation of income derived by resident entities, individuals and non-residents; taxation of business income, investment income, capital and transactions; business taxes and other charges, tax incentives and exemptions; and international aspects, including tax treaties. There is a final section on tax administration.

**Argentina: adjustment for inflation in Argentine income tax law.**
*See* item no. 637.

# Trade and Commerce

**777   Anglo-Argentine commercial relations: a private sector view, 1922-43.**
Paul B. Goodwin. *Hispanic American Historical Review*, vol. 61, no. 1 (Feb. 1981), p. 29-51.
A study of the lively debates within the British Chamber of Commerce in Buenos Aires, which 'represented the multiple interests of British enterprise': importers, local manufacturers and retailers, *estancieros* and directors of public utilities. The Chamber opposed Argentine tariff protection and was alarmed at Britain's waning competitiveness with the United States and Germany. Includes discussion of the 1929 D'Abernon mission and the 1933 Roca-Runciman Treaty. 'Import interests, consistently on the defensive from the mid-1920s, were destined never to win significant trade concessions from Argentina.' The author argues against the dependency theory, insisting that 'the Argentine Government was master in its own house'.

**778   The Anglo-Argentine connection, 1900-1939.**
Roger Gravil.   Boulder, Colorado; London: Westview Press, 1985. 267p. bibliog. (Dellplain Latin American Studies, no. 16).
An impressive study of Anglo-Argentine trade relations, especially Argentina's meat and grain exports to Great Britain, its chief trading partner before 1914. The work contains valuable analyses of Argentine agricultural production, the 'big four' Argentine-owned grain export-houses, British exports to Argentina, Argentine tariffs and Anglo-American rivalries. The 1933 Roca-Runciman Treaty (which the author deplores – he is generally critical of British trade policies), caused much Argentine resentment and encouraged the emergence of Peronism which removed Britain from its former privileged position. There are many tables in the text and a statistical appendix.

779 **Anglo-Argentine trading arrangements.**
Ursula Wassermann. *Journal of World Trade Law*, vol. 16, no. 4
(July-Aug. 1982), p. 366-69.

The 1825 Treaty of Amity and Commerce 'formed the basis for Anglo-Argentine financial and commercial relations for over a hundred years'; it was replaced in 1933 by the Roca-Runciman Treaty. The author reviews British investment and finance before the Falklands War, after which both countries froze the other's assets. In 1982 Argentina ranked thirty-seventh among Britain's trade partners; however, 'indirect relations in terms of invisibles remain of considerable importance'.

780 **Argentina – economic cooperation with the Federal Republic of Germany and the European Community: problems and prospects.**
Guido Ashoff, Klaus Esser. Berlin: German Development Institute,
1985. 153p. bibliog. (Occasional Papers, no. 84).

Part one examines Argentine political and economic developments since redemocratization and their implications for economic cooperation with the Federal Republic of Germany. German exports still largely consist of 'other products', especially armaments; 'hardly any of Argentina's exporting industries can compete with their counterparts' in Germany. Part two deals with relations between Argentina and the European Community. Since 1970 Argentina has lost much of the EC's market for its agricultural exports and no trade or cooperation agreement currently exists; the chief obstacles are the EC's agricultural policy and Britain's stance over the Falkland Islands issue.

781 **Argentina's foreign trade.**
Carlos M. Gabel. *Journal of World Trade Law*, vol. 2 (Nov.-
Dec. 1968), p. 663-83.

A survey of the legal provisions affecting Argentina's foreign trade in the twentieth century, focusing on the period since 1946. In 1968 the country's exports of primary products were comparatively diversified despite the 'tightening of its foreign markets'. Eleven tables are included.

782 **Argentine-Brazilian economic integration: an early appraisal.**
Luigi Manzetti. *Latin American Research Review*, vol. 25, no. 3
(1990), p. 109-40. bibliog.

In July 1986 Presidents Raúl Alfonsín and José Sarney signed the Argentina-Brazil Economic Integration Pact (ABEIP). The article describes previous integration efforts, the main provisions of the Pact (especially its all-important first protocol creating a customs union for a number of capital goods), and an appraisal of the structural, financial and administrative problems encountered so far. There are nine tables of statistics of bilateral trade, 1975-88. See also Daniel Chudnovsky, 'Economic integration between Argentina and Brazil: capital goods as a starting point', *Development and South-South Cooperation*, vol. 4, no. 7 (Dec. 1988), p. 105-13. bibliog; and *On Argentine-Brazilian economic integration* (item no. 792).

783 **British mercantile houses in Buenos Aires, 1810-1880.**
Vera Blinn Reber.   Cambridge, Massachusetts: Harvard University
Press, 1979. 203p. maps. bibliog.

An economic study of the organization and operations of British import and export houses in Buenos Aires during the period, with many interesting details on the social life of the merchants. The author also considers their impact on the Argentine economy, and defends them from accusations of 'imperialism': 'Although merchants acted in nearly every case from self-interest, the overall effect on Argentina was positive'. The merchants repatriated little capital to England and the drain on Argentine capital was not significant.

784 **British retail trade in Argentina, 1900-40.**
Roger Gravil.   *Inter-American Economic Affairs*, vol. 24, no. 2
(autumn 1970), p. 3-26.

By 1900 'Buenos Aires had developed into a highly sophisticated market led by an upper class clientele who knew European consumption standards and demanded that British department stores should match them'. The article is based on Department of Overseas Trade reports and the archives of two major Buenos Aires stores, Gath & Chaves and Harrods.

785 **The commercial relations between the United States and Argentina.**
Paul DeWitt.   *Southwestern Political and Social Science Quarterly*,
vol. 11, no. 2 (Sept. 1930), p. 156-72.

Commercial and diplomatic relations between the two countries during the nineteenth century were relatively uneventful. Two bilateral commercial treaties were signed in 1853: the Treaty of Friendship, Commerce and Navigation and the Treaty for the Free Navigation of the Rivers Paraná and Uruguay. Between 1850 and 1880, trade was generally favourable to Argentina; in the latter year it exported (mostly raw hides and skins) three times as much as it imported; between 1880 and 1910 'merchandise trade was, generally, and sometimes overwhelmingly, favorable to the United States'. The article also discusses the effects of United States tariff laws. The United States' lack of banking facilities and modest levels of investment in Argentina were hindrances to its export trade to Argentina before 1914.

786 **Exchange control and the Argentine market.**
Virgil Salera.   New York: Columbia University Press, 1941. 283p.
bibliog.

Since 1899, Argentina 'has successively experienced fourteen years of the gold standard, thirteen years of uncontrolled inconvertible paper, another two years of the gold standard, still another biennium of uncontrolled inconvertible currency, and finally, since 1931, two distinct types of exchange control'. The book considers the effects of this fluctuating system of exchange control on British bilateral trade with Argentina, 1899-1937.

787 **From import substitution to exports: the manufacturing exports experience of Argentina and Brazil.**
Simón Teitel, Francisco E. Thoumi. *Economic Development and Cultural Change*, vol. 34, no. 3 (April 1986), p. 455-90.
Argentina's and Brazil's import-substitution manufacturing policies were 'a preamble to the export stage, providing the learning required before reaching out for markets abroad'. Since the 1960s both countries have been successfully exporting natural-resource-based manufactures and skill-based metalworking products, assisted by an easing of protectionist measures.

788 **Guía de exportadores e importadores argentinos / Directory of Argentine exporters and importers.**
Edited by Telmo G. Mirat. Buenos Aires: Editorial Scott, 1990. 16th ed. 186p. map.
This guide is 'compiled with the purpose of giving foreign traders and manufacturers a basic reference source to locate appropriate trading partners in Argentina'. It comprises four sections: a survey of foreign-trade institutions (government agencies, banks, business and industrial associations, trade publications and services such as customs brokers, transport companies and cargo agents); information for business visitors; a directory of exporters (names and addresses, classified by product, p. 67-147) and a directory of importers, agents and representatives (39p.). Also useful is the bimonthly *Comments on Argentine trade* (Buenos Aires: American Chamber of Commerce in Argentina, 1920- ).

789 **Major companies of Argentina, Brazil, Mexico and Venezuela 1982.**
Edited by S. J. Longrigg. London: Graham & Trotman, 1981. 3rd ed. 518p.
An alphabetical directory of 514 major industrial and commercial companies, including a number of foreign firms, supplying the following information: address, senior executives, principal activity, agencies, branch offices, plants and warehouses, subsidiary and associate companies, financial information (capital, turnover, loans, profits, reserves, deposits), principal shareholders and number of employees.

790 **Market guide: Latin America. January 1990.**
New York: Dun & Bradstreet International, 1990. 2 vols. maps.
The directory of Argentina's producers of goods and services is included on pages 1-80 of volume two, and is alphabetical by city or town and listing address, type of product, estimated financial strength and rating.

791 **The merchants of Buenos Aires, 1778-1810: family and commerce.**
Susan Migden Socolow. Cambridge, England; New York: Cambridge University Press, 1978. 253p. maps. bibliog. (Cambridge Latin American Studies, 30).
A predominantly social study of the rich and successful wholesale merchants of Buenos Aires at the end of the colonial era: their origins, training, commercial ventures, lifestyle, religious participation and political and social awareness. There is a revealing chapter on the role of marriage and kinship in the formation of commercial alliances. Twelve important familes are examined, and there is a case-study of one particular

221

merchant, Gaspar de Santa Coloma. For the following period, see Karla Robinson, 'The merchants of post-independence Buenos Aires', in *Hispanic-American essays in honor of Max Leon Moorhead*, edited by William S. Coker (Pensacola, Florida: Perdido Bay Press, 1979, p. 111-32).

792  **On Argentine-Brazilian economic integration.**
Daniel Chudnovsky, Fernando Porta. *CEPAL Review*, no. 39 (Dec. 1989), p. 115-34. bibliog.

In November 1988 the governments of Argentina and Brazil strengthened their 1986 treaty (see *Argentine-Brazilian economic integration: an early appraisal*) by signing a Treaty of Integration, Cooperation and Development. This sets a period of ten years for forming a common market between the two countries by establishing a preferential trade agreement (customs union) and gradually dismantling reciprocal trade barriers. Together, the two countries account for more than half of Latin America's manufacturing product. The article summarizes trade flows between them during the past ten years. Argentina exports agro-food products to Brazil and imports industrial manufactures, 'almost always with a negative balance'. The author adds a warning: 'the macroeconomic imbalances [of each country] are of such magnitude that they can neutralize integration schemes of any kind'.

793  **Petty capitalism in Spanish America: the pulperos of Puebla, Mexico City, Caracas, and Buenos Aires.**
Jay Kinsbruner.  Boulder, Colorado; London: Westview Press, 1987. 159p. bibliog. (Dellplain Latin American Studies).

A descriptive economic and social profile of *pulperos* (small retail grocers) between 1750 and 1850, focusing on store (*almacén*) ownership and management and town council regulations governing their commerce. Buenos Aires had the greatest number of grocery stores in relation to population: 457 in 1813 (a ratio of 1:94), 502 in 1824 (1:120).

794  **The Uruguayan-Argentinian Trade Co-operation Agreement.**
Daniel Ferrere.  *Journal of World Trade Law*, vol. 18, no. 4 (July-Aug. 1984), p. 320-34.

In 1974 the two countries signed a trade cooperation agreement (Convenio Argentino-Uruguayo de Cooperación Económica, CAUCE – the acronym means 'riverbed' in Spanish), which the author considers a 'flagrant and open violation' of the essential rules of the Latin American Free Trade Association (1960). The agreement exempts more than 950 Uruguayan products from tariffs and restrictions but has had little impact until now on Argentine exports. In 1982 the two countries signed an agricultural version of CAUCE.

795  **Wool trade and commercial networks in Buenos Aires, 1840s to 1880s.**
Hilda Sábato.  *Journal of Latin American Studies*, vol. 15, no. 1 (May 1983), p. 49-81.

During the forty-year period, Argentina became one of the chief suppliers of wool to the expanding wool markets. 'Most of this wool was grown in the fertile sheep-runs of the richest province in the country, and was sent to Europe through its capital city and port, Buenos Aires.' The article describes the international market (there was competition from Australia and the Cape), and the commercial network (export houses, consignment agents, middlemen and the wool warehouses). 'Sheep-raising expanded rapidly throughout the province, pushing cattle southwards and invading the best lands.'

**Commercial arbitration in Argentina.**
*See* item no. 642.

**Doing business in Argentina.**
*See* itcm no. 755.

**Summary of business conditions in Argentina.**
*See* item no. 765.

# Industry

## General

796  **Antecedentes para la historia de la industria argentina.** (The beginnings of industry in Argentina.)
Juan Carlos Nicolau.   Buenos Aires: Talleres Gráficos Lumen, 1968. 192p.

This is a perceptive short history of early Argentine industry, written by a professional engineer. The first section, p. 15-67, deals with colonial regional industries and the questions of labour, transport and legislation. The second and larger section discusses aspects of industry from 1810 to 1835, when the main industrial activities were directed towards food, clothing and housing: the revolutionary government's support for early industrial endeavour; military arms manufactures; meat-salting, hide-curing and small manufacturing industries; provincial industries including Cuyo's wine and mining (and the northwest's sugar), which were affected by free trade and the competition from imported goods; population and labour supply; and investment.

797  **Cincuenta años de industrialización en la Argentina, 1930-1980: desarrollo y perspectivas.** (Fifty years of industrialization in Argentina, 1930-1980: development and prospects.)
Adolfo Dorfman.   Buenos Aires: Ediciones Solar, 1983. 618p.
(Biblioteca 'Dimensión Argentina').

A detailed study of Argentina's industrial development and the decline of heavy industry in the 1970s through a combination of domestic factors. Separate chapters examine industry's natural-resource base (raw materials, agricultural and mineral resources), capital and foreign investment, exports and industrial policy. There are also studies of specific key industries – metallurgical, chemical, oil, automobile, home products, machinery, paper and cement. A continuation of the author's *Historia de la industria argentina* (q.v.).

798 **Dependency, the credit market, and Argentine industrialization, 1860-1940.**
Donna J. Guy. *Business History Review*, vol. 58, no. 4 (winter 1984), p. 532-61.

Describes the development of Argentine industry in terms of the role of foreign investment, local credit structures and 'intraclass disputes as manifested in the political struggle to control scarce credit'. The author concludes that dependency theory is inadequate to explain industry's reliance on foreign capital: it was due 'much more to local Argentine institutions – the Commercial Law [of 1862], the stock market, and the government inspection bureau – than to any pressures from abroad'. See also the author's 'Carlos Pellegrini and the politics of early Argentine industrialization, 1873-1906', *Journal of Latin American Studies*, vol. 11, no. 1 (May 1979), p. 123-44.

799 **Financing Argentine industrial corporate development in the aftermath of the first Perón regime.**
David K. Eiteman. In: *Money and politics in Latin America.* Edited by James W. Wilkie. Los Angeles: UCLA Latin American Center Publications, University of California, 1977, p. 41-91. (Statistical Abstract of Latin America. Supplement Series, vol. 7).

Reviews aspects of the corporate financing policies of fifty large Argentine-owned industrial enterprises, 1955-66, a period of rapid growth in the industrial sector but also of 'rapid inflation and chaotic political conditions', analysing their sources and use of funds, working-capital turnover and balance sheets. The author finds that the largest source of funds was the owners' own equity, channelled mainly into increasing assets.

800 **Historia de la industria argentina.** (A history of Argentine industry.)
Adolfo Dorfman. Buenos Aires: Solar / Hachette, 1970. 2nd ed. 398p. bibliog. (Biblioteca 'Dimensión Argentina').

A classic history of industry from colonial times to 1935, with nearly ninety-six tables. All aspects and sectors of industry are discussed and the treatment is chronological, much of the text being taken up with long lists of companies in particular industries. There is a chapter on the industrial census of 1913. Argentina was still largely an agricultural producer in 1930 and only a small part of its produce was exported. A chronological history from precolonial times to 1961 is Antonio Váquer (et al.), *Historia de la ingeniería en la Argentina* (Buenos Aires: Editorial Universitaria de Buenos Aires, 1968. 441p.). Useful for the colonial period are Pedro Santos Martínez, *Las industrias durante el virreinato, 1776-1810* (Buenos Aires: Editorial Universitaria de Buenos Aires, 1969. 162p.); and Guillermo Fúrlong Cárdiff, *Las industrias en el Río de la Plata desde la colonización hasta 1778* (Buenos Aires: Academia Nacional de la Historia, 1978. 157p.).

801 **Incomplete industrialization: an Argentine obsession.**
Juan Carlos Korol, Hilda Sábato. *Latin American Research Review*, vol. 25, no. 1 (1990), p. 7-30. bibliog.

'The subject of industrialization has become almost an obsession with Argentines. The image of a belated, weak, incomplete, and truncated process of industrialization has become associated with the frustrated destiny of Argentina.' The authors examine the most influential Argentine academic literature on the subject of industrialization, particularly that produced during the 1950s and 1960s.

802 **Industrialization of Latin America.**
Edited by Lloyd J. Hughlett. New York: McGraw-Hill, 1946. 508p.
An undocumented text summarizing the development and current status of Latin American industries. Sections on Argentina may be found within chapters on the following: cement, chemical, communications, fishing, food, leather, metalworking, mining, paint and varnish, petroleum, pharmaceutical, power, publishing, pulp/paper/ lumber, sugar, textile and transportation. Also useful for the period is George Wythe, *Industry in Latin America*, 2nd ed. (New York: Columbia University Press, 1949, 387p.), which contains a chapter on Argentina, p. 79-127, dealing with industrial resources, leading manufacturing industries and national economic policy. Both works were reprinted by Greenwood Press, New York (1970, 1969).

803 **Síntesis histórica del desarrollo industrial argentino.** (A concise history of industrial development in Argentina.)
José Panettieri. Buenos Aires: Ediciones Macchi, 1969. 110p. bibliog. (Colección Humanidades. Temas de Historia. Serie I: Trabajos Originales, 2).
A useful chronological summary of industrial history, 1870 to 1965, intended for students and the general reader, containing twenty-five statistical tables.

804 **The struggle of Argentina within the new international division of labor.**
Lawrence R. Alschuler. *Canadian Journal of Development Studies*, vol. 1, no. 2 (1980), p. 219-41. bibliog.
An examination of the industrial strategies of five administrations, from Perón in 1946 to the end of Onganía's presidency in 1970, focusing on 'multinational penetration' and the 'promotion of non-traditional exports through domestic manufacturing without hindering the traditional agro-export sector'. The author's own conclusion is clear: 'It appears that Argentina has only stabilized its subordinate role within the international division of labor and at the expense of increasing denationalization, industrial concentration, technological and financial dependence, unemployment, and income inequality.'

# Industrialists

805 **The Argentine industrial bourgeoisie: economic strategies and alliances after the fall of Perón.**
Judith Teichman. *NS/NorthSouth: Canadian Journal of Latin American Studies*, vol. 8, no. 16 (1983), p. 1-20.
The author discusses the 'attitudes and political alliances' of the industrial bourgeoisie from the fall of Perón in 1955 to the military coup which brought Onganía to power in 1966, from the perspective of the trade associations representing the textile and metallurgy sectors: the Argentine Industrial Union (UIA) and its arch-rival, the General Economic Confederation (CGE). The UIA was export-oriented and consistently hostile towards the labour movement; the CGE was Peronist and pro-labour. The same author has also made a study of the textile and metallurgical trade

associations during the Perón regime: 'Interest conflict and entrepreneurial support for Perón', *Latin American Research Review*, vol. 16, no. 1 (1981), p. 144-55. An earlier study of 100 industrialists from the UIA and the more interior-based Confederation of Industry is John W. Freels, 'Industrialists and politics in Argentina: an opinion survey of trade association leaders', *Journal of Inter-American Studies and World Affairs*, vol. 12, no. 3 (July 1970), p. 439-54.

806 **Entrepreneurship in Argentine culture: Torcuato di Tella and S.I.A.M.**
Thomas C. Cochran, Rubén E. Reina. Philadelphia: University of Pennsylvania Press, 1963. 338p. bibliog.

Written by a historian and a sociologist, this is 'neither a biography nor a business history in the conventional sense' but a study of the 'strong, paternalistic' entrepreneurial leadership of Italian-born Torcuato di Tella, father of sociologist Torcuato S. di Tella and economist Guido di Tella and founder in 1911 of the huge industrial complex Sociedad Industrial Americana de Maquinarias (S.I.A.M.). After di Tella's death, S.I.A.M. 'moved gradually in the direction of United States management practices'.

807 **Immigrant entrepreneurs, manufacturing and industrial policy in the Argentine, 1922-28.**
Colin M. Lewis. *Journal of Imperial and Commonwealth History*, vol. 16, no. 1 (Oct. 1987), p. 77-108.

Examines the extent to which immigrant industrial entrepreneurs influenced industrial growth and the formulation of economic policy during the presidency of Marcelo T. de Alvear, largely through the campaign for tariff protection mounted by the industrialists' association, the Unión Industrial Argentina. The author concludes that the 1923 tariff deepened the Argentine industrial base.

808 **The industrialists of Argentina.**
Gustavo Polit. In: *Latin America: reform or revolution? A reader.* Edited by James Petras, Maurice Zeitlin. Greenwich, Connecticut: Fawcett Publishers, 1968, p. 399-430. (Political Perspectives Series).

This is a useful summary of the literature coupled with a criticism of the self-interest of landowners and industrialists and of foreign (especially United States) investment in Argentine industry: as Argentine industry has developed, 'it has increased its relationship with landholders and foreign capital'.

809 **Politics in a nondemocratic state: the Argentine industrial elite.**
James Petras, Thomas Cook. In: *Latin America: from dependence to revolution.* Edited by James Petras, Thomas Cook. New York; London; Sydney; Toronto: John Wiley, 1973, p. 176-92.

A profile of Argentine industrial executives, their problem-solving techniques and political attitudes, which reveals that 'nondemocratic forms of representation evoke substantial support from the industrial elite over the short run especially as a bulwark of private property'. This chapter is preceded by the same authors' 'Dependency and the industrial bourgeoisie: attitudes of Argentine executives toward foreign economic investment and U.S. policy', p. 143-75, which finds that Argentine executives (especially, not surprisingly, those working for foreign firms) are more favourable towards foreign investment.

# Manufacturing

810 **Absentee entrepreneurship and the dynamics of the motor vehicle industry in Argentina.**
María Beatriz Nofal. New York; Westport, Connecticut; London: Praeger, 1989. 268p. map. bibliog.
An investigation into the unsatisfactory performance of the motor-vehicle industry from the mid-1950s to 1983, analysing its development, government regulation, production, labour and location, and exports. The author concludes that 'automotive manufacturing in Argentina is still strongly oriented towards production for the domestic market, a market relatively small in size, stagnant, and protected from competition of finished vehicle imports through tariffs and nontariff barriers'.

811 **Argentina.**
Ricardo J. Soifer. *World Development*, vol. 12, nos 5/6 (May/June 1984), p. 625-44. bibliog.
This is a contribution to a special issue on 'Exports of technology by newly-industrializing countries', examining Argentine exports of technology since 1965. Argentina was Latin America's industrial leader in the 1950s, but lost ground to Brazil and Mexico whilst maintaining the region's highest per capita manufacturing product. Argentina is a well-established technology exporter, mainly to the Latin American market (Peru, followed by Bolivia, Paraguay and Cuba). In terms of value, the most important exports are pipeline construction, the industrial sector, research (especially nuclear) facilities, oil refineries, water resources and hydroelectricity, transportation and public health.

812 **The challenge by domestic enterprises to the transnational corporations' domination: a case study of the Argentine pharmaceutical industry.**
Daniel Chudnovsky. *World Development*, vol. 7, no. 1 (Jan. 1979), p. 45-58.
Argentina is one of the world leaders in the manufacture of drugs and six pharmaceutical companies are among the country's top fifteen firms. The relatively low foreign participation in Argentina's pharmaceuticals market (57 per cent in 1972) has been achieved by Argentine firms' product differentiation, transfer of technology, reliance on non-patent sources and investment in R&D. There are several references to Argentina, especially p. 220-3, in Gary Gereffi, *The pharmaceutical industry and dependency in the Third World* (Princeton, New Jersey: Princeton University Press, 1983. 291p.).

813 **The diffusion and production of numerically controlled machine tools, with special reference to Argentina.**
Daniel Chudnovsky. *World Development*, vol. 16, no. 6 (June 1988), p. 723-32. bibliog.
Argentina's machine-tool industry developed rapidly during the 1950s and 1960s and reached its high point in 1973; however, the industry contracted with the military government's deindustrialization policy after 1976. The implementation of the Austral Plan in 1985 led to a growing demand for machine tools and more than 4,000 were made in 1986. Today the most important Latin American market is Brazil. The first numerically controlled lathes were manufactured in 1979; see Staffan Jacobsson, 'Technical change and industrial policy: the case of computer numerically controlled lathes in Argentina, Korea and Taiwan', *World Development*, vol. 13, no. 3 (March 1985), p. 353-70.

814 **Foreign investment and technology transfer: the tire industry in Latin America.**
Peter J. West. Greenwich, Connecticut; London: JAI Press, 1984. 303p. bibliog. (Contemporary Studies in Economic and Financial Analysis, vol. 31).
A study of the growth and organization of the tyre industry in Argentina, Chile, Peru and Venezuela. Chapter 8 includes consideration of foreign investment and structural organization in Argentina's industry (p. 139-44) and chapter 12 is a case-study of FATE, the nationally owned tyre manufacturer. The first tyre-sales subsidiaries in Argentina were established by Dunlop (1911), Goodyear and Firestone (1915) and US Rubber (1917); Goodyear and Firestone both established manufacturing plants close to Buenos Aires in 1931. In 1980 the four major manufacturers were Goodyear, Firestone, FATE and Pirelli, all 100 per cent foreign-owned except FATE.

815 **Henry J. Kaiser and the establishment of an automobile industry in Argentina.**
Norbert MacDonald. *Business History*, vol. 30, no. 3 (July 1988), p. 329-45.
Henry Kaiser, head of the huge Kaiser industrial empire, visited Argentina in 1954, at a time when Perón was inviting foreign investment in industry. In 1956 the first jeep rolled off the assembly lines of Industrias Kaiser Argentina (IKA, sited in Córdoba), a corporate merger between Kaiser and Industrias Aeronáuticas y Mecánicas del Estado (IAME). With 8,500 employees, IKA became Argentina's largest single automobile manufacturer. IKA's market share dropped from two-thirds in the 1950s to 25-30 per cent by the mid-1960s; in 1967 the French company Renault bought out IKA and changed its name to IKA-Renault.

816 **Production functions, foreign investment and growth: a study based on the Argentine manufacturing sector, 1946-1961.**
Jorge M. Katz. Amsterdam; London: North-Holland, 1969. 203p. bibliog. (Contributions to Economic Analysis, 58).
A very technical statistical study of 'the sources and nature of economic growth' in the Argentine manufacturing sector. Three useful chapters describe the results of a cross-section inter-industry analysis of fifteen specific industries (labour productivity in

relation to output, unit labour costs, gross margins, prices and employment), the relation between the market performance of different industries and the prevailing degree of business concentration, and the distribution of the benefits of productivity growth among the various factors of production.

817 **Rates of return to physical capital in manufacturing industries in Argentina.**
Amalio Humberto Petrei. *Oxford Economic Papers*, new series, vol. 25, no. 3 (Nov. 1973), p. 378-404. bibliog.

An estimate of the rates of return to physical capital in Argentina's manufacturing industries, 1961-67, based on a random sample of some 600 private-sector corporations. Over the period as a whole the net private rate of return averaged about 0.11; there was a tendency for investment 'to move toward the areas where high rates of return prevailed'.

818 **The rise and fall of the Argentine motor vehicle industry.**
Rhys O. Jenkins. In: *The political economy of the Latin American motor vehicle industry.* Edited by Rich Kronish, Kenneth S. Mericle. Cambridge, Massachusetts: MIT Press, 1984, p. 41-73.

A chronological account of the development of the Argentine automobile industry from 1916, when Ford set up one of its earliest overseas assembly plants in Buenos Aires. Significantly, no Argentine government before 1959 had succeeded in getting a major company to move from local assembly to totally local manufacture. The motor industry was one of the key sectors of Frondizi's development programme and foreign capital began to flow into Argentina on a massive scale after 1959; foreign control was 'virtually complete' by 1968. But the Argentine industry, which in the early 1960s appeared to have at least as much potential as the Brazilian and Mexican industries, signally failed to expand like the other two after 1970. The author blames Argentina's virtually stagnant worker productivity, the lack of new investments, the slackening of domestic demand and the high price of vehicles which 'ensured that cars remained a luxury consumer good'. See also *Reflections on Argentine auto workers and their unions*, in the same work.

819 **Technology generation in Latin American manufacturing industries.**
Edited by Jorge M. Katz. New York: St. Martin's Press; London: Macmillan, 1987. 549p. bibliog.

Contains six chapters on Argentine industries: Philip Maxwell on the Acindar Steelplant in Rosario (p. 119-53); Jorge M. Katz (et al.) on Ducilo Argentina, a rayon plant and subsidiary of the United States DuPont company, on the outskirts of Buenos Aires; Julio Fidel and Jorge Lucángeli on the cigarette industry; Guillermo Vitelli on the construction industry; Ruth Pearson on the cement industry; and Eduardo Ablin and Katz on Argentina's international sale of industrial plants and engineering work.

# Energy and mining

**820 The Argentine petrochemical industry.**
*Bank of London and South America Quarterly Review*, vol. 3, no. 2
(April 1963), p. 58-69.
Petrochemicals have been produced in Argentina since 1943, when the Dirección
General de Fabricaciones Militares began to produce toluene on a limited scale.
Output in 1963 was limited to toluene, isopropanol, carbon sulphide, carbon black and
phenol. The article describes the promotion scheme established in 1961, plants and
projects in existence and being built, and future prospects. The main sites of
petrochemical plants were Zárate-Campana, La Plata, San Lorenzo and Córdoba.

**821 Breve historia minera de la Argentina.** (A short history of mining in
Argentina.)
Edmundo F. Catalano.   Buenos Aires: Ediciones Depalma, 1984.
274p. maps.
A valuable chronological history from the colonial period to 1980, sparsely illustrated
and with a full contents list but no index. The Spanish crown was never very interested
in industrial minerals; the post-revolutionary government established the first mineral
law in 1813. Until as late as 1900, the minerals industry was devoted almost entirely to
the extraction of precious metals. The mining sector today is relatively underdeveloped, despite a rich variety of mineral deposits. Iron ore is the chief mineral
extracted, followed by copper, lead, zinc, tin, gold, silver and uranium.

**822 Energy alternatives in Latin America.**
Edited by Francisco Szekely.   Dublin: Tycooly International
Publishing, 1983. 168p. (Natural Resources and the Environment
Series, vol. 9).
Contains a case-study, 'Charcoal siderurgy in Argentina', p. 120-31, which also deals
with the industry in Brazil. Altos Hornos Zapla (founded 1945) has five blast furnaces,
and Altos Hornos Güemes one; they use charcoal as a fuel and reducing-agent in the
production of pig iron, which constitutes one of Argentina's most important industrial
sectors. There was one other plant under construction at the time of writing.

**823 The Frondizi contracts and petroleum self-sufficiency in Argentina.**
Gertrud G. Edwards.   In: *Foreign investment in the petroleum and
mineral industries*.   Edited by Raymond F. Mikesell.   Baltimore,
Maryland; London: Johns Hopkins University Press for Resources for
the Future, Inc., 1971, p. 157-88.
The Frondizi government (1958-62) sought to increase domestic oil production in order
to reduce imports and save foreign exchange; between 1958 and 1961, contracts were
signed permitting private companies to carry out a programme of oil exploration,
development and drilling 'more extensive than could be immediately accomplished by
Yacimientos Petrolíferos Fiscales', the state company. Later governments nullified
these contracts in 1963 and renegotiated some of them in 1967.

824 **Mineral industries of Latin America.**
Pablo Velasco.   Washington, DC: US Bureau of Mines, Division of
International Minerals, Staff, Branch of Latin America and Canada,
1988. 134p. maps. bibliog. (Mineral Perspective).
There is a section on Argentina, p. 9-12. The country is self-sufficient in energy
resources (petroleum, gas, coal and uranium); it is also the third-largest producer of
crude petroleum and gas in Latin America, and ranks fourth in the world production of
boron minerals. Production of mineral commodities in 1985 was dominated by the
industrial minerals, which represented 98 per cent of total output, with metals
accounting for the rest. However, 'mining in Argentina continued to be an industry of
only marginal importance'. Slightly more detail, though more dated, is contained in
Velasco's 'The mineral industry of Argentina', in *Bureau of Mines Minerals Yearbook
1983* (1983, p. 1-12).

825 **Nuclear power in developing countries: an analysis of decision making.**
James Everett Katz, Onkar S. Marwah.   Lexington, Massachusetts;
Toronto: Lexington Books, 1982. 373p.
Includes case-studies of Argentina, Brazil, Mexico, Venezuela and Cuba. Argentina's
Comisión Nacional de Energía Atómica was created in 1950 and today the country has
the most advanced nuclear-power programme in Latin America. Its first reactor,
Atucha I, of the heavy-water-pressure type, 110 kilometres up the river Paraná from
Buenos Aires, was completed in 1974 under contract with the German Siemens
company; a second reactor, Embalse, built at Río Tercero in the province of Córdoba
under contract with Atomic Energy of Canada AECL, began generating in 1984. The
two reactors have a combined capacity of 1005MWe and were producing 13.4 per cent
of the country's electricity in 1987. A third reactor, Atucha II, also of the heavy-water
type, is expected to be completed by 1995. A short recent summary of Argentina's
nuclear programme is 'Datafile: Argentina', *Nuclear Engineering International*, vol. 34,
no. 414 (Feb. 1989), p. 52-4.

826 **Nuclear proliferation prospects for Argentina.**
Daniel Poneman.   *Orbis*, vol. 27, no. 4 (winter 1984), p. 853-80.
Discusses the history of Argentina's nuclear energy programme and its security
implications. Argentina has the capacity to build a nuclear explosive but has not signed
the non-proliferation treaty and 'reserves the right to conduct peaceful nuclear
explosions'. The Comisión Nacional de Energía Atómica has a shrewd policy 'of
touting the nuclear benefits of fission without compromising its military potential'.

827 **Oil and nationalism in Argentina: a history.**
Carl E. Solberg.   Stanford, California: Stanford University Press,
1979. 245p. map. bibliog.
A historical analysis of Argentine petroleum politics and the development of the state
company, Yacimientos Petrolíferos Fiscales (YPF), from 1907, when oil was first
discovered in Patagonia, to the mid-1970s, but focusing on government oil policies
during the formative decades before 1930. The book seeks to link the rise of Argentine
economic nationalism with the question of the foreign-owned oil companies Standard
Oil and Royal Dutch Shell. Conflicts between YPF and oil-producing provinces in the
interior are also dealt with. The book's central character is General Enrique Mosconi,
YPF's dynamic director who reorganized the company in the 1920s. See also the same

author's 'YPF: the formative years of Latin America's pioneer state oil company, 1922-39', in *Latin American oil companies and the politics of energy*, edited by John D. Wirth (Lincoln, Nebraska; London: University of Nebraska Press, 1985, p. 51-103).

828 **Oil and politics in Latin America: nationalist movements and state companies.**
George Philip.    Cambridge, England: Cambridge University Press, 1982. 577p. maps. bibliog. (Cambridge Latin American Studies, 40).
Chapters 8 and 19 (p. 162-81 and 401-28) deal with Argentina: the development of nationalism and the internal factors which led to the nationalization of the oil industry. The first chapter discusses the private oil companies 1907-28; the early history of oil nationalism and Yacimientos Petrolíferos Fiscales, 'the first effective state oil company in Latin America', which, between 1922 and 1935, fought both for a share of the domestic market and 'to wrest control of as much potentially oil-bearing Argentine soil as possible from state governments and transnational companies'; and the 1935 law which stopped further concessions being granted. The second chapter takes the story to 1979. For each government after 1930, 'the needs of YPF were considered to be at best secondary to other political or economic objectives', and private investment into the industry was welcomed.

**The evolution of petroleum contracts in Argentina – issues of the foreign investor's legal protection.**
*See* item no. 644.

# Agriculture

829 **Agrarian structures in Latin America: a resumé of the CIDA Land Tenure Studies of: Argentina, Brazil, Chile, Colombia, Ecuador, Guatemala, Peru.**
Edited by Solon L. Barraclough, in collaboration with Juan Carlos Collarte. Lexington, Massachusetts: Lexington Books, D.C. Heath, 1973. 351p. maps. (Studies in the Economic and Social Development of Latin America).
The volume is based on country studies prepared by the Inter-American Committee for Agricultural Development. The original, full Argentine study was entitled *Land tenure conditions and socio-economic development of the agricultural sector: Argentina* (Washington, DC: Pan American Union, 1965. 141p.); it was directed by Arthur Domike and made extensive use of data from the 1960 agricultural census. In this 1971 summary, the chapter on Argentina, p. 61-82, investigates land ownership and land-tenure structure, 'with particular attention to determining the incidence of *latifundios* and *minifundios*, and the economic and social performance of the various tenure systems', agricultural development and government programmes and policy. Finally, the report suggests policy alternatives. 'Virtually no government aid has been extended to the thousands of *minifundistas* and farm workers whose economic situation was, and still is, even worse than that of the commercial tenants.' IACAD also produced an *Inventory of information basic to the planning of agricultural develpment in Latin America: Argentina* (1964. 114p.).

830 **La agricultura aborigen argentina.** (Aboriginal agriculture in Argentina.)
Lorenzo R. Parodi. Buenos Aires: Editorial Universitaria de Buenos Aires, 1966. 48p. bibliog. (Cuadernos de América, 4).
Part one describes the pre-Hispanic Indians' agricultural implements, and methods of cultivation, irrigation and harvesting. Part two lists six categories of cultivated plants. The conquistadors quickly recognized the value of Indian plants; nearly thirty species of domestic plants survive from before the conquest, notably maize, potatoes and

sweet potatoes, calabashes, tomatoes, garlic, peanuts, beans and mandioca. There are forty-five text illustrations, mostly of plants, and four pages of plates.

831 **La agricultura y la ganadería argentina en el período 1930-1960.**
(Agriculture and livestock-rearing in Argentina, 1930-1960.)
José Alfredo Martínez de Hoz (h.). Buenos Aires: Editorial Sudamericana, 1967. 123p. (Biblioteca de Orientación Económica).

This is a basic chronological study of the agricultural economy and of agricultural production during the thirty-year period, and deliberately ignores questions of colonization, land ownership and tenure. No tables are included but useful statistical data appear throughout the text. The author, who was Agriculture Minister in 1963 as well as being Finance Minister 1976-81, recommends diversification of production, increased exports and higher investment; a short earlier version appeared in item no. 11 (q.v.). Another study of the period is Arthur S. Morris, 'Factors in changes of the Argentine pampas farm economy', *Oxford Agrarian Studies*, new series, vol. 3, no. 1 (1974), p. 50-67.

832 **Agricultural credit in the Province of Buenos Aires, Argentina, 1890-1914.**
Jeremy Adelman. *Journal of Latin American Studies*, vol. 22, no. 1 (Feb. 1990), p. 69-87.

Direct and formal financial services for agriculture were scarce at the time. Farmers could obtain bank credit, but mostly from informal lenders (rural merchants and suppliers) who were willing to take the risk because they earned profits on the purchase and sale of agricultural produce which the loans themselves created. 'Two decades of phenomenal agricultural expansion owed little directly to banks.' For a discussion of agricultural credit in the following decade and a half, see Joseph S. Tulchin, 'El crédito agrario en la Argentina, 1910-1926', *Desarrollo Económico*, vol. 18, no. 71 (Oct.-Dec. 1978), p. 381-408.

833 **The agricultural development of Argentina: a policy and development perspective.**
Darrell F. Fienup, Russell H. Brannon, Frank A. Fender. New York; Washington, DC; London: Frederick A. Praeger, 1969. 437p. maps. bibliog. (Praeger Special Studies in International Economics & Development. Bench Mark Studies on Agricultural Development in Latin America, 3).

This is a detailed study, supported by the Ford Foundation and based on 1963-64 data, of agricultural performance and government policies. The authors conclude that 'there is no question about the stagnation of Argentine agriculture over the past twenty-five years' – manifested in the under-utilization of resources, an unequal land-distribution structure, the absence of an effective land tax, declining productivity, low prices, high costs, inefficient marketing, poor training and the lack of a coherent agricultural policy – and make a series of recommendations in eight key problem areas.

834 **Argentine meat and the British market: chapters in the history of the Argentine meat industry.**
Simon G. Hanson. Stanford, California; London: Oxford University Press, 1938. 294p. bibliog.

'England was the first great nation to experience a need for imported meat', and the development of Argentina's frozen-meat industry became intimately connected with the British market. Argentina's livestock was 'improved by the continued heavy import of British blooded animals, moved on British-owned railways to British-equipped and financed plants, from which the finished product was shipped to England', for many years the only important market for animal products. This is a classic history of the meat trade both in the pre-refrigeration era (to about 1880) and afterwards.

835 **Argentine plains and Andean glaciers: life on an estancia, and an expedition into the Andes.**
Walter Larden. London: T. Fisher Unwin, 1911. 320p. map.

The author's brother first went to work in Argentina in 1868. Twice, in 1888-89 and 1908-9, Larden visited him on the farm where he worked, Estancia Santa Isabel in southern Santa Fe province. The estate, which belonged to the United Estancias Company and one-third of which was let out to Italian colonists, raised cattle, sheep and horses, and grew alfalfa. On his second visit he hardly recognized the place: 'Alas, for the change. Prosperity had come, and romance had gone forever.' The work, which has become a classic description of 'camp' (rural) life at the turn of the century, was reprinted as *Estancia life: agricultural, economic, and cultural aspects of Argentine farming* (Detroit, Michigan: Blaine Ethridge, 1974).

836 **Argentine sugar politics: Tucumán and the Generation of Eighty.**
Donna J. Guy. Tempe, Arizona: Arizona State University, Center for Latin American Studies, 1980. 162p. map. bibliog.

A history of the Tucumán sugar industry between 1862 and 1914 (production, marketing, taxation, government incentives and labour), the mixed effects of provincial politics on its development, and the rivalry between export-oriented interests (such as the meat-packers) and local sugar industrialists (sugar failed to break beyond the domestic market). So-called 'sugar politics' was to blame for many of the province's political intrigues and rebellions during the period. A later episode in Tucumán's sugar history is described in Daniel J. Greenberg, 'Sugar depression and agrarian revolt: the Argentine Radical Party and the Tucumán *cañeros*' strike of 1927', *Hispanic American Historical Review*, vol. 67, no. 2 (May 1987), p. 301-27.

837 **Cash crop production and family labour: tobacco growers in Corrientes, Argentina.**
Marit Melhuus. In: *Family and work in rural societies: perspectives on non-wage labour.* Edited by Norman Long. London; New York: Tavistock Publications, 1984, p. 61-82. bibliog.

The tobacco growers of Corrientes are peasant sharecroppers dependent on a landowner for access to land; their crop, Turkish or dark tobacco, is sold to the international tobacco companies. The rent the landlord receives is determined by the price of tobacco and the productivity of each production unit dependent upon him.

Tobacco production is highly labour-intensive and the production unit is the family household.

838  **Cattle raising in the Argentine northeast: Corrientes, c.1750-1870.**
Thomas Whigham. *Journal of Latin American Studies*, vol. 20, no. 2 (Nov. 1988), p. 313-35.
The province of Corrientes is not as readily associated with cattle ranching as the more southerly provinces, yet it possesses excellent pastures. During the period under review it managed to export a portion of its hides and cattle byproducts, but faced stiff opposition from Buenos Aires, which 'had little desire for products that its own ranches could supply in abundance'. Although Paraguay took some of the province's animal products, '*porteño* intransigence . . . together with unfavourable geography, was ultimately responsible for the relatively poor showing of Correntino stockraising'.

839  **Dairying in Argentina.**
Arthur S. Morris. *Revista Geográfica* (Mexico), no. 76 (June 1972), p. 103-20. maps. bibliog.
A description of the historical origins of dairying, recent trends in production, demand and supply, and some regional characteristics of the industry. Dairying 'was almost an afterthought for the holders of beef-producing estancias '. Today's dairy farms, concentrated in the Argentine Midwest (the western border of Buenos Aires, eastern Córdoba and western Santa Fe), are large, 'a one-hundred hectare farm being common in the western areas, and larger farms no rarity'. The industry has expanded significantly since 1937 and has been helped by the 'all-important organization of production and marketing via cooperatives'.

840  **Distribution of flax production in Argentina.**
George F. Deasy. *Economic Geography*, vol. 19, no. 1 (Jan. 1943), p. 45-54. map.
At the time of writing, Argentina was the most important flaxseed-producing country in the world; it had for many years supplied 40 to 50 per cent of the world's annual output of linseed. Flax ranked fourth among Argentine crops after alfalfa, wheat and maize. In parts of the provinces of Entre Ríos, Santa Fe and Buenos Aires, flax was the most important crop, occupying nearly three-quarters of the cultivated land in some districts. The article chiefly describes the flax-growing regions and conditions for cultivation.

841  **Evolución histórica del régimen de la tierra pública, 1810-1916.** (The historical development of the system of public land ownership in Argentina, 1810-1916.)
Miguel Angel Cárcano. Buenos Aires: EUDEBA, 1972. 3rd ed. 459p. bibliog. (Biblioteca del Universitario. Temas/Derecho).
This is a fundamental treatise on the history and legal aspects of public agricultural-land policy from colonial times to about 1955, with emphasis on the provincial land laws of Buenos Aires, Santa Fe, Entre Ríos, Córdoba and Corrientes, described in detail with extracts. There is an appendix of national and provincial land laws from the period 1950-70, compiled by María Susana Taborda Caro.

842  **The failure of small farmer settlement in Buenos Aires province, Argentina.**
Arthur S. Morris.    *Revista Geográfica* (Mexico), no. 85 (June 1977), p. 63-77. bibliog.

Agricultural colonies as an institution made no headway in Buenos Aires province. The standard explanation for the lack of successful owner-operator small farms in Latin America is the mentality of the *latifundista*, but this cannot be applied to late-nineteenth-century Buenos Aires province, where there was a diversity of farming. The author's own explanation is that 'interprovincial differences in the level of protection given to small farmers are one factor but should not be overemphasized as all provinces were negligent. An important matter is the time-space diffusion of the *colonia agrícola*, starting from central Santa Fe and Entre Ríos and arriving at Buenos Aires province in changed form, when conditions allowed a tenant rather than owner-operator farm to be the norm'. Three exceptions are given of successful German colonies in the districts of Baradero, Olavarría and Tornquist.

843  **Historia de las aguadas y el molino.** (A history of water engines and watermills in Argentina.)
Noel H. Sbarra.    Buenos Aires: Editorial Universitaria de Buenos Aires, 1973. 2nd ed. 191p. (Biblioteca Cultural. Colección Argentina).

Sixteen plates illustrate this history of early hydraulic engineering for drinking and irrigation purposes. The dump-bucket (*balde volcador*) was invented by the Frenchman Carlos Enrique Pellegrini (father of Carlos Pellegrini, president 1890-92) in 1853; another Frenchman, Adolfo Sourdeaux, sank Argentina's first artesian well in 1862; and the water windmill was introduced by Miguel Lanús in 1880.

844  **Historia de las vaquerías de Río de la Plata, 1555-1750.** (A history of cattle raising in the River Plate, 1555-1750.)
Emilio A. Coni.    Buenos Aires: Editorial Devenir, 1956. 2nd ed. 93p. (Colección Los Pequeños Grandes Libros).

A brief summary of the formative years of the cattle industry in the River Plate region, the early wild herds, the rise of the *estancia* and the phenomenon of the gaucho. See also *El Gaucho: Argentina-Brasil-Uruguay*. The work was republished by Platero in 1979.

845  **Historia de los saladeros argentinos.** (A history of Argentina's meat-salting plants.)
Alfredo J. Montoya.    Buenos Aires: Editorial Raigal, 1956. 107p. bibliog. (Colección Campo Argentino, 4).

A well-written history of the salt-meat industry in the provinces of Buenos Aires and Entre Ríos, based on travel accounts, published documents and archival material. Dried beef (*charqui* or 'jerky', known as *tasajo* when salted) was first exported to the slave plantations in Brazil and Cuba. The first *saladero* was probably founded at Quilmes, near Buenos Aires, in 1795, but Montoya says that Robert Staples established the first plant at Ensenada in 1810. Meat-salting was overtaken by the introduction of refrigeration – the first *frigorífico* was built by Eugenio Terrasón at San Nicolás in 1882 – and the *saladeros* had disappeared by 1908.

846 **Historia del alambrado en la Argentina.** (A history of wire fencing in Argentina.)
Noel H. Sbarra.    Buenos Aires: Editorial Universitaria de Buenos Aires, 1964. 2nd ed. 119p. map. bibliog.

One of the most important developments in the history of Argentina's stockraising industry was the introduction in 1846 of wire fencing by Richard Black Newton (1801-98), a British rancher. Newton originally used fine English steel wire to protect his farmhouse near Chascomús from marauding animals; in 1855 he (or it may have been Francisco Halbach, the Russian consul in Buenos Aires) was the first to use fencing to encircle his entire *estancia*. The ñandubay tree was first used for fence-posts. The book describes the spread of wire fencing throughout the country, with appropriate quotations from travellers' accounts.

847 **Historia económica de la ganadería argentina.** (An economic history of the livestock industry in Argentina.)
Horacio C. E. Giberti.    Buenos Aires: Ediciones Solar, 1981. 3rd ed. 275p. (Biblioteca Dimensión Argentina).

The book follows six chronological periods of development: the introduction of cattle to the region in the 1550s, the first wild herds and the beginnings of the hide industry (1600-1750), the colonial cattle *estancia* and the gaucho cattle-hand (1750-1810), the *saladero* (meat-salting plant, 1810-50), the European demand for wool and the rise of the sheepraising industry (1850-1900), and the *frigorífico* (refrigeration plant, after 1900). The author was president of the Instituto Nacional de Tecnología Agropecuaria.

848 **The history and present state of the sheep-breeding industry in the Argentine Republic.**
Herbert Gibson.    Buenos Aires: Ravenscroft and Mills, 1893. 297p. maps.

The dedication informs us that the author was the son of Thomas Gibson, who introduced Improved Merino and long-woolled sheep to Argentina. His book is 'intended alike for the prospective colonist . . . and for the sheep-farmer already come to the country, with a view to assist him in the selection of his stock and in the manner of breeding them at a profit'. The book is a valuable source of information on the sheep industry at the time; the last chapter describes twelve sheep-breeding estates owned by the Gibson family. There are thirteen photographs.

849 **La industria de semillas en la Argentina.** (The seed industry in Argentina.)
Eduardo Jacobs, Marta Gutiérrez.    Buenos Aires: Centro de Investigaciones Sociales sobre el Estado y la Administración, 1986. 242p. bibliog. (Documentos del CISEA, 85).

A description of the development, structure, financing and marketing of the seed industry (predominantly maize, sorghum, sunflower seeds, wheat and soybeans), with case-studies of six important seed producers. In the 1970s, a number of large Argentine chemical and pharmaceutical firms acquired some of the leading United States seed companies operating in the country.

## Agriculture

850 **The integration of the highland peasantry into the sugar cane economy of northern Argentina, 1930-43.**
Ian Rutledge. In: *Land and labour in Latin America.* Edited by Kenneth Duncan, Ian Rutledge, with the collaboration of Colin Harding. Cambridge, England: Cambridge University Press, 1977, p. 205-28. maps. (Cambridge Latin American Studies, 26).

Describes the recruitment of highland Indians as labour for the sugar-cane plantations in the provinces of Salta and Jujuy, which by 1930 had begun to expand more rapidly than those in the traditional sugar province of Tucumán. Apart from the peasantry of Salta and Jujuy themselves, the sugar mills (*ingenios*) also recruited seasonal labour for the six-month harvest (*zafra*) from the neighbouring province of Catamarca and from Bolivia. The mills obtained their work-force 'by coercion, and they accomplished this by monopolizing the lands on which the Indians lived and worked and using their political power to dragoon the population into working for them'.

851 **Introducción a la pesca argentina: su rol en la economía nacional y mundial.** (An introduction to Argentina's fishing industry: its role in the national and international economies.)
Milcíades Espoz Espoz. Mar del Plata, Argentina: Fundación Atlántica, 1985. 336p. bibliog.

A detailed study of the fishing industry using abundant statistical data from the 1960s: the fishing grounds, ports and fleets; fish products (their industries, work-force and marketing); and fishing policy and legislation. Catches increased by 87 per cent in the period 1970-81, mostly destined for the export market since domestic consumption is very low. Argentina netted nearly half a million tons of fish in 1982. In 1970 the country was fortieth in the world in terms of total tonnage caught; by 1983 it occupied twenty-ninth place.

852 **Jesuit ranches and the agrarian development of colonial Argentina, 1650-1767.**
Nicholas P. Cushner. Albany, New York: State University of New York, 1983. 206p. map. bibliog.

This is the third volume in the author's trilogy concerning Jesuit agricultural activity in colonial South America; the first two dealt with Peru and Ecuador. He focuses here on Jesuit farms and ranches in the marginal provinces of Tucumán and Córdoba from 1650 to the expulsion of the Jesuits in 1767: land acquisition and distribution, the organization, working and financial management of the estates, trade routes and the mule trade (the Jesuits' most lucrative activity) linking the littoral with the mines of Upper Peru, and agricultural production and labour (including slave labour, which the Jesuits relied on increasingly). The Jesuits' farming enterprises were highly successful, but they were enclave profit-making concerns and contributed little to (but were too small to harm) the regional economies. The classic history of the Jesuits during the colonial period is Magnus Mörner, *The political and economic activities of the Jesuits in the La Plata region: the Hapsburg era* (Stockholm: Library and Institute of Ibero-American Studies, 1953. 254p.).

853 **Land tenure, hazards, and the economy: viticulture in the Mendoza oasis, Argentina.**
Richard A. Hansis. *Economic Geography*, vol. 53, no. 4 (Oct. 1977), p. 368-71. bibliog.

A case-study of the Delfino family, which first came to Mendoza in 1898. The father began work as a *contratista*, 'a labor arrangement in which the land was supplied by the owner while the vineyard was planted by the *contratista*'. He later bought his own small vineyard on which one of his sons worked; his other son worked as a *contratista* on another vineyard. At the time of writing, the price of grapes was going down relative to the costs of production and living; this, combined with the deteriorating environment (inadequate water supply, waterlogging and soil salinization) would probably force the Delfino sons to 'migrate to the city to search for low paying jobs'. See also Arthur S. Morris, 'The development of the irrigation economy of Mendoza, Argentina', *Annals of the Association of American Geographers*, vol. 59, no. 1 (March 1969), p. 97-115, which describes water provision to Mendoza's vineyards and fruit and vegetable farms.

854 **Modern cattle breeds in Argentina: origins, diffusion and change.**
Morton D. Winsberg. Lawrence, Kansas: University of Kansas, Center of Latin American Studies, 1968. 59p. maps. bibliog. (Occasional Publications, 13).

In 1966 there were an estimated forty-six million head of cattle in Argentina and its herds were 'among the most scientifically managed in the world'. Around 1826 an Englishman, John Miller, introduced the first pure-bred animal, a shorthorn bull called Tarquin, to his *estancia* thirty-five miles south of Buenos Aires. The second phase of pure-breds, also shorthorns, was introduced in 1856. The author surveys the geographical concentrations and changes in popularity of the modern cattle breeds, and reviews the history of the modern beef trade since 1914. 'Though frequently condemned, in at least one respect the system of large scale absentee landownership which grew to such importance in Argentina during the nineteenth century and continues to be inept today, facilitated the conversion of herds from creole to modern breeds.' The same author describes the second most popular breed of cattle in 'The introduction and diffusion of the Aberdeen Angus in Argentina', *Geography*, vol. 55, no. 2 (April 1970), p. 187-95.

855 **Politics and beef in Argentina: patterns of conflict and change.**
Peter H. Smith. New York; London: Columbia University Press, 1969. 292p. bibliog.

An expert chronological examination of the Argentine beef industry between 1900 and 1946. The author uses the 'social, economic, and political conflicts experienced by and within' the industry to show how the challenge to Argentina's traditional landholding aristocracy came not so much from the 'surging urban class' as from 'intra-class conflict' within the rural sector itself. He does this by analysing each of the five beef interest groups, the first three upper-class, the last two urban and lower-class: packing-house managers, breeders, fatteners, consumers in Buenos Aires and packing-house workers. They are seen in relation to each other (the beef producers successfully excluded the two lower-class groups from the decision-making process) and to other vital sectors of the economy (especially wheat producers, labour leaders and industrialists).

856   The prairies and the pampas: agrarian policy in Canada and Argentina,
1880-1930.
Carl E. Solberg.   Stanford, California: Stanford University Press,
1987. 297p. bibliog. (Comparative Studies in History, Institutions, and
Public Policy).

A comparative study of both countries' agricultural development (colonization, land-
tenure and settlement patterns, tariffs, technology, transport, agricultural policy and
production), in which the author tries to answer the question of 'why Canada surged
ahead while Argentina stagnated and declined? Why did wheat agriculture in the
prairies and the pampas, regions whose economic history began along parallel lines,
diverge in such different directions?' After 1910 Canada surpassed Argentina in wheat
exports and in the quality and quantity of wheat production. He points to Canada's
'solid institutional structure' established by its grain growers and blames Argentina's
'decades of neglect [that] left pampa farming in no position to expand production' and
an agricultural marketing system 'left in the hands of grasping grain merchants'. In
addition, many of Argentina's immigrant farmers rented farms on short-term contracts,
expecting to return to Europe, and lacked the Canadian farmers' commitment to the
land.

857   Revolution on the pampas: a social history of Argentine wheat, 1860-
1910.
James R. Scobie.   Austin, Texas: University of Texas Press, 1964.
206p. maps. bibliog. (Institute of Latin American Studies. Latin
American Monographs, 1).

A richly documented and superbly written account of the evolution of Argentina from
an importer of wheat in the 1870s to the world's third-largest exporter of wheat thirty
years later: 'Behind this economic accomplishment lies the social history of an
agricultural heartland, the pampas. The predominance of the city and the province of
Buenos Aires, the absentee land-tenure system, the poverty and ignorance of the
sparse rural population, the heavy Italianization of the country, are all part of the story
of Argentine wheat.' There are chapters on the land, immigration, the wheatgrower's
life, the growing and marketing of wheat, and government farm policies. After 1895
there was 'a definite shift from colonization and small owner-farmers to the much
larger units of extensive tenant farming'.

858   The River Plate beef trade.
J. Colin Crossley, Robert Greenhill.   In: *Business imperialism, 1840-
1930: an inquiry based on British experience in Latin America.*   Edited
by D. C. M. Platt.   Oxford: Clarendon Press, 1977, p. 284-334. map.

This is a study of the Argentine beef trade after 1885 (fresh, salted, frozen, chilled,
jerked, corned and beef extract), based mainly on company archives and government
documents. Argentina's first four refrigerated meat-packing plants (*frigoríficos*) all
began production between 1883 and 1886 and concentrated on frozen mutton; after
1907 frozen beef represented 51 per cent of all Argentina's meat exports, compared
with one per cent in 1897; by 1910 chilled-beef exports surpassed frozen beef, a trend
reversed after 1918, when corned-beef exports rose. The author includes a case-study
of the leading producer of corned beef and extract, Liebig's Extract of Meat Company
(1865), which had factories around Buenos Aires and in Entre Ríos and Uruguay.

859    **Rural production and labour in late colonial Buenos Aires.**
    Samuel Amaral.   *Journal of Latin American Studies*, vol. 19, no. 2
    (Nov. 1987), p. 235-78.

A detailed examination of the management and operation of a colonial *estancia* – that
of Clemente López Osornio in the Magdalena district, sixty miles southeast of Buenos
Aires – between 1785 and 1795, based on an analysis of the estate inventories and
accounts. The *estancia* produced live cattle for the domestic beef market rather than
hides for export, and was profitable. The supply of free labour was steady but seasonal
demand for it was uncertain; slaves were therefore kept to meet the labour
requirements during these seasonal periods of low demand

860    **The sheep and wool industry in Argentina.**
    T. E. Hore.   *Quarterly Review of Agricultural Economics* (Canberra),
    vol. 10, no. 4 (Oct. 1957), p. 196-204. map.

At the time of writing, Argentina had the third-largest sheep population in the world
and was the fourth-largest producer of wool, after Australia, the Soviet Union and
New Zealand. Wool was responsible for ten per cent of the country's export income
and ranked third after meat and grain as an export commodity. The article describes
the sheep-rearing regions (pampas, Mesopotamia and Patagonia), the main breeds of
sheep, sheep numbers and wool production, the woollen and worsted industries, wool
exports and future prospects. There are five tables.

861    **The states of the River Plate: their industries and commerce. Sheep-
    farming, sheep-breeding, cattle-breeding, and meat-preserving;
    employment of capital; land and stock, and their values; labour and its
    remuneration.**
    Wilfrid Latham.   London: Longmans, Green, 1868. 2nd ed. 381p.
    map.

The long title amply describes the contents; the core chapters (p. 61-238) relate to
sheep-farming, the diseases of sheep, 'the science of high-class sheep-breeding', the
beef industry, agricultural crops and 'the River Plate as a field for the employment of
cattle land labour'. There is a statistical appendix by the former chargé d'affaires in the
River Plate, F. Clare Ford. Latham, himself a sheep-breeder in the region for twenty-
five years, was anxious 'to check the decadence, and raise the type of our flock'; his
remedy was 'to increase the size of the sheep by crossing with large true-shaped rams';
it was also essential 'that the rams should not run with the flock'.

862    **The story of the Forestal.**
    Agnes H. Hicks.   London: The Forestal Land, Timber and Railways
    Company, 1956. 102p.

The Argentine branch of the Forestal was registered in London in 1906 after acquiring
the Compañía Forestal del Chaco, which had been established in 1902. The early
history of the company in Argentina is closely connected with the quebracho industry
(see *The quebracho region of Argentina*). In 1913 it absorbed the Santa Fé Land
Company (a log and extract producer) and the Argentine Quebracho Company, and
expanded into cattle-ranching. In 1931 the Argentine assets (the Forestal also had
extract and tanning factories in England, the United States, Rhodesia and Kenya) were

transferred to a locally registered company, La Forestal Argentina, which in 1956 was operating only one quebracho-based plant, Quebracho Fusionados (Chaco province), at which it was 'determined to carry on production . . . the Chaco . . . is said to contain enormous untapped resources of quebracho'.

863 **Tea – a new agricultural industry for Argentina.**
Norman R. Stewart. *Economic Geography*, vol. 36, no. 3 (July 1960), p. 267-76. map.

China tea was introduced to five north Argentine provinces in 1924. Today production is restricted to the Mesopotamian provinces of Misiones and Corrientes; in 1950, these humid, subtropical provinces produced nearly two-and-a-half million pounds of finished tea from 3,500 acres farmed almost entirely by foreign colonists. The domestic market for tea is relatively small; the indigenous *yerba mate*, sometimes called Paraguayan tea, is much more popular. The article describes planting, growing, picking, processing and marketing.

864 **Trade, exchange rate, and agricultural pricing policies in Argentina.**
Adolfo Sturzenegger, with the collaboration of Wylian Otrera and the assistance of Beatriz Mosquera. Washington, DC: World Bank, 1990. 314p. bibliog. (World Bank Comparative Studies. The Political Economy of Agricultural Pricing Policy).

A detailed study, with a statistical appendix of 150 tables, of the impact of trade and exchange-rate policies between 1961 and 1985 on the production of wheat, corn, sorghum, soybeans, sunflower seeds and beef. The authors find that direct price intervention reduced producer prices for all six commodities. By the early 1980s, Argentine agriculture 'had lost much of its importance': beef exports were negligible, corn and wheat exports accounted for less than ten per cent of world trade, and the only substantial trade was in soybeans and soybean products. See also Lucio G. Reca, *Argentina: country case study of agricultural prices, taxes, and subsidies* (1980. 72p. World Bank Staff Working Papers, no. 386), which analyses the pricing policy applied to seven agricultural products, 1950-75. For a number of years the United States Department of Agriculture's Foreign Agricultural Service produced valuable periodical reports on Argentina's agricultural and livestock industries; examples are its surveys of the fruit industry (1942, 1958 and 1959), cotton and fishing (1962), wheat and meat (1960, 1963). It also produced general surveys, a good example of which is: John N. Smith, *Argentine agriculture: trends in production and world competition* (the Department's Economic Research Service, 1968. 178p. ERS-Foreign 216).

865 **Water management & agricultural development: a case study of the Cuyo region of Argentina.**
Kenneth D. Frederick. Baltimore, Maryland; London: Johns Hopkins University Press for Resources for the Future, Inc., 1975. 187p. map.

The semi-arid Cuyo region (the provinces of Mendoza and San Juan), is one of the world's major producers of wine grapes and wine; irrigation is essential since the annual rainfall averages only eight inches in Mendoza and four in San Juan. Until the 1940s surface water was adequate for agriculture's needs; since then, as Pierre R. Crosson's introduction tells us, 'the rise in demand has been met by pumping water from wells and building infrastructure designed to increase the usable supply of surface water'; however, groundwater tables are falling at an alarming rate. The author examines the economic, political and institutional conditions determining the current pattern of water use: direct and indirect government regulation such as credit policy, tax incentives and electric-power rates, and policy towards the grape-wine industry. He concludes that 'changes in the laws, institutions, pricing policies, and research efforts to reflect the importance and social costs of water would alter sharply the region's development'.

866   **Wheat growing in the Argentine Republic.**
William Goodwin.   Liverpool, England: Northern Publishing
Company, 1895. 75p.

This classic short account was written 'with the idea of supplying to the Grain Trade [in England] some data not easily obtainable . . . because the subject is of considerable interest to many investors in Argentine securities and to those who are connected with Agriculture in other parts of the world and want to know what sort of competition they have to meet'. The author focuses on wheat farming in Santa Fe province, on land tenure and government policy, and on the general economics of wheat growing. In 1888 he was commissioned by the Buenos Ayres Great Southern Railway and Buenos Ayres and Rosario Railway companies to report upon 'the advisability of fostering the grain trade of the Argentine Republic by building elevators with the view of introducing the United States system of selling grain according to classification'.

# Transport and Communications

## General

867 **Airlines of Latin America since 1919.**
R. E. G. Davies.   London; New York: Putnam, 1984. 698p. maps.
bibliog.

Air transport in Argentina first got under way when an Englishman, Major Shirley H. Kingsley, formed the River Plate Aviation Company in 1919. Chapters 27-29 (p. 543-92) refer to Argentina: the early mail airlines, the opening-up of Patagonia and the historic first flight across the Andes to Chile (1929), the creation of joint-stock companies, the state corporation Aerolíneas Argentinas and the military line LADE in the 1940s, Transcontinental and Austral in the 1950s, and the arrival of the first jet airliners in 1959. There are numerous illustrations and ten route-maps.

868 **Automotores norteamericanos, caminos, y modernización urbana en la Argentina, 1918-1939.** (United States motor vehicles, roads and urban modernization in Argentina, 1918-1939.)
Raúl García Heras.   Buenos Aires: Libros de Hispanoamérica, 1985. 141p. bibliog.

A study of roadbuilding projects in Argentina and the evolution of competition between motor vehicles (chiefly imported from the United States) and other means of transport (buses, lorries, taxis and *colectivos* [micro-buses], but especially the British-owned railway and tramway companies), set against a background of Argentina's commercial relations with Britain and the United States during the period.

869 **Aviación comercial argentina (1945-1980).** (Argentine commercial aviation, 1945-1980.)
Pablo Luciano Potenze. Buenos Aires: Ediciones El Cronista Comercial, 1987. 388p. maps. bibliog.

A fascinating chronological history of commercial aviation, illustrated with fifty-eight black-and-white photographs and many tables and graphs. Raúl Larra's *La conquista aérea del desierto* (Buenos Aires: Ediciones Anfora, 1979. 142p.) is another good history from the first flights in 1914 to 1973. Antoine de Saint-Exupéry's *Vol de nuit* (*Night flight*, 1932), is a classic impressionistic account of the French author's experiences as a pilot on early Argentine airmail routes.

870 **The development of Argentina's four state fleets.**
Pedro C. M. Teichert. In: *Economic policy revolution and industrialization in Latin America.* Edited by Pedro C. M. Teichert. New York: Greenwood Press, 1975, p. 162-76. bibliog.

A history of the country's four state merchant-shipping fleets in 1957: the State Tanker Fleet (Yacimientos Petrolíferos Fiscales, the oldest and largest, formed after the First World War to carry Argentina's oil), State Overseas Fleet (Flota Argentina de Navegación de Ultramar, British-owned until 1931 and nationalized in 1949), State Fleet (Flota Mercante del Estado, created 1941) and State River Fleet (Flota Argentina de Navegación Fluvial, created 1944 to increase transport facilities along Argentina's rivers). The fleets' current tonnage, earnings records and total values are given.

871 **Edward A. Hopkins and the development of Argentine transportation and communication.**
Victor L. Johnson. *Hispanic American Historical Review*, vol. 26, no. 1 (Feb. 1946), p. 19-37.

Hopkins (1822-91), a native of Pennsylvania, first did business in Paraguay before settling permanently in Argentina in 1854. His first project was the establishment of a regular passenger-freight steamboat service on the river Paraná. Steam navigation and railway construction were his chief enterprises and he was instrumental in providing Argentina with its telegraph service, but his dream of setting up a steamship line from the United States to Buenos Aires remained unfulfilled. 'He failed to achieve many of his goals, but in his failure he drew attention to things that needed to be done.'

872 **The growth of the shipping industry in the Río de la Plata region, 1794-1860.**
Clifton B. Kroeber. Madison, Wisconsin: University of Wisconsin Press, 1957. 194p. maps. bibliog.

Between 1794 and 1860, foreign trade and river shipping in the River Plate increased steadily, despite 'the long period of disorder and hostilities'. Governments encouraged early steamboating activities by providing monopoly concessions and subsidizing navigational aids that private parties could never finance. Buenos Aires remained the centre of the shipping industry (its chief rival in the region was Montevideo), profiting by its direct contact with the main overland routes, the river trade and foreign shipping. The book contains thirteen tables but no illustrations. The beautifully produced *Historia marítima argentina*, edited by Laurio H. Destéfani (Buenos Aires: Cuántica Editora, 1982-90. 10 vols) is a history of naval shipping and activities.

873 **Highways improvements and agricultural production: an Argentine case study.**
Fred Miller. *Traffic Quarterly*, vol. 22 (July 1968), p. 397-418. map.
The author studied an unpaved section of National Highway 35 which passed through a semi-arid agricultural zone producing cattle, sheep and grain, between the cities of Bahía Blanca, Buenos Aires province, and Santa Rosa, capital of La Pampa province. He concluded that highway improvements would not lead to a substantial increase in agricultural production because access was adequately provided for by a railway and the system of dirt roads.

874 **Historia del colectivo.** (The story of the *colectivo*.)
Horacio N. Casal. Buenos Aires: Centro Editor de América Latina, 1971. 111p. (La Historia Popular. Vida y Milagros de Nuestro Pueblo, 21).
In the late 1920s city transport was dominated by British trams, the British-built underground (*subte*) and a few omnibuses; the taxi service was poor. In October 1928 the first *taxi-colectivo* (micro-bus) service, carrying seven passengers, was inaugurated. This is a social, not a technical, history, documenting the *colectivos'* battle for survival. Today these brightly coloured, privately run buses are a common sight in Buenos Aires and other Argentine cities. Thirty-seven illustrations are included.

875 **History of the telephone and telegraph in the Argentine Republic, 1857-1921.**
Victor M. Berthold. New York: The author, 1921. 38p. bibliog.
Argentina had a land and submarine telegraph link with Montevideo (1866) before it had practically any land telegraph. Private companies installed the first local and international telephone lines; seventy-one private companies were granted concessions between 1881 and 1913. The government's reluctance to enter the telephone field was due to the high number of private telephones in the country: 111,000 in 1920, 42 per cent of the total telephones in South America. Two companies, the United River Plate Telephone Company (1886) and Sociedad Cooperativa Telefónica (1887), are described. The text of the current Telephone Rate Law (1920) is given, as are telegraph statistics for 1912-19. See also Ramón de Castro Esteves, *Historia de correos y telégrafos de la República Argentina* (Buenos Aires: Talleres Gráfico de Correos y Telégrafos, 1934-38. 2 vols), and Ricardo T. Mulleady, *Breve historia de la telefonía argentina: 1856-1956* (Buenos Aires: Kraft, 1957. 70p.).

876 **Rastrilladas, huellas y caminos.** (Trails, tracks and roads.)
Enrique M. Barba. Buenos Aires: Editorial Raigal, 1956. 102p. map. bibliog. (Colección Campo Argentino, 5).
A useful short history of early road routes within the country and across the Andes to Peru and Chile, ending in 1943, when Argentina had 65,194 kilometres of roads. Ramón J. Cárcano's *Historia de los medios de comunicación y transporte en la República Argentina* (Buenos Aires: Lajouane, 1893. 2 vols) deals entirely with the colonial era.

877 **The role of the telegraph in the consolidation and expansion of the Argentine Republic.**
John E. Hodge. *The Americas*, vol. 41, no. 1 (July 1984), p. 59-80.
Before the national telegraph network was created in 1891 under the supervision of the Administración Central de los Telégrafos Nacionales, an arm of the postal service, for over thirty years there were several systems often operating at cross-purposes: government, provincial, private, railway and military. A national telegraph law was enacted in 1875, amplified by the telegraph code of 1892. The telegraph's role in the development of the National Meteorological Office is noted. Argentina participated in the International Telegraph Convention from 1888. The author concludes that the telegraph played a significant role in 'civilizing and unifying the country, over immense distances'. The question of competition from the telephone ('already a major factor in urban communication by the 1890s') is not discussed.

878 **Shipbuilding in Argentina.**
*Shipping World & Shipbuilder*, vol. 17, no. 3984 (March 1982), p. 121-7.
Argentina's foreign trade is mostly seaborne – about 97 per cent of exports and 84 per cent of imports – but only 20 per cent of cargo is carried in Argentine ships. Altogether, Argentina has 148 shipbuilding and boatbuilding companies, but only 25 are capable of building large ships. This short article describes three shipbuilders: the state-owned Astilleros Argentinos Río de la Plata (ASTARSA) and Astilleros Fábricas Navales del Estado (AFNE, with the largest shipyard and strong links with the Navy), and the private Astilleros Alianza. See also the short article on ports and shipbuilding in *Fairplay International Shipping Weekly* (24 May 1990), p. 22-31.

879 **South American packets: the British Packet Service to Brazil, the River Plate, the West Coast (via the Straits of Magellan) and the Falkland Islands, 1808-80.**
J. N. T. Howat. York, England: Postal History Society in association with William Sessions, 1984. 283p. maps. bibliog.
In 1823 British Foreign Secretary George Canning introduced a monthly Admiralty sailing-packet service to Buenos Aires, 'so as to provide a regular, dependable means of direct communication with the consuls in the states bordering the River Plate'; they carried mail, goods and passengers. After 1832 Buenos Aires was served by a branch packet (steamboat from 1851) via Rio de Janeiro and Montevideo. The book emphasizes the sailboat and steamboat companies (successively Post Office, Navy, Royal Mail Steam Packet Company and their privately owned rivals), their sailings (there are detailed tables), and British postal agencies and their postmarks. There is a chapter on the branch packet to the Falkland Islands, 1852-80.

880 **South Atlantic seaway: an illustrated history of the passenger lines and liners from Europe to Brazil, Uruguay and Argentina.**
N. R. P. Bonsor. Jersey, Channel Islands: Brookside Publications, 1983. 525p. maps. bibliog.
An illustrated history of seventy-one shipping lines flying eleven flags, dominated by twenty-two Italian, seventeen British, eleven French and two Argentine companies; only one, the Italian Costa Line, was still running a passenger service at the time of

publication. The lines are described in chronological order of founding, from the British Royal Mail Steam Packet Company, 1851, to Empresas Líneas Marítimas Argentinas, 1962: history, fleet list, ships' activities, changes of name and ports.

881   **Trade and trading links in western Argentina during the viceroyalty.**
David J. Robinson. *Geographical Journal*, vol. 136, no. 1 (March 1970), p. 24-41. maps. bibliog.

Describes the local and regional communication systems centred on the city of Mendoza from 1776 to 1810, 'a period during which patterns were established that were to endure until the twentieth century'. The trails were usually little more than tracks along which cattle, horses and waggons were driven. The chief regional arteries were the all-important link with Buenos Aires by way of San Luis, the routes northwards to San Juan and La Rioja, and the trans-Andean passes. A table shows distances between staging-posts on the Mendoza to Buenos Aires trail.

882   **Valor económico de los puertos argentinos.** (Argentine ports: their economic importance.)
Ricardo M. Ortiz.   Buenos Aires: Editorial Losada, 1943. 242p.
(Biblioteca de Estudios Económicos).

Clearly a well-researched history, though unillustrated and undocumented, of the economic importance of Argentina's ports (especially the major international ports of Buenos Aires, Rosario, La Plata and Bahía Blanca, and the Paraná-Uruguay river ports), their management and legal regulation, and competition from the railways. Robert Veitch, in his *Down Argentine way (light and heavy)* (Buenos Aires: Emecé, 1946. 305p.), a hotchpotch of 'pen pictures' on many aspects of life in Argentina, is aimed mainly at 'men connected with the sea' and contains some useful first-hand information on shipping in the River Plate estuary.

883   **La victoria de las alas: historia de la aviación argentina.** (Winged victory: the story of aviation in Argentina.)
Angel María Zuloaga.   Buenos Aires: Librería y Editorial 'El Ateneo', 1948. 386p. bibliog.

A history of civil, military and naval aviation, from the first balloon flight in 1908, beautifully illustrated with photographs and paintings.

# The railways

884   **British-owned railways in Argentina: their effect on economic nationalism, 1854-1948.**
Winthrop R. Wright.   Austin, Texas; London: University of Texas Press, 1974. 305p. maps. bibliog. (Institute of Latin American Studies. Latin American Monographs, 34).

Although the British-owned railways transformed Argentina 'from a backward rural country into a modern food producer', an increasing number of Argentines began to view them 'as instruments of foreign domination and as tokens of retrogression and strangulation of Argentina's economic development'. This strain of economic nationalism was a factor in the rise of Juan Domingo Perón, who nationalized some 16,000 miles of British lines in 1948. The author identifies four stages of railway development: British control (1852-90), state regulation (1890-1930), competition from the automobile (1930-43) and the negotiations to nationalize the railways (1943-48).

885　**British railways in Argentina, 1857-1914: a case study of foreign investment.**
Colin M. Lewis.　London: Athlone Press, 1983. 259p. maps. bibliog. (University of London. Institute of Latin American Studies. Monographs, 12).

Essentially a financial history of British railways, focusing on the largest companies, the broad-gauge (5' 6") Pampean lines: the Buenos Ayres Great Southern, Buenos Ayres and Ensenada Port, Central Argentine, Buenos Ayres Western and Buenos Ayres and Pacific. The author, an economic historian, considers 'the problems and profits of railway operations, the expectations of a "modernizing elite" and the 'factors promoting and perpetuating a community of interest among apparently disparate groups'.

886　**British steam on the pampas: the locomotives of the Buenos Aires Great Southern Railway.**
D. S. Purdom.　London; New York: Mechanical Engineering Publications, 1977. maps.

A historical and technical study of the 'great steam locomotives which had run and in some cases are still running' on the largest of the old British-owned railways (1861), now renamed the Ferrocarril General Roca. The author was the company's chief mechanical engineer until 1951. The text is illustrated with fifty locomotive-class diagrams, 1924-67, which are listed in the table at the end of the volume. The classic history of the Buenos Ayres Great Southern Railway, compiled by colleagues from the notes of the Danish-born former assistant chief of the company's drawing office, is William Rögind, *Historia del Ferrocarril Sud, 1861-1936* (Buenos Aires: Establecimiento Gráfico Argentino, 1937. 692p.).

887　**The Central Argentine Railway and the economic development of Argentina, 1854-1881.**
Paul B. Goodwin.　*Hispanic American Historical Review*, vol. 57, no. 4 (Nov. 1977), p. 613-32. map.

Until the opening in 1870 of the British-owned Central Argentine Railway between Rosario and Córdoba, transport was provided by 'caravans of carts and trains of mules that were tortuously slow and expensive'. In the 1850s Rosario was a minor port; while construction proceeded in the 1860s the city's population more than tripled. The railway 'created demand and was the prime mover in economic development'; it became a great railway 'once it was able to draw ever-increasing amounts of traffic from the northwest and Cuyo'.

888 **Los ferrocarriles en la Argentina: un enfoque geográfico.** (The railways
of Argentina: a geographical survey.)
Juan A. Roccatagliata. Buenos Aires: Editorial Universitaria de
Buenos Aires, 1987. 276p. maps. bibliog. (Temas de EUDEBA).
A region-by-region history and discussion of the present conditions of Argentine
railways, with useful recent statistical data.

889 **Foreign capital, local interests and railway development in Argentina:
French investments in railways, 1900-1914.**
Andrés M. Regalsky. *Journal of Latin American Studies*, vol. 21,
no. 3 (Oct. 1989), p. 425-52.
After 1900 competition was opened up to new railway investment groups. Three
French railway companies established themselves in the pampas: the Ferrocarril
Provincia de Santa Fé, Compañía General de Ferrocarriles en la Provincia de Buenos
Aires, and the Ferrocarril de Rosario a Puerto Belgrano. The first of these, also the
oldest group, was the only line to survive the 1890 financial crisis, owing to its
'projection towards regions that . . . were far from the zones of influence of other
companies'; the second partially succeeded in building a network with branches; the
third, limited to only one line and very exposed to competition, failed completely. The
article demonstrates 'the limitations inherent in the idea of competing with the great
British companies by means of isolated lines'.

890 **Historia de los ferrocarriles en la Argentina.** (A history of Argentine
railways.)
Horacio Juan Cuccorese. Buenos Aires: Ediciones Macchi, 1969.
159p. maps. bibliog. (Colección Humanidades. Temas de Historia, I.
Serie 1: Trabajos Originales).
An outstanding economic history of Argentina'a railways from the 1850s to their
nationalization in 1948. Other contemporary Argentine histories are notorious for their
bias and/or superficiality; a notable example is Raúl Scalabrini Ortiz's fiercely
nationalistic *Historia de los ferrocarriles argentinos* (Buenos Aires: Editorial Plus Ultra,
1964. 4th complete ed.). On Scalabrini Ortiz, see Mark Falcoff, 'Raúl Scalabrini Ortiz:
the making of an Argentine nationalist', *Hispanic American Historical Review*, vol. 52,
no. 1 (Feb. 1972), p. 74-101.

891 **Hostage private companies under restraint: British railways and
transport co-ordination in Argentina during the 1930s.**
Raúl García Heras. *Journal of Latin American Studies*, vol. 19, no. 1
(May 1987), p. 41-7.
During the 1930s the British-owned railways were at the mercy of Argentina's
economic and transport-coordination policies; the British government did not want to
antagonize the Argentine authorities, who virtually held the railways hostage 'as a
bargaining card during the 1936 Anglo-Argentine trade negotiations and in September
1939 to secure the access of Argentina's beef to the British market'. The same author
describes the run-up to nationalization negotiations in 'World War II and the frustrated
nationalization of the Argentine British-owned railways, 1939-1943', *Journal of Latin
American Studies*, vol. 17, no. 1 (May 1985), p. 135-55.

892 **The politics of rate-making: the British-owned railways and the Unión Cívica Radical, 1921-1928.**
Paul B. Goodwin. *Journal of Latin American Studies*, vol. 6, no. 2 (Nov. 1974), p. 257-87.
Relations between Radical Party governments and the British-owned railways were marked by suspicion: 'long years of intimate association with the oligarchy had tainted the companies in Radical eyes'. This article examines Radical railway policies between the crucial election years 1921 and 1928. Tensions increased when financial difficulties forced the railway companies to raise their tariffs in 1921-22 and 1928. President Alvear had been more conciliatory towards the foreign companies but Yrigoyen, although not hostile to railway capital *per se*, 'seized upon the rates question and used it to his party's advantage'. This is a summary of the author's book, *Los ferrocarriles británicos y la UCR, 1916-1930* (Buenos Aires: Ediciones La Bastilla, 1974. 320p.).

893 **The railroad and Argentine national development, 1852-1914.**
Raymond H. Pulley. *The Americas*, vol. 23, no. 1 (July 1966), p. 63-75.
The expansion of railways in Argentina beween 1852 and 1914 was 'indeed phenomenal': total track mileage rose from a mere seven miles in 1857 (this was the Ferrocarril Oeste line from the centre of Buenos Aires to the village of Floresta) to 20,726 in 1914. The railways were the essential element in the spectacular development of the Argentine economy after 1880 and 'in the welding of the country into an effective political unit': 'In addition to transporting crops to port at harvest time, the railway assisted national development by carrying into the hinterland many of the 2,110,000 immigrants.'

894 **Railway expansion in Latin America: descriptive and narrative history of the railroad systems of Argentina, Peru, Venezuela, Brazil, Chile, Bolivia and all other countries of South and Central America.**
Frederic M. Halsey. New York: The Moody Magazine and Book Co., 1916. 170p. maps.
The chapter on Argentina, p. 7-31, briefly describes the history and current operating conditions of seventeen railway companies. There are twelve photographs and a folding map of the trans-Andine route to Valparaíso.

895 **Railway in the desert: the story of the building of the Chubut Railway and the life of its constructor Engineer E. J. Williams.**
Kenneth Skinner. Wolverhampton, England: Beechen Green Books, 1984. 137p. map.
The Ferrocarril Central Chubut was constructed between 1886 and 1888 under the supervision of *ingeniero* Edward Jones Williams, who had been born in Durham, England. The line was financed by English capital and employed Welsh labourers. It ran from Puerto Madryn to the Welsh colony, and incidentally gave birth to the commercial town of Trelew, the important aluminium-manufacturing town of Madryn and the oil centre of Comodoro Rivadavia. An extension to Gaimán was completed in 1909. After Perón nationalized the railways in 1948 the Chubut line 'was allowed to fall into decay under the competition of increased motor transport and improved roads'; when the author visited Chubut in 1974 the Trelew railway station had been converted

into a museum and library, and 'the great station at Madryn had been taken over by itinerant peons as a "squat"'.

896 **Railways of the Andes.**
Brian Fawcett. London: George Allen & Unwin, 1963. 328p. maps. bibliog.

Chapter five, p. 87-109, deals with the financing, construction and rolling stock of the trans-Andine railway between Mendoza and Valparaíso, built by the Buenos Ayres and Pacific Railway to replace existing mule transport. The first section, from Juncal to Los Andes (Chile), was finished in 1906, the third and final section in 1910; the line from Mendoza to the Upsallata Pass, a distance of 57 kilometres, was completed in 1891. The government purchased the Argentine section in 1939 and in 1947 this became part of the Ferrocarril Nacional General Belgrano. More than 600 miles to the north is the lesser-known metre-gauge railway, called in Spanish Ramal C14, between Salta and Antofagasta on the Chilean side. See H. R. Stones, 'Northern Transandine', *Railway Magazine*, vol. 124, no. 929 (Sept. 1978), p. 428-31. In 1980 Chile closed its side of the line.

897 **Railways of South America. Part I: Argentina.**
George S. Brady. Washington, DC: Government Printing Office for US Department of Commerce, Bureau of Foreign and Domestic Commerce, 1926. 267p. maps. (Trade Promotion Series, no. 32).

A detailed history of Argentina's railway lines, with over fifty illustrations and numerous statistical tables, covering 'the development of the line, the mileage, operating officials, the right of way, number of employees, motive power and rolling stock, repair shops and equipment'.

898 **Regional development and transportation in Argentina: Mendoza and the Gran Oeste Argentino Railroad, 1885-1914.**
William J. Fleming. New York; London: Garland Publishing, 1987. 218p. maps. bibliog. (South American and Latin American Economic History).

Before the construction of the Argentine Great Western Railway (1885), Mendoza's local economy, based on agriculture and stock-raising, maintained close links with Chile and other central and northern Argentine provinces. The railway linked Mendoza directly with the coastal markets and brought an influx of Spanish and Italian immigrants who began to develop the local wine industry, so radically altering the structure and orientation of Mendoza's economy.

899 **A sleeping giant awakes.**
*Railway Gazette International*, vol. 137, no. 10 (Oct. 1981), p. 824-6. map.

In three parts: an interview with the president of Argentine railways (Ferrocarriles Argentinos), who describes how the national railways were 'emerging as a slimmed down giant fit to fight the unrestricted competition on Argentina's highways', by standardizing diesel motive power, computerizing seat reservations and wagon control, and electrifying suburban and main lines; how the Buenos Aires underground railway (*subte*) was planning new lines and extensions; and a survey of rolling-stock and component manufacturers.

900 **South American steam.**
M. H. J. Finch. Truro, England: Barton, 1974. 96p. maps.
A pictorial survey of South American railways containing 135 photographs taken by the author between 1967 and 1969, half of them of British-built locomotives. Argentina occupies nearly half of the book (p. 9-44): fifty-five locomotives, mostly 'on shed' in Buenos Aires, Rosario and Bahía Blanca and belonging to the Generals Roca, Urquiza and Belgrano state lines, are shown. There is also a brief description of the railway described in item no. 901.

901 **Steam on the Río Gallegos.**
H. R. Stones. *Railway Magazine*, vol. 127, no. 968 (Dec. 1981), p. 572-5. map.
Described as the world's most southerly railway, the 75-centimetre-gauge Red Ferrocarril Industrial de Río Turbio, opened 1951, is a state industrial line operated by the Argentine Coal Board (Yacimientos Carboníferos Fiscales) and used exclusively to transport good low-grade coal to the port of Río Gallegos 160 miles away. The article describes, with five photographs, the history of the line and its locomotives, and mining operations.

902 **World of South American steam.**
Roy Christian, Ken Mills. Felton, California: Big Trees Press, 1974. 136p. maps.
Contains a description (p. 54-91) of six Argentine lines (Generals Mitre, San Martín, Roca, Urquiza and Belgrano, and the Ferrocarril Patagónico), illustrated with over sixty photographs of steam (and two electric) engines, five maps and rosters which list builders, dates of construction and the numbers of many locomotives. There are also short descriptions, p. 92-8, with eight more photographs, of the Salta–Antofagasta trans-Andine line and the line linking the Río Turbio coal mine with the port of Río Gallegos (see item no. 901).

# Employment and Income

903 **The Buenos Aires mini-enterprise sector.**
Arthur J. Mann, Jacques R. Delons. *Social and Economic Studies*,
vol. 36, no. 2 (June 1987), p. 41-67. bibliog.
The article describes self-employed workers in the mini-enterprise sector – defined as
businesses of from one to five persons engaged in the production and/or distribution of
goods and services – in the Buenos Aires metropolitan area in late 1980. The sector
was a main provider of employment among the area's 9.8 million residents (the
proportion of self-employed persons rose from 18.5 per cent in 1974 to 23.1 per cent in
1980) and was concentrated in the service, construction and transport subsectors. The
study is based on a survey of 854 workers and employees, their incomes (above
average), educational qualifications (also above average) and expectations ('relatively
high degrees of satisfaction'), and on the *Encuesta permanente de hogares* (Instituto
Nacional de Estadística y Censos, October 1980).

904 **The fall of labor's share in income and consumption: a new 'growth
model' for Argentina?**
Adriana Marshall. In: *Lost promises: debt, austerity, and development
in Latin America*. Edited by William L. Canak. Boulder, Colorado:
Westview Press, 1989, p. 47-65. bibliog.
A study of labour's falling income and its impact on manufacturing production and the
consumer market. The wage policies (wage freezes accompanied by liberalized prices)
introduced by the last military régime, 1976-83, caused a drastic fall in real wages;
labour's participation in the gross national product declined from 50.6 per cent in 1970
to 39.3 per cent in 1983. However, there was an increase in the concentration of
personal income between 1975 and 1981: 'the ten per cent in the highest income class
had a considerable gain'. The participation of labour in total private consumption
stood at 57 per cent in 1970 and reached a maximum of 70 per cent in 1975; after 1976

it was generally less than 50 per cent and labour increasingly lost its spending power: in 1983 total consumption per capita was some 7 per cent below its level of 1970, and in 1985 food consumption was below the levels of 1970-80. Between 1975 and 1985, the production of clothing, textiles and leather goods was among the most sensitive to the drop in the consumption of low-income households; these sectors declined at the rate of almost 5 per cent; in only a very few cases were 1984 production levels comparable to those of the early 1970s.

905 **Hours of work in Buenos Aires, 1914-1936.**
*Monthly Labour Review*, vol. 49, no. 4 (Oct. 1939), p. 962-3.
The average working week in Buenos Aires was reduced by 8.08 hours between 1914 and 1938 – from 53.57 to 45.49 hours. The eight-hour day and forty-eight-hour week became effective in 1929, and the Saturday half-holiday in 1932. However, the computation of average working hours was complicated by the fact that the 1929 law excluded certain industrial groups such as agriculture and domestic service. This brief article discusses a number of other categories of worker and tabulates the annual average hours of work.

906 **Income distribution in Argentina.**
Alberto Fracchia, Oscar Altimir. *Economic Bulletin for Latin America*, vol. 11, no. 1 (1966), p. 106-31.
These are the results of a study sponsored by Argentina's National Development Council (Consejo Nacional de Desarrollo) and the United Nations Economic Commission for Latin America. The statistical appendix tabulates the distribution of personal income for all categories of salaried, waged, self-employed, property-investor and retired persons. In the 1950s 'a significant deterioration occurred in the distribution of income in Argentina. The lowest 60 per cent of all income recipients decreased their share in total income. The next higher groups lost, but the loss was small. The top 10 per cent achieved a substantial increase in its share of the total'. Also valuable on income distribution between 1950 and 1960 are Clarence Zuvekas, 'Economic growth and income distribution in postwar Argentina', *Inter-American Economic Affairs*, vol. 20, no. 3 (winter 1966), p. 19-38; and Richard Weisskoff, 'Income distribution and economic growth in Puerto Rico, Argentina, and Mexico', *Review of Income and Wealth*, vol. 16, no. 4 (Dec. 1970), p. 303-32.

907 **Industrial development and the blue-collar worker in Argentina.**
Richard P. Gale. *International Journal of Comparative Sociology*, vol. 10, nos 1-2 (March-June 1969), p. 117-50. bibliog.
The author looks at the case of the blue-collar worker, especially the car worker, in his work and non-work environments, examining labour recruitment and the workplace, standard of living and consumption, education, kinship and political attitudes. 'Born of immigrants who settled in one of three major urban centers – Buenos Aires, Rosario, or Córdoba – he is likely to be a second generation industrial worker'; 'politically, [he] is an "*hijo de Perón*", brought into national participation during the decade of Perón's rule which ended in 1955'. He has completed six years of primary schooling and the first segment of secondary school; as for religion, he 'may be "*católico por tradición*", a Catholic by tradition'. In the same issue see also William H. Form, 'Occupational and social integration of automobile workers in four countries: a comparative study', p. 95-116, which includes a study of blue-collar workers from the Industrias Kaiser car plant in Córdoba.

908 **Labor control and discrimination: the contratista system in Mendoza, Argentina, 1880-1920.**
Ricardo D. Salvatore. *Agricultural History*, vol. 60, no. 3 (summer 1986), p. 52-80.

The period 1880-1920 was one of dramatic transformations in the national and regional economies. The equally dramatic growth of viticulture in Mendoza generated a new set of labour relations between landowners and immigrant workers, known as the *contratista* system, a 'regime of land tenure and labour relations that allowed native landowners to plant and cultivate vineyards in their holdings with the combined labor force of immigrant and creole workers'. For the creole élite, the system served as a solution to the scarcity of labour. But the system itself 'imposed a hierarchy into the labor force along ethnic lines'. Immigrants took the role of farmers and managers, while creole workers were limited to the role of seasonal wage labourers; the system therefore aggravated the discrimination against native-born workers. There were two types of contract under the system: the *contrato de cultivación*, by which the landowner gave to a *contratista* and his family a plot of land to be planted with vines, and the *contrato de cultivo*, by which a *contratista* agreed to take care of the vineyard in return for a certain amount of money per hectare per year.

909 **Labor relations in Argentina, Brazil, and Chile.**
Robert J. Alexander. New York: McGraw-Hill, 1962. 411p. bibliog. (Publication of the Wertheim Committee).

The chapter on Argentina, p. 139-234, is a thorough analysis of labour conditions and labour relations from 1890, and covers such topics as the recruitment and commitment of industrial manpower (training, promotion, incentives and wage levels), collective bargaining, workers' living conditions, social security and health insurance. He is in no doubt that Perón 'tried to substitute government dictation for collective bargaining' and 'sought to forestall many of the grievances of the laboring man through labor legislation and social security'. Governments after 1955 'did not evolve a consistent policy toward the knottiest problem of post-Perón Argentina – labor-management relations'.

910 **Labour markets and wage growth: the case of Argentina.**
Adriana Marshall. *Cambridge Journal of Economics*, vol. 4, no. 1 (March 1980), p. 37-60. bibliog.

An examination of labour markets and their influence on the rate of growth of wages between 1955 and 1972, 'a new phase in the development of Argentine capitalism'. The period was one of excess labour supply; real wages were maintained at a practically constant level while productivity continued to increase. The author also examines three types of wage differentials: between different sectors, skills and industries. Inter-industry wage differentials tended to widen; 'this tendency was *attenuated* by labour market forces, by trade union practices and, occasionally, by government policy measures. The three factors worked in the same direction'. See also the same author's 'Immigrant workers in the Buenos Aires labor market', *International Migration Review*, vol. 13, no. 3 (fall 1979), p. 488-501.

911 **Modernization and the working class: the politics of legitimacy.**
Carlos H. Waisman. Austin, Texas: University of Texas Press, 1982.
244p. (The Dan Danciger Publication Series).
An inquiry into 'some of the factors that contribute to the legitimation of capitalism by
the industrial working class [and] the crisis brought about by the irruption of the
working class into the political system'. He examines the cases of Disraelian Britain,
Bismarckian Germany and Peronist Argentina. The emphasis is on the last and is
based on fieldwork carried out 1966-67 by the author and others among the
'established working class' (sugar-cane workers in Tucumán) and among 'new workers'
(recent migrants from the northeast to the cities of Buenos Aires and Rosario). The
first group's 'degree of centrality was high . . . and their exposure to marginalization
processes was also high'; the second group 'had a low level of integration into the
working class . . . and most lived in shantytowns in large urban areas'.

912 **Monetarism, employment and social stratification.**
Ricardo Lagos, Víctor E. Tokman. *World Development*, vol. 12,
no. 1 (Jan. 1984), p. 43-65. bibliog.
The authors compare the occupational changes that occurred as a result of monetarist
economic policies applied in Argentina after 1976 and Chile after 1973. The 1950s and
1960s had seen an increase in the proportion of industrial employment in both
countries. After 1976 there was a fall in the proportion of Argentina's industrial wage-
earners, 'structural demobilization' or insufficient productive employment for the
supply of labour available, a rise in the number of unemployed and a decline in the
workers' negotiating power.

913 **The settlement of labour disputes in Argentina.**
Efrén Córdova, Geralso von Potobsky, Antonio Vázquez Vialard.
*International Labour Review*, vol. 104, nos 1-2 (July-Aug. 1971),
p. 77-96.
This is a history and current review of labour legislation, unfair legal practices,
individual disputes and collective bargaining, compulsory arbitration, and strikes and
lockouts. The number of labour disputes remained fairly constant between 1946 and
1966; a table lists the number of strikes and stoppages in Buenos Aires between 1962
and 1969.

914 **State corporatism in Argentina: labor administration under Perón and
Onganía.**
Paul G. Buchanan. *Latin American Research Review*, vol. 20, no. 1
(1985), p. 61-95.
A sophisticated comparison of the methods used by the Perón (1946-55) and Onganía
(1966-70) governments to control organized labour. For each régime, the author looks
at the internal labour administration (in Perón's case the Secretaría de Trabajo y
Previsón Social, in Onganía's case the Ministerio de Economía y Trabajo), its
personnel and branch allocations (general funds earmarked for centralized agencies in
the national labour administration). The total number of employees in centralized
agencies of Perón's Labour ministry remained relatively stable throughout his régime,
while Onganía's ministry was headed by professional economists with previous
experience in private enterprise, public administration or higher education. Branch

allocations under Perón slowly decreased; under Onganía they were even lower: 'national labor administration was financially a low priority of the regime'.

915  **Trends of real wages in Argentina (1880-1910).**
Roberto Cortés Conde.  Cambridge, England: University of Cambridge, Centre of Latin-American Studies, 1976. 45p. (Working Papers, 26).

This study of urban wages is based on official figures and the records of the firm of Bagley Brothers, which produced crackers and *hesperedina*, a drink made from the skin of bitter oranges. The author makes use of an article by the former United States Consul, William I. Buchanan ('La moneda y la vida en la República Argentina', *Revista de Derecho, Historia y Letras*, 1898), which analysed the firm's cash books to 1890 and its series of wages for 1880-1903. He found that real wages reached a peak in 1899 and declined after 1900 with a slight improvement from 1910-12.

916  **Wages and salaries by occupation and industry in Argentina.**
In: *Labor Developments Abroad.*  Washington, DC: US Department of Labor, May 1966, p. 1-5.

Wage rates kept pace with living costs between 1960 and 1965, thanks to collective-bargaining contracts. 'Base wages for industrial workers by the year 1965 were, on the average, more than triple such wages in 1960. For technicians and administrators, increases in the average base salary were about half those of industrial workers.' Tables show the average hourly base rates and monthly salaries for thirty-four selected industries and occupations in the Buenos Aires federal capital.

**International encyclopaedia for labour law and industrial relations.**
*See* item no. 646.

**The law and practice of labor arbitration in Argentina.**
*See* item no. 647.

# Trades Unions and the Labour Movement

917 **Argentina, from anarchism to Peronism: workers, unions and politics, 1855-1985.**
Ronaldo Munck, with Ricardo Falcón, Bernardo Galitelli. London; Atlantic Highlands, New Jersey: Zed Books, 1987. 261p. bibliog.
Seventeen chronological chapters chart the development of the Argentine labour movement from its mid-nineteenth-century origins in artisan guilds, mutual-aid societies and immigrants imbued with European Socialism. The book is well researched and the authors employ a loosely Marxist methodology although they insist that theirs is 'not a propagandist work'. The book is filled with the long history of workers' clashes with government and employers alike; indeed, the emphasis is on class and worker 'resistance': strike activity, inter-union struggles and the 'insertion' of labour in national politics. The upsurge in labour militancy in the early twentieth century was influenced overwhelmingly by anarchists and syndicalists: since the time of Perón the history of the labour movement has been dominated by its relationship with the economic-nationalist movement.

918 **Argentina 1976-1982: labour leadership and military government.**
Pablo A. Pozzi. *Journal of Latin American Studies*, vol. 20, no. 1 (May 1988), p. 111-38.
This is a useful summary of labour activity during the period and of the leading tendencies within the movement (listed in the glossary at the end). The author is highly critical of the labour leadership's 'tendency towards bureaucratisation' and of its 'role as intermediary between the rank and file and the dictatorial state': on the one hand 'it put a brake on working-class struggle, making an effort to channel it through the *Proceso*', on the other it failed to take a more combative stance towards the military and its 'collaborationism' eventually '[contributed] towards the regime's objectives towards the organised labour movement'.

919 **The Argentine labor movement, 1930-1945: a study in the origins of Peronism.**
David Tamarin. Albuquerque, New Mexico: University of New Mexico Press, 1985. 273p. bibliog.

The work focuses on the 'tortuous evolution' of organized labour and the origins of Perón's labour-based support. Battles between syndicalists, anarchists, socialists and communists for control of the labour movement allowed Perón to win the support of the non-communist faction of the national labour federation (Confederación General del Trabajo, founded in 1930) which accepted government intervention in the economy and rejected cooperation with communist unions on ideological grounds. Perón took control of the movement through 'appeasement and cooptation' and eventually won over the communists as well. Special attention is paid to the CGT's dominant railway unions, above all the Unión Ferroviaria's ideological and personal struggles with weaker unions within the CGT. 'Perón seized upon long-standing labor grievances and the movement's already established inclination to seek governmental solutions as the vehicles by which he subordinated labor to his offices.'

920 **Argentine unions, the state & the rise of Perón, 1930-1945.**
Joel Horowitz. Berkeley, California: University of California, Institute of International Studies, 1990. 284p. (Research Series, 76).

The book centres upon a detailed examination of five unions which in 1936 comprised 39 per cent of all union members: the Federación Obreros y Empleados Telefónicos (syndicalist), Federación Empleados de Comercio (socialist-controlled), Unión Obreros y Empleados Municipales (also socialist), Unión Ferroviaria (the largest and most powerful union, which dominated the Confederación General del Trabajo), and the Unión Obrera Textil (socialist-controlled). The five unions 'differed in ideology, in the type of workers they represented, and in their responses to the challenges of the Neo-Conservative era and the military régime that took power in 1943'. They were all based in Buenos Aires, since provincial unions played very minor roles in the labour movement of the 1930s.

921 **La formación del sindicalismo peronista.** (The evolution of Peronist trades unionism.)
Edited by Juan Carlos Torre. Buenos Aires: Editorial Legasa, 1988. 358p. (Ensayo Crítico).

The volume consists of the editor's introduction and nine essays on the labour movement between 1935 and 1955 by a group of Argentine and foreign scholars, including Joel Horowitz and Walter Little. They consider the growth and structure of the labour movement, collective bargaining, state–labour relations and the role of the Confederación General del Trabajo.

922 **Labor in Latin America: comparative essays on Chile, Argentina, Venezuela and Colombia.**
Charles Bergquist. Stanford, California: Stanford University Press, 1986. 397p. maps.

The long chapter on Argentina, p. 81-190, provides a detailed and well-written analysis of the labour movement from 1880 to 1955, including an excellent case-study of the meat-packing workers and their unions. There is a brief postscript to 1976.

923 **Labor, nationalism, and politics in Argentina.**
Samuel L. Baily. New Brunswick, New Jersey: Rutgers University
Press, 1967. 241p. bibliog.

A scholarly but slightly dated history of the 'ideological role of labor', its relation with the state and the rise of working-class nationalism. The book is based chiefly on interviews and labour newspapers and covers the years 1890-1957. The author contrasts the 'liberal' nationalism of the first two generations of immigrants with the 'creole' nationalism of workers who migrated to the cities from the interior and 'sought political power primarily through Perón'. The book is concerned chiefly with the 1946-55 period when a third strand, labour nationalism, aided and abetted the rise of Perón but was later rejected by him. See also the same author's 'The Italians and the development of organized labor in Argentina, Brazil, and the United States, 1880-1914', *Journal of Social History*, vol. 3, no. 2 (winter 1969-70), p. 123-34.

924 **Labor unrest in Argentina, 1887-1907.**
Roberto P. Korzeniewicz. *Latin American Research Review*, vol. 24,
no. 3 (1989), p. 71-98. bibliog.

The article is based on a detailed reading of newspapers since official labour statistics were not compiled until 1907. It analyses the geographical distribution of strikes, 60 per cent of which revolved around wage claims, and the impact of organized labour and the labour market on the forms of action taken by workers in manufacturing industries. During the period, 53 per cent of all recorded strikes occurred in the city of Buenos Aires and its suburbs, 24 per cent elsewhere in the province of Buenos Aires, 14 per cent in the province of Santa Fe and 11 per cent in other provinces. The same author's 'The labour movement and the state in Argentina, 1887-1907', *Bulletin of Latin American Research*, vol. 8, no. 1 (1989), p. 25-45, focuses on anarchism, which was 'not as prevalent within the labour movement as studies of the period have generally maintained'; see also *The limitations of ideology in the early Argentine labour movement: anarchism in the trade unions, 1890-1920.*

925 **Labour conflicts under the second Peronist regime, Argentina, 1973-76.**
Elizabeth Jelin. *Development and Change*, vol. 10, no. 2 (April
1979), p. 237-57. bibliog.

A comprehensive study of the strikes and stoppages that took place under the second Peronist régime (May 1973 to March 1976), their causes and nature, frequency and intensity, and the increasingly repressive responses of the Ministry of Labour. The industrial workers tended to strike over statutes and job-classification issues and, increasingly, for parity with other workers; the public-sector workers struggled for 'recognition of their condition as wage workers'. There was a clash between 'two disconnected social forces: the bureaucratic union organization whose possibilities rest[ed] on a docile labour force . . . and new sectors of the working class with active experience of participating in decentralized, direct working-class struggle, and unable to accept populist unionism although they define[d] themselves politically as Peronists'.

926 **Latin American labor organizations.**
Edited by Gerald Michael Greenfield, Sheldon L. Maram. New York; Westport, Connecticut; London: Greenwood Press, 1987. 929p. bibliog.

The section on Argentina by Lisbeth Haas (p. 1-24) begins with a useful history of labour organizations. The directory proper lists thirty such organizations founded between 1857 and 1945, from the Agrarian Federation of Argentina to the Workers' Federation of Río Gallegos. There is an average of ten lines on each organization; not surprisingly, the General Confederation of Labour (CGT, founded in 1930) merits two pages, and there is one page each on the Regional Argentine Labour Federation (the country's first major labour organization, 1901), the National Federation of Construction Workers (1936) and the Railway Workers' Union (1922). See also A. P. Coldrick, Philip Jones, *The international directory of the trade union movement* (London: Macmillan, 1979, p. 1041-52).

927 **The limitations of ideology in the early Argentine labour movement: anarchism in the trade unions, 1890-1920.**
Ruth Thompson. *Journal of Latin American Studies*, vol. 16, no. 1 (May 1984), p. 81-99.

'Argentina is widely quoted, along with Spain, as one of the countries where anarchist and/or anarcho-syndicalist ideology and practice dominated the labour movement.' The author proceeds to show that the importance of anarchism has been exaggerated. The Federación Obrera Regional Argentina (FORA, founded 1901) was an anarchist union federation; its great rival was the syndicalist Unión General de Trabajadores, superseded in 1909 by the Confederación General de Trabajadores. In 1915 most of FORA's members renounced anarcho-communism and formed the more moderate FORA IX, the dominant federation between 1915 and 1920; it eclipsed FORA V, formed by those remaining faithful to the old FORA. The article includes a case-study of the Confederación de Ferrocarrileros, the general railwaymen's union and the largest single union in Argentina before 1920, which was politically non-aligned.

928 **El movimiento obrero argentino.** (The Argentine labour movement.)
Julio Godio. Buenos Aires: Editorial Legasa, 1987-89. 3 vols.

An expert chronological history of the labour movement from 1870 to 1943, by a leading Argentine scholar. Another good descriptive history is by Sebastián Marotta, a former trade-union leader: *El movimiento sindical argentino: su génesis y desarrollo* (Buenos Aires: Ediciones Libera, 1960-70. 3 vols), covering the period 1857-1935.

929 **Occupational community and the creation of a self-styled elite: railroad workers in Argentina.**
Joel Horowitz. *The Americas*, vol. 42, no. 1 (July 1985), p. 55-81.

During the 1930s, Argentina's two railway unions, La Fraternidad (founded 1887) and the Unión Ferroviaria (1922), were the dominant labour organizations in the country; 'their members considered themselves the elite of the working class'. This article considers the case of the Unión Ferroviaria, which was very successful in obtaining and maintaining better conditions for its members through collective bargaining. Two factors, the strategic nature of the industry and the sense of community created by the UF's chain of cooperatives and mutual-aid societies, contributed to the strength of the union. Although no closed shop existed, sixty per cent of eligible workers were paid-up members in 1941.

930 **The political, economic, and labor climate in Argentina.**
David R. Decker. Philadelphia: University of Pennsylvania, Wharton School, Industrial Research Unit, 1983. 131p. map. bibliog. (Multinational Industrial Relations Series 0149-0818. No. 4: Latin American Studies, 4f).

The first two chapters summarize political history, the political parties and key aspects of the economy. The third and best chapter supplies information (to 1982) on employment, labour unions and labour law. The appendix constitutes a directory of labour organizations in basic industries.

931 **Reflections on Argentine auto workers and their unions.**
Judith Evans, Paul Heath Hoeffel, Daniel James. In: *The political economy of the Latin American motor vehicle industry.* Edited by Rich Kronish, Kenneth S. Mericle. Cambridge, Massachusetts: MIT Press, 1984, p. 133-59.

The authors examine 'the activity and organization of rank-and-file auto workers both on a wider political level and on the more immediate shop floor level', from 1955 to 1980. The first stage in the industry's growth, 1955-67, was characterized by relatively high wages, full employment and tranquil labour relations. By 1967 the period of 'seemingly limitless expansion of the auto industry' was coming to an end and there developed a high level of militancy in the Córdoba and Buenos Aires plants until 1972. The return of Peronism in 1973 increased the combativeness of the auto workers; after the 1976 military coup, the level of activity naturally declined but 'resistance . . . persisted'. The chapter focuses on three Córdoba auto unions: the moderate SMATA (Motor Mechanics' Union) and two militant unions in the Fiat plants of Concord and Materfer, SITRAM (Sindicato de Trabajadores de Materfer) and SITRAC (Sindicato de Trabajadores de Concord).

932 **Resistance and integration: Peronism and the Argentine working class, 1946-1976.**
Daniel James. Cambridge, England: Cambridge University Press, 1988. 301p. bibliog. (Cambridge Latin American Studies, 64).

A major contribution to the history of the modern Argentine labour movement, the result of fifteen years' work which effectively summarizes a number of the author's important earlier articles. It makes extensive use of interview material, union archives and newspapers, and even analyses popular tango lyrics. It focuses on the relationship between Peronism and the working class and between the rank-and-file and its undemocratic and hierarchical union leadership in the period between the first and second Peronist administrations, 1955-73.

933 **The silversmiths of Buenos Aires: a case study in the failure of corporate social organization.**
Lyman L. Johnson. *Journal of Latin American Studies*, vol. 8, no. 2 (Nov. 1976), p. 181-213.

The article describes the unsuccessful attempts by Buenos Aires silversmiths to create their own guild between 1615 and 1810. The author has made two other pioneering studies of craftsmen's guilds in colonial Buenos Aires: 'The entrepreneurial reorganization of an artisan trade: the bakers of Buenos Aires, 1770-1820', *The Americas*, vol. 37, no. 2 (Oct. 1980), p. 139-60; and 'Francisco Baquero: shoemaker and organizer', in *Struggle and survival in colonial America*, edited by David G. Sweet, Gary B. Nash (Berkeley, California; Los Angeles; London: University of California Press, 1981, p. 86-101). See also his 'The role of apprenticeship in colonial Buenos Aires', *Revista de Historia de América*, no. 103 (Jan.-June 1987), p. 7-30.

934 **Sindicalismo y peronsimo: los comienzos de un vínculo perdurable.**
(Trades unionism and Peronism: the beginnings of a permanent relationship.)
Hugo del Campo. Buenos Aires: Consejo Latinoamericano de Ciencias Sociales, 1983. 273p. bibliog. (Biblioteca de Ciencias Sociales. CLACSO, 5).

An analysis of the labour movement before and under Perón. The author considers that the resurgence of the labour movement after 1955 proves that 'the links forged during the period 1943-46 between the labour movement and Peronism were long-lasting'. Another good history of the ideological evolution of the labour leadership between the World Wars and the origins of the massive worker support for Perón in 1943-45 is by a Japanese scholar: Hiroshi Matsushita, *Movimiento obrero argentino, 1930-1945: sus proyecciones en los orígenes del peronismo* (Buenos Aires: Siglo Veinte, 1983. 347p.).

935 **Los sindicatos en el gobierno, 1973-1976.** (Trades unions and the government, 1973-1976.)
Juan Carlos Torre. Buenos Aires: Centro Editor de América Latina, 1983. 166p. bibliog. (Biblioteca Política Argentina, 30).

A description of the strained relations between the unions and the administrations of Juan and Isabel Perón, May 1974 to March 1976, by the leading Argentine expert on the labour movement. Disaffection with the government culminated in the first-ever general strike under a Peronist government, in May 1975.

# Statistics

936　**La actividad estadística en la República Argentina, 1550-1983.** (Statistics in Argentina, 1550-1983.)
Buenos Aires: Instituto Nacional de Estadística y Censos, 1983. 146p.
A brief history of official statistical activities, with special attention paid to the present-day national statistical service, which is coordinated by the Instituto Nacional de Estadística y Censos (INDEC): its structure, areas of activity (population, agricultural and economic censuses; statistical surveys and indexes, etc.), links with international bodies, and the training of officers. There is a list of the publications of INDEC and its predecessors since 1887 (mainly since 1960), and a province-by-province directory of official statistical agencies.

937　**Anuario estadístico agropecuario argentino, 1930-1984: producción-comercio-precios-insumos.** (Argentine statistical yearbook of agriculture and livestock farming, 1930-1984: production, commerce, prices and inputs.)
Edited by Enrique Román.　Buenos Aires: Centro de Estudios de Comercialización Agropecuaria y Agroindustrial, 1984. 2 vols.
A total of 497 pages in two ring-binders. Volume one contains the statistics of agricultural production, marketing and prices, volume two livestock.

938　**Anuario estadístico de la República Argentina.** (Statistical yearbook for Argentina.)
Buenos Aires: Instituto Nacional de Estadística y Censos, 1950- .
annual.
Contains detailed statistics on all aspects of the economy – resources, industry, public finance and foreign trade. A quarterly *Boletín estadístico trimestral* (1947- ) contains demographic and social statistics, agriculture and fishing, industry, trade, finance, construction and transport. A monthly *Estadística mensual* is also published (1973- ),

267

listing consumer prices, construction costs, wages, labour demand, and exports and imports.

939 **Argentina en las urnas, 1916-1989.** (Argentina at the polls, 1916-1989.) Rosendo Fraga, with the collaboration of Gabriela Malacrida. Buenos Aires: Editorial Centro de Estudios Unión para la Nueva Mayoría, 1989. 245p. (Colección Análisis Político, 2).

Part one is a detailed analysis of the national election results of 14 May 1989. Part two reproduces the provincial results of all presidential elections since 1916 with other data on more recent elections, including the last four elections for national deputies and the gubernatorial election of 1987.

940 **Argentina: social sectors in crisis.** Washington, DC: World Bank, 1988. 104p. map. (World Bank Country Study).

The findings of a World Bank Mission to Argentina in November and December 1986, published here in mainly statistical form, covering education, health care and housing. Political instability and economic crises after 1976 reduced the living standards of an increasing section of the population. Despite President Alfonsín's social emergency programmes, this report identifies 'critical problems in the organization and targeting of social services . . . as well as serious weaknesses in the capacity to mobilize and maintain the funds needed for their provision'.

941 **Catálogo de estadísticas publicadas en la República Argentina.** (Catalogue of Argentine statistics.) Lelia I. Boeri. Buenos Aires: Instituto Torcuato di Tella, Centro de Investigaciones Económicas, 1966. 2nd ed. 2 vols.

A catalogue of publications from a total of forty-three national, provincial and municipal statistical bodies, published during the previous twenty years, and their main features: area coverage, dates, frequency and form of tabulation. The publications cover every imaginable type of social and economic activity, including employment, cost of living, production, trade, transport and communications, finance and taxation.

942 **Economic survey of Latin America and the Caribbean.** Santiago, Chile: United Nations Economic Commission for Latin America and the Caribbean, 1948- . annual.

Tables showing twenty indicators of Argentina's 'economic evolution' occupy pages 125-50 of the 1988 edition, published in 1989. Comparisons with earlier years are made.

943 **Estadísticas históricas argentinas: compendio 1873-1973.** (A compendium of historical statistics for Argentina, 1873-1973.) Vicente Vázquez-Presedo. Buenos Aires: Academia Nacional de Ciencias Económicas, Instituto de Economía Aplicada, 1988. 431p.

This is a summary 'with new figures and some corrections' of the compiler's earlier *Estadísticas históricas argentinas, 1875-1914 (comparadas)* (Buenos Aires: Ediciones Macchi, 1971. 2 vols). A total of 256 tables covering population, education, production (agriculture, industry, mining, energy, transport and communications), foreign trade, finance and miscellaneous.

944  **A guide to Latin American and Caribbean census material: a bibliography and union list.**
Edited by Carole Travis.  London: British Library; Standing Conference of National and University Libraries; Institute of Latin American Studies, University of London, 1990. 739p.

The chapter on Argentina by Alan Biggins, p. 1-94, contains a brief summary of census-taking, a list of contents and a full chronological bibliography of over 240 censuses of every description published since the first national census (1869). In addition, locations are provided for thirty-six national, special and public libraries in the United Kingdom. Statistical surveys (*encuestas*), population estimates and other more general statistical material are not included. A useful short description of Argentine national population censuses between 1869 and 1970 may be found in *The handbook of national population censuses: Latin America and the Caribbean, North America, and Oceania*, edited by Doreen S. Goyer and Elaine Domschke (Westport, Connecticut: Greenwood Press, 1983, p. 41-9).

945  **Relevamiento estadístico de la economía argentina, 1900-1980.**
(Statistical survey of the Argentine economy, 1900-1980.)
Edited by Banco de Análisis y Computación, Consultora de Investigaciones Económicas y Estadísticas.  Buenos Aires: Banco de Análisis y Computación, 1982. 772p. bibliog.

In two sections: part one contains global statistics (national accounts, foreign trade, the public sector, finance and employment); part two reproduces statistics for the following sectors: agriculture and fishing, mining, construction, manufacturing industries and services.

946  **Statistical abstract of Latin America.**
Los Angeles, California: UCLA Latin America Center Publications, 1956- . annual.

Statistics for Argentina are contained in general or separate tables under the following broad headings, with further subdivisions: geography and land tenure; transportation and communication; population, health and education; church, state and crime; working conditions, migration and housing; industry, mining and energy; sea and land harvests; foreign trade; financial flows; national accounts, government policy and finance, and prices. The coverage extends back to 1970 or even 1960; the latest figures in the 1989 volume (1145p.) refer to 1987. There is a detailed subject index at the back of the volume. The publication is based on a wide range of solid international sources and official country statistics.

947  **Statistical yearbook for Latin America and the Caribbean.**
Santiago, Chile: United Nations Economic Commission for Latin America and the Caribbean, 1973- . annual.

Argentina appears in general tables under the following headings: (part one) social development, economic growth, domestic prices, external trade, external financing; (part two) population and national accounts (domestic prices, balance of payments, external financing/indebtedness/trade, natural resources and production of goods, infrastructure services, employment and social conditions. The 1989 edition (1990, 770p.) publishes figures to 1983; comparative figures are given to 1970, sometimes 1960.

948 **Women of the world: Latin America and the Caribbean.**
Elsa M. Chaney.   Washington, DC: US Department of Commerce, Bureau of the Census, 1984. 173p. map. bibliog.

One of the regional handbooks on 'Women of the world' produced by the National Statistics on Women project of the Office of Women in Development, US Agency for International Development. The handbook consists chiefly of tables of figures from the 1960s onwards, in two or three area sections (Argentina is to be found in most of the tables headed 'South America') and covering: population distribution and change, literacy and education, women in economic activity, marital status and living arrangements, and fertility and mortality.

# Urbanization and Housing

## General

949 **Argentina: a mature urbanization pattern.**
Alejandro B. Rofman. *Cities*, vol. 2, no. 1 (Feb. 1985), p. 47-54.
map.

Argentina is the second most urbanized country in Latin America, with around eighty per cent of its population living in urban centres of more than 2,000 inhabitants. The article describes the historical development of Argentina's cities, the urban regional pattern (dominated by the centre-littoral and the country's primate city, Buenos Aires), economic influences on demographic trends (the recent example is migration to oil towns and new industrial sites), and the current low rate of urbanization (in 1980 the centre-littoral had a lower proportion of the population than in 1970, and population growth in Buenos Aires is now actually static).

950 **Argentina's urban system and the economic crisis.**
Mabel Manzanal. *Cities*, vol. 5, no. 3 (Aug. 1988), p. 260-7. map.

In recent decades, a slowing of population growth in many of Argentina's largest cities has been matched by steady population growth in small and intermediate-sized urban centres. The author suggests the economic reasons for these changes: 'a decline in industrial activity and a decrease in industrial waged labour'.

951 **The Argentine system of cities: primacy and rank-size rule.**
César A. Vapñarsky. In: *Urbanization in Latin America: approaches and issues*. Edited by Jorge E. Hardoy. Garden City, New York: Anchor Press, 1975, p. 369-89.

Between 1869 and 1900 Argentina's urban pattern was characterized by low 'closure' and low interdependence; since 1900 Buenos Aires has retained its primacy and the other cities have conformed to the rank-size rule. Buenos Aires is 'one of the most extreme examples of primacy in the world – that is, in 1960 it had 6,700,000

271

inhabitants, more than ten times the population of Rosario, the second Argentine city'. An analysis of four nodal city subsystems in 1947 (Central region, Northwest, Comahue, Northeast) reveals the local primacy of one or more cities.

952   **The city-idea in Argentina: a study in evanescence.**
Richard M. Morse.   *Journal of Urban History*, vol. 2, no. 3 (May 1976), p. 307-30.
Argentine literature provides rich material for 'tracing the decomposition of the city-idea because an overriding dichotomy between Buenos Aires and the "interior" has dominated Argentine history for two centuries'. The author examines the following writers for references to 'allogenetic' Buenos Aires, where an alien culture has been transplanted to a new environment: Francis Bond Head (*Rough notes taken during some rapid journeys across the pampas and among the Andes*, 1828 [q.v.]); Domingo F. Sarmiento (*Facundo*, 1845 [see item no. 278], and *Argirópolis*, 1850); José Hernández (*Martín Fierro*, 1872-79, see item no. 1051); Lucio Vicente López (*La gran aldea*, 1884); Jorge Luis Borges (*Fervor de Buenos Aires*, 1923); Ricardo Güiraldes (*Don Segundo Sombra*, 1926 [see item no. 1049]); Eduardo Mallea (*Historia de una pasión argentina*, 1937 [see item no. 530], *Fiesta en noviembre*, 1938, and *La bahía del silencio*, 1940); Leopoldo Marechal (*Adán Buenosayres*, 1948); and Julio Cortázar (*Rayuela*, 1963).

953   **La ciudad argentina en el período precensal (1516-1869).**
(The Argentine city, 1516-1869.)
Jorge E. Hardoy, Luis A. Romero.   *Revista de la Sociedad Interamericana de Planificación*, vol. 5, no. 17 (March-June 1971), p. 16-39. bibliog.
A chronological study of the economic and social development of Argentine cities before the taking of the first national census in 1869. Includes a review of sources for urban history, including travel accounts, maps and iconography. Poorly documented but a useful introduction.

954   **La ciudad pampeana: geografía urbana, geografía histórica.** (The cities of the pampas: an urban and historical geography.)
Patricio H. Randle.   Buenos Aires: Editorial Universitaria de Buenos Aires, 1969. 146p. maps. bibliog. (Temas de EUDEBA: Geografía).
In five chapters: the early development of towns and cities in the province of Buenos Aires 1779-1879, two theoretical chapters on urban formation, and two twentieth-century case-studies: towns immediately north of the Salado river and the Campo de Mayo district. There are sixty-five plates, mostly town plans showing clearly the traditional *domero* (grid) pattern of development. The author has produced a complementary *Atlas: geografía histórica de la pampa anterior* (q.v.).

955 **Claves políticas del problema habitacional argentino, 1955-1981.**
(Political causes of the housing problem in Argentina, 1955-1981.)
Oscar Yujnovsky. Buenos Aires: Grupo Editor Latinoamericano,
1984. 411p. (Colección Estudios Políticos y Sociales).

A study of housing interest-groups and the effects of government housing policies on housebuilding, the housing market, housing services and housing conditions. Two appendices list major housebuilding firms and housing organizations, and there is a statistical appendix. The main problems are identified as a housing shortage in some regions and low population density in others, the frequent flooding of certain occupied areas, the lack of basic services such as water, sewerage and public transport, and environmental pollution. The fault lies in 'an economic and social system which permits lucrative property speculation'. An essential journal for urban studies is *Medio ambiente y urbanización* (Buenos Aires: Instituto Internacional de Medio Ambiente y Urbanización, 1983- . four issues a year). Its chief editor is the well-known scholar Jorge Hardoy. Each issue usually includes one or more articles on Argentina and there is now a regular brief 'Sección Argentina'. Recent numbers have contained articles on flooding, shanty-towns, public health, the conservation of historic towns, and the environment.

956 **Historia de la ciudad argentina.** (A history of the city in Argentina.)
Amílcar Razori. Buenos Aires: Imprenta López, 1945. 4 vols. in 3.
maps.

An exhaustive history of early city growth: pre-colonial Indian settlements, the colonial Jesuit reductions, the opening up of the Indian frontier, and 'spontaneous' and 'conscious' urban formation. Volumes one and three include maps and city plans. There are four detailed indexes of personal names, Indian tribes, frontier forts and towns.

957 **New towns in eighteenth century northwest Argentina.**
David J. Robinson, Teresa Thomas. *Journal of Latin American Studies*, vol. 6, no. 1 (May 1974), p. 1-33. maps.

Urban development in Argentina's Northwest was stagnant until steady population growth accompanied by increased immigration and the creation of the Viceroyalty of the River Plate in 1776 integrated the region economically with the rest of the country. During the eighteenth century, twenty-two new towns were established, all in the Cuyo region except for two in the old province of Tucumán and the new intendancy of Salta. Their purpose was to achieve administrative and social control over a large number of inhabitants and to act as defences against Indian attacks. One-third of the article considers the new town of Nueva Orán, Salta, founded in 1794.

958 **El proceso de urbanización en la Argentina.** (The process of
urbanization in Argentina.)
Gino Germani. *Revista Interamericana de Ciencias Sociales*, segunda
época, vol. 2, no. 3 (1963), p. 287-345. bibliog.

A synthesis of previous studies on urbanization together with an original analysis of primary data, especially censuses, for the period 1869-1947, reviewing internal migration and foreign immigration, and social and economic factors. Thirty tables and four graphs are included.

959 **Regional urbanization and agricultural production in Argentina: a comparative analysis.**
Jorge Balán. In: *Urbanization in contemporary Latin America: critical approaches to the analysis of urban issues.* Edited by Alan Gilbert, Jorge E. Hardoy, Ronaldo Ramírez. Chichester, England; New York: John Wiley, 1982, p. 35-58. maps. bibliog.

Examines the urbanization process in Tucumán and Mendoza provinces, 1870-1914. The two areas had similar colonial settlement histories and were both oriented towards their regional sugar and wine industries. After 1880, differences emerged. In Tucumán, rapid urban growth was followed by a slowing of rural growth, whereas in Mendoza rural [with urban] growth continued. Mendoza's local economy was more dynamic than Tucumán's and 'rural Mendoza was more deeply penetrated by urban values and institutions, and had greater contact with the outside world'.

960 **Urban planning in the Argentine: the Buenos Aires Province experience.**
Rodolfo Makobodzki. *Journal of the Royal Town Planning Institute* (London), vol. 58, no. 5 (May 1972), p. 201-8. maps.

Part one of this undocumented study describes Argentina's recent urban-planning history: Perón's two National Economic Plans (1947 and 1953), the creation in 1958 of the Consejo Federal de Inversiones ('to regulate the structure of development and investment') and its incorporation in the National Planning and Development System (CONADE, 1966), which provided for eight regional development boards; and provincial and municipal planning structures. Part two evaluates the planning process in Buenos Aires province, particularly the work of the Urban Development Board (1967) within four designated 'operational areas'.

961 **Villeros y villas miseria** [sic]. (Shanty-towns and shanty-dwellers.)
Hugo E. Ratier. Buenos Aires: Centro Editor de América Latina, 1971. 113p. (Vida y Milagros de Nuestro Pueblo. La Historia Popular, 60).

In 1955, there were 80,000 people living in shanty-towns; by 1970 the estimate was ten times as many (700,000 in the province of Buenos Aires, 200,000 in the capital city itself). The author, a sociologist, criticizes the shanty 'eradication' plans after 1955. An uneven, popularized account, whose thirty-four photographs perhaps speak more loudly than the text.

962 **The working class and state housing policy: Argentina, 1976-1981.**
Oscar Yujnovsky. *Comparative Urban Research*, vol. 11, nos 1-2 (1985), p. 52-69. bibliog.

Describes three different examples of state housing policy. The National Mortgage Bank (Banco Hipotecario Nacional), grants thirty-year mortgages with three per cent annual interest, mainly to middle-class house-buyers; when the Bank increased monthly repayments in 1980, protest marches were held throughout the country. The National Housing Fund (FONAVI), a dependency of the Ministry of Urban Development and Housing, is directed towards lower-income groups, and specializes in social welfare. There have been various programmes for the elimination ('eradication') of shanty-towns (the euphemistically named *villas de emergencia*) in the city of Buenos

Aires, but evictions have been carried out forcibly and, in most cases, 'gave rise to new *villas* located in other parts of metropolitan Buenos Aires'.

# Buenos Aires

963  **Avenida de Mayo: legendary avenue of Buenos Aires.**
Germinal Nogués. *Américas*, vol. 27, no. 3 (March 1975), p. 12-18.
The Avenida de Mayo, running east–west from the Plaza de Mayo to the Plaza del Congreso, was the first of Buenos Aires's grand avenues (inaugurated 1894). This article describes the history of the avenue in its transport (the first cars, 1888, the first omnibus, 1904, the underground, 1913); its notable buildings (the *La Prensa* newspaper, 1896, the Gothic-Roman Pasaje Barolo, Buenos Aires's second skyscraper, the first lift installed in a building, 1898); and its hotels, cafés, office blocks, bookshops, theatres and (now-vanished) carnivals. Important features of the Plaza de Mayo and Plaza del Congreso are also described.

964  **Buenos Aires.**
Carlos Mouchet.   In: *Great cities of the world: their government, politics and planning.*   Edited by William A. Robson, D. E. Regan. London: George Allen & Unwin, 1972. 3rd ed. bibliog.
Volume one, p. 240-69, of this revised and enlarged edition describes the capital city's municipal powers and functions (mainly covering 'the fields of police and public order, taxation and the regulation and administration of the public domain'), municipal organization and management, finance, relations with the federal government, municipal planning and development, and administrative boundary problems and jurisdictional conflicts. The capital is governed by special legislation laid down by the national government, while the other municipalities of the province of Buenos Aires are governed by provincial charter law.

965  **Buenos Aires anteayer: testimonios gráficos de una ciudad, 1854-1910.**
(The Buenos Aires of yesteryear: the record of a city in photographs, 1854-1910.)
José María Peña.   Buenos Aires: Manrique Zago Ediciones, 1981. 191p.
A beautiful collection of photographs, selected by the author, recording different aspects of the city's life in its development from *la gran aldea* (the 'great village') to a modern metropolis.

966  **Buenos Aires, Argentina's melting-pot metropolis.**
Jules B. Billard, photographs by Winfield Parks.   *National Geographic Magazine*, vol. 132, no. 5 (Nov. 1967), p. 662-95. maps.
A brief tour of the city illustrated with thirty colour photographs: restaurants, the docks, housing, traffic, the Plaza de Mayo and its famous public buildings (Casa Rosada [government house], the Cabildo [colonial town council], Cathedral), the Plaza

del Congreso, San Telmo, La Boca and other quarters of the city, the underground, theatres, sports clubs, and an interview with the mayor.

967 **Buenos Aires: 1800-1830: su gente.** (The people of Buenos Aires, 1800-1830.)
Susana R. Frías, César A. García Belsunce (et al.). Buenos Aires: Emecé Distribuidora, 1976. 256p. maps.
A well-illustrated study of population change in the city and surrounding rural districts, based largely on censuses. Two further volumes in the same series deal with health and medicine, crime, education and social welfare: Frías and Abelardo Levaggi, *Buenos Aires, 1800-1830: salud y delito* (1977. 297p.) and Frías, Belsunce (et al.), *Buenos Aires, 1800-1830: educación y asistencia social* (1979. 388p.).

968 **Buenos Aires: 400 years.**
Edited by Stanley R. Ross, Thomas F. McGann. Austin, Texas: University of Texas Press, 1982. 192p. maps.
The papers of a 1980 conference sponsored by the University of Texas and the Municipality of Buenos Aires and held at the Library of Congress, to commemorate the second, and permanent, founding of the city by Juan de Garay in 1580. In two parts: 'The historical city' includes Jonathan Brown and Susan M. Socolow (commercial, social and spatial development 1740-1830s), James R. Scobie (nineteenth-century economic and political development), Mark Szuchman (the city's role in the country's political, economic and intellectual life); while 'The contemporary city' includes Richard J. Walter (social and economic growth 1910-80), Merlin H. Forster (intellectual and cultural life), Roberto Etchepareborda (possible future evolution) and Joseph S. Tulchin ('how to know the city'); finally, there are two 'perceptions' by Argentines living abroad.

969 **Buenos Aires: historia de cuatro siglos.** (Buenos Aires: four centuries of history.)
Edited by José Luis Romero, Luis Alberto Romero. Buenos Aires: Editorial Abril, 1983. 2 vols. maps. bibliog.
A magnificently produced volume on urban history (political, economic, demographic, cultural), running to over 1,000 pages, consisting of more than sixty essays by forty-seven well-known scholars, mostly Argentine but including also some foreign specialists. The work is divided into seven chronological sections: the foundations 1536-80, the colonial city 1580-1806, the 'Jacobin city' 1806-20, the 'creole city' 1820-52, the 'patrician city' 1852-80, the 'bourgeois city' 1880-1930, and the 'city of the masses' (since 1930). There is also a detailed chronology.

970 **Buenos Aires: plaza to suburb, 1870-1910.**
James R. Scobie. New York: Oxford University Press, 1974. 323p. maps. bibliog.
The period under review saw the population of the city of Buenos Aires grow through immigration from 180,000 to 1,300,000. The author of this magnificent urban history points to three forces which had most effect on the city's development: the construction of the port, the city's position as hub of the country's railway network, and the 'commercial-bureaucratic' functions which Buenos Aires performed as entrepôt and administrative centre after it was designated federal capital in 1880. The

book also examines housing, transportation and a number of social themes, including the family and education. Forty-nine contemporary photographs and twelve maps and plans are included.

971 **La ciudad indiana: Buenos Aires desde 1600 hasta mediados del siglo XVIII.** (City of the Indies: Buenos Aires from 1600 to the middle of the eighteenth century.)
Juan Agustín García. Buenos Aires: Estrada, 1900. 375p.

A classic history of colonial Buenos Aires by a prominent sociological thinker, examining property, commerce, administration and institutions, the family and religion. The title refers to the city's colonial nature. See also Rómulo Zabala, Enrique de Gandía, *Historia de la ciudad de Buenos Aires* (Buenos Aires: Municipalidad de Buenos Aires, 1936-37. 2 vols), for the period 1536-1800. Ezequiel Martínez Estrada's *Cabeza de Goliat: microscopía de Buenos Aires* (Buenos Aires: Nova, 1957. 3rd ed. 320p.), contains eighty-seven vignettes on the city, its institutions and characters.

972 **Housing solutions for Buenos Aires' invisible poor.**
David Welna. *Grassroots Development*, vol. 12, no. 1 (1988), p. 2-7.

Two kinds of dwellings are commonly available to 205,000 of Buenos Aires's poor residents: *conventillos*, decrepit former mansions on the south side of the city, subdivided into single-room tenements (an estimated 45,000 live in them); and so-called 'family hotels', run-down boarding houses that let out expensive rooms by the week, 'with no contractual obligations on either side and no protection from eviction for the tenants' (an estimated 60,000). A third way is to illegally occupy ('squat' in) vacant buildings (an estimated 100,000). This article describes the work of two housing groups: Grupo Habitat, an organization which is trying to change the legislation governing such issues as landlord–tenant agreements, and the Buenos Aires Tenants' Centre (CIBA), which provides low-cost services and helps contest arbitrary evictions. Both groups have formed tenants' groups and devised self-help renovation pro-grammes. See also Elizabeth Jelin, 'Buenos Aires: class structure, public policy and the urban poor', in *Cities in crisis: the urban challenge in the Americas*, edited by Matthew Edel and Ronald G. Hellman (New York: City University of New York, Bildner Center for Western Hemisphere Studies, 1989, p. 91-101).

973 **Inquiry into the social effects of urbanization in a working-class sector of Greater Buenos Aires.**
Gino Germani. In: *Urbanization in Latin America*. Edited by Philip M. Hauser. New York: Columbia University Press, International Documents Service, 1961, p. 206-33.

A case-study of Isla Maciel, a working-class district in the Avellaneda suburb of Buenos Aires. The district was formed of two distinct zones: an urbanized sector of modest houses inhabited by city-born residents or migrants of long standing, and a *villa miseria* (shanties), occupied mostly by new migrants from the interior, especially northeast, provinces. The degree of 'social disorganization' in the shanties was high, with prostitution and alcoholism the most prevalent problems, caused by economic difficulties and the primitive housing conditions.

974 **Moving the capital of Argentina: a further example of utopian planning?**
Alan Gilbert. *Cities*, vol. 6, no. 3 (Aug. 1989), p. 234-42. maps.

The idea of moving the federal capital is not new, but in May 1987 Congress approved a law to re-establish it 800 kilometres to the southwest, centred on the twin towns of Viedma and Carmen de Patagones, Río Negro province. The aim was to stimulate development in Patagonia and to slow the growth of Buenos Aires; at the same time, 15,000 key government workers would be transferred to create a new élite civil service in the new city, so ending years of inefficient government bureaucracy. President Alfonsín's choice of Viedma was made without extensive research, and 'both the urban design and the basic aims underlying the project [incorporated] too many grandiose elements'; the project was shelved by the incoming Peronist government.

975 **Neighborhood associations in Buenos Aires: contradictions within contradictions.**
Juan Silva, Frans J. Schuurman. In: *Urban social movements in the Third World*. Edited by Frans J. Schuurman. London: Routledge, 1988, p. 45-61. bibliog.

After 1976 a shortage of rented property and forced eviction of squatters through 'eradication' laws to permit highway construction through their areas led, because of suppression by the military, to only limited protests by *sociedades de fomento* and *juntas vecinales* (neighbourhood associations), the history of which dates back to 1936. The movement was revived after 1983. Case-studies are provided of three types of squatter settlements, a *villa de emergencia* (Retiro, in the city centre), a more regulated *asentamiento* (Barrio Argentino, in the municipality of Merlo), and an established *barrio* (the Quilmes-west district). The authors describe the associations' relations with local and national government and with each other (geographical separation, political rivalry and limited resident participation). In 1986 there were eleven *villas* in the federal capital (home to 19,400 persons), with an umbrella organization, the Consejo de Demandantes. A national federation of community cooperatives, the Movimiento Comunitario, was formed in 1987.

976 **Population and space in eighteenth century Buenos Aires.**
Lyman L. Johnson, Susana Migden Socolow. In: *Social fabric and spatial structure in colonial Latin America*. Edited by David J. Robinson. Ann Arbor, Michigan: University Microfilms International for the Department of Geography, Syracuse University, 1979, p. 339-68. (Dellplain Latin American Studies, 1).

The city's population censuses are studied to show the numerical patterns of growth and their effect on population density, housing and household composition, and occupations. During this period, the total population increased almost fourfold. The authors conclude that Buenos Aires did not have a stable, permanent population, and that the flow of immigrants 'had a negative impact on the occupational opportunities and potential for social mobility available to the native-born population'. While the city centre became more densely populated and more ethnically diverse, the outlying areas 'continued to be rural, creole and poor'.

977 **The spatial evolution of Greater Buenos Aires, Argentina, 1870-1930.**
Charles S. Sargent. Tempe, Arizona: Arizona State University,
Center for Latin American Studies, 1974. 164p. maps. bibliog.

A well-illustrated history of the transformation of the surrounding countryside and
towns into city, and of the inner city of Buenos Aires, analysing the part played by
various factors in that growth: the development of pampas agriculture and the export-
based economy, the city as commercial entrepôt and administrative capital, and the
spread of the railway network. Land development and speculation are also considered,
especially in the formative period before 1870, as well as transport, municipal services,
residential density, employment opportunities and the changing social status of the
suburbs.

# Other cities

978 **Growing up in cities: studies of the spatial environment of adolescence in
Cracow, Melbourne, Mexico City, Salta, Toluca, and Warszawa.**
Edited by Kevin Lynch. Cambridge, Massachusetts; London: MIT
Press; Paris: Unesco, 1977. 177p. maps. bibliog.

Las Rosas, on the outskirts of Salta, has 'an exceptionally well-defined physical setting,
backed by low open hills' and the appearance of a 'hopeful and active community'. Its
residents are 'nearly all lower middle class', mixed in occupations and status but mostly
employed in local government. Nine boys and girls aged eleven to fourteen were
interviewed by Antonio Battro and an architect, Eduardo Ellis, about their image of
the city, their favourite places, their homes, their use of time and space and their
conceptions of physical change, beauty and ugliness.

979 **The historic geography of Tucumán.**
Oscar Schmeider. *University of California Publications in Geography*,
vol. 2, no. 12 (12 June 1928), p. 359-86. maps.

A study of pre-Columbian and colonial Tucumán city and province, based on
secondary sources: the early explorations and Spanish settlements (the first successful
foundation was San Miguel de Tucumán, 1565), the colonization of the interior
valleys, and the economic life during the colonial period. See also Madaline W.
Nichols, 'Colonial Tucumán', *Hispanic American Historical Review*, vol. 18, no. 4
(Nov. 1938), p. 461-85.

980   **The legal and institutional organization of metropolitan Rosario, Argentina.**
Raúl Oscar Basaldúa, Oscar Moreno.   In: *Latin American urban research. Vol. 2: Regional and urban development policies: a Latin American perspective.*   Edited by Guillermo Geisse, Jorge E. Hardoy.   Beverley Hills, California; London: Sage Publications, 1972, p. 189-228. maps.

Rosario's population grew rapidly with large influxes of immigrants between 1870 and 1920; the 1940s and 1950s saw intense industrial development and today the city is an important port and industrial centre, mainly in the area of metallurgy. 'Rosario's disorderly growth has produced well-known deficiencies, among which are serious defects in the network of highways, access roads, and railways, location of important industries in residential areas, and insufficient urban services.' In 1969 a new municipal agency, 'which has as its principal objective integration of areawide planning and programming', was created. The volume also contains a chapter on 'The Argentine national plan for eradicating *villas de emergencia*', by Carlos Tobar, p. 221-8.

981   **Mendoza: land use in the adobe city.**
Arthur S. Morris.   In: *Morphology of towns.*   Edited by C. S. Yadav. New Delhi: Concept, 1987, p. 61-79. (Concept's International Series in Geography, no. 3. Perspectives in Urban Geography, vol. 10).

Virtually all of Mendoza was destroyed by the 1861 earthquake, but the colonial tradition of adobe single-floor houses was retained in the rebuilding of the city. Since 1944, the use of adobe bricks has been forbidden and only anti-seismic materials allowed. The 'apparently patternless' inner city is predominantly residential, interspersed with a few small shops and industries. In the 1970s 10,500 new housing units were built around the adobe city, nearly all financed by the Banco Hipotecario Nacional (National Mortgage Bank); the net effect of this expansion was 'to bring into being a sprawl of single houses, with very few flats, all around the city, leaving the adobe area intact'. There is a general absence of 'zoning' in general and of planning control over urban land use in the city and there are no local community action groups; on the other hand, shanty-towns are uncommon in Mendoza (one per cent of the population in 1960).

982   **Salta, an early commercial center of Argentina.**
G. M. Wrigley.   *Geographical Review*, vol. 2, no. 2 (Aug. 1916), p. 116-33. maps.

Salta, lying between two rivers and 'in the midst of marshes and swamps', was founded as a strategic site and centre of the mule trade between Lima and Buenos Aires. In the nineteenth century it was connected to the Atlantic economy by the building of the railway link south through Tucumán. By the twentieth century the province's main activity was 'still her staple of three centuries ago – livestock, the tropical frontier product'. Its population in 1915 was nearly 30,000.

983   Secondary cities of Argentina: the social history of Corrientes, Salta, and
      Mendoza, 1850-1910.
      James R. Scobie, completed and edited by Samuel L. Baily.   Stanford,
      California: Stanford University Press, 1988. 276p. maps.

The late James Scobie had completed the first five chapters of this splendid book and
drafted the remaining five; Samuel Baily revised the remaining sections but without
making any additional research. The development of the three cities was similar: in the
early colonial period, they were local commercial centres – Mendoza traded with
Chile, Salta with Bolivia and Corrientes with Paraguay; by 1850 all three cities had
nearly identical populations of 7,000 to 8,000. Yet, after 1850, 'Mendoza grew rapidly,
Corrientes stagnated, and Salta fell somewhere in between'. Each city's historical
development is described and major aspects of their urban setting compared: the
composition and class structure of the population, the impact of immigration on the
upper classes, residential patterns, work and employment, and leisure and social
activities.

# Education

**984 Argentina and the brain drain: some perspectives from expatriates in the United States.**
David L. McKee. *International Migration*, vol. 23, no. 4 (Dec. 1985), p. 453-9. bibliog.

This article is based on a survey of eighty-nine Argentine health-care professionals and physical scientists living in the United States, whom the author had asked to provide details concerning their primary reasons for staying abroad. Forty-three cited educational considerations and forty that their move was work-oriented. Several respondents mentioned the unfavourable political climate in Argentina; a small number had entered the United States accompanying their parents as small children. Most of the expatriates held Argentine degrees.

**985 Argentina: higher education and political instability.**
Nick Caistor. In: *Education in Latin America*. Edited by Colin Brock, Hugh Lawlor. London: Croom Helm, 1985, p. 183-92.

The study begins in the watershed year of 1966, 'when the armed forces first broke into the campus of Buenos Aires claiming as is their wont that the university was a breeding ground for "subversion"'. The Onganía régime banned all political activity and student unions, repealed university autonomy and appointed its own rectors and deans, and generally made higher education as 'apolitical' as possible. With the return of Peronism in 1973, student militants and young Peronist academics were thrust into the running of the universities, where student work 'often degenerated into endless political debate'. Up to 2,000 university lecturers were sacked in the first three months after the 1976 coup, and the most suspect faculties, sociology, psychology and education itself, were closed down. This was part of a campaign of physical repression against 'subversive cells' and Marxist ideology. University autonomy was revoked, funds and student numbers cut, and private universities encouraged (some excellent universities are the result, it must be said). Education in general was decentralized and returned to the provinces. The author ends by contrasting the Argentine and British systems of higher education and by listing the problems facing the new university authorities after 1983.

986 **The Argentine professorate: occupational insecurity and political interference.**
Daniel J. Socolow. *Comparative Education Review*, vol. 17, no. 3 (Oct. 1973), p. 375-88.

Over 400 academics from the national universities of Buenos Aires, Tucumán, Rosario and del Sur (Bahía Blanca) and representing four disciplines (science, agronomy, economics and humanities), were surveyed beginning in 1969, three years after the Onganía government's clash with the universities and two years after autonomy had been restored. The author studied the characteristics of those preoccupied with job insecurity, the professors' income and socioeconomic background, and the implications of instability for research and training and for the growth of a full-time professorate. Younger, part-time, better-paid, foreign-trained professors from the economics and agronomy faculties tended to be slightly less concerned about job insecurity.

987 **Aspectos ocultos de la educación en la Argentina: políticas de inversión y productividad, 1900-1970.** (The hidden face of education in Argentina: investment policies and productivity, 1900-1970.)
Carlos Escudé. Buenos Aires: Editorial El Coloquio, 1975. 281p. bibliog.

This is a detailed study of the productivity returns of seventy years of investment in primary and secondary education. Much of the material in the main chapters is theoretical; statistical details are contained in the appendices. The author concludes that, while investment in education is necessary, there is obviously an upper limit, and he is critical of the fact that most of the education budget is spent not on teachers but on the huge educational bureaucracy. He is in favour of giving more resources to secondary education (especially for capital projects) and improving technical education.

988 **Cultural imperialism and educational centralism in Argentina.**
Ray Edward Johnson. *Revista/Review Interamericana*, vol. 10, no. 2 (summer 1980), p. 205-19.

The title should not deter the would-be reader. The article is an attack on educational centralism and a useful summary of nineteenth-century Argentine educational thought. Argentine educationalists, most prominent of whom was Domingo F. Sarmiento, adopted European and North American theories and techniques with the motive of increasing central governmental control over education 'to the near total exclusion of all indigenous influences'. He also considers the influences of positivist and sociological thought, and those sections of the 1853 Constitution which relate to education. The characteristics of centrally administered national education, fostered by national plans, are 'teacher licensing, inspections, examinations, master curricular schedules with compulsory courses, censorship of materials, directed political positions incorporated in school programs, and regulation of all non-affiliated parochial and private institutions by the central government'.

989 **Education and employment: the case of the industrial sector in Argentina.**
Juan C. Tedesco. *Prospects*, vol. 9, no. 1 (1979), p. 105-13.
Argentina has almost entirely eliminated illiteracy from its industrial work-force. During the 1960s there was a sharp drop in the proportion of workers who had not completed seven years of basic schooling. A large part of the educationally backward category consisted of labour coming in from neighbouring countries. However, there were still workers 'with a level of formal education lower than that which is theoretically supposed to fit the type of the post in question'. A number of recommendations for pre-service and in-service training programmes is put forward. The author has published two important books: *Educación y sociedad en la Argentina (1880-1945)* (Buenos Aires: Ediciones Solar, 1986. new ed. 285p.); and, with two others, *El proyecto educativo autoritario: Argentina, 1976-1982* (Buenos Aires: FLACSO, 1983. 305p.).

990 **Education and social change: the Argentine case.**
David Nasatir. *Sociology of Education*, vol. 39, no. 2 (spring 1966), p. 167-82.
In 1963 the author interviewed a sample of 1,700 university and non-university students and asked them about 'their job aspirations, the manner in which they would characterize an ideal job, and their opinions concerning the responsibilities of educated members of the society at large'. He found that Argentine students were far more vocationally oriented than their North American counterparts. The work was reprinted in *Education and development: Latin America and the Caribbean*, edited by Thomas J. La Belle (Los Angeles: University of California, Latin American Center, 1972, p. 683-700).

991 **Education, human resources and development in Argentina.**
Paris: Organisation for Economic Co-operation and Development, 1967-68. 2 vols. map.
This planning document is the result of studies carried out in 1965-66 by the OECD's Programme on Human and Scientific Resources for Development in collaboration with the Argentine National Development Council (CONADE). It looked at the internal efficiency of the educational system and the demand for and supply of subject skills in the employment market, analysed occupational and educational data for 1960 (although some of the figures refer back as far as 1910), and made forecasts. Volume one is the general report, volume two the methodology and statistical appendices. The report identified one of the most serious problems as 'wastage' – high dropout and truancy rates, which have consistently plagued Argentine education.

992 **Education in Argentina, 1890-1914: the limits of oligarchical reform.**
Hobart A. Spalding. *Journal of Interdisciplinary History*, vol. 3, no. 1 (1972), p. 31-61.
Educational reformers 'steeped in Positivistic principles' made real improvements in school conditions and teaching methods, and education reached more pupils than ever before during the period. Although new specializations were introduced to the curriculum, the élite 'had little interest in industry or commerce . . . A strong anti-intellectual current existed within it'. But 'socio-economic factors, the inefficient use of resources, and a recalcitrant government prevented changes from passing much beyond

the qualitative stage', perhaps because the government saw the potential impact of mass education: 'the areas of highest literacy constantly produced the largest anti-elite vote after the introduction of the secret ballot in 1912'.

993　**Educational technology in Argentina.**
Roberto Ronchi. *Programmed Learning and Educational Technology*, vol. 17, no. 3 (Nov. 1980), p. 201-9. bibliog.

In June 1979 there were fifty-two institutions working in the area of educational technology (ET), twenty in Buenos Aires and the rest spread throughout fifteen of the twenty-four provinces. Sixteen centres were devoted exclusively to ET, the main two being the Centro Nacional de Tecnología Educativa, founded in 1948, and Santa Fe's provincial ET centre; seventeen organizations incorporated ET significantly, and a further eighteen partly, into their programmes. The most widely used media were correspondence courses, radio, television, personal contact, audiovisual media, tape recording, courses and short seminars, one case of the use of the telephone and only one case of the use of the computer, although the University of Belgrano's Institute of Educational Research had recently created a Centre for Cybernetic Pedagogy which was 'trying to apply scientific control to the process of learning through the use of computers'. Argentina had no open university, even though 'because of its size the nation needs to use distance education'.

994　**The encyclopedia of comparative education and national systems of education.**
Edited by T. Neville Postlethwaite.　Oxford; New York: Pergamon Press, 1988, 627p. bibliog. (Advances in Education).

'Argentina', by Michael A. Petty, p. 101-6, is a short but useful description of the goals of the education system (officially stated in terms of 'integral education' and with emphasis on the system's democratization), the structure and size of the various levels of education, administration and finance, the conditions of teachers, educational research and major problems. The contribution on Argentina by Emilio Fermín Mignone in *International encyclopedia of higher education*, editor-in-chief Asa S. Knowles (San Francisco; Washington, DC; London: Jossey-Bass, 1977, vol. 2, p. 465-71) is based on 1976 data.

995　**The engineering profession and economic development in Argentina.**
Enrique Oteiza.　Geneva: International Institute for Labour Studies, 1963. 53p.

The author, then executive director of the Instituto Torcuato di Tella, considers the large-scale emigration of Argentine engineers to the United States. Industrial, mining and civil engineers, poorly paid and 'in a subordinate position' at home, found work in the United States because there was a shortfall of engineers in the host country; in Argentina the proportion of engineering to all university graduates was 12.5 per cent (compared with 10 per cent in the United States) and only half the active engineers who had graduated in 1962 (7,000) were working in industry. Another version was published as 'Emigration of engineers from Argentina: a case of Latin American "brain drain"', *International Labour Review*, vol. 92, no. 6 (Dec. 1965), p. 445-59. See also *Modernization for emigration: the medical brain drain from Argentina*.

996   **The formation of the Argentine public primary and secondary school system.**
      John E. Hodge.   *The Americas*, vol. 44, no. 1 (July 1987), p. 45-65.

The government of Bartolomé Mitre (1862-68) was unable to make more than 'woefully modest' progress in education because of its limited resources; schools in the provinces were said to be in a 'dismal state'. One achievement was the creation in 1863 of the prototype of the Argentine *colegio nacional* (secondary school), the Colegio Nacional de Buenos Aires. Like Mitre, Domingo F. Sarmiento, the great educator-president (1868-74), placed the greatest emphasis on primary studies and literacy. The first of three vitally important education laws enacted during this period, providing 'the framework within which the elementary schools system could develop in the twentieth century', was Law 463 (1871), which stimulated primary education and created the normal school, or teacher-training college, the first of these being the Escuela Normal de Paraná (see *Yankee teachers and the founding of Argentina's elementary school system*). Law 1420 (1884) stipulated that primary education was to be coeducational, free and compulsory, and it created the Consejo Nacional de Educación. Law 2737 (1890) was a qualifying law obliging the provinces to devote more funds to primary education.

997   **Freedom in the Argentine universities before and after the Perón regime.**
      Juan Mantovani.   In: *The Year Book of Education 1959*.   London: Evans, 1959, p. 405-15.

Many university teachers were removed from their posts on political grounds between 1943 and 1946 and the two university laws of 1947 and 1953 brought higher education under the power of the state. The universities began their recovery during the first days of October 1955 after Perón had been removed; their self-government was restored and dismissed professors reinstated. 'Since the beginning of 1958, all the universities of the country are rejoicing in their right of self-government.' Their autonomy was short-lived, however, as a military government again intervened in the universities in 1966. See also William L. Munger, 'Academic freedom under Perón', *Antioch Review*, vol. 7, no. 2 (June 1947), p. 275-90.

998   **Historia de la educación argentina.** (A history of education in Argentina.)
      Manuel Horacio Solari.   Buenos Aires: Editorial Paidós, 1972. 2nd rev. ed. 243p. bibliog. (Biblioteca del Educador Contemporáneo. Serie Mayor, vol. 26).

This is perhaps the best-known general history of Argentine education, but although the first edition was published as long ago as 1949, this second edition still does not take the story beyond 1947. The treatment is chronological; there are many quotations from contemporary documents and there is, unusually for Argentine books, an index, but there are no statistical tables.

999  **Historia de la Universidad de Buenos Aires.** (A history of the University
of Buenos Aires.)
Tulio Halperín Donghi.  Buenos Aires: Editorial Universitaria de
Buenos Aires, 1962. 227p. bibliog. (Biblioteca de América).

A brief introduction to Argentina's second-oldest national university, inaugurated in
1821. (The University of Córdoba was founded as early as 1613.) It was originally
structured as six departments: preparatory studies, exact sciences, medicine, law,
religion and elementary education. After the federalization of the city of Buenos Aires
in 1880 the university was formally nationalized. This is primarily an institutional
history; the bibliography cites a mere ten works but the volume does have a name
index.

1000  **International handbook of education systems.**
Edited by J. Cameron, Robert Cowen (et al.).  Chichester, England;
New York: John Wiley, 1984. 3 vols. map.

The chapter on Argentina in volume three (Asia, Australasia and Latin America),
p. 565-99, describes the various levels of the education system (pre-primary, primary,
secondary, higher, commercial, vocational, adult, non-formal and teacher training),
central administration and finance, and development and planning (including
curriculum theory and planning institutions). The same text, but with slightly variant
statistics, appears as *Argentina* (London: British Council, 1978. 22p.).

1001  **Modernization for emigration: the medical brain drain from Argentina.**
Alejandro Portes, Adreain A. Ross.  *Journal of Interamerican
Studies & World* Affairs, vol. 18, no. 4 (Nov. 1976), p. 395-422.
bibliog.

In 1970, Argentina was a net exporter of professionals; from 1950 to 1964 over 5,000
emigrated to the United States, with physicians representing the single largest
contingent (1,475 between 1950 and 1970). The author interviewed twenty-four young
physicians planning to emigrate to that country and compared them with a second
sample of thirty-three who had decided to stay and work as interns (*residentes*) in
public hospitals. Opportunities for employment were cited as the main reason for
emigrating, even though there was a deficit of trained professionals in neglected areas
of Argentina's interior. Those who stayed foresaw problems of adaptation in the
United States and displayed 'emerging nationalist values'. See also item no. 995.

1002  **Recent developments in the social sciences in Argentina.**
Virginia Leonard.  *The Americas*, vol. 40, no. 4 (April 1984),
p. 560-7.

The author sampled research in the social sciences being carried out in six national and
private universities ('is there any research going on in provincial universities?'), and
lists, without addresses, the most active of the small research institutes, foremost of
which is the Instituto Torcuato di Tella. A diverse range of topics was being studied,
often from an interdisciplinary point of view; social class divisions and the economy
were the favourite topics ('above all, social scientists are interested in Argentine
subjects which they often see as "problems"'). Argentine researchers are more likely

to look to Europe for interpretations, theories and models, 'especially to the neo-Marxism and structuralism of the French'.

1003 **Sociology and reality in Latin America: the case of Argentina.**
Norberto Rodríguez Bustamante. *International Social Science Journal*, vol. 31, no. 1 (1979), p. 86-97.
Half of the article is devoted to a discussion of the social sciences in Latin America since 1940, and the ideological (especially Marxist) bias that has bedevilled the discipline of sociology. He then examines the case of the Sociology Department of the University of Buenos Aires between 1966 and 1974. In 1966, with Onganía's intervention in the universities, large numbers of the academic and research staff of the Department and Institute of Sociology resigned, including their director Gino Germani. Thus was 'demolished the edifice of theory and effective practice in scientific research which had marked the period 1957-66'. From now on there was 'outright politicization of the student body, along Peronist lines, with a strong nationalist bias'; sociology was 'supplanted by practical politics', its original syllabus was dismembered and courses were used to create 'a general climate for ideological and political recruitment'. By 1973, the curriculum was burdened with 'the study of problems and subjects associated with populist politics at municipal, provincial and national levels'. Ironically, between 1966 and 1973 enrolment in the Sociology Department soared from 533 to 1,542 students.

1004 **Student politics in Argentina: the University Reform and its effects, 1918-1964.**
Richard J. Walter. New York; London: Basic Books, 1968. 236p. bibliog. (Student Movements – Past and Present, 2).
In 1918 a series of student strikes in the city of Córdoba led to the University Reform movement which established the principle of student participation in the university administrative councils not only in Argentina but throughout Latin America. 'With the Reform, the Argentine universities were changed from oligarchically controlled institutions of limited enrollment to schools more representative of all the Republic's citizens, especially of the middle sectors.' The author examines the development of student political activity in Argentina. During the period, 'most student groups were idealistic and nationalistic and assumed a generally leftist position'; in the long run, they 'have not been so important in bringing about changes on the national level'. The author provides more material on the Argentine social context of the Reform in 'The intellectual background of the 1918 University Reform in Argentina', *Hispanic American Historical Review*, vol. 49, no. 2 (May 1969), p. 233-53. Mark J. Van Aken, in 'University Reform before Córdoba', *Hispanic American Historical Review*, vol. 51, no. 3 (Aug. 1971), p. 447-62, cites earlier, international manifestations of student activism.

1005 **Students and the political system of the University of Buenos Aires.**
Ronald C. Newton. *Journal of Inter-American Studies*, vol. 8, no. 4 (Oct. 1966), p. 533-56.
The chapter begins with a description of the University's internal political system. The University statute of 1958 conferred self-government upon the ten faculties scattered about the city. Student participation in the running of the University (known as *cogobierno*) operated at two levels: faculty councils and the Superior Council of the University. The 'ineffectuality' of the students' extra-mural political role in times of

crisis is noted. A two-page preface outlines events since Onganía deposed the civilian government of Arturo Illia in June 1966 and issued a law abolishing political activity within the University. See also the study by David Nasatir which demonstrates the greater interest in politics shown by university students than non-university youth of a comparable age: 'University experience and political unrest of students in Buenos Aires', *Comparative Education Review*, vol. 10, no. 2 (June 1966), p. 273-81; also in *Student politics*, edited by S. M. Lipsett (New York: Basic Books, 1967, p. 318-31, and in *Education and development: Latin America and the Caribbean*, edited by Thomas J. La Belle (Los Angeles: University of California, Latin American Center, 1972, p. 701-12).

1006 **Ten years of change at the University of Buenos Aires, 1956-66: innovations and the recovery of autonomy.**
Gilda L. de Romero Brest. In: *World Year Book of Education 1972/73*. London: Evans, 1972, p. 124-36.
The author describes the University's ten years of reconstruction, 'principally aimed at recovering its autonomy', from the fall of the Perón régime to the military coup in 1966 which again brought state interference in university affairs. The reforms affected the following areas: student participation, teaching staff, courses, research, the campus, extension activities, the University Press (EUDEBA), vocational guidance and student welfare, and secondary schools associated with the University. The same chapter appears in *Universities facing the future*, edited by W. R. Niblett and R. F. Butts (San Francisco: Jossey-Bass, 1972, p. 124-36).

1007 **Yankee teachers and the founding of Argentina's elementary school system.**
J. Fred Rippy. *Hispanic American Historical Review*, vol. 24, no. 1 (19 Feb. 1944), p. 166-9.
The founders of Argentina's state primary schools were assisted by teachers from the United States. Between 1871 and 1886 more than thirty *escuelas normales* (teacher-training schools) were inaugurated in almost every part of the country. The first normal school, at Paraná, was opened in 1871 with a New Englander, George Stearns, as director. Some thirty to forty women teachers from the United States were employed during the twenty years following 1871 either in women's or mixed normal schools. The story of sixty-five teachers, mostly women, who worked in Argentina's state schools between 1869 and 1916, is told in Alice Houston Luiggi, *65 valiants* (Gainesville, Florida: University of Florida Press, 1965. 191p.). See also Arturo Andrés Roig, 'The Paraná Normal School', *Américas*, vol. 25, no. 4 (April 1973), p. 11-13.

# Science and Technology

1008 **Benjamin Apthorp Gould and the founding of the Argentine national observatory.**
John E. Hodge. *The Americas*, vol. 28, no. 2 (Oct. 1971), p. 151-75.
Gould (1824-96) was a United States astronomer who wanted to map and catalogue the heavens in the Southern Hemisphere and thought that the Argentine city of Córdoba was on an ideal latitude. He won the support of President Domingo F. Sarmiento and established an observatory in 1870-71. He was a pioneer of planetary photography and the preparation of star catalogues using cameras; his famous 'Uranometria' was reissued as *Atlas de la uranometria argentina que contiene las estrellas del hemisferio sud* (Buenos Aires, 1905). He returned to the United States in 1885 and was succeeded as director by his long-time assistant, Juan M. Thome, a native of Pennsylvania. See the same author's 'Juan M. Thome, Argentine astronomer from the Quaker state', *Journal of Interamerican Studies and World Affairs*, vol. 13, no. 2 (April 1971), p. 215-29. He continued Gould's pioneering work between 1885 and 1908, and managed to secure adequate funding from enlightened President Julio A. Roca during the economic crises of the 1890s. The Observatory's third director, Charles D. Perrine (1909-36), was also an American.

1009 **Biotechnology in Europe and Latin America: prospects for co-operation.**
Edited by Bernardo Sorj, Mark Cantley, Karl Simpson. Dordrecht, Netherlands; Boston, Massachusetts; London: Kluwer Academic Publishers for the Commission of the European Communities, 1989. 223p.
Part one deals with biotechnology in Europe, part two Latin America. Chapter 2.1, by José La Torre and Sara Bartfeld de Rietti, examines Argentina's National Biotechnology Programme (created in 1982 as an 'advisory, co-ordinating and financing unity' subsidiary to the National Department of Science and Technology), its structure, financing, vocational training, and international cooperation. 'Argentina has

a long tradition in biosciences (with three Nobel Prizes) as well as an important pharmaceutical and biochemical industry.'

1010   **La ciencia en la Argentina.** (Science in Argentina.)
José Babini.   Buenos Aires: Editorial Universitaria de Buenos Aires, 1963. 97p. (Biblioteca de América. Libros del Tiempo Nuevo, 10).
An abridged and updated edition of *La evolución del pensamiento científico en la Argentina* (Buenos Aires: La Fragua, 1954. 249p.). By a foremost writer on scientific affairs, this is a regrettably short and undocumented but valuable starting-point for the study of Argentine scientific advancement (including the principal scientific figures) from the colonial period: mathematics, medicine, physics and chemistry, earth sciences, biology, juridical science and the 'cultural' sciences (philosophy, history, sociology). It also considers the teaching of science and scientific institutions (universities, museums, observatories, the Consejo Nacional de Investigaciones Científicas y Técnicas [CONICET, founded 1958]). The author's wife, Rosa Diner de Babini, compiled a *Cronología científica argentina* (Buenos Aires: Ediciones Marymar, 1982), covering 1501-1960.

1011   **The incomplete transmission of a European image: physics at Greater Buenos Aires and Montreal, 1890-1920.**
Lewis Pyenson.   *Proceedings of the American Philosophical Society*, vol. 122, no. 2 (April 1978), p. 92-114.
In 1865 the University of Buenos Aires was expanded to establish a department of exact sciences, and in 1891 a new faculty of exact, physical and natural sciences was created there. An Academy of Sciences was founded at Córdoba in 1869, although the most important scientific work at Córdoba came from the Observatory (see *Benjamin Apthorp Gould and the founding of the Argentine national observatory*). The turning-point came in 1904, when 'vast resources were committed to bring physics to the National University of La Plata'; an institute of physics was formed, becoming a school in 1909 under the German Emil Hermann Bose, the 'pioneer of modern physics in Argentina'. Before 1914 some twenty German scholars formed the teaching staff (including that of the physics department) of the National Institute for Secondary School Teachers in Buenos Aires. Throughout the first half of the twentieth century Argentina 'remained a magnet for hundreds of German scientists', although the First World War created a vacuum that was not filled for several decades. See also item no. 1012.

1012   **Physics and politics in Latin America – a personal experience.**
L. M. Falicov.   *Science and Public Affairs: Bulletin of the Atomic Scientists*, vol. 26, no. 9 (Nov. 1970), p. 8-10, 41-5.
An undocumented introduction to the history of the physical sciences in Argentina together with observations based on the author's teaching experience in the country (he was the first Argentine to gain a doctorate in theoretical physics, 1958). As with the earlier development of the science (see item no. 1011), modern physics began in the 1930s with the arrival of German scientists. Before the 1950s 'the physical sciences were a branch of engineering, and very poorly developed at that'. An institute of physics was created in San Carlos de Bariloche in 1952 and schools of physics were established in the national universities. With the 1966 coup, all physicists emigrated *en masse*. 'Science in Argentina currently presents an overall picture of desolation . . .

291

Physics and chemistry at the University of Buenos Aires have returned to the level of the 1930s.'

1013  **The power of ideology: the quest for technological autonomy in Argentina and Brazil.**
Emmanuel Adler.   Berkeley, California; Los Angeles; London: University of California Press, 1987. 398p.

A comparison of the two countries' science and technology policies 1966-72, their venture into computers in the mid-1970s, and their 'quest for nuclear autonomy'. Chapter five provides a useful account of the role of the state in science-policy formation; the evolution of the Instituto Nacional de Tecnología Agropecuaria (1956), Instituto Nacional de Tecnología Industrial (1957) and Consejo Nacional de Investigaciones Científicas y Técnicas (1958); the 'means' of policy implementation (capital equipment, technical assistance, foreign patents, technology transfer, direct foreign investment); and the management of knowledge (training and research, information-retrieval systems). Despite developing a quite sophisticated electronics industry in the 1950s, Argentina, unlike Brazil, failed to diversify into computers. The opposite happened in the nuclear industry. The two countries were structurally similar but local institutional and ideological determining factors were different in each case.

1014  **Science and technology in Latin America.**
Edited by Christopher Roper, Jorge Silva.   London; New York: Longman / Latin American Newsletters, 1983. 363p. maps. (Longman Guide to World Science and Technology).

The chapter on Argentina, p. 1-22, consists of a short introductory essay followed by a directory of institutions (unfortunately without addresses), under these headings: national policies and financing; science and technology at government and academic level; industrial; agricultural and marine; medical; nuclear; aerospace; military; meteorology, environmental pollution and astrophysics; technical information services; international cooperation; societies and professional associations; national and provincial universities.

**From military rule to liberal democracy in Argentina.**
*See* item no. 597.

# Literature

## General

**1015 Alternate voices in the contemporary Latin American narrative.**
David William Foster. Columbia, Missouri: University of Missouri
Press, 1985. 163p. bibliog.

Focuses on works that are 'not predominantly available in English translation, by
choosing categories that do not evoke prevailing literary norms': Rodolfo Walsh's
*Operación masacre* (Buenos Aires: Jorge Alvarez, 1969), 'easily the most authentic
example of documentary narrative in Latin American fiction', recreating the killing of
a group of innocent citizens in La Plata in June 1956; the narrative technique of Eva
Perón's *La razón de mi vida* (Peuser, 1951; translated as *Evita by Evita: Eva Duarte
Perón tells her own story* [New York: Proteus Publishing, 1978]); the 'demythification
of Buenos Aires in the Argentine novel of the seventies' (Enrique Medina, Reina
Roffé, Héctor Lastra, Jorge Asís), a longer version of which appeared in *Chasqui*,
vol. 10, no. 1 (1980); and Marta Lynch's political novel *La penúltima versión de la
Colorada Villanueva* (Sudamericana, 1978).

**1016 Argentina.**
Pablo Medina. *Phaedrus: an International Annual of Children's
Literature*, vol. 10 (1984), p. 37-44. bibliog.

Argentina is an important producer of children's literature. This article discusses the
history of children's books and magazines (the longest-running is *Billiken*, founded
1919) and children's publishers; it also lists twenty representative modern works.
Federica Domínguez Colavita's 'The current state of children's literature in Argentina',
*Children's Literature*, vol. 7 (1978), p. 169-80, reviews writers, publishers, research on
children's literature and professional organizations. Graciela Rosa Gallelli, in
*Panorama de la literatura infantil-juvenil argentina* (Buenos Aires: Editorial Plus Ultra,
1985. 187p.), analyses 380 works for children published 1950-84.

1017  **Argentine letters and the *peronato*: an overview.**
Martin S. Stabb.  *Journal of Interamerican Studies and World Affairs*,
vol. 13, nos 3-4 (July-Oct. 1971), p. 434-55.

Perón meddled relatively little in literary activity until the late 1940s, after which 'the peronato began to take on an increasingly totalitarian shape'. Discusses the pro-Peronist journals *Argentina* and *Sexto Continente*, the seizure of *La Prensa*, the politically neutral *Contorno* group (see *Contorno: literary engagement in post-Peronist Argentina*), Ernesto Sábato and Ezequiel Martínez Estrada (both of whom had 'ambiguous views of Peronism'), and other prose writers of the period.

1018  **The Argentine novel in the nineteenth century.**
Myron I. Lichtblau.  New York: Hispanic Institute in the United States, 1959. 225p. bibliog.

A chronological review which covers José Mármol's *Amalia* (generally agreed to be the first Argentine novel); the historical novels of Vicente Fidel López; the development of the romantic novel (Miguel Cané, women novelists Juana Manuela Gorriti, Eduarda Mansilla de García and Rosa Guerra); the 1870s novelists Juan B. Alberdi, Eduardo L. Holmberg and Luis V. Varela; the realist novels of Lucio Vicente López and Paul Groussac; novels of immigration and the financial crisis of the 1890s; and naturalism (Eugenio Cambaceres, Juan Antonio Argerich). The bibliography includes a valuable chronological list of novels.

1019  *Contorno*: **literary engagement in post-Peronist Argentina.**
William H. Katra.  Cranbury, New Jersey: Fairleigh Dickinson University Press; London; Toronto: Associated University Presses, 1988. 170p. bibliog.

Although only ten issues of *Contorno* were published between 1953 and 1959 (a 'golden age of Argentine cultural activity'), this Marxist journal was one of the most important literary and sociopolitical journals of the century. It provided a platform for a number of *engagé* middle-class writers who are now leading figures: David Viñas, Tulio Halperín Donghi, Noé Jitrik, Adolfo Prieto and Juan José Sebreli. An extensive up-to-date bibliography of writers associated with the journal is included.

1020  **Currents in the contemporary Argentine novel: Arlt, Mallea, Sábato, and Cortázar.**
David William Foster.  Columbia, Missouri: University of Missouri Press, 1975. 155p. bibliog.

Analyses Roberto Arlt's *Los siete locos* (1929), Eduardo Mallea's *La bahía del silencio* (1940), Ernesto Sábato's *Sobre héroes y tumbas* (1961), and Julio Cortázar's *Rayuela* (1963). The final chapter contains brief comments on the works of Leopoldo Marechal, Antonio di Benedetto, Daniel Moyano, María Esther de Miguel, Pedro Orgambide and Manuel Puig.

1021 **Detective fiction from Latin America.**
Amelia S. Simpson. Teaneck, New Jersey: Fairleigh Dickinson
University Press; London; Toronto: Associated University Presses,
1990. 218p. bibliog.

The River Plate (chapter 1, p. 29-61) is the 'source of the first as well as the most' *literatura policial*; the other main producers are Brazil, Mexico and Cuba. The chapter describes the history of the genre and analyses five representative texts: the use of satire to comment on social and ethical issues (short stories by Eduardo Ladislao Holmberg, 'La bolsa de huesos', 1896, and Enrique Anderson Imbert's 'El General hace un lindo cadáver', 1956); unsolved crimes stressing 'real-world sociopolitical contexts over literary and philosophical considerations' (José Pablo Feinmann's *Ultimos días de la víctima* [Legasa, 1979] and Ricardo Piglia's short story 'La loca y el relato del crimen', 1975); and 'history as mystery' (Rodolfo Walsh's *Operación masacre*, 1975; see also *Alternate voices in the contemporary Latin American narrative*).

1022 **Historia de la literatura argentina: ensayo filosófico sobre la evolución de la cultura en el Plata.** (A history of Argentine literature: a philosophical essay on the evolution of culture in the River Plate.) Ricardo Rojas. Buenos Aires: Kraft, 1957. 4th ed. 9 vols.

A monumental history, first published in 1917, which attempts to show the cyclical development of a national cultural heritage. The volumes follow four themes: gaucho, colonial, 'proscribed' (mainly exile) and modern literature. Also valuable are Rafael Alberto Arrieta (ed.), *Historia de la literatura argentina* (Buenos Aires: Ediciones Peuser, 1958-60. 6 vols) and the *Historia de la literatura argentina* (Buenos Aires: Centro Editor de América Latina, 1980. 5 vols).

1023 **Jewish issues in Argentine literature: from Gerchunoff to Szichman.**
Naomi Lindstrom. Columbia, Missouri: University of Missouri
Press, 1989. 205p. bibliog.

Attempts to show the diversity of Jewish-Argentine literature with a historical overview and concentration on eight works published between 1910 and 1977: Alberto Gerchunoff, *Los gauchos judíos* (1919, 'rhapsodizing a Jewish new world' [see item no. 417]); César Tiempo, *Sabatión argentino* (1933, urban experience); Bernardo Verbitsky, *Es difícil empezar a vivir* (1941, social realism); David Viñas, *Dar la cara* (1962, middle-class Jewish life); José Rabinovich, *El violinista bajo el tejado* (1970, realist rhetorical poetry); José Isaacson, *Cuaderno Spinoza* (1977, poetry); Marcos Ricardo Barnatán, *El laberinto de Sión* (1970, borrowing from the Kaballah); and Mario Szichman, *Los judíos del mar dulce* (1971, Jewish-Argentine history). The 'postface' surveys Jewish-Argentine writing during the military dictatorship, 1976-83.

1024 **Knives and angels: women writers in Latin America.**
Edited by Susan Bassnett. London: Atlantic Highlands, New Jersey:
Zed Books, 1990. 202p.

Contains four studies of Argentine women writers: John King, 'Victoria Ocampo (1890-1979): precursor', p. 9-25; Susan Bassnett, 'Speaking with many voices: the poems of Alejandra Pizarnik', p. 36-51; Catherine Boyle, 'Griselda Gambaro and the female dramatist: the audacious trespasser', p. 145-57; and Nissa Torrents, 'One woman's cinema: interview with María Luisa Bemberg', p. 171-5.

1025 **The last happy men: the generation of 1922, fiction, and the Argentine reality.**
Christopher Towne Leland. Syracuse, New York: Syracuse University Press, 1986. 198p. bibliog.

A survey of a particular literary era, the 1920s, which produced two antagonistic literary movements: the Boedo Group (called after the Buenos Aires quarter of the same name), 'the champion of social change, the working class, and art at the service of the coming revolution'; and Florida (named after the 'street of elegance and taste'), the 'aesthetic vanguard, dedicated to art and its redefinition'. The representative authors of these movements (Eduardo González Lanuza, Eduardo Mallea, Enrique González Tuñón, Elías Castelnuovo, Alvaro Yunque and Leónidas Barletta) are discussed, along with three key works of the period: Roberto Mariani's *Cuentos de la oficina* (1926), Roberto Arlt's *El juguete rabioso* (1925) and Ricardo Güiraldes's *Don Segundo Sombra* (1926). There is a postscript on the 1930s, which marked the end of the 'age of the last men to be happy in quite the same way in this century'.

1026 **Latin American women writers: yesterday and today.**
Edited by Yvette E. Miller, Charles M. Tatum. Pittsburgh, Pennsylvania: Latin American Literary Review, 1977. 199p.

The volume contains two substantial chapters on Argentine writers: Esther A. Azzario, 'María Angélica Bosco and Beatriz Guido: an approach to two Argentinian novelists between 1960 and 1970', p. 59-67, which discusses four of Bosco's novels dealing with upper-middle-class women, and three of Guido's which deal with the effects of the political climate upon the family; and Corina S. Mathieu, 'Argentine women in the novels of Silvina Bullrich', p. 68-74, which analyses Bullrich's projection of the 'warmth and sensitivity of the feminine soul' in *Tres novelas* (1966), *Mañana digo basta* (1968), *Entre mis veinte y treinta años* (1970) and *Mal don* (1973). Bullrich and Marta Lynch are treated in Ana Kaminsky, 'The real circle of iron: mothers and children, children and mothers, in four Argentine novels', *Latin American Literary Review*, vol. 4, no. 9 (fall-winter 1976), p. 77-87. See also H. Ernest Lewald, 'Aspects of the modern Argentine woman: the fiction of S. Bullrich and M. Lynch', *Chasqui*, vol. 5, no. 3 (1976), p. 19-26.

1027 **Literary expressionism in Argentina: the presentation of incoherence.**
Naomi Lindstrom. Tempe, Arizona: Arizona State University, Center for Latin American Studies, 1977. 89p.

A study of four writers of the period 1915-40 whom the author considers 'expressionists' even though the movement as such never existed in Argentina: Roberto Arlt, Armando Discépolo, Jorge Luis Borges and Macedonio Fernández.

1028 **The portrayal of immigration in nineteenth century Argentine fiction (1845-1902).**
Evelyn Fishburn. Berlin: Colloquium Verlag, 1981. 259p. bibliog. (Bibliotheca Ibero-Americana. Band 29).

A close analysis of both major and minor novels: the pre-immigration novel (1845-80), and the anti-immigrant (1880-90) and pro-immigrant (1890-1902) novels of the immigration period. The first group is represented by Domingo F. Sarmiento's *Facundo* (1845, see item no. 278) and Juan B. Alberdi's *Peregrinación de luz del día* (1871); the second by Antonio Argerich's *Inocentes o culpables* (1884), Eugenio

Cambaceres's *En la sangre* (1887), and Julián Martel's *La bolsa* (1891); the third by Adolfo Saldías's *Bianchetto* (1896), Francisco Grandmontaigne's *Teodoro Foronda* (1896) and Francisco Sicardi's *Libro extraño* (1894). The appendix summarizes immigration history. See also Gladys S. Onega, *La inmigración en la literatura argentina, 1880-1910* (Buenos Aires: Editorial Galerna, 1969. 220p.).

1029 **Social realism in the Argentine narrative.**
David William Foster. Chapel Hill, North Carolina: University of North Carolina Department of Romance Languages, 1986. 159p. (North Carolina Studies in the Romance Languages and Literatures, 227).

A study of a rather neglected literary period, 1930-50, and a group of novelists inspired 'by the Russian revolution, Soviet communism, international Marxism, and the need to respond critically . . . to the various mechanisms of repression and the frustration of personal and collective aspirations during the period'. One chapter is devoted to Raúl Scalabrini Ortiz's influential *El hombre que está solo y espera* (q.v.). Other writers treated are Bernardo Kordon, Leónidas Barletta, Luis María Albamonte, José Rabinovich, Bernardo Verbitsky, Max Dickmann, Carlos Ruiz Daudet, Elías Castelnuovo, Alvaro Yunque, Alfredo Varela, Josefina Marpon and Juan Goyanarte.

1030 *Sur*: **a study of the Argentine literary journal and its role in the development of a culture, 1931-1970.**
John King. Cambridge, England: Cambridge University Press, 1986. 232p. bibliog. (Cambridge Iberian and Latin American Studies).

*Sur* is acknowledged to be Latin America's most important literary review. Founded in 1931 by Victoria Ocampo, it is an 'elegant fusion of fiction, poetry, philosophy, plastic arts, history and social commentary'. The author places the journal 'within the very specific development of Argentine letters' and the wider context of 'developments within Argentine and world history to which the magazine was forced to respond' (the internal conflicts within *Sur*'s brand of liberalism in reaction to fascism, communism, the Second World War and Peronism). Borges, the journal's greatest Argentine contributor, is treated in some detail.

1031 **Women's voices from Latin America: interviews with six contemporary authors.**
Evelyn Picon Garfield. Detroit, Michigan: Wayne State University Press, 1985. 188p. bibliog.

Interviews which serve as an introduction to the 'lives, careers, and creative expressions of six accomplished writers', including Griselda Gambaro (p. 53-71), whose plays present mankind 'in its more grotesque dimensions': 'impotence, passivity, and suffering' mark her characters; Elvira Orphée (p. 97-113): 'the majority of Orphée's creatures are orphans, social outcasts, and humiliated victims suffering from some kind of acute deficiency'; Marta Traba (p. 115-40), who is concerned with human rights and life in the city ghetto; and Luisa Valenzuela (p. 141-65), known for her 'focussing on eroticism and death'.

# Biography and criticism of major writers

## Roberto Arlt (1900-42)

1032 **The prose works of Roberto Arlt: a thematic approach.**
Jack M. Flint. Durham, England: University of Durham, 1985. 93p.
bibliog. (Durham Modern Languages Series, HM4).
Explores the themes of alienation, anguish, self-abasement, sexuality and politics in
Arlt's works. His *Los siete locos* (1929, its sequel is *Los lanzallamas*, 1931) was
translated by Naomi Lindstrom as *The seven madmen* (Boston, Massachusetts:
Godine, 1984); it is the story of a group of madmen who plot to destroy Buenos Aires.

## Adolfo Bioy Casares (1914- )

1033 **Adolfo Bioy Casares: satire & self-portrait.**
Alfred J. MacAdam. In: *Modern Latin American narratives: the
dreams of reason.* Edited by Alfred J. MacAdam. Chicago,
Illinois: University of Chicago Press, 1977, p. 29-36. bibliog.
A study of two of Bioy's novels. *La invención de Morel* (1940) is a first-person
narrative in which a man fleeing from political persecution seeks refuge on an island
supposed to be the epicentre of a fatal disease; its inhabitants are images reflected by
cameras operated by the tides; translated by Ruth L. C. Simms in *The invention of
Morel, and other stories* (Austin, Texas: University of Texas Press, 1961). *Plan de
evasión* (1945) takes the form of letters written from a penal colony; translated by
Suzanne Jill Levine, *A plan for escape* (New York: Dutton, 1975).

1034 **The novels and short stories of Adolfo Bioy Casares.**
David P. Gallagher. *Bulletin of Hispanic Studies*, vol. 52, no. 3 (July
1975), p. 247-66.
Analyses the 'comic masterpieces' *Plan de evasión* and *La invención de Morel* ('the
island is, I think, as important for Bioy as the labyrinth is for Borges'), *El sueño de los
héroes* (1954, translated by Diana Thorold as *The dream of the hero* [London: Quartet,
1987]) and *Diario de la guerra del cerdo* (1969, *Diary of the war of the pig*, translated
by Gregory Woodruff and Donald A. Yates [New York: McGraw-Hill, 1972]). A
fourth work, *Dormir al sol*, has been translated by Suzanne Jill Levine: *Asleep in the
sun* (New York: Persea Books, 1978). Bioy also wrote a number of books in
collaboration with Jorge Luis Borges, notably *Seis problemas para Don Isidro Parodi*
(1942, *Six problems for Don Isidro Parodi*, translated by Norman Thomas di Giovanni
[New York: Dutton; London: Allen Lane, 1981]).

# Jorge Luis Borges (1899-1986)

**1035  Borges and his fiction: a guide to his mind and art.**
Gene H. Bell-Villada.   Chapel Hill, North Carolina: University of
North Carolina Press, 1981. 292p. bibliog.
An assessment of Borges's fiction in a historical literary context, paying special
attention to three works: *Ficciones* (1944 and 1956, *Fictions*, translated by Anthony
Kerrigan, Alastair Reid and others [New York: Grove Press; London: Weidenfeld &
Nicolson, 1962]); *El hacedor* (1960, *Dreamtigers*, translated by Mildred Boyer, Harold
Morland [Austin: University of Texas Press, 1964]); and *The Aleph and other stories,
1933-1969*, edited and translated by Norman Thomas di Giovanni (New York: Dutton,
1970).

**1036  In memory of Borges.**
Edited by Norman Thomas di Giovanni.   London: Constable, 1988.
128p.
The texts of the first five Jorge Luis Borges lectures sponsored by the Anglo-Argentine
Society of London: a personal memoir by the editor and lifelong translator and friend
of Borges; Borges largely answering questions from his audience; Graham Greene on
meeting Borges; H. S. Ferns on Anglo-Argentine relations; Alicia Jurado on R. B.
Cunninghame Graham; and Mario Vargas Llosa on Borges's fiction.

**1037  Jorge Luis Borges.**
Edited and with an introduction by Harold Bloom.   New York; New
Haven, Connecticut; Philadelphia: Chelsea House Publishers, 1986.
256p. bibliog. (Modern Critical Views).
A 'representative selection of the best criticism so far devoted to the writings of the
Argentine master': the editor's introduction and fifteen essays printed in chronological
order of publication, including Jaime Alazraki, James E. Irby, Emir Rodríguez-
Monegal and John Sturrock.

**1038  Jorge Luis Borges.**
D. P. Gallagher.   In: *Modern Latin American literature*.   Edited by
D. P. Gallagher.   London; Oxford; New York: Oxford University
Press, 1973, p. 74-121.
A masterly short assessment of the themes and devices in Borges's fiction, with
particular emphasis on the 1942 short story 'La muerte y la brújula' ('Death and the
compass') from *Ficciones*.

**1039  Jorge Luis Borges: a literary biography.**
Emir Rodríguez Monegal.   New York: E. P. Dutton, 1978. 502p.
bibliog.
An affectionate and revealing biography and criticism of the works by a friend of
Borges. The biography is organized around an analysis of the texts; both stop in the
1960s, when Borges was 'discovered', and are treated in psychoanalytical terms.

1040   **The mythmaker: a study of motif and symbol in the short stories of Jorge Luis Borges.**
Carter Wheelock.   Austin, Texas; London: University of Texas Press, 1969. 190p. bibliog.
Explores the literary origins of the use of symbolism in Borges's stories, including *El Aleph*, *Ficciones*, *El hacedor*, *Historia de la eternidad* (1936), *Inquisiciones* (1925) and *Otras inquisiciones* (1952).

1041   **Paper tigers: the ideal fictions of Jorge Luis Borges.**
John Sturrock.   Oxford: Clarendon Press, 1977. 227p. bibliog.
Paper tigers are figments of the imagination which recur in Borges's writings as 'symbols of the achievements and frustrations of working only with words'. This is an analytical study of his short stories, especially of the earlier, 'more intricate ones', *Ficciones* and *El Aleph*. The other key Borgesian works are: *El libro de arena* (1975, *The book of sand*, translated by Norman Thomas di Giovanni [New York: Dutton, 1977]); *El informe de Brodie* (1970, *Doctor Brodie's report*, translated by di Giovanni [New York: Dutton: 1972]); *Labyrinths: selected stories and other writings*, edited by Donald A. Yates and James E. Irby (New York: New Directions, 1964); and *Selected poems, 1923-1967*, edited and translated by di Giovanni (New York: Delacorte, 1972).

# Julio Cortázar (1914-84)

1042   **The final island: the fiction of Julio Cortázar.**
Edited by Jaime Alazraki, Ivar Ivask.   Norman, Oklahoma: University of Oklahoma Press, 1978. 199p. bibliog.
Contains a chronology of Cortázar's career, a short story ('Second time around') and two lectures on modern literature by Cortázar himself, and critical essays on his short stories and novels by the editor and eleven other contributors.

1043   **Julio Cortázar.**
Evelyn Picon Garfield.   New York: Frederick Ungar, 1975. 164p. bibliog. (Modern Literature Monographs).
A chronology, an extended interview, and two main chapters which analyse the writer's novels and short stories: *Bestiario* (1951), *Final del juego* (1956) and *Las armas secretas* (1959), all three translated by Paul Blackburn as *The end of the game, and other stories* (New York: Random House, 1963); *Historia de cronopios y famas* (1962, *Cronopios and famas*, translated Paul Blackburn [New York: Pantheon Books, 1969]); *Todos los fuegos el fuego* (1966, *All fires the fire, and other stories*, translated by Suzanne Jill Levine [New York: Pantheon, 1973]); *Los premios* (1960, *The winners*, translated by Elaine Kerrigan [New York: Pantheon, 1965]); *Rayuela* (1963, *Hopscotch*, translated by Gregory Rabassa [New York: Pantheon, 1966]); *62: modelo para armar* (1968, *62, a model kit*, translated by Gregory Rabassa [New York: Pantheon, 1972]); *Libro de Manuel* (1973, *A manual for Manuel*, translated by Gregory Rabassa [New York: Pantheon, 1978]); and the two biographical collages: *La vuelta al día en ochenta mundos* (1967, *Around the day in eighty worlds*, translated by

Thomas Christensen [San Francisco: North Point Press, 1986]); and *Ultimo round* (1969, not yet translated).

1044 **The novels of Julio Cortázar.**
Steven Boldy. Cambridge, England: Cambridge University Press, 1980. 220p. bibliog. (Cambridge Iberian and Latin American Studies).
A study of the four major novels: *Los premios* (a metaphysical and existential story of sinister happenings and a mutiny on board an ocean liner); *Rayuela* (Cortázar's best-known work, the story of a bohemian intellectual in Paris and Buenos Aires, peopled by 'monsters, doubles, and dualism', which may be read normally or following a random order); *62: modelo para armar*, and the politically committed *Libro de Manuel*. Cortázar's most recent works are: *Un tal Lucas* (1979, *A certain Lucas*, translated by Gregory Rabassa [New York: Knopf, 1984]); *Octaedro* and *Alguien anda por ahí* (1974 and 1978, *A change of light and other stories*, translated by Gregory Rabassa [New York: Knopf, 1980]); *Queremos tanto a Glenda* (1981, *We love Glenda so much and other tales*, translated by Rabassa [New York: Knopf, 1983]).

# Esteban Echeverría (1805-51)

1045 **Esteban Echeverría.**
Edgar C. Knowlton. Bryn Mawr, Pennsylvania: Dorrance, 1986. 125p.
Biographical details of this romantic poet and utopian socialist are followed by an examination of the narrative poems (*Los consuelos*, 1834, and *Rimas*, 1837, which includes the famous *La cautiva*, 'The captive woman'), *El dogma socialista* (1846), his posthumous allegorical novel of the Rosas régime, *El matadero* (1871, *The slaughter house*, translated by Angel Flores [New York: Las Américas, 1959]), and miscellaneous prose.

# Macedonio Fernández (1874-1952)

1046 **Macedonio Fernández.**
Naomi Lindstrom. Lincoln, Nebraska: Society of Spanish and Spanish-American Studies, 1981. 138p. bibliog.
Fernández was a radical innovator, yet he was not interested in seeing his own works into print and twelve of his eighteen books were not published until after his death. Large portions of his *oeuvre* 'consist partly or wholly of statements on metaphysics, esthetics and social theory'. This is a study of his place in the literary vanguard of the 1920s and a close textual analysis of passages from his writings. He is still largely unknown outside Argentina perhaps because 'he was too much ahead of his time'.

1047 **Macedonio Fernández and the Spanish American new novel.**
Jo Anne Engelbert. New York: New York University Press, 1978.
216p. bibliog. (A Center for Inter-American Relations Book).
This is essentially a study of his posthumous novel, *Museo de la novela de la eterna*
(1967). The author has edited *Macedonio: selected writings in translation* (Fort Worth,
Texas: Latitudes Press, 1984. 124p.), reviewing which the *Handbook of Latin
American Studies* (q.v.) describes Fernández as 'a pre-Dadaist whose metaphysical
games with space, time, narrative form and language inspired Borges, Cortázar and
other "River Plate" writers'.

## Manuel Gálvez (1882-1962)

1048 **Manuel Gálvez.**
Myron I. Lichtblau. New York: Twayne, 1972. 152p. bibliog.
(Twayne's World Author Series. TWAS 203).
A biographical and critical study of 'one of the most important figures of the modern
Argentine novel because of his realistic portrayal of the social fabric of Argentine life'.
It focuses on the major works: *Nacha Regules* (1919, translated by Leo Ongley [New
York: Dutton, 1922], the story of a prostitute) and *Miércoles santo* (1930, *Holy
Wednesday*, translated by Warre B. Wells [New York: Appleton; London: John Lane,
1934]). See also Jefferson Rea Spell, 'City life in the Argentine as seen by Manuel
Gálvez', in his *Contemporary Spanish-American fiction* (Chapel Hill, North Carolina:
University of North Carolina Press, 1944, p. 15-63).

## Ricardo Güiraldes (1886-1927)

1049 **Ricardo Güiraldes and *Don Segundo Sombra*: life and works.**
Giovanni Previtali, foreword by Adelina del Carril de Güiraldes,
preface by Jorge Luis Borges. New York: Hispanic Institute in the
United States, 1963. 225p. bibliog.
A comprehensive study of Güiraldes's life and of his classic novel *Don Segundo
Sombra* (1926, *Don Segundo Sombra: shadows on the pampas*, translated by Harriet de
Onís [New York: Farrar & Rinehart, 1935, later editions]), the story of a boy
befriended by an old gaucho.

1050 **The Spanish American regional novel: modernity and autochthony.**
Carlos J. Alonso. Cambridge, England: Cambridge University Press,
1990. 212p. bibliog. (Cambridge Studies in Latin American and
Iberian Literature).
A study of three Spanish-American *novelas de la tierra*. Chapter three, p. 79-108,
examines *Don Segundo Sombra* and in particular the novel's treatment of 'knowledge,
property and writing' and 'the metaphor of "taking stock" that rules the novel'. Nature
'serves as a backdrop against which to highlight the transcendental quality of human
work'.

# José Hernández (1834-86)

1051 **Personal destiny and national destiny in Martín Fierro.**
Alfredo A. Roggiano. *Latin American Literary Review*, no. 5 (1974),
p. 37-49.
*Martín Fierro* is the quintessential gaucho epic, the greatest Spanish-American poem of
the nineteenth century. The first part (the 'Ida' ['going-out']), published in 1872, tells
of a *payador* (gaucho minstrel) conscripted to fight the pampa Indians, who deserts,
finds his home in ruins, becomes an outlaw and joins the Indians. In the second part,
*La vuelta de Martín Fierro* ('The return'), published in 1879, Martín Fierro escapes
from Indian captivity and is reunited with his sons. The classic translation (there have
been several others) is by Walter Owen: *The gaucho, Martín Fierro* (London:
Shakespeare Head Press; New York: Farrar & Rinehart, 1936. 326p.). There is
surprisingly little on Hernández in English; see the brief 'Poem of the pampas', by
Evelio A. Echevarría, *Américas*, vol. 29, vol. 4 (April 1977), p. 2-5.

# Leopoldo Lugones (1874-1938)

1052 **The dissonant legacy of modernismo: Lugones, Herrera y Reissig, and
the voices of modern Spanish American poetry.**
Gwen Kirkpatrick. Berkeley, California; Los Angeles; London:
University of California Press, 1989. 294p. bibliog. (Latin American
Literature and Culture).
A study of two Modernist poets, Lugones and the Uruguayan Julio Herrera y Reissig,
but emphasizing the former. Chapters 3-5 assess Lugones's early writings, French-
influenced attempts to 'incorporate art, politics, and personal justification within one
pattern', especially the 'subversion, irony and parody' of *Los crepúsculos del jardín*
(1905), and *Lunario sentimental* (1909). A final chapter traces the legacy of Modernism
in three contemporary poets, including Alfonsina Storni. There is no English
translation of his work.

1053 **Leopoldo Lugones.**
John Eugene Englekirk. In: *Edgar Allan Poe in Hispanic Literature*.
Edited by John Eugene Englekirk. New York: Instituto de las
Españas en los Estados Unidos, 1934, p. 278-304.
Examines the influence of Poe – themes of mystery and horror – in Lugones's writings:
*Las montañas de oro* (1897), *Los crepúsculos del jardín* (1905), *Lunario sentimental*
(1909), *El libro fiel* (1912), *Cuentos fatales* (1924) and *Las fuerzas extrañas* (1906).

1054 **Leopoldo Lugones: the short stories.**
Joan E. Ciruti. *Inter-American Review of Bibliography*, vol. 25
(1975), p. 134-49.
Lugones is not fully appreciated for the more than 100 short stories which he wrote
throughout his life. In fact, he is one of the originators of the *cuento fantástico*, a genre
which has flourished in Argentina. This article analyses his major collections of short

stories: *Las fuerzas extrañas* (1906), *Cuentos* (1916), *Cuentos fatales* (1924) and *Filosofícula* (1924). The first collection is preoccupied with 'the occult, the inexplicable, the powers beyond man's control or comprehension', and includes five science-fiction stories.

# Eduardo Mallea (1903-82)

1055 **Eduardo Mallea.**
H. Ernest Lewald. Boston, Massachusetts: Twayne, 1977. 118p. bibliog. (Twayne's World Authors Series. TWAS 433).
Mallea was a prolific writer of novels, short stories and essays, who first attracted attention with his *Cuentos para una inglesa desesperada* ('Stories for a desperate Englishwoman', 1926). He was editor of the Literary Supplement of *La Nación* and a member of the *Sur*-Florida group. His works reflect a search for the authentic Argentina (see item no. 530), and his characters are 'cerebral, hermetic, and anguished, they yearn to transcend their sterile condition in order to communicate and commune'.

1056 **The writings of Eduardo Mallea.**
John H. R. Polt. Berkeley, California: University of California Press, 1959. 132p. bibliog. (University of California Publications in Philology, 54).
Six chapters examine Mallea's search for the 'visible' and 'invisible' Argentina, his treatment of characters (especially the role of the individual), structure and literary style. Much of his work is set in his native Bahía Blanca. English translations are: *La bahía del silencio* (1940, *The bay of silence*, translated by Stuart Edgar Grummon, [New York: Knopf, 1944]); and *Fiesta en noviembre* (1938), *Todo verdor perecerá* (1941) and *Chaves* (1953), translated by Harriet de Onís (et al.) as *All green shall perish and other novellas and stories* (New York: Knopf, 1966), with separate editions published by Calder & Boyars, London, 1967, 1969 and 1970.

# José Mármol (1817-71)

1057 **The poetry of José Mármol.**
Stuart Cuthbertson. *University of Colorado Studies. Series A: General studies*, vol. 35 (1935), p. 79-276.
This Romantic poet is best known for his great novel *Amalia* (first complete edition 1855, *Amalia: a romance of the Argentine*, translated by Mary J. Serrano [New York: Dutton, 1919]), written while in exile in Montevideo during the Rosas dictatorship; it is the tragic love story of a couple in hiding from Rosas. Cuthbertson here studies the versification of Mármol's *Cantos del peregrino* (1846), which tells of a sea-voyage round the coasts of South America, and *Armonías* (1851-44), combining romantic lyrical verse with political invective against Rosas. He was influenced by Spanish poets but is 'far more cosmopolitan' than is generally thought.

# Ezequiel Martínez Estrada (1895-1964)

1058 **A call to authenticity: the essays of Ezequiel Martínez Estrada.**
James Maharg. University, Mississippi: Romance Monographs,
1977. 203p. bibliog. (Romance Monographs, 26).
Martínez Estrada is best remembered and read (but little outside his own country) as
an essayist. He published twenty-eight essays at regular intervals from 1933 until his
death in self-imposed exile in Cuba, apart from some 350 contributions to journals,
more than 300 of which can accurately be described as short essays. Three are studied
in detail: *Radiografía de la pampa* (1933, see *X-ray of the pampa*), *La cabeza de Goliat:
microscopía de Buenos Aires* (1940, 'on the abominations of Buenos Aires', the 'head
of Goliath'; see *La ciudad indiana: Buenos Aires desde 1600 hasta mediados del siglo
XVIII*), and the 'historico-sociological' *Sarmiento* (1946).

1059 **Prophet in the wilderness: the works of Ezequiel Martínez Estrada.**
Peter G. Earle. Austin, Texas: University of Texas Press, 1971.
254p. bibliog. (Texas Pan American Series).
An examination of his major pampean/urban essays and short stories: *Radiografía de la
pampa* (1933), *Muerte y transfiguración de Martín Fierro* (1948), and *La cabeza de
Goliat* (1940); the historical *Sarmiento* (1946); and the poetry. His *Sábado de gloria*
(1956) and *Cuatro novelas* (1968) have been translated by Leland H. Chambers as
*Holy Saturday and other stories* (Pittsburgh, Pennsylvania: Latin American Literary
Review Press, 1988).

# Manuel Mújica Láinez (1910-84)

1060 **The persistence of human passions: Manuel Mújica Láinez's satirical
neo-modernism.**
George O. Schanzer. London: Tamesis Books, 1986. 153p. bibliog.
(Colección Támesis. Serie A: Monografías, 119).
Mújica Láinez has written more than fifty works, twenty of them novels or collections
of short stories. This is primarily a study of his fiction, with a sideways look at his
essays, biography and poetry: his popular 'saga of Buenos Aires' published between
1949 and 1957 (*Aquí vivieron, Misteriosa Buenos Aires, Los ídolos, La casa, Los
viajeros, Invitados en El Paraíso*); his 'universalist' phase, including *Bomarzo* (1962:
*Bomarzo, a novel*, translated by Gregory Rabassa [New York: Simon & Schuster,
1969]), made into an opera 1967, set in sixteenth-century Italy; *El unicornio* (1965, *The
wandering unicorn*, translated by Mary Fitton [Toronto: Lester & Orpen Dennys,
1982]), based on a French folk legend; and later works.

# Silvina Ocampo (1903- )

1061 **The mad double in the stories of Silvina Ocampo.**
Patricia N. Klingenberg. *Latin American Literary Review*, vol. 16,
no. 32 (July-Dec. 1988), p. 29-40. bibliog.
Silvina Ocampo is a novelist, poet and painter, the sister of Victoria Ocampo and the
wife of Adolfo Bioy Casares. Four collections of stories (*Autobiografía de Irene* (1948),
*La furia* (1959), *Las invitadas* (1961) and *Los días de la noche* (1970)) have been
translated by Daniel Balderston as *Leopoldina's dream* (Toronto: Penguin Books,
1988).

# Victoria Ocampo (1890-1979)

1062 **Victoria Ocampo: against the wind and the tide.**
Doris Meyer, with a selection of essays by Victoria Ocampo,
translated by Doris Meyer. New York: George Braziller, 1979. 314p.
bibliog.
Victoria Ocampo, the eldest of six daughters of an aristocratic family, is 'the most
famous woman of letters in twentieth-century Latin American literature', the author of
more than ten volumes of essays and a dozen shorter works, founder and director of
the literary review *Sur* (see *Sur: a study of the Argentine literary journal and its role in
the development of a culture, 1931-1970*), and the friend of famous writers and
musicians the world over. She was also a feminist and scandalizer of society, hence the
subtitle. None of her works has so far been translated into English. She also wrote a
biography of the Indian poet Tagore (1961); a study of their two meetings and long
correspondence is *In your blossoming flower-garden: Rabindranath Tagore and Victoria
Ocampo*, by Ketaki Kushari Dyson (New Delhi: Sahitya Akademi, 1988. 477p.). See
also her autobiographical *Testimonios* (Buenos Aires: Sur, 10 series, 1935-77).

# Alejandra Pizarnik (1936-72)

1063 **Alejandra Pizarnik: a profile.**
Edited, with an introduction, by Frank Graziano. Durango,
Colorado: Logbridge-Rhodes, 1987. 143p. bibliog.
Pizarnik was a poet and painter who committed suicide at the age of thirty-six. Her
very short surrealist poems, sometimes consisting of only two or three lines, are
preoccupied with the themes of death and absence. This is a compilation of her poetry,
prose and journals, together with some of her photographs and drawings. See also
Thorpe Running, 'The poetry of Alejandra Pizarnik', *Chasqui*, vol. 14, nos 2-3 (Feb.-
May 1985), p. 45-55; and *Knives and angels: women writers in Latin America* (see item
no. 1024).

# Manuel Puig (1934- )

**1064  The necessary dream: a study of the novels of Manuel Puig.**
Pamela Bacarisse.  Cardiff: University of Wales Press, 1988. 285p.
bibliog.

Intended for students and teachers of literature, this is a detailed critique of Puig's
seven novels 'with recourse to fields such as psychology, feminism, Argentine politics,
myth, camp literature and pop culture'. His novels are filled with references to popular
culture, especially Hollywood films: *La traición de Rita Hayworth* (1968, *Betrayed by
Rita Hayworth*, translated by Suzanne Jill Levine [New York: Dutton, 1971], the pitiful
story of a provincial homosexual); *Boquitas pintadas* (1969, *Heartbreak tango: a serial*,
translated by Levine [New York: Dutton, 1973], three young girls and a woman in love
with a condemned man; the title is taken from a Gardel tango song); *The Buenos Aires
affair* (1973, *The Buenos Aires affair: a detective novel*, translated by Levine [New
York: Dutton, 1976], the psychological drama of a frustrated and unfulfilled couple);
*El beso de la mujer araña* (1976, *The kiss of the spider woman*, translated by Thomas
Colchie [New York: Knopf, 1979], the dialogue between two prisoners, a homosexual
and a political activist; made into a successful film); *Pubis angelical* (1979, *Pubis
angelical*, translated by Elena Brunet [New York: Random House, 1986], the reminiscences of a political refugee in a Mexico City hospital); *Maldición eterna a quien lea
estas páginas* (1980, *Eternal curse on the reader of these pages*, written in English [New
York: Random House, 1982]); and *Sangre de amor correspondido* (1984, *Blood of
requited love*, translated Jan L. Grayson [New York: Vintage Books, 1984], a story of
sexual politics in Brazil, where Puig now lives).

**1065  Suspended fictions: reading novels by Manuel Puig.**
Lucille Kerr.  Urbana, Illinois: University of Illinois Press, 1987.
266p.

A close reading of *La traición de Rita Hayworth*, *Boquitas pintadas*, *The Buenos Aires
affair* and *El beso de la mujer araña*. Also useful is Norman Lavers, *Pop culture into
art: the novels of Manuel Puig* (Columbia, Missouri: University of Missouri Press,
1988. 70p.), confined to *Traición*, *Beso* and *Maldición*. Two recent translated works
are: *Misterio del ramo de rosas* (1988, *Mystery of the rose bouquet*, translated by Allan
Baker [London: Faber & Faber, 1988]) and *Bajo un manto de estrellas* (1982, *Under a
mantle of stars: a play in two acts*, translated by Ronald Christ [New York: Lumen
Books, 1985]).

# Ernesto Sábato (1911- )

**1066  Ernesto Sábato.**
Harley D. Oberhelman.  New York: Twayne, 1970. 165p. bibliog.
(Twayne's World Authors Series. TWAS 123).

A biography and critical study of Sábato's ten volumes of essays and his two great
psychological novels: *El túnel* (1948, *The outsider*, translated by Harriet de Onís [New
York: Knopf, 1950] also translated as *The tunnel* by Margaret Sayers Peden [New
York: Random House, 1988], the growing madness of an artist who has murdered his

mistress), and *Sobre héroes y tumbas* (1961, *On heroes and tombs*, translated by Helen R. Lane [Boston, Massachusetts: Godine, 1981], a woman kills her criminal-lunatic father, symbol of the degenerate Argentine aristocracy).

# Alfonsina Storni (1892-1938)

1067 **Alfonsina Storni.**
Sonia Jones. Boston, Massachusetts: Twayne, 1979. 149p. bibliog. (Twayne's World Authors Series. TWAS 519).
An excellent study of the poetry, prose and plays. Storni was born in Switzerland but moved to Argentina with her family when a young girl; she became a teacher, published her first poems in 1911 and was the first woman to join the 'Nosotros' literary circle in 1916. She drowned herself when ill with cancer. An anthology, with a short biographical and critical assessment, is *Alfonsina Storni, Argentina's feminist poet: the poetry in Spanish with English translations*, edited by Florence Williams Talamantes (Los Cerillos, New Mexico: San Marcos Press, 1975. 67p.); two other collections of selected poems have been published by Amana Books (Brattleboro, Utah, 1986), edited by Dorothy Scott Loos, and White Pine Press (Franconia, New York, 1987), edited by Marion Freeman.

1068 **Alfonsina Storni: from poetess to poet.**
Rachel Phillips. London: Tamesis Books, 1975. 131p. bibliog.
A feminist reading of Storni's poetry and theatrical works. 'Her work falls obviously into a tripartite division: first the poems from 1916 to 1925, not without their own inner development, but overweighted with subjective lyricism, and with banalities of love and unsatisfactory experiences. Then the plays, more sophisticated and varied; lastly the two volumes of 1934 and 1938 [in which] she declares herself free of literary and personal conventions.'

# Luisa Valenzuela (1938- )

1069 **Luisa Valenzuela: from *Hay que sonreír* to *Cambio de armas*.**
Sharon Magnarelli. *World Literature Today*, vol. 58, no. 1 (winter 1984), p. 9-13.
Valenzuela's novels centre on 'three intricately related preoccupations: language, women, and politics. Her work is clearly an attempt to free language and women from the shackles of society'. Two differing works are examined: *Hay que sonreír* (1966, with *Los heréticos* (1967) translated by Hortense Carpentier and Jorge Castillo as *Clara: thirteen short stories and a novel* [New York; London: Harcourt Brace Jovanovich, 1976], in which a provincial girl becomes a prostitute in Buenos Aires); and *Cambio de armas* (1982, *Other weapons*, translated by Deborah Bonner [Hanover, New Hampshire: Ediciones del Norte, 1985], a political love story involving an ambassador). See also the special issue of *Review of Contemporary Fiction* devoted to Valenzuela (vol. 6, no. 3 [fall 1986]). Her other works in English translation are: *Aquí pasan cosas raras* (1983, *Strange things happen here: twenty-six short stories and a*

*novel*, translated by Helen Lane [New York: Harcourt Brace Jovanovich, 1979]); *Cola de lagartija* (1983, The lizard's tale, translated by Gregory Rabassa, [New York: Farrar, Straus, Giroux, 1983]); and an anthology, *Open door* (Berkeley, California: North Point Press, 1988).

# Anthologies

1070  **Argentine anthology.**
Compiled by María Susana Weissmann de Ferdkin, in collaboration with Elizabeth Dall, Rosa Clarke de Armando, Charles W. Yates.
London: Oxford University Press, 1948. 91p.
In three sections: nine 'folklore-legends-fables' by six writers including Joaquín V. González, Carlos O. Bunge and Juan B. Ambrosetti; 'Scenes and portraits', eight rural vignettes by Ricardo Rojas, R. B. Cunninghame Graham ('La pampa' from his collection *Rodeo*), Domingo F. Sarmiento and others; and fifteen miscellaneous 'Essays and sketches' by Nicolás Avellaneda, Bartolomé Mitre, W. H. Hudson, Miguel Cané (from his autobiography *Juvenilia*), Ricardo Güiraldes (from *Don Segundo Sombra*), Eduardo Wilde and others. The introduction and preface are in Spanish.

1071  **Argentine anthology of modern verse.**
Edited and with a preface by Patricio Gannon    Buenos Aires:
Francisco A. Columbo, 1942. 73p.
Fifteen poets writing after 1900 are represented chronologically by one or two poems each: Leopoldo Lugones ('Sonnet', 'The withered rose'), Enrique Larreta, Baldomero Fernández Moreno, Enrique Banchs, Rafael Alberto Arrieta, Pedro Miguel Obligado, Alfonsina Storni ('Epitaph for my tomb'), Conrado Nalé Roxlo, Ricardo E. Molinari, José Pedroni, Francisco Luis Bernárdez, Leopoldo Marechal ('Madrigal in silva'), Eduardo González Lanuza, Jorge Luis Borges ('General Quiroga drives in coach to death', 'A patio'), and Roberto Ledesma. A parallel text is provided.

1072  **Celeste goes dancing, and other stories: an Argentine collection.**
Edited by Norman Thomas di Giovanni, translated by Norman
Thomas di Giovanni and Susan Ashe.    London: Constable, 1989.
184p.
A wide variety of short narratives, many translated here for the first time, by fourteen contemporary writers: Silvina Ocampo, Adolfo Bioy Casares, Isidoro Blaisten, Fernando Sánchez-Sorondo, Estela dos Santos (the title story), Alberto Vanasco, Marcos Aguinis, Eduardo Gudiño-Kieffer, Lilian Heer, Fernando Sorrentino, Angel Bonomini, Jorge Asís, Abelardo Castillo and Santiago Sylvester.

1073  **Contemporary Argentine poetry: an anthology.**
Compiled and translated by William Shand.    Buenos Aires:
Fundación Argentina para la Poesía, 1969. 275p.
An 'objective' selection of 107 poets from 'the last forty years of Argentine poetry with the central aim of presenting the live poets'. Each poet is accorded between one and six poems; those best represented include Jorge Luis Borges, Ricardo E. Molinari,

**Literature.** Biography and criticism of major writers

Leopoldo Marechal, Enrique Molina, Silvina Ocampo, Alejandra Pizarnik and María Elena Walsh.

1074   **The Faber book of contemporary Latin American short stories.**
Edited by Nick Caistor.   London; Boston, Massachusetts: Faber & Faber, 1989. 188p.

Includes three Argentine writers: Isidoro Blaisten, 'Uncle Fernando', translated by Cynthia Ventura, first published in the *Journal of Literary Translation* (see the 'Argentine feature section' in vol. 18 [spring 1987] of this journal, edited by Norman Thomas di Giovanni); Daniel Moyano, exiled in Spain since 1976, 'Aunt Lila', translated by the editor, first published in *Index on Censorship*; and Luisa Valenzuela, 'Up among the eagles', translated by Margaret Sayers Peden, from *Open door* (Berkeley, California: North Point Press, 1988).

1075   **Landscapes of a new land: fiction by Latin American women.**
Edited by Marjorie Agosín.   Buffalo, New York: White Pine Press, 1989. 194p.

The anthology contains twenty-two stories, four by Argentine writers: Alicia Steimberg, 'Cecilia's last will and testament', translated by Christopher Towne Leland; Luisa Valenzuela, 'The snow white guard', translated by Sharon Magnarelli; Silvina Ocampo, 'The servant's slaves' translated by Susan Bassnett; and Elvira Orphée, 'The beguiling ladies', also translated by Leland.

1076   **Latin American revolutionary poetry: a bilingual anthology.**
Edited and with an introduction by Robert Márquez.   New York; London: Monthly Review Press, 1974. 505p.

Presents poetry 'written in the context of the broad struggle for national liberation and the achievement of sovereign independence': three poems by Enrique Molina, four by Juan Gelman (who founded the radical literary journal and publishing house El Pan Duro in 1954) and a long surrealist narrative poem by Víctor García Robles ('Sepa lo que pasa a lágrima viva y con malas palabras').

1077   **Lives on the line: the testimony of contemporary Latin American authors.**
Edited and with an introduction by Doris Meyer.   Berkeley, California; Los Angeles; London: University of California Press, 1988. 314p. bibliog.

Four extracts by Argentine writers, together with brief biographical essays, are included: Jorge Luis Borges, 'Maturity', translated by Norman Thomas di Giovanni, from *The Aleph and other stories*; Victoria Ocampo, 'Woman's past and present', translated by Doris Meyer, from *Testimonios*, 7th series, 1962-67 (Editorial Sur, 1967); Julio Cortázar, 'Letter to Roberto Fernández Retamar', translated by Jo Anne Engelbert, from *Casa de las Américas* (Havana), no. 45 (1967); and Luisa Valenzuela, 'A legacy of poets and cannibals: literature revives in Argentina', translated by Lori M. Carlson, previously unpublished.

1078    **The modernist trend in Spanish-American poetry: a collection of**
        **representative poems of the Modernist movement and the reaction.**
        Translated into English verse with a commentary by G. Dundas
        Craig.    Berkeley, California: University of California Press, 1934.
        347p. bibliog.

Contains poems by Leopoldo Lugones ('El solterón', 'A los ganados y las mieses',
'Desdén', 'Lied de la boca florida'), Alfonsina Storni ('Carta lírica a otra mujer') and
Jorge Luis Borges ('Calle desconocida', 'La guitarra').

1079    **Other fires: short fiction by Latin American women.**
        Edited by Alberto Manguel.    London: Picador, 1986. 217p.

Includes seven Argentine poems, all translated by the editor, with brief biographies of
the authors: Marta Lynch ('Latin lover'), Alejandra Pizarnik ('The bloody countess'),
Angélica Gorodischer ('Man's dwelling place'), Vlady Kociancich ('Knight, death and
the devil'), Silvina Ocampo ('Two reports'), Lilianer Heker ('The stolen party') and
Beatriz Guido ('The usurper').

1080    **The Penguin book of Latin American verse.**
        Edited by E. Caracciolo-Trejo.    Harmondsworth, England: Penguin
        Books, 1971. 425p.

The section on Argentina, p. 3-46, contains the original text, with plain prose
translations, of poems by Esteban Echeverría (from *La cautiva*), José Hernández
(from *Martín Fierro*), Leopoldo Lugones, Baldomero Fernández Moreno, Enrique
Banchs, Oliverio Girondo, Ezequiel Martínez Estrada, Ricardo E. Molinari, Jorge
Luis Borges, Enrique Molina, Edgar Bayley, Alberto Girri and Raúl Gustavo Aguirre.

1081    **Tales from the Argentine.**
        Edited, with a foreword by Waldo Frank, translated from the Spanish
        by Anita Brenner.    New York: Farrar & Rinehart, 1930. 268p.

A selection of material which is 'both typical and good writing': Roberto J. Payró,
'Laucha's marriage' and 'The devil in Pago Chico' (from *Pago chico*, 1908); Leopoldo
Lugones, 'Death of a gaucho' (from *La guerra gaucha*, 1905); Lucio V. López,
'Holiday in Buenos Aires' (from *La gran aldea*, 1884), Domingo F. Sarmiento, 'The
private life of Facundo' (see item no. 278); Ricardo Güiraldes, 'Rosaura' (from
*Rosaura*, 1922); and Horacio Quiroga, 'The return of Anaconda' (from *Los
desterrados*, 1926; Quiroga was born in Uruguay but 'is the leading literary master of
the aboriginal forest of North Argentina').

1082    **The web: stories by Argentine women.**
        Edited and translated by H. Ernest Lewald.    Washington, DC: Three
        Continents Press, 1983. 170p.

A compilation of one or two poems by each of the following: Luisa Mercedes
Levinson, Silvina Ocampo, Silvina Bullrich, María Angélica Bosco, Syria Polletti,
Beatriz Guido, Marta Lynch, Amalia Jamilis, Eugenia Calny, Luisa Valenzuela,
Cecilia Absatz and Reina Roffé.

# The Arts

## General

1083　**La cultura en Buenos Aires hasta 1810.** (Culture in Buenos Aires to 1810.)
José Luis Trenti Rocamora.　Buenos Aires: Universidad de Buenos Aires, Departamento de Acción Social Universitaria, 1948. 156p. bibliog. (Serie Divulgación de Nuestra Historia. Cuaderno, no. 2).

A comprehensive summary of culture and the arts during the colonial period: education, literature, journalism, printing and publishing, architecture, painting, sculpture, silverwork, engraving, theatre, music and medicine. Twenty-nine plates are included.

1084　**Cultural policy in Argentina.**
Edwin R. Harvey.　Paris: Unesco, 1979. 92p. (Studies and Documents on Cultural Policies).

An uncritical survey in a series intended 'to show how cultural policies are planned and implemented'. Nine chapters describe the administrative structure of state cultural bodies; culture's federal or regional nature; international cultural cooperation; cultural legislation; finance for the arts; protection of the country's cultural heritage; assistance for creative activities and the social and legal status of artists, writers and composers; cultural institutions and media (theatre, music, publishing, libraries), and the mass media.

1085 **El Di Tella y el desarrollo cultural argentino en la década del sesenta.**
(The Di Tella Institute and Argentine cultural development in the
1960s.)
John King. Buenos Aires: Ediciones de Arte Gaglianone, 1985.
309p. bibliog. (Colección Ensayo).

The Instituto Torcuato di Tella, founded in 1958, is one of the foremost centres of social and economic research in Latin America. The institute became an important cultural centre when a Centro de Artes Visuales was created around the art collection of the founder of the SIAM Di Tella enterprise (see item no. 806). A Centro de Experimentación Audiovisual (theatre) and a Centro Latinoamericano de Estudios Musicales soon followed. One of the most significant cultural experiments of the 1960s ended with the economic collapse of SIAM Di Tella and the menacing cultural climate under Onganía. For a summary in English see the same author's 'El Di Tella and Argentine cultural development in the 1960s', *Bulletin of Latin American Research*, vol. 1, no. 1 (Oct. 1981), p. 105-12.

1086 **Historia social y cultural del Río de la Plata, 1536-1810.** (A social and
cultural history of the River Plate, 1536-1810.)
Guillermo Fúrlong Cárdiff. Buenos Aires: Tipográfica Editora
Argentina, 1969. 3 vols. maps. bibliog.

A virtual encyclopaedia, with hundreds of illustrations, of the cultural and social history of Argentina, Bolivia, Paraguay and Uruguay. Volume one (754p.) deals with the fine and manual arts, volume two (505p.) with the pure, applied, natural and moral sciences, volume three (575p.) with social and cultural history. There is unfortunately no index.

1087 **The National Arts Fund of Argentina.**
Roberto Etchepareborda. *Cultures* (Paris), vol. 7, no. 3 (1980),
p. 31-48. bibliog.

The National Arts Fund was founded in 1958 with the aim of 'advancing credit and complementary economic support for cultural activities'. The article describes the Fund's structure, financing methods, activities and achievements. Between 1959 and 1973 it published fifty numbers of a *Bibliografía argentina de artes y letras*, a bold experiment in quasi-national bibliography which recorded 23,000 publications published in Argentina and abroad.

1088 **The redemocratization of Argentine culture, 1983 and beyond: an
international research symposium at Arizona State University,
February 16-17, 1987.**
Edited by David William Foster. Tempe, Arizona: Arizona State
University Press, Center for Latin American Studies, 1989. 67p.

An editorial and five essays on the 'impact of repression on literature and on the intellectual scene and the literary response to it' during and after the last military administration, by Marcos Aguinis (novelist and director of Argentina's National Programme of Cultural Democratization), Javier Torre (director of the important Centro Cultural General San Martín, Buenos Aires), Andrés Avellaneda (a summary of *Censura, autoritarismo y cultura: Argentina 1960-1983* [q.v.]), Beatriz Sarlo (professor of literature at the University of Buenos Aires), and Emil Volek (professor of Spanish, Arizona State University).

# Visual arts

1089 **Argentina.**
Manuel Mújica Láinez. Washington, DC: Pan American Union, 1961. 74p. bibliog. (Art in Latin America Today).
A useful introduction (p. 1-16), with fifty-four rather unclear illustrations, to the history of Argentine painting and sculpture, emphasizing the twentieth century. A virtual catalogue of modern painters is Aldo Pellegrini, *Panorama de la pintura argentina contemporánea* (Buenos Aires: Paidós, 1967. 214p. 64 plates). More comprehensive, especially for the colonial and nineteenth-century periods, is Romualdo Brughetti, *Historia del arte en la Argentina* (Mexico City: Editorial Pormaca, 1965. 223p. 48 plates).

1090 **Art in Argentina.**
Jorge Glusberg. Milan, Italy: Giancarlo Politi Editore, 1986. 142p.
The most up-to-date history of modern art since 1970, with 121 black-and-white photographs. The first chapter (p. 7-25) is a history of painting from 1700. Other chapters deal with pop and systems art; the CAYC (Centre of Art and Communication) Group, founded 1971, a 'concrete expression of the theory of Systems Art'; other experimental artists; the post-figurative movement; and New Image painting.

1091 **Arte argentino hoy: una selección de 48 artistas.** (Art in Argentina today: 48 selected artists.)
Rafael Squirru. Buenos Aires: Ediciones de Arte Gaglianone, 1983. 201p. (Colección Unión Carbide).
A gallery of painters (in the main) representing a variety of styles. Each artist receives four pages containing a critical biographical essay, a list of major exhibitions and prizes, and a large colour reproduction. A similar celebration of fifty painters and eleven sculptors is an exhibition catalogue, *Arte argentino contemporáneo* (Madrid: Museo Español de Arte Contemporáneo, 1976), introduced by Rafael Squirru and Jorge Romero Brest.

1092 **El arte de los argentinos.** (Art of the Argentines.)
José León Pagano. Buenos Aires: The author, 1937-40. 3 vols.
A classic history of painting, sculpture and engraving from earliest times. Volume three considers the artisitic production of the interior provinces. A one-volume synthesis is *Historia del arte argentino: desde los aborígenes hasta el momento actual* (Buenos Aires: Editorial L'Amateur, 1944. 507p.). An unillustrated revision by the author's son in encyclopaedic form was issued as *El arte de los argentinos* (Buenos Aires: Editorial y Librería Goncourt, 1981. 231p.).

1093   **Artesanías argentinas tradicionales / Traditional Argentine crafts.**
Perla Bardin.   Buenos Aires: Achala Ediciones, 1981. 107p. map.
A basic bilingual descriptive text by an Argentine potter is illustrated by forty-five
photographs, two-thirds of them in colour, showing the following crafts: silverware,
weaving, basketry, religious imagery, musical instruments, pottery, leather, wood and
masks.

1094   **Buenos Aires y sus esculturas.** (Buenos Aires and its sculptures.)
Photographs by Eduardo Frías and Jorge Salatino, text by Eduardo
Baliari, José Barcia (et al.).   Buenos Aires: Manrique Zago, 1981.
2nd ed. 214p.
A beautifully produced folio volume illustrating public sculpture in the city of Buenos
Aires: over 130 works by ninety-six sculptors extolling important figures from the fields
of science, education, art, literature, politics and diplomacy. An English translation of
the text is included on pages 189-212.

1095   **A century and a half of painting in Argentina.**
Alberto Prando.   *Texas Quarterly*, vol. 3, no. 1 (spring 1960),
p. 74-88.
In the nineteenth century 'we find only solitary artists, whose greatest charm lies in the
primitive flavor of their works': Emeric Essex Vidal (an English artist – 'our first
painters were foreigners', see item no. 126), Carlos Enrique Pellegrini (watercolourist
and portrait painter), Fernando García del Molino (portraits), Carlos Morel ('the first
Argentine who fully deserves the title of painter', pampa customs and gauchos),
Prilidiano Pueyrredón ('the next native-born Argentine prominent in the history of
Argentine art', landscapes and portraits), Cándido López (oils of the 'colorful epic of
the Paraguayan War') and other more recent painters.

1096   **Contemporary art in Latin America.**
Gilbert Chase.   New York: Free Press; London: Collier-Macmillan,
1970. 292p. bibliog.
A general survey of contemporary plastic arts and architecture in Latin America.
Argentine painting is reviewed on pages 127-69: cubist, figurative, abstract,
neofigurative, geometrical, optical and pop. 'Argentina owes its priority and prestige in
the modern art movement of Latin America largely to the pioneer work of Emilio
Pettoruti in painting and Pablo Curatella Manes in sculpture.' The brief section on
Argentine architecture, p. 257-60, considers Amancio Williams and the Teatro San
Martín (built 1961).

1097   **40 dibujantes argentinos.** (Argentine drawing: 40 artists.)
Buenos Aires: Ediciones Actualidad en el Arte, 1987. 343p.
Six prominent critics provide the one-page critical biographies (mentioning exhibitions
and prizes) of forty contemporary exponents of the art of drawing, illustrated with
black-and-white reproductions.

1098 **40 escultores argentinos.** (Forty Argentine sculptors.)
Buenos Aires: Ediciones Actualidad en el Arte, 1988. 333p.

Identical in format to the previous item: eight critics have written the critical introductions (parallel Spanish/English text) to the black-and-white illustrations of contemporary sculptors. See also the series *Escultores argentinos del siglo XX* (Buenos Aires: Centro Editor de América Latina, 1982- ), each volume of which discusses the work of a number of sculptors.

1099 **Diccionario de artistas plásticos en la Argentina.** (A dictionary of plastic arts in Argentina.)
Vicente Gesualdo, Aldo Biglione, Rodolfo Santos.    Buenos Aires: Editorial Inca, 1988. 2 vols.

Contains biographical and critical information on 5,000 Argentine artists and foreign artists working in the country, from earliest times to the present day. It covers painting, sculpture, drawing, engraving, book illustration, cartooning, pottery, silverwork and architecture, and includes 111 colour and 20 black-and-white illustrations. Also valuable is Adrián Merlino's *Diccionario de artistas plásticos de la Argentina, siglos XVIII-XIX-XX* (Buenos Aires: Imprenta de Jorge J. Batmalle, 1954. 433p.), which emphasizes contemporary artists.

1100 **Enciclopedia del arte en América.** (Encyclopaedia of art in Latin America.)
Vicente Gesualdo.    Buenos Aires: Editorial Bibliográfica Argentina (OMEBA), 1969. 5 vols.

Volumes 1-2 are introductions to the history of art. 'Argentina' (vol. 1, p. 1-92), describes pre-Columbian art, architecture, painting, sculpture and silverwork. Volumes 3-5, Biographies, contain many entries on Argentine artists.

1101 **Global new waves in 80s [sic]: Argentina.**
Guillermo González Riuz.    *Graphic Design* (Tokyo), no. 17 (March 1980), p. 38-58.

A milestone in Argentine graphic art was the formation in 1948 of a group known as Arte Concreto Invención. This article (bilingual English-Japanese text) considers twelve individual graphic artists and partnerships from the present generation. It is generously illustrated with photographs of posters, labels and packaging, book and magazine designs, symbols and logotypes.

1102 **Grafik-Design in Argentinien – Graphic design in Argentina – Graphic-design en Argentine.**
Marcelo Varela, Laura Lazzaretti.    *Novum Gebrauchsgraphik*, no. 58 (Feb. 1987), p. 4-11.

Graphic design was given a boost by the formation in the late 1970s of a group of young trained artists, the Asociación de Diseñadores Gráficos de Buenos Aires. This article shows selected graphic designs from a collection of the group's work, entitled *ADG2*, published in 1985: posters, brochures, pictograms, symbols, lettering, book covers, packaging and signage systems. The text is in English, German and French.

1103   **Iconografía de Buenos Aires: la ciudad de Garay hasta 1852.** (Images
       of Buenos Aires, 1628-1852.)
       Bonifacio del Carril, Aníbal G. Aguirre Saravia.   Buenos Aires:
       Municipalidad de la Ciudad de Buenos Aires, 1982. 256p. bibliog.

A well-indexed catalogue of 324 general or partial views in paintings and drawings of
the city founded by Juan de Garay: buildings, churches, houses, streets, squares, and a
few human characters. A fully researched but unillustrated chronological history of
some eighty painters active in Buenos Aires, 1810 to the present, is Carlos Antonio
Arcán González, *La pintura en Buenos Aires* (Municipalidad de la Ciudad de Buenos
Aires, 1981. 243p.).

1104   **Imágenes del Río de la Plata: crónica de la fotografía rioplatense, 1840-
       1940.** (Images of the River Plate: a chronicle of River Plate
       photography, 1840-1940.)
       Amado Bécquer Casaballe, Miguel Angel Cuarterolo.   Buenos
       Aires: Editorial del Fotógrafo, 1983. 95p. bibliog.

An excellent collection of historic photographs beginning with the United States
pioneer Charles de Forest Fredricks who worked in Argentina in the 1850s; they depict
the Paraguayan War and the Conquest of the Desert, and scientific and press
photography. The informative text also describes the evolution of photography in
Argentina. For the work of ten contemporary photographers see *Fotógrafos argentinos
del siglo XX* (Buenos Aires: Centro Editor de América Latina, 1982. 256p.).

1105   **Man of La Boca.**
       Osiris Chiérico.   *Américas*, vol. 30, no. 5 (May 1978), p. 30-4.

Benito Quinquela Martín was one of the leading artists of the 1910s and 1920s. His
early life was hard but he later won the patronage of President Marcelo T. de Alvear.
He is famous for his paintings of the dockyards of the La Boca district of Buenos Aires
where he lived; there is a museum to him there. He also decorated buildings, buses
and the underground railway with murals. Five of his works are reproduced.

1106   **80 años de pintura argentina: del pre-impresionismo a la novísima
       figuración.** (Eighty years of painting in Argentina: from pre-
       Impressionism to the new wave.)
       Córdova Iturburu.   Buenos Aires: Ediciones Librería La Ciudad,
       1978. 243p. bibliog.

A catalogue of artists, with their dates, who are representative of fourteen artistic
periods and movements, arranged chronologically. There are forty-six colour and
eighty-two black-and-white illustrations.

1107   **Patriotism and popular culture in the Falkland/Malvinas conflict: the
       view from Buenos Aires.**
       J. Laurence Day.   *Studies in Latin American Popular Culture*, vol. 3
       (1984), p. 152-61.

Describes the often humorous 'pop art and mass media messages' that were directed at
the general Argentine public during the Falklands War: popular art, posters, magazine
covers and flyers. Great Britain (especially Prime Minister Margaret Thatcher) and

United States Secretary of State Alexander Haig were the targets of most of the caricatures in posters, cartoons and on magazine covers. German, Irish and American communities in Buenos Aires supported the Argentine cause and also produced patriotic popular art.

1108 **Platería sudamericana.** (South American silverwork.)
Alfredo Taullard. Buenos Aires: Peuser, 1941. 285p. bibliog.

Chapters 6-8 (p. 49-84) refer to the River Plate, with particular emphasis on *mate*-drinking gourds and spoons, and gaucho silverware. Chapter nine describes silver mines in northern Chile and Argentina (La Rioja). Many of the 387 illustrations are of River Plate (especially Argentine) silverwork. Another beautifully illustrated work, with an English text, is Adolfo Luis Ribera, Héctor H. Schenone, *Platería sudamericana de los siglos XVII-XX* (Munich, Germany: Hirmer Verlag, 1981. 454p.).

1109 **Political graffiti and wall painting in Greater Buenos Aires: an alternative communication system.**
Lyman G. Chaffee. *Studies in Latin American Popular Culture*, vol. 8 (1989), p. 37-60.

In Buenos Aires 'one quickly becomes sensitized to the ubiquitousness of political street propaganda in its various manifestations – graffiti, wall painting, posters, murals, banners, stickers, and street demonstrations'. The article describes the sectarian origins of graffiti and wall painting (mainly the Radical and Peronist parties, competing for space), the main themes since 1983 (elections, the referendum on the Beagle Channel dispute, the Austral Plan, the divorce issue, Peronist in-fighting, student politics), and the main areas where they are found. Twelve examples are illustrated. On poster art, see the same author's 'Poster art and political propaganda in Argentina', in vol. 5 (1986), p. 78-89 of the same journal.

1110 **Tejidos y ponchos indígenas de Sudamérica.** (Indigenous textiles and ponchos from South America.)
Alfredo Taullard. Buenos Aires: Editorial Guillermo Kraft, 1949. 174p. map. bibliog.

Five of the nine chapters (p. 95-128) and many of the 280 photographs refer to the weaving of ponchos, *chiripás* (gaucho leggings) and textiles in northern Argentina (Catamarca, Santiago del Estero, Tucumán, Córdoba, La Rioja, Jujuy, Salta and the Calchaquí Valley.). There are many text illustrations of looms, motifs and weaving techniques. Contains a good glossary and a chapter on wool dyes.

# Architecture

**1111  Amancio Williams.**
Edited by Jorge Silvetti.  New York: Rizzoli International
Publications for Harvard University, Graduate School of Design,
1987. 63p. bibliog.
Amancio Williams was born in Buenos Aires in 1913 and has always lived and worked
in his native city. He is an influential exponent of the Modern Movement and his most
famous work is a bridge-like house built for his father Alberto (a musician who
founded the Buenos Aires Conservatorio de Música) in Mar del Plata. This is an
exhibition catalogue of both his built work and (mainly) his 'projects', many of them
unrealized.

**1112  Argentina: monumentos históricos y arqueológicos.** (Historic and
archaeological monuments of Argentina.)
Mario J. Buschiazzo.  Mexico City: Instituto Panamericano de
Geografía e Historia, Comisión de Historia, 1959. 174p. bibliog.
(Monumentos Históricos y Arqueológicos, 11).
A history and catalogue chiefly of historic monuments (churches, monasteries, town
halls, *estancias*), with chapters on their restoration and legislation. See also Carlos
Vigil, *Los monumentos y lugares históricos de la Argentina* (Buenos Aires: Editorial
Atlántida, 1948. 460p.), organized by province.

**1113  Arquitectos argentinos durante la dominación hispánica.** (Argentine
architects during the Spanish colonial period.)
Guillermo Fúrlong Cárdiff.  Buenos Aires: Editorial Huarpes, 1946.
427p. bibliog. (Cultura Colonial Argentina, 4).
A chronological, well-documented history (1536-1810), with many photographs,
drawings, plans and cross-sections, especially valuable for its discussion of Jesuit
architecture in Misiones province. Over 1,190 architects and buildings are listed in the
index.

**1114  Arquitectos de Buenos Aires.** (Architects of Buenos Aires.)
Sixteen works presented by Jorge Glusberg.  Buenos Aires: Espacio
Editora, 1979. 141p. (Colección del Centro de Documentación de
Arte y Arquitectura para América Latina).
Based on exhibitions in Antwerp and Paris of the works of sixteen architects completed
or projected during the 1970s, illustrated with photographs and drawings: a hospital,
school, embassy, auditorium, a number of apartment blocks, and commercial, sports
and television centres.

1115  **Arquitectura argentina contemporánea: panorama de la arquitectura argentina, 1950-63.** (A panorama of contemporary Argentine architecture, 1950-63.)
Francisco Bullrich.  Buenos Aires: Ediciones Nueva Visión, 1963.
163p. (Colección Arquitectura Contemporánea).

The author, a noted architect, surveys modern architecture and its antecedents since 1910. Argentine architecture is well represented in its 300 illustrations, and in the same author's *Arquitectura latinoamericana, 1930-1970* (Buenos Aires: Sudamericana, 1969. 222p.) and *New directions in Latin American architecture* (London: Studio Vista, 1969. 128p.): see p. 30-4 and thirty photographs on Argentine architecture at the back of the last book).

1116  **Arquitectura en la Argentina.** (Architecture in Argentina.)
Edited by María Angélica Correa.  Buenos Aires: Editorial Universitaria de Buenos Aires, 1982. 10 vols.

Ten slim books on Argentina's architecture through the ages, by region, written by experts and reasonably well illustrated.

1117  **La arquitectura en la Argentina, 1930-1970.** (Architecture in Argentina, 1930-1970.)
Federico F. Ortiz, Ramón Gutiérrez.  Buenos Aires: Hogar y Arquitectura, [197-?] 70p.

A chronological description of Argentine, mostly Buenos Airean, architecture – town and country houses, apartments, public buildings and offices – with 196 photographs and plans. Useful for the preceding period is Mario J. Buschiazzo, *La arquitectura en la República Argentina, 1810-1930* (Buenos Aires: Filmediciones Valero, 1976. 82p. colour slides).

1118  **La arquitectura tradicional de Buenos Aires, 1536-1870.**
(The traditional architecture of Buenos Aires, 1536-1870.)
Vicente Nadal Mora.  Buenos Aires: Editorial Nadal Mora, 1977.
3rd ed. 278p. bibliog.

An affectionate re-creation of the fast-disappearing colonial architecture of Buenos Aires ('a city which does not care about its past') through 158 of the author's own drawings of façades, doors, ironwork (gates, balconies and window grilles), ceramic tiles and well-heads. There is an index by architectural feature and by address of the buildings illustrated.

1119  **Art nouveau in Buenos Aires.**
Hernández Rosselot.  *Connoisseur*, vol. 189, no. 759 (May 1975), p. 54-61.

Argentina's most important art-nouveau architect was Julián García Núñez, a disciple of Antonio Gaudí of Barcelona. Art-nouveau ironwork was mostly produced by foreign craftsmen. Unfortunately, most of the art-nouveau houses have been or are in the process of being demolished. The article reviews the history of the movement in Buenos Aires and illustrates it with six surviving examples.

1120  **La casa porteña.** (The Buenos Aires house.)
Blas Matamoro.  Buenos Aires: Centro Editor de América Latina,
1971. 114p. (Vida y Milagros de Nuestro Pueblo. La Historia
Popular, 63).
A brief introduction to the changing styles of town-house architecture in Buenos Aires,
1850-1930, illustrated with twenty-four plates and five floor-plans.

1121  **The changing face of Latin American architecture: conversations with
ten leading architects.**
Damián Bayón, Paolo Gasparini, translated by Galen D. Greaser.
Chichester, England; New York; Brisbane, Australia; Toronto:
J. Wiley, 1979. 254p.
Includes an interview with the Italian-born Argentine architect Clorindo Testa, whose
most famous works are the Civic Centre and Ministry buildings in Santa Rosa (capital
of La Pampa province, 1955), the Bank of London and South America (in partnership,
1960-66), the National Library (also in partnership, still unfinished) and a number of
regional hospitals. For more detail, see Jorge Glusberg, *Clorindo Testa, pintor y
arquitecto* (Buenos Aires: Ediciones Summa, 1983. 103p.).

1122  **El Congreso de la Nación Argentina / The Argentine National
Congress.**
Edited by Manrique Zago.  Buenos Aires: Manrique Zago
Ediciones, 1985. 215p. bibliog.
A photographic celebration of the architecture and internal decoration of the National
Congress building, begun in 1898 and inaugurated in 1906. The work of the Congress
and its various technical departments is also described. A parallel Spanish/English text
is provided.

1123  **Eduardo Catalano: buildings and projects.**
Camillo Gubitosi, Alberto Izzo.  Rome: Officina Edizioni, 1978.
166p. bibliog.
Catalano was born in Buenos Aires and educated in the United States, and was
professor of architecture at the Massachusetts Institute of Technology 1956-77. His
works show a 'sense of order, clarity, simplicity in construction, and a passion for
geometry', using long spans and cantilevers. His two major Argentine creations were
the City Auditorium and United States Embassy in Buenos Aires; since then, he has
designed public buildings in the United States. This is chiefly (p. 33-159) an illustrated
catalogue of his works. There is a parallel Italian/English text.

1124  **Estancia houses: Argentinian revivals of about 1900.**
Francisco Bullrich.  *Architectural Review*, vol. 131, no. 780
(Feb. 1962), p. 121-6.
Nineteenth-century *estancia* houses followed the Spanish tradition modified in an
Argentine way. After 1870, more elaborate two-storey houses began to be built. The
*estancia* house reached its heyday in the 1920s, uniting traditional styles with mediaeval
Gothic, pure English, Scottish baronial and French château influences. A well-
illustrated guide to fifty representative *estancia* houses is *Nuestras estancias/Argentine*

321

*ranches: cincuenta estancias representativas de la República Argentina* (Buenos Aires:
Casa Pardo, 1968. 258p.).

1125 **International handbook of contemporary developments in architecture.**
Edited by Warren Sanderson. Westport, Connecticut; London:
Greenwood Press, 1981. 623p. bibliog.

The chapter on Argentina, by Elizabeth D. Harris, p. 99-109, is an excellent summary
of developments since 1900. Modern architecture began with Le Corbusier's visit to
Argentina in 1929 and 'remained in [his] shadow through the 1940s', reflected in the
work of Amancio Williams and the so-called Austral Group. In the 1950s, three
tendencies emerged: Formalism, Brutalism and a return to natural materials. In the
1960s, concrete and an interplay between architecture and sculpture predominated.
The essay is confined largely to Buenos Aires architecture but briefly mentions the
work of Miguel Angel Roca (see *Miguel Angel Roca*) in Argentina's second-largest
city, Córdoba; it also discusses the work of Clorindo Testa.

1126 **Latin American architecture since 1945.**
Henry-Russell Hitchcock. New York: Museum of Modern Art,
distributed by Simon & Schuster, 1955. 203p.

The works of six Argentine architects are illustrated, including the only construction by
Le Corbusier in the Americas, a house in La Plata. 'In Argentina there has been little
development beyond what has been called the "false dawn" of modern architecture
there some ten years ago . . . Business buildings and apartment houses in considerable
quantity maintain at their best the median level of Latin American work in these
fields.' Curiously, some of the best Argentine work was done in Uruguay, notably by
Spanish-born Antonio Bonet in the holiday resort of Punta Ballena.

1127 **Miguel Angel Roca.**
Jorge Glusberg, Oriol Bohigas. London: Academy Editions, 1981.
160p. bibliog.

Miguel Angel is an architect, painter, writer and university professor. His designs and
buildings, many of them executed in Córdoba, are 'paradigms of a Post-Modern
poetics': residential blocks, community centres, low-rise housing developments, office
blocks, shopping arcades, banks, churches, hospitals, university blocks and public
parks. A parallel English/Spanish text is accompanied by many illustrations (twenty-
four in colour).

1128 **1930-1950: arquitectura moderna en Buenos Aires.** (Modern
architecture in Buenos Aires, 1930-1950.)
Sandro Borghini, Hugo Salama, Justo Solsona. Buenos Aires:
Universidad de Buenos Aires, Facultad de Arquitectura y Urbanismo,
1987. 124p.

A teaching text illustrating eighteen works (mainly apartment blocks) by thirteen
Rationalist architects in Buenos Aires, consisting chiefly of drawings of façades and
floor-plans by Faculty architectural students, with a technical commentary, biographies
of the architects and five appendices.

1129  **La ornamentación en la arquitectura de Buenos Aires, 1800-1900.**
(Decoration in the architecture of Buenos Aires, 1800-1900.)
José Xavier Martini, José María Peña.  Buenos Aires: Universidad
de Buenos Aires, Facultad de Arquitectura y Urbanismo, Instituto de
Arte Americano e Investigaciones Estéticas, 1966-67. 2 vols.
The text (p. 7-64) is followed by sixty-four black-and-white plates, many of them full-
page. The two sections cover: styles in chronological order (colonial, post-colonial,
neoclassical, neo-Gothic, Italianate, 'academic', utilitarian and nouveau) and materials
(ceramic, mortar, iron and other metals, stone, marble, slate, wood and glass).

# Cartoons and comic strips

1130  **From Mafalda to Los Supermachos: Latin American graphic humor as
popular culture.**
David William Foster.  Boulder, Colorado; London: Lynne Rienner,
1989. 119p.
A collection of illustrated essays which have appeared elsewhere in slightly different
form. Four Argentine examples are discussed. Uruguayan-born Hermenegildo Sábat is
best known as the principal editorial cartoonist for the Buenos Aires daily *Clarín* and
for his popular collection of fifty cartoons accompanied by Gardel tango lyrics, *Al
troesma con cariño* (Buenos Aires: Siglo Veintiuno, 1971); his political cartoons 1971-
75 were collected in *Seré breve* (Editorial La Garza, 1975). Roberto Fontanarrosa
draws one-frame or one-strip cartoons, and has created two characters, *Boogie, el
aceitoso* (Ediciones de la Flor, 1974- ) and a 'paradigmatic gaucho', El Renegau (*Las
aventuras de Inodoro Pereyra ¡El Renegau! Poema telúrico de Fontanarrosa*, 1974).
*Mafalda* (see *Mafalda: an Argentine comic strip*) is the third example. Finally, two
satirical magazines, *Sol de Noche* and *Superhumor* (1979); the latter is a subsidiary or
parallel publication of *Humor Registrado* (Ediciones de la Urraca, 1978- , banned
briefly in late 1982).

1131  **Historia del humor gráfico y escrito en la Argentina.** (A history of
graphic and written humour in Argentina.)
Oscar E. Vázquez Lucio.  Buenos Aires: EUDEBA, 1985-87. 2 vols.
A chronological history from 1801 to 1985, illustrated with hundreds of examples of
cartoons, comic strips and verbal humour from over 450 satirical magazines (notably
*Caras y Caretas, Cascabel, Crítica, Don Quijote, El Mosquito, El Mundo, Hortensia,
Humor Registrado, Patoruzú, Rico Tipo, Satiricón* and *Tía Vicenta*) and daily
newspapers (*La Prensa, La Nación, Clarín, La Razón*). There are detailed indexes.

1132 **Las historietas.** (Comics in Argentina.)
Alberto Bróccoli, Carlos Trillo. Buenos Aires: Centro Editor de
América Latina, 1972. 107p. bibliog. (Vida y Milagros de Nuestro
Pueblo. La Historia Popular, 77).
A well-illustrated history of comics and comic strips, from 1897 to the 1960s. The very
first comics were translations of American and European products; the first truly
Argentine comic was the weekly *Viruta y Chicharrón* (1912). Seventy-eight examples
are illustrated. See also Carlos Trillo, Guillermo Saccomano, *Historia de la historieta
argentina* (Buenos Aires: Ediciones Record, 1980), a more anecdotal history of comics
and cartoons from 1900.

1133 **Mafalda: an Argentine comic strip.**
David William Foster. *Journal of Popular Culture*, vol. 14, no. 3
(winter 1980), p. 497-508.
Mafalda is the comic-strip creation of Quino (the pseudonym of Joaquín Salvador
Lavado). She is 'a little girl, about eight or nine years old, who lives with her solidly
middle-class family in an unspecified section of Buenos Aires'. The strips, which are a
'remarkably accurate representation of metonymic details of Argentine bourgeois daily
life', appeared originally in Argentine and Uruguayan newspapers and magazines;
more than ten collections have been published since 1967. Ten individual strips of
between two and six panels are illustrated and commented upon.

1134 **'Quino' after *Mafalda*: a bittersweet look at Argentine reality.**
Claudia Cairo Resnick, Paula K. Speck. *Studies in Latin American
Popular Culture*, vol. 2 (1983), p. 79-87.
Quino's *Mafalda* strip was criticized by both Left and Right elements in Argentina; in
1973 he stopped drawing *Mafalda* and moved to Italy. He now produces 'one-time'
cartoon panels and sequences of between one and four panels, six of which are
reproduced. Quino's sharpest criticisms are aimed at the curtailment of freedom of
expression, but they are not entirely political: they cover a variety of topics, 'from
marriage through inflation to the bureaucracy'.

1135 **Social commentary in Argentine cartooning: from description to
questioning.**
Naomi Lindstrom. *Journal of Popular Culture*, vol. 14, no. 3 (winter
1980), p. 509-23.
Examines the social content manifest in Argentine cartoons published in mass-
audience magazines since the 1940s: Guillermo Divito's weekly humour magazine *Rico
Tipo* (founded 1944), which appealed to lower-middle-class readers, and whose
principal cartoonists were Oski (Oscar Conti), Landrú (Juan Carlos Columbres) and
Divito himself (he created the famous *chicas* [girls] cycle); and the 'new wave' humour
of the 1950s (*Esto Es*, *Qué*, *Potpurrí*, *Avivato* and, especially, *Tía Vicenta*). The
individual artists Fontanarrosa and Quino are also discussed.

# Music and dance

## General

1136 **Enciclopedia de la música argentina.** (Encyclopaedia of Argentine music.)
Rodolfo Arizaga. Buenos Aires: Fondo Nacional de las Artes, 1971. 371p. bibliog.
The alphabetical entries (p. 35-332) refer to composers, performers, conductors, musicologists and music critics. There is a chronological musical index, 1580-1960s, a list of Argentine operas, 1877-1969, and a discography.

1137 **The encyclopedia of opera.**
Edited by Leslie Orrey. London: Pitman, 1976. 376p.
The short but informative entry on Argentina is by Malena Kuss, p. 23-4. Opera was introduced to Argentina by Italian companies as early as 1823 and a regular opera season established in 1825. The first fully 'ethnic' opera, Pascal de Rogatis's *Huemac* (1916), was influenced by pre-Columbian traditions. Argentina has the 'strongest tradition of native opera in Latin America', but productions have declined over the last twenty years. A recent study of the Italian contribution to the growth of opera in Buenos Aires is John Rosselli, 'The opera business and the Italian immigrant community in Latin America, 1820-1930: the case of Buenos Aires', *Past and Present*, no. 127 (May 1990), p. 155-82.

1138 **The guitarist singer of pre-1900 gaucho literature.**
Richard Pinnell. *Revista de Música Latino-Americana / Latin American Music Review*, vol. 5, no. 2 (fall/winter 1984), p. 243-62. bibliog.
The guitar or *vihuela* was used by itinerant gauchos to accompany improvised ballads. Concolorcorvo, in his *El Lazarillo* (see item no. 119), is the first chronicler to mention the guitar. The tour de force of the gaucho balladeer (*payador*) was the *payada de contrapunto*, a contest in which two singer-guitarists supplied alternate verses. References to the *payador* in Argentine and Uruguayan literature are made, with some texts and lyrics reproduced. Unfortunately, the article barely mentions guitar technique; for this see Segundo N. Contreras, *La guitarra argentina: apuntes para su historia y otros artículos* (Buenos Aires: Castro Barrera, 1950. 76p.).

1139 **Historia de la música en la Argentina, 1536-1851.** (A history of music in Argentina, 1536-1851.)
Vicente Gesualdo. Buenos Aires: Libros de Hispanoamérica, 1978. 2nd ed. 3 vols. bibliog.
A comprehensive history of both classical and popular music: opera, light opera, symphonies, ballet, folklore, composers and movements. Based on published works, newspapers, travellers' accounts and archive material. There are over 400 musical

examples; the illustrations are of rather poor quality. The author has published a one-volume summary: *La música en la Argentina* (Buenos Aires: Editorial Stella, 1988. 288p.).

1140 **La historia del Teatro Colón, 1908-1968.** (The history of the Colón
Theatre, 1908-1968.)
Roberto Caamaño. Buenos Aires: Editorial Cinetea, 1969. 3 vols.
The Colón Theatre is Latin America's greatest opera house; it opened on 25 May 1908
with a production of *Aida*. This is a lavishly illustrated history of its construction,
architecture, performances and performers, management and artistic departments,
including a detailed list of each season's operas, ballets, concerts and plays. Another
celebratory work is *El Teatro Colón: cincuenta años de gloria, 1908-1958* (Buenos
Aires: J. Héctor Matera, 1958. 194p.). Caamaño has written a short account in
English: 'The Colón Theater in Buenos Aires', *Inter-American Music Bulletin*, vol. 54
(July 1966), p. 1-10. An entertaining account of the planning and construction of the
theatre is John E. Hodge, 'The construction of the Colón Theater', *The Americas*,
vol. 36, no. 2 (Oct. 1979), p. 235-55. See also A. R. Williams, 'Eighty years of
elegance and excellence', *Américas*, vol. 39, no. 5 (Sept.-Oct. 1987), p. 14-19.

1141 **Latin American Music Review.**
vol. 6, no. 1 (spring/summer 1985).
Contains a special obituary celebration of the famous Argentine composer Alberto
Ginastera (1916-83), edited by Malena Kuss, p. 80-107: Gilbert Chase, 'Remembering
Ginastera'; Carleton Sprague Smith on Ginastera's *Duo for flute and oboe* (1945);
Robert Stevenson on Ginastera's arrangement of an organ toccata by Domenico Zipoli
('some recollections about the career of a master composer'); and W. Stuart Pope, of
music publishers Boosey & Hawkes, 'The composer-publisher relation: chronicle of a
friendship'. See also the important article by Gilbert Chase, 'Alberto Ginastera:
Argentine composer', *Musical Quarterly*, vol. 43, no. 4 (Oct. 1957), p. 439-60, which
mentioned early (later 'withdrawn') works omitted from his 1980 article in the *New
Grove dictionary of music and musicians* (q.v.), vol. 7, p. 387-90.

1142 **Music in Latin America: an introduction.**
Gerard Béhague. Englewood Cliffs, New Jersey: Prentice-Hall,
1979. 369p. map. bibliog. (Prentice-Hall 'History of Music' Series).
Argentine music is covered in all five chapters of this classic history: sacred music of
the colonial period (p. 54-6), musical nationalism and Romantic academicism
(Alberto Williams, Juan José Castro, Luis Gianneo, Alberto Ginastera, p. 105-10, 212-
20), abstract 'countercurrents' before 1930 (p. 240), 1930s and 1940s neo-Classicism
and the twelve-tone music of Juan Carlos Paz (p. 272-7), and music since 1950
(Ginastera, Paz and younger composers, p. 328-40).

1143 **La música argentina durante el período de la organización nacional.**
(Music in Argentina during the nineteenth century.)
Mario García Acevedo.   Buenos Aires: Ediciones Culturales
Argentinas, 1961. 115p. (Biblioteca del Sesquicentenario. Colección
Textos).

A short, unpretentious history of music after national unification, 1852 to 1910,
containing interesting material on nineteenth-century composers, opera, musical
education and musical theatre. It was published under the auspices of the Ministerio de
Educación y Justicia.

1144 **Músicos argentinos durante la dominacíon hispánica.** (Music in
Argentina during the colonial period.)
Guillermo Fúrlong Cárdiff.   Buenos Aires: Huarpes, 1945. 203p.
(Cultura Colonial Argentina, 2).

Thirty-six detailed chapters on musicians and musical instruments from the conquest to
1810: sacred, indigenous and Negro music, dance and theatre. Eighteen plates, mainly
of cathedral organs, are included as well as two musical examples.

1145 **The new Grove dictionary of music and musicians.**
Edited by Stanley Sadie.   London: Macmillan, 1980. 20 vols. bibliog.

Volume one includes a succinct entry ('Argentina', p. 564-71) on art music (colonial,
1800-1930, since 1930) and folk music (sources and collections, indigenous, mestizo
and creole) by Gerard Béhague and Isabel Aretz respectively. (Aretz, a noted
Venezuelan musicologist of Argentine birth, earns her own entry, p. 563-4.) 'Tango'
(volume 18, p. 563-5), by Béhague, is a masterful short summary which devotes
fifteen lines to the 'extraordinary figure' of Carlos Gardel (who does not have a
separate article).

1146 *Rock nacional* **and dictatorship in Argentina.**
Pablo Vila.   *Popular Music*, vol. 6, no. 2 (May 1987), p. 129-48.
bibliog.

'National rock' music emerged as a 'counter-culture and a social movement' between
1976 and 1983. It attracted mass attendance at concerts and gave rise to hundreds of
official and underground fan magazines. This is a study of the movement based on
interviews and the magazines' correspondence columns. The leading musicians were
Charly García, Fito Páez and León Gieco. The movement's eclectic musical features
are analysed in the same author's 'Argentina's *rock nacional*: the struggle for
meaning', *Latin American Music Review*, vol. 10, no. 1 (June 1989), p. 1-28. See also
two articles in *Popular Music Perspectives*, no. 2 (1985): Ramón Pelinski, 'From tango
to "rock nacional": a case study of changing popular music taste in Buenos Aires',
p. 287-95; and Marcela Hidalgo, Omar García Brunelli and Ricardo D. Salton, 'The
evolution of rock in Argentina' [since 1965], p. 296-303. A longer study in Spanish is:
Alfredo Beltrán Fuentes, *La ideología autoritaria del rock nacional* (Buenos Aires:
Centro Editor de América Latina, 1989. 111p.).

1147 **'We blew it after all': the Argentine musical group Les Luthiers.**
David William Foster. *Studies in Latin American Popular Culture*,
vol. 5 (1986), p. 135-43.

Les Luthiers are a famous six-member group founded in the 1970s, whose main base of operations is Buenos Aires's Teatro Liceo. Their appearance is studiously refined (black tie and tails); their instruments grotesquely constructed from the 'flotsam and jetsam of the modern technological world'; their music a satirical blend of patriotic, operatic, folkloric, classical, ballad and popular styles; their performances punctuated by 'unacceptable gestures and body movement'; their purpose to ridicule social pretensions and the entire tradition of classical and ceremonial music. Three examples of their routines are given.

# Folk music and dance

1148 **Compendio de danzas folklóricas argentinas.** (Compendium of
Argentine folk dances.)
Haydée S. B. de Pérez del Cerro, Raquel Nelli. Buenos Aires:
Imprenta López, 1953. 2 vols. bibliog.

The history and choreography of 37 traditional folk dances, with 115 illustrations of dance-steps and the *zapateo* (foot-stamping).

1149 **Dances of Argentina.**
A. L. Lloyd. London: Max Parrish, published under the auspices of
the Royal Academy of Dancing and the Ling Physical Education
Association, 1960. 40p. bibliog. (The Traditional Dances of Latin
America, 2).

Part one provides a brief history of four dances (the *carnavalito*, a 'round dance for as many as will', *chacarera* and *escondido*, for couples, and *bailecito*, a graceful handkerchief square dance for two couples), their music (which 'consists in the main of a mixture of Spanish popular music and the music of the aboriginal Indians'), instruments (guitar, *quena* [flute], *charango* [small guitar], *bombo* and *caja* [drums]) and costumes. Part two describes the dance steps, with coloured drawings of positions and costumes. The author was a celebrated historian of British folk-song.

1150 **Danzas folklóricas argentinas: estudio integral.** (Folk dances of
Argentina: a complete study.)
Eleanora Luisa Benvenuto, costume drawings by Luis Diego
Pedreira. Buenos Aires: Cesarini Editores, 1962. 361p.

The first seven chapters are introductory. Individual chapters then describe in detail the characteristics, history, music and lyrics, choreography and costumes of twenty-three important dances. There are many choreographic drawings, and indexes to steps and *zapateo* figures.

1151 **Las danzas populares argentinas. Vol. 1.** (Popular dances of
Argentina. Volume one.)
Carlos Vega. Buenos Aires: Dirección General de Cultura, Instituto
de Musicología, 1952. 780p. maps. bibliog.

A comprehensive history, classification and choreographic guide, only one volume of
which was published, describing individual dances (*malambo*, *solo inglés* and
*campana*), collective dances (*danza de las cintas*, *carnavalito*) and the many dances for
couples. There are 138 figures in the text, 35 musical examples and 18 plates. The
studies of the dances were also issued in individual pamphlets, published by Julio Korn
in 1952.

1152 **Danzas tradicionales argentinas.** (Traditional dances of Argentina.)
Joaquín López Flores. Buenos Aires: Editorial Record, 1949. 336p.

A description of the music and choreography of twenty dances, including the varieties
of the *mudanza* figure, and discussion of the gaucho's traditional costume, music and
song and use of the guitar. The work is well illustrated with diagrams of dance figures.

1153 **El folklore musical argentino.** (The folk music of Argentina.)
Isabel Aretz. Buenos Aires: Ricordi Americana, 1952. 271p. bibliog.
(Manuales Musicales Ricordi).

A classic introduction to folk music, still in print. Part one describes music,
instruments, lyrics and dance choreography; part two discusses song, dance and *tocatas*
(instrumental 'calls'). Ninety-one musical examples (scored for folk instruments) are
provided, with thirty-three diagrams and eight plates.

1154 **Manual de danzas regionales argentinas del folklore argentino: método
de enseñanza práctica.** (Manual of Argentine regional folk-dances: a
practical teaching method.)
Antonio Cisneros Lugones. Rosario, Argentina: Librería y Editorial
Ruiz, 1962. 4th ed. 78p.

Instructions on the performance of eighty-six dances, with diagrams and verbal calls.
Nineteen dances are described fully with music (arranged for piano); a further five are
supplied with music and brief choreographies; the rest are treated more sketchily. Nine
folk instruments are described and illustrated.

1155 **La música de proyección folklórica argentina.** (Folk music in
Argentina.)
Ariel Gravano. *Folklore Americano*, no. 35 (Jan.-June 1983),
p. 5-71.

A good synthesis of folk-music history, research and movements, with a passionate
plea for a recognition and strengthening of the country's *patrimonio folklórico*.
Contains valuable material on the folk boom of the 1960s, the first Festival Nacional de
Folklore de Cosquín (1961) and the major musicians of the past thirty years: Los
Abalos, Atahualpa Yupanqui, Los Chalchaleros, Los Fronterizos and Los Cantores de
Quilla Huasi.

1156 **Música tradicional argentina: Tucumán, historia y folklore.**
(Traditional music of Argentina: Tucumán, history and folklore.)
Isabel Aretz-Thiele.   San Miguel de Tucumán, Argentina:
Universidad Nacional de Tucumán, 1946. 743p. map. bibliog.

The *Handbook of Latin American Studies* (q.v.) describes this as 'probably the most complete and well-documented study of the folk music of a region of comparable size ever made in Latin America'. It covers both music and dance and is illustrated with 795 musical examples, 18 pieces scored for piano, and 26 pages of photographs.

# The tango

1157 **El bandoneón: retrato de un instrumento unilateralmente conocido.**
(The bandoneón: portrait of a unilaterally known instrument.)
Clara Meierovich.   *Heterofonía* (Mexico City), vol. 18, no. 2 [no. 89]
(April-June 1985), p. 5-38.

The *New Grove dictionary of music and musicians* (q.v.) devotes only ten lines to this instrument, a 'square-built button accordion or concertina invented in the 1840s by Heinrich Band of Krefeld . . . It has been used since about 1900 as a solo instrument in tango orchestras in Argentina, Uruguay and Brazil. Early models had more than 88 notes; the South American instrument usually has 38 keys or buttons for the high and medium registers and 33 for the lower register'. This article describes its early history (including, very briefly, its mechanical construction, tuning and note formation), introduction in the River Plate, notable interpreters, an interview with the virtuoso Alejandro Barletta, the musical text of two works by René Marino Moreno, and a list of works for the instrument by eighteen composers.

1158 **La historia del tango.** (The history of the tango.)
Compiled by Juan Carlos Martini Real.   Buenos Aires: Ediciones
Corregidor, 1976-85. 18 vols. (Serie Mayor).

Partly chronological, partly thematic, this is the definitive history (over 3,500 well-illustrated pages) of the tango, its interpreters, music and instruments.

1159 **El libro del tango: crónica & diccionario, 1850-1977.** (The book of the tango: chronicle and dictionary, 1850-1977.)
Horacio Ferrer.   Buenos Aires: Editorial Galerna, 1977. 2 vols.

The book opens with an appreciation of tango specialist Ferrer. The 'chronicle' summarizes tango history. The alphabetical dictionary section (p. 235-763) covers everything related to the tango (history, musicians, *lunfardo*, and much more) and contains hundreds of photographs.

1160   **The life, music and times of Carlos Gardel.**
Simon Collier.   Pittsburgh, Pennsylvania: University of Pittsburgh
Press, 1986. 340p. bibliog. (Pitt Latin American Series).
Gardel (1890-1935) was born in Toulouse, France, and christened Charles Romuauld
Gardes. With Uruguayan-born José Razzano (later his business manager) he formed a
famous vocal folk duo (1911-18) but switched to the tango in the 1920s. His records
and films made him 'Latin America's first (and in many ways greatest) superstar of
light entertainment'. He was killed in a plane crash. This book, the only biography in
English, focuses on Gardel's private life and artistic career. There are extracts of his
song lyrics but no musical examples.

1161   **Popular culture as a source for the historian: the tango in its era of La
Guardia Vieja.**
Donald S. Castro.   *Studies in Latin American Popular Culture*, vol. 3
(1984), p. 70-85.
A study of the first stage of the tango's historical development, 1870-1917. The
following period of tango history is treated by the same author's 'Popular culture as a
source for the historian: the tango in its Epoca de oro, 1917-1943', *Journal of Popular
Culture*, vol. 20, no. 3 (winter 1986), p. 45-71, which analyses a number of song lyrics
which show Buenos Aires 'reality' (sexual relations, women's fashions, unemployment,
poor housing, labour strikes, prostitution) and compares the most famous vocalists.
For commentaries on Gardel's lyrics, see Castro's 'Popular culture as a source for the
historian: why Carlos Gardel?', *Studies in Latin American Popular Culture*, vol. 5
(1986), p. 144-62. His 'The soul of the people: the tango as a source for Argentine
popular history', *ibid.*, vol. 9 (1990), p. 279-95, contains a useful annotated, selected
bibliography.

1162   **The tango: its origins and meaning.**
Russell O. Salmon.   *Journal of Popular Culture*, vol. 10, no. 4
(spring 1977), p. 859-66.
A provocative article on the history and social significance of the tango dance and song
lyrics, and the tango in literature (notably Manuel Puig's *Heartbreak tango*) and film
(Bertolucci's *Last tango in Paris*). The 'narcotic effect' of tango music 'isolates and
insulates the individual', the tango dance 'typifies the Argentine propensity for
introspective musing on oneself'. Most challenging of all: 'In its exaggerated posturing
it is *kitsch*, *cursi* [showy] or camp; in any man's language it is gaudy, garish and tacky.
Rather than an expression of erotic exuberance, the tango expresses the existential
anguish of existence.'

1163   **Tango: theme of class and nation.**
Julie M. Taylor.   *Ethnomusicology*, vol. 20, no. 2 (May 1976),
p. 273-91. bibliog.
A study of the social significance of the tango's song and dance elements: the
environment which produced the tango ('to dance a tango is to feel oneself a part of
the land, a part of Argentina'), the moral and emotional content of its lyrics and
dance, and the Gardel myth. The songs are grouped into eight representative themes
(sadness, moping, the stupidly innocent, the cuckold, the mother, the dance-hall girl
become prostitute, the 'dream of social mobility' and 'return to the barrio' [city
quarter]). The author notes that the tango, considered 'the epitome of degradation' in

331

the 1880s, has become an entirely urban form, and that tango enthusiasts around the world are 'exclusively male'.

# Theatre

1164 **Argentine New Theatre: the coming of age of popular tradition.**
Claudia Kaiser-Lenoir. *Theatre Research International*, vol. 14, no. 2 (summer 1989), p. 165-74
New Theatre continues the tradition of the early River Plate theatre 'which drew its language, characters and themes from the immediate environment': eighteenth-century plays such as *El amor de la estanciera*, the nineteenth-century gaucho cycle, the *sainete criollo* and the more recent *grotesco criollo*. The New Theatre's 'collective creations' since the 1960s, mostly produced outside the commercial circuit, are 'polemical and dialectical' compared with the traditional theatre's 'celebratory and integrational' works.

1165 **The Argentine Teatro Independiente, 1930-1955.**
David William Foster. York, South Carolina: Spanish Literature, 1986. 143p.
Teatro Independiente was 'one of the most creative enterprises in Latin American theatrical history' after the low period of 1910-30. The movement began when Leónidas Barletta founded the Teatro del Pueblo in 1930. This is not so much a history of independent theatre groups as a close analysis of the 'theatrical semiology' of some of the movement's principal texts: Roberto Arlt's *Trescientos millones* (1932) and *La isla desierta* (1938), Samuel Eichelbaum's *Un guapo del 900* (1940), Carlos Gorostiza's *El puente* (1949), Conrado Nalé Roxlo's *Judith y las rosas* (1956), Osvaldo Dragún's *Historias para ser contadas* (1957), and a brief consideration of the texts of five minor playwrights. The dramatists of the Teatro Independiente 'saw in nonnaturalistic strategies one way to refute accepted masks of identity and to probe underlying levels of feeling and motivation'.

1166 **The Argentine theatre and the problem of national identity: a critical survey.**
John E. Lyon. *Latin American Theatre Review*, vol. 5, no. 2 (spring 1972), p. 5-18. bibliog.
The preoccupation with national identity in the Argentine theatre can be traced back to 1810. Since 1940 there have been three tendencies: the Universalists (whose greatest exponent outside the field of drama is Jorge Luis Borges) such as Atilio Betti, Julio Imbert, Omar del Carlo and Alberto de Zavalía; the theatre of myth and legend (Rodolfo Kusch, Bernardo Canal Feijóo); and the theatre of social polemic (Carlos Gorostiza, Osvaldo Dragún, Andrés Lizárraga, Agustín Cuzzani, Roberto Cossa, Ricardo Halac).

1167  **Behind Spanish American footlights.**
Willis Knapp Jones.   Austin, Texas: University of Texas Press, 1966.
609p. bibliog.
Six of the thirty-two chapters deal with Argentina and the River Plate (p. 77-82) and
cover: the origins of drama to 1812; the beginnings of Argentine national drama (1812-
1936); Florencio Sánchez; the 'gringa' (foreign immigrant) theme in River Plate drama
(1884-1931, epitomized by Florencio Sánchez's *La gringa*, 1904); well-known
twentieth-century Argentine dramatists; and some forty contemporary playwrights.

1168  **Breve historia del teatro argentino.** (A brief history of Argentine
theatre.)
Edited by Luis Ordaz.   Buenos Aires: Editorial Universitaria de
Buenos Aires, 1962-64. 6 vols. (Serie del Siglo y Medio, 36, 39, 43, 46,
50, 53).
The best single history of the theatre, which includes some extracts of plays. For a
concise summary see his collaborative, oversize and well-illustrated *Historia del teatro
argentino* (Buenos Aires: Centro Editor de América Latina, 1982. 408p.). Also
valuable, but unindexed, is Raúl Héctor Castagnino, *Literatura dramática argentina,
1717-1967* (Buenos Aires: Editorial Pleamar, 1968. 208p.).

1169  **Cocoliche: the art of assimilation and dissimulation among Italians and
Argentines.**
Ana Cara-Walker.   *Latin American Research Review*, vol. 22, no. 3
(1987), p. 37-67.
Cocoliche is a dramatic character invented during an improvised pantomime
performance of the first Argentine gaucho play acted in the circus ring, Eduardo
Gutiérrez's *Juan Moreria* (1884). By extension the term has come to refer to the
'mixed' way of talking of Italian immigrants. The famous incident between the gaucho
and the Italian in José Hernández's poem *Martín Fierro* is often cited as a cocoliche-
like 'interaction'. The article describes examples of *cocoliche* speech, notably the pun,
and examples of *cocoliche* in *sainetes* and other plays, short stories and popular songs.
For the text of *Juan Moreira*, see *Three plays of the Argentine: Juan Moreira, Santos
Vega, The witches' mountain*, edited by Edward Hale Bierstadt (New York: Duffield,
1920).

1170  **Diccionario de autores teatrales argentinos, 1950-1980.** (A dictionary of
Argentine playwrights, 1950-1980).
Perla Zayas de Lima.   Buenos Aires: Editorial Rodolfo Alonso,
1981. 188p. bibliog.
Contains bio-bibliographical information on more than 300 contemporary playwrights
who have had their works produced in Argentina or abroad, arranged in one
alphabetical sequence. See also the *Diccionario teatral del Río de la Plata* by Tito Livio
Foppa (Buenos Aires: Argentores, 1961. 1046p.), which consists of a biographical
dictionary of playwrights (p. 43-704) followed by essays on various aspects of the
theatre. Zayas de Lima has recently published *Diccionario de directores y escenógrafos
del teatro argentino* (Buenos Aires: Galerna, 1990: 394p.).

1171 **The dramatic works of William Shand.**
John Walker. *NS/NorthSouth: Canadian Journal of Latin American Studies*, vol. 9, no. 17 (1984), p. 75-84.

William Shand was born in Scotland in 1902 and has been a resident of Buenos Aires since 1938. He has produced a steady stream of drama, fiction and poetry; he was almost forty before he began to write in Spanish. His 'simple and spare' farces and extravaganzas are concerned with family relationships, human degradation, the Nazi-Jewish question and political corruption. For an examination of Shand's fiction, see the same author's 'The real fictional world of William Shand', *Bulletin of Latin American Research*, vol. 2, no. 1 (Oct. 1982), p. 43-50.

1172 **Dramatists in revolt: the new Latin American theater.**
Edited by Leon F. Lyday, George W. Woodyard. Austin, Texas: University of Texas Press, 1976. 275p. bibliog. (Texas Pan American Series).

Contains four chapters on Argentine playwrights: Alyce de Kuehne, 'The spectacular in the theater of Agustín Cuzzani' (social farces), p. 37-58; Donald L. Schmidt, 'The theater of Osvaldo Dragún' (expressionist), p. 77-94; Sandra Messinger Cypess, 'The plays of Griselda Gambaro' (theatre of cruelty), p. 95-109; and Merlin H. Forster, 'The theater of Carlos Gorostiza' (realism, fantasy and the absurd), p. 110-19.

1173 **The evolution of the *sainete* in the River Plate area.**
Amthony M. Pasquariello. *Latin American Theatre Review*, vol. 17, no. 1 (fall 1983), p. 15-24.

The *sainete*, a one-act play on contemporary manners, was invented by a Spanish dramatist, Ramón de la Cruz, at the end of the eighteenth century. The first River Plate example is the anonymous *El amor de la estanciera*, performed some time between 1780 and 1795. An attempt to discredit the *sainete* was the anonymous *El examen de los sainetes* (1805 or 1806), itself now ironically considered a classic of the genre. These were the only two extant colonial *sainetes* until four more were discovered and published in 1950. The plots of all six *sainetes* are described with extracts.

1174 **Florencio Sánchez and the Argentine theatre.**
Ruth Richardson. New York: Instituto de las Españas en los Estados Unidos, 1933. 243p. bibliog.

Florencio Sánchez (1875-1910), one of the great figures of River Plate drama, was born in Montevideo but lived for many years in Buenos Aires and had many of his plays performed and published there. Part one of this book discusses the Argentine theatre between 1747 and 1900, describes Sánchez's life and analyses his works. It was reprinted by the Gordon Press, New York, in 1975. For the plays in English see *Representative plays of Florencio Sánchez*, translated by Willis Knapp Jones (Washington, DC: Pan American Union, General Secretariat, 1961. 326p.).

1175    **Griselda Gambaro's theatre of the absurd.**
Tamara Holzapfel.    *Latin American Theatre Review*, vol. 4, no. 1
(fall 1970), p. 5-11.

Griselda Gambaro (or Gámbaro, as this author calls her) was born in 1928 and began
her career as a short-story writer. Her first dramatic work was a prize-winning two-act
play, *Las paredes* (1963). Her plays incorporate psychological cruelty and physical
violence and are characterized by 'desolation, defeat and disintegration'. The article
analyses three of her most significant works: *El desatino* (1965), *Los siameses* and *El
campo* (both 1967).

1176    **Historia de nuestros viejos teatros.** (The history of our old theatres.)
Alfredo Taullard.    Buenos Aires: Imprenta López, 1932. 500p.

A history of theatre buildings, their most famous performances (both drama and
opera) and performers, from the colonial period – the first-ever theatre, *La Ranchería*
was opened in 1778 but long since demolished – to the inauguration of the Colón
Theatre in 1908. There are illustrations of interiors and portraits of actors and singers.

1177    **Open Theatre revisited: an Argentine experiment.**
Edith E. Pross.    *Latin American Theatre Review*, vol. 18, no. 1 (fall
1984), p. 83-94.

Teatro Abierto was a showcase for contemporary theatre conceived by a group of
playwrights led by Osvaldo Dragún and Roberto Durán. Like United States Open
Theater, it emerged as a reaction against commercialized theatre, dealt with non-
realistic material, was concerned with social and political issues and involved audience
participation. This article describes the mixed fortunes of Teatro Abierto's first three
seasons, 1981-83.

1178    **Power, myths, and aggression in Eduardo Pavlovsky's theater.**
Charles B. Driskell.    *Hispania*, vol. 65, no. 4 (Dec. 1982), p. 570-9.

Eduardo Pavlovsky, a professional psychoanalyst, is also one of Argentina's
outstanding avant-garde playwrights. He 'admits a tremendous debt to Beckett and
Pinter, but his themes are Argentine, and relevant to universal problems'. The article
discusses three recent plays: *La mueca* (1970), in which 'four young self-appointed
"artists" clandestinely enter the well-appointed apartment of a married couple who are
away at the movies'; *El señor Galíndez* (1973), his most popular play, a study in
torture; and *Telarañas* (1976), an exploration of violent family relationships 'as an
allegory of national and universal realities'.

1179    **Theatre of dissent: three young Argentine playwrights.**
Virginia Ramos Foster.    *Latin American LiteraryReview*, vol. 4,
no. 2 (spring 1971), p. 45-50.

Three young 'socially-committed' dramatists burst upon the scene during the 1970
season. The author analyses their first plays: *Hoy napalm hoy: motivación en un acto*
by Víctor de los Solares; *Hablemos al calzón quitado* by Guillermo Gentile; and *Una
noche con el señor Magnus e hijos* by Ricardo Monti. The last two have become
established playwrights.

1180   **The world's illogic in two plays by Argentine expressionists.**
Naomi E. Lindstrom.   *Latin American Theatre Review*, vol. 4, no. 8
(spring-summer 1976), p. 83-8.
Discusses Roberto Arlt's posthumous *El desierto entra a la ciudad* (1952), a study of a
community 'modeled along the lines of Roman government circles but located in 1942';
and Armando Discépalo's *Entre el hierro* (1910), in which a clever young woman
marries a 'dim-witted lout' and ends by killing him. Both plays depict 'an
expressionistic universe not to be set to rights by the use of reason'.

# Film

1181   **Argentine cinema.**
Edited by Tim Barnard.   Toronto: Nightwood Editions, 1986. 177p.
bibliog.
A collection of essays prepared to accompany a retrospective of Argentine cinema at
the Ontario Film Institute. Many of the papers are extracts from lengthier works. The
editor, a film promoter, writes on 'Popular cinema and populist politics'; Fernando
Birri on 'The roots of documentary realism' (a slightly edited version of his interview in
*Cinema and social change in Latin America* [q.v.]) and 'For a nationalist, realist,
critical and popular cinema'; Alfonso Gumucio Dagrón on censorship 1950-83; Octavio
Getino (co-director of *La hora de los hornos*) on the 'Third Cinema' (in particular, the
radical film collective Cine Liberación); Julio Cortázar on Jorge Cedrón (director of
*Operación masacre*, 1972); Edgardo Cozarinsky on Borges in/and/on cinema; an
interview with Borges; and a 'Report on the state of Argentine cinema' by Jorge
Ventura, secretary-general of the Argentine Film-workers' Union. Finally, there is a
chronology of Argentine cinema, 1896-1985, by the editor.

1182   **Catálogo del nuevo cine argentino, 1987/88.** (Argentine film catalogue,
1987/88.)
Compiled by Daniel López.   Buenos Aires: Instituto Nacional de
Cinematografía, 1989. 198p.
A chronological register of eighty-two Argentine feature films 'the shooting of which
started on or after January 1st, 1987, and until the end of 1988', not all of which have
been released; also included are short- and medium-length films and documentaries.
For each film the catalogue provides production credits, summary of plot (in Spanish
and English), foreign distributor, film format and length. There are lists of films
entered in national and international festivals, and indexes by film, director and
production company. The same compiler has also issued a catalogue of films for 1984-
86 (1987. 282p.).

1183    **Cine argentino: diccionario de realizadores contemporáneos.**
(A dictionary of contemporary Argentine film directors.)
Jorge Abel Martín.    Buenos Aires: Instituto Nacional de
Cinematografía, 1987. 210p.

Biographical data are provided on 175 directors active 1970-86, including their filmographies and international prizes, illustrated with portraits and film stills. The author also compiles *Cine argentino* (published by Legasa), an annual catalogue of Argentine films similar to that in item no. 1182, and has written a biography of a major Argentine film director: *Los films de Leopoldo Torre Nilsson* (Buenos Aires: Corregidor, 1980. 168p.).

1184    **Cinema and social change in Latin America: conversations with filmmakers.**
Edited by Julianne Burton.    Austin, Texas: University of Texas
Press, 1986. 302p. bibliog. (Special Publication).

The volume includes an interview with Fernando Birri, founder of the Documentary Film School in the Universidad Nacional del Litoral (Santa Fe), pioneer of the New Latin American Cinema movement and director of major neorealist films such as *Tire dié* ('Throw me a dime', 1960), *La pampa gringa* (1963) and *Los inundados* ('Flooded out', 1962).

1185    **The connection: three essays on the treatment of history in the early Argentine cinema.**
Jorge Miguel Couseló, translated and introduced by E. Bradford
Burns.    *Journal of Latin American Lore*, vol. 1, no. 2 (winter 1975),
p. 211-30.

A study of three pioneering films of the silent era, 'whose goals were to interpret and teach the Argentine past': *Mariano Moreno y la Revolución de Mayo* (directed by Enrique García Velloso, 1915, only a few stills remain of the film which was destroyed in a fire in the 1930s); *El último malón* ('The last Indian rebellion', Alcides Greca, 1917, a love story within a documentary of the 1904 Mocoví rebellion in Santa Fe province); and *El misionero de Atacama* (Clemente Onelli, 1922, a romantic reconstruction of Indian civilization in eighteenth-century northern Chile).

1186    **Film industries in Latin America: dependency and development.**
Jorge A. Schnitman.    Norwood, New Jersey: Ablex Publishing
Corporation, 1984. 134p. bibliog. (Communication and Information
Science).

A work which examines the economic, political and cultural factors affecting the growth of national film industries, including the production, exhibition and distribution of films, protectionism and censorship. Chapter four (p. 27-47) considers Argentina and Mexico between 1930 and 1980, and there are references to the early Argentine cinema in general chapters two and three.

1187 **The garden of forking paths: Argentine cinema.**
Edited by John King, Nissa Torrents. London: British Film Institute, 1988. 144p. bibliog.

A volume of essays prepared to accompany a season of Argentine films at the National Film Theatre, London, in 1988-89. John King considers the social and political context of Argentine cinema; Simon Collier discusses the films of the tango singer Carlos Gardel; Jorge Miguel Couseló, Ana López, Nick Caistor and Nissa Torrents review cinema history from the beginning of the sound era (1930-87); Nissa Torrents and Sheila Whitaker interview the female directors Beatriz Guido and María Luisa Bemberg; and John King interviews Bebe Kamin, director of *Los chicos de la guerra* (1984). Finally, there are filmographies of the twenty directors featured in the NFT season.

1188 **Historia del cine argentino.** (A history of the Argentine cinema.)
Jorge Miguel Couseló, Mariano Calistro (et al.). Buenos Aires: Centro Editor de América Latina, 1984. 190p. bibliog.

A richly illustrated history of commercial film-making from the silent era to the present day (1897-1983), with a chronology and list of international prizes won by Argentine films since 1937. See also Domingo di Núbila, *Historia del cine argentino* (Buenos Aires: Editorial Cruz de Malta, 1959, vol. 1 only published); and José Agustín Mahieu, *Breve historia del cine nacional, 1896-1974* (Buenos Aires: Alzamor, 1974. 141p.). The first fifty years of a major film company which made hundreds of films (including the first sound film, *¡Tango!*, 1933) is Claudio España, Miguel Angel Rosado, *Medio siglo de cine: Argentina Sono Film, S.A.C.I.* (Buenos Aires: Editorial Abril / Heraldo del Cine, 1984. 345p.).

1189 **Magical reels: a history of cinema in Latin America.**
John King. London; New York: Verso, published in association with the Latin America Bureau, 1990. 266p. bibliog. (Critical Studies in Latin American Culture).

This is a history of Latin American cinema which concentrates on providing an artistic analysis of the most important films against a background of the political environment and economics of film-making, making this a good complementary work to Schnitman's study (q.v.). Argentine cinema is described in chapters one (silent era, p. 8-14), two (from sound to the 'New Cinema', 1930-50s, p. 36-41) and four (recent decades to 1983, p. 79-103).

1190   **National identity in Argentine films.**
E. Bradford Burns.   *Americas*, vol. 27, nos 11-12 (Nov.-Dec. 1975),
p. 4-10.

Many early Argentine films before the 1940s were introspective reconstructions of
Argentine history, searching for the 'roots of Argentine nationality'. Their chief
subjects were the Indian, the gaucho and the tango. Argentina's first professional film
director, José Agustín Ferreyra, 'freely drew inspiration from the growing exaltation of
the gaucho', and made a cycle of films about the pampas. The early 1940s saw the end
of this 'informal period peopled with self-taught, bohemian filmmakers . . . whose
films to a large extent addressed a popular market'; films henceforth became
'organized, commercialized, and directed toward a new market, the growing middle
class'.

# Folklore

1191 **Bottles of water on the road: material symbols of an Argentine popular saint's cult.**
Kathleen L. Figgen. *Women's Studies International Forum*, vol. 9, no. 3 (1986), p. 281-5. bibliog.
The sides of Argentine roads are 'dotted by bottles of water, discarded automobile and truck tires, and anonymously constructed roadside niches laden with plastic flowers, candles, figurines, post-cards, snowstorm paper weights, medallions and coins'. These are manifestations of the popular religious cult to La Difunta Correa, a regional popular saint in northwestern Argentina 'whose fame and miraculous power spread nationally during the turbulent 70s'. The legend has it that she died of exposure while following behind her soldier-husband; her young child was found still alive and clinging to her breasts three days after her death. There is also a general discussion of folk religion and popular religious cults.

1192 **Costumbres tradicionales argentinas.** (Traditional customs of Argentina.)
Isabel Aretz. Buenos Aires: Editorial Raigal, 1954. 221p. bibliog. (Biblioteca de Etnografía y Folklore. Serie 'Cara al Campo').
A description of customs related to popular music and dancing, of two types: pagan customs (carnivals, ritual animal round-ups, popular and work songs, serenades and farewell songs), and religious festivals and ceremonies. The work contains twenty-two photographs and sixty-five musical examples.

1193   **Cuentos folklóricos de la Argentina.** (Folk tales of Argentina.)
Edited by Susana Chertudi.   Buenos Aires: Ministerio de Educación
y Justicia, Instituto Nacional de Filología y Folklore, Instituto
Nacional de Antropología, 1960-64. 2 vols. bibliog.
Each volume (255p., 226p.) contains 100 folk tales, some written partially in dialect,
grouped by theme and commented upon by the editor. There are also indexes by tale
type and a brief lexicon. Additional folk tales collected by the editor are to be found
in: 'Cuentos folklóricos de la Argentina: nueva serie', *Folklore Americano*, no. 32
(Dec. 1981), p. 9-92.

1194   **Diccionario de creencias y supersticiones (argentinas y americanas).**
(Dictionary of beliefs and superstitions [Argentine and Latin
American].)
Félix Coluccio.   Buenos Aires: Corregidor, 1983. 473p. bibliog.
An alphabetical dictionary, from *abejas* (in Corrientes a swarm of bees near a ranch is
a bad omen) to *zupay* (the Devil in northern Argentina). Although well documented,
unfortunately the many quotations are not attributed to the works cited in the
bibliography. Twenty illustrations are included.

1195   **Diccionario folklórico argentino.** (Dictionary of Argentine folklore.)
Félix Coluccio.   Buenos Aires: Editorial Plus Ultra, 1981. 3rd ed.
712p. maps. bibliog.
Subtitled 'with related terms, other Latin American terms, and an appendix of Latin
American folklorists and folklore institutions', this is a comprehensive lexicon in single
alphabetical order, listing all types of customs and traditions including legends, myths,
popular medicine, food, children's games, musical instruments, work implements,
dances, entertainments, religious and pagan festivals, popular speech and *lunfardo*.
The many words of Indian origin, mostly from Quechua, relate to flora and fauna.
Musical examples are included.

1196   **Fábulas argentinas. ('El hombre dijo a la oveja . . .').** (Argentine
fables. ['The man said to the ewe . . .'].)
Godofredo Daireaux.   Buenos Aires: Ediciones Agro, 1945. 199p.
A compilation consisting of 163 fables, mostly concerning animals. In the fable of the
title, the man tells the ewe: 'I will protect you!', keeps her in a pen, takes her lambs
away and hits the ungrateful animal on the head when she tries to escape.

1197   **Fiestas y celebraciones en la República Argentina.** (Festivals and
celebrations of Argentina.)
Félix Coluccio, with the collaboration of Susana B. C. de Regis, María
Isabel Coluccio.   Buenos Aires: Plus Ultra, 1978. 2nd ed. 292p.
bibliog. (Colección Nuestro Folklore).
This is a calendar of over 200 popular and traditional folk festivals, celebrations, fairs
and markets, which does not claim to be exhaustive. Arranged chronologically from
January to December, the events are described as follows: date, where held, how long
it lasts, reason for celebration and traditions associated with the event (music,
costumes, extracts of lyrics).

Folklore

1198 **Folklore argentino.** (Argentine folklore.)
José Imbelloni, Bruno C. Jacovella (et al.). Buenos Aires:
Editorial Nova, 1959. 397p. maps. bibliog. (Humanior: Biblioteca
del Americanista Moderno, 6. Sección E: Culturas de la Argentina,
6).

A splendid introduction on the theory of folklore by Imbelloni is followed by nine
expert essays on regional folklore, popular verse and superstitions (Bruno C. Jacovella),
folk tales and legends (Susana Chertudi), customs (Augusto Raúl Cortázar), folk
medicine (Armando Vivante), clothing and adornments (María Delia Millán de
Palavecino), transportation (Félix Coluccio), cultural areas of the country (Enrique
Palavecino) and indigenous place-names (Ricardo L. J. Nardi).

1199 **Historia del folklore argentino.** (A history of Argentine folklore.)
Juan Alfonso Carrizo. Buenos Aires: Ministerio de Educación,
Instituto Nacional de la Tradición, 1953. 187p.

This is a good synthesis of Argentine folklore for students. It discusses folklorists, folk
institutions and publications, folklore in art, folksong, folk music and dance, legends
and superstitions, games, regional traditions, folk vocabulary and folk crafts. A reprint
('second edition') was issued by Ediciones Dictio in 1977. The author has written a
number of books on Argentine regional folksong.

1200 **El mito, la leyenda y el hombre: usos y costumbres del folklore.**
(Myths, legends and man: folklore usages and customs.)
Félix Molina-Téllez. Buenos Aires: Editorial Claridad, 1947. 298p.
(Colección Arco Iris. Segunda Serie, vol. 1).

A useful description of myths, animals and plants in folklore, popular festivals, folk
magic and indigenous cultures, with a chapter on Indian mythology in the Chaco and
Santiago del Estero. There are twenty-four photographs and four plates of
*chacosantiagueño* ceramic designs.

1201 **Reseña histórico-descriptiva de antiguas y modernas supersticiones del
Río de la Plata.** (A description of the ancient and modern superstitions
of the River Plate region.)
Daniel Granada. Buenos Aires: Editorial Guillermo Kraft, 1947.
438p.

A classic descriptive history of superstitions relating to flora and fauna, geographical
features, food, burial, fire, natural phenomena, 'autosuggestion', medicine, ghosts,
magic and witchcraft, and many others.

1202 **Supersticiones y leyendas: región misionera – valles calchaquíes – las
pampas.** (Superstitions and legends of Misiones, the Calchaquí Valley
and the Pampas.)
Juan B. Ambrosetti. Buenos Aires: Ediciones Siglo XX, 1976. 140p.
bibliog.

This is the latest reprint of a pioneering study first published in 1917: the edition is
'considerably enlarged with previously unpublished pages, an appendix with supplementary notes and a biography of the author by E. M. S. Danero'. It describes and

342

comments upon the superstitions of three areas: Misiones, the Calchaquí Valley (province of Salta) and the pampas region. A few legends from Misiones only are included. The bibliography is of Ambrosetti's writings.

# Food and Drink

1203    **Así cocinan los argentinos. How Argentina cooks.**
Alberto Vázquez-Prego.    Buenos Aires: Librería 'El Ateneo'
Editorial, 1979. 351p. bibliog.
A total of 333 recipes from all regions of the country and representing many traditions.
They were 'prepared with an average of four hungry people in mind' and are grouped
according to fifteen categories: beef pots, broths and soups; thick soups: *locro* (maize
and meat stew) and *humita* (sweet corn and vegetables); pies or turnovers
(*empanadas*); roasts and grills; marinades and dressings; vegetables and stuffings; pies,
tarts and puddings; breaded fritters and croquettes; omelettes and scrambles; pickled
meats and vegetables; pasta and sauces; stews and casseroles; sauces; desserts and
preserves; and mate tea recipes. The text is parallel Spanish–English and there are no
illustrations.

1204    **The book of Latin American cooking.**
Elizabeth Lambert Ortiz.    London: Robert Hale; New York: Alfred
A. Knopf; Toronto: Random House, 1984. 336p.
The chapter on the River Plate describes a number of Argentine recipes (twenty are
listed in the index) under the following headings: hors-d'oeuvres and appetizers, soups,
fish and shellfish, meats, poultry, substantial dishes, vegetables and salads, breads and
desserts, sauces and drinks.

1205    **Fortifying a vintage industry.**
Dereck H. N. Foster.    *Américas*, vol. 40, no. 2 (March/April 1988),
p. 30-5.
Argentina is the world's fifth-largest producer of wine, with Mendoza the most
important wine-producing province, followed by San Juan, Río Negro, La Rioja,
Catamarca and Salta. Home consumption of fine wines remains a steady two litres per
head a year but exports are vital for the industry's survival. This article provides a brief
history of the wine industry and its present characteristics. The author is the wine and

food columnist for the *Buenos Aires Herald*; his book, *The noble wines of Argentina*, is awaiting publication.

1206 **Our favourite recipes from Argentina.**
Compiled and edited by Gillian Peiro.    London: Omni Plus, 1988.
33p.

Twenty-two recipes are included: two soups; a starter (stuffed courgettes); pies (*empanadas*), croquettes and mint sauce; main dishes (*asado,* beef roasts, and *humita,* sweet corn and vegetables); and six recipes for sweets (including *alfajores,* maize-flour biscuits with a filling of *dulce de leche,* milk-jam).

# Sport and Recreation

1207    **Argentina's 'philatelic annexation' of the Falklands.**
Peter J. Beck.    *History Today*, vol. 33, no. 2 (Feb. 1983), p. 39-44.
bibliog.

Argentina has 'regarded stamp issues as an integral part of its propaganda campaign to recover the Malvinas, for map stamps offered an easy method of "annexing" the islands which it lacked the power to secure in reality.' As early as 1884 the Argentine government, to British protests, issued a stamp showing the Falkland Islands as part of its national territory, and in 1936 a new one-peso stamp featured a map of South America 'upon which Argentine territory, including the Falklands, was shaded in a chocolate brown colour'. The article concentrates upon the 1930s, when Argentina also used the International Postal Union as an international platform for its territorial claim. Eight stamps and one postcard, 1933-83, are illustrated.

1208    **Catálogo histórico descriptivo de sellos postales de la República Argentina.** (Historical descriptive catalogue of Argentine postage stamps.)
Alfredo Taullard.    Buenos Aires: Sociedad de Comerciantes en Sellos Postales de Buenos Aires, 1932. 327p.

The province of Corrientes first adopted the adhesive postage stamp in 1856; Buenos Aires and Córdoba followed suit in 1858. This classic early catalogue describes and illustrates (with current values) the varieties of stamp issues to 1932. A beautifully produced bilingual history of the Argentine postal service and its postage stamps in relation to the country's development is Walter Björn, Ludovico Bose and Julio C. Sáenz, *Sellos postales argentinos con historia / Argentine postage stamps and history* (Buenos Aires: Manrique Zago, 1981. 192p.).

1209   **Del truquiflor a la rayuela: panorama de los juegos y entretenimientos argentinos.** (From brag to hopscotch: a panorama of games and amusements in Argentina.)
Jorge Páez.   Buenos Aires: Centro Editor de América Latina, 1971. 115p. (La Historia Popular. Vida y Milagros de Nuestro Pueblo, 57).
An interesting sketch of aboriginal ball games, card games, board games, games of chance and children's games, with twenty-four illustrations.

1210   **The demise of the gaucho and the rise of equestrian sport in Argentina.**
Richard W. Slatta.   *Journal of Sport History*, vol. 13, no. 2 (summer 1986), p. 97-110.
The first part describes the gaucho's traditional equestrian contests, based on nineteenth-century first-hand accounts: *cinchada* (a tug-of-war between two horses tied tail-to-tail), *pechando* (head-on clashes), *pialar* (lassoing of a horse), *pato* (a kind of mounted rugby), and *maroma* (jumping onto the back of a wild horse or steer). After 1880, the landowning élite 'replaced these practices with organized, civilized pato and imported rodeo, polo, and thoroughbred racing'. A mere two-and-half pages are devoted to these modern equestrian sports.

1211   **From soccer to war in Argentina: preliminary notes on sports-as-politics under a military regime (1978-1982).**
Alberto Ciria.   In: *Latin America and the Caribbean: geopolitics, development and culture.*   Edited by Arch R. M. Ritter.   Ottawa: Canadian Association for Latin American and Caribbean Studies, 1984, p. 80-95. bibliog.
Soccer was professionalized in the 1930s. Between 1943 and 1976 there were numerous instances of soccer's mixing with politics and vice versa. The author examines in particular the *futbolización* ('soccerization') of the 1978 World Cup in Argentina, the 1982 Falklands War and the 1982 World Cup in Spain, and looks at an 'opinion leader' (soccer radio commentator José María Muñoz) and a 'role model' (manager César Luis Menotti, 'who led the Argentine squad to victory in 1978 but failed to do an encore in 1982'). See also Ariel Scher, Héctor Palomino, *Fútbol: pasión de multitudes y de elites: un estudio institucional de la Asociación de Fútbol Argentino (1934-1986)* (Buenos Aires: CISEA, 1988. 245p.), also a study of the link between football and politics. See also: Joseph L. Arbena, 'Generals and *goles*: assessing the connection between military and soccer in Argentina', *International Journal of the History of Sport*, vol. 7, no. 1 (May 1990), p. 120-39.

1212   **Hoofbeats from the pampas.**
Gustavo Levene.   *Américas*, vol. 40, no. 6 (Nov.-Dec. 1988), p. 27-31.
Polo, invented by British cavalry officers in India, was introduced to Argentina some time between 1874 and 1876. It is the country's second most popular sport after soccer. Argentina's polo ponies (about 70,000 head) and 6,000 registered players are now the best in the world. Every November, 30,000-40,000 spectators watch the Argentine Open at the home of polo, the Cancha de la Victoria grounds in Palermo, Buenos Aires. The sport's greatest attraction is the Americas Cup, played between Argentina and the United States. Despite high earnings, it is still an amateur sport. Some of the

best ponies were raised by the late Héctor Barrantes and his wife Susan, mother of the Duchess of York. See J.-C. Suarès, 'Prime polo ponies: Hector Barrantes raises the world's best, in Argentina', *Connoisseur*, vol. 219, no. 925 (Feb. 1989), p. 66-73.

1213 **Juegos y deportes entre los indios del Río de la Plata.** (Games and sports of the Indians of the River Plate.)
Emilio Alberto Breda. Buenos Aires: Ediciones Theoria, 1962. 34p. bibliog.

An interesting miscellany of games and sports practised by the Indians of Argentina, Paraguay and Uruguay: football, *pelota*, hockey, boxing, swimming, foot-racing, horse-racing, cards, dice, children's games and games used as training for war.

1214 **Orígenes de los deportes británicos en el Río de la Plata.** (The origins of British sports in the River Plate.)
Eduardo A. Olivera. Buenos Aires: Talleres Gráficos Argentinos L. J. Rosso, 1932. 128p.

Most of Argentina's (and the world's) sports were introduced by British residents. Eight chapters describe the early contests between British sportsmen in the following sports: cricket (introduced at the time of the British invasion of 1806), soccer (the Buenos Aires Football Club was founded in 1867), rugby (also organized by the Buenos Aires Football Club and first played in 1873), rowing (1857), swimming (1863), athletics (1807), horse-racing (Buenos Aires Racing Club, 1826), polo (1874), lawn tennis (1880), golf (early 1880s) and rackets (1866).

1215 **Postal images of Argentine *próceres*: a look at selective myth-making.**
David Bushnell. *Studies in Latin American Popular Culture*, vol. 1 (1982), p. 91-105.

Examines the changing popularity of national heroes on Argentine stamps. The earliest stamps, 1858-62, featured only versions of the national shield; from 1864 to 1867 all issues bore the portrait of Bernardino Rivadavia, 'greatest of all the founders of Argentine liberalism'; San Martín and a number of other 'liberal favorites' appeared after 1867; in the twentieth century, stamp issues dedicated to liberal figures have become relatively fewer. Five anti-liberal figures have appeared, including Eva Perón. Of thirty foreign figures on Argentine stamps, the United States leads the field. The study is based on the standard Argentine stamp catalogue, *1976/77 sellos postales de la República Argentina* (Buenos Aires: Imprenta Mercur, 1976).

1216 **Soccer in Argentina: a lecture.**
Alberto Noguera. *Journal of Sport History*, vol. 13, no. 2 (summer 1986), p. 147-52.

The text of a brief but interesting lecture by the President of the San Lorenzo Soccer Club. He touches on the early amateur origins of the sport in Argentina, its professionalization in the 1930s, and some of the notable clubs. Between 1931 and 1969, five teams dominated the league: Boca Juniors and River Plate (the two great Buenos Aires rivals), Independiente and Racing Club (the next two great rival clubs, from the Avellaneda district of Buenos Aires province and San Lorenzo, Almagro suburb of Buenos Aires city). The author considers that the 1930s to the 1950s were soccer's (and the tango's) finest years; now 'violence is one reason the good days of soccer have passed'; but the media 'continue to create the mystique of national soccer' and it plays a vital role in Argentine culture, with soccer clubs acting as neighbourhood organizations. A good early history of soccer, containing annual statistics of league competitions, is Alonso Rey, *El fútbol argentino* (Buenos Aires: Ediciones Nogal, 1947. 250p.). Argentina won the World Cup in 1978 and 1986; see Colin Malam's *World Cup Argentina* (London: William Collins, 1978. 128p.).

1217   **A study of Argentine soccer: the dynamics of its fans and their folklore.**
Marcelo Mariò [sic] Suárez-Orozco.   *Journal of Psychoanalytic Anthropology*, vol. 5, no. 1 (winter 1982), p. 7-28. bibliog.
An analysis of the verbal aggression of soccer fans with a review of the literature on soccer psychology. The author also describes a 'typical journey to the soccer stadium' of Boca Juniors on a Sunday afternoon, and the 'verbal duels' of the rival fans. The Argentine soccer fan 'has plenty of anxieties to vent, especially about his masculinity'. The author makes many interesting (and unprintable) observations, concluding that other social scientists have overlooked 'the salient feature of machismo, inherent in the Argentine data, that the hypermanly macho is afraid of being homosexually attacked' by the opposing fans. A good recent study of the Argentine soccer fan is Juan José Sebreli, *Fútbol y masas* (Buenos Aires: Editorial Galerna, 1981. 198p.). The early classic is Julio Mafud, *Sociología del fútbol* (Buenos Aires: Editorial Americalee, 1967. 151p.), chiefly theoretical and with only partial references to Argentina.

1218   **Toros y toreros en el Río de la Plata.** (Bulls and bullfighters in the River Plate.)
Gori Muñoz.   Buenos Aires: Schapire, 1970. 141p. map. bibliog. (Colección Historia, 5).
The earliest reference to bullfighting in Argentina dates from 1609. This is a short history of bullrings, bullfights and bullfighters. The sport was officially banned in Argentina (and Uruguay) in 1856 but bullfights continued sporadically into the early twentieth century (there is a reference here to a *corrida* in Bahía Blanca as late as 1950).

1219   **Trout fishing in Argentina: probably the world's best.**
Jeremy Main, photographs by José Azel.   *Connoisseur*, vol. 219, no. 924 (Jan. 1989), p. 60-7. map.
Trout and salmon were introduced to Andean rivers and the Patagonian lakes from the United States and Europe in 1905. The best fishing area in Argentina is a fifty-mile-long zone of the Andean foothills centred on the ski and summer resort of San Carlos de Bariloche. This article describes the author's fishing trip which started 100 miles north of Bariloche on the Malleo river, then proceeded south to San Martín de los Andes and the Desaguadero river in Los Alerces National Park, and finished up on the river Grande and Lake San Ricardo in Tierra del Fuego.

# Libraries and Librarianship, Archives and Museums

1220 **Archivo Histórico de la Ciudad de Buenos Aires.** (The Historical Archive of the city of Buenos Aires.)
James Baer. *Latin American Research Review*, vol. 21, no. 3 (1986), p. 137-43. bibliog.

The Archive is a depository for documents dealing with the government of the capital city and 'has gathered thousands of items dealing with the day-to-day administration of Buenos Aires between 1856 and 1909', a key period in the growth of the city and the nation. The article describes the organization of the archives and lists works by twelve historians, notably James R. Scobie and Samuel L. Baily, which have made extensive use of the Archive's census information, city statistics and contemporary sources.

1221 **Bibliotecas argentinas durante la dominación hispánica.** (Libraries in Argentina during the colonial period.)
Guillermo Fúrlong Cárdiff. Buenos Aires: Editorial Huarpes, 1944. 180p. (Cultura Colonial Argentina, 1).

The introductory text (p. 13-84) is a history of colonial libraries (chiefly of religious orders and individuals) which stresses that European books were widely distributed in Argentina despite the monopoly of the Spanish Crown. The last 100 pages contain inventories of the private libraries of eight notable collectors. There is a biobibliographical sketch of Fúrlong, a prolific Jesuit intellectual historian of the River Plate area, by José Torre Revello, himself a distinguished historian and bibliographer.

1222   **Buenos Aires: la Biblioteca Nacional.** (Buenos Aires: the National
       Library.)
       Arundell Esdaile.   In: *National libraries of the world: their history,
       administration and public services.*   Completely revised by F. J.
       Hill.   London: Library Association, 1957, 2nd ed., p. 326-34. bibliog.

Describes the National Library's history and present services. The library was founded
in 1796 when the Bishop of Buenos Aires, Manuel Azamor y Ramírez, bequeathed his
'famous and costly library to the favour of the Holy Church, and for public education
and instruction'. The revolutionary government established the Biblioteca Pública in
1810; it became the Biblioteca Nacional in 1884 and moved to its present building,
originally intended for the National Lottery, in 1904.

1223   **Contribución al estudio histórico del desarrollo de los servicios
       bibliotecarios de la Argentina en el siglo XIX.** (Contribution to the
       study of the historical development of library services in Argentina
       during the nineteenth century.)
       María Angeles Sabor Riera.   Resistencia, Argentina: Universidad
       Nacional del Nordeste, Secretaría de Coordinación Popular y
       Extensión Universitaria [and] Dirección de Bibliotecas, 1974-75.
       2 vols. bibliog.

An excellent synthesis of the voluminous and frequently contradictory literature on
libraries between 1810 and 1910. The work describes the development of the National
Library and its great director Paul Groussac (1885-1929), the towering figure of
Sarmiento and his support for school and public libraries, the growth of university
libraries and the beginnings of modern librarianship before 1910. No comparable
history for twentieth-century libraries has been written.

1224   **La enseñanza de la bibliotecología en la facultad de Filosofía y Letras.**
       (The teaching of librarianship in the Faculty of Philosophy and
       Letters, University of Buenos Aires.)
       Stella Maris Fernández.   *Bibliotecología y Documentación* (Buenos
       Aires: Asociación de Bibliotecarios Graduados de la República
       Argentina), vol. 1, no. 2 (July-Dec. 1979), p. 5-30.

The first course in librarianship was run in 1909-10 but the formation of the Faculty's
School of Librarianship in 1922 'marks the beginning of systematic library education in
Argentina'. The chequered history of the school is charted through its four phases
under directors Ricardo Rojas, Augusto Raúl Cortázar, Josefa E. Sabor (see *Libraries
in Argentina*) and Roberto Juarroz (now also a famous poet). Its chief rival has been
the library school of the Museo Social Argentino, from which Carlos Víctor Penna
graduated (see *La obra bibliotecológica de Carlos Víctor Penna*). This article is
incidentally an excellent short review of twentieth-century Argentine librarianship in
general.

1225 **Evolución de la bibliotecología en la Argentina.** (The development of librarianship in Argentina.)
J. Federico Finó, Luis A. Hourcade. *Universidad* (Santa Fe), no. 25 (1952), p. 265-301.

A wide-ranging study of the development of librarianship since 1757: library literature, catalogues and bibliography, congresses and legislation, training, and institutes and associations.

1226 **Guía de bibliotecas argentinas.** (Guide to Argentine libraries.)
Compiled by Carlos Alberto Giuffra. Buenos Aires: Comisión Nacional Argentina para Unesco, Fundación Interamericana de Bibliotecología Franklin, 1967. 334p.

A total of 2,718 libraries is included: specialized (subdivided by area of interest) and general (by type: national, public, private, school, university, and so on). Within each category the libraries are further subdivided by province. Data include: address, date of founding, director, hours of opening, specialization, catalogues, cataloguing rules and classification, stock, staff, publications, and number of readers.

1227 **Guía de las bibliotecas universitarias argentinas.** (Guide to Argentine university libraries.)
Universidad Nacional del Sur [Bahía Blanca], Centro de Investigación Bibliotecológica. Buenos Aires: Casa Pardo, 1976. 3rd ed. 207p.

The latest comprehensive guide to 189 libraries in twenty-six universities, sponsored by the Junta de Bibliotecas Universitarias Nacionales (JUBIUNA). Among the information provided are size of collection, catalogues and hours of opening.

1228 **Guía de los archivos de Córdoba.** (Guide to the archives of Córdoba.)
Aurelio Z. Tanodi. Córdoba, Argentina: Universidad Nacional de Córdoba, Dirección General de Publicaciones, 1968. (Facultad de Filosofía y Humanidades. Escuela de Archiveros. Collectanea Archivistica, 3).

A survey of thirty major government, university and ecclesiastical archives in the province – mainly the city – of Córdoba: brief history, address, opening hours, catalogues and other publications. The author is founder and director of a major training school for archivists, the Centro Interamericano de Formación de Archiveros, based in the Universidad Nacional de Córdoba, which since 1974 has published the *Boletín interamericano de archivos* (from 1982 the *Anuario interamericano de archivos*).

1229 **A guide to selected diplomatic archives of South America.**
Ron L. Seckinger. *Latin American Research Review*, vol. 10, no. 1 (spring 1975), p. 127-53. bibliog.

On p. 130-2 the author describes the Archivo General de la Nación (the national archives) and Archivo General del Ministerio de Relaciones Exteriores y Culto (the foreign-office archive, whose diplomatic correspondence for 1810-60 has been transferred to the former). The information provided is: address, opening hours, admission requirements, collections, research conditions (for example, both archives are cold in winter) and useful hints.

1230  **Historia del libro y de las bibliotecas argentinas.** (A history of books
and libraries in Argentina.)
Nicanor Sarmiento.   Buenos Aires: Imprenta Luis Veggia, 1930.
158p.
This is predominantly a history of libraries to 1929, with references to printing,
publishing and bibliography. The second half of the book mostly describes twentieth-
century library associations and congresses; the author was President of the Asociación
Nacional de Bibliotecarios.

1231  **Latin America in basic historical collections: a working guide.**
Russell H. Bartley, Stuart L. Wagner.   Stanford, California: Hoover
Institution Press, 1972. 217p. bibliog. (Hoover Institution
Bibliographical Series, 51).
A publication providing researchers 'with concise descriptive statements and
bibliography on major archives, libraries and special collections germane to the study
of Latin American history'. The section on Argentina, p. 70-1, describes the Archivo
General de la Nación, Biblioteca Nacional, Biblioteca del Congreso, Museo Mitre,
Museo Histórico and archives in Córdoba and Mendoza.

1232  **Libraries in Argentina.**
Josefa E. Sabor, translated by Savina Roxas.   In: *Encyclopedia of
library and information science.*   Edited by Allen Kent, Harold
Lancour.   New York: Marcel Dekker, 1968, vol. 1, p. 520-9.
bibliog.
A concise history of libraries and librarianship by a distinguished Argentine librarian:
early development (including nineteenth-century national bibliographies), the present-
day library situation (structure, library education, library literature, research and
professional associations), the development of documentation centres, and future
prospects.

1233  **Museología argentina: guía de instituciones y museos.** (A guide to the
museums of Argentina.)
Adolfo Enrique Rodríguez.   Buenos Aires: Colegio de Museólogos
de la República Argentina, 1978. 2nd ed. 248p.
A directory of 419 national, provincial, municipal and private museums, arranged by
province and then by city or town, indicating address, date of foundation, dependency,
major collecting areas and director. Also mentioned are a number of related
institutions such as professional associations and training schools.

1234  **The Museum of the City of Buenos Aires: art fairs, wedding gowns and
chamber pots.**
Virginia W. Leonard.   *Studies in Latin America Popular Culture,*
vol. 5 (1986), p. 163-71.
The primary role of the Museum (founded 1968) is to 'preserve the architectural
landmarks [notably Beaux-Arts pieces] of the Southern and Northern Cathedral districts
of Buenos Aires', in which it is located. The director is a professional architect. The
Museum is also dedicated to the popular culture of the city, and it organizes a Sunday

flea market, a crafts fair and an arts fair, sponsors art competitions and conducts guided tours. The article gives examples of recent exhibitions, including (hence the title) wedding dresses and chamber pots. There are eleven illustrations.

1235 **The National Library of Argentina.**
Horació H. Hernández. In: *Encyclopedia of library and information science.* Edited by Allen Kent. New York; Basel, Switzerland: Marcel Dekker, 1985, vol. 39, supplement 4, p. 48-52.

The author, a director of the National Library in the early 1980s, describes its early history, present administration and services, and the new building which has been under construction for the past twenty years.

1236 **La obra bibliotecológica de Carlos Víctor Penna.** (The library career of Carlos Víctor Penna.)
Horacio Jorge Becco. San Miguel de Tucumán, Argentina: Universidad Nacional de Tucumán, Biblioteca Central, 1981. 62p. bibliog. (Cuadernos Ciencia de la Documentación. Serie 3: La Bibliografía, no. 2).

Penna is the greatest figure in Argentine international librarianship. He first came to prominence as the head of library studies in the Museo Social Argentino (1942), but he 'was essentially made for international work' and in 1951 he joined Unesco as director of its Centro Regional en el Hemisferio Occidental (Havana), which in 1954 created the famous Pilot Public Library for Latin America, in Medellín, Colombia. In 1964 Penna became head of Unesco's Libraries Division and in 1967 established a mobile Curso Audiovisual de Bibliotecología, which reached out to provincial librarians in a number of countries, including Argentina. Penna retired in 1971 and became an international consultant.

1237 **Regional research in Argentina: a critical evaluation of the archives and libraries of Mendoza province.**
William. J. Fleming. *The Americas*, vol. 35, no. 1 (July 1978), p. 110-20, 131.

Describes the collections and facilities of thirteen major and minor libraries and archives 'in or near the city center of Mendoza', and assesses their research potential for historians of the colonial and national periods.

1238 **Repertorio de bibliotecas especializadas y centros de información.**
(Directory of special libraries and information centres.)
Buenos Aires: Secretaría de Planeamiento, Dirección General de Coordinación Administrativa, Area Biblioteca, 1979. 89p.

Gives essential information on 748 libraries, including certain libraries of an encyclopaedic and general nature such as the National Library and university central libraries, arranged by province and city. There are indexes by institution, subject and library publications.

1239  **World guide to library schools and training courses in documentation / Guide mondial des écoles de bibliothécaires et documentalistes.**
London: Bingley; Paris: Unesco, 1981. 2nd ed. 549p.

The section on Argentina, p. 18-35, lists fourteen library schools (four in the city of Buenos Aires, two more in the province of Buenos Aires, two in Córdoba, and one each in the Chaco, Misiones, San Juan and Santa Fe). The data supplied are: address, date of founding, level of teaching, qualifications awarded, admission requirements, length of course, teaching staff, and library. The text is in French.

# Books and Publishing

1240 **Argentina: climbing back.**
Herbert R. Lottman. *Publishers' Weekly*, vol. 237, no. 7 (16 Feb. 1990), p. 33-43.

There is 'evidence of a return to stability in the book trade and a new optimism among publishers, who are learning how to survive in a crisis. Some of them are on their way to becoming market leaders, not only in their own country but throughout the Spanish-speaking world'. The article features a number of major publishers: Emecé, Sudamericana, Javier Vergara, Ediciones de la Flor, Atlántida, Sigmar (a children's publisher), Médica Panamericana (medical) and El Ateneo (which has a large bookstore on Florida Street in the heart of Buenos Aires). The sixteenth annual Buenos Aires International Book Fair was held in April 1990. See also the same author's 'Argentina: a book world, a world away', *Publishers' Weekly*, vol. 220, no. 12 (18 Sept. 1981), p. 100-13, 116-19.

1241 **La ciudad y los libros: excursión bibliográfica al pasado porteño.** (The city and the books: a bibliographical excursion to old Buenos Aires.)
Rafael Alberto Arrieta. Buenos Aires: Librería del Colegio, 1955. 207p. bibliog.

A nostalgic, discursive look at the world of publishing and books in nineteenth-century Buenos Aires – the Biblioteca Pública (the early National Library), publishers, bookshops, literary salons, private libraries and the literary generation of 1880. A good selective bibliography is included.

1242 **Desarrollo de la industria editorial argentina.** (The development of the publishing industry in Argentina.)
Eustasio Antonio García.    Buenos Aires: Fundación Interamericana de Bibliotecología Franklin, 1965. 186p. bibliog.

Combines a detailed history of the book trade from 1601 to 1964 (p. 43-54, 131-53) with a good statistical overview of the present state of the industry. In 1964 there were some 280 establishments associated with publishing, 160 of them commercial publishers, and about 1,500 bookshops throughout the country. In 1962, 3,323 book titles were published, just behind Mexico but a long way behind Brazil. García stresses the beneficial impact of the Spanish Civil War which drove a number of dynamic publishers to Argentina (see *Spanish immigration in Argentina*). The years 1936-47 saw the foundation of the Sociedad de Editores Argentinos (1938), the first national Book Fair (1943) and the first publishing legislation. He ends with the hope that a national 'book law' will soon be introduced.

1243 **La edición de libros en Argentina.** (Book publishing in Argentina.)
Raúl H. Bottaro.    Buenos Aires: Editorial Troquel, 1964. 103p. bibliog.

A study of the recent history of publishing since 1943 and an analysis of current book production (compared also with that of other countries), the competition from other mass media, the domestic and international book market, the lack of official protection given to the industry (the author cites piracy, copyright and paper production) and the need for a publishing law.

1244 **Libreros, editores e impresores de Buenos Aires: esbozo para una historia del libro argentino.** (Booksellers, publishers and printers in Buenos Aires: a brief history of books in Argentina.)
Domingo Buonocore.    Buenos Aires: Bowker Editores, 1974. 260p. bibliog.

An affectionate dip into the past, by a distinguished former librarian and bibliographer, reprinted from the 1944 edition published by El Ateneo. The title says it all. There is a name index.

1245 **La politique de l'édition du livre en Argentine.** (The policy of book publishing in Argentina.)
Pierre Lagarde.    Toulouse, France: Service de Publications de l'Université de Toulouse – Le Mirail, 1981. 226p. bibliog. (Travaux de l'Université de Toulouse – Le Mirail. Série A, Tome XV-1980).

The most up-to-date work on the history of publishing (to 1977, emphasizing the twentieth century), the present structure of the industry (including printing and the question of copyright), the marketing of books, and publishing legislation. He confines his study to the major commercial houses (Editorial de la Universidad de Buenos Aires, Centro Editor de América Latina, Losada, Sudamericana, Emecé and Paidós). Legislation is analysed in some detail, and the text of the proposed 'ley del libro' (book law), in gestation since 1973, is given.

1246 **Recent Jewish publishing in Argentina: a mixed blessing.**
Barry Walfish. *Judaica Librarianship*, vol. 4 no. 1 (fall 1987 – winter 1988), p. 62-7. bibliog.

A steady stream of works on the Jewish community of Argentina (which celebrated its centenary in 1988) has been appearing since the restoration of democracy in 1983. Many of the works are in Yiddish. The author, a librarian at the University of Toronto, analyses these recent materials from the point of view of acquisition by a library, criticizing the poor quality of reproduction, paper and binding. Finally, he lists sixty-five recent Yiddish works published in Argentina and recommends Argentine and other Latin American book dealers who export Judaica.

**Historia del libro y de las bibliotecas argentinas.**
*See* item no. 1230.

# Mass Media and Censorship

1247 **Academic press censorship under military and civilian regimes: the Argentine and Brazilian cases, 1964-1975.**
Peter T. Johnson. *Luso-Brazilian Review*, vol. 15, no. 1 (summer 1978), p. 3-35.
Describes censorship under the three military régimes of Onganía, Levingston and Lanusse, and the civilian régimes of Illia, Cámpora, and the two Peróns. The scholarly presses of both countries experienced 'controlled as well as relatively free conditions' under both types of régime. The Onganía years probably affected scholarship and publishing the most. In the absence of legal censorship, publishers resorted to various forms of self-censorship. The article is slightly stronger on Brazilian examples.

1248 **Argentina: Perón's legacy of censorship.**
Marvin Alisky. In: *Latin American media: guidance and censorship.* Edited by Marvin Alisky. Ames, Iowa: Iowa State Univesity Press, 1981, p. 166-91. map. bibliog.
Argentina enjoyed press and broadcasting freedom for decades before 1943. Perón 'left a negative imprint upon the public life of Argentina both politically and journalistically'. After 1955 the media were not interfered with but the 'surrounding economic and political chaos inhibited editors into degrees of self-censorship'. The military governments made censorship official from 1966 to 1973. Under Perón and his widow, 1973-76, the media were technically free; after 1976 the military government again stifled press freedom.

1249 **Argentine literary journalism: the production of a critical discourse.**
Francine Masiello. *Latin American Research Review*, vol. 20, no. 1 (1985), p. 27-60.
Discusses selected Argentine literary reviews of the independent Left, during four periods after 1945: the early avant-garde (*Nosotros*, *Sur*, *Martín Fierro* and *Proa*), the 'artistic subjectivity' of the 1950s (*Centro*, *Ciudad* and *Contorno*), the 'breakdown of

359

the writer's authority' in the 1960s (*Hoy en la Cultura, El Escarabajo de Oro, Nuevos Aires* and *La Gaceta Literaria*), and the 'death of the author', 1970-74 (*Nuevos Aires* again and *Los Libros*).

1250 **Censura, autoritarismo y cultura: Argentina, 1960-1983.** (Censorship, authoritarianism and culture: Argentina, 1960-1983.)
Andrés Avellaneda. Buenos Aires: Centro Editor de América Latina, 1986. 2 vols. (Biblioteca Política Argentina).

A chronology, reproducing original documents, which traces the permeation of censorship through all the media of communication (especially journalism, literature, cinema, the theatre and popular song), from 1960 to 1983. The work is based extensively on extracts from daily newspapers, notably *La Nación* and *La Prensa*.

1251 **Content analysis of news in three Argentine dailies.**
Paul R. Hoopes. *Journalism Quarterly*, vol. 43, no. 3 (autumn 1966), p. 534-7.

Analyses the treatment of foreign news in Argentina's 'prestige dailies', *La Prensa, La Nación* and the *Buenos Aires Herald*, from 1 November 1963 to 31 January 1964, and finds that all three, and especially the *Herald*, printed more foreign news than comparable United States and other Latin American newspapers.

1252 **Defense of freedom.**
Editors of *La Prensa*. London; New York: T. V. Boardman, 1952. 315p.

*La Prensa*, founded in 1869, is Argentina's oldest surviving daily newspaper. It was expropriated by President Juan Domingo Perón in 1951 and not returned to its owners until 1955. Part one of this book describes the history of the newspaper and the steps taken by Perón to destroy its outspokenness. Part two consists of twenty-six editorials printed in the newspaper between 1934 and 1951 on the general subject of freedom of the press.

1253 **Magazines & masks: *Caras y Caretas* as a reflection of Buenos Aires, 1898-1908.**
Howard M. Fraser. Tempe, Arizona: Arizona State University, Center for Latin American Studies, 1987. 257p. bibliog.

*Caras y Caretas* was Argentina's 'most popular family magazine' at the turn of the century. It combined current affairs with social notes, satirical humour, poetry, fiction and essays. This is an anthology, with a good introduction, of facsimile photographs and other material selected from over 2,110 issues between 1898 and 1908, reflecting 'the flowering of Buenos Aires' during the Belle Epoque.

1254 **Media and politics in Latin America: the struggle for democracy.**
Edited by Elizabeth Fox. London; Newbury Park, California;
Beverly Hills, California; New Delhi: Sage Publications, 1988. 193p.
bibliog. (Communication and Human Values).

Three chapters are of Argentine interest: Elizabeth Fox, 'Nationalism, censorship and transnational control', p. 36-44 (all media, 1880-1979); Heriberto Muraro, 'Dictatorship and transition to democracy: Argentina 1973-86', p. 116-24; and Oscar Landi, 'Media, cultural processes and political systems', p. 138-47 (the end of the military régime and Alfonsín).

1255 **Organizational mortality in the newspaper industries of Argentina and Ireland: an ecological approach.**
Glenn R. Carroll, Jacques Delacroix. *Administrative Science Quarterly*, vol. 27, no. 2 (June 1982), p. 169-98. bibliog.

An analysis of the survival of nineteenth-century Argentine and Irish newspapers according to their age and in the context of the 'social environment', which finds that they were more likely to close down in their early stages. The theme is developed in the same authors' 'Organizational foundings: an ecological study of the newspaper industries of Argentina and Ireland', in a later issue of the same journal, vol. 28, no. 2 (June 1983), p. 274-91.

1256 **El periodismo argentino: amplia y documentada historia desde sus orígenes hasta el presente.** (Argentine journalism: a complete, documentary history from its origins to the present day.)
C. Galván Moreno. Buenos Aires: Editorial Claridad, 1944. 520p.
bibliog. (Biblioteca de Escritores Argentinos. Obras de Autores Clásicos y Contemporáneos, 14).

The best history of Argentine newspapers and journalism, from colonial times to the 1940s. Good on provincial newspapers but stronger on Buenos Aires titles. Describes legislation, news agencies and relationships with other communications media. Two other solid histories of journalism, also published during the 1940s, are: Juan Rómulo Fernández, *Historia del periodismo argentino* (Buenos Aires: Talleres Gráficos de Macagno, Landa y Cía, 1943. 405p.); and Oscar R. Beltrán, *Historia del periodismo argentino: pensamiento y obra de los forjadores de la patria* (Buenos Aires: Editorial Sopena Argentina, 1943. 359p.).

1257 **The press in Argentina, 1973-8; with additional material for 1979-81.**
Andrew Graham-Yooll. London: Writers and Scholars Educational Trust, distributed by *Index on Censorship*, 1984. 184p.

A day-by-day chronology of the Argentine press and its efforts to preserve 'liberal values in times of political and economic crisis', May 1973–December 1981. The chapters for 1973-78 are reprinted without change from the first edition (1979). An appendix lists political publications on sale in Buenos Aires, 1973-76. The historical introduction is by Walter Little.

1258 **Radiodifusión en la Argentina.** (Radio in Argentina.)
Jorge Eduardo Noguer. Buenos Aires: Editorial Bien Común, 1985.
543p. bibliog.

A history of radio in Argentina. See also Washington Duranga, José María Pasquini Durán, *Precisiones sobre la radio a partir de casos en Argentina* (Buenos Aires: Ediciones Paulinas, 1988. 222p.), a call for the introduction of national radio legislation with case-studies of the organization and broadcast output of eight radio stations in the provinces of Buenos Aires, Córdoba, Chaco, Corrientes and Santiago del Estero.

1259 **Las revistas literarias argentinas, 1893-1967.** (Argentine literary reviews, 1893-1967.)
Héctor René Lafleur, Sergio D. Provenzano, Fernando P. Alonso.
Buenos Aires: Centro Editor de América Latina, 1969. 2nd ed. 351p.
(Biblioteca de Literatura. Literatura Argentina. Obras de Referencia).

A detailed history of literary reviews (and generations) during four periods: the 'first vanguard' (1893-1914), the 'new generation' (1915-30), the 1940s and the 1950s. A directory section in each chapter lists each review's directors, dates of publication and chief contributors. Twenty-four plates reproduce some of the journals' covers.

1260 **The role of two newspapers in the assimilation of Italians in Buenos Aires and São Paulo, 1893-1913.**
Samuel L. Baily. *International Migration Review*, vol. 12, no. 3 (fall 1978), p. 321-40.

Both cities had 'so many Italian language newspapers of every conceivable type'. This is an evaluation of two with the largest circulation and generally acknowledged to be the most influential: *La Patria degli Italiani* of Buenos Aires and *Fanfulla* of São Paulo. *La Patria*, whose predecessor was founded in 1876, was a 'liberal, anti-clerical, and moderately anti-monarchist' morning daily with a maximum circulation of 40,000, making it the third-largest newspaper of any kind in Argentina. Both papers campaigned against the social assimilation of Italian immigrants within their host communities.

1261 **The Socialist press in turn-of-the-century Argentina.**
Richard J. Walter. *The Americas*, vol. 37, no. 1 (July 1980), p. 1-24.

Surveys the best-known, most widely distributed and most influential Socialist newspapers of the period: *La Vanguardia*, *El Obrero* and *La Montaña*. *La Vanguardia*, founded in 1895, became the official organ of Argentina's Socialist Party, formed the following year. *El Obrero* (1890-92) was the 'first publication to introduce and to apply Marxist ideas systematically to Argentine conditions'. *La Montaña* (founded 1897) was famed for its 'relentless and sometimes ruthless' attacks on the Party's national leadership.

1262   **The sound of one hand clapping: a preliminary study of the Argentine press in a time of terror.**
Robert Cox.   Washington, DC: Woodrow Wilson International Center for Scholars, 1980. 28p. (Latin American Program. Working Paper, 83).

An unbiased consideration of the press, mainly since 1976, by a former editor of the *Buenos Aires Herald*, which discusses the principle of press freedom and Argentina's history of censorship since 1943, the 'crucial breakdown' in press responsibility under the Peróns, and the conduct of the press during the 'dirty war' after 1976. 'With a few honourable exceptions' (the *Herald*, *La Prensa*, Jacobo Timerman's *La Opinión* – see item no. 623 – and some provincial newspapers), Argentine newspapers failed to speak out against human-rights violations by both the guerrillas and the military.

1263   **A state of fear: memories of Argentina's nightmare.**
Andrew Graham-Yooll.   London: Eland; New York: Hippocrene Books, 1986. bibliog.

The author was for ten years news editor of the *Buenos Aires Herald* until forced into exile in England. His book, first published as *Portrait of an exile* (London: Junction Books, 1981), is an account of the often terrifying experience of being an investigative reporter during the early years of the military backlash against left-wing terrorism.

1264   **25 años de TV argentina.** (Twenty-five years of television in Argentina.)
Gregorio Santos Hernando.   Buenos Aires: Editorial Herpa, 1977. 357p.

A detailed, chronological history of the development of television in Argentina. A national Television Centre was established in 1930, just three years after the invention of the medium, and the first experimental broadcasts begun. However, it was not until 1944 that a closed-circuit programme was beamed to a small number of receivers. The first official broadcasts began at the end of 1951. The book ends in 1976, before the introduction of colour television in time for the relaying of the World Cup in 1978.

1265   **The wild oats they sowed: Latin American exiles in Europe.**
Andrew Graham-Yooll.   *Third World Quarterly*, vol. 9, no. 1 (Jan. 1987), p. 246-53.

An examination of the publications of Argentine (and a few Uruguayan and Chilean) journalists and writers exiled in Europe (chiefly Spain) after 1976. Despite the title, there is much interesting information on Argentine exile journalism in Mexico and Venezuela, including the account of a heated debate between an exiled journalist and a novelist who had stayed in Argentina on whether or not exiles were privileged and should return.

# Encyclopaedias, Directories and Biographical Dictionaries

## Encyclopaedias and directories

1266 **The Americas review.**
Saffron Walden, England: World of Information; Edison, New Jersey: Hunter Publishing, 1979- . annual.

This economic and business report has undergone three changes of title; it was last called *Latin America & Caribbean review*. The chapter on Argentina has been contributed by Jimmy Burns of the *Financial Times* since 1985. It occupies pages 23-9 of the 1990 edition: a review of the current political and economic situation, a country profile (political system, main cities and towns, media, external trade, agriculture, industry, energy, membership of international organizations), a two-page business guide (practical guidance on entry requirements, transport, telecommunications, banking), and a business guide (hotels, car hire, useful organizations).

1267    **Argentina: a chronology and fact book, 1516-1973.**
Compiled and edited by Russell H. Fitzgibbon.    Dobbs Ferry, New
York: Oceana Publications, 1974. 148p. bibliog. (World Chronology
Series).

The historical chronology is on pages 1-28. A series of documents is reproduced on
pages 29-129: extracts from foreign travel writing (Darwin, Caldcleugh, Koebel and
others), the writings of nineteenth-century statesmen (Mitre, Sarmiento), and
twentieth-century official documents (for example, the 1944 GOU [United Officers'
Group] manifesto, and extracts from the 'Blue Book'). The appendices list national
rulers since 1810, seventeen eminent Argentines, and area and population statistics.

1268    **Argentina and Perón, 1970-75.**
Edited by Lester A. Sobel.    New York: Facts on File, 1975. 167p.
map.

Compiled from Facts on File's weekly coverage of world events, this is a chronology,
by year and several main themes, of the period 'just preceding Perón's return, the brief
interval of his resumption of power, the events surrounding his death and the period
that followed when his widow succeeded him as president and tried to rule an
increasingly disturbed nation'. Name and subject indexes are included.

1269    **De Perón a Videla.** (From Perón to Videla.)
Andrew Graham-Yooll.    Buenos Aires: Editorial Legasa, 1989. 557p.

This is a detailed chronology of the period from 19 September 1955 (when Perón was
ousted) and 31 March 1976 (when the last military junta seized power – an appendix
reproduces its early communiqués). Further appendices list some cabinet ministers
1955-76, victims of political violence 1975, a chronology of journalism and the press
1973-76 (see also item no. 1257) and representative political journals and newspapers
1973-76. See also Alonso Gerardo López, *1930-1980, cincuenta años de historia
argentina: una cronología básica* (Buenos Aires: Editorial de Belgrano, 1982. 414p.),
which covers the period from General Uriburu's coup of 6 September 1930 to a year
later than the title indicates, the beginning of General Galtieri's administration on
22 December 1981.

1270    **Diccionario histórico argentino.** (Historical dictionary of Argentina.)
Edited by Ricardo Piccirilli, Francisco L. Romay, Leoncio Gianello.
Buenos Aires: Ediciones Históricas Argentinas, 1953-54. 6 vols.
bibliog.

A well-written and accurate dictionary, predominantly biographical but also covering
administrative titles, events, places, organizations, religion, folklore, plants, and many
other subjects. There are full cross-references and most entries, usually one page in
length, have a short bibliography appended. However, the work is not illustrated.

**Encyclopaedias, Directories and Biographical Dictionaries.**
Encyclopaedias and directories

1271 **Enciclopedia de la literatura argentina.** (Encyclopaedia of Argentine literature.)
Edited by Pedro Orgambide, Roberto Yahni. Buenos Aires: Editorial Sudamericana, 1970. 639p.

A reliable source of information on authors. There are entries under the titles of classic works (*Amalia*, *Martín Fierro*, etc.) but the choice of entries under themes and movements is inconsistent. Also useful is the earlier *Diccionario de la literatura latinoamericana: Argentina* (Washington, DC: Pan American Union, 1960-61. 2 vols). For translations see Jason Wilson, *An A-Z of modern Latin American literature in English translation* (London: University of London, Institute of Latin American Studies, 1989. 95p.).

1272 **The Falkland Islands dispute in international law and politics: a documentary sourcebook.**
Raphael Perl, with an historic chronology and bibliography by Everette E. Larson. London; Rome; New York: Oceana Publications, 1983. 722p. map. bibliog.

The introduction, p. 1-85, considers the theory of acquisition and loss of territory under customary international law; British, Argentine and United States policy on sovereignty over the Falkland Islands; recent historical precedents and a historical chronology. The texts of fifty-two documents are then reproduced, from the papal bull of Alexander VI (1493) to the Resolution of the United Nations General Assembly (November 1982). Documents 24-51 are from the period April-November 1982.

1273 **Gran enciclopedia argentina.** (Grand encyclopaedia of Argentina.)
Edited by Diego Abad de Santillán. Buenos Aires: Ediar Soc. Anon. Editores, 1956-64. 9 vols. maps. bibliog.

Subtitled 'everything on Argentina, arranged alphabetically: geography and history, place names, biography, science, arts, literature, law, economy, industry and commerce, institutions, flora and fauna, folklore and local terms'. There are many illustrations, some in colour.

1274 **Guerrilla and terrorist organisations: a world bibliography and directory.**
Peter Janke, with Richard Sim. Brighton, England: Harvester Press, 1983. 531p. map. bibliog.

The section on Argentina, p. 419-30, contains a two-page introduction followed by a directory of ten guerrilla groups active between 1963 and 1976, from the Alianza Anticomunista Argentina to the Brigadas Rojas del Poder Obrero. Most space is devoted to the best-known groups, the Montoneros and the Ejército Revolucionario del Pueblo. See also Charles A. Russell, James F. Schenkel, James A. Miller, 'Urban guerrillas in Argentina: a select bibliography', *Latin American Research Review*, vol. 9, no. 3 (1974), p. 53-92.

1275  **Historical dictionary of Argentina.**
Ione S. Wright, Lisa M. Nekhom.  Metuchen, New Jersey;
Scarecrow Press, 1978. 1113p. maps. bibliog. (Latin American
Historical Dictionaries, no. 17).

Easily the biggest and best of Scarecrow Press's series of Latin American historical dictionaries, with about 3,000 entries covering historical figures, events, organizations and concepts, but not ignoring other aspects of Argentine culture such as geography, literature, folklore and education. An Argentine translation, *Diccionario histórico argentino*, with revisions by Fernando Ruiz, was published by Emecé in 1990.

1276  **Latin America: a guide to illustrations.**
A. Curtis Wilgus.  Metuchen, New Jersey; London: Scarecrow Press,
1981. 250p. bibliog.

A useful reference-aid to illustrations on Latin American themes in 'comparatively recent – and hence readily available' encyclopaedias, books and periodicals. References to the River Plate and Argentina are listed under historical period and relate to archaeology, environment, politics, cities/towns/villages, society, culture, religion, economy, transport and communications, and miscellaneous.

1277  **Latin America and Caribbean contemporary record.**
New York; London: Holmes & Meier, 1983- . annual.

Part one of volume five, covering 1985-86, edited by Abraham F. Lowenthal and published in 1988, contains eleven general essays on current issues. In part two, the country-by-country review, 'Argentina' by Gary W. Wynia (p. B3-B21), contains a political-economic review of the period (Austral Plan, congressional elections of November 1985, labour politics, the future of Peronism, human rights, foreign policy and future prospects), and a statistical profile.

1278  **Latin American economic and social serials.**
Committee on Latin America (COLA).  London: Clive Bingley;
Hamden, Connecticut: Archon Books, 1969. 189p.

The first of three directories of Latin American serials, together with their locations in selected libraries in the United Kingdom, compiled by a committee of British librarians. This lists 122 Argentine titles. COLA produced two further guides: *Latin American history with politics – a serials list*, edited by C. J. Koster (Farnborough, England: Gregg International Publishers, 1973. 165p.), listing 138 Argentine titles; and *Literature with language, art and music*, edited by Laurence Hallewell (London: COLA, 1977. 152p.), listing 197 Argentine titles. See also the *Historical periodicals directory. Vol. 4: Latin America and the West Indies*, edited by Eric H. Boehm, Barbara H. Pope and Marie S. Ensign (Santa Barbara, California; Denver, Colorado; Oxford; ABC-Clio, 1985. 157p.), which registers details of 220 Argentine periodicals in the field of history 'in its broadest sense'. The firm of Fernando García Cambeiro (Cochabamba 244, 1150 Buenos Aires), recommended as a supplier for all Argentine publications, occasionally produces a useful checklist of selected current serials.

**Encyclopaedias, Directories and Biographical Dictionaries.**
Encyclopaedias and directories

1279 **Latin American newspapers in United States libraries: a union list.**
Compiled by Steven M. Charno. Austin, Texas; London: University
of Texas Press for the Conference on Latin American History, 1968.
619p.
Lists a total of 5,000 Latin American newspapers held by seventy libraries with Latin
American or area-studies collections. Nearly 300 Argentine titles are listed alphabetically under thirty-nine cities and towns. Data for each title are periodicity, date of
founding, occasional supplementary note, and citation of library holdings.

1280 **Latin American serial documents: a holdings list. Volume 5: Argentina.**
Compiled by Rosa Quintero Mesa. New York; London: R. R.
Bowker, 1971. 693p. bibliog.
An alphabetical catalogue of 'as many serial documents as could be identified':
publications of the judicial, executive and legislative branches, national museums,
national libraries, national universities, agricultural experiment stations and govern-
ment-financed autonomous agencies. Excluded are newspapers, publications of inter-
American or international organizations, and publications of scientific and cultural
institutions independent of national government. Holdings statements are given for
eighteen United States and Canadian libraries, including the Library of Congress and
New York Public Library.

1281 **Political parties of the Americas: Canada, Latin America, and the West
Indies.**
Edited by Robert J. Alexander. Westport, Connecticut; London:
Greenwood Press, 1982. 2 vols. bibliog. (Greenwood Historical
Encyclopedia of the World's Political Parties).
The chapter on Argentina, by John T. Deiner (vol. 1, p. 52-89), provides a useful
twelve-page historical sketch of the 'role' and 'range' of political parties and the
Peronist movement, and an alphabetical directory of thirty-four parties under their
English names, with cross-references from Spanish names and merged parties. See also
Ciarán O'Maoláin (ed.), *Latin American political movements* (Harlow, England:
Longman; New York: Facts on File, 1985. 287p.), a directory of information on forty-
three Argentine political parties and alliances, guerrilla movements, pressure groups
and 'other legal and illegal organizations currently active'.

1282 **Primer directorio de fundaciones de la República Argentina / First
Argentine foundation directory.**
Buenos Aires: Fundación José María Aragón, 1980. 277p. bibliog.
Includes a total of 581 private or semi-private foundations, most of them founded since
1960, arranged by province; two-thirds (397) are in the federal capital and a further
fifty-three in the province of Buenos Aires. Each entry gives the organization's
address, date of registration, purpose, activities, financial data and board members.
There is a subject index to area of activity: general (64 entities), community
development and assistance (159), education (122), research (186), health (64), art and
culture (76), religion (35), sports and tourism (11) and wildlife and pet protection (2).
A table lists the top twenty-five foundations in terms of net assets; a supplement
listing 227 new and amended entries was published in 1982.

1283 **Publicaciones periódicas argentinas registradas para el Sistema Internacional de Datos sobre Publicaciones Seriadas (ISDS).**
(Argentine serials registered with the ISDS.)
Buenos Aires: Consejo Nacional de Investigaciones Científicas y Técnicas, Centro Argentino de Información Científica y Tecnológica, 1981. 217p.

Contains minimal data on 1,457 titles which have been registered with the International Serials Data System and allocated International Standard Serial Numbers. A first supplement recording amendments and 340 new titles was published in 1983. Also useful is Eduardo F. Ferreira Sobral, *Publicaciones periódicas argentinas, 1781-1969. Tomo 1* (Buenos Aires: Ministerio de Agricultura y Ganadería, 1971. 771p.), providing basic information on 9,081 titles of all types.

1284 **South America, Central America and the Caribbean 1991.**
London: Europa Publications, 1990. 3rd ed. 702p. maps. bibliog.

The section on Argentina (p. 51-77) begins with summaries of the history and economy of the country by Harold Blakemore, revised by Guillermo Makin and Sue Cunningham respectively. This is followed by a five-page statistical survey and the detailed directory under these headings: constitution, government, legislature, political organizations, diplomatic representation, judicial system, religion, press, publishers, radio and television, finance, trade and industry, transport, tourism, power (including atomic power), defence and education.

1285 **The world of learning 1991.**
London: Europa Publications, 1990. 41st edition. 1987p.

The directory for Argentina, p. 52-70, provides vital information on the following types of organizations: academies, learned societies, research institutes, libraries and archives, museums, national and private universities, colleges, and schools of art and music.

# Biographical dictionaries

1286 **Argentines of to-day.**
Edited by William Belmont Parker. New York: Hispanic Society of America, 1920. 2 vols. (Hispanic Notes and Monographs, vol. 5).

A dictionary of 420 'representative' people born after 1850 and alive in 1920, selected from all parts of the country and from all classes and professions: 'thus artists, authors, statesmen, soldiers, sailors, merchants, clergymen, teachers and men of affairs are all to be found here'. Printed in large, attractive type with a photograph of most subjects. The entries are in no logical order, but there is an alphabetical index at the end of volume two. There is a later reprint (New York: Kraus Reprint Corporation, 1967).

**Encyclopaedias, Directories and Biographical Dictionaries.**
Biographical dictionaries

1287 **Diccionario biográfico argentino.** (Biographical dictionary of
Argentina.)
Enrique Udaondo. Buenos Aires: Imprenta y Casa Editora 'Coni',
1938. 1151p.

A publication sponsored by the Institución Mitre, containing 3,200 entries for
personalities active 1800-1920, complementing the same compiler's *Diccionario
biográfico colonial argentino* (Buenos Aires: Editorial Huarpes, 1945. 980p.), which
covers the colonial period to 1810. Udaondo collaborated with others to produce
*Grandes hombres de nuestra patria* (Buenos Aires: Editorial Pleamar, 1968. 3 vols),
consisting of over 300 biographies of 'military men, journalists, doctors, lawyers,
writers, sportsmen, scientists and priests'; printed in good-size type with many
portraits. Jacinto R. Yaben's *Biografías argentinas y sudamericanas* (Buenos Aires:
Editorial 'Metropólis', 1938-40. 5 vols) contains mostly military and naval biographies.

1288 **Diccionario biográfico de mujeres argentinas.** (Biographical dictionary
of Argentine women.)
Lily Sosa de Newton. Buenos Aires: Editorial Plus Ultra, 1986.
3rd ed. 716p. bibliog.

This enlarged and updated edition provides biographical accounts and anecdotal
information on some 1,700 famous Argentine women, past and present, from all walks
of life, but chiefly artists, educationalists, professionals, and the wives, mothers, sisters
or daughters of famous men.

1289 **Diccionario biográfico de políticos argentinos.** (Biographical dictionary
of Argentine politicians.)
Germinal Nogués. Buenos Aires: Grupo Editorial Planeta, 1989.
245p. bibliog.

This dictionary was compiled partly through a questionnaire survey of over 650
biographees active between 1930 and 1989. Although some of the important
contemporary political names are here (Menem, Alfonsín, the Peróns), many previous
presidents are conspicuously absent, and the value of this dictionary lies in the
numerous less well-known figures included.

1290 **Diccionario biográfico del campo argentino.** (Biographical dictionary of
the Argentine countryside.)
Jorge Newton. Buenos Aires: The author, 1972. 436p.

Published to complement the compiler's (with his wife Lily Sosa de Newton) *Historia
de la Sociedad Rural en el centenario de su fundación* (Buenos Aires: Editorial y
Librería Goncourt, 1966. 381p.), this provides information on the 'men who most
influenced the development of agricultural and livestock activities' in Argentina:
principally *hacendados*, *ganaderos*, colonizers, and presidents and other officials of
rural societies.

1291   **Diccionario biográfico italo-argentino.** (Biographical dictionary of Italian-Argentines.)
Dionisio Petriella, Sara Sosa Miatello.   Buenos Aires: Asociación Dante Alighieri, 1976. 771p. bibliog.

Contains 1,186 biographies of native-born Italians and first-generation Argentines of Italian parentage who have made a noteworthy contribution to national life. There is an index by profession. See also Petriella's *Los italianos en la historia de la cultura argentina* (Buenos Aires: Asociación Dante Alighieri, 1979. 365p.), which includes biographical entries on a further 330 names.

1292   **Index to Spanish American collective biography.**
Sara de Mundo Lo.   Boston, Massachusetts: G. K. Hall, 1981-85. 4 vols.

A handbook of 'general biographical dictionaries, specialized biographical dictionaries for fields or professions . . . and general and subject encyclopedias', indicating locations in selected United States and Canadian libraries. Volume four, 'The River Plate Republics' (1985, 388p.), records 934 annotated entries for Argentina, p. 3-156, in thirty-three subject areas from aeronautics to women. There are indexes by author, short title, biographee and place.

1293   **Nuevo diccionario biográfico argentino (1750-1930).** (New biographical dictionary of Argentina, 1750-1930.)
Vicente Osvaldo Cutolo.   Buenos Aires: Editorial Elche, 1968-85. 7 vols. bibliog.

The most complete single biographical dictionary for Argentina. The entries occupy densely printed double columns filling 5,053 pages. Each entry gives date and place of birth and death, education, career, major publications, and a short bibliography of previous biographies.

1294   **Presidentes argentinos.** (Presidents of Argentina.)
Edited by Gustavo Gabriel Levene, Alberto Palcos, Boleslao Lewin, Ricardo Rodríguez Molas, Félix Luna.   Buenos Aires: Compañía General Fabril Editora, 1961. 299p. (Creaciones Gráficas).

Brief biographical sketches of twenty-seven presidents from Rivadavia to Frondizi, 1826 to 1962, with portraits.

1295   **Quién es quién en América del Sur: diccionario biográfico argentino, 1982-1983.** (Who's who in South America: a dictionary of Argentine biography, 1982-1983.)
Edited by Pablo Raúl Vitaver.   Buenos Aires: Publicaciones Referenciales Latinoamericanas, 1982. 917p.

Sponsored by over fifty business enterprises and limited to 6,000 Argentine professionals and businessmen, although claiming to include also scientists, industrialists, ambassadors, political leaders, clergymen, judges, members of the armed forces and academics, artists, writers and journalists. For astrologists there is an index by date of birth.

**Encyclopaedias, Directories and Biographical Dictionaries.**
Biographical dictionaries

1296 **Quién es quién en la Argentina: biografías contemporáneas.** (Who's who in Argentina: contemporary biographies.)
Buenos Aires: Kraft, 1968. 9th ed. 1038p.
The ninth edition (the first was published in 1939) provided the following information about distinguished living Argentines: profession, date of birth, family, education, career, publications, clubs, private and professional addresses.

1297 **Quién es quién en la sociedad argentina.** (Who's who in Argentine society.)
Buenos Aires: Ediciones Elite, 1982. 753p.
Lists biographical information about 'professionals, artists, scientists and businessmen', including profession, date and place of birth, family, education, career, awards and private address.

1298 **River Plate personalities: a biographical dictionary.**
John S. Lamb.   Buenos Aires: Sociedad Anónima Imprenta Lamb & Cía, 1939. 351p.
Some 500 flattering biographies of prominent personalities from government and business – native Argentines and a large number of foreign residents, many of them British. The publication was apparently financed by subscription. An earlier edition was published in 1937.

1299 **Spanish American women writers: a bio-bibliographical sourcebook.**
Edited by Diane E. Marting.   New York; Westport, Connecticut; London: Greenwood Press, 1990. 645p. bibliog.
Each entry provides biographical and career information, major themes of the writer's work, a survey of criticism and a select bibliography of works by (including translations) and about the author. The Argentine writers included are Silvina Bullrich, Sara Gallardo, Griselda Gambaro, Juana Manuela Gorriti, Marta Lynch, Silvina and Victoria Ocampo, Olga Orozco, Alejandra Pizarnik, Syria Poletti, Alfonsina Storni, Marta Traba, Luisa Valenzuela and (briefly) the Chiriguano Indian writer Facundina.

1300 **Who's who in Latin America. Part 5: Argentina, Paraguay, and Uruguay.**
Edited by Ronald Hilton.   Stanford, California: Stanford University Press; Chicago: A. N. Marquis; London: Oxford University Press, 1950. 3rd rev. ed. 358p.
'Only figures whose prominence has been proved over a fairly long period of time have been included.' The Argentine section (p. 1-194) contains over 1100 biographies of politicians and public figures, professionals, artists and writers, members of the armed forces, lawyers, journalists, engineers, agronomists and physicians. The first edition was published in 1935.

# Bibliographies

1301 **An annotated bibliography of Latin American sport: pre-conquest to the present.**
Compiled by Joseph L. Arbena. New York; Westport, Connecticut; London: Greenwood Press, 1989. 324p. (Bibliographies and Indexes in World History, 17).

There are references to Argentina in the general chapters on indigenous traditions and the colonial era. The main section for modern Argentine sport (p. 137-80) contains 190 entries in single alphabetical order. The compiler surprisingly found no items on rugby or cricket.

1302 **Argentina, 1875-1975: población, economía, sociedad. Estudio temático y bibliográfico.** (Argentina, 1875-1975: population, economy and society. Subject study and bibliography.)
Sergio Bagú. Mexico City: Universidad Nacional Autónoma de México, 1978. 159p. (Facultad de Ciencias Política y Sociales. Centro de Estudios Latinoamericanos. Serie Bibliografías, 3).

The general introduction surveys statistical and other official and non-official reference sources for the subjects in question. Under headings for population, economy and society, there is an introduction to the subject and a survey of the literature; some of the entries are annotated. The index is by author.

1303 **Argentine literature: a research guide.**
David William Foster. New York; London: Garland, 1982. 2nd rev. ed. 778p. (Garland Reference Library of the Humanities, vol. 338).

A new expanded edition of the *Research guide to Argentine literature* (1970), which lists (but does not annotate) 9,209 bibliographies, dissertations, monographs and articles in two sections: general references (thirty subsections dealing with various forms, themes and periods), and authors (critical works on seventy-three novelists, essayists, poets and dramatists). Borges receives the most entries (1,058), followed by Sarmiento (826), Cortázar, (610) and José Hernández (525). There is an index of critics.

1304   **Bibliografía argentina: catálogo de materiales argentinos en las bibliotecas de la Universidad de Buenos Aires / Argentine bibliography: a union catalog of the Argentine holdings of the libraries of the University of Buenos Aires.**
Boston, Massachusetts: G. K. Hall, 1980. 7 vols.

The Instituto Bibliotecológico, a coordinating body for the libraries of the University of Buenos Aires, maintains union card catalogues of the complete holdings of the University's seventeeen central and fifty-six faculty and departmental libraries, and for books and pamphlets printed in Argentina and occasionally abroad. This large-format catalogue reproduces about 11,000 cards from the latter catalogue, in author order with cross-references, covering all subjects.

1305   **Bibliografía argentina de ciencias sociales / Argentine bibliography of the social sciences.**
Edited by Corina Tiribelli de Seoane.   Buenos Aires: Fundación José María Aragón, 1982- . annual.

This is the Argentine contribution to Unesco's *International bibliography of the social sciences*. The Aragón Foundation aims, but unfortunately fails, to record all Argentine monographs, reports and journal articles in the social sciences, published by public, private and international organizations throughout the country. The 1989 compilation listed over 150 items, under 19 subject headings, with author and subject indexes.

1306   **Bibliografía básica de arqueología americana.** (Basic bibliography of Latin American archaeology.)
José Alcina Franch.   Madrid: Instituto de Cooperación Iberoamericana, 1985. 475p. (Ediciones Cultura Hispánica).

This is a new edition of a work first published in 1960. The section on Argentina contains 430 entries (unannotated), arranged under general works and by eight principal regions. There are also references to Argentina under general South America.

1307   **Bibliografía bibliotecológica argentina (hasta 1967).** (Bibliography of Argentine library literature, to 1967.)
Nicolás J. Matijevic.   Bahía Blanca, Argentina: Universidad Nacional del Sur, Centro de Documentación Bibliotecológica, 1969. 354p.

Contains 2,539 items under 77 headings covering all aspects of librarianship, including library management and buildings, archives, bibliography, printing and book production, incunabula, reading, copyright and audiovisual material. There is an author index. Atilio Peralta compiled the supplements: *Bibliografía bibliotecológica argentina, 1968-1969* (1970, 108 entries); four supplements with a further 281 references covering 1970-1975, in the Centro's *Documentación Bibliotecológica*, nos 3-7/8 (1972-1977/78); and *Bibliografía bibliotecológica argentina, 1976-1977* (1980, 75 references). Two international indexes to library literature contain occasional references to Argentina: *Library & information science abstracts* (London: Library Association, 1969- . monthly with annual cumulation); and *Library literature* (Bronx, New York: H. W. Wilson, 1921- . bimonthly with annual cumulation).

1308   **Bibliografía de bibliografías argentinas, 1807-1970.** (Bibliography of Argentine bibliographies, 1807-1970.)
       Abel Rodolfo Geoghegan.   Buenos Aires: Casa Pardo, 1970. 130p.

A modestly styled 'preliminary edition' which lists 452 bibliographies, many of them annotated, by subject according to the Dewey Decimal Classification. This is the first such list since Narciso Binayán's 'Bibliografía de bibliografías argentinas', *Revista de la Universidad de Buenos Aires*, año 16, vol. 43, no. 143 (Oct.-Dec. 1919), p. 114-49, which listed 164 titles.

1309   **Bibliografía de viajeros a la Argentina.** (Bibliography of travel literature on Argentina.)
       Susana Santos Gómez.   Buenos Aires: Fundación para la Educación, la Ciencia y la Cultura, 1983. 2 vols.

This exhaustive bibliography of 650 pages lists a total of 4,395 entries: 2,673 individual travel accounts, 1,500 works about travellers, 146 anthologies and 76 bibliographies and bibliographies of bibliographies. Few of the items are annotated but there are 515 detailed footnotes. There is an index of names but unfortunately not of places. The British made the greatest contribution to Argentine travel literature in the nineteenth century and their accounts are a valuable source for historians. Useful surveys are José E. Uriburu, *La República Argentina a través de las obras de los escritores ingleses* (Buenos Aires: Claridad, 1948. 211p.); Samuel S. Trífilo, 'A bibliography of British travel books on Argentina: 1810-1860', *The Americas*, vol. 16, no. 2 (Oct. 1959), p. 133-43, which also mentions travellers before 1810; and Scott Myers, 'A survey of British literature on Buenos Aires during the first half of the nineteenth century', *The Americas*, vol. 44, no. 1 (July 1987), p. 67-79.

1310   **Bibliografía del folklore argentino.** (Bibliography of Argentine folklore.)
       Edited by Augusto Raúl Cortázar.   Buenos Aires: Fondo Nacional de las Artes, 1965-66. 2 vols. (Bibliografía Argentina de Artes y Letras. Compilaciones Especiales, 21/22, 25/26).

Volume one lists 923 books arranged under 58 headings according to the Universal Decimal Classification; some entries are annotated briefly or their contents listed, and there is an author index. Volume two lists 1,504 articles from 56 different journals, with an author-title index, and also includes a subject index to both volumes.

1311   **Bibliografía filosófica argentina (1900-1975).** (Bibliography of Argentine philosophy, 1900-75.)
       Celina Ana Lértora Mendoza, with the collaboration of Matilde Isabel García Losada.   Buenos Aires: Fundación para la Educación, la Ciencia y la Cultura, 1983. 359p.

The first Argentine bibliography of twentieth-century philosophy, which aims at comprehensiveness (books, edited works and articles from an impressive 242 journals from the Americas and Europe) and promises future supplements. It contains 5,182 unannotated entries listed under ten broad philosophical disciplines and a further 143 subheadings. There are author and subject indexes.

1312 **Bibliografía geográfica referida a la República Argentina (primera contribución).** (Bibliography of the geography of Argentina. Part one.)
Raúl Rey Balmaceda.   Buenos Aires: GAEA: Sociedad Argentina de Estudios Geográficos, 1975. 648p. (Serie Especial, no. 11, vols I-II).

Contains a total of 9,222 items published anywhere in the world between 1955 and 1969, with author, subject and place indexes. It is continued by *Bibliografía geográfica argentina (segunda contribución)* (1983. 2 vols), listing 21,806 monographs, articles and doctoral dissertations published 1970-79. Both in turn continue Oscar Adolfo Uriondo, *Bibliografía geográfica referente a la República Argentina; primera contribución* (Buenos Aires: Talleres Gráficos 'Junior', 1964. 110p.), containing 2,295 works published 1825-1967.

1313 **Bibliografía iberoamericana de administración local.** (Bibliography of local government in Latin America.)
Enrique Orduña Rebollo.   Caracas: Asociación Venezolana de Cooperación Intermunicipal; Madrid: Instituto de Estudios de Administración Local, 1983. 811p.

An unannotated bibliography of 10,177 items under eight general subject headings, including municipal law, public services, housing, and relations between local, regional and federal governments. Some 117 items refer to Argentina. The indexes are by author and subject and geographical.

1314 **Bibliografía jurídica de América Latina (1810-1965).** (Bibliography of the law of Latin America, 1810-1965.)
Alberto Villalón-Galdames.   Santiago, Chile: Editorial Jurídica de Chile, 1969. 2 vols. 487p.

Volume one, 'Argentina, Bolivia', contains an Argentine section (p. 219-434) of 2,591 unannotated entries in single alphabetical author order. Volume two is the index to the first volume.

1315 **Bibliografía para el estudio de la población de la Argentina.** (Bibliography for the study of population in Argentina.)
M. Martha Accinelli, María S. Müller, Edith A. Pantelides.   Buenos Aires: Centro de Estudios de Población, 1978. 83p. (Cuadernos del CENEP, 3).

A selective bibliography, covering 1930-70, which includes references to books, articles, reports and conference papers, but not official publications such as censuses and statistical yearbooks. It is useful for Argentine material but there are omissions in the English-language literature.

1316  **La bibliografía reciente sobre la cuestión Malvinas.** (Recent writing on the Falklands/Malvinas dispute.)
Roberto Etcehpareborda.  *Inter-American Review of Bibliography*, vol. 34, no. 1 (1984), p. 1-52; vol. 34, no. 2 (1984), p. 227-88.
A valuable two-part bibliographical essay, unashamedly pro-Argentine, which considers the wide range of publications published on the Falklands dispute since the 1982 war. For further British and Argentine sources on both the sovereignty issue and the war see the *Atlantic Ocean* (1985) volume in the World Bibliographical Series by H. G. R. King.

1317  **Bibliografía sobre el impacto inmigratorio masivo en la Argentina (1850-1930).** (Bibliography on the impact of mass immigration to Argentina, 1850-1930.)
Edited by Hernán Asdrúbal Silva.  In: *Bibliografía sobre el impacto del proceso inmigratorio masivo en el Cono Sur de América: Argentina–Brasil–Chile–Uruguay.*  Mexico City: Instituto Panamericano de Geografía e Historia, 1984, p. 9-109. (Serie Inmigración, vol. 1).
A four-page introduction to the subject is followed by 2,795 unannotated entries in alphabetical author order, a subject index and a list of abbreviations used. Categories include geographical distribution and rural/urban spread of immigration, immigrants' country of origin, and political, economic, social and cultural aspects of immigration.

1318  **Bibliografía teológica comentada del área iberoamericana.** (Annotated theological bibliography of Latin America.)
Buenos Aires: Asociación Interconfesional de Estudios Teológicos, Instituto Superior Evangélico de Estudios Teológicos, 1973- . annual.
This is an index to books and to articles published in over 450 periodicals from the Americas and Europe. Each annual volume contains 7,000-8,000 entries. Apart from the purely theological subjects treated, there is wide coverage of related areas – economic, political, social, cultural, educational, psychological, philosophical and legal.

1319  **Bibliographic guide to Latin American studies.**
Boston, Massachusetts: G. K. Hall, 1979- . annual.
A catalogue produced by merging the annual accessions of the Latin American Collection of the University of Texas, Austin, with additional entries from the Library of Congress 'for thorough subject coverage'. The unannotated entries are listed in one alphabetical dictionary sequence of authors, titles, series and subjects. There are usually two, occasionally three, annual volumes. It serves as a supplement to the *Catalog of the Latin American Collection of the University of Texas at Austin* (published 1966-77 in 39 vols with four supplements of 19 vols).

Bibliographies

## 1320  A bibliography of Latin American bibliographies.
Arthur E. Gropp.   Metuchen, New Jersey: Scarecrow Press, 1968.
515p.

A list of 7,210 monograph items published before 1964, grouped first under 69 subject headings and then by country, with a detailed index. This work is complemented by the same compiler's *A bibliography of Latin America bibliographies published in periodicals* (Scarecrow Press, 1976. 2 vols), which listed 9,715 items to 1965. Three five-year supplements have been published by Scarecrow Press: Arthur E. Gropp, *A bibliography of Latin American bibliographies: supplement* (1971), records 1,416 monographic bibliographies published 1965-69; Daniel Raposo Cordeiro (ed.), *A bibliography of Latin American bibliographies: social sciences & humanities* (1979), lists 1,750 items published as monographs (1969-74) or periodical articles (1966-74); Haydée Piedracueva (ed.), *A bibliography of Latin American bibliographies, 1975-1979: social sciences and humanities* (1982), refers to 2,122 monographic and periodical items appearing 1975-79. Since 1980 Lionel V. Loroña has produced for the Seminar on the Acquisition of Latin American Library Materials (the sponsor of earlier volumes) an annual *Bibliography of Latin American and Caribbean bibliographies*, currently published by the University of New Mexico's General Library, Albuquerque. None of the above bibliographies is annotated.

## 1321  British bulletin of publications on Latin America, the Caribbean, Spain and Portugal.
London: Hispanic and Luso-Brazilian Council, 1949- . two issues a
year.

A useful source of information on English-language works published anywhere in the world but mainly in the United Kingdom and the United States. Recent books are listed and annotated by the Council's librarian; the selection of unannotated periodical and newspaper articles has for many years been supplied by the noted bibliographer A. J. Walford. In the April 1990 issue, there are nine monographic and twenty-two periodical entries for Argentina; there are also sections on the Falkland Islands and Antarctica.

## 1322  The Catholic Left in Latin America: a comprehensive bibliography.
Therrin C. Dahlin, Gary P. Gillum, Mark L. Grover.   Boston,
Massachusetts: G. K. Hall, 1981. 410p.

A bibliography, 'comprehensive for the years 1960-1978', in two parts: general and country-by-country. The section on Argentina, p. 151-62, contains 145 entries under the following headings: general, agrarian reform, Catholic change and social change, Catholic Church and the state, Catholic clergy, Christian Democracy, communism, documents, economic development, education, labour and labouring classes, liberation, Marxism, Nationalism, politics, revolution, Socialism, and violence.

1323   **Education in Latin America: a bibliography.**
Ludwig Lauerhass, Vera Lúcia Oliveira de Araújo Haugse.   Los
Angeles: University of California, UCLA Latin American Center
Publications; Boston, Massachusetts: G. K. Hall, 1980. 431p. (UCLA
Latin American Center. Reference Series, vol. 9).

This unannotated bibliography has a broad coverage of mostly Latin American
material, emphasizing works published during 1945-75. The section on Argentina,
p. 151-90, arranges the entries under five main headings: serials and reference sources,
education in general, in-school education, out-of-school education and special
programmes, and educational planning and administration.

1324   **Guía bibliográfica de las artes visuales en la Argentina, siglo XX.**
(Bibliographic guide to visual arts in Argentina, 20th century.)
Alberto Collazo, Jorge Glusberg.   Buenos Aires: Centro de Arte y
Comunicación, 1983. 99p.

An unannotated listing of 106 items, with an addendum of 36 works published in 1982;
these are arranged under twelve thematic headings and there is a combined
author/institutional/place index.

1325   **Guide to the law and legal literature of Argentina, Brazil and Chile.**
Edwin M. Borchard.   Washington, DC: Government Printing Office,
1917. 523p.

Not a simple list of titles but a discussion of major works published during the previous
few decades, under fifteen categories. Its supplement is: Helen L. Clagett, *A guide to
the law and legal literature of Argentina, 1917-1946* (Washington, DC: Library of
Congress, 1948. 180p.).

1326   **A guide to the official publications of the other American republics. I:
Argentina.**
Edited by James B. Childs.   Washington, DC: Library of Congress,
1945. 124p. (Latin American Series, 9).

Not a full listing of official publications since 1810; instead, it centres upon 'the present
scene both as to agencies and publications stressing informational potentialities and
giving wherever possible brief data about the development of agencies and
publications'. Subdivided by legislative, executive and judicial branches, with a general
introduction and index. A two-volume reprint of all the country volumes in the series
was issued by Johnson Reprint Corporation (New York) in 1964.

1327   **Handbook of Latin American art / Manual de arte latinoamericano: a
bibliographic compilation.**
Edited by Joyce Waddell Bailey.   Santa Barbara, California;
Denver, Colorado; Oxford: ABC-Clio, 1984-86. 3 vols.

Volume one, entitled 'General references and art of the nineteenth and twentieth
centuries', has two sections on Argentina: the first (p. 124-38) under five broad
headings (art in general, exhibitions, collections, museums, art media and studies, and
art history by region), the second focusing on individual artists and art forms. Volume
two, 'Art of the colonial period', includes a section on Argentina, p. 313-49.

1328    **Handbook of Latin American studies.**
Cambridge, Massachusetts, 1936-51; Gainesville, Florida, 1952-78;
Austin, Texas: University of Texas Press, 1979- . annual.
This is the classic general bibliography for Latin American studies. It is prepared by 'a
number of scholars for the Hispanic Division of the Library of Congress', who
annotate monographs and periodical articles in either English or Spanish according to
preference. Since volume 27 (1965) it has appeared in alternate Humanities and Social
Sciences volumes. The former covers art, film, history, language, literature, music and
philosophy; the latter covers anthropology, economics, education, geography,
government and politics, international relations and sociology. Argentina usually
appears as a country subdivision and there were 244 specific Argentine references in
volume 49. Each volume also contains a section on bibliography and general works,
and author and subject indexes. There is a cumulative author index to volumes 1-28.

1329    **HAPI: Hispanic American Periodicals Index.**
Edited by Barbara G. Valk.    Los Angeles: University of California,
UCLA Latin American Center, 1970- . annual.
Publication began in 1977 with a volume indexing articles published in 1974. In 1984 a
retrospective three-volume set was issued for the years 1970-74, thereby continuing
coverage from the *Index to Latin American periodical literature, 1929-1960* (Boston,
Massachusetts: G. K. Hall, 1962. 8 vols) and its two supplements for 1961-65 (1968, 2
vols) and 1966-70 (1980, 2 vols). The index covers some 250 key journals (mainly
political, economic, social and cultural) published specifically on Latin America
throughout the world. It is arranged by subject (including book reviews) and author.
References to the major subjects for Argentina are to be found under that country's
name; in addition, there are some 175 'see also' references.

1330    **Historia y bibliografía de las primeras imprentas rioplatenses, 1700-
1850: misiones del Paraguay, Argentina, Uruguay.** (History and
bibliography of the early printed books of the River Plate: the
Paraguayan missions, Argentina, Uruguay.)
Guillermo Fúrlong Cárdiff.    Buenos Aires: Editorial Guarania (vol.
1); Librería del Plata (vols 2-3); Librería Huemul (vol. 4), 1953-75.
The author, assisted by Juan E. Pivel Devoto, Efraím Cardozo and Manuel Selva,
provides a wealth of bibliographical information on early printing in the Jesuit
reductions (where Argentine printing began), Buenos Aires, Córdoba and Montevideo. The volumes are predominantly listings of titles, with informed commentary.

1331    **El indio en la llanura del Plata: guía bibliográfica.** (Bibliographical
guide to the Indian in the River Plate.)
P. Meinrado Hux.    La Plata, Argentina: Provincia de Buenos Aires,
Dirección General de Escuelas, Archivo Histórico 'Ricardo Levene',
1984. 262p.
A single author-alphabetical sequence containing 5,159 unannotated references,
complemented by a very detailed subject index. There is an annexe of 499 references
to maps (separate or in other works) and a place index.

1332 **Jorge Luis Borges: an annotated primary and secondary bibliography.**
David William Foster. New York; London: Garland, 1984. 328p.
(Garland Reference Library of the Humanities, vol. 439).
The bibliography consists of about 1,500 monographic and periodical entries
emphasizing critical works of Borges's short fiction and essays over the last forty years.
In fifteen sections: works by Borges; general studies; general studies of the poetry,
fiction and essays; criticism on specific texts; special topics; Borges and other writers
and literatures; commentaries by other writers; negative criticism; interviews;
chronology, biography and memorabilia; collections of articles; bibliographies and
review surveys.

1333 **Latin America: a guide to economic history, 1830-1930.**
Edited by Roberto Cortés Conde, Stanley J. Stein. Berkeley,
California; London: University of California Press, 1977. 685p.
The section on Argentina by Tulio Halperín Donghi (p. 49-162) includes a detailed
introduction followed by a bibliography of 1,066 works organized under ten headings
and annotated in Spanish. Included are monographs, government publications,
periodical articles and conference reports. There is an author (but no subject) index.

1334 **Latin America: a guide to the historical literature.**
Edited by Charles C. Griffin, J. B. Warren. Austin, Texas:
University of Texas Press, 1971. 700p. (Conference on Latin
American History. Publication, 4).
A very selective but valuable annotated bibliography compiled by a team of subject
experts. Material on Argentina may be found in three general chapters, a chapter on
international relations since 1830, and in the sections devoted to Colonial Latin
America ('Río de la Plata' by John Lynch, 98 entries); Independence ('Río de la Plata'
by David Bushnell, 48 entries); Latin America since independence ('Argentina, 1828-
1910', by Joseph Criscenti, 165 entries; and 'Argentina, twentieth century', by Samuel
L. Baily, 257 entries).

1335 **Latin America and the Caribbean: a bibliographical guide to works
in English.**
S. A. Bayitch. Coral Gables, Florida: University of Miami Press;
Dobbs Ferry, New York: Oceana Publications, 1967. 943p.
(University of Miami School of Law. Interamerican Legal Studies,
vol. 10).
This is an expanded version of a work first published in 1961. In two main parts: by
subjects (subdivided by area – Latin America, Caribbean, Central America) and by
country (the section on Argentina, p. 299-336, contains brief references under eighty-
five headings). The coverage is overwhelmingly of twentieth-century titles.

1336 **Latin America: social sciences information sources, 1967-1979.**
Robert L. Delorme. Santa Barbara, California; Oxford: ABC-Clio, 1981. 262p.

Contains 416 titles referring to Argentina – including monographs, articles and chapters in edited books – in alphabetical order. The same editor has produced two supplements: *Latin America, 1979-1983: a social science bibliography*, issued by ABC-Clio in 1984, containing 171 references to Argentina; and *Latin America, 1983-1987: a social science bibliography* (New York: Greenwood Press, 1988), listing 265 entries on Argentina.

1337 **Latin American history: a guide to the literature in English.**
R. A. Humphreys. London; New York; Toronto: Oxford University Press, 1958. 197p.

This guide, which remains useful, lists works on Argentina to 1810 under these headings: reference works, periodicals, general histories, land and environment, ancient peoples and cultures, and the Spanish empire and its fall. Argentina's modern period is covered on pages 73-6 (wars of independence) and since 1830 (p. 111-17, eighty-three references).

1338 **Latin American play index.**
Herbert H. Hoffman. Metuchen, New Jersey; London: Scarecrow Press, 1983-84. 2 vols.

The two volumes provide access to a total of about 3,300 plays by 1,000 dramatists, listed by author and play title. Included are plays published as 'stand-alone' works, in collections, in anthologies and in periodicals. Most of the collections and anthologies covered in volume one appear also in the *Handbook of Latin American studies* (q.v.); for each of these, the HLAS volume and entry number are supplied.

1339 **Latin American urbanization: a guide to the literature, organizations and personnel.**
Martin H. Sable. Metuchen, New Jersey: Scarecrow Press, 1971. 1077p.

The bibliography is in four parts, subdivided by thirty subject fields: 'aesthetics and humanities'; economics, industry and commerce; government and law; and urbanization as a phenomenon and research field. A directory section follows, subdivided by country. There are author and subject (including country and place) indexes to the bibliography and an index to the directory.

1340 **Libros argentinos: ISBN.** (Current Argentine books.)
Buenos Aires: Cámara Argentina del Libro, 1984- . every two years.

Argentina has a strong and versatile publishing industry but has no current national bibliography. The last attempt, a *Boletín bibliográfico nacional*, produced by the National Library, ceased publication in the 1960s. This is its nearest equivalent, a catalogue produced by the national publishers' association of books, official publications and educational materials recently registered for International Standard Book Numbers. In 1984 a first catalogue was produced, of titles published during 1982, and in 1985 a volume covering 1982 and 1983 titles. A cumulative volume for 1982-86 appeared in 1987 (721p.); this lists over 28,000 titles arranged according to the

Universal Decimal Classification (twenty-three broad subject headings, 190 further subdivisions); it contains author and title indexes and a useful list of publishers. Bimonthly updates to the catalogue are listed in the 'Información bibliográfica' section of the Cámara's journal *Lea: libros de edición argentina*. See the section on Argentina in 'Latin American national bibliography', by Hensley C. Woodbridge with the research assistance of Jane Larkin, in *Encyclopedia of library and information science*, edited by Allen Kent (New York; Basel, Switzerland: Marcel Dekker, 1983, vol. 36, supplement 1, p. 277-83); the chapter on Argentina in *Guide to current national bibliographies of the Third World*, by G. E. Gorman and J. J. Mills (London: Hans Zell, 1987. 2nd rev. ed.); and in Marcelle Beaudiquez, *Bibliographic services throughout the world: supplement 1983-1984* (Paris: Unesco, 1987. 319p. PGI-87/WS/4).

1341 **Modern Latin American art: a bibliography.**
Compiled by James A. Findlay.   Westport, Connecticut: London: Greenwood Press, 1983. 301p. (Art Reference Collection, no. 3).
The section on Argentina, p. 40-79, contains references to 443 items in twelve categories, including design, graphic arts, painting, photography and sculpture. Monographs and exhibition catalogues are emphasized.

1342 **Peronism and the three Perons: a checklist of material on Peronism and on Juan Domingo, Eva, and Isabel Peron and their writings in the Hoover Institution Library and Archives and in the Stanford University Libraries.**
Compiled by Laszlo Horvath.   Stanford, California: Hoover Institution, Stanford University, 1988. 170p.
An unannotated inventory of the Hoover Institution's collection of books, pamphlets, offprints and archival material, some of which is extremely rare. The entries are arranged according to works about and by each of the Peróns. See also *Eva Perón: books, articles, and other sources of study: an annotated bibliography*, compiled by Gabriela Sonntag (Madison, Wisconsin: University of Wisconsin-Madison, Memorial Library, 1983. 55p. Seminar on the Acquisition of Latin American Library Materials. Bibliographical Series, 7), which lists 374 entries (130 books, 232 articles) by and about Eva Perón, including speeches and legislation, and is confined to items traced in United States libraries and mainly published before 1979.

1343 **Protestantism in Latin America: a bibliographical guide.**
Edited by John H. Sinclair.   South Pasadena, California: William Carey Library, 1976. 414p.
A selective, mostly annotated, bibliography arranged by country with an author index. It includes theses but excludes 'printed minutes, reports, minor denominational publications and missionary promotional material'. Two sections on Argentina (p. 121-9, 308-12) list ninety-six entries: bibliography, general background, Protestantism in general, denominational history, Baptist, Disciples of Christ, indigenous churches, Lutheran, Mennonite, Methodist and Waldensian. A preliminary edition was published in 1967. See also Carlos A. Bisio, *Contribución bibliográfica para el estudio de las iglesias cristianas evangélicas en Argentina* (Buenos Aires: Instituto Bibliográfico 'Antonio Zinny', 1982. 120p.).

1344    **Selected annotated bibliography on the climates of Paraguay, Uruguay and Argentina.**
Mary L. Rice. *Meteorological Abstracts and Bibliography*, vol. 3, no. 3 (March 1952), p. 243-90.
There are 141 references to Argentina: monographs and articles published between 1876 and 1952, mostly in Spanish and English, under sixteen subjects, including atmospheric composition, structure and dynamics; pressure systems, fronts and air masses; radiation; temperature; wind; fog, clouds and hydrometeors; hydrometeorology; and climatology.

1345    **Soils of Argentina.**
Compiled by Commonwealth Bureau of Soils, Rothamsted Experimental Station. Farnham Royal, England: Commonwealth Agricultural Bureaux, 1977. 15p. (Annotated Bibliography, no. SG1838).
Contains 189 annotated entries covering the published literature for 1936-75, under nine headings with an author index.

1346    **The Spanish of Argentina and Uruguay: an annotated bibliography for 1940-1978.**
Jack Emory Davis. Berlin; New York; Amsterdam: Mouton, 1982. 360p. (Jana Linguarum. Series Maior, 105).
A comprehensive bibliography totalling 1,227 entries, with very detailed annotations and notes, covering all types of material. In four main sections: lexicography, semantics and etymology subdivided by: general, specific provinces or regions, specific fields, individual words and phrases (including *lunfardo*), the language of individual authors, *lunfardo* and *lunfardesco*, gaucho and *gauchesco*, place-names and personal names; inter-language influence (indigenous, Spanish and other European languages, African and Hebrew); phonology and phonetics; grammar; and miscellaneous studies. An index of authors is added.

1347    **Teatro hispanoamericano: una bibliografía anotada / Spanish American theatre: an annotated bibliography.**
Richard F. Allen. Boston, Massachusetts: G. K. Hall, 1987. 633p. (A Reference Publication in Latin American Studies).
A bibliography of dramatic works, all in their original Spanish-language editions, with an indication of locations in United States libraries. For Argentina, 607 works are listed (p. 14-144): anthologies and collections, plays written by an individual playwright or two or more authors, plays representing a historical movement and theatrical groups, collections from national and local theatre organizations, and theatre festivals.

1348　Temas de Buenos Aires: contribución bibliográfica y hemerográfica.
(A bibliography of books and articles on Buenos Aires.)
Edited, with notes and an introduction, by Mario Tesler.　Buenos
Aires: Empresa Nacional de Telecomunicaciones, 1982. 419p.

An alphabetical list of 1,221 entries, most of them annotated and many in great detail, covering all aspects of the city's history and institutions, with a subject index.

1349　**Women authors of modern Hispanic South America: a bibliography of literary criticism and interpretation.**
Sandra Messinger Cypess, David R. Kohut, Rachelle Moore.
Metuchen, New Jersey: Scarecrow Press, 1989. 155p.

Lists unannotated references to 169 modern women authors, including 68 from Argentina (p. 13-60). Every literary genre is catered for: drama, poetry, prose, the novel and the short story. Critical works are registered in the form of monographs, collections of essays, periodical articles, conference proceedings and doctoral dissertations. See also Lynn Ellen Rice Cortina's *Spanish-American women writers: a bibliographical checklist* (New York; London: Garland, 1983. 292p.), an unannotated list of the works of 308 Argentine women authors (p. 3-43), but with minimal bibliographical details (many dates are lacking).

1350　**Women in Spanish America: an annotated bibliography from pre-conquest to contemporary times.**
Meri Knaster.　Boston, Massachusetts: G. K. Hall, 1977. 696p.

The best single source of references on women, mainly of secondary material (books, chapters, articles and pamphlets), with some theses, travel accounts and memoirs. There are references to Argentine women under 'South America' within broad subject headings: biography and autobiography, the arts, literature, mass media and folklore, education, magic, religion and ritual, ethnography, community studies, marriage and the family, human sexuality, reproduction and health, psychology, economic life, law, female delinquency and penal institutions, employment legislation, history (four periods), political and twentieth-century revolutionary movements, women's liberation, and miscellaneous. Also useful, with some more up-to-date references, is K. Lynn Stoner, *Latinas of the Americas: a source book* (New York; London: Garland, 1989).

# Indexes

There follow three separate indexes: authors (personal and corporate); titles; and subjects. Title entries are italicized and refer either to the main titles, or to other works cited in the annotations. The numbers refer to bibliographical entries, not to pages. Individual index entries are arranged in alphabetical sequence.

## Index of Authors

### A

Abad de Santillán, D. 449, 1273
Abel, C. 764
Ablin, E. 819
Abstatz, C. 1082
Accinelli, M. M. 1315
Ackerman, K. J. 536
Ackerman, W. V. 57
Acuña, J. H. 11
Acuña, M. L. 576
Adams, R. 521
Adelman, J. 832
Adler, E. 1013
Agor, W. H. 659
Agosín, M. 620, 1075
Aguilar, A. 552
Aguinis, M. 1072, 1088
Aguirre, R. G. 1080
Aguirre Saravia, A. G. 1103
Agulla, J. C. 525
Akers, C. E. 104
Alazraki, J. 1037, 1042
Alberdi, J. B. 480, 485
Albert, B. 299
Albiano, N. 559
Alcina Franch, J. 1306
Alexander, R. J. 23, 310, 909, 1281
Alhadeff, P. 570, 708, 728
Alisky, M. 1248
Allen, R. F. 1347
Alonso, C. J. 1050
Alonso, F. P. 1259
Alschuler, L. R. 727, 804

Alsina, J. A. 367
Altimir, O. 906
Alvarez Suárez, A. E. 480
Amadeo, S. P. 627
Amaral, S. 859
Ambrosetti, J. B. 1070, 1202
American Chamber of Commerce in Argentina 788
Amnesty International 614, 624
Amos, A. J. 71
Andreu, J. 390
Andrews, G. R. 436
Andrews, J. 117
Andrien, P. E. 65
Anglade, C. 732
Anglo-Argentine Society (London) 1036
Antoine, C. 615
Aparicio, F. de 39
Ara, G. 29
Aramburu, R. H. 213
Aranovich, F. C. 639
Arbena, J. L. 1211, 1301
Ardila, R. 562
Areán González, C. A. 1103
Aretz, I. 1145, 1153, 1156, 1192
Aretz-Thiele, I. *see* Aretz, I.
Arizaga, R. 1136
Arlt, R. 1032, 1100
Armstrong, W. 554, 708
Arrieta, R. A. 259, 1022, 1071, 1241

Ashe, S. 1072
Ashoff, G. 780
Asís, J. 1072
Asociación de Diseñadores Gráficos de Buenos Aires 1102
Asociación Interconfesional de Estudios Teológicos 1318
Aspe Armella, P. 740
Astiz, C. A. 581, 583
Astrada, C. 479
Athey, L. 618
Atkins, G. P. 609
Automóvil Club Argentina 91
Avellaneda, A. 1088, 1250
Avellaneda, N. 1070
Avni, H. 412
Azara, F. de 143
Azel, J. 1219
Azéma, M. A. 151
Aznar, L. 476
Azpiazu, D. 727
Azzario, E. A. 1026

### B

Babini, J. 11, 1010
Bacarisse, P. 1064
Backhouse, H. 145
Baer, J. 1220
Bagú, S. J. 527, 1302
Bailey, J. P. 396
Bailey, J. W. 1327

Baily, S. L. 371, 403, 923, 983, 1260, 1334
Baker, A. 1065
Balán, J. 959
Balderston, D. 1061
Baliari, E. 1094
Baliño, T. J. J. 767
Balmori, D. 532
Balossi, E. C. 543, 556
Banchs, E. 1071, 1080
Banco Central 771
Banco de Análisis y Computación 945
Barabino, A. 457
Barager, J. R. 259, 306, 572
Barba, E. M. 876
Barbera, M. 753
Barcia, J. 464, 1094
Bardin, P. 1093
Bardoni, A. L. 193
Barletta, A. 1157
Barnard, T. 1181
Barnes, J. 309
Barr, R. R. 615
Barraclough, S. 829
Barrett, K. R. E. 173
Barrett, R. Le M. 173
Bartfeld de Rietti, S. 1009
Barth, F. 234
Bartlett, D. 175
Bartlett, J. 175
Bartley, R. H. 1237
Bartolomé, M. A. 433
Basaldúa, R. O. 980
Bassnett, S. 1024, 1075
Battolla, O. C. 101
Bayitch, S. A. 1335
Bayley, E. 1080
Bayón, D. 1121
Beaudiquez, M. 1340
Beaumont, J. A. B. 132
Becco, H. J. 1236
Beck, P. J. 690, 1207
Bécquer Casaballe, A. 1104
Beerbohm, J. 102
Beeson, T. 506
Béhague, G. 1142, 1145
Bellisio, N. B. 211
Bell-Villada, G. H. 1035
Beltrán, O. R. 1256
Beltrán, V. R. 600
Beltrán Fuentes, A. 1146

Bemberg, M. L. 1187
Bendersky, M. J. 638
Bennassar, B. 390
Bennett, J. 616
Bennett, W. C. 235
Benson, E. P. 228, 237
Benvenuto, E. L. 1150
Berelson, B. 326
Bergmann, J. F. 75
Bergquist, C. 922
Bernárdez, F. L. 1071
Berryman, P. 507
Berthold, V. M. 875
Besio Moreno, N. 328
Bestene, J. O. 401
Bethell, L. 285, 288-9, 295, 711
Beveraggi Allende, A. M. 762
Beveraggi Allende, W. 11
Beverina, J. 267
Beyer, C. 82
Biagini, H. E. 474
Biblioteca Nacional 1340
Bidart Campos, G. J. 631, 635, 641
Biedma, J. J. 82
Bienen, H. 608
Bierstadt, E. H. 1169
Biggins, A. 944
Biglione, A. 1099
Biles, R. E. 663
Billard, J. B. 966
Binayán, N. 1308
Bioy Casares, A. 1033-4, 1072
Bird, J. B. 224
Birnbaum, A. M. 95
Birnbaum, S. 95
Birri, F. 1181, 1184
Bishop, P. 701
Bisio, C. A. 1343
Bitbol, A. 643
Björn, W. 1208
Blackburn, P. 1043
Blackwelder, J. K. 518
Blaistein, I. see Blaisten, I.
Blaisten, I. 1072, 1074
Blakemore, H. 51, 1284
Blanksten, G. I. 317
Blanpain, R. 646
Blaustein, A. P. 630
Bleiler, E. F. 235
Bloom, H. 1037

Boehm, E. H. 1278
Boeri, L. I. 941
Bohigas, O. 1127
Boldy, S. 1044
Bonner, D. 1069
Bonsor, N. R. P. 880
Boole, S. 9
Borchard, E. M. 1325
Borges, J. L. 29, 441, 1035, 1038, 1040-1, 1049, 1071, 1073, 1077-8, 1080
Borghini, S. 1128
Borzone de Manrique, A. M. 461
Bosch, B. 442
Bosco, M. A. 1082
Bose, L. 1208
Bottaro, R. H. 1243
Bourne, B. F. 122
Bousquet, J.-P. 621
Bown, W. L. 201
Box, B. 100
Box, P. H. 296
Boyer, M. 548, 1035
Boyle, C. 1024
Brackenridge, H. M. 142
Bradt, H. 94
Brady, G. S. 897
Brailovsky, A. 754
Brannon, R. H. 833
Braslavsky, C. 540
Braunstein, S. 618
Breda, E. A. 1213
Brenner, A. 1081
Brett, M. T. 561
Bridges, E. L. 171
Brisk, W. J. 641
Bróccoli, A. 1132
Brock, C. 985
Brooman, F. 771
Browman, D. L. 216, 335, 511
Brown, J. C. 262, 968
Brown, L. C. 489
Browning, W. E. 504
Bruce, J. 33
Brughetti, R. 29, 1089
Brunet, E. 1064
Bruno, C. 499
Bruno, M. 741
Bryce, J. 167
Buchanan, P. G. 914
Buchanan, W. I. 915

Doorn, J. van 611
Dorfman, A. 428, 797, 800
Dornbusch, R. 729, 740-1
Dostal, W. 433
Draguns, J. G. 566
Driskell, C. B. 1178
Drut, R. 555
Du Toit, B. M. 337
Dubois, M. E. 522
Dun & Bradstreet
    International 790
Duncan, K. 850
Duncan, T. 716
Dunning, J. S. 214
Duprez, P. 341
Duranga, W. 1258
Durland, W. D. 64
Durrell, G. 183
Dyson, K. K. 1062


E

Earle, P. G. 1059
Echevarría, E. A. 1051
Echeverría, E. 480, 1045,
    1080
Economic Commission for
    Latin America and the
    Caribbean 718, 942,
    947
Economist Intelligence
    Unit 717
Eddy, P. 704
Edel, M. 972
Edelstein, J. 566
Eder, P. J. 652
Edwards, G. G. 823
Edwards, S. 746
Egan, E. W. 10
Eidt, R. C. 377, 402
Eisenmann, E. 207
Eiteman, D. K. 799
Elazar, D. J. 416
Elbow, G. 75
Elkin, J. L. 411, 418
Elliott, B. 6
Elliott, C. M. 355
Elliott, L. E. 146
Engelbert, J. A. 1047,
    1077
Englekirk, J. E. 1053
English, A. J. 602

Enns, A. W. 500
Ensign, M. S. 1278
Ensinck, O. L. 375
Epstein, E. C. 743
Eriksson, N. 348
Erize, F. 180
Ernesto Tornquist & Cía
    720
Escalante, R. 198
Escobar, R. T. 452
Escudé, C. 570, 668, 672,
    987
Escudero, J. C. 546
Esdaile, A. 1222
España, C. 1188
Espínola, J. C. 384
Espoz Espoz, M. 851
Esser, K. 780
Essorio y Florit, M. 643
Etchepareborda, R. 679,
    968, 1087, 1316
Ethell, B. 703
Etzrodt, W. 649
Europa Publications
    1284-5
Evans, C. 227
Evans, J. 931
Evans, P. B. 538
Even-Shoshan, I. 418


F

Facts on File 1268
Fainboim, H. 553
Fainboim, M. 769
Falcoff, M. 304, 890
Falcón, R. 917
Falicov, L. M. 1012
Falkner, T. 109
Fanelli, J. M. 741
Fargosi, A. E. 642
Farré, L. 472
Fasano-Filho, U. 736
Fawcett, B. 896
Feijóo, M. del C. 349
Feldman, D. L. 613
Fender, F. A. 833
Fennell, L. C. 659
Ferguson, J. H. 31
Fernández, F. A. 552
Fernández, J. 229, 242
Fernández, J. A. 586

Fernández, J. R. 1256
Fernández, M. 1046-7
Fernández, S. M. 1224
Fernández Distel, A. A.
    215
Fernández Moreno, B.
    1071, 1080
Ferns, H. S. 246, 570, 675,
    715, 1036
Ferrari, G. E. 287, 671
Ferreira Sobral, E. F. 1283
Ferrer, A. 591, 713, 723,
    726
Ferrer, H. 1159
Ferrere, D. 794
Feruglio, E. 69
Fester, G. A. 226
Fidel, J. 819
Fienup, D. F. 833
Fifer, J. V. 688
Figgen, K. L. 1191
Figueira, R. 83
Fillol, T. R. 730
Financial Times Business
    Information 759
Finch, M. H. J. 267, 900
Findlay, J. A. 1341
Finó, J. F. 1225
Fischer, S. 741
Fishburn, E. 1028
Fisher, J. 621
Fitton, M. 1060
Fitzgibbon, R. H. 1267
Flanz, G. H. 630
Fleming, W. J. 55, 898,
    1237
Flichman, G. 732
Flint, J. M. 1032
Flora Patagónica 186
Flores, A. 1045
Flores, María see Main,
    M.F.
Fock, N. 225, 509
Fodor, J. 251, 728
Fogarty, J. 570, 708, 716
Fontanarrosa, R. 1130
Foppa, T. L. 1170
Ford, A. G. 251, 723
Ford, J. P. 751
Form, W. H. 907
Forster, M. H. 968, 1172
Fortin, C. 732
Foster, D. H. N. 17, 1205
Foster, D. W. 448, 469,

391

Greenup, R. 305
Gregoratti, H. D. 326
Gregory, S. 624
Griffin, C. C. 1334
Gropp, A. E. 1320
Grover, M. L. 1322
Grummon, S. E. 1056
Grupo de Oficiales Unidos (GOU) *see* United Officers' Group
Guarnieri, J. C. 453-4, 460
Gubitosi, C. 1123
Gudiño-Kieffer, E. 1072
Guedalla, P. 147
Guerrino, A. A. 563
Guido, B. 1079, 1082, 1187
Güiraldes, A. 441
Güiraldes, R. 1049-50, 1070, 1081
Guirao, M. 461
Gumucio Dagrón, A. 1181
Gunther, J. 22
Gurevitz, N. 81
Gurrieri, J. 378
Gusinde, M. 510, 513
Gutiérrez, M. 849
Gutiérrez, R. 1117
Guy, D. J. 364, 539, 648, 798, 836

## H

Hadfield, W. 106
Haigh, R. M. 281
Haigh, S. 130
Hall, D. 92
Hall, E. 24
Hallewell, L. 1278
Halperín Donghi, T. 255, 282, 590, 728, 999, 1333
Halsey, F. M. 894
Hammerton, J. A. 164
Hanrahan, B. 701
Hansis, R. A. 853
Hanson, S. G. 834
Harbinson, W. A. 309
Harding, C. 850
Hardoy, J. E. 56, 951, 953, 955, 959, 980
Hargreaves, C. 94

Harloff, E. 660
Harris, E. D. 1125
Harris, M. S. 475
Harrison, G. R. 28
Harteneck, López & Cía 765
Harvey, E. R. 1084
Hasbrouck, A. 291
Hastings, M. 699
Hauger-Klevene, J. H. 543, 556
Haugse, V. L. O. de A. 1323
Hauser, P. M. 973
Havighurst, R. J. 522
Hawkes, J. G. 192
Head, F. B. 129
Heath, D. B. 521
Heer, L. 1072
Helg, A. 483
Hellman, R. G. 972
Henderson, P. 299
Hendrie, A. 769
Hennessy, A. 681
Hermitte, E. 335
Hernández, A. 555
Hernández, H. H. 1235
Hernández, J. 1051, 1080
Herron, F. 160
Hester, T. R. 234
Hewko, J. 639
Hicks, A. H. 862
Hidalgo, M. 1146
Hilger, M. I. 243
Hill, F. J. 1222
Hilton, R. 1300
Hilton, S. E. 668, 674
Hirst, W. A. 2
Hispanic and Luso-Brazilian Council 1321
Hitchcock, H.-R. 1126
Hjerting, J. P. 192
Hodge, J. E. 877, 996, 1008, 1140
Hodges, D. C. 575
Hoefer, H. 92, 96
Hoeffel, P. H. 931
Hoffman, H. H. 1338
Hoffmann, F. L. 314, 696
Hoffmann, O. M. 696
Holbo, P. S. 478
Holdich, T. H. 152
Holland, W. J. 182
Hollander, N. C. 365

Holzapfel, T. 1175
Honeywell, M. 692
Honsa, V. 448
Hoopes, P. R. 1251
Hore, T. E. 860
Hornos, A. 12
Horowitz, I. L. 372, 415
Horowitz, J. 920-1, 929
Horvath, L. 1342
Hourcade, L. A. 1225
Howard, G. D. 233
Howat, J. N. T. 879
Hudson, W. H. 110, 115, 177, 200, 1070
Hughlett, L. J. 802
Humphreys, R. A. 268, 303, 1337
Hunt, J. C. 25
Hunter, J. M. 346
Huret, J. 153
Hutchinson, B. 537
Hutchinson, T. J. 107
Hux, P. M. 1331
Hyams, E. 187

## I

Ibarra Grasso, D. E. 221
Iglesias Echegaray, A. 612
Ilsley, L. L. 628
Imaz, J. L. de 519, 581, 590
Imbelloni, J. 1198
Imperiale, G. 357
Ingenieros, J. 480
Iñigo Carrera, H. 358
Iñigo Carrera, N. 421
Inkeles, A. 515
Instituto de Desarrollo Económico y Social 731
Instituto Geográfico Militar 44, 78, 85-6, 90
Instituto Nacional de Estadística y Censos (INDEC) 903, 936, 938
Instituto Nacional de Tecnología Agropecuaria (INTA) 84

393

397

Phillips, J. C. 131
Phillips, R. 1068
Piccirilli, R. 284, 1270
Piedracueva, H. 1320
Pike, F. B. 490
Pilkington, J. 94
Pinnell, R. 1138
Pion-Berlin, D. 600
Pivel Devoto, J. E. 1330
Pizarnik, A. 1063, 1073,
1079
Platt, D. C. M. 570, 708,
728, 757, 858
Platt, R. S. 50
Podestá, C. 216
Polit, G. 808
Pollard, G. C. 238
Polletti, S. 1082
Pollono, D. 555
Polt, J. H. R. 1056
Poneman, D. 826
Pope, B. H. 1278
Pope, W. S. 1141
Porta, F. 792
Portantiero, J. C. 302, 729
Portes, A. 1001
Porth, J. S. 603
Portnoy, A. 618
Postlethwaite, T. N. 994
Potash, R. A. 604-5
Potenze, P. L. 869
Potobsky, G. von 913
Potter, A. L. 293
Pozzi, P. A. 918
Pozzo, A. 9
Prando, A. 1095
Prebisch, R. 728
*La Prensa* 1252
Preston, D. A. 336
Previtali, G. 1049
Price Waterhouse 755
Prichard, H. H. 170
Proctor, R. 124
Prohaska, F. 41
Pross, E. E. 1177
Provenzano, S. D. 1259
Puget, J. 567
Puig, M. 1064-5
Puiggrós, R. 580
Pulley, R. H. 893
Puppo, G. 222
Purdom, D. S. 886
Pyenson, L. 1011
Pyle, J. 332

# Q

Queiro Trajalli, I. 571
Quevedo, Lafone 232
Quino *see* Lavado, J.S.
Quintero Ramos, A. M.
772
Quiroga, H. 1081

# R

Rabassa, G. 1043-4, 1060,
1069
Rabossi, E. 482
Raithelhuber, J. 189
Rama, A. 591
Ramella, F. 403
Ramírez, R. 959
Ramos, J. 743
Ramos, V. A. 88
Randall, L. 721
Randle, P. H. 79, 81, 954
Ranis, P. 659
Rapoport, M. 668, 676
Ratier, H. E. 557, 961
Ravignani, E. 632
Razori, A. 956
Reber, V. B. 783
Reca, L. G. 864
Recchini de Lattes, Z. L.
327, 329, 340-1, 351,
355, 373
Regalsky, A. M. 889
Regan, D. E. 964
Regis, S. B. C. de 1197
Reich, P. 344
Reid, A. 1035
Reina, R. E. 534, 806
Reinharz, J. 411
Remmer, K. L. 584
Rennic, Y. F. 253
Resnick, C. C. 1134
Revill, W. 149
*Revista de Jurisprudencia
Argentina* 651
Rey, A. 1216
Rey Balmaceda, R. C. 38,
1312
Reyburn, M. F. 514
Reyburn, W. D. 514
Ribera, A. L. 1108

Ricci, J. 462
Rice, D. 707
Rice, M. L. 1344
Richardson, R. 1174
Rickard, F. I. 73
Ricketts, M. 309
Ridgely, R. S. 201, 214
Ringuelet, R. A. 210, 213
Rippy, J. F. 758, 1007
Ritter, A. R. M. 1211
Roberts, C. 267
Robertson, J. P. 121
Robertson, M. 166
Robertson, W. P. 121
Robertson, W. S. 257
Robinson, A. 547
Robinson, D. J. 881, 957,
976
Robinson, K. 791
Robson, W. A. 964
Roccatagliata, J. A. 38, 888
Rock, D. 249, 251, 288,
297, 477, 597, 711, 728
Rodríguez, A. E. 1233
Rodríguez, C. A. 746
Rodríguez, M. 265
Rodríguez, N. J. 421
Rodríguez Braun, C. 729
Rodríguez Bustamante, N.
1003
Rodríguez Molas, R. 446,
1294
Rodríguez Monegal, E.
1037, 1039
Rodríguez-Novás, J. 636
Rögind, W. 886
Römer, R. A. 528
Roffé, R. 1082
Rofman, A. B. 949
Rogers, G. C. 617
Roggiano, A. A. 1051
Rohrlich-Leavitt, R. 361
Roig, A. A. 479, 1007
Rojas, R. 480, 1022, 1070
Román, E. 937
Romay, F. L. 1270
Romero, F. 479, 485
Romero, J. L. 260, 969
Romero, L. A. 953, 969
Romero Brest, G. L. de
1006
Romero Brest, J. 1091
Ronchi, R. 993
Rondina, R. V. D. 193

399

# Index of Titles

413

**R**

El radicalismo: ensayo sobre su historia y doctrina 576

Radiodifusión en la Argentina 1258

Radiografía de la pampa 36, 1058-9

Railway expansion in Latin America: descriptive and narrative history of the railroad systems of Argentina, Peru, Venezuela, Brazil, Chile, Bolivia and all other countries of South and Central America 894

Railway in the desert: the story of the building of the Chubut Railway and the life of its constructor Engineer E. J. Williams 895

Railways of the Andes 897

Railways of South America. Part I: Argentina 896

Ramón writes 30

Rastrilladas, huellas y caminos 876

Rayuela 952, 1020, 1043-4

La Razón 1131

La razón de mi vida 1015

Real Argentine: notes and impressions of a year in the Argentine and Uruguay 164

Records of the Scottish settlers in the River Plate and their churches 502

Recruitment of candidates in Mendoza Province, Argentina 586

Redemocratization of Argentine culture, 1983 and beyond: an international research symposium at Arizona State University, February 16-17, 1987 1088

Reform and reaction in the Platine provinces, 1810-1852 283

Region versus nation: Cuyo in the crosscurrents of Argentine development, 1861-1914 55

Regional development and transportation in Argentina: Mendoza and the Gran Oeste Argentino Railroad, 1885-1914 898

Regional disparities and policy in modern Argentina 66

Relevamiento estadístico de la economía argentina, 1900-1980 945

Religion in Latin American life and literature 489

Religion, revolution, and reform: new forces for change in Latin America 490

Repertorio de bibliotecas especializadas y centros de información 1238

Repertorio de legislación argentina, años 1862-1970: leyes y decretos nacionales. Actualizados hasta diciembre de 1970 651

Report of an Amnesty International mission to Argentina, 6-15 November 1976 624

Report of journeys across the Andes and pampas of the Argentine Provinces 128

Report on the situation of human rights in Argentina 625

Representative plays of Florencio Sánchez 1174

República Argentina 90

La República Argentina a través de las obras de los escritores ingleses 1309

República Argentina: red caminera principal 91

Research guide to Argentine literature 1303

Reseña histórico-descriptiva de antiguas y modernas supersticiones del Río de la Plata 1201

Resistance and integration: Peronism and the Argentine working class, 1946-1976 932

La restauración nacionalista 484

Return of Eva Perón, with The killings in Trinidad 325

Return to Río de la Plata: response to the return of exiles to Argentina and Uruguay 378

Reversal of development in Argentina: postwar counterrevolutionary policies and their structural consequences 730

Review of Contemporary Fiction 1069

Review of the River Plate 731

Las revistas literarias argentinas, 1893-1967 1259

Revolution before breakfast: Argentina 1941-1946 305

Revolution on the pampas: a social history of Argentine wheat, 1860-1910 857

Ricardo Güiraldes and Don Segundo Sombra: life and works 1049

Rico Tipo 1131-5

Rimas 1045

Rivadavia y su tiempo 284

River and the people 165

River Plate personalities: a biographical dictionary 1298

River Plate republics: a

# Index of Subjects

## A

433

on stamps 1207
Falkland Islands dispute
689-98, 1272
bibliography 1316
*see also* Falklands War
Falklands War (1982) 249,
261, 592, 594, 598,
616, 685, 699-707,
1107, 1211
Famantina mines 117
Family history 533
Family law 636
Family life 3, 24, 387, 528
Family networks 532
Family planning 326, 345
Family relations 529
Farmers' revolt (1912) 294
Farrell, Edelmiro J. 300
Fascism 300, 578
Fashion 397
FATE 814
Fauna 3, 6, 15-16, 39, 43,
92, 116, 170, 174,
194-214, 1273
Federación Empleados de
Comercio 920
Federación Indígena del
Chaco 431
Federación Obrera
Regional Argentina
927
Federación Obreros y
Empleados
Telefónicos 920
Federal Code of Civil and
Commercial
Procedure 642
Federal finances 275
Federal government 627,
656-8
Federal Investment
Council *see* Consejo
Federal de Inversiones
Federal Republic of
Germany 780
Fehily, Thomas 407
Feinmann, José Pablo 1021
Feminist movement 347,
349, 352, 354, 360,
1062
Fernández, Macedonio
1027, 1046-7
Ferreyra, José Agustín
1190

Ferrocarril Central Chubut
895
Ferrocarril de Rosario a
Puerto Belgrano 889
Ferrocarril General Mitre
902
Ferrocarril General Roca
886, 900, 902
Ferrocarril General San
Martín 902
Ferrocarril Nacional
General Belgrano 896,
900, 902
Ferrocarril Nacional
General Urquiza 900,
902
Ferrocarril Oeste 893
Ferrocarril Patagónico 902
Ferrocarril Provincia de
Santa Fé 889
Ferrocarriles Argentinos
899
Fertility rates 326, 333-4,
345, 948
Festival Nacional de
Folklore de Cosquín
1155
Festivals 6, 1197, 1200
Fiat 753, 931
Field Museum of Natural
History, Chicago 245
Field, Thomas 407
Figueiredo, João 674
Film 1181-90, 1328
*see also* Censorship
Film directors 1183
*see also by name*
*Filosofía cristiana* 474
Finance 2, 8, 11, 14, 34,
270, 299, 709-10, 712,
717, 731, 751-66, 1284
statistics 938, 941, 945-7
Financial crisis (1890)
103-4, 889
Financial institutions 763,
769
Finland 679
Firestone 814
Fiscal policy 756
Fishes 204-5, 208, 210, 213
Fishing industry 802, 851,
864
statistics 938, 945-6
Five-year plans 66

Fjords 62
Flax production 840
Flemish merchants 141
Flora 3, 6, 15-16, 39, 92,
116, 170, 185-93, 1273
Florida group [literary
movement] 1025, 1055
Flota Argentina de
Navegación de
Ultramar 870
Flota Argentina de
Navegación Fluvial
870
Flota Mercante del Estado
870
Folk literature 508-14,
1193
Folk music and dance
1148-56, 1192, 1199
Folk religion 1191-2
Folklore 29, 1191-1202,
1273, 1275
bibliography 1310
FONAVI *see* National
Housing Fund
Fontanarrosa, Roberto
1130, 1135
Fontezuelas 224
Food and drink 3, 17, 27,
1203-6
Food consumption 554,
720, 904
Food industry 796, 802
Foot Indians 427
Football 1213
*see also* Soccer
FORA *see* Federación
Obrera Regional
Argentina
Ford 818
Ford, F. Clare 861
Ford Foundation 833
Foreign debt 717, 726,
744-7, 762
Foreign exchange 324, 750,
752
Foreign investment 251,
644, 720, 725, 727-8,
798, 808-9, 814, 1013
Foreign Investments Law
(1976) 639, 752
(1949-71) 754
(1973) 754
Foreign news 1251

442

violations 507, 1262
Humanist socialists 489
Humid Pampa 45, 47, 50
  occupation phases 59, 61
*Humita* 1203, 1206
Hunger 554
Hunter-gatherers 217, 234,
  424
Hunting 145
*Hyacinth* [ship] 126
Hydraulic engineering 843
Hydroelectricity 811
Hydrography 39, 43
Hyperinflation 326, 726,
  739

I

IAME *see* Industrias
  Aeronáuticas y
  Mecánicas del Estado
Iconography
  feline 228
Idealism 471
IGM *see* Instituto
  Geográfico Militar
Iguazú Falls 26, 97-9, 172
IKA *see* Industrias Kaiser
  Argentina
Illia, Arturo 1005, 1247
Illiteracy 989
Illustrations
  guide to 1276
Imbert, Julio 1166
IMF *see* International
  Monetary Fund
Immigrants 332, 570, 908,
  923, 980
  Arabs 157, 388, 401
  Boer 157
  English 138, 154
  European 61, 167, 372,
    376
  French 374
  Irish 19, 138, 154, 392,
    396, 407
  Jewish 411-19
  Russian 157
  Scottish 138, 155, 157,
    181
  Spanish 157
  Swedish 157

Swiss 294
  *see also other*
    *nationalities by name*
Immigration 8, 16, 33,
  107-8, 252, 289, 329,
  334, 337, 341, 367-80,
  534-5, 970, 983
  bibliography 1317
  British 132, 396
  European 139
  from outside Americas
    387-410, 435-40
  from South America
    381-6
  illegal 381
  Jewish 411-19
  *see also* Immigrants;
    Welsh settlers
Immigration controls 381
Import controls 752
Import substitution 787
Import tariff policy 275,
  649, 777-8, 787, 807
Importers
  directory 788
Imports 14, 725
Inca horizon 215
Inca influence 219, 238
Income 903-16
  *see also* Per capita
    income; Salaries;
    Wages
Income distribution 295,
  732, 906
Income tax 775-6
Incomes policy 323
Inconvertible paper money
  714, 786
INDEC *see* Instituto
  Nacional de
  Estadística y Censos
Independence 268, 272-86,
  471, 480
  movement (1810) 481
Indian organizations 431,
  433
Indian population 16, 62,
  135, 221, 420-34
  bibliography 1331
  blood groups 547
  conquered 291
  Patagonia 122, 179
  sports 1213
  *see also by tribes*

Indian tribute 271
Industrial expansion 302,
  737, 907
Industrial law 653
Industrial parks 66
Industrial relations 646
Industrialists 805-9
Industrialization 25, 254,
  301, 364, 801
  (1870-1914) 252
  (1880-1930) 372
  since 1914 708
Industrias Aeronáuticas y
  Mecánicas del Estado
  815
Industrias Kaiser
  Argentina 815, 907
Industry 1-3, 6-7, 11,
  15-16, 26, 33-4, 38-9,
  43, 49, 51, 60, 139,
  144, 275, 324, 391,
  397, 709-10, 712, 720,
  796-804, 1273, 1284
  key sectors 752
  statistics 938, 946-7
  *see also by sector*
Infectious diseases 561
Inflation 320, 324, 637,
  736, 748-50, 761
  anti-inflationary
    policies 740-1
Infrastructure 65
  communications 79
Ingeniero Jacobacci 162
Ingenieros, José 471, 478,
  480, 483, 485-6
Initiation ceremony 423,
  510
Insecticides 545
Insects 177, 204-5
In-service training 989
Institución Mitre 1287
Institute of Current World
  Affairs, New York 160
Institute of Educational
  Research, Belgrano
  993
Institute of Virology,
  Córdoba 195
Instituto Bibliotecológico
  1304
Instituto del Aborigen 428
Instituto Geográfico
  Militar 78, 85-6, 90

445

Ports and harbours 8, 14, 152, 758, 878, 882, 970, 980
Portugal 686
Portuguese colonists 265
Posadas 99, 172
Positivism 471-3, 475, 477, 480, 988, 992
Posters 1101-2, 1107, 1109
Potatoes 192
Potosí 269
Potosí intendancy 270
Pottery *see* Artefacts; Arts and crafts
Prairies 856
Prebisch, Raúl 742
Preferential trade agreement 792
Prehistory 1, 215-45
Presbyterians 502
Presidential elections (1946) 305 (1973) 323
Presidents 1294 (1880-1910) 287
Press 16, 33, 139, 656, 1257, 1284
*see also* Censorship; Journalism; Newspapers; Publishing
Pressure groups 569, 1281
Price controls 752, 864
Price stabilization 737, 750
Price Waterhouse 755
Prices 717, 720, 748-9, 761, 864
statistics 937, 946-7
Prieto, Adolfo 1019
Primary education 987, 996, 1000, 1007
Primary sources 307, 328
*see also* Archives; Historical documents
Prince of Wales's visit (1925) 34
Printing 1230, 1240-6, 1330
Private international law 636
Privateering 274
Professional women 361
Professors 986, 997
Profits 320
Programme on Human and

Scientific Resources for Development 991
Pronunciation 468
Prostitution 539, 973
Protectionism *see* Import tariff policy
Protestant Waldensians 387, 1343
Protestantism 488, 494, 498, 500, 503-4, 506
bibliography 1343
Protomedicato 551
Proverbs 470
Provincial industries 796
Provincial politics 298
Provincial tax systems 774
Psychiatric disorders 560, 566
Psychiatry 563, 620
Psychoanalysis 542, 567
Psychology 542, 562
Psychoses 560
Puberty 541
Public debt 275
Public health 811
Public land ownership 841
Public-sector finance 710
Public services 11
Publishing 405, 1230, 1240-6, 1284, 1340
need for law 1242-3, 1245
*see also* Censorship
Puelche Indians 59, 266
Puerto Bueno 161
Puerto Madryn 99, 895
Pueyrredón, Juan Martín de 274
Pueyrredón, Prilidiano 1095
Puig, Manuel 1020, 1064-5, 1162
*Pulperos see* Retail grocery
Pumas 173, 177, 183
Puna 237
Punta Arenas 105, 159, 170
Punta Ballena 1126

Quebracho Fusionados 862
Quebracho tree 64, 862

Quebrada de Humahuaca 216, 223
Quechua language 453, 460, 466
Querandí Indians 59, 266
Quevedo, Lafone 232
Quilmes 502
Quino *see* Lavado, Joaquín Salvador
Quinquela Martín, Benito 1105
Quiroga, Juan Facundo 278

Rabinovich, José 1023, 1029
Race 8
Racial discrimination 437
Racism 436, 483
Radbone, James 158
Radical Party 290, 293-4, 298-7, 311, 593, 892 (1890-1916) 252 (1890-1964) 576
Radicalism 489
Radio broadcasting 1258, 1284
Radiocarbon dating 217, 231
Railway Workers' Union 926
Railways 7-8, 37, 144, 146-7, 152, 162, 376, 758, 884-902, 970, 982
Ramakrishna Mission 150
Ramal C14 896
Ramírez, Pedro Pablo 300
Ramos Mejía, Francisco 485
Ramos Mejía, José María 485
Ranching 3, 167
Raw materials 797
Rawson 154, 170, 393
Razzano, José 1160
Real wages 910, 915
Recipes 1203-4, 1206
*Reconquista* (1806) 267
Reconquista, river 67
Recreation 6-7, 17, 24, 33, 1207-19

Cooperation and
Development (1988)
792
Treaty of Peace and
Friendship (1984) 684
Treaty of Tordesillas
(1494) 686
Trekking 94
Trelew 895
Tres Arroyos 394
Tribunal Mayor de
Cuentas [Royal
Auditing Agency] 271,
655
Tribute 271
Trout fishing 1219
Tucumán Province 73, 107,
148, 153, 162, 232,
376, 380, 388, 431,
836, 850, 982
economic growth 264
history 979
urbanization 959
Tumours 555
Turks 388
Tyre industry 814


U

UF see Unión Ferroviaria
Ugarte, Manuel 471
UIA see Argentine
Industrial Union
Ukrainian immigrants 395,
409
UN Conference on Trade
and Development 742
UN Economic Commission
for Latin America
742, 906
UN Educational, Social
and Cultural
Organization 1236,
1305
UN General Assembly
Resolution (1982) 1272
UNCTAD see UN
Conference on Trade
and Development
Underdevelopment 733
Unemployment 912
Unesco see UN

Educational, Social
and Cultural
Organization
Unidades básicas see
Women's centres
Unión Cívica Radical see
Radical Party
Unión Ferroviaria 919-20,
929
Unión Industrial Argentina
see Argentine
Industrial Union
Unión Obrera Textil 920
Unión Obreros y
Empleados
Municipales 920
Unions see Trades unions
United Estancias Company
835
United Nations 311, 1272
see also UN
organizations by name
United Officers' Group
1944 manifesto 1267
United Provinces of the
Río de la Plata 130,
132, 142, 284
United Provinces of South
America 286
United River Plate
Telephone Company
875
United States of America
33, 150, 273-4, 321,
413, 616, 661, 688,
694, 862
Argentine attitudes to
305
Argentine immigrants
357, 368, 984, 995,
1001
Constitution (1787) 627
influence 302
investment 251
protective tariffs 669,
725, 785
relations with Argentina
667-70, 680, 682, 684,
687, 725
see also US
Universidad de Belgrano
993
University autonomy
985-6, 997

University libraries 1223,
1227
University of Buenos Aires
985-6, 999, 1003,
1005-6, 1011, 1304
Press (EUDEBA) 1006,
1245
University of Córdoba 999,
1004, 1011, 1228
University of La Plata 1011
University of Texas
Latin American
Collection 1319
University Reform
movement 1004
Upper Canada 129
Upper class 516, 519
Upper Peru 268, 271, 852
Upsallata Pass 128-9, 133,
135, 896
Uranium 821, 824
Urban Development
Board 960
Urban lifestyle 326
Urban migration 327, 370
Urban planning 67, 960
Urban poor 524, 972
Urbanization
38-9, 327, 340, 949-62
bibliography 1339
Buenos Aires 963-77
cities other than BA
978-83
maps 79
see also cities by name
Uriburu, General 147, 583
coup (1930) 1269
Urn burials 219, 225
Urquiza, Justo José de
118, 123, 125, 273, 285
Uruguay 8, 31-2, 46, 121,
164, 198, 264, 283,
285, 381, 569, 620,
678, 685-6, 743, 1086
bureaucracy 322
churches 497
demography 326, 333
Uruguay, river 46, 114,
138, 233
ethnography 240
Uruguayan-Argentinian
Trade Co-operation
Agreement 794
US Agency for

# Map of Argentina

This map shows the more important towns and other features.

MAJOR CITIES
1. San Salvador de Jujuy
2. Salta
3. San Miguel de Tucumán
4. Catamarca
5. Santiago del Estero
6. Resistencia
7. Corrientes
8. La Rioja
9. Córdoba
10. Santa Fe
11. Paraná
12. Rosario
13. San Juan
14. Mendoza
15. San Luis
16. La Plata
17. Mar del Plata
18. Bahía Blanca
19. Santa Rosa
20. San Carlos de Bariloche
21. Viedma
22. Rawson
23. Comodoro Rivadavia
24. Río Gallegos
25. Ushuaia